Discovering Christ In Leviticus

Discovering Christ

In Leviticus

Donald S. Fortner

Go *publications*

Go Publications
3 South Parade, Seascale, Cumbria, CA20 1PZ, ENGLAND.

ISBN 978-1-908475-22-0

This book is dedicated to

Pastor Clay Curtis

Sovereign Grace Baptist Church
Ewing, New Jersey

Table of Contents

Chapter	Passage	Page
Foreword by Peter L. Meney		11
1. God Demands And Gives Holiness		13
2. How Can A Sinner Come To God?	1:1-9	21
3. Faith In Christ	1:4, 5	29
4. The Sacrifices Of The Poor	1:10-17	35
5. Turtledoves Or Pigeons	1:14-17	43
6. 'He Shall Kill The Bullock'	1:5	49
7. The Meat Offerings	2:1-16	55
8. The Oblation Of Firstfruits	2:12-16	67
9. The Salt Of God	2:13	73
10. The Peace Offerings	3:1-17	79
11. Things Pertaining To Peace	3:1-17	89
12. Christ The Sin Offering	4:1-35	99
13. The Trespass Offering And The Cross	5:1-6:7	109
14. Restitution Made Or The Lord Revealed	5:15-6:7	117
15. Ever-Burning Fire	6:8-13	125
16. 'It Is Most Holy'	6:8-7:15	131
17. God's People God's Priests	6:14-23	137
18. The Sacrifice That Could Not Be Eaten	6:24-30	145
19. The Priests' Portion	7:1-10	153
20. 'There Is One Law'	7:7	161
21. 'The Law Of Consecrations'	7:11-38	169
22. 'An Holy Priesthood'	8:1-36	177
23. The Urim And The Thummim	8:6-9	185
24. The Beauty And Glory Of Our Priest	8:7-9	197
25. 'The Thing Which The LORD Commanded'	8:1-36	205
26. The Efficacy Of The Blood	8:14-30	211

27. 'On The Eighth Day'	9:1-10:7	221
28. The Revelation Of God's Glory	9:22-24	231
29. Nadab And Abihu: The Worship Of God	10:1-20	241
30. Strange Fire: Counterfeit Religion	10:1-3	251
31. Sacrifice, Submission, Stedfastness, Sobriety	10:1-11	257
32. A Possessed People	11:1-47	267
33. Fallen Man An Unclean Thing	12:1-8	275
34. The Law Of Leprosy	13:1-14:59	283
35. He Who Has The Plague Is Clean	13:12-17	291
36. 'In The Day Of His Cleansing'	14:1-59	299
37. 'A Running Issue'	15:1-33	311
38. The Day Of Atonement	15:1-34	319
39. The Scapegoat	16:1-34	327
40. The Blood	17:1-16	333
41. 'Abominable Customs'	18:1-30	345
42. Holiness	19:1-37	353
43. Doing Justice	19:35, 36	365
44. Biblical Separation	20:1-27	375
45. God's Priests And God's Priest	21:1-24	387
46. 'Profane Not My Holy Name'	22:1-33	399
47. 'Shall Be Perfect To Be Accepted'	22:21	411
48. Inspiration To Worship	22:31-33	419
49. The Chain Of Grace	22:31-33	425
50. 'The Feasts Of The LORD'	23:1-44	433
51. 'The Sabbath Of Rest'	23:1-3	443
52. 'The Lord's Passover'	23:4, 5	453
53. 'The Feast Of Unleavened Bread'	23:6-8	459
54. The Feast Of Firstfruits	23:9-14	467
55. The Feast Of Pentecost	23:15-22	475
56. The Feast Of Trumpets	23:23-25	483
57. The Feast Of Atonement	23:26-32	489
58. The Feast Of Tabernacles	23:33-44	495
59. The Golden Candlestick	24:1-4	503
60. The Table Of Shewbread	24:5-9	511
61. The Death Of A Blasphemer	24:10-23	519
62. The Year Of Jubilee	25:8-13	529
63. The Sabbath That Remains	25:1-22	537
64. Let Us Start Over	25:8-17	545

65. Is It Safe And Wise To Trust The Lord?   25:18-22   551
66. Strangers And Sojourners With God   25:23-34   559
67. Christ Our Kinsman Redeemer   25:25-28   565
68. God's Slaves   25:35-55   569
69. A Blessing And A Curse   26:1-46   575
70. The Old Store And The New   26:1-20   583
71. Public Worship   26:1-4   595
72. A Call To Voluntary Consecration   27:1-34   607

Index Of Bible Verses   617

Discovering Christ In Leviticus

Foreword

Moses' third book, the Book of Leviticus, is full of the Lord Jesus Christ. In the tabernacle we see Christ, in the priesthood we see Christ, in the sacrifices and the diverse offerings, our Saviour can be traced in type, picture, symbol and figure by all who have eyes to see.

In this present work, our author, Pastor Don Fortner, is keen not to let pass unnoticed any opportunity to discover Christ. Herein lies the value and usefulness of this new work *Discovering Christ in Leviticus*.

When the Master told His listeners they should 'search the scriptures', He was speaking of the Old Testament and said, 'they are they which testify of me'. Specifically, he declared, 'Moses ... wrote of me' and here in these twenty-seven chapters of Leviticus we rejoice to find confirmation of Jesus' statement as our Lord is portrayed to an eminent degree by His servant Moses.

Leviticus contains very little by way of history and differs noticeably in this respect from Genesis and Exodus. Yet the Voice of Jehovah echoes and re-echoes throughout the book when clear commands and precise conditions for approaching God are set forth. Here God tells His people how and when and where He will meet with them. Men and women should take note of this. If we would know God we must come by the way He prescribes.

God told Jeremiah, 'ye shall seek me, and find me, when ye shall search for me with all your heart. And I will be found of you, saith the LORD'. Leviticus shows us how. God will be sought after by men but He shall be found only in the place He specifies, only by the way He determines and only through the blood of a perfect sacrifice. That sacrifice is His Son, Jesus Christ.

Throughout Leviticus we are constantly reminded of this book's divine origin and authority. The LORD, the Living Word, frequently addresses His servant with the words, 'And the LORD called unto Moses, and spake unto him'. We see this in chapter one verse one, and in similar fashion some fifty more times. This is absolutely God's enduring word and while the sacrifices and rituals have long since ceased, the Truth behind the types is today as meaningful and important for a proper understanding of the Gospel as it was when it was first spoken.

Last year shortly after completing this book Pastor Fortner passed into the presence of His Lord and Saviour. We are indebted to him for this labour of love on behalf of the church of Christ. It is also appropriate to acknowledge the contribution of his dear wife, Shelby, in its editing and checking. It is our prayer that the Lord use these pages from the pen of His faithful servant to encourage the Lord's sheep and challenge those yet outside of the fold of God. May our friend's burden to lift up his Saviour in the written and preached word continue to meet with success.

Peter L. Meney
Sovereign Grace Church,
Great Falls, Montana

Chapter 1

God Demands And Gives Holiness

The book of Exodus concludes with the setting up of the tabernacle for the worship of God. This was the place where God met with his chosen people, the place of divine worship, the place whence the Lord God gave out his word to his people. This tabernacle, being a picture of our dear Saviour, the Lord Jesus Christ, the incarnate God, was made exactly according to the pattern God gave to Moses. The book of Leviticus gives us the prescribed ordinances and ceremonies of divine worship.

John Gill tells us the book of Leviticus was written by Moses 2514 years after the creation, about 1490 years before the coming of Christ. The various sacrifices, rites, and ceremonies here described were typical of Christ, and shadows of those good things to come by him for the everlasting salvation of our souls.

Three Historical Events

There are only three historical events mentioned in the whole book of Leviticus. But those three historical events are very instructive. The first historical event recorded in this book is the consecration of Aaron and his sons as the priests of Israel in chapters 8 and 9. There is a twofold type here.

First, the Aaronic priesthood represents the priesthood of our Lord Jesus Christ. Aaron, as the High Priest of Israel, foreshadowed the Lord

Jesus Christ, our great High Priest before God. He was divinely chosen, equipped, anointed, approved, and accepted. Only Aaron could make atonement in the holy of holies, because he represented Christ our great High Priest who alone could and would put away sin by the sacrifice of himself (Hebrews 7:23-28).

Second, Aaron's sons represent the church and kingdom of God, as that 'holy priesthood' of believers who serve God in the holy place day and night (1 Peter 2:5-9). Everything about these priests typifies and represents believing sinners in this world. These men were specifically chosen by God, portraying our election unto salvation. They were God's priests because of their relationship to Aaron. Believers are made priests unto God because of our relationship to the Lord Jesus Christ. They wore the garments of the priesthood. God's priests today wear the garments of their priesthood, too, the garments of salvation, the righteousness of Christ. Aaron's sons were accepted as priests because of a slain sacrifice. We are accepted because of Christ's sacrifice. They were anointed with holy anointing oil and washed with pure water. Believers are anointed with the Holy Spirit and washed in the pure water of free grace by the Word of God in the new birth. Aaron's sons were men who deliberately and voluntarily consecrated themselves to God. Believers are people who deliberately and voluntarily consecrate themselves to God. As Aaron's sons lived continually upon the sacrifice of God's altar, God's sons live continually upon Christ. As they served God and his people all the days of their lives, so God's 'holy priesthood' today serves him and his people continually.

The second historic event recorded in Leviticus is the death of Nadab and Abihu by the hand of God for offering 'strange fire before the LORD' (Leviticus 10:1-7). Let all who would worship God understand the powerful lesson set before us in chapter 10. If we would worship God and find acceptance with him, we must come to him with that which he has provided, Christ alone, and no mixture of anything with Christ (Leviticus 10:1-3). God is sanctified, that is, honoured, only by Christ; and the only way he can be sanctified by fallen, sinful men and women is by faith in Christ.

The third historic event recorded in the book of Leviticus is the stoning of Shelomith's son for blasphemy (Leviticus 24:10-16). Those who blaspheme the name of God, cursing and denying him as God alone, shall be destroyed by him. Though this unnamed wretch had a

Hebrew mother, his father was an Egyptian; and he preferred both the gods and the people of Egypt to the God of Glory and his people. He was stoned by the people themselves because they judged him worthy of death. In like manner, though our hearts may break and cause us to weep as we behold lost rebels today under the wrath of God, when the Lord God executes his righteous judgment upon the damned in eternity, all shall consent and say 'Amen' to it.

All the rest of the book is taken up with the ceremonial laws God gave to Israel by Moses concerning their sacrifices and offerings, meats and drinks, and different washings. By these things God set Israel apart as a people for himself and distinguished them from other people and nations. All these things were shadows of those good things to come, which are ours in Christ. This book is called Leviticus because it is primarily about the Levitical priesthood (Hebrews 7:11).

The Message

We do not have to guess about the central, dominant message of the book of Leviticus. It is plainly stated in chapters 19 and 20. 'And the LORD spake unto Moses, saying, Speak unto all the congregation of the children of Israel, and say unto them, Ye shall be holy: for I the LORD your God am holy ... And ye shall be holy unto me: for I the LORD am holy, and have severed you from other people, that ye should be mine' (Leviticus 19:1, 2; 20:26).

The message of Leviticus is this: God demands holiness and God gives what he demands in Christ. All the types and ceremonies, laws and sacrifices, priests and holy things spoken of in these twenty-seven chapters show us that our only way of access to God is Christ. But, blessed be his holy name, we do have access to God by Christ, because we have that holiness which God demands in him, by his obedience and blood (John 14:6; Hebrews 10:14-22).

Holiness

'And ye shall be holy unto me: for I the LORD am holy, and have severed you from other people, that ye should be mine ... And the LORD spake unto Moses, saying, Speak unto all the congregation of the children of Israel, and say unto them, Ye shall be holy: for I the LORD your God am holy'.

This is both the command of God and the promise of God to his people. God commands us to be holy. Without holiness no one shall see the Lord (Hebrews 12:14). But that holiness without which we cannot see God is not something we perform. It is something God gives.

The Lord God declares to his chosen, covenant people that they shall be a holy people; not partially holy, not mostly holy, but entirely holy. This is not a recommendation, but a declaration. It is a declaration of grace made to a specific people.

The word 'holy' has two distinct meanings. Both definitions of the word must be understood and applied here. To be holy is to be separate, distinct, peculiar, separated and severed from all others. And to be holy is to be pure or purified.

The Lord God here declares to his Israel, to all who stand before him as his covenant people, 'You shall be separate, distinct, peculiar, separated and severed from all others; pure and purified before me'. We know this is the intent and meaning of this statement by comparing Scripture with Scripture (Exodus 19:6; Leviticus 11:44; 20:7; 1 Thessalonians 4:7; 1 Corinthians 6:9-11; Titus 2:11-14; 1 Peter 2:7-10).

The Lord God almighty, by the work of his sovereign, free, distinguishing grace, takes such things as us, such things as he finds in the dung heap of fallen humanity, and makes them holy. God makes sinners holy by the total removal of all sin and guilt from them and the imputation of righteousness to them in free justification by the precious blood of Christ (2 Corinthians 5:17). He makes us holy in sanctification, i.e. our regeneration. He makes us holy by imparting holiness to us i.e. creating a new, holy nature in us. And he makes us holy by his almighty grace (Romans 7:14-23; 2 Peter 1:4; 1 John 3:9). Furthermore, we shall be made holy in resurrection glory, when our very bodies are changed into the likeness of his glorious body (Romans 8:28-30; Ephesians 5:25, 26; Jude 1:24, 25; 1 Corinthians 15:20-28; 49-58).

Without a doubt, the Scriptures teach us that God requires holiness and God gives holiness to his people; but what is this holiness? Because we are so universally inundated with false, freewill, works-religion from our youth up, we commonly think that holiness has something to do with what we do. We tend to think of holiness in connection with austere, weird behaviour. We tend to think that 'holy' people are people who look and act as if they were weaned on dill pickles and bathe daily in embalming fluid.

We are that little city girl we have all heard about, who on her first visit to the country saw a mule looking over a fence at her with his long, sad face. She had never seen a mule before, and she said, 'I don't know what you are, but you must be a Christian you look just like Grandpa'.

Holiness is commonly associated with grimness, strangeness, oddness, something ugly and unappealing. And, frankly, as I have heard it described from the pulpit and read about it in the writings of men, I must acknowledge such thoughts are justified. But that is not holiness. That is nothing but religious self-righteousness and religious delusion.

The Word of God speaks of holiness in a quite different way. The Bible speaks of holiness as a beautiful and delightful thing. Four times we are called to worship God in the beauty of holiness (1 Chronicles 16:29; 2 Chronicles 20:21; Psalm 29:2; 96:9).

Wholeness

Holiness has something to do with wholeness. Holiness means wholeness, completion, entirety, perfection of being. There are no degrees to it. Either we are whole or we are broken and un-whole, complete or incomplete, perfect or imperfect. As a general rule, when reading the Bible, if you will think wholeness every time you read the word holiness, you will get a better picture of what holiness is.

That is what the Lord is talking about in Leviticus. He says to his covenant people, 'You shall be whole, because I am whole'. God is complete. He is perfect. There is no blemish in his character. He exists in perfect harmony with himself. He is perfect in beauty. He is perfect wholeness. He looks upon his chosen in great, boundless grace, and says, 'You, too, shall be whole'.

I am not suggesting that holiness does not involve separation, distinctness, and peculiarity. It certainly does. What I am saying is this: wholeness is that which separates God's elect from a ruined race. Wholeness, the blessed wholeness of grace and righteousness in Christ, is our separateness, distinctness, and peculiarity.

Nothing is more desirable, nothing more beautiful, and nothing more rare than wholeness. We long to be a whole people. The whole book of Leviticus, indeed the whole Word of God tells us how that God demands this wholeness and gives it to poor, helpless, broken, ruined sinners. He declares, 'I am the LORD that healeth thee'. Then he heals us by the sacrifice of his dear Son. It is written, 'with his stripes ye are healed' (Isaiah 53:5). God almighty heals the broken, ruined state and condition of his people by five things described in this great book of Leviticus: sacrifice, priesthood, atonement, restoration, liberty.

Sacrifice (Leviticus 1-7)

In chapters 1-7, God gave Moses specific instructions about the sacrifices and offerings by which his people would be allowed to approach him. In these five sacrifices, Israel was ceremonially provided with everything needed to make them whole or holy. These sacrifices represent the Lord Jesus Christ, in and by whom the Lord God gives us everything needed to make us whole, complete, and holy before him (Colossians 2:9, 10).

The burnt offering shows us the way to God (1:1-17). We must come to God by faith in Christ, who was consumed by the fire of God's wrath as our Substitute. Let it ever be remembered that our Lord Jesus Christ is that Burnt Offering who, being consumed by the fire of God's wrath, did in turn consume the fire of God's wrath for his people. Because his fury was poured out like fire upon our Substitute (Nahum 1:6), he declares, 'Fury is not in me' (Isaiah 27:4).

The meat offering portrays the character of Christ, the God-man (2:1-16). He who is our Substitute is most holy unto the Lord. It also speaks of our consecration to God by faith in Christ.

The peace offering speaks of the Lord Jesus Christ, who is our Peace (3:1-17). Christ alone can reconcile God and man. Christ alone can speak peace to the guilty conscience. Christ alone is our Peace.

The sin offering, of course, represents Christ our Substitute (4:1-35). Without the shedding of blood there is no remission of sin. There is no forgiveness with God except by the merits of a suitable, slain sin offering; and that Sin Offering is Christ.

The trespass offering sets before us a picture of Christ's atonement (5:1-6:7). Our Lord Jesus Christ made atonement for the sins of his people by paying our debt to the full satisfaction of divine justice.

Priesthood (Leviticus 8-10)

Here is depicted our un-wholeness, our brokenness. Sin has separated us from God. We cannot, in and of ourselves, come to him, approach him, and find acceptance with him. How, then, can we come to God and find acceptance with him? We must have a priest, a mediator, a daysman, an advocate. This God has provided in Christ.

None but God's Priest, the Lord Jesus Christ, can represent us before the holy Lord God, make sacrifice for us in the presence of God, and bring to us the blessing of God. But, there is more, our great High Priest, the Lord Jesus Christ, is so great, so meritorious, so effectual, so worthy that he also makes us priests unto God! Yes, it is true!

Atonement (Leviticus 11-16)
The Lord Jesus is our great High Priest; but a priest is useless without a sacrifice. Christ is both our Priest and our sin-atoning Sacrifice, the Lamb of God who has taken away our sins! He has, by his one great sacrifice for sin, forever put away all the sins of all his people (Isaiah 53:6, 9-11; Hebrews 9:26; 1 John 3:5).

Restoration (Leviticus 17-24)
Leviticus 17-24 shows us typically that which is the result of Christ's sin-atoning sacrifice as our Substitute. Because Christ has made atonement for us and put away our sins by the sacrifice of himself, God almighty sends his Spirit in omnipotent, saving grace and restores us to himself, reconciles us, and brings us into fellowship with him as the sons of God, causing us to walk with him in the obedience of faith, and worshipping him. He says, 'I am the Lord your God, which have separated you from other people' (20:24). In other words, he says to you and me, as we come to him through the sacrifice of Christ, 'I am yours and you are mine'. Even now, he owns us as his! He declares, 'And ye shall be holy unto me: for I the LORD am holy, and have severed you from other people, that ye should be mine' (20:26). The only thing left is that liberty for which Paul longed, when he cried, 'O wretched man that I am. Who shall deliver me from the body of this death?'

Liberty (Leviticus 25-27)
Leviticus 25 opens with the blowing of the jubilee trumpet. I can hardly wait. Soon, Christ shall come again. Then liberty, the glorious liberty of the sons of God! Then, blessed be his name, we shall be made whole!

That is what our heavenly Father says to us. He sees our hurt, our shame, our heartache, our brokenness due to our horrid sin, and our longing to be whole; and he says, 'You are mine'. But it is not all. Our God declares, 'You will be healed, made whole. You shall be holy. I will see to it. All your blemishes will be removed. All your deformities will be corrected. All your faults will be fixed. You shall be whole, for I am whole'. That is what the book of Leviticus is about. That is what the Bible is about (Jude 1:24, 25). It is what God's amazing grace in Christ does. It makes sinners whole and makes sinners free.

Chapter 2

How Can A Sinner Come To God?

And the LORD called unto Moses, and spake unto him out of the tabernacle of the congregation, saying, Speak unto the children of Israel, and say unto them, If any man of you bring an offering unto the LORD, ye shall bring your offering of the cattle, even of the herd, and of the flock. If his offering be a burnt sacrifice of the herd, let him offer a male without blemish: he shall offer it of his own voluntary will at the door of the tabernacle of the congregation before the LORD. And he shall put his hand upon the head of the burnt offering; and it shall be accepted for him to make atonement for him. And he shall kill the bullock before the LORD: and the priests, Aaron's sons, shall bring the blood, and sprinkle the blood round about upon the altar that is by the door of the tabernacle of the congregation. And he shall flay the burnt offering, and cut it into his pieces. And the sons of Aaron the priest shall put fire upon the altar, and lay the wood in order upon the fire: And the priests, Aaron's sons, shall lay the parts, the head, and the fat, in order upon the wood that is on the fire which is upon the altar: But his inwards and his legs shall he wash in water: and the priest shall burn all on the altar, to be a burnt sacrifice, an offering made by fire, of a sweet savour unto the LORD.

Leviticus 1:1-9

How can a sinner come to God? That is the question I want to answer in this study. How can I, a guilty, vile, base sinner, deserving God's holy wrath, come to the thrice holy Lord God and find acceptance with him? Are you interested?

The Way to God

Here we see that there is a way whereby sinners may indeed come to God and find acceptance with him. Thank God, there is a way! However, and this is of vital importance and must be understood, the only way sinners can come to God, the only way you and I can draw near to him is by faith in the Lord Jesus Christ. There is no acceptance with God upon the footing of religious ritualism or our own works of righteousness. If we would be saved, if we would find acceptance with God, we must come to him like the publican of old, confessing our sins and trusting the merits of the Lord Jesus Christ. It is written, 'Believe on the Lord Jesus Christ, and thou shalt be saved'. Salvation is looking to Christ, as the children of Israel looked to the brazen serpent. Salvation is coming to Christ (Hebrews 7:25). Salvation is leaning on Christ, trusting Christ, resting in Christ. Christ is Salvation. He is the Way. There is no other.

The only way a sinner can come to God is by Christ, the Way. The only door by which we can come into the presence of the holy Lord God is Christ, the Door. This is the doctrine of the entire Bible. I want to show it to you from the book of Leviticus. If we would worship God, if we would find acceptance with him, we must come to him, call upon him, worship him in the way he has prescribed, trusting Christ, the Sacrifice that he has accepted, as our only acceptance with him.

Christ the Theme

The book of Leviticus is one of the least read books of the Bible. Yet, it is pre-eminently the book in which God speaks directly to man. Andrew Bonar pointed out, no book in the Bible 'contains more of the very words of God than Leviticus'.

On the surface, the things spoken of in these twenty-seven chapters may seem to have no apparent message or relevance for us today. After all, the book is called 'Leviticus'. It is all about the functions of the priests of the Levitical order. The whole book is about Levitical laws, ceremonies, and priestly functions that have been abolished for more than two thousand years. What do these things have to do with us? It has everything to do with us, because the entire book of Leviticus is about Christ and the salvation God gives to sinners in him.

In Old Testament times, this was the first book Jewish children were taught to study, as we teach the young to read John or Romans. You see, Leviticus deals directly with all of the major issues in a believer's relationship with God, especially those involving sin and atonement. These are matters of great importance to the souls of men in every age.

Be Holy
The purpose of Leviticus is echoed in verses such as 11:44, 45, 19:2, and 20:26: 'Ye shall be holy, for I the Lord your God am holy'. The word 'holy' appears more often in the book of Leviticus than in any other book of the Bible. The book of Leviticus both calls God's people to be holy, and shows us how sinners are made holy by Christ. It declares that God's elect shall be made holy in Christ by the mighty operations of his grace.

The Burnt Offering
In chapters 1-7, God gave Moses specific instructions about the sacrifices and offerings by which his people would be allowed to approach him. The first of these is the burnt offering (1:1-17). The burnt offering speaks of God's wrath and Christ's substitution in the place of His people.

A Sinner Coming
Here is a sinner coming to God (vv. 1-4).

> And the LORD called unto Moses, and spake unto him out of the tabernacle of the congregation, saying, Speak unto the children of Israel, and say unto them, If any man of you bring an offering unto the LORD, ye shall bring your offering of the cattle, even of the herd, and of the flock (Leviticus 1:1, 2).

The Lord spoke to the children of Israel through Moses to teach them of their need of a Mediator. It is as though he had said, 'No sinner can see my face or hear my voice, but by a Mediator. I will not speak to, nor will I be spoken to by man, except through a Mediator'.

The fact that the sinner comes to the door of the tabernacle with an offering is, in itself, a declaration of a desperate need. Only sinners need a sacrifice.

> If his offering be a burnt sacrifice of the herd, let him offer a male without blemish: he shall offer it of his own voluntary will at the door of the tabernacle of the congregation before the LORD (Leviticus 1:3).

We are told four things about the one who brings the offering:

1. The offering was brought to 'the door of the tabernacle'

The altar of brass was near the door of the tabernacle, facing it. This was the first thing that met the worshipper's eye as he approached the tabernacle. Here the priest met him and led him with his sacrifice to the altar. The object in bringing the sacrifice was to get access to God. The door of access had been blocked by sin. It could not be opened without a sacrifice. Christ is that Sacrifice for sin, by which the way has been opened for sinners to come to God. He points to his blood atonement and says to needy sinners, 'Behold, I set before you an open door' (Hebrews 10:19-22).

2. The offering was brought by a person 'of his own voluntary will'

God demands a willing heart; and God gives the willing heart. This is the warrant of the Gospel. 'Whosoever will, let him come.' There must be a willing heart or else God is not worshipped. It is true, none are willing to come to Christ, none are willing to trust his atoning work, except those who are made willing by him in the day of his power.

This is wonderful. Are you willing to go yonder to the Altar? Are you willing to trust Christ? Do you reply, 'Yes, I am willing to be saved by Christ alone'. Then you may come. Leviticus 1:3 says nothing about your feelings, your experiences, or your worth. It speaks only of a willing heart, a soul willing to be bathed in the blood of Christ. Are you willing to be saved by him? If you are, that is God's work in you. God demands a willing heart. That makes it your responsibility. But only God can give a willing heart. That makes this a work of divine sovereignty and free grace (Romans 9:15, 16).

3. The offering was brought for acceptance with God

The phrase, 'he shall offer it of his own voluntary will', might be translated, 'he shall offer it in order to be accepted'. Reading it that way, it refers to an act of faith. We come to God, trusting Christ alone for acceptance with him. His blood is our only atonement for sin. His righteousness is our only righteousness before God.

We see this stated emphatically in the fourth verse. The sinner who comes to God trusting Christ finds acceptance with God in and by him (v. 4). 'And he shall put his hand upon the head of the burnt offering; and it shall be accepted for him to make atonement for him'.

Not only was the worshipper required to acknowledge his need of a sacrifice to gain acceptance with God, he must personally identify himself with the sacrifice. 'He shall put his hand upon the head of the burnt offering.' This suggests a transfer of sin from the sinner to the sacrifice. It portrays a confession of sin. It is also a declared approbation or approval of God's ordinance, an implicit agreement with divine justice. And it speaks of faith. The word used for 'put' is a very strong word. It means 'lean'. We come to God leaning upon Christ alone.

4. 'And it shall be accepted for him to make atonement for him'

Glorious Gospel! Believing sinners, by believing on the Lord Jesus Christ, receive atonement and find acceptance with God. Our faith does not make atonement or give us acceptance. But, believing Christ, we receive atonement and acceptance. Christ was accepted for us; and we are accepted for him. By faith in him we receive the atonement and discover acceptance, as the love of God is shed abroad in our hearts by the Holy Ghost (Romans 5:5-11; Ephesians 1:3-6).

The Sacrifice

Here is the Sacrifice by which sinners find acceptance with God (vv. 3, 5-9). The one Sacrifice by which you and I can come to God and find acceptance with him is the Lord Jesus Christ, God's own dear Son. He is the One of whom this burnt offering speaks.

> If his offering be a burnt sacrifice of the herd, let him offer a male without blemish: he shall offer it of his own voluntary will at the door of the tabernacle of the congregation before the LORD (Leviticus 1:3).

Anyone can execute wrath. In fact, God executes his wrath by all creation. But only God's Priest, the Lord Jesus Christ, can make atonement and bring mercy. Christ is both the sacrificing Priest and the Sacrifice offered for sin.

And he shall kill the bullock before the LORD: and the priests, Aaron's sons, shall bring the blood, and sprinkle the blood round about upon the altar that is by the door of the tabernacle of the congregation. And he shall flay the burnt offering, and cut it into his pieces. And the sons of Aaron the priest shall put fire upon the altar, and lay the wood in order upon the fire: And the priests, Aaron's sons, shall lay the parts, the head, and the fat, in order upon the wood that is on the fire which is upon the altar: But his inwards and his legs shall he wash in water: and the priest shall burn all on the altar, to be a burnt sacrifice, an offering made by fire, of a sweet savour unto the LORD (Leviticus 1:5-9).

Everything had to be done 'before the Lord'. Only the priest could offer the blood. Atonement can be made only by God's Priest. Mercy can come only through God's Priest. The sacrifice spoken of here is a burnt sacrifice (v. 3). Here is a sacrifice which had to be consumed by the fire of God, a sacrifice upon which God poured out his wrath, before the sinner could find acceptance with him. That sacrifice is Christ.

The sacrifice had to be a male from the herd, portraying Christ, the last Adam, the God-man, by whom righteousness has been brought in and by whom sin has been put away. Being from the herd, it was a Sacrifice of God's own providing.

The burnt offering must be a sacrifice without blemish. If he would make atonement for sin, our Sacrifice must be holy. He is the holy Lord God; and he is the holy Man. As such, he is able to offer a sacrifice to God worthy of God's holiness, justice, and truth. The Lord Jesus Christ, if he would present his church as a spotless bride; holy, unblameable, and unreproveable before God, must first himself be without blemish.

The sacrifice had to be killed before the Lord (v. 5). A blameless, holy life is not enough to make atonement for sin. A holy life could never open the door of access to God for poor sinners. Oh, no! Blood must be shed. Christ must die. He must die before the Lord. Our

Saviour's death was God's work. His was a sacrifice made to God, before God, and for God. Atonement and the redemption by atonement are God's works alone.

Then the blood of the sacrifice must be sprinkled by God's priest (v. 5). The blood sprinkled in heaven is redemption accomplished (Hebrews 9:12). The blood sprinkled upon the heart is redemption applied (Hebrews 9:14).

We are told the sacrifice must be flayed and cut in pieces (v. 6). This speaks of the believing sinner's confession and contrition before the Lord. Justice requires complete exposure of our souls, portrayed in the skinning of this sacrifice. Justice demands the deliberate slaughter of the criminal. The hewing of this sacrifice shows us the excruciating torments due to us because of our sin. God's sword, like Abraham's knife, spares not the sacrifice (Zechariah 13:7).

Note that everything about the sacrifice was done by divine order.

And the sons of Aaron the priest shall put fire upon the altar, and lay the wood in order upon the fire: And the priests, Aaron's sons, shall lay the parts, the head, and the fat, in order upon the wood that is on the fire which is upon the altar (Leviticus 1:7, 8).

The inwards (the intestines) and the legs of the sacrifice had to be washed. You cannot separate Christ (God's Sacrifice) from his people. The washing of the animal's intestines and legs speaks of us. Though redeemed by the blood of Christ, though our sins are atoned, we must be washed by his Spirit in what is called 'the washing of regeneration and renewing of the Holy Ghost' (Titus 3:5), by the 'washing of water by the Word' (Ephesians 5:26).

The Sacrifice God requires and accepts is that Sacrifice which is 'a sweet savour unto the Lord' (v. 9). 'But his inwards and his legs shall he wash in water: and the priest shall burn all on the altar, to be a burnt sacrifice, an offering made by fire, of a sweet savour unto the LORD'. The whole sacrifice was placed on the altar and offered to God. The whole sacrifice was consumed with the fire of God's wrath. The sacrifice was a sweet savour unto the Lord. Christ is that Sacrifice (Ephesians 5:2). 'Thanks be unto God for his unspeakable gift.'

Chapter 3

Faith In Christ

And he shall put his hand upon the head of the burnt offering; and it shall be accepted for him to make atonement for him. And he shall kill the bullock before the LORD: and the priests, Aaron's sons, shall bring the blood, and sprinkle the blood round about upon the altar that is by the door of the tabernacle of the congregation.

Leviticus 1:4, 5

The picture we have before us is that of a guilty Israelite during the days of the Levitical priesthood. The man was a sinner before God. Atonement must be made for his sins in the way that God had appointed. The sinner goes out to his fields and selects a lamb or a young calf to be his sacrifice of atonement. He brings his sacrifice to the priest and the priest inspects it to be sure it is a perfect sacrifice suitable for atonement. The guilty man lays his hands upon the animal's head. Then the sacrificial animal is slain. The priest takes the blood and sprinkles it upon the altar that is by the door of the tabernacle.

What does this all mean? What is the significance of this solemn ceremony? Why was it done? There are many lessons to be gathered from the various sacrifices of the Old Testament. The burnt offering, the meat offering, the peace offering, and the sin offering all have a distinct reference to some aspect of the atoning work of Christ. If in the minds of the priest and the worshipper they did not signify that one great Sacrifice who was to come, the Lord Jesus Christ, then they were mere empty rituals. Indeed, this is what they became during the days of Isaiah (Isaiah 66:3). All those elaborate ceremonies and sacrifices of the Old Testament were designed by God to point men to Christ, the true atonement and propitiation of sin. I want to show you the typical meaning of one part of this divinely prescribed ceremony of the Levitical era; portraying faith in Christ.

Here are two things of utmost importance. Without these two things you will perish: first is the precious blood of Christ and second is faith in that blood. Even in Leviticus these were the two essential elements in the sacrifices of the ceremonial law. Both are set before us in Leviticus 1:4, 5. 'He shall put his hand upon the head of the offering.' Here is the sinner expressing faith in the atoning blood of God's appointed sacrifice. 'He shall kill the bullock before the Lord.' Here is the picture of the death of Christ, God's sacrifice for sin.

God will never receive or accept anyone, except through a Sacrifice. God Almighty requires blood, either yours or that of a substitutionary sacrifice. But this is the marvel of God's wonderful grace. God has provided himself a Sacrifice for human sin! Behold, the Lamb of God! Jesus Christ, God's own well-beloved Son is the Sacrifice, the only Sacrifice God will accept. Christ is the Sacrifice God appointed and set apart. The Lamb of God was inspected by the high priests of Israel and found to be without spot or blemish. This Lamb was slain by the very men for whom he died, under the wrath of God, and accepted by God himself as a sweet-smelling savour.

The Sacrifice was provided. He was slain under the penalty of the law. And God has accepted him. Yet, there is one essential thing remaining without which you will die. You must lay your hands upon the head of God's sacrifice. This is an act of faith. Isaac Watts wrote,

> My faith doth lay her hand
> On that dear head of Thine,
> While like a penitent I stand,
> And there confess my sin.
>
> My soul looks back to see
> The burdens Thou didst bear,
> When hanging on the cursed tree,
> And hopes her guilt was there.

Believing, we rejoice
To see the curse remove;
We bless the Lamb with cheerful voice,
And sing His bleeding love.

Faith in Christ is symbolized in the Old Testament by a man laying his hands on the head of the sacrificial lamb. This is the one thing you must do. You must lay your hands of faith upon the head of Christ, God's Sacrifice for sin. When a man came and laid his hands upon the head of the sacrifice, it meant four things to him.

Confession
Picture the man. He is standing beside the sacrifice at the door of the tabernacle before God's priest; he lays both of his hands upon the head of that innocent animal. What does it mean? It means, first, that he is making a solemn, sincere, and public confession. This is what we do when we come to God, leaning upon Christ. We are making a confession to him.

Laying my hands upon the head of God's Sacrifice, I confess my sins. 'If we confess our sins, he is faithful and just to forgive us our sins, and to cleanse us from all unrighteousness' (1 John 1:9). This was the thing foremost in the mind of the ancient Jew when he brought a sacrifice of any kind before the Lord. He was acknowledging his sin. The only reason I need a sacrifice is because I am a sinner (Leviticus 16:21). So, too, you and I must come to God confessing our sin. Those who lay their hands on Christ acknowledge their sinfulness.

Sin must be confessed. I am a sinner by birth. I am a sinner by choice. I am a sinner by practice. All I am and do is marred by sin. Like the leper, everything I touch I defile. All is stained by sin.

And we must confess our sin sincerely. Sin with us is more than a theory. We have tasted its bitter poison. We have known and felt the evil of sin. God's Lamb is given as a sacrifice for sinners. The righteous, the innocent, and the good have no need of him; and they cannot have him. The Saviour is provided for none but sinners. Here is our true place. We lean heavily upon the Saviour because we are sinners. We plead guilty to the dreadful indictment of God's holy law; and we are therefore glad to lay our hands upon the Sacrifice for sin.

This act is also a confession of impotence. Not only am I a sinner, I am a helpless sinner. There is nothing I can do to help myself. I must have Christ as a sacrifice for my sin. I cannot keep God's law for myself. I cannot make atonement for my past sins. I cannot hope to gain acceptance with God by my future obedience. Christ is precious to us, because we cannot do without him. If I am not accepted before God upon the merits of Christ's righteousness and shed blood, I am a damned man, utterly without hope!

We must have the blood of Christ as an atonement and covering for our sin. Something must cover us to keep the eye of God from seeing our sin. The blood of Christ so thoroughly covers us that God beholds no blemish in us! I stand before God laying my hands upon the head of Christ, leaning my entire soul upon him, because I am an impotent man.

Laying my hands upon the head of God's Sacrifice, I confess I deserve to die. When a man brought his calf, or goat, or lamb and put his hands upon its head, he knew the poor creature must die. By this act, he confessed he deserved to die. As the innocent lamb fell in the dust in pain, struggling, bleeding, dying, the man confessed, 'This is what I deserve from the hand of God. Death is my due'. If ever you come to see this, you will lean hard upon Christ, and acknowledge that the death he died you deserved to die (Psalm 51:1-4). If God had been pleased to send me to hell, it would be no more than I deserve. He would have been both righteous and just in doing it. But, instead, he poured out my hell upon his Son! 'The chastisement of our peace was upon him, and with his stripes we are healed' (Isaiah 53:5).

Come, sinner, lay your hands upon Christ's head in humble, sincere confession. 'I am a guilty sinner, unable to do anything to help myself, and worthy of eternal damnation. But I trust Christ to save me.'

Repentance

Second, when a man laid his hands upon the head of the sacrifice, he was saying, 'I accept and bow to God's remedy for sin, I repent'. When a sinner comes to trust Christ, he confesses and acknowledges his acceptance of God's salvation. That is the essence of true repentance. Repentance is, in its essence, taking sides with God.

Laying my hands of faith upon Christ I testify to God and to all men that I believe God and bow to his plan and purpose of salvation by a substitute (Romans 5:12-21). But there is more. Having accepted the gospel of substitution, I accept, bow to, and receive the substitute himself. Salvation is not in a plan. It is in a person. Salvation is not in the doctrine of substitution. It is in the Divine Substitute. We rest our souls not upon a doctrine, but upon the Lord Jesus Christ himself. We cast ourselves entirely upon him. We receive him.

Only those who receive Christ are saved by Christ. It is true, our salvation is God accepting and receiving us in Christ; and acceptance of our souls in Christ is eternal, from everlasting (Romans 8:29, 30; Ephesians 1:3-6). 'The works were finished from the foundation of the world' (Hebrews 4:3). Yet, we must receive the Lord Jesus Christ. We must bow to, embrace, and receive him by faith (John 1:11-13). Faith in Christ is just as necessary for our eternal salvation as our Saviour's death upon the cursed tree as our Substitute.

Transference
Thirdly, when the sinner laid his hands on the head of the sacrifice, he was expressing faith in a marvellous transference (Leviticus 16:21). In a typical sense, that man's sin and guilt were transferred from him to the innocent lamb and that lamb's innocence and perfection were transferred to him. The whole thing was done in anticipation of our Lord's death at Calvary.

When a sinner comes to Christ by faith accepting him as Saviour, he is saying, 'I agree with the mighty and mysterious transaction that took place long ago on Calvary's brow'. This mighty transaction took place and was completed when the Son of God stood in our place at Calvary (2 Corinthians 5:21). God Almighty made his Son sin for us; and he has made us the very righteousness of God in his Son. By faith we simply accept the finished work, adding nothing to it. Laying my hands upon the head of my Redeemer, I rest my soul upon this mighty transaction trusting the complete efficacy of God's Sacrifice.

Identification
In the last place, laying my hands of faith upon the head of Christ, there is identification between the sinner and the Substitute. I think that if the man's heart was right, and he was not a mere ritualist, as he watched that lamb struggle, and bleed, and die, his eyes must have welled with tears. He must have said in his heart, 'That death is mine'. Now, child of God, come lay your hands upon the head of our Substitute, and

identify yourself with him. His death is our death, and now we cannot die again (2 Corinthians 5:14; Galatians 2:20).

Can you grasp this? If you are a believer, if you trust him, when Christ died you died. 'I am crucified with Christ, nevertheless I live.' 'Ye are dead and your life is hid with Christ in God.' In the person of your Substitute you paid your debt to God's law. When Christ arose, being accepted of God, you arose in him. As Christ is now a sweet-smelling savour to God, you are a sweet-smelling savour, 'accepted in the beloved'. Blessed be God, there is a real identification here. Christ and God's elect are one. Believing sinners and their Substitute are one. This union, this identification is both real and eternal. We are one with him, one with Christ, and complete in him. John Kent wrote,

> 'Twixt Jesus and the chosen race
> Subsists a bond of sovereign grace,
> That hell, with its infernal train,
> Shall ne'er dissolve nor rend in vain

In him dwelleth all the fulness of the Godhead bodily. And ye are complete in him, which is the head of all principality and power (Colossians 2:9, 10).

But of him are ye in Christ Jesus, who of God is made unto us wisdom, and righteousness, and sanctification, and redemption: That, according as it is written, He that glorieth, let him glory in the Lord (1 Corinthians 1:30, 31).

Chapter 4

The Sacrifices Of The Poor

And if his offering be of the flocks, namely, of the sheep, or of the goats, for a burnt sacrifice; he shall bring it a male without blemish. And he shall kill it on the side of the altar northward before the LORD: and the priests, Aaron's sons, shall sprinkle his blood round about upon the altar. And he shall cut it into his pieces, with his head and his fat: and the priest shall lay them in order on the wood that is on the fire which is upon the altar: But he shall wash the inwards and the legs with water: and the priest shall bring it all, and burn it upon the altar: it is a burnt sacrifice, an offering made by fire, of a sweet savour unto the LORD. And if the burnt sacrifice for his offering to the LORD be of fowls, then he shall bring his offering of turtledoves, or of young pigeons. And the priest shall bring it unto the altar, and wring off his head, and burn it on the altar; and the blood thereof shall be wrung out at the side of the altar: And he shall pluck away his crop with his feathers, and cast it beside the altar on the east part, by the place of the ashes: And he shall cleave it with the wings thereof, but shall not divide it asunder: and the priest shall burn it upon the altar, upon the wood that is upon the fire: it is a burnt sacrifice, an offering made by fire, of a sweet savour unto the LORD.

Leviticus 1:10-17

I once read a story about a little boy, ten or eleven years old, whose sister needed a blood transfusion. The doctor explained that she had the same disease the boy had recovered from two years earlier. Her only chance for recovery was a blood transfusion from someone who had previously beaten the disease. Since the two children had the same rare blood type, the boy was the ideal donor. 'Would you give your blood to Mary?' the doctor asked. Johnny hesitated. His lower lip began to quiver. Then he smiled and said, 'Sure, for my sister'.

Soon the two children were wheeled into the hospital room. Mary was pale and thin. Johnny was robust and healthy. Neither spoke, but when they met, Johnny grinned. As the nurse put the needle into his arm, Johnny's smile faded. He watched the blood flow through the tube. When the ordeal was almost over, the boy's shaky voice broke the silence. 'Doctor, when do I die?'

Only then did the doctor realise why Johnny had hesitated, why his lip had quivered when he agreed to donate his blood. He thought giving his blood to his sister meant giving up his life. In that brief moment he had made a great, momentous decision, and was willingly resolved to lay down his life for the sister he dearly loved.

In fact, though he thought it was necessary, Johnny did not have to die to save his sister. However, you and I have a condition far more serious than Mary's. It required the blood of God's own Son, the Lord Jesus Christ, to cure us.

It is written, 'Christ died the just for the unjust, that he might bring us to God. With his stripes we are healed'. The Lord of glory poured out his life's blood unto death at Calvary as the Lamb of God, that he might redeem us from the curse of the law and give us eternal life. Christ died that we might live. Why? Because he loved us with an everlasting love; and 'having loved his own which were in the world, he loved us to the end'. Willingly, voluntarily, the Son of God laid down his life for the people he loved, his chosen bride, his church, his sister, his spouse, his beloved (Romans 5:6-11; 2 Corinthians 5:21; Galatians 3:13, 14).

I want us to look again at our Lord's great sacrifice, asking God the Holy Spirit to make his work real and effectual to our hearts.

In this first chapter of Leviticus, the Lord God describes the sacrifices of burnt offerings by which sinners drew near to God in the typical, ceremonial worship of the legal dispensation.[1] In the first nine

---

[1] In the Old Testament, those who worshipped God did not trust those sacrifices they brought to the tabernacle to give them access to and acceptance with God. That would

verses of this chapter, the Lord God gave instructions concerning the burnt-offering sacrifice of bullocks. In verses 10-17 we read about the sacrifices of the flocks and the fowls. These sacrifices were the sacrifices of the poor.

These burnt offerings, like all the sacrifices of the Old Testament, typified our Lord Jesus Christ, God's one, great, effectual, sin-atoning Sacrifice, by whose blood we have been redeemed.

Sacrifices of the Flocks
In verses 10-13, the Holy Spirit describes the sacrifices of the flocks, taken from the sheep or the goats. Let us read these verses again.

> And if his offering be of the flocks, namely, of the sheep, or of the goats, for a burnt sacrifice; he shall bring it a male without blemish. And he shall kill it on the side of the altar northward before the LORD: and the priests, Aaron's sons, shall sprinkle his blood round about upon the altar. And he shall cut it into his pieces, with his head and his fat: and the priest shall lay them in order on the wood that is on the fire which is upon the altar: But he shall wash the inwards and the legs with water: and the priest shall bring it all, and burn it upon the altar: it is a burnt sacrifice, an offering made by fire, of a sweet savour unto the LORD. (Leviticus 1:10-13)

The worship of God is not a spectator sport. The worshipper was actively involved in the sacrifice, picturing the believer's faith in Christ and confession of guilt before God.

Here the victims offered from the flocks must be either from the sheep or from the goats.

One cannot help noticing there are many different sacrifices by which Christ and his redemptive work are portrayed in the Old Testament. In this one chapter, bullocks, sheep, goats, turtledoves and pigeons are all used as types of Christ. Why so many types?

No one type could ever accurately portray our Saviour. Yet, as John Gill points out, each of these sacrifices were very good and fit types and

---

have been idolatry. Those who worshipped God in that typical age, worshipped God trusting Christ, the Lamb of God, represented, typified, and pictured in those sacrifices.

emblems of the sinner's Substitute. The bullock, or young ox, portrayed both our Redeemer's strength and labour. The sheep, like our Lord, is harmless, innocent, and patient.

The goat is also a proper type of Christ, both because it is stronger than the sheep and because it is commonly looked upon as a dirty, unclean animal. Though our Lord had no sin and did no sin, he was thought to be a sinner and accused of horrid evils. Indeed, he came here in the likeness of sinful flesh, and was made to be sin for us, having all the sins of God's elect made his, that he might justly die under the penalty of God's holy law for sin.

Turtledoves and Pigeons

The turtledove and the pigeon beautifully portray our Saviour's meekness, humility, and grace, as well as the peace he brings to his people. The offering from the flocks could be either a sheep or a goat. Those who were wealthier in Israel offered sacrifices of bullocks or oxen unto the Lord for burnt-offerings. The princes in Israel all offered such sacrifices (Numbers 7). Those who were poorer offered sheep or goats. The poorest of the people offered turtledoves or pigeons.

God is no respecter of persons, and even in the law he took great care to show that he is no respecter of persons. The upper class, the middle class, and the poor, all have access to and acceptance with the Lord God through the merits of Christ. In Christ there is neither Jew nor Gentile, male nor female, learned nor unlearned, rich nor poor; but Christ is all and in all.

The Saviour of the world is equally within the reach of sinners among all people. Our great High Priest welcomes sinners under the broad, wide phrase, 'Him that cometh unto me' (John 6:37). No sound is sweeter to the ears of our Aaron than the sound of a sinner, great or small, coming to God by him.

These sacrifices of the flocks also point to our Lord Jesus Christ as the Lamb of God. The lamb stands out in Scripture as the eminent sacrifice of the Old Testament age, and rightly so. The morning and evening sacrifice, the every day sacrifice, and the every year passover sacrifice portrayed to Israel that which Isaiah declared. 'He was led as a lamb to the slaughter' (Isaiah 53:7). All the priests of Israel proclaimed exactly the same thing that all the prophets of God proclaimed. Pointing in their ceremonies and sacrifices to the Lord

Jesus Christ, they said, every morning, every evening, every year, 'Behold, the Lamb of God that taketh away the sin of the world'.

The place of sacrifice for the lambs is distinctly described in verse eleven. 'And he shall kill it on the side of the altar northward before the LORD: and the priests, Aaron's sons, shall sprinkle his blood round about upon the altar'.

There is a distinction made here which was not made regarding the sacrifices from the herds. The sacrifice from the flocks must be killed 'on the north side of the altar'. Psalm 48 gives us the reason for this.

> Great is the LORD, and greatly to be praised in the city of our God, in the mountain of his holiness. Beautiful for situation, the joy of the whole earth, is mount Zion, on the sides of the north, the city of the great King. God is known in her palaces for a refuge (Psalm 48:1-3).

The Lord Jesus Christ, our sin offering, was killed by the priests of Israel in Jerusalem, in Mount Zion, which was on 'the sides of the north'. Specifically, our Saviour was crucified on Mount Calvary, which is on the northwest side of Jerusalem, at precisely the spot where the morning sacrifice had been slaughtered every day for hundreds of years!

Do you not stand in awe and utter amazement when you realise how precise the Scriptures are in prophecy and in type? Any man who denounces the book of God as a myth, a book of religious fables, and denies its infallibility, inerrancy, and inspiration reveals nothing by his words but insolence, rebellion, and enmity of heart against God. He prefers wilful ignorance rather than acknowledge the Almighty.

Unlike the bullock (v. 6), there was no requirement that the sheep and goats be flayed. Flaying the bullock portrayed the helplessness of the sinner stripped and naked, without a covering, before the holy Lord God. But the sheep and goat are naturally helpless, defenceless animals. Our attention is fixed rather on the slaughter of the victim by the knife, hewing the animal in pieces and making it ready for the fire.

Thus, when the Lord God cried, 'Awake, O sword, against my shepherd, and against the man that is my fellow ... smite the shepherd, and the sheep shall be scattered. (Zechariah 13:7), our Saviour, the Lamb of God, was pierced to his very soul, smitten indeed of God, when the Almighty poured out the fire of his holy wrath upon our Surety's head.

Both the worshipper and the priests performed the ceremonial ritual of sacrificing the burnt-offering with great reverence, carefully observing the order God prescribed.

> And he shall cut it into his pieces, with his head and his fat: and the priest shall lay them in order on the wood that is on the fire which is upon the altar: But he shall wash the inwards and the legs with water: and the priest shall bring it all, and burn it upon the altar: it is a burnt sacrifice, an offering made by fire, of a sweet savour unto the LORD (Leviticus 1:12, 13).

The same honour was given to the sacrifices of the poor as was given to the sacrifices of the rich, because the only thing that gave either sacrifice significance and importance was the great antitype they represented, the Lamb of God.

John Trapp, on verse 12 regarding the dividing of the sacrifice, says gospel preachers 'must rightly divide the Word of God (2 Timothy 2:15) and evidently set forth Christ crucified (Galatians 3:1)'.

The washing of the inward parts and legs speaks of our Saviour's righteousness and purity, both inwardly and outwardly.

The sacrificial laws were very simple and crystal clear. But we must not allow ourselves to be taken up with the ceremony. It is not the ceremony that made atonement, but the sacrifice.

Understand what I am saying. It is not the meekness and humility of Christ that saves us, but the meek and humble Lamb of God, our Lord Jesus Christ. It is not the righteousness of Christ that saves us, but Christ who is our righteousness. It is not substitution that that saves us, but Christ our Substitute. It is not the sovereignty of Christ that saves us, but Christ our sovereign God. Again, understand me. We do not separate the work of Christ from the person of Christ. But the work of Christ is not the object of our faith. Christ is! The work of Christ is not our Saviour. Christ is!

In verses 14-17, the Holy Spirit describes the offerings of the fowls, the sacrifices of turtledoves and young pigeons, young doves, unto the Lord. We shall consider this sacrifice more specifically in the next chapter but for the moment let us summarise a few points.

And if the burnt sacrifice for his offering to the LORD be of fowls, then he shall bring his offering of turtledoves, or of young pigeons. And the priest shall bring it unto the altar, and wring off his head, and burn it on the altar; and the blood thereof shall be wrung out at the side of the altar: And he shall pluck away his crop with his feathers, and cast it beside the altar on the east part, by the place of the ashes: And he shall cleave it with the wings thereof, but shall not divide it asunder: and the priest shall burn it upon the altar, upon the wood that is upon the fire: it is a burnt sacrifice, an offering made by fire, of a sweet savour unto the LORD (Leviticus 1:14-17).

The dove, too, was a beautiful type of our Saviour (Song of Solomon 2:12; 5:12) in its meekness and humility, chastity and purity, tenderness and peace. It was the dove that brought the olive branch back to Noah in the ark, declaring that wrath was done, judgment was over, the storm had ended. And it is the voice of Christ in the gospel that comes in the springtime of grace declaring peace to guilty sinners upon the ground of justice satisfied!

Turtledoves and pigeons were bountiful in the land of Israel, so bountiful that any man, no matter how poor, could easily lay hold on one and bring it to God. The doves were free for the taking. What a picture! The Lord Jesus Christ is a bountiful, plenteous Redeemer, with whom is plenteous redemption. He is such a large, bountiful Saviour that any poor sinner in all the world may lay hold on him and bring God Almighty the very Sacrifice he requires.

Though we have nothing to offer God, he bids us come and buy without money and without price. Like the dove in Israel, the Lord Jesus Christ is free for the taking.

A Violent Death

The turtledove was slaughtered violently. The priest wrung off its neck, squeezed out its blood, and cut it into pieces. Then the priest burned it with fire. Thus, the Lord of glory was slaughtered under the violence of God's holy, unmitigated wrath when he was made sin for us! Our Lord Jesus Christ was slain by our hands and slain by the purpose and justice of God.

41

Sweet-smelling Savour

Like the bullock and the lamb, the sacrifice of the dove was a sweet-smelling savour unto God, a sacrifice accepted. That is what Christ has done for us (Ephesians 5:2).

The great sacrifice of our Lord Jesus Christ is the glorious theme of Scripture from beginning to end. He is the one in whom alone and by whom alone sinners have hope. From the dawn of time to the end of time, all who trust God trust him who is the Seed of the woman, by whose death upon the cursed tree, God Almighty is just and the Justifier of all who believe.

Adam and Eve worshipped God through a blood sacrifice in the Garden. Abraham offered these very same sacrifices unto the Lord (Genesis 15:9, 10). Abraham spoke of our Lord Jesus Christ as both God and the Lamb, by whose sacrifice God would deliver his chosen from the sentence of death.

I pray God the Holy Spirit will grant you grace to lay hold on Christ, the Lamb of God. He is a Lamb slain, a turtledove near at hand. He is free for the taking. Bring this Sacrifice to God and find acceptance with him forever. He will be for you a perpetual sweet-smelling savour before God, and he will make you a perpetual sweet-smelling savour to God (Ecclesiastes 9:7).

Chapter 5

Turtledoves Or Pigeons

And if the burnt sacrifice for his offering to the LORD be of fowls, then he shall bring his offering of turtledoves, or of young pigeons. And the priest shall bring it unto the altar, and wring off his head, and burn it on the altar; and the blood thereof shall be wrung out at the side of the altar: And he shall pluck away his crop with his feathers, and cast it beside the altar on the east part, by the place of the ashes: And he shall cleave it with the wings thereof, but shall not divide it asunder: and the priest shall burn it upon the altar, upon the wood that is upon the fire: it is a burnt sacrifice, an offering made by fire, of a sweet savour unto the LORD.

Leviticus 1:14-17

Sinners cannot come to God without a sacrifice. We all know that. God has stamped this fact upon the consciences of all men by creation. Every man in the world knows that God is, that God is both holy and just, and that he will punish sin (Romans 1:18-20). Everyone knows by nature that God demands righteousness and satisfaction (Romans 2:14, 15). Every man knows by nature, because God has stamped it indelibly upon his conscience, that sin demands blood atonement. It is for this reason that throughout history, in all parts of the world, civilized and barbaric, men and women have attempted to appease the wrath of God and ease their consciences of guilt by blood sacrifices.

This natural God consciousness, from which no man in this world can ever completely escape, is never a saving knowledge of God, but always condemning. The depravity of man's heart and his heart enmity against God perverts his judgment and always turns him away from light into darkness. In obstinate rebellion, he holds or holds down and suppresses the truth of God in unrighteousness, and turns the truth of God into a lie, changing 'the glory of the incorruptible God into an image made like unto corruptible man' (Romans 1:23-25).

Four Undeniable Facts

Still, these are facts known by all men. The heathen know them and you know them. No matter how sternly you try to suppress them, you know these are facts from which you cannot escape.

1. God is holy, righteous and just. He must and will punish sin.
2. We are sinners, guilty and under the curse of God.
3. God demands both righteousness and satisfaction.
4. We shall meet God in judgment.

If you think about these things without Christ, they torment your soul. So, you try to put them out of your mind. But they keep gnawing at you. You will never be able to find the answer to the demands these things make upon your conscience until you learn from God's own Word why these things are so, and how the great and glorious Lord God who made you can forgive your sin completely and make you completely and perfectly righteous, without sin.

Are you interested in these things? Would you like to have your conscience pacified? What would you give to be able to think honestly about yourself, your sin, God Almighty, righteousness, judgment, and eternity all without fear?

From the very beginning God has demanded satisfaction for sin; and from the very beginning he has declared that he would get satisfaction from a substitute, by blood atonement. From the very beginning the Lord God promised he will forgive sin; but he has also declared he will forgive sin only by blood atonement. It is written, 'without shedding of blood is no remission' (Hebrews 9:22).

The holy Lord God demands blood atonement; and he provides what he demands in Christ. That is what is taught in the typical sacrifices he demanded of Israel under the Mosaic law, as they are described in Leviticus chapter 1. I want to show you from the book of God what God teaches us about the glorious work of our great God and glorious

Saviour, Jesus Christ, in the typical sacrifices of turtledoves or pigeons spoken of in Leviticus 1:14-17.

The sacrifices of burnt offering could be a sacrifice chosen from the herd or from the flock or from the fowls. If it was a sacrifice from the herd it must be a male without blemish. If it was taken from among the sheep or the goats it also had to be a male without blemish.

However, if the sacrifice offered was from the fowls it may be male or female; and there was no requirement it must be without blemish. That was not by accident but by divine decree. In order to save us, the holy Lamb of God, a male who was taken from a woman and the Seed of woman, must be made to be sin for us (2 Corinthians 5:21).

Old Testament Examples

All who ever knew God came to him with a blood sacrifice. Believing God, Adam (Genesis 3:15, 21), Abel (Genesis 4:3-5), Noah (Genesis 8:20-22), Abraham (Genesis 15:9-11; 22:8), and Moses (Exodus 12:1-13), all believed the promise God made in Genesis 3:15 and offered typical sacrifices which by divine institution represented the Lord Jesus Christ, the Lamb of God.

They did not trust those sacrifices that typified Christ. Those sacrifices could never take away sin (Hebrews 10:1-14). Thy were not heathen. They were taught of God.

They trusted Christ. God did not save sinners in the Old Testament either by their works or by their legal sacrifices and ceremonies which were typical. God did not save his elect in the Old Testament in a different way. They were saved as we are by grace alone through faith alone, in, with, and by Christ alone. They were not saved on credit. Christ is the Lamb of God slain from the foundation of the world (Revelation 13:8; Hebrews 4:3).

If you and I would find atonement and righteousness, if we would find acceptance with God, we must, like those ancient believers, look to Christ, the Lamb of God. We must believe on the Son of God (Romans 3:19-26; 8:1-4).

This gospel message of blood atonement and substitutionary redemption is taught in Leviticus 1:14-17, in typical sacrifices of turtledoves or pigeons.

Types of Christ

These sacrifices, the turtledoves and the pigeons, are distinct eminent types of the Lord Jesus Christ as our Saviour (v. 14). The Lord Jesus Christ in his manhood always identified himself with the poor and needy because he came here to redeem and save poor, needy, helpless, destitute, bankrupt sinners. Men and women who have nothing to offer God (Luke 2:21-30).

Turtledoves and pigeons are held out in Holy Scripture as excellent, eminent types of our Saviour. The dove is not only the epitome of humility, meekness, devotion, and purity, it is also the constant emblem of peace and reconciliation. It is recognised as such the world over; but that fact is really insignificant.

The dove is held before us in Holy Scripture as the type, picture, and symbol of peace, of Christ who is our peace. After our Lord Jesus Christ had, by the sacrifice of himself, completely and forever exhausted the wrath of God for his people, he sent the Holy Spirit, the Dove of Heaven, to his church, declaring reconciliation by blood atonement (Acts 2). This is what was symbolized in our Lord's baptism (Matthew 3:13-17).

When the time of love comes for the calling of Christ's redeemed ones he sends the Dove of heaven with the olive branch of peace declaring justice is satisfied, wrath is gone, judgment is over, and reconciliation is accomplished. This is the gospel, and what the blood of Christ speaks to the believing conscience (Hebrews 9:14).

Violently Slaughtered

As the dove was slain by the priest, with one violent stroke, so the Lord Jesus Christ, our all-glorious Saviour, was slain by the violent stroke of God's holy wrath when he bore our sins in his own body on the cross (v. 15). If we did not understand by divine revelation what this scene represented, it would be an abhorrent thing to behold. But, blessed be our God, we understand what was portrayed here. God explained it to us plainly by his prophet Isaiah.

> Yet it pleased the LORD to bruise him; he hath put him to grief: when thou shalt make his soul an offering for sin, he shall see his seed, he shall prolong his days, and the pleasure of the LORD shall prosper in his hand. he shall see of the travail of his

soul, and shall be satisfied: by his knowledge shall my righteous servant justify many; for he shall bear their iniquities' (Isaiah 53:10, 11).

This thing was done before the Lord. And the dove's blood was squeezed from its slaughtered body not upon the altar, but over the side of the altar for all to see. There it ran down to the ground beneath the altar and symbolically spoke for God's elect beneath the altar (Revelation 6:9), those for whom the blood was shed.

Like the blood of Abel, the blood of the slain dove cried from the ground. Just as Abel's blood cried out for vengeance upon Cain who had murdered him, the blood of the dove, the blood of Christ, cries out from the altar of God. But Christ's blood speaks better things than the blood of Abel. Our Saviour's blood cries out perpetually for the forgiveness of those very sinners by whose hands, and for whose sins he was slain.

Sin Put Away

As this slain dove's entrails, its crop, were ripped out and its feathers plucked out and thrown away on the east side of the altar in the place of ashes (v. 16), our blessed Saviour has by the sacrifice of himself forever put away our sins.

Notice it was not the priest, but the sacrificing sinner who plucked off the crop with the feathers and cast it all by the place of ashes out of God's sight. We have absolutely nothing to do with the putting away of our sins, yet when we come to God trusting Christ, we do by faith cast them away. The crop refers to the entrails, the waste, the dung, the filth of the animal, typifying our sins. The feathers are the dove's covering, picturing our righteousnesses. Both have been forever cast away. The Lord God has cast away our sins and we have cast away our defiled works and self-righteousness.

Burnt Sacrifice

Like this dove, the Lord Jesus Christ was burned upon the altar of God, precisely as God himself ordained (v. 17). The dove had to be split, but not divided. Though its body was violently split down the middle, it was not to be divided or torn into two pieces. Remember, this, as all the sacrifice, was done by divine order exactly as God commanded because it represented Christ crucified for us by the determinate counsel of God.

When he died in our place, our Saviour's soul was separated from his body; but his humanity was not divided from his deity. Though he was forsaken by his Father as our Substitute when he was made sin for us, he was never divided from him as the Son of God. The union of the holy Trinity can never be broken. And, though our Redeemer died for us and has gone away into heaven, he can never be separated from his church, which is his body, 'the fulness of him that filleth all in all'. He said, 'Lo, I am with you alway'.

After the worshipper had split the dove of sacrifice, the priest took and burned it upon the altar. This slain dove, like our Lord Jesus, our crucified Redeemer, was 'a burnt sacrifice, an offering made by fire, of a sweet savour unto the Lord'. 'Christ also hath loved us, and hath given himself a sacrifice to God for a sweet smelling savour' (Ephesians 5:2).

When we read of these sacrifices, may God the Holy Spirit always remind us what they meant and send us to our knees with thanksgiving, praise, and rejoicing for God-given faith to believe the gospel here proclaimed. Since God has accepted the sacrifice, he has accepted the sinner for whom the sacrifice was made. Since God has accepted Christ, he has forever accepted those for whom Christ died. Since God has accepted the sinner's Substitute, he has forever, immutably, completely accepted every sinner who trusts his dear Son, because the Substitute and the sinner for whom he died are one; perfectly, completely, absolutely, and forever one.

How absolute is this union? Hear what God says in his Word and rejoice and give glory to God. Is Christ called the Dove? He calls his church 'My Dove'. Is the Lord Jesus called the Lily? He calls his church 'a lily'. We delight to say to him, 'Behold, thou art fair, my Beloved'. With equal, yea, with infinitely greater delight, he says to us, 'Behold, thou art fair, my love'. Is our Saviour the Son of God? We are the sons of God in him. Is this Man 'THE LORD OUR RIGHTEOUSNESS'? He declares that the name of his church is 'The Lord our righteousness'!

Oh, how sweet the gospel is to poor, needy sinners. Blessed Son of God, we are the sin you were made, and you are our Righteousness. We the death you died, and you are our Life. You have taken from us all that we are and all that was ours; and you have given to us all that you are and all that is yours (2 Corinthians 5:17-21).

Chapter 6

'He Shall Kill The Bullock'

And he shall kill the bullock before the LORD: and the priests, Aaron's sons, shall bring the blood, and sprinkle the blood round about upon the altar that is by the door of the tabernacle of the congregation.

Leviticus 1:5

The death of our Lord Jesus Christ was absolutely essential. The sacrifice for sin must be slain. It is only through the blood, which he shed at Calvary for human guilt that poor, guilty sinners can have the remission of sins. That is the thing set before us in the typical ceremony described in Leviticus 1:5.

Verse four is a picture of faith in Christ. 'And he shall put his hand upon the head of the burnt offering; and it shall be accepted for him to make atonement for him'. Here is a sinner coming to God with a sin offering, the offering God required. He puts his hands on the same head on which the Lord God laid his hands, symbolically agreeing to all that God has done. God and the believing sinner meet at the same place. Both are satisfied by the same sacrifice. That blood which satisfies the justice of the thrice-holy God satisfies the conscience of the believing sinner.

The words, 'He shall put his hand upon the head', are stronger in the original text than they appear in our translation. They can be translated, 'He shall lean his hand upon the head'. The very same words are used in Psalm 88:7. 'Thy wrath lieth (or leaneth) hard upon me'. Do you see the picture? Believing sinners lean their souls upon the same Sacrifice that God Almighty leaned his wrath.

Once the sinner had symbolically laid his sins upon the head of the sacrifice, he stepped aside, leaving his sins upon the appointed victim. He has done what God required him to do. Now, he can go home rejoicing, saying, 'I have put my hand upon the head of God's sacrifice. It shall be accepted for me to make atonement for me'. 'Blessed is the man to whom the Lord will not impute sin.'

But more than this is needed for atonement, forgiveness of sin, and justification before God. Believing God in itself will never atone for sin. The bullock must be killed. That is the typical picture given in verse five. 'And he shall kill the bullock before the LORD: and the priests, Aaron's sons, shall bring the blood, and sprinkle the blood round about upon the altar that is by the door of the tabernacle of the congregation'.

In this chapter I want to show you both the necessity and the benefits of Christ's death upon the cursed tree as our all-glorious Substitute and Saviour.

The Man
We are specifically told that the man who brought the sacrifice was to kill it before the Lord. This is a picture of the execution of divine wrath. It is proper that the man himself, the sinner, kill the animal because there are many executioners of divine wrath. Indeed, all things shall prove to be executioners of God's holy wrath upon the damned. As heaven, earth, and hell combined to execute the Lamb of God, so heaven, earth, and hell shall together execute the wrath of God upon the unbelieving soul forever.

The Priest
The man must kill the beast of sacrifice; but only the priest appointed by God himself could make atonement and dispense mercy on the basis of atonement made (Numbers 6:24-26). Only the priest can bestow pardon in the name of God. None but the Lord Jesus Christ, God's great High Priest could make atonement for our sins. None but Christ, God's great High Priest, can dispense mercy to and bestow pardon upon needy sinners.

50

The animal must be killed before the Lord. What an awesome sight, solemn and instructive in every detail. The priest catches the blood, the warm blood of life, the blood of the slain bullock in one of the bowls of the altar. All eyes are upon the priest and the blood, as he brings the sacrificed life to God.

Andrew Bonar wrote, 'It is as if the living soul of the sinner were carried in its utter helplessness and in all its filthiness and laid down before the Holy One'.

Then the blood is sprinkled. The priest takes the blood of the slain animal and sprinkles it 'round about upon the altar'. The life of the sacrifice has been taken away. The sinner stands, as it were, naked before God. There is no covering of his sin. He deserves the death symbolized in the animal's slaughter, death by the law of God, a violent death, death in the presence of the Lord, death for the punishment of sin, death for the satisfaction of holiness, wrath, justice, and truth.

As the blood on the door of the house on the night of the Lord's passover in Egypt represented the death of the firstborn in the house, so here, the blood on the altar represents the death of the sinner for whom the sacrifice is made. Thus, we are told that the Lord of Glory, the Son of God, our most blessed Christ, 'poured out his soul unto death' as our Substitute.

Notice, the blood is poured out and sprinkled both upon and 'round about' the altar. It is on all sides; north, south, east, and west, for all to see. Hear the voice of the Saviour's blood upon the altar. It cries out to sinners everywhere, 'Look unto me and be ye saved, all the ends of the earth'. The Lord Jesus Christ is God's appointed Sacrifice for sin. He is the only Sacrifice for sin. He is the infinitely meritorious and effectual Sacrifice for sin. He is the Sacrifice for sinners everywhere.

In all its details the slaying of the sacrificial bullock, as described in Leviticus 1:5, was typical of the death of Christ for us at Calvary.

Necessary

First, understand that the death of Christ as a sacrifice for sin was absolutely necessary. Many things were very important about the sacrifices of the Old Testament. But no atonement was made until the victim was slain. Even so, the Lamb of God must be slain in order to make an atonement for sin. 'It behooved him to suffer.' Had he not died, he would not have a people with him in glory (John 12:24).

Atonement and the remission of sins are not in the life of the sacrifice, but in its death (Leviticus 17:11; Hebrews 9:22). The question is sometimes raised, 'Why was it necessary and essential for Christ to die?' Many answers are given in the Scriptures.

Jesus Christ, the Lamb of God, must die in order to fulfil the types and prophecies of the Old Testament Scriptures. The Word of God overflows with statements about the death of Christ. It was as much a subject of Old Testament prophecy as it is of New Testament declaration. The most instructive Old Testament type of redemption by Christ is that of the Passover lamb (Exodus 12:13).

The Lord God declares, 'When I see the blood, I will pass over you'. God's eye resting on the blood is evidence that a substitutionary lamb has been slain and guarantees the life of the sinner. This is atonement. David prophesied that through his death, and only through his death, Christ would establish his universal kingdom (Psalm 22:1, 22, 25-28). Isaiah tells us that the death of the Lamb is the source of his conquest and the cause of his reward (Isaiah 53:12).

As the death of Christ was the subject of the Old Testament types and prophecies, it is the theme of the New Testament as well. There is no redemption and remission of sins but by the Son of God pouring out his life's blood as an atoning sacrifice for sin (Hebrews 9:12). Redemption and the remission of sin is not accomplished by the life of Christ, the example of Christ, our repentance toward Christ, our faith in Christ, or our obedience to Christ. Sin must be purged away by the blood of Christ, 'in whom we have redemption through his blood, the forgiveness of sins'. 'The blood of Jesus Christ, God's Son, cleanseth us from all sin.'

The death and shed blood of Christ is the centre of all true Gospel preaching. It is the essential element of the ordinances of the gospel. Baptism is a confession of faith in the death of Christ, 'the fulfilment of all righteousness'. The Lord's Supper is a remembrance of the Lord's death. 'This is my blood in the New Testament, which is shed for many for the remission of sins.'

Never forget, child of God, we are redeemed to God by the blood of Christ. The Sacrifice must be slain. Blood must be shed. The blood of Christ will be the theme of our songs in heaven, and it ought to be here.

Above all, the sacrifice must be slain, or God could never have justified any sinner. No sinner ever could be saved, accepted, forgiven, pardoned, and justified in the sight of God if Jesus Christ had not been slain as the Substitute of sinners (Romans 3:24-26). Only through the sin-atoning sacrifice of his own dear Son can the holy Lord God be 'a just God and a Saviour' (Isaiah 45:21).

Death is the result and penalty of sin. Once Christ had our sins laid upon him, once he who knew no sin was made sin for us, he must die. Nothing could satisfy the law and justice of God but death. The death of Christ is the only way possible for God to save sinners. Without the shedding of his blood, without the death of God's darling Son, salvation is not possible.

There are things even God cannot do. God cannot lie. God cannot forgive sin without satisfaction. God cannot punish sin again, once satisfaction has been made. The death of Christ was absolutely necessary to give peace to a guilty conscience (Hebrews 9:14).

Infinite and Effectual
Second, I want you to see that the death of Christ is infinite in its merit, and effectual in its purpose and power. This gives peace and comfort to my heart and soul. Since Jesus Christ has paid the great debt I owed to the law of God, I am freed from the debt and justified before the law. 'He that is dead is freed from sin' (Romans 6:7). The atoning sacrifice of Christ means complete redemption is fully accomplished.

Those typical sacrifices of the law we read about in the book of Leviticus could never put away sin. But, when our Lord was fastened to the tree and cried, 'It is finished', he finished the transgression and made an end of sin and brought in an everlasting righteousness (Hebrews 10:1-4; Colossians 2:13, 14).

All that Christ intended to do in his great sacrificial atonement, he has done. How do we know the death of Christ is effectual? I know Christ cannot fail in his work because I know he is God. To deny the efficacy of his blood is to deny our Saviour is God! His sacrifice is of infinite value, of infinite merit, and infinite in its efficacy, completely efficacious in its design. I know the death of Christ is effectual because he is the perfect man, the God-man Mediator. 'He knew no sin.' 'He shall not fail.'

Furthermore, I know the sacrifice of Christ is effectual because of the substitutionary character of his death. The death of Christ was as much an act of divine justice as it was an act of divine mercy. Christ voluntarily laid down his life for us. The Son of God took the place of his people upon the cross and our Lord was triumphant in his death. I know the sacrificial death of Christ is effectual because of his covenant engagements. He came into the world in our flesh to fulfil his own agreements with the Father as our Surety in the covenant of grace. I know the death of Christ is effectual, because God has testified that it is. Our Lord himself said, 'It is finished'. He was raised again the third day as a testimony of completed justification (Romans 4:25). He is seated in heaven now because his work is gloriously effectual (Hebrews 10:10-14). He cannot fail!

Calvary School
In the third place, the sacrificial death of Christ gives us the best instruction about the weightiest matters. The best school of theology in the world is the school at Mount Calvary. There is no school like Calvary School! Come to Calvary. Sit down at the foot of the cross. Behold there the Lamb of God and learn of him.

Here we learn that God is holy, we learn that God is just, we learn that sin is infinitely evil, we learn that God is infinitely gracious and 'he delighteth in mercy'. Here we learn the infinite character of God's love, we learn how that a man is justified with God, and how human sin is put away. Here we learn how to love one another and how to give. Here we learn how to live and serve our God.

Let those who choose to do so remain in the dark school of bondage found at Sinai. God's children are taught at Calvary and find all motivation at Calvary.

Motivation
In the last place, the death of Christ is the great source of inspiration and the motive of obedience in a believer's life. Did the Son of God die for me? Then I must surely consecrate myself entirely to him (Romans 12:1, 2). His death inspires me to seek his will, his honour, and his glory in every aspect of my life. Nothing has a greater power to inspire my heart with love for Christ than the realization of his dying love for me (2 Corinthians 5:14; 1 John 4:19). The only motive needed to constrain a believer to obey the Lord is this: 'He died for you'. Surely the knowledge of Christ's sacrifice for sin ought to inspire us to seek the salvation of sinners.

Chapter 7

The Meat Offerings

And when any will offer a meat offering unto the LORD, his offering shall be of fine flour; and he shall pour oil upon it, and put frankincense thereon: And he shall bring it to Aaron's sons the priests: and he shall take thereout his handful of the flour thereof, and of the oil thereof, with all the frankincense thereof; and the priest shall burn the memorial of it upon the altar, to be an offering made by fire, of a sweet savour unto the LORD: And the remnant of the meat offering shall be Aaron's and his sons': it is a thing most holy of the offerings of the LORD made by fire. And if thou bring an oblation of a meat offering baken in the oven, it shall be unleavened cakes of fine flour mingled with oil, or unleavened wafers anointed with oil. And if thy oblation be a meat offering baken in a pan, it shall be of fine flour unleavened, mingled with oil. Thou shalt part it in pieces, and pour oil thereon: it is a meat offering. And if thy oblation be a meat offering baken in the fryingpan, it shall be made of fine flour with oil. And thou shalt bring the meat offering that is made of these things unto the LORD: and when it is presented unto the priest, he shall bring it unto the altar. And the priest shall take from the meat offering a memorial thereof, and shall burn it upon the altar: it is an offering made by fire, of a sweet savour unto the LORD. And that which is left of the meat offering shall be Aaron's and his sons': it is a thing most holy of the offerings of the LORD made by fire. No meat offering, which ye shall bring unto the LORD, shall be made with leaven: for ye shall burn no leaven, nor any honey, in any offering of the LORD made by fire. As for the oblation of the firstfruits, ye shall offer them unto the LORD: but they shall not be burnt on the altar for a sweet savour. And every oblation of thy meat offering shalt thou season with salt; neither shalt thou suffer the salt of the covenant of thy God to be lacking from thy meat offering: with all thine offerings thou shalt offer salt. And if thou offer a meat offering of thy firstfruits unto the LORD, thou shalt offer for the meat offering of thy firstfruits green ears of corn dried by the fire, even corn beaten out of full ears. And thou shalt put oil upon it, and lay frankincense thereon: it is a meat offering. And the priest shall burn the memorial of it, part of the beaten corn thereof, and part of the oil thereof, with all the frankincense thereof: it is an offering made by fire unto the LORD.

Leviticus 2:1-16

In the first five chapters of Leviticus the Lord God gave the children of Israel his requirements for the various offerings they brought to him under the law. In chapter one burnt offerings; in chapter two meat offerings; in chapter three peace offerings; in chapter four sin offerings; in chapter five trespass offerings.

As we read about these offerings, we should always look for the Lord Jesus in them. They were given to Israel to be types and pictures of our blessed Saviour. The fruits of the earth, the fine flour, the oil and frankincense, and the daily lamb of the Israelite all pointed to him and had their fulfilment in him. As we read this portion of the book of God, we should do so praying for God the Holy Spirit to enlighten the eyes of our minds and hearts in the knowledge of him who loved us and gave himself for us. As required in the law, in this day of grace may all our offerings to God, by faith in Christ, have no leaven of works mingled with the all-perfect oblation of our Saviour. Seek nothing, bring nothing, depend upon nothing, know nothing, but Christ and him crucified. He alone is our atonement, righteousness, sanctification, peace, and acceptance with God.

Giving Thanks
These 16 verses of Inspiration are all about giving thanks to God. The meat offerings were offerings of thanksgiving to God. We ought to be very interested in that. May God ever make us a thankful people!

It is always discourteous when a person does not have the manners and common decency to say, 'Thank you', when someone has been kind to them, done something for them, or given something to them. It is an altogether greater evil in us that you and I need to be reminded to say, 'Thank you', to God our Saviour for wondrous grace richly bestowed upon us. Yet, we do need to be reminded in everything to give thanks.

This is a matter of great importance. The heart of all true worship is giving thanks. Only thankful hearts worship God. Only thankful souls serve him. Others may fear him. Others may pay tribute to him in one way or another. But only the thankful worship and serve him.

In this second chapter of Leviticus the Lord God gave Moses specific rules about meat offerings. There were other meat offerings required in the law. But these meat offerings were specifically offerings of thanksgiving to the Lord our God. These offerings were freewill offerings, offered voluntarily without compulsion of law. They represented a man voluntarily giving up himself to God with a thankful, willing heart. Still, though they were freewill offerings, they must be offered in the way God prescribed.

As the burnt-offering represented the value of Christ's work in the Father's estimation as our sin-atoning Substitute, giving 'himself for us, an offering and a sacrifice to God for a sweet smelling savour' (Ephesians 5:2), so the meat-offerings set forth our Saviour's perfect human character and conduct. They are clearly linked with his obedience to God as our Representative, by which he finished the work of bringing in an everlasting righteousness for us. This was the will of the Father that Christ came to perform, both the putting away of sin and the bringing in of an everlasting righteousness. He said, 'My meat is to do the will of him that sent me and to finish his work' (John 4:34). This work was completed by his obedience unto death (John 17:1-5; 19:30).

Our Lord's obedience, weaving out a righteous garment for us, was performed during his earthly life as a perfect man, as Jehovah's perfect, righteous Servant, but his righteousness could not be our righteousness except obedience in death put away our sins. Hence, the burnt offering is first made, then the meat offering, by which we celebrate full redemption, complete forgiveness, and perfect justification. What reason we have for thanksgiving to our God! 'O give thanks unto the LORD; call upon his name: make known his deeds among the people'

(Psalm 105:1). 'Praise ye the LORD. O give thanks unto the LORD; for he is good: for his mercy endureth forever' (Psalm 106:1).

The meat offering was always presented along with the burnt offering, or some other animal sacrifice, to show the connection between the pardon of sin and consecration to the Lord. The moment we receive the pardon of sin we become, experimentally, the property of our Redeemer. 'Ye are not your own, for ye are bought with a price' (1 Corinthians 6:19, 20). When Boaz bought Ruth, he claimed her inheritance. When the Lord Jesus Christ, our Kinsman-Redeemer, bought us, he bought all we are and all we possess.

Yet, as said before, the meat offerings, like the burnt offerings, speak of our Lord Jesus Christ, by whom alone our sacrifices of praise and thanksgiving are accepted with God (Hebrews 13:15; 1 Peter 2:5).

Cain's Offering
Cain brought a meat offering to the Lord and was rejected precisely because he did not bring a blood offering with his meat offering. Why did God have no respect for Cain and his offering? Why was Cain rejected? Why did the Lord God refuse to accept Cain's offering? The answer is declared throughout Holy Scripture. God will not and cannot accept the best of our sacrifices without blood atonement. Sin must be pardoned before we can bring the holy Lord God anything.

Bloodless Offering
Though the meat offering was a bloodless sacrifice, it was always connected with blood.

> And when any will offer a meat offering unto the LORD, his offering shall be of fine flour; and he shall pour oil upon it, and put frankincense thereon' (Leviticus 2:1).

There is nothing in the meat offering that even hints of sin. Our sins were dealt with in the burnt offering, in the sin-atoning sacrifice of Christ, and were thereby completely and forever put away. The meat offering portrays sinners perfect in the sight of God, accepted by the merits of Christ's blood.

It was not a bloody sacrifice, but consisted of fine flour, thoroughly sifted. It had no bran at all in it. There was nothing rough or uneven in it, speaking of both the perfect holiness and righteousness of our Saviour and of our perfect righteousness before God in him. That which is true of him is true of his church. We are accepted in him.

There was nothing coarse, rough, or uneven in the human nature of the Lord Jesus. Look at him through the whole course of his humiliation. There is nothing in him but fine flour. Nothing moved him from his purpose or caused him to hesitate in his course. Nothing prevented him from his obedience. Nothing kept him from doing good.

In all his person and character our blessed God-man Mediator is perfect. He is perfectly gracious and perfectly just, perfectly holy and perfectly kind, perfect in love and yet without compromise. Circumstances had no effect upon him. Company did not alter him. Sorrow did not deter him. Praise did not puff him up. Our Lord was always elevated by his very character above all that surrounded him.

These things cannot be said of any of his disciples. In all other men, however great the church or the world may judge them to be, there are serious defects and infirmities. Even their strongest points are counter-balanced by some humiliating weakness. Christ alone could declare, 'The Father hath not left me alone ... I do always those things that please him ... Which of you convinceth me of sin?' (John 8:29, 46). God the Father twice burst heaven open to exclaim, 'This is my beloved Son, in whom I am well pleased' (Matthew 3:17; 17:5).

That is not the case with us. Even our very best attempts to live for his glory display in the most glaring way that there is much bran and little evenness in us. John, who loved him well, and who was perhaps the most humble of all the disciples, desired the highest place in the kingdom for himself. Peter, willing to die with Jesus, afterwards denied and forsook him. Paul, who was caught up to the third heaven, had to live with a constant thorn in his flesh lest he be exalted above measure. How often, in preaching the gospel, doing that by which I strive hardest to serve immortal souls and honour our God, I have needlessly spoken something by which I have hurt or offended one of the Lord's children and dishonoured my God! In prayer I often find myself speaking routinely, making selfish requests, and meaningless repetitions! How much more our weaknesses are manifest in lesser matters.

This meat offering, the fine flour, speaks of Christ, the Bread of Life. His flesh is meat indeed. All who eat this Bread have life in themselves! He is the Bread that satisfies God and the Bread that satisfies our souls.

Baked Offering

The meat offering was a baked offering.

> And he shall bring it to Aaron's sons the priests: and he shall take thereout his handful of the flour thereof, and of the oil thereof, with all the frankincense thereof; and the priest shall burn the memorial of it upon the altar, to be an offering made by fire, of a sweet savour unto the LORD: And the remnant of the meat offering shall be Aaron's and his sons': it is a thing most holy of the offerings of the LORD made by fire (Leviticus 2:2, 3).

It was an offering made by fire unto the Lord. It might be baked in an oven (v. 4), or in a pan if a man had no oven (v. 5), or in a frying pan, an earthen fry pan, if the worshipper were poorer still (v. 7). No matter what instrument was used or who offered it, the fine flour was thoroughly baked. Every particle of it was exposed to the fire.

Again, the reference to our all glorious Redeemer is obvious and clear. Our great Saviour cried out in his hot distress, 'I am poured out like water, and all my bones are out of joint; my heart is like wax; it is melted in the midst of my bowels. My strength is dried up like a potsherd, and my tongue cleaveth to my jaws, and thou hast brought me into the dust of death' (Psalm 22:14, 15).

The fire was burning very fiercely when he who had always done those things that pleased his Father uttered the wail of a breaking heart: 'My God, my God, why hast thou forsaken me?' (Matthew 27:46).

Mingled Offering

The meat offering was an offering mingled, or mixed, and anointed with oil. First, it was mingled with oil.

> And if thou bring an oblation of a meat offering baken in the oven, it shall be unleavened cakes of fine flour mingled with oil, or unleavened wafers anointed with oil (Leviticus 2:4).

> And if thy oblation be a meat offering baken in the fryingpan, it shall be made of fine flour with oil (Leviticus 2:7).

Oil is the well-known symbol of the Holy Spirit in Scripture. When the angel announced to the virgin the birth of the promised Messiah, he said to her, 'The Holy Ghost shall come upon thee, and the power of the Highest shall overshadow thee; therefore also that holy thing which shall be born of thee shall be called the Son of God' (Luke 1:35).

Though the Lord Jesus was the seed of the woman, he was not the seed of the man, but as the angel said to Joseph, 'That which is conceived in her is of the Holy Ghost' (Matthew 1:20). His entire nature was perfectly holy, unlike our nature, which 'is enmity against God; for it is not subject to the law of God, neither indeed can be' (Romans 8:7).

This oil mingled with flour also speaks of us. The oil in the flour speaks of the Holy Spirit in us. It is only by the Spirit in us that we worship and serve our God. Yet, and be sure you do not miss this, the Spirit in us and his work in us have nothing whatever to do with our acceptance with God. That is what the burnt-offering was all about. The work of the Holy Spirit in us contributes nothing to the work of Christ for us, but only makes it manifest. The coming and gift of the Holy Spirit in the new birth is the fruit of acceptance, not the cause.

The meat offering was also an offering anointed with oil.

And if thou bring an oblation of a meat offering baken in the oven, it shall be unleavened cakes of fine flour mingled with oil, or unleavened wafers anointed with oil (Leviticus 2:4).

The unleavened wafers of fine flour were anointed with oil. When the Lord Jesus came up out of the watery grave of baptism, John 'saw the Spirit of God descending like a dove, and lighting upon him' (Matthew 3:16). Then 'Jesus being full of the Holy Ghost, returned from Jordan, and was led by the Spirit into the wilderness' and 'returned in the power of the Spirit into Galilee' to proclaim 'the Spirit of the Lord is upon me, because he hath anointed me to preach the gospel to the poor' (Luke 4:1, 14, 18). Peter tells us that 'God anointed Jesus of Nazareth with the Holy Ghost and with power' (Acts 10:38).

If the blood of sacrifices under the law availed to put away sin ceremonially, 'How much more shall the blood of Christ, who through the eternal Spirit offered himself without spot to God, purge your conscience from dead works to serve the living God?' (Hebrews 9:14).

Frankincense Offering

The meat offering was an offering with frankincense. 'And when any will offer a meat offering unto the LORD, his offering shall be of fine flour; and he shall pour oil upon it, and put frankincense thereon' (v. 1).

The meat-offering was not only anointed with oil, frankincense was also added. The word 'frankincense' is derived from a verb which means 'to be white or to make white'. David used this word when he cried out, 'Wash me, and I shall be whiter than snow' (Psalm 51:7). It is also the word God used when He said, 'Though your sins be as scarlet, they shall be as white as snow' (Isaiah 1:18).

The word translated frankincense[2] occurs twenty times in the Old Testament, and was closely connected with the holy anointing oil, a type of the Holy Ghost (Exodus 30:34). It was placed upon the twelve loaves that were ever in the presence of God on the tables of shewbread (Leviticus 24:5-8). Where sin was in question it could not be used (Leviticus 5:11; Numbers 5:15). Yet, it speaks of the relation between Christ, our Bridegroom, and his bride (Song of Solomon 3:6; 4:6, 14).

The bride, the church, speaks of Christ, saying, 'Who is this that cometh out of the wilderness like pillars of smoke, perfumed with myrrh and frankincense, with all powders of the merchant?' (Song of Solomon 3:6). The Lord Jesus says to his bride, his church, 'Until the day break, and the shadows flee away, I will get me to the mountain of myrrh, and to the hill of frankincense' (Song of Solomon 4:6). Again, he says, 'Spikenard and saffron; calamus and cinnamon, with all trees of frankincense; myrrh and aloes, with all the chief spices' (Song of Solomon 4:14). Frankincense also speaks of the perpetual intercession of Christ in heaven (1 John 2:1, 2).

Unleavened Offering

The meat offering must be an offering made without leaven or honey.

No meat offering, which ye shall bring unto the LORD, shall be made with leaven: for ye shall burn no leaven, nor any honey, in any offering of the LORD made by fire (Leviticus 2:11).

---

[2] In Exodus 30 we find that frankincense with its strong perfume and sweet odour was kept by the altar. It was strictly forbidden for anyone to attempt to imitate it or use it for any other purpose.

Leaven is a symbol of evil and hypocrisy. Honey was forbidden[3] to teach us that whatever is sweet to nature must be disowned, if we would walk after the example of Christ who pleased not himself (Romans 15:3; Matthew 16:24; Luke 9:59-62; John 6:63).

Leaven and honey were also forbidden, perhaps primarily forbidden, because these things were commonly used by the heathen in their idolatrous sacrifices. God's people must not follow the way of idolaters. Our worship of our God must be regulated by his Word alone.

> Take heed to thyself that thou be not snared by following them, after that they be destroyed from before thee; and that thou inquire not after their gods, saying, How did these nations serve their gods? Even so will I do likewise. Thou shalt not do so unto the LORD thy God: for every abomination to the LORD, which he hateth, have they done unto their gods; for even their sons and their daughters they have burnt in the fire to their gods. What thing soever I command you, observe to do it: thou shalt not add thereto, nor diminish from it (Deuteronomy 12:30-32).

Salt Offering

The meat offering, like all the offerings of the Old Testament, was an offering seasoned with salt.

> And every oblation of thy meat offering shalt thou season with salt; neither shalt thou suffer the salt of the covenant of thy God to be lacking from thy meat offering: with all thine offerings thou shalt offer salt (Leviticus 2:13).

Salt preserves and arrests the spread of corruption. It is used throughout the Scriptures as a symbol of the everlasting covenant of redemption and grace by which we are saved. Salt is also used as a description of God's people in this world. 'Ye are the salt of the earth',

---

[3] Honey is sweet in the mouth, but bitter in the belly when too much is eaten (Proverbs 25:16). So it is with all self-righteous religion. So it is, too, with all the additions men make to the worship of God such as skits, plays, entertainment, adornments, vestments, religious garb and a show of religious ritualism and symbolism.

said our Master to his disciples. 'But if the salt have lost his savour, wherewith shall it be salted? It is thenceforth good for nothing, but to be cast out, and to be trodden under foot of men' (Matthew 5:13). Paul admonishes, 'Let your speech be always with grace, seasoned with salt' (Colossians 4:6).

Like the frankincense, the salt was not brought by the worshipper. The salt was provided by the priest. It is Christ our great High Priest who preserves us with the salt of his grace. The covenant of grace is a covenant of salt, secured by God our Saviour. We are useful only by the salt of grace. We are secured and kept by the salt of God.

God's Offering
Though given to and primarily consumed by man, the meat offering was an offering offered to the Lord.

> And he shall bring it to Aaron's sons the priests: and he shall take thereout his handful of the flour thereof, and of the oil thereof, with all the frankincense thereof; and the priest shall burn the memorial of it upon the altar, to be an offering made by fire, of a sweet savour unto the LORD: And the remnant of the meat offering shall be Aaron's and his sons': it is a thing most holy of the offerings of the LORD made by fire. And the priest shall take from the meat offering a memorial thereof, and shall burn it upon the altar: it is an offering made by fire, of a sweet savour unto the LORD. And that which is left of the meat offering shall be Aaron's and his sons': it is a thing most holy of the offerings of the LORD made by fire (Leviticus 2:2, 3, 9, 10).

The meat offering was a voluntary thank offering made by grateful men, according as the Lord had prospered them. The priests in the tabernacle and temple were sustained by the sacrifices of the people. The sacrifices made were considered most holy by the Lord, because they were sacrifices made to him. So, too, that which we give to and do for others, in the name of Christ, is accepted of God as a sweet savour before him (Philippians 4:18; Hebrews 6:10; 13:15; 1 Peter 2:5).

The meat offering was a gift of thanks, a tribute of praise, offered by the forgiven sinner to God. God symbolically granted forgiveness of sins through the burnt offering; and the worshipper responded by giving to God his tribute of thanks and praise. It was an act of dedication and consecration to God as Saviour and covenant King. It expressed not only thankfulness but also devotion to the Lord.

How much more ought we who are born of God and taught of God give praise and thanks to him incessantly, in word, in deed, in sacrifice to him, to his people, and to his cause while we live in this world. The Lord our God has forgiven us of all sin. He assures us of forgiveness through the sacrifice of Christ, our Saviour. He has saved us. Let us never forget to say, 'Thank you', to him.

What is expected of us? What is the tribute we are called to bring, to give to the Lord?

> I beseech you therefore, brethren, by the mercies of God, that ye present your bodies a living sacrifice, holy, acceptable unto God, which is your reasonable service. And be not conformed to this world: but be ye transformed by the renewing of your mind, that ye may prove what is that good, and acceptable, and perfect, will of God (Romans 12:1, 2).
>
> By him therefore let us offer the sacrifice of praise to God continually, that is, the fruit of our lips giving thanks to his name. But to do good and to communicate forget not: for with such sacrifices God is well pleased (Hebrews 13:15, 16).

What is our tribute? To live for Christ and dedicate ourselves entirely to him. To obey him, confess him and to do good to others in his name. Why? Because 'the love of Christ constraineth us'.

That word, 'constrains', means literally, 'leaves me no choice'. Paul is saying, 'I have no choice but to respond to the love of Christ with my whole being, to say thank you, thank you, thank you'.

When we serve Christ, when we share God's love with others by loving them, when we come to the house of God to worship him and give of our means to support the gospel, we do not do it begrudgingly. We do it with thankful, willing hearts, because we really have no choice. It is our tribute! It is our 'THANK YOU' to our God.

Chapter 8

The Oblation Of Firstfruits

As for the oblation of the firstfruits, ye shall offer them unto the LORD: but they shall not be burnt on the altar for a sweet savour. And every oblation of thy meat offering shalt thou season with salt; neither shalt thou suffer the salt of the covenant of thy God to be lacking from thy meat offering: with all thine offerings thou shalt offer salt. And if thou offer a meat offering of thy firstfruits unto the LORD, thou shalt offer for the meat offering of thy firstfruits green ears of corn dried by the fire, even corn beaten out of full ears. And thou shalt put oil upon it, and lay frankincense thereon: it is a meat offering. And the priest shall burn the memorial of it, part of the beaten corn thereof, and part of the oil thereof, with all the frankincense thereof: it is an offering made by fire unto the LORD.

Leviticus 2:12-16

The resurrection of our Lord Jesus Christ is a fact which cannot be reasonably disputed. It is a revealed fact, an historical fact, and an indispensable fact. The Lord Jesus Christ, the God-man Mediator, who put away our sins by the sacrifice of himself, is risen from the dead. Rejoice! He has ascended up on high, leading captivity captive, conquering death, hell, and the grave. He is exalted King of kings and Lord of lords.

This risen, exalted, almighty Christ has empowered and commanded his church to preach the gospel to all men, making known to all both the fact and, more importantly, the meaning of his resurrection.

The resurrection of Christ was as plainly and clearly prophesied in the Old Testament Scriptures as were his incarnation, obedience, and death as our covenant Surety (Psalm 16:9-11; Isaiah 26:19; 53:10-12). His resurrection was portrayed in the typical sacrifices of the Old Testament. That is what is represented in 'the oblation of the firstfruits' spoken of in Leviticus 2:12-16. Here, we are given a clear, instructive picture of our Lord's resurrection, of our own resurrection, and of faith in and consecration to the risen Christ.

Not Burned

As for the oblation of the firstfruits, ye shall offer them unto the LORD: but they shall not be burnt on the altar for a sweet savour' (Leviticus 2:12).

This oblation was not to be burned on the altar. Without question, these firstfruits were offered as a voluntary acknowledgement of God's goodness in providing his people with daily bread. They are included in the meat offerings described in this chapter because they were freewill offerings of thanksgiving, gratitude, and praise. They certainly speak much concerning both the worshipper and his property.

However, you will notice the firstfruits here described were brought to the altar because they primarily represented and typified the Lord Jesus Christ in his resurrection glory. There is no burning here. His burning is over. His suffering is done. His sacrifice has been made and accepted. Justice is fully satisfied. Sin is gone! Yet, as we shall see, there is always the reminder of his suffering and death as our Substitute.

Seasoned with Salt

And every oblation of thy meat offering shalt thou season with salt; neither shalt thou suffer the salt of the covenant of thy God to be lacking from thy meat offering: with all thine offerings thou shalt offer salt' (Leviticus 2:13).

Salt represents preservation and security. Salt indicates corruption removed and prevented. Salt speaks of covenant grace (Numbers 18:19; 2 Chronicles 13:5). It was used in past times as a symbol of friendship.

God Almighty, in all his fulness and in all he does, is ours in Christ. Though we were once, at heart, enmity against the Almighty, he has brought us to himself in a covenant of everlasting friendship. In Christ God sups with man and man sups with God (Revelation 3:20). He blesses us in our souls, in our homes, in our fields, and in our store. In all things, God says, 'Say ye to the righteous, It shall be well with him' and 'there shall no evil happen to the just'. God our Father has made even the beasts of the field and the fowls of the air to be our friends (Job 5:23; Hosea 2:18; Romans 8:28). By requiring that all sacrifices be offered with salt, the Lord God declared that the satisfaction he has in the sacrifice of Christ, the burnt offering, is unchanging, abiding, eternal, and indestructible, and that he will forever remain faithful to his purpose, his promise, his covenant, and his people for Christ's sake.

Green Ears of Corn

And if thou offer a meat offering of thy firstfruits unto the LORD, thou shalt offer for the meat offering of thy firstfruits green ears of corn dried by the fire, even corn beaten out of full ears' (Leviticus 2:14).

These green ears of corn represent our Lord Jesus Christ (John 12:24). They had to be 'green ears', portraying our Saviour who was cut off, like green ears of corn, in the prime of his life. The words might be translated 'ears of the best kind'. That is our Saviour. He is Alpha and Omega. He is the perfect God, the perfect Man, the perfect Sacrifice, the perfect Saviour!

These ears of corn were to be 'dried by the fire'. Though there is no blood in these offerings of praise, there is always a reminder of it. Our thanksgiving and worship, our gifts and sacrifices, our firstfruits of thanksgiving are offered and accepted because of what Christ endured as our Substitute to put away our sins (Psalm 22:14; 102:4).

This is a picture of the Man of Sorrows. All his life long, he was being dried in the fire. It is true, he did not make atonement but by his blood in his death upon the cursed tree; but everything he endured as a Man and in anticipation of being made sin, dried up his life and withered his physical frame. At thirty-three years old he appeared to be a man fifty!

Then, these ears of corn had to be 'beaten out'. Andrew Bonar suggested that this 'represents the bruises and strokes whereby he was prepared for the altar'. 'For it became him, for whom are all things, and by whom are all things, in bringing many sons unto glory, to make the captain of their salvation perfect through sufferings' (Hebrews 2:10).

Christ the Firstfruits

In all these things, Christ is the Firstfruits. Firstfruits imply that many more shall follow. He is the Firstfruits. Those that follow are like the firstfruits. The full harvest conforms to the firstfruits (Romans 8:28-30; Philippians 3:10, 21). The Scriptures do not leave us in the dark about these types and pictures. Rather, God the Holy Spirit has given us full instruction concerning these sacrifices and their significance, these oblations of the firstfruits.

First and foremost, as we have seen, the firstfruits speak of our Lord Jesus Christ in his resurrection glory (1 Corinthians 15:20-23). Then, the firstfruits represent our regeneration, our spiritual resurrection with Christ (James 1:18; Romans 8:22, 23; 16:5).

The Apostle Paul spoke of one of his beloved friends, Epaenetus, as 'the firstfruits of Achaia unto Christ'. That means, he was the first one in Achaia who was born of God and brought to Christ. Being born of God the Holy Ghost, we now have the firstfruits of eternal life and heavenly glory (Romans 8:22, 23). If we have the firstfruits of the Spirit; grace, eternal life, everlasting salvation in Christ, peace, pardon, justification, and acceptance with God, what will heavenly glory be?

The oblation of the firstfruits was also a picture of believers honouring God with their substance (Proverbs 3:5-10). Giving, like the offering of the firstfruits, is an act of faith. God deserves and demands the firstfruits. All offerings to the Lord our God must be of the first and best. To offer otherwise is mockery. We are to bring our God our best, only our best (Malachi 1:14). God's gift of his Son, our all-glorious Christ, to which the firstfruits oblation pointed, is his gift of the best. Christ is the first and the best. He was offered upon the altar of God as an offering in the prime of life, and he is the sin-cleansing sacrifice of fire (Hebrews 9:14). Dare we bring him anything less to such a Saviour than our best?

Giving God the firstfruits is a declaration that all is his. Giving him the firstfruits is an act of faith. We must give him the first and best of all things, our time, labour, money, and life, trusting our Father to provide the rest. He has promised he shall (Exodus 34:23, 24).

The oblation of the firstfruits was also a picture of the believing sinner's hope of his own resurrection glory with Christ (1 Corinthians 15:23; Revelation 14:4). When we stand before God with Christ in glory there will still be yet more to come. After the firstfruits of the resurrection comes the reconciliation of all things and eternity with Christ.

Accepted Oblation

> And thou shalt put oil upon it, and lay frankincense thereon: it is a meat offering. And the priest shall burn the memorial of it, part of the beaten corn thereof, and part of the oil thereof, with all the frankincense thereof: it is an offering made by fire unto the LORD (Leviticus 2:15, 16).

The smoke and the frankincense ascend up to heaven, declaring that all is accepted: first the Lord Jesus Christ himself, then his redeemed and all that is ours. Our blessed Saviour passed through the suffering, the fire, and the flame. Only then was he received up into heaven. Now, because we are one with him, we are treated as if we had ourselves passed through the suffering, fire, and flame of God's holy wrath and justice, because in union with our dear Saviour we truly did pass through the suffering, fire, and flame of God's holy wrath and justice with him. In Christ we are accepted of God: accepted because he is accepted, and accepted as he is accepted, forever accepted.

That is the meaning of 'the oblation of the firstfruits'. And that is the message of the resurrection (Romans 4:25-5:2; 1 Thessalonians 4:13-18; 1 Corinthians 15:51-58; Revelation 20:6).

Chapter 9

The Salt Of God

And every oblation of thy meat offering shalt thou season with salt;
neither shalt thou suffer the salt of the covenant of thy God to be lacking
from thy meat offering: with all thine offerings thou shalt offer salt.

Leviticus 2:13

Our Lord Jesus Christ was truly the prince of preachers. His preaching
was never scholarly, eloquent, or entertaining. It was plain, powerful,
and persuasive; simple, instructive, and enlightening. He found
common, ordinary, everyday things with which men and women were
familiar and used them to illustrate and portray great, heavenly, gospel
truths. By the use of the most common things of ordinary life, the Lord
Jesus taught eternity bound sinners the gospel of God.

Following the Master's example, I want to display the glorious
gospel of God set forth in this verse of Inspiration, using salt as it is
used here to set forth the way of life, salvation, and acceptance with the
holy Lord God by Christ Jesus. One of the most common things in the
world is salt. And salt is used of God in this portion of Scripture to teach
sinners how to come to him by faith in Christ.

An Illustration
In 2 Kings 2 we are given an illustration of salt's usefulness. Without
question, in healing the dead and deadly waters of Jericho, Elisha was
typical of our dear Saviour, the Lord Jesus Christ, the Healer of all our
death, all our barrenness, and all our bitter waters. Elisha healed these

deadly waters by casting salt into them, and went toward Bethel. Some children from Bethel mocked God's prophet as he passed by resulting in their sudden judgment.

Those children, as John Gill rightly tells us, were not what we commonly think of as 'little children'. They were old enough to be out by themselves in a large group. They certainly knew right from wrong. They tauntingly took notice of Elisha's baldness, and they were sufficiently aware to know he was a prophet. When they scorned Elisha, the prophet of God cursed them for their mockery (2 Chronicles 36:16) and two she bears suddenly appeared and tore them to pieces. As Gill put it, 'from a malignant spirit in them, (they) mocked at him as such'. Being 'taught by their idolatrous parents, they had an aversion' to God's prophet and mocked him. Elisha was undeterred by the mockery of these children and by the judgment of God upon them.

Salt is here set before us as an emblem of the gospel and of the grace of God proclaimed in the gospel. The same gospel by which God saves his elect brings everlasting destruction upon those who despise it (2 Corinthians 2:14-16). What shall hell be like for those men and women who bring their own sons and daughters into the bottomless pit by teaching them to mock God, his Son, his gospel, and those men who faithfully preach it. No mortal can imagine.

Judgment

Salt is sometimes used in the Scriptures as an instrument of divine judgment. The first time we see the word salt is in Genesis 14:3. There we read of the Salt Sea, probably the Dead Sea. It was Siddim, the place where Sodom and Gomorrah once stood. The next time we see the word salt is in Genesis 19:26. There Lot's wife was turned into a pillar of salt. Ezekiel, Jeremiah, and Zephaniah all tell us of God's judgment upon lands, making them perpetually barren by giving them over to salt (Ezekiel 47:11; Jeremiah 17:6; Zephaniah 2:9). David tells us that the Lord God turns the fruitful land into barrenness which is interpreted in the margin as saltiness (Psalm 107:34).

The fact that salt is set before us in the Scriptures as an instrument of judgment shows us it is representative of the gospel, the grace of God proclaimed in the gospel, and our Lord Jesus Christ, who soon shall come to sit in judgment over all the earth (2 Corinthians 2:14-16; 5:10, 11; Luke 2:34).

Salt for Sacrifices

We are told that the Lord God required that every sacrifice offered to him be offered with salt.

> And every oblation of thy meat offering shalt thou season with salt; neither shalt thou suffer the salt of the covenant of thy God to be lacking from thy meat offering: with all thine offerings thou shalt offer salt (Leviticus 2:13).

It is taken for granted that all true Israelites would bring their oblations and offerings of different kinds to God; and they did. True Israelites still do. But how is this to be done? That is the point. We should say with Paul, 'Lord, what wilt thou have me to do?' Then we might add another question. 'How will you have me do it?' Will-worship is not acceptable with God. If we bring God what he does not ask it will not be received. We only present to him what he requires. We must present it to him in his own way, for he is a jealous God.

In this one verse (Leviticus 2:13), the Lord God three times expressly commands that with the meat offerings and all other offerings his worshippers were to offer salt. Does the great God that made heaven and earth talk about salt? Does he condescend to such minute details of his service as to declare that the lack of a handful of salt renders a sacrifice unacceptable? Does the holy, Lord God assert that the presence of salt is absolutely necessary to any sacrifice being received by him? He does indeed.

Again, we see here that salt is an emblem of grace and of the Lord Jesus. Our only acceptance with God is Christ. We cannot worship God, we cannot serve God, we cannot offer God anything, until first our souls are healed by the salt of his saving grace in Christ.

Other Things Required

As we read this second chapter of Leviticus, we see that other things were also required in connection with the sacrifices brought to God's altar. The people's sacrifices were imperfect. They had to have frankincense when they offered their sacrifice to God. God did not smell sweet savour in the bullock, or the ram, or the lamb unless sweet spices were added. The best performances of our hands must not appear before his throne without the merit of Christ's blood and righteousness.

There must be that mixture of myrrh, and aloes, and cassia, with which the garments of our Prince are perfumed, to make our sacrifices a sweet savour to the Most High.

They also had to bring oil with their sacrifices. That oil was typical of the blessed Spirit of God. What is the use of a sermon if there is no unction in it? What is unction but the Holy Ghost? What is prayer without the anointing that comes of the Holy Spirit? What is praise unless the Spirit of God is in it to give it life, that it may rise to heaven? That which goes to God must first come from God. We need the oil. We must have the oil. We cannot serve God without it. But only God can give us his oil, his Spirit, and his grace in Christ.

Then came a third requisite; salt. If you read the preceding verses, you will see how the Lord forbade them to present any honey: no leaven and no honey!

No meat offering, which ye shall bring unto the LORD, shall be made with leaven: for ye shall burn no leaven, nor any honey, in an offering of the LORD made by fire. As for the oblation of the firstfruits, ye shall offer them unto the LORD: but they shall not be burnt on the altar for a sweet savour' (Leviticus 2:11, 12).

God does not ask for sweetness, he asks for salt. Not honey, but salt must be added to all the sacrifices we present before the living God.

Do not come to God's altar as a hypocrite, with honey. Come to God with honesty and sincerity. Serve God with honesty and sincerity. God will not accept honey at his altar; but he requires salt, the bitter salt of a broken spirit, a broken and contrite heart!

Covenant of Salt

Salt is used in Scripture with reference to God's covenant. God's covenant with Aaron was a covenant of salt; and God's covenant with David was a covenant of salt (Numbers 18:19; 2 Chronicles 13:5). And, blessed be our all-gracious God, we have acceptance with him in Christ by a covenant of salt, an everlasting, immutable covenant of salt. We come to God, not on the footing of works but on the footing of grace in an everlasting covenant of salt. The salt of the covenant is purifying salt, justifying, sanctifying grace. The salt of the covenant is preserving salt, keeping grace.

Communion

Salt is also a token of communion. In ancient times, salt was shared between men who were sworn friends. Once a man took a little salt from another and ate it, he was committed never to harm his friend.

Christ is our Salt and he is God's Salt, 'the salt of the covenant of thy God'. We serve God in union with Christ. We serve God in fellowship with him, seeking his will and his glory. We serve God in fellowship of his people. We serve God in the Spirit, by the Spirit of his grace, in harmony with God himself, as friends committed to one another.

God's Provision

Salt, like grace, is God's provision not man's production. God only accepts what God provides (Genesis 22:8): Christ's righteousness, his atoning blood, his intercession, his grace. Our Lord Jesus Christ heals like salt and preserves like salt. Our Lord Jesus Christ saves from corruption, cleanses us from filth, and purifies His people.

Salt was never to be omitted in the offerings of God. Christ is 'the salt of the covenant of thy God'. Salt figuratively sets forth the Lord Jesus Christ and the free grace of God in him. God's requirement of salt was intended to show in type and picture the importance and preeminence of Christ, his person, his blood, and his righteousness in all things.

Where Christ is not, there is no sweet-savour. It is his blood which gives a fragrancy and a perfume to our most holy things. If Christ is the salt of the covenant of our God, and with all our offerings he is first and last presented, both the Alpha and Omega, in our view as he is in the view of God our Father, then is that Scripture blessedly fulfilled which the Lord delivered by the prophet:

> In mine holy mountain in the mountain of the height of Israel, saith the Lord God, there shall all the house of Israel, all of them in the land, serve me. There will I accept them, and there will I require your offerings, and the first fruits of your oblations, with all your holy things. I will accept you with your sweet savour; and ye shall know that I am the Lord (Ezekiel 20:40-42).

The Lord Jesus Christ is our sweet-smelling savour, our Sacrifice, our Salt before God (Ephesians 5:2).

Christ crucified is Salt for God's altar and Salt for the gospel table. Let this Salt be sprinkled everywhere, on everything, always, and unsparingly. Salt heals. Salt cures. Salt purifies. Salt makes things tasty and savoury.

Job asks, 'Can that which is unsavoury be eaten without salt?' (Job 6:6). Our poor souls can never be accepted of God but in, with, and by Christ Jesus our Saviour. Our souls cannot be cured and preserved from everlasting corruption but by the Lord Jesus. So take God's Salt and come to God. In Christ, with Christ, God will accept you as a sacrifice of a sweet-smelling savour.

Chapter 10

The Peace Offerings

And if his oblation be a sacrifice of peace offering, if he offer it of the herd; whether it be a male or female, he shall offer it without blemish before the LORD. And he shall lay his hand upon the head of his offering, and kill it at the door of the tabernacle of the congregation: and Aaron's sons the priests shall sprinkle the blood upon the altar round about ... And the two kidneys, and the fat that is upon them, which is by the flanks, and the caul above the liver, with the kidneys, it shall he take away. And the priest shall burn them upon the altar: it is the food of the offering made by fire for a sweet savour: all the fat is the LORD'S. It shall be a perpetual statute for your generations throughout all your dwellings, that ye eat neither fat nor blood.

Leviticus 3:1-17

And this is the law of the sacrifice of peace offerings, which he shall offer unto the LORD. If he offer it for a thanksgiving, then he shall offer with the sacrifice of thanksgiving unleavened cakes mingled with oil, and unleavened wafers anointed with oil, and cakes mingled with oil, of fine flour, fried. Besides the cakes, he shall offer for his offering leavened bread with the sacrifice of thanksgiving of his peace offerings. And of it he shall offer one out of the whole oblation for an heave offering unto the LORD, and it shall be the priest's that sprinkleth the blood of the peace offerings. And the flesh of the sacrifice of his peace offerings for thanksgiving shall be eaten the same day that it is offered; he shall not leave any of it until the morning ... Moreover the soul that shall touch any unclean thing, as the uncleanness of man, or any unclean beast, or any abominable unclean thing, and eat of the flesh of the sacrifice of peace offerings, which pertain unto the LORD, even that soul shall be cut off from his people.

Leviticus 7:11-21

Speak unto the children of Israel, saying, He that offereth the sacrifice of his peace offerings unto the LORD shall bring his oblation unto the LORD of the sacrifice of his peace offerings ... He among the sons of Aaron, that offereth the blood of the peace offerings, and the fat, shall have the right shoulder for his part. For the wave breast and the heave shoulder have I taken of the children of Israel from off the sacrifices of their peace offerings, and have given them unto Aaron the priest and unto his sons by a statute forever from among the children of Israel.

Leviticus 7:29-34

The book of Leviticus begins with a description of five sacrifices that God ordained for the Israelites. The sacrifices, of course, are pictures of our Lord Jesus Christ and the redemption he accomplished for us at Calvary by the shedding of his blood.

These sacrifices were ordinances of worship ordained and directed by the Lord God himself. The poor, needy sinner came to God with the symbolic sacrifice God required. In the sacrifice, representing the Lord Jesus and his sacrifice, he found both acceptance with God by blood atonement, and mercy, grace and blessedness heaped upon him by God's free grace. The sacrifice was real but prefigured the grace that flows to believing sinners through the precious blood of Christ. Each of the sacrifices represented God's provision for the deep needs of fallen men and women. Each one displayed different aspects of our Saviour's accomplishments at Calvary.

Burnt Offerings

Chapter 1 speaks of atonement. We are sinners in need of atonement, and acceptance with God. That is what is represented in the burnt offerings described in chapter one. The burnt offerings pictured the acceptance of guilty sinners by the holy Lord God through the merits of Christ. God's acceptance of his people is complete. He accepts us as a whole, all of us, all our parts. As the burnt offering was consumed by fire in its entirety, so the Lord Jesus Christ was accepted as our Substitute and consumed in all his holy being by the fire of God's holy, just wrath against sin, and we are accepted of God for Christ's sake. The burnt offering declares, to every believing sinner, 'accepted in the Beloved'.

Meat Offerings
Chapter 2 shows the meat offerings of thanksgiving and consecration. Fallen man, being estranged and alienated from God, has within his soul a desperate need of consecration to God. Man needs to give himself up to God. He strives to find ways of doing so; but there is no rest in his soul until he gives himself up entirely to God by faith in Christ and devotion to Christ.

Here we see man bringing back to God the very stuff of which we are made, our staple food, bread. This portrays the believer's response to the mercy, love and grace of God in Christ, the believer's proper response to blood atonement. Just as our Saviour gave himself to God entirely as our sin-atoning sacrifice, believers give themselves entirely to God in Christ. The meat offering is the believer coming to God by Christ, full of gratitude and saying, 'I am not my own. I have been bought with the price of Christ's precious blood. Now I am God's'.

Peace Offerings
Still there is another universal need in fallen men. We need peace; peace within, peace with one another, and peace with God. The fact is, men can never have peace within or peace with one another, not real peace, until we have peace with God. That is what is portrayed in Leviticus 3. Here the holy Lord God describes for us the ceremonial, highly symbolical, typical peace offerings, which of course portray Christ our Peace.

Without question, God's elect, though redeemed by the blood of Christ and devoted to the will and glory of God, still live in a world of hurt. We are often caught up in temptations, trials, and troubles. We must, as long as we live in this world, as the Apostle Paul tells us in Romans 8, face and deal with trouble and persecution, famine and nakedness, peril and sword. Yet, in the midst of all these things, our Lord says, 'My peace give I unto you'.

As you read this third chapter of Leviticus, may God the Holy Ghost, who gave us these instructive pictures of our dear Saviour, make his message in this portion of Holy Scripture a source of comfort and joy and peace to help you through your day of adversity in this world.

One Way

As with the burnt offerings, the peace offerings could be either a calf, or a lamb, or a goat. The worshipper had to identify himself with the sacrifice. Laying his hands upon the animal's head he acknowledged his guilt, confessed his sins, and expressed his faith in God's sacrifice for sin, the Lord Jesus Christ. The innocent victim had to be slain, slain by the worshipper. The blood had to be sprinkled, sprinkled by the priest. In other words, there is only one way to God, the blood of Christ.

And if his offering be a goat, then he shall offer it before the LORD. And he shall lay his hand upon the head of it, and kill it before the tabernacle of the congregation: and the sons of Aaron shall sprinkle the blood thereof upon the altar round about. And he shall offer thereof his offering, even an offering made by fire unto the LORD; the fat that covereth the inwards, and all the fat that is upon the inwards, And the two kidneys, and the fat that is upon them, which is by the flanks, and the caul above the liver, with the kidneys, it shall he take away. And the priest shall burn them upon the altar: it is the food of the offering made by fire for a sweet savour: all the fat is the LORD'S. It shall be a perpetual statute for your generations throughout all your dwellings, that ye eat neither fat nor blood (Leviticus 3:12-17).

Let me show you four things about the peace offerings, four things that distinguish these from the other offerings.

The Fat

In the last part of verse 16 we see what appears to be an unusual requirement. There we are told, 'All the fat is the LORD'S'. What is the significance of that statement? In the burnt offering the entire animal was consumed in the fire. In the peace offering, God provides detailed instructions concerning the parts of the body that are to be burned. Then, in verse 16, we read, 'All fat is the Lord's'. Why?

In our culture the word 'fat' has negative connotations. Our ideal male and female forms are slender and thin. No one wants to be called 'fat'. But in most cultures and in most of the world's history, that has not been the case. Because most people in the history of the world lived in poverty, only the prosperous could become fat. Those who were a bit heavy tended to be those who were most prosperous.

I am told by our friends who have spent some time in Africa and New Guinea that this is the case. In the poor, tribal societies found in those parts of the world, if your wife looks like a fashion model, other men feel sorry for you. To call a child 'very fat' is a great compliment to the parents. In poor countries, when a person attains a measure of wealth, his waistline almost always increases.

In the Old Testament, the Jews had a similar attitude about fat. In fact, the word 'fat' is commonly used in the Bible in positive ways. Here are two examples.

> And take your father and your households, and come unto me: and I will give you the good of the land of Egypt, and ye shall eat the fat of the land (Genesis 45:18).

Here Pharaoh promised Joseph 'the good of the land of Egypt and the fat of the land'. The 'fat of the land' refers to the best of the land, the best produce of the land. Fat represented abundance and prosperity.

> All the best of the oil, and all the best of the wine, and of the wheat, the firstfruits of them which they shall offer unto the LORD, them have I given thee (Numbers 18:12).

The word translated 'best' here is the same Hebrew word elsewhere translated 'fat'. Wine has no fat in it. But the 'fat of the wine' is the best wine, the finest wine.

This is the reason all fat of the sacrifices in Leviticus 3 belonged to the Lord. The fat represented that which was good, indeed, that which was best. James puts it this way,

> Every good gift and every perfect gift is from above, and cometh down from the Father of lights, with whom is no variableness, neither shadow of turning (James 1:17).

If we would enjoy peace in this world, two things are essential. First, we must recognise that the singular source of all that is good is our God and look to him alone for it. All saving goodness (Ephesians 1:3-6; 1 Corinthians 1:30), all spiritual goodness, all providential goodness (Romans 8:28), and all eternal goodness comes from our God.

Second, realising that all we have comes from God and belongs to God, we must, with grateful, willing hearts, give all back to him again. If we would have peace in this world we must recognise there is nothing good in our lives except what comes from God. We do not deserve what we have. We have not earned what we have. All that we are and all that we have comes from our heavenly Father and rightfully belongs to him. It is God alone who makes us to differ from others (1 Corinthians 4:7).

This is a basic requirement for peace. If we try to hold onto what we have and protect ourselves from losing what we have, then the more we have the more we will fret and worry about it. If we can hold what we have, everything we have in this world, lightly and with confidence that God is both sovereign and good, we will enjoy peace.

Offerings Eaten
In Leviticus 3:16 we are told that this peace offering was 'a food offering'. In Leviticus 7:15-18 we are told that the sacrifice of the peace offering had to be eaten.

> And the flesh of the sacrifice of his peace offerings for thanksgiving shall be eaten the same day that it is offered; he shall not leave any of it until the morning. But if the sacrifice of his offering be a vow, or a voluntary offering, it shall be eaten the same day that he offereth his sacrifice: and on the morrow also the remainder of it shall be eaten: But the remainder of the flesh of the sacrifice on the third day shall be burnt with fire. And if any of the flesh of the sacrifice of his peace offerings be eaten at all on the third day, it shall not be accepted, neither shall it be imputed unto him that offereth it: it shall be an abomination, and the soul that eateth of it shall bear his iniquity (Leviticus 7:15-18).

This is the only offering that was to be eaten by the one who brought it. Remember, the fat was given to God and burned on the altar. The breast and the right shoulder were given to the priest. The rest was to be eaten by the worshipper and could be shared with anyone who was ceremonially clean before the Lord. Surely, there is much to be gleaned from this. Here we see the Lord God himself, the Lord Jesus Christ our great High Priest, and the redeemed sinner all feeding together upon, and finding satisfaction with, the same sacrifice.

What a great, glorious, effectual sacrifice Christ is. It is the sin-atoning blood of Christ, and that alone, which gives satisfaction to the holy Lord God. 'He is the propitiation for our sins'. The Lord Jesus Christ, our great High Priest, finds satisfaction in his own sacrifice (Isaiah 53:9-11; Hebrews 12:2). And believing sinners find satisfaction in him, ever eating his flesh and drinking his blood by faith (Psalm 73:25, 26; John 4:13, 14; 6:48, 53-55; Psalm 17:15).

All who are clean before God feed upon the same sacrifice: the worshipper, the priest, and the priests' sons. But God required that the peace offering was to be eaten within two days.

The worshipper was to begin eating it on the day it was offered. This is what that means. Peace with God commences in the soul as soon as we apprehend the accomplishment of redemption by faith. The efficacy of Christ's sacrifice does not wait for our faith. Thank God for that! But peace, soul satisfaction, commences when faith apprehends the efficacy of the sacrifice. Peace comes to the soul when Christ, the Peace Offering, is trusted (Romans 5:1).

Also, all of the sacrifice had to be eaten before the third day. Why? The third day is resurrection day. If we would have peace in this world, we must live by faith, ever feeding upon Christ, until our days in this world of woe are ended, until our change comes (Romans 8:17-21, 28-39).

Only the Clean
Only those who stood clean before the Lord were allowed to eat the sacrifice.

But the soul that eateth of the flesh of the sacrifice of peace offerings, that pertain unto the LORD, having his uncleanness upon him, even that soul shall be cut off from his people. Moreover the soul that shall touch any unclean thing, as the uncleanness of man, or any unclean beast, or any abominable unclean thing, and eat of the flesh of the sacrifice of peace offerings, which pertain unto the LORD, even that soul shall be cut off from his people (Leviticus 7:20, 21).

If a person had any uncleanness upon him, he could not feast upon God's sacrifice. But is not the Lord Jesus Christ a Fountain opened for the unclean? Is he not specifically said to be the Friend of sinners? Did he not come to save sinners? Most certainly he did. But the sinner who comes to God with his burnt offering, the blood of Christ, his meat offering, the righteousness of Christ, and his peace offering, the Lamb of God, is clean before the Lord. He has no uncleanness upon him. Christ makes sinners holy, righteous, fit, worthy to feast in his house.

Priests' Portion

Leviticus 7:29-34 tell us that the breast and the right shoulder were the priests' portion.

> Speak unto the children of Israel, saying, He that offereth the sacrifice of his peace offerings unto the LORD shall bring his oblation unto the LORD of the sacrifice of his peace offerings. His own hands shall bring the offerings of the LORD made by fire, the fat with the breast, it shall he bring, that the breast may be waved for a wave offering before the LORD. And the priest shall burn the fat upon the altar: but the breast shall be Aaron's and his sons'. And the right shoulder shall ye give unto the priest for an heave offering of the sacrifices of your peace offerings. He among the sons of Aaron, that offereth the blood of the peace offerings, and the fat, shall have the right shoulder for his part. For the wave breast and the heave shoulder have I taken of the children of Israel from off the sacrifices of their peace offerings, and have given them unto Aaron the priest and unto his sons by a statute forever from among the children of Israel (Leviticus 7:29-34).

The breast being the meat closest to the heart, speaks of affection, the love of God in Christ. The right shoulder represents both strength and majesty. The priests ate them both. What is the meaning of this?

There is no peace for anyone in this world until he is enabled by the grace of God to believe and to trust, the Lord Jesus Christ. Our Saviour is Zion's glorious King and Priest, in whom alone all the love of God and all the omnipotence of the Almighty is found. He who is God our Saviour is both God full of compassion and the God of omnipotent ability, God mighty to save. Peace is found in trusting him (Psalm 62:3, 4, 11, 12). If we would have peace, we must be convinced that he who is God our Saviour is God full of compassion, one who loves us, and God almighty, one who is able to save. Everything we might otherwise fear is under his total control.

Without this confidence in God our Saviour, without this confidence in Christ, we are easily overwhelmed by our circumstances. We live in a world that seems out of control. How often men and women are brought into such straits that they think, 'I just can't take any more'. How sad, how very sad! The Lord Jesus has promised to all who trust him, 'Peace I leave with you, my peace I give unto you ... Let not your heart be troubled, neither let it be afraid' (John 14:27).

It is this peace, the peace of God that passes understanding, that is set forth in the peace offerings. It is this peace that God gives to sinners as we trust his Son and feed upon him. It is this peace, the peace that Christ gives, which the world can neither understand nor take away. May God be pleased to make it yours and mine, for Christ's sake.

Chapter 11

Things Pertaining To Peace

And if his oblation be a sacrifice of peace offering, if he offer it of the herd; whether it be a male or female, he shall offer it without blemish before the LORD. And he shall lay his hand upon the head of his offering, and kill it at the door of the tabernacle of the congregation: and Aaron's sons the priests shall sprinkle the blood upon the altar round about. And he shall offer of the sacrifice of the peace offering an offering made by fire unto the LORD; the fat that covereth the inwards, and all the fat that is upon the inwards, And the two kidneys, and the fat that is on them, which is by the flanks, and the caul above the liver, with the kidneys, it shall he take away. And Aaron's sons shall burn it on the altar upon the burnt sacrifice, which is upon the wood that is on the fire: it is an offering made by fire, of a sweet savour unto the LORD. And if his offering for a sacrifice of peace offering unto the LORD be of the flock; male or female, he shall offer it without blemish. If he offer a lamb for his offering, then shall he offer it before the LORD. And he shall lay his hand upon the head of his offering, and kill it before the tabernacle of the congregation: and Aaron's sons shall sprinkle the blood thereof round about upon the altar. And he shall offer of the sacrifice of the peace offering an offering made by fire unto the LORD; the fat thereof, and the whole rump, it shall he take off hard by the backbone; and the fat that covereth the inwards, and all the fat that is upon the inwards, And the two kidneys, and the fat that is upon them, which is by the flanks, and the caul above the liver, with the kidneys, it shall he take away. And the priest shall burn it upon the altar: it is the food of the offering made by fire unto the LORD. And if his offering be a goat, then he shall offer it before the LORD. And he shall lay his hand upon the head of it, and kill it before the tabernacle of the congregation: and the sons of Aaron shall sprinkle the blood thereof upon the altar round about. And he shall offer thereof his offering, even an offering made by fire unto the LORD; the fat that covereth the inwards, and all the fat that is upon the inwards, And the two kidneys, and the fat that is upon them, which is by the flanks, and the caul above the liver, with the kidneys, it shall he take away. And the priest shall burn them upon the altar: it is the food of the offering made by fire for a sweet savour: all the fat is the LORD'S. It shall be a perpetual statute for your generations throughout all your dwellings, that ye eat neither fat nor blood.

Leviticus 3:1-17

As we look again at the peace offerings in Leviticus 3, bear in mind that the Hebrew word for 'peace offering' is always used in the plural, the one exception is in Amos 5:22. Perhaps the closest equivalent in English would be 'things pertaining to peace'.

Allow me to tell you a true story about a family of believers who knew something about things pertaining to peace, who knew something about the peace of God which is found in Christ Jesus. John and Betty Stam and their family found peace in the midst of indescribably more extreme stress than most of us will ever experience.

John and Betty met in Bible college in 1930. They were both in their mid-twenties. Betty grew up in China where her parents were missionaries. She returned to China in 1931. John soon followed. In a little less than two years, in October 1933, they were married.

Fourteen months later, communist insurgents under the command of Mao Tse-tung captured the town where John, Betty, and their infant child, Helen, lived. The Stams were arrested. Early on December 8, 1934, the soldiers discussed how they would kill baby Helen. A poor Chinese farmer stepped forward, pleading for the child's life. The soldiers replied, 'We won't kill the child, if you are willing to die in her place'. The farmer agreed. The soldiers shot and killed him.

The next morning, the soldiers forced John and Betty to leave their house without Helen. They stripped the couple down to their underwear and marched them through the streets, mocking them. As a crowd formed, the Stams were sentenced to death. A Chinese doctor, until this time afraid to speak up, made a last-minute plea for their lives. The communists asked if he was a Christian. When he openly professed Christ as his Lord, they killed him. Then John and Betty were ordered to their knees. John was beheaded with a sword. Betty grabbed him to hold him, and she, too, was beheaded.

When Betty's parents were informed of her death, they replied by telegraph to the staff of China Inland Mission, 'Deeply appreciate your consolation. Sacrifice seems great, but not too great for him who gave himself for us. Experiencing God's grace. Believe wholeheartedly Romans 8:28.'

Betty Stam's parents knew the peace of God and found strength and comfort in his free grace in Christ and in his wise, adorable, good providence. They knew that no matter what the circumstances, even in death, we are 'more than conquerors through him who loved us'.

Betty's sister, Helen, for whom the baby had been named, wrote to her bereaved parents, 'Dearest Daddy and Mother, you don't need to hear me say how much we love you and are thinking of and praying for you in these days ... I have such a radiant picture of Betty and John standing with their palms of victory before the Throne, singing a song of pure joy that I cannot break lose and cry about it as people expect. Crying seems to be too petty for a thing that was so manifestly in God's hands alone; but my heart is very, very sore for you'.

It is this peace, the peace of God that passes understanding that is set forth in the peace offerings. The peace offerings were not offerings made to obtain peace. Peace was obtained for us by the sin-offering Christ Jesus. These peace offerings portrayed the enjoyment of peace made by the blood of his cross. It is this peace, found only in Christ, obtained only by faith in him, that inspired those who worshipped God to bring their peace offerings. It is this peace that God gives to sinners as we trust his Son and feed upon him. It is this peace, the peace that Christ gives, which the world can neither understand nor take away, 'the peace of God which passeth all understanding' (Philippians 4:7). May God be pleased to make it yours and mine, for Christ's sake.

In the seventeen verses of Leviticus 3, God the Holy Spirit shows us things pertaining to this peace from the typology of the peace offerings.

In Romans 4:25 we are told that the Lord Jesus Christ 'was delivered for', or because of, 'our offences and was raised again for', or because of, 'our justification'. Then, in chapter five, the apostle Paul declares the result of this.

> Therefore being justified by faith, we have peace with God through our Lord Jesus Christ: By whom also we have access by faith into this grace wherein we stand, and rejoice in hope of the glory of God (Romans 5:1, 2).

It is this peace arising from our justification by the finished work of Christ that is pictured in the typical peace offerings of the ceremonial law. These offerings might be taken from the herd (vv. 1-5), or the flock (vv. 6-11), or the goats (vv. 12-17).

From the Herd
The peace offering might be an offering from the herd (vv. 1-5).

> And if his oblation be a sacrifice of peace offering, if he offer it of the herd; whether it be a male or female, he shall offer it without blemish before the LORD (Leviticus 3:1).

The peace offerings are set before us in direct connection with the burnt offerings and the meat offerings. The redeemed sinner gladly lifts his heart in praise to God because God has given him peace by the blood of Christ (Psalm 116:16, 17). Andrew Bonar wrote ...

> The connection is simply this: a justified soul, devoted to the Lord in all things, spontaneously engages in acts of praise and exercises of fellowship, for the soul has been accepted and is at peace with God.

You will notice that the animal sacrificed for a peace offering could be either male or female. When I read that, I cannot help asking, 'Why?' The reason appears to be that the burnt offering pictured atonement, atonement by Christ, the Lamb of God and the Son of God, our God-man Mediator. The peace offering pictured the result of the atonement, peace with God, which flows to all believers, male and female, through the accomplishments of Christ at Calvary.

The sacrifice could be either male or female, but it must be 'without blemish' because it represents the holy Lamb of God, that One who knew no sin though he was made sin for us, the altogether lovely One in whom the Father delights. Were he not perfect we could never have peace. He who is the sinners' Substitute must be both infinite and perfect else he could not satisfy the demands of God for us.

> And he shall lay his hand upon the head of his offering, and kill it at the door of the tabernacle of the congregation: and Aaron's sons the priests shall sprinkle the blood upon the altar round about (Leviticus 3:2).

By laying his hand upon the head of the sacrifice the believing sinner both identified himself with the victim and pointed to Christ as the source of his peace, saying, my peace cannot be found in me but only in my sin-atoning Substitute. So it is with us. Peace is found entirely outside ourselves in the person and work of Christ.

We cannot cross the threshold of the sanctuary, we cannot enter into the presence of the Almighty except by the blood of Christ that speaks better things than the blood of Abel. Abel's blood cried for wrath and vengeance. Christ's blood says, 'Peace'. 'Being justified, by faith we have peace with God through our Lord Jesus Christ. By whom also we have access by faith into this grace' being completely and perfectly justified, 'wherein we stand, and rejoice in hope of the glory of God'.

> And he shall offer of the sacrifice of the peace offering an offering made by fire unto the LORD; the fat that covereth the inwards, and all the fat that is upon the inwards, And the two kidneys, and the fat that is on them, which is by the flanks, and the caul above the liver, with the kidneys, it shall he take away (Leviticus 3:3, 4).

Those portions of the animal offered for a peace offering were to be set aside from what was to be burned unto the Lord. They were considered the richest portions of the animal and were those nearest its heart.

We come to God not as sinners to be reconciled but as sinners who are reconciled. As we come to hold fellowship with the eternal God in holy worship, like those before his throne in heaven, what can we bring him except the deepest, richest love of our hearts? Our very loins were once filled with pain when sin laid heavy upon us (Isaiah 21:3, 4). Now, where once we knew nothing but pain and turmoil, the peace of God and the joy of the Lord reign within. As our Lord Jesus Christ, who is our Peace, offered himself as our Substitute to God's holy law and justice with every depth of affection, with every feeling of love, with every desire of compassion, so we must 'worship him in spirit and in truth'.

> And Aaron's sons shall burn it on the altar upon the burnt sacrifice, which is upon the wood that is on the fire: it is an offering made by fire, of a sweet savour unto the LORD (Leviticus 3:5).

Let us never fail to recognise and give thanks to God for him who offered himself as 'an offering made by fire, of a sweet savour unto the Lord'. We have peace only because the Son of God endured and extinguished the fire of God's holy wrath. Such a sacrifice as the Lord Jesus Christ is demands our hearts! Shall not the heat of his love for us melt our hearts for Christ, as the fire of God's wrath melted his very soul for us?

Nothing regarding the worship of God was random, unplanned, or haphazard in the Mosaic age. Neither shall it be today. If we worship God, we must do so 'after the due order', with care, diligence, and preparation. That portion of the peace offering to be burnt must be burnt 'on the altar upon the burnt sacrifice, which is upon the wood that is on the fire'. There is a distinct reference here to the daily sacrifice, which typified full atonement by the blood of Christ.

The message to us seems obvious. Our daily fellowship and communion with God, our daily worship, praise, and thanksgiving must be that which arises fresh to God from a fresh sense of Christ's sacrifice for us. 'By him therefore let us offer the sacrifice of praise to God continually, that is, the fruit of our lips giving thanks to his name' (Hebrews 13:15).

From the Flock

The peace offering could also come from the flock of sheep (vv. 6-11).

> And if his offering for a sacrifice of peace offering unto the LORD be of the flock; male or female, he shall offer it without blemish (Leviticus 3:6).

Do not fail to notice how frequently the words 'without blemish' are used in connection with the offerings. Surely, this is intended to teach us how the sacrifices offered to and accepted by God point to our Lord Jesus Christ who is the infinite delight of his Father (Isaiah 42:1; Matthew 3:17; 17:5).

The frequent repetition of the words 'without blemish' also is designed to teach us that our God, being infinitely and perfectly delighted with his Son, is also infinitely and perfectly delighted with all his people in his Son, and for the sake of his Son, who are made by him to be 'without blemish' in his sight.

> The LORD thy God in the midst of thee is mighty; he will save, he will rejoice over thee with joy; he will rest in his love, he will joy over thee with singing (Zephaniah 3:17).

Can you get hold of this? Nothing can be more unspeakably delightful to the believing sinner's heart than this. The holy Lord God has satisfied, totally and forever satisfied, all his holy demands for us in the sacrifice of his own dear Son as our Substitute. He who pardons sin by Christ is truly 'a just God and a Saviour'.

> If he offer a lamb for his offering, then shall he offer it before the LORD. And he shall lay his hand upon the head of his offering, and kill it before the tabernacle of the congregation: and Aaron's sons shall sprinkle the blood thereof round about upon the altar (Leviticus 3:7, 8).

The lamb was just as fully accepted as the calf, because the value is not in the type but in Christ the antitype. Atonement was not made by these animal sacrifices. They only pointed to the Lamb of God who alone took away the sins of his people by the sacrifice of himself (John 1:29; Romans 8:1-4).

> And he shall offer of the sacrifice of the peace offering an offering made by fire unto the LORD; the fat thereof, and the whole rump, it shall he take off hard by the backbone; and the fat that covereth the inwards, and all the fat that is upon the inwards, And the two kidneys, and the fat that is upon them, which is by the flanks, and the caul above the liver, with the kidneys, it shall he take away (Leviticus 3:9, 10).

'The rump' was considered the very richest portion of the lamb. The teaching here is plain enough. Only our best is to be offered to God. If we worship God, we will give him our best: the best of our affections, the best of our time, the best of our labour, the best of our gifts. With David, let us resolve, 'I will not offer the Lord that which doth cost me nothing' (Malachi 3:6-11).

> And the priest shall burn it upon the altar: it is the food of the offering made by fire unto the LORD (Leviticus 3:11).

There is a different expression used here. Instead of the sacrifice being called 'a sweet savour' it is called 'the food of the offering made by fire unto the Lord'. This represents both the holy Lord God and the believing sinner feeding upon and finding satisfaction in the sacrifice of Christ. The Lord Jesus Christ, our crucified, risen, exalted, accepted Saviour satisfies all the demands of God and satisfies all the needs of our poor souls.

From the Goats
The peace offering might also be a sacrifice from the goats (vv. 12-17).

> And if his offering be a goat, then he shall offer it before the LORD. And he shall lay his hand upon the head of it, and kill it before the tabernacle of the congregation: and the sons of Aaron shall sprinkle the blood thereof upon the altar round about (Leviticus 3:12, 13).

The goat is set before us here in the same way as the turtledove in chapter one. It was the sacrifice of the poor. The goat represents our Lord Jesus Christ as one taken out of the flock for the salvation of the rest. One is killed and the rest are spared. Thus, the sacrifice is a picture of substitutionary redemption (Psalm 89:19; John 11:47-52; 1 Peter 3:18; 2 Corinthians 5:21).

And he shall offer thereof his offering, even an offering made by fire unto the LORD; the fat that covereth the inwards, and all the fat that is upon the inwards, And the two kidneys, and the fat that is upon them, which is by the flanks, and the caul above the liver, with the kidneys, it shall he take away. And the priest shall burn them upon the altar: it is the food of the offering made by fire for a sweet savour: all the fat is the LORD'S (Leviticus 3:14-16).

The sacrifice was fully accepted for the believing sinner. So, too, our Lord Jesus Christ, the Lamb slain from the foundation of the world, is fully accepted for God's elect and we accepted, fully and forever accepted in him!

It shall be a perpetual statute for your generations throughout all your dwellings, that ye eat neither fat nor blood (Leviticus 3:17).

It is my prayer that you who read these lines have and live in that peace of God which passes all understanding flowing from the sacrifice of our Lord Jesus Christ. If not before, may God give it to you now by working in you that faith in Christ which only he can give, as I call your attention to three things in verse 17.

First, we read 'all the fat is the Lord's'. Clearly, the fat, as we have seen, represents the best. Let us ever give God our best.

Second, this statute was not for one or two generations, and was not for the house of God alone, but throughout the generations of God's people on this earth, and to be observed in all our dwellings. Obviously, we are no longer to observe the rituals of the law. 'Christ is the end of the law.' But we are to worship God in exactly the same way those saints of old worshipped him, by faith in Christ.

Moreover, we are to worship him not merely in the house of God at the appointed time of public worship, but in our homes. Our homes are to be sanctuaries of worship. In other words, we are to live as redeemed sinners, devoted to Christ, our God and Saviour.

Third, in all things, we are to remember and honour the blood, the precious blood of Christ, by which we have been redeemed. Realising our utter dependence upon the blood of Christ let us ever cast the crown of his grace at the feet of our all-glorious Saviour, in constant remembrance of his blood atonement to the everlasting praise of his worthy name!

And the very God of peace sanctify you wholly; and I pray God your whole spirit and soul and body be preserved blameless unto the coming of our Lord Jesus Christ. Faithful is he that calleth you, who also will do it (1 Thessalonians 5:23, 24).

Chapter 12

Christ The Sin Offering

And the LORD spake unto Moses, saying, Speak unto the children of Israel, saying, If a soul shall sin through ignorance against any of the commandments of the LORD concerning things which ought not to be done, and shall do against any of them: If the priest that is anointed do sin according to the sin of the people; then let him bring for his sin, which he hath sinned, a young bullock without blemish unto the LORD for a sin offering ... And he shall take away all the fat thereof, as the fat of the lamb is taken away from the sacrifice of the peace offerings; and the priest shall burn them upon the altar, according to the offerings made by fire unto the LORD: and the priest shall make an atonement for his sin that he hath committed, and it shall be forgiven him.

Leviticus 4:1-35

Why did the Lord Jesus Christ have to die upon the cursed tree to save his people from their sins? Leviticus 4 gives the answer to that question. This is the message of the sin offering given in this chapter. Blessed be his holy name, the God of Glory, the God against whom we have sinned, is a God who 'delighteth in mercy'. He forgives sin. He forgives sin freely. He forgives sin fully. He forgives sin forever. Our God is a great forgiver! But the holy Lord God, just and true, cannot and will not forgive sin except through the merits of Christ's shed blood as our great sin offering (1 John 1:7-2:2). That is the message of Leviticus 4. That is what God taught Moses and the children of Israel when he gave them the law of the sin offering.

What joy ought to flood our hearts when we read in the book of God that he 'delighteth in mercy'. The holy Lord God against whom we have sinned delights in mercy and forgives sin (Psalm 130:3-8). He says, 'I, even I, am he that blotteth out thy transgressions for mine own sake, and will not remember thy sins' (Isaiah 43:25).

Unknown Sin

The Scriptures speak of a specific sin for which we must be forgiven, a sin about which none are aware, or even suspicious, until they are born of God, a sin that must be acknowledged, confessed, atoned for, and forgiven. Leviticus 4 is all about atonement for unknown sin.

In the Old Testament everywhere we read the words 'sin offering' an equally acceptable translation would be 'sin'. Our translators very properly translated the Hebrew word 'sin offering' because the context is referring to an offering for sin. But God the Holy Ghost tells us plainly that these sin offerings represented the Lord Jesus Christ who was made sin for us. (Compare Isaiah 53:10 and 2 Corinthians 5:21). So, as we read this fourth chapter of Leviticus and come to the words 'sin offering', we should think 'sin', remembering that the sin offering is pointing to him who was made sin for us that we might be made the righteousness of God in him. I want to simply declare to you the message of this chapter. This chapter is about Christ the sin offering.

The Sin Offering

The offering described in this chapter is specifically called 'a sin offering', not a trespass offering. This distinction is commonly overlooked, but it ought not be. There is a clear distinction made between the sacrifice for a sin offering and the sacrifice for a trespass offering. The sin offering is discussed in Leviticus 4:1-35. The trespass offering is discussed in Leviticus 5:1-6:7.

The distinction is made for a reason. It is ever the short-sighted tendency of human flesh to judge the character of a person by what he does. God judges the character of a person by what he is. He sees the sin that is in us and declares it is what we are. The trespasses we commit are but the fruit of what we are. Sin is our nature, what we are. Trespasses are our deeds of evil and the fruits of our corrupt nature. Religion only deals with the fruits of sin, our trespasses. But God deals with both what we are and what we do. He deals with what we are first. He first convinces us of what we are, then corrects what we do.

As we read the 35 verses of Leviticus 4, we find no mention of any particular act of sin. We see the priest, the whole congregation, the ruler, and the common man all standing before God confessing themselves sinners; but no mention is made of any act of sin. In the trespass offering, however, specific acts of sin are dealt with but specific persons are not mentioned.

The Experience of Forgiveness
There are five distinct things involved in the experience of forgiveness. I stress the experience of forgiveness because the accomplishment of forgiveness and the experience of it are two separate, distinct things. Our sins were blotted out, put away and forgiven when Christ died at Calvary as our Substitute. But we cannot know anything about the experience of forgiveness until God the Holy Ghost convinces us of the accomplishment of redemption by revealing Christ in us.

First, sin must be made known and 'come to his knowledge' (v. 23). If there is no known need, there can be no sacrifice.

> When the sin, which they have sinned against it, is known, then the congregation shall offer a young bullock for the sin, and bring him before the tabernacle of the congregation (Leviticus 4:14).

This has reference to Holy Spirit conviction (John 16:8-11). Sin cannot be confessed and the experience of it cannot be known until we have been made to know our own sin, not just our sinful acts, but our very nature. We must see ourselves in the mirror of God's holy law (Luke 18:13; Romans 7:9).

Second, sin must be confessed. 'Lay his hand upon the bullock's head' (vv. 4, 24, 29, 33; Proverbs 28:13; 1 John 1:9).

Third, sin must be judged. 'Kill the bullock'. The sinner must kill the sin offering with his own hands, identifying himself with the guilt for the Saviour's blood. Thereby he declared both his heart enmity toward God – he identified himself with the guilt of crucifying the Son of God – and the justice of God in punishing him for sin.

Fourth, sin judged in Christ is sin atoned. 'The priest shall make atonement for him' (v. 26; Romans 5:10, 11).

Fifth, sin confessed, judged, and atoned for is sin forgiven. 'It shall be forgiven him' (v. 26; Ephesians 1:7; Colossians 1:14). This forgiveness is instant, complete, unending, and assured.

The Sacrifice Offered

Now, look at the sacrifice of the sin offering. Here we see the great work of our Lord Jesus Christ, the great sin offering, by whom our sins have been put away. Here, in the sacrificial sin offering, we see the glorious gospel doctrine of substitution. The Lord Jesus Christ was made sin for us (2 Corinthians 5:21).

Our Saviour's character is set before us in the requirements given for the sin offering. The sacrifice for the priest must be a bullock without blemish (v. 3). The sacrifice of the congregation must also be a young bullock without blemish (v. 14). The sacrifice of the ruler must be a kid of the goats without blemish (v. 23). The sacrifice of the common people must be a kid of the goats or a lamb of the sheep, a female, without blemish (v. 28).

The sin offering, unlike the burnt offering, the meat offering, and the trespass offering, was not optional. This sacrifice must be made and the sacrifice must be without blemish before the Lord. He who is our substitute must have no obligations of his own. He cannot pay my debt, if he owes anything for himself. The Lord Jesus Christ could not be our sin offering were he not the holy Lamb of God. He who redeemed us from the curse of the law died for us as 'the just for the unjust', a perfect sacrifice, a mortal sacrifice, and a sacrifice of infinite worth.

With each sacrifice there was a ceremonial laying on of hands. The sinner laid his hands on the head of the victim portraying his confession of sin; but it portrayed more than that. Merely confessing sin cannot change anything. This act showed the great, mysterious, glorious work of God in the transference of sin from the sinner to the Lord Jesus Christ, the sinner's Substitute (Isaiah 53:4-11; 2 Corinthians 5:21).

> My countless sins transferred to Him,
> Shall never more be found,
> Lost in His blood's atoning stream
> Where every crime is drowned!

But there was no atonement made, no forgiveness granted, no blessing pronounced until the victim was slain (vv. 4, 15, 24, 29). As soon as sin was transferred, the victim was slain. I thank God for Christ incarnate. I delight to see our Lord living in righteousness as our representative, obeying the righteous precepts of God's holy law for us. I endeavour to follow my Lord's example. I rejoice in Christ's glorious exaltation and sovereign dominion. But the message of God revealed in Holy Scripture is first and foremost 'Christ crucified'! 'It is the blood that maketh atonement for the soul.'

The whole work of atonement once the animal was publicly slain was done out of the view of the common man, 'before the Lord'. It was a work done out of sight, performed by the priest within the tabernacle. This means three things. First, atonement is God's work. 'When I see the blood, I will pass over you.' Second, atonement is totally outside of ourselves. Third, atonement must be received by faith, by believing the Word of God.

The Symbolism of the Offering

This fourth chapter sets before us the glorious efficacy of Christ's precious blood beautifully symbolized in the sin offering. The precious blood of Christ is effectual, sin-atoning, justice-satisfying blood.

As soon as the victim was slain, the priest carefully collected the blood. The animal was slain in the court of the Israelites. There it lay at the foot of the brazen altar where the priest caught its blood in a bowl. He goes into the court of the priests, past the golden altar of incense which stood in the holy place and proceeds to dip his finger in the bowl. Now he sprinkles the blood seven times towards the veil which concealed the Holy of Holies. The veil, made of very expensive tapestry must, over the years, have gradually come to look very much like a vesture dipped in blood. Seven times towards the veil the blood of the sin offering is sprinkled by the priest.

Why did he begin there? It was to show that our approach to God, our acceptance with God, and our communion with God is by blood. The veil, of course, was not then rent. It showed that the way of access to God was not then revealed. The sprinkling of the blood showed that the only thing that could open the way of access to God was blood; that the blood when perfectly offered, sprinkled seven times, would rend the veil.

The blood of Christ has fulfilled the type to the letter. When our Lord Jesus sprinkled perfectly as it were, seven times, his own heart's blood upon the veil, he cried, 'It is finished', and 'the veil of the temple was rent in twain from the top to the bottom'.

Through the perfect offering of our Saviour's precious blood we have access with boldness into this grace wherein we stand (Romans 4:25-5:2). We who have faith in that blood of our Substitute have intimate communion with the living God. We come near to the mercy seat and talk with him who dwells between the cherubim, as a man talks with his friend.

Next, the priest backed away from the veil to the golden altar of incense, adorned with four horns of gold, pointing to the four corners of the earth from whence God's elect must be gathered. Dipping his finger in the basin again he smears each of the four horns of the altar until each glowed crimson in the light of the golden candlestick.

The horn is indicative of strength. Why was the blood put upon horns of the altar? That altar of incense was typical of prayer, and especially of the intercession of Christ. The blood on the horn showed that the force and power of Christ's all-prevailing intercession lies in the blood. Thank God for those blood smeared horns!

> The Father hears Him pray,
> His dear anointed One,
> He cannot turn away
> The presence of His Son!

With the bowl of blood still in his hands, the priest continues to move backward, as it were, from God to the people, until he gets to the great brazen altar where the burnt offerings were consumed with fire. There he pours out all the rest of the blood before the people. What does that represent? The only ground and basis of our acceptance before God is the shed blood of Christ.

Do you get the picture? Blood is everywhere. A blessed sight! Blood sprinkled on the veil. Blood spilled on the golden altar. Blood smeared on the horns of the altar. Blood poured out and blood all over the priest. Hear of what the blood speaks and rejoice: expiation has been made. Justice is satisfied. Sin is forgiven. The sinner is accepted.

One Peculiar Sin
The sacrifice of Christ, our sin offering, is one sacrifice for all our sins, one sacrifice by which all sin is forgiven. But here in Leviticus 4, the sacrifice points to one peculiar sin, one sin that identifies the great crime of all the human race, a sin of which all are guilty and all are ignorant until they are born of God and taught of God. It is specifically identified in Leviticus 4 as a sin of ignorance, hidden from the one who is guilty of it.

Yet, it is the sin of the whole congregation, the sin of the priest, the sin of each individual, the sin of the ruler, against the commandment of God. What is this unknown sin? Our Saviour tells us plainly. When the Spirit of God comes in the mighty, saving operations of his grace, he convinces chosen, redeemed sinners 'of sin because they believe not on me' (John 16:9). As soon as you are given faith in Christ, you are convinced, made aware of, and confess your unbelief, like the publican, crying, 'God be merciful to me a sinner' (Luke 18:13). And as soon as you confess your sin, offering to God his offering for sin, Christ Jesus, you are forgiven of all sin.

The Shame of the Ordeal
The sin offering sets before us something of the horrid shame our Lord Jesus Christ endured as our Substitute, when he was made sin for us and suffered all the hell and ignominy of God's holy wrath for our sin. Look what had to be done with the carcass of the slain sacrifice. Once the fat was burned before the Lord, the carcass, with the dung, was carried forth without the camp and burned. We read ...

As it was taken off from the bullock of the sacrifice of peace offerings: and the priest shall burn them upon the altar of the burnt offering. And the skin of the bullock, and all his flesh, with his head, and with his legs, and his inwards, and his dung, Even the whole bullock shall he carry forth without the camp unto a clean place, where the ashes are poured out, and burn him on the wood with fire: where the ashes are poured out shall he be burnt (Leviticus 4:10-12).

The priest takes the carcass of the sacrifice and carries it without the camp, a procession of some four miles, to the place where the ashes were poured out; and there he burns the whole thing, not on an altar, but on the ground. What a picture of utter humiliation, shame, and sorrow. What a picture this is of what Christ endured for us. I can almost hear the cry ascending up to heaven, reverberating throughout the camp of Israel, 'My God! My God! Why hast thou forsaken me?'.

Perhaps our Lord Jesus was referring to this in Matthew 24:28. 'For wheresoever the carcase is, there will the eagles be gathered together.' Perhaps the carcass here refers to our Lord Jesus Christ, who was slain for our sins, and the eagles refer to chosen sinners like you and me who flee to him for salvation and life. If so, the lesson is this: Christ crucified is the great magnet by which God draws chosen sinners to himself.

Whether this is the teaching of this particular verse or not, it is the teaching of Holy Scripture (John 12:32; 1 Corinthians 1:21-23). It is our Saviour's teaching in Luke 17:37 where he makes a similar statement. 'Wheresoever the body is, thither will the eagles be gathered together'. Notice the use of the definite article. Our Lord said, 'Wheresoever *the* body is' – not wheresoever bodies are – 'thither will the eagles be gathered together'. Also, notice he speaks of eagles in the plural, and not of buzzards or vultures.

'The body' of the one slain is our Lord Jesus Christ. 'The eagles' are God's elect who are gathered to him in faith. We find this teaching elsewhere in Holy Scripture (Deuteronomy 32:8-12; Job 9:25, 26) as well as the teaching of our Saviour here. God's elect are spoken of in the Scriptures as eagles. His church is given 'the wings of the eagle, that great eagle', and we gather to him (Revelation 12:14). 'They that wait upon the Lord shall renew their strength; they shall mount up with wings as eagles' (Isaiah 40:31).

Wherever Christ crucified is set forth in the preaching of the gospel, wherever the crucified Christ is revealed to men by the power and grace of his Spirit through the preaching of the gospel, there his elect will be gathered unto him 'in the day when the Son of man is revealed'.

Christ's eagles 'gather' to him who is their food. He is the one upon whom we live. He is to us life eternal. The body of our slain Saviour, Christ crucified, is the meeting-point of his elect. He is the great magnet drawing needy souls, like eagles to the carcass. He said, 'I, if I be lifted up from the earth, will draw all men unto me'.

God our Creator, in the book of Job, says of the eagle, his creature, 'She abideth upon the rock from thence she seeketh the prey; her eyes behold afar off ... where the slain are, there is she'. God our Saviour here tells us, 'As the eagles gather round the body, so the souls of men, chosen, redeemed, and called by my grace, are gathered unto me'. Keen and swift as eagles for the prey are God's elect for Christ crucified. These are the words of our blessed Saviour. Let not one of them fall to the ground. 'Wheresoever the body is, thither will the eagles be gathered together.'

The eagle is a bird of prey. In all birds of prey, we are told, there is great sense of smell. Added to its sense of smell, the eagle has a ravenous appetite. Compelled by hunger and its sense of smell, it flies quickly, at every opportunity, to its feast. But the eagle is not a vulture. It does not ordinarily feed on dead things but living prey. And the crucified Christ, upon whom our souls feed, though once slain as our substitute, is alive for evermore.

If Christ has given us life in himself, if he has made us alive by his grace, he gives us a continually increasing appetite and hunger for himself. Does he not? Do you not hunger for him, for his grace, for his embrace, for his face, for his righteousness, for his blood, for his presence? Hungering for him, his eagles fly to the place where he is, like famished birds hastening to the prey. They fly with eager anticipation to his house, his Word, his ordinances, and his throne of grace.

As David longed for the waters of Bethlehem when he was thirsty, oh, let our souls long for Christ. 'As the hart panteth after the water brooks', so he longed for his God. May the same be true of you and me. Oh, for grace to have our souls hungering for Christ crucified day and night! As the eagles gather together unto the prey, so should we be found feasting upon Christ crucified relentlessly. In him, in his glorious excellencies is everything our souls need. His name is our Salvation and High Tower. His blood is our atonement. His righteousness is our dress. His perfections are our delight. His promises are our meditation. His grace is our assurance. His visits are our sweet memories. His presence is our joy. His strength is our comfort. His glory is our ambition. His coming is our hope. His company forever is our heaven!

Crave him! Crave him! Like birds of prey crave their food, let us crave our Saviour. If we have tasted that the Lord is gracious, let us feast upon him. May God give us an insatiable, constant, ever-increasing hunger for Christ, a hunger for everything he is, for everything he gives, for everything he has done, for everything that belongs to him, touches him, and smells of him; a hunger that graciously forces us ever to fly to him, like an eagle to the prey! Wherever Christ is, there will his people fly, as eagles to the prey and as doves to their windows (Isaiah 60:8).

God will have blood, either yours or Christ's. Sin must be punished. Justice must be satisfied. But there is forgiveness with God! He 'delighteth in mercy'! 'The blood of Jesus Christ his Son cleanseth us from all sin.'

How shall we who are now forgiven of all sin through the precious blood of Christ respond to this message? Fly to him like eagles to the carcass.

> We have an altar, whereof they have no right to eat which serve the tabernacle. For the bodies of those beasts, whose blood is brought into the sanctuary by the high priest for sin, are burned without the camp. Wherefore Jesus also, that he might sanctify the people with his own blood, suffered without the gate. Let us go forth therefore unto him without the camp, bearing his reproach. For here have we no continuing city, but we seek one to come. By him therefore let us offer the sacrifice of praise to God continually, that is, the fruit of our lips giving thanks to his name (Hebrews 13:10-15).

'Let us go forth unto him' by faith. Let us go forth unto him alone, 'without the camp, bearing his reproach', by baptism identifying ourselves with him and his gospel. 'Let us go forth unto him' as pilgrims in this world seeking our home with him, offering the sacrifices of praise and thanksgiving unto our God continually!

Chapter 13

The Trespass Offering And The Cross

And if a soul sin, and hear the voice of swearing, and is a witness, whether he hath seen or known of it; if he do not utter it, then he shall bear his iniquity ... And it shall be, when he shall be guilty in one of these things, that he shall confess that he hath sinned in that thing: And he shall bring his trespass offering unto the LORD for his sin which he hath sinned, a female from the flock, a lamb or a kid of the goats, for a sin offering; and the priest shall make an atonement for him concerning his sin ... Then it shall be, because he hath sinned, and is guilty, that he shall restore that which he took violently away, or the thing which he hath deceitfully gotten, or that which was delivered him to keep, or the lost thing which he found, Or all that about which he hath sworn falsely; he shall even restore it in the principal, and shall add the fifth part more thereto, and give it unto him to whom it appertaineth, in the day of his trespass offering. And he shall bring his trespass offering unto the LORD, a ram without blemish out of the flock, with thy estimation, for a trespass offering, unto the priest: And the priest shall make an atonement for him before the LORD: and it shall be forgiven him for any thing of all that he hath done in trespassing therein.

Leviticus 5:1-6:7

In the fourth chapter of Leviticus the Lord God gave Moses and the children of Israel the law of the sin-offering. Primarily, that law dealt with the corruption of our nature and the necessity of us being brought by the grace of God to acknowledge and confess our need of Christ as our Substitute, who was portrayed in the sin offerings. The trespass offering and the sin offering, though similar and very closely connected,[4] are distinct in many ways.

Like the sin offering, the trespass offering was required by God, teaching us that the only way sinners can approach the holy Lord God and find forgiveness and acceptance with him is through the blood atonement of the Lord Jesus Christ, our Substitute.

In all the offerings three things stand out prominently. Let us not neglect these three things or pass over them lightly. First, sin and its acknowledgement. Second, blood atonement and substitution. Third, grace atonement and forgiveness by the blood. Here are four distinctions between the sin-offering and the trespass-offering.

Substitution and Satisfaction
First, the sin offering emphasized substitution, while the trespass offering emphasized satisfaction. These two aspects of our Lord's redemptive work are vital. It was not only necessary that a substitute be found who was willing to suffer all the wrath of God for us, additionally, that substitute must be one who could and would satisfy the infinite righteousness and justice of God for all his people. Blessed be the Lord our God, he has found such a substitute in the Lord Jesus Christ. 'By mercy and truth iniquity is purged' (Proverbs 16:6; Job 33:24; Psalm 89:14, 19).

The Lord Jesus Christ, by his blood atonement as our Substitute made complete satisfaction to God for our sins. He satisfied the purpose of God, the law of God, the righteousness of God, and the justice of God. 'He shall see of the travail of his soul and be satisfied.'

Sinners and Sins
Second, the sin-offering dealt with the sinner, while the trespass-offering dealt with his sins. God's law requires that we love God with all our heart, soul, mind, and strength, and our neighbour as ourselves.

---

[4] In Leviticus 5:11, 12, though the law here is talking about the trespass-offering, the sacrifice offered is called '*a sin offering*'. Both the sin-offering and the trespass-offering were required sacrifices, sacrifices which the Lord God demanded. Whereas, the burnt-offering (acceptance with God), the meat-offering (consecration to God), and the peace-offering (peace with God) were optional, free-will sacrifices of gratitude and praise.

Any act done against God or man is trespass against God. If we wrong God or man by what we do, we trespass or transgress the law of God.

The law of the typical trespass offering tells us five things about sin: 1. All sin is against God. This chapter talks about sins, all sorts of sins; sins of ignorance, uncleanness, deceit, theft, and sins in the holy things of the Lord. All are described as trespasses against God. It is obvious that David understood this when he confessed his sin in the matter of Uriah.

> Have mercy upon me, O God, according to thy lovingkindness: according unto the multitude of thy tender mercies blot out my transgressions. Wash me thoroughly from mine iniquity, and cleanse me from my sin. For I acknowledge my transgressions: and my sin is ever before me. Against thee, thee only, have I sinned, and done this evil in thy sight: that thou mightest be justified when thou speakest, and be clear when thou judgest (Psalm 51:1-4).

Let me give a brief explanation of some of the specific acts of sin described in Leviticus 5 and 6. I mention these only because the reading of the text in our English translation is not as clear as it could be.

> And if a soul sin, and hear the voice of swearing, and is a witness, whether he hath seen or known of it; if he do not utter it, then he shall bear his iniquity (Leviticus 5:1).

This verse is talking about perjury before one of the judges of the people. It is not talking about hearing profanity. And it is not telling us that we ought to go around gossiping about evil to which we are eye or ear witnesses. We ought to cover the faults of others, not expose them. But in a court of law, if called as a witness, a man was (and is) required to tell the truth, no matter how dearly he loved the person on trial.

> Or if a soul swear, pronouncing with his lips to do evil, or to do good, whatsoever it be that a man shall pronounce with an oath, and it be hid from him; when he knoweth of it, then he shall be guilty in one of these (Leviticus 5:4).

This is talking about one who makes rash vows, either of doing evil or of doing good, vows pronounced with an oath, invoking the name of God. Let us pray that the Lord God set a watch before our mouths and keep the door of our lips (Psalm 141:3). 'Be not rash with thy mouth, and let not thine heart be hasty to utter any thing before God: for God is in heaven, and thou upon earth: therefore let thy words be few' (Ecclesiastes 5:2).

If a soul sin, and commit a trespass against the LORD, and lie unto his neighbour in that which was delivered him to keep, or in fellowship, or in a thing taken away by violence, or hath deceived his neighbour (Leviticus 6:2).

This gives specific specimens of fraud; lying, deception, theft. The word translated 'fellowship' would be better translated 'dealing'. It is talking about deceiving someone in business. Whatever the trespass is, it is against God, a violation of his law, a denial of his right to be God.

2. Sin is a costly thing. It is costly afterwards in life, costly in the misery it brings in death, costly in eternity in hell. It was by a price of infinite cost that the Lord Jesus Christ redeemed his elect from sin.

3. Sin brings us into debt at the bar of God.

4. Sin's debt must and shall be paid. 'The wages of sin is death.'

5. The only way we can be forgiven our sins and our debt be paid is by the sacrifice of Christ, our sin-atoning, justice-satisfying Substitute.

The trespass offering was required, not because of what the man was, but because of what he had done. The sin offering was required because of what he was. In requiring the sin offering, the Lord mentioned specific people as sinners but made no mention of their sins. Here, he makes no mention of anyone in particular, but deals with acts of sin, trespasses, wilful sins, and sins of ignorance. That mention is made regarding sins of ignorance tells us we are all incompetent to determine what is and is not sin. C. H. Mackintosh observed ...

It is a very grave error to suppose that, provided a man acts up to the dictates of his conscience, he is all right and safe. The peace which rests upon such a foundation as this will be eternally destroyed when the light of the judgment-seat shines upon the conscience.

Fallen man is totally unable to assess the evil he has done, how much less the evil he is! We call light darkness and darkness light and think we are right. We call good evil and evil good convinced our judgment is sound. It is not. A man can be unclean or do an unclean thing, and not know it, but he is still guilty (vv. 2, 3). A person can speak rashly with his mouth and be ignorant of it, but he is still guilty (v. 4). Verse 17 tells us that a man can violate the law of God and be unaware of his trespass – how often we do – but he is still guilty.

Read verse 15 and come face to face with this shocking truth: we often, in ignorance, commit trespass and sin in the worship and service of God. Even our holy things are polluted!

If a soul commit a trespass, and sin through ignorance, in the holy things of the LORD; then he shall bring for his trespass unto the LORD a ram without blemish out of the flocks, with thy estimation by shekels of silver, after the shekel of the sanctuary, for a trespass offering (Leviticus 5:15).

Be not rash with thy mouth, and let not thine heart be hasty to utter any thing before God: for God is in heaven, and thou upon earth: therefore let thy words be few (Ecclesiastes 5:2).

But here is the good news of the gospel given in the legal type of the trespass offering: all manner of sin is forgiven by our great God! Thank God for our Aaron, our High Priest, the Lord Jesus Christ, who has borne the iniquity of our holy things!

And if a soul sin, and commit any of these things which are forbidden to be done by the commandments of the LORD; though he wist it not, yet is he guilty, and shall bear his iniquity. And he shall bring a ram without blemish out of the flock, with thy estimation, for a trespass offering, unto the priest: and the priest shall make an atonement for him concerning his ignorance wherein he erred and wist it not, and it shall be forgiven him (Leviticus 5:17, 18).

Five times, the Lord God declares, 'It shall be forgiven'. I think it is safe to assume 'It shall be forgiven'.

Three things are vital. No one will have forgiveness without these three things: 1. The sinner must be convinced of his sin. 2. The sinner must confess his sin. 3. Atonement must be made for the sinner and his sin. Blessed be God, where these three things are found, forgiveness is sure (Isaiah 43:25; 44:22; 48:9; Jeremiah 50:20; Acts 13:38, 39).

It is God against whom we have sinned, who made atonement for sin, convinces us of sin, and convinces us of atonement, satisfaction, and forgiveness by the sacrifice of his Son, the Lord Jesus Christ.

Blood and Money

Third, the sin offering was an offering of blood only, while the trespass offering required both blood and money. Whether a man robbed God in worship or his neighbour by fraud, the Lord God required 'He shall make amends for the harm that he hath done ... He shall restore that which he took violently away'. This was to be done by adding to his blood sacrifice the priest's 'estimation by shekels of silver, after the shekel of the sanctuary' (v. 15). To this, 'the fifth part' more was added (5:15, 16; 6:5, 6). The measurement of the silver by which atonement was made was not man's measure, but God's, 'the shekel of the sanctuary'. In other words, God's demands were measured out by God himself, exacted by God, and paid to God. Here is the measurement of the sanctuary, 'The precious blood of Christ'.

Restitution Required

Fourth, in the sin-offering no restitution was required; but in the trespass-offering restitution was made and a fifth part added.

What does that mean? Read Genesis 47 and you will see. The first time these words 'fifth part' are used in Scripture is in Genesis 47. Perhaps you know the story. Pharaoh was king over Egypt and Joseph was his prime minister. Before the seven years of famine Pharaoh was possessor of the land and the people were his servants. Yet, they were, in a sense, somewhat independent of him until Joseph did something for the people in Pharaoh's name. We read,

> When that year was ended, they came unto him the second year, and said unto him, we will not hide it from my lord, how that our money is spent; my lord also hath our herds of cattle; there is not ought left in the sight of my lord, but our bodies, and

our lands: Wherefore shall we die before thine eyes, both we and our land? Buy us and our land for bread, and we and our land will be servants unto Pharaoh: and give us seed, that we may live, and not die, that the land be not desolate. And Joseph bought all the land of Egypt for Pharaoh; for the Egyptians sold every man his field, because the famine prevailed over them: so the land became Pharaoh's. And as for the people, he removed them to cities from one end of the borders of Egypt even to the other end thereof. Only the land of the priests bought he not; for the priests had a portion assigned them of Pharaoh, and did eat their portion which Pharaoh gave them: wherefore they sold not their lands. Then Joseph said unto the people, Behold, I have bought you this day and your land for Pharaoh: lo, here is seed for you, and ye shall sow the land. And it shall come to pass in the increase, that ye shall give the fifth part unto Pharaoh, and four parts shall be your own, for seed of the field, and for your food, and for them of your households, and for food for your little ones. And they said, thou hast saved our lives: let us find grace in the sight of my lord, and we will be Pharaoh's servants. And Joseph made it a law over the land of Egypt unto this day, that Pharaoh should have the fifth part; except the land of the priests only, which became not Pharaoh's (Genesis 47:18-26).

The fifth part was a declaration by the forgiven sinner that he now belonged to God by another claim, the claim of redemption.

Know ye not that the unrighteous shall not inherit the kingdom of God? Be not deceived: neither fornicators, nor idolaters, nor adulterers, nor effeminate, nor abusers of themselves with mankind, nor thieves, nor covetous, nor drunkards, nor revilers, nor extortioners, shall inherit the kingdom of God. And such were some of you: but ye are washed, but ye are sanctified, but ye are justified in the name of the Lord Jesus, and by the Spirit of our God ... What? know ye not that your body is the temple of the Holy Ghost which is in you, which ye have of God, and ye are not your own? For ye are bought with a price: therefore glorify God in your body, and in your spirit, which are God's (1 Corinthians 6:9-11, 19, 20).

This added fifth part also tells us that both God against whom the trespass was made and the man who was injured by it were gainers in the end. Here is the glory of the cross. 'Where sin abounded, grace did much more abound.' The trespass offering declares, 'Because sin abounded, grace did much more abound'. I have chosen my words deliberately. Both God and man have gained more by the forgiveness of sin through the blood of Christ than was lost by the sin and fall of our father Adam. The holy Lord God has gained more by redemption than ever he lost – if I may be permitted to use such language – by the Fall. The Lord God reaps a richer harvest of glory in the fields of grace than he could ever have reaped in the garden of innocence (Ephesians 1:3-14; 2:7). The sons of God raise a loftier song of praise around the empty tomb of the crucified Christ than we could ever have raised in the garden of Eden. The injury done by sin has not only been perfectly atoned for and remedied by the blood of Christ, but God has gained by the cross the praise of the glory of his grace (Psalm 76:10).

This is a stupendous truth. God, the eternal, Triune, holy Lord God, has gotten himself great gain by the work accomplished by our all-glorious Christ at Calvary!

Who could have conceived such a thing? When we see man and the creation over which he was lord laid in a heap of ruins at the feet of Satan, how could we ever imagine that from those ruins the great God of glory would gather a crown for his holy head which could not be gotten in any other way? Let every knee bow to the crucified Son of God and every tongue confess his praises forever. He deserves it! Let the crucified Christ hold all the affection of our hearts. He deserves it!

Not only is it true that God is the gainer by the Fall, we are too! Martin Luther understood what I am trying to say to you. He said, with regard to Adam's sin in the Garden, 'O blessed Fall'! Had there been no fall, no sin, no condemnation, we could never have known the wonders of redemption. Had there been no fall, no sin, no condemnation, we could never have known the glories of grace. Therefore, we most gladly say to our Lord Jesus Christ, as the Egyptians said to Joseph, 'Thou hast saved our lives: we have found grace in the sight of our lord, and we will be thy servants forever'.

Chapter 14

Restitution Made Or The Lord Revealed

If a soul commit a trespass, and sin through ignorance, in the holy things of the LORD; then he shall bring for his trespass unto the LORD a ram without blemish out of the flocks, with thy estimation by shekels of silver, after the shekel of the sanctuary, for a trespass offering: And he shall make amends for the harm that he hath done in the holy thing, and shall add the fifth part thereto, and give it unto the priest: and the priest shall make an atonement for him with the ram of the trespass offering, and it shall be forgiven him ... If a soul sin, and commit a trespass against the LORD, and lie unto his neighbour in that which was delivered him to keep, or in fellowship, or in a thing taken away by violence, or hath deceived his neighbour; Or have found that which was lost, and lieth concerning it, and sweareth falsely; in any of all these that a man doeth, sinning therein: Then it shall be, because he hath sinned, and is guilty, that he shall restore that which he took violently away, or the thing which he hath deceitfully gotten, or that which was delivered him to keep, or the lost thing which he found, Or all that about which he hath sworn falsely; he shall even restore it in the principal, and shall add the fifth part more thereto, and give it unto him to whom it appertaineth, in the day of his trespass offering. And he shall bring his trespass offering unto the LORD, a ram without blemish out of the flock, with thy estimation, for a trespass offering, unto the priest: And the priest shall make an atonement for him before the LORD: and it shall be forgiven him for any thing of all that he hath done in trespassing therein.

Leviticus 5:15-6:7

Blessed is that enlightened soul who, by the grace of God, is able to see Christ in the Old Testament as well as in the New. Blessed are those eyes that behold the Lord Jesus Christ in all the promises, precepts, and prophecies of the Old Testament, as well as in the proclamations of the New. Blessed are those hearts that can see the beauty and glory of Christ in the ordinances, types, and shadows of the law, as well as in the shining light of the gospel.

It is a sad fact, but a fact it is, that most who read the Bible and most who preach and teach from it see nothing in the Old Testament but historic facts, legal precepts, carnal ceremonies, and moral ethics. To the vast majority of the religious people I know, the Old Testament is a sealed book without meaning or message. They simply cannot unlock it because they do not have the key. They are like those Isaiah describes in Isaiah 6. Seeing, they see not. Hearing, they hear not. Understanding, they understand not the things written in Old Testament Scripture.

The key to the Old Testament is Christ. What a great blessing it is to have the key. Yet, there is no room for boasting here. If we see, hear, and understand the Scriptures, it is because God has graciously caused the light of his glory and grace to shine in our hearts by his Spirit. It is because we have been taught of God. It is because the Lord God has opened our understanding that we might understand the Scriptures (Luke 24:45). It is written, 'Blessed are your eyes, for they see: and your ears, for they hear' (Matthew 13:16).

Nowhere is man's spiritual blindness more evident than in the things written about the Mosaic law and the Levitical sacrifices. Reading the things written by various commentators about the laws of restitution given in Exodus 21-23 and the requirement of restitution to make atonement here in the book of Leviticus, I was as amazed as I was disappointed to see so very few make even a gospel application of them, much less give a gospel interpretation.

The law of God requiring restitution for any wrong done by one person to another and the sacrifices requiring restitution for atonement were not intended merely to teach a moral precept of restitution. Rather, these things were written to teach by precept and by picture that the Lord Jesus Christ would, by his great work of redemption, turn the tables and make a full restitution of all things to the everlasting praise and glory of the Triune God. They all testify of that which is written of him in Psalm 69:4. 'Then I restored that which I took not away' (Acts 3:18-21; Ephesians 2:4-7).

Glory Revealed

God's prophet Isaiah declared that the glory of the Lord would be revealed in our Lord Jesus Christ and his accomplishments of redemption as our Surety (Isaiah 40:1-5). The glory of the Lord is the Lord Jesus Christ, the incarnate God-man, our Mediator, our Surety, our Substitute, our Saviour. Christ is the embodiment of 'the glory of the LORD', but he is more. The Lord Jesus Christ is essentially and emphatically 'the glory of the LORD', for in him dwells all the fulness of the Godhead bodily. When Isaiah said, 'the glory of the LORD shall be revealed', he spoke prophetically of the incarnation of Christ. He was saying, 'God the Son shall come in human flesh possessing all the glory of the glorious God; and in him, God shall be seen of all men, for this man is God'. God's glory was revealed in his Son when he was sent here on the mission of mercy to redeem and save his people. Yet, the meaning of Isaiah's words is fuller still.

The glory of the Lord is displayed in the attributes of his being. His glory is that which sets him apart from all his creatures and identifies him as God over all, blessed forever. Isaiah declared that the glory of God, all the glory of all his attributes, would be revealed in the accomplishments of Christ at Calvary.

David said, 'The heavens declare the glory of God', and they do, but only in part. Great as the glory of God revealed in the heavens is, believing sinners see a display of that glory so great, so stupendous, and so wonderful that the glory of his wisdom and power in creation pales into insignificance by comparison. The glory of the cross, the glory of the Lord revealed in the crucified Christ, the glory of the Lord revealed in the salvation of poor, fallen, helpless, doomed, damned sinners, that is the glory of the Lord! Sin had blinded us to the glory of God; but grace reveals it far more fully in our crucified Saviour than it could ever have been known otherwise. The glory of God is revealed in the gospel but it is hidden from them that are lost ...

In whom the God of this world hath blinded the minds of them which believe not, lest the light of the glorious gospel of Christ, who is the image of God, should shine unto them. For we preach not ourselves, but Christ Jesus the Lord; and ourselves your servants for Jesus' sake. For God, who commanded the light to shine out of darkness, hath shined in our hearts, to give the light of the knowledge of the glory of God in the face of Jesus Christ (2 Corinthians 4:4-6).

Look to Christ, the crucified, risen, exalted saving Christ, and behold the glory of God. In him and by him restitution has been made and both God and man have gained more in him than ever was lost by the sin and fall of Adam, for in him 'the glory of the LORD is revealed'.

Wisdom and Knowledge
I see in the cross of Christ the glory of the Lord's wisdom and knowledge more fully than it could ever have been seen in any other way.

O the depth of the riches both of the wisdom and knowledge of God! how unsearchable are his judgments, and his ways past finding out! For who hath known the mind of the Lord? or who hath been his counsellor? Or who hath first given to him, and it shall be recompensed unto him again? For of him, and through him, and to him, are all things: to whom be glory forever. Amen (Romans 11:33-36).

Adam saw the wisdom of God in creation more clearly than any man has seen it or could see it since the fall. But Adam did not and could not see the glory of God's wisdom in redemption until he experienced it.

I know, cavilling will-worshippers cry, 'If that is true, if God has ordained all things, then let us sin that grace may abound'. Do not be so foolish. Though it is the wisdom of God that ordained sin, it is the justice of God that punishes it. Believing hearts do not challenge God's wisdom. We adore it.

Here is the glory of God's wisdom. It is written, 'By mercy and truth iniquity is purged' (Proverbs 16:6). But iniquity could never be purged and truth maintained, unless some way known only to infinite wisdom is found to do it, unless some infinitely wise arrangement could be made to both satisfy the infinite rigid requirements of truth while exercising absolute mercy. Righteousness and peace could never have kissed each other had not God in infinite wisdom found a way to make it happen. The glory of God's wisdom is revealed in that way. It is called substitution. Salvation by a Substitute of infinite worth makes it possible and certain that iniquity shall be purged by mercy and by truth. Behold the cross of Christ and sing ...

> Surely his salvation is nigh them that fear him; that glory may dwell in our land. Mercy and truth are met together; righteousness and peace have kissed each other. Truth shall spring out of the earth; and righteousness shall look down from heaven (Psalm 85:9-11).

Mercy, Love, and Grace

In the cross of our Lord Jesus Christ the glory of the Lord's mercy, love, and grace is revealed. I do not suggest that the love of God is not revealed in other ways, in other acts of his goodness, or in other places. It is. I am certain that Adam, before the fall, knew God's love in benevolence, goodness, and sweet communion. He knew the love of God as his Creator, his Maker, and his Companion, just as the holy angels know it. But Adam did not know and could not know the glory of God's love. Indeed, it would not have been possible for anyone to know the glory of God's love had there been no fall. The glory of God's love is revealed in the cross of our Lord Jesus Christ.

We read of God's everlasting, electing love and we rejoice. We give thanks to our God for his eternal, adopting love (Jeremiah 31:3; 1 John 3:1). But the glory of the love of God is revealed at Calvary (John 3:16; Romans 5:6-8; 1 John 3:16; 4:9, 10). The Son of God loved me and gave himself for me.

Love is known by its deeds. But love is also known by comparison. Those who vainly imagine they are wiser than God would tell us God loves all men. Others among them would have us believe the love of God would have been more greatly revealed had there been no entrance of sin into the world. But it was the wisdom of God that ordained the entrance of sin into the world. That wisdom is displayed here. By the sin and fall of our father Adam and the ruin of all the human race in him, the Lord God shows the glory of his love in saving some.

121

If the Lord God had kept all from sinning, or if he had saved all, how could we know the intensity, devotion, and freeness of his love for us? Love is displayed by these two things, self-sacrifice and comparison. I know the love of God because he loved me and gave himself for me; and I know the love of God, the glory of his love, because he loved me. If God loved every creature as he loves his elect, where can we see the glory of his love? But once a sinner is made to see that the Lord God has loved him and loved him immutably from all eternity, passing by many more noble, more useful, more appealing than him, then the chosen, redeemed, called sinner sees the surpassing glory of the love of God in the face of Christ, and is conquered by his love. We see the glory of God's love in the fact that it is discriminating love. 'We love him, because he first loved us' (1 John 4:19). Horatius Bonar wrote:

> O love of God, how strong and true!
> Eternal, and yet ever new,
> Uncomprehended and unbought,
> Beyond all knowledge and all thought!

> We read Thee best in Him Who came
> To bear for us the cross of shame;
> Sent by the Father from on high,
> Our life to live, our death to die!

> O love of God, our shield and stay,
> Through all the perils of our way:
> Eternal love, in thee we rest,
> Forever safe, forever blest!

Truth, Justice, and Holiness

As I behold the Son of God hanging upon the cursed tree, made to be sin, bearing all the terror of God's holy wrath, forsaken of God and slain, I see the glory of God's absolute truth, inflexible justice, and immaculate holiness.

In Christ crucified, the glory of God's justice is revealed as it could not be revealed in any other way. Adam knew the threat of justice before he fell. Sinners in hell know the severity of God's justice. We see tokens of justice every day. Justice demands punishment, a just and righteous punishment for every offense. Justice demands a victim. No pleadings, no tears, no repentance, no works of restitution can turn away the sword of justice. Mercy may implore leniency and love beg for pardon, but justice is unaffected and unbending. Justice 'will by no means clear the guilty'. But God, in infinite wisdom and love, found a way to both punish the sinner and forgive him.

Behold the glory of God's justice in the face of his darling Son, when he was made to be sin for us! Believing sinners are justified freely by the grace of God through the redemption that is in Christ Jesus (Romans 3:25, 26).

When the holy Lord God looks on the shed blood of his darling Son, he says, 'Enough!' Here the glory of God's justice is revealed. Oh, how holy, how just, how true the God of glory must be! When the holy Lord God found sin on his own beloved Son, he spared him not. When God the Son bore the wrath of God in his own body, in his soul, and in his heart on the cursed tree, he satisfied the justice of God. God, the holy Lord God will, for he must, punish sin. Justice demands it.

Sovereignty and Goodness
In the cross of our Lord Jesus Christ, in the face of our crucified Redeemer, in the redemption accomplished by God our Saviour at Calvary, we see the glory of the Lord's universal sovereignty and absolute goodness revealed, and revealed in such full splendour as it could never have been known otherwise.

When Moses asked the Lord to show him his glory, he said 'I will make all my goodness to pass before thee; and I will be gracious to whom I will be gracious'. Here is the glory of God's sovereign goodness, the glory of his grace. God is gracious. God will be gracious to whom he will be gracious. God makes even the wrath of man to praise him and work for the good of his chosen (Psalm 76:10). Satan, who dared imagine he could thwart the purpose of the Almighty, led a rebellion in heaven, and leads the rebellion of men and demons on earth and in hell, yet he is but the servant of our God to accomplish his purpose of grace toward his elect.

God's glory is great in salvation, indescribably greater than ever it could have been had Adam not fallen, had sin never entered into the world, had the Lord Jesus Christ not died at Calvary, had he not saved his people from their sins. This is what the laws and sacrifices of restitution tell us. Behold the cross of our Lord Jesus Christ and understand when you hear the Son of God cry, 'It is finished', that restitution has been made and the glory of God is revealed.

If the glory of God is most fully and perfectly revealed in the salvation of sinners, how that fact ought to inspire poor, needy sinners with hope. Surely, if God is glorified in saving sinners, he would be glorified in saving me! I will, upon that ground, like David of old, sue for mercy. 'For thy name's sake, O Lord, pardon mine iniquity; for it is great' (Psalm 25:11).

Chapter 15

Ever-Burning Fire

And the LORD spake unto Moses, saying, Command Aaron and his sons, saying, This is the law of the burnt offering: It is the burnt offering, because of the burning upon the altar all night unto the morning, and the fire of the altar shall be burning in it. And the priest shall put on his linen garment, and his linen breeches shall he put upon his flesh, and take up the ashes which the fire hath consumed with the burnt offering on the altar, and he shall put them beside the altar. And he shall put off his garments, and put on other garments, and carry forth the ashes without the camp unto a clean place. And the fire upon the altar shall be burning in it; it shall not be put out: and the priest shall burn wood on it every morning, and lay the burnt offering in order upon it; and he shall burn thereon the fat of the peace offerings The fire shall ever be burning upon the altar; it shall never go out.

Leviticus 6:8-13

Fire is used throughout the Scriptures as an emblem of God's purity, holiness and justice. It was so from the very beginning. When the Lord God drove Adam and Eve out of the Garden of Eden he set 'Cherubim and a flaming sword which turned every way to keep the way of the tree of life' (Genesis 3:24). When Abraham offered sacrifice to God who revealed himself in 'smoking furnace and a burning lamp' (Genesis 15:17, 18) he carried fire with him to the altar of sacrifice (Genesis 22). God poured out fire and brimstone from heaven upon Sodom. When the Lord God revealed himself to Moses, he spoke to him out of a bush that burned with fire (Exodus 3). When God gave his law at Sinai, the mount was filled with fire. Nadab and Abihu were killed by the hand of the Lord because they burned 'strange fire' on God's altar (Leviticus 10). Hell is a place of horrible torment, a pit of everlasting, unquenchable fire.[5] Our God is a consuming fire. In the camp of Israel on the altar of God fire burned continually. It is written, 'The fire shall ever be burning upon the altar; it shall never go out'.

Never imagine there is redundancy in the Word of God. Everything written in the book of Inspiration is written according to divine purpose. In the first five chapters of Leviticus the Lord gave Moses specific instructions about how the burnt offering, the meat offering, the peace offering, the sin offering, and the trespass offering were to be made. Here, in chapters 6 and 7, he gives instructions again about those same offerings. In the first five chapters the instructions were for the people who brought the offerings. In these two chapters the instructions were given specifically to the priests, to Aaron and his sons.

In this portion of Scripture the primary thing set before us is the ever-burning fire upon the altar. 'The fire shall ever be burning upon the altar; it shall never go out.' The fire burning upon the altar is an instructive picture of the holy justice of God which must be satisfied. God the Holy Ghost gives us the message of this passage in 2 Corinthians 5:18-21.

The Fire upon the Altar

And the LORD spake unto Moses, saying, Command Aaron and his sons, saying, This is the law of the burnt offering: It is the

---

[5] Through the ages multitudes, both religious and profane, have brought forth countless arguments to fritter away the fact of the everlasting damnation of unbelieving rebels in hell, but the fact stands as it is plainly revealed in Holy Scripture. 'The wicked shall be turned into hell' (Psalm 9:17). 'Who among us shall dwell with the devouring fire? Who among us shall dwell with everlasting burnings?' (Isaiah 33:14). Troubling and horrible as the fact of eternal damnation is, God's elect know with certainty that soon our Lord Jesus shall be 'revealed from heaven with his mighty angels in flaming fire taking vengeance on them that know not God and obey not the gospel of the Lord Jesus Christ, who shall be punished with everlasting destruction from the presence of the Lord and from the glory of his power'. In that day and for all eternity he shall be 'glorified in his saints' and 'admired in all them that believe' (2 Thessalonians 1:6-10).

burnt offering, because of the burning upon the altar all night unto the morning, and the fire of the altar shall be burning in it (Leviticus 6:8, 9).

Here the Holy One of Israel speaks again from the holy place, revealing the horror of his wrath against sin and the perfection of his justice which demands its punishment. God's infinite justice, burning against sin, is displayed in the fire burning on the altar of the tabernacle.

This fire was never to be extinguished. In these five verses, the Lord God tells us three times that the fire was never to be put out by man or allowed to burn out on its own. Why? Because 'every one of his righteous judgments endure forever' (Psalm 119:160). The fire burned all through the night as an emblem of the sleeplessness of hell, the burning wrath of God against all iniquity, and the all-seeing eye of divine righteousness that watches over the earth.

In the pit of the damned they have no rest, no respite, no relief from the wrath of God. And the holy eyes of the holy Lord God ever behold the sons of men upon the earth. He whose eyes are a flaming fire constantly watches over his creation, beholding the sons of men.

In the book of God, we read concerning the damned that the smoke of their torments ascends forever. The fire and brimstone of hell produces a smoke ever rising to God, the holy angels, the redeemed in Glory, and the Lamb upon his throne (Revelation 14:10, 11, 18).

All through the night the fire burned upon the altar. It could be seen by all the camp of Israel. The wise believing father might well have taken his children to their tent's door before going to bed and pointing to the fire have said, 'Children, do you see that fire? Do you smell that smoke? Except you find refuge in the Lamb of God, so shall the fire of God's wrath consume you forever'.

But, blessed be God, that fire represented something far greater than God's holy and just wrath. It represented the way of escape. Can you see the victim burned upon the altar, the lamb consumed by the fire, whose life feeds the flames? That is Christ dying under the awful wrath of God in the place of sinners who deserve to die. Christ's suffering and death, upon which the Triune God had his holy eye from eternity, was perpetually held forth in the camp of Israel in the fire burning upon the altar. There the love and justice of God met together in perfect unison. Righteousness and peace perpetually kissed each other. Mercy and truth embraced each other. Beholding the fire on the altar, the believing Israelite could sleep peacefully through the night knowing that God in Christ is both a just God and a Saviour!

The Priest's Linen Garments
The Lord commanded his priest to put on his linen garments.

> And the priest shall put on his linen garment, and his linen breeches shall he put upon his flesh, and take up the ashes which the fire hath consumed with the burnt offering on the altar, and he shall put them beside the altar (Leviticus 6:10).

We do not have to guess what these linen garments represented. The priest's linen garment with his linen breeches portrayed purity, holiness, and righteousness.

> And to her was granted that she should be arrayed in fine linen, clean and white: for the fine linen is the righteousness of saints (Revelation 19:8).

In this suit of purity the priest was a type and emblem of Christ our Redeemer in his perfect purity, divine and human, coming to perform the work of atonement as our Substitute. In this suit of pure, white linen, the priest was to take the ashes of the burnt sacrifice off the altar and lay them for a while beside the altar so that all Israel might see that the flame of justice had not spared the sacrifice. There, the ashes lying beside the altar portrayed our crucified Saviour in the tomb, and declared, 'Justice has found its object. The lightning of God's holy wrath has struck the lightning rod and shall not strike again'.

Blessed be the God of all grace, he has made our Priest's holy linen garments ours! Believing on the Lord Jesus Christ, God's elect are made the righteousness of God in, with, and by him who was made sin for us. In Revelation 19:8 the word 'righteousness' can read the righteousnesses of saints – plural, and not the righteousness – singular of saints. The righteousness that is ours in Christ is, like our Saviour's, a plural righteousness: righteousness imputed in justification and righteousness imparted in regeneration.

The Priest's Other Garments
Then, God's priest was required to take off his linen garments and put on his other garments.

> And he shall put off his garments, and put on other garments, and carry forth the ashes without the camp unto a clean place (Leviticus 6:11).

Coming out of the sanctuary the priest has put aside his linen garments and is wearing his other garments. He takes off the garments that had been ceremonially polluted by sin and puts on his holy, priestly garments to carry the ashes of the sacrifice away to a clean place. The Valley of Ashes (Jeremiah 31:40) was used for this purpose. The Valley of Ashes was southwest of the city of Jerusalem, a ditch at the foot of Mount Calvary (Hebrews 9:12; 10:9-23).

Our great Saviour, who bore our sin in his own body on the tree, wears another garment now. That body in which he was made to be sin for us, that body in which he bore our iniquities, that body in which he was made a curse for us has now been made a glorious body. He has cast off and cast away our sins. He has carried his blood into a clean place, having by the merit of his blood obtained eternal redemption for us (Romans 4:25-5:11).

The Fuel for the Fire
Because the fire on the altar was never to be put out or allowed to go out, it had to have a constant supply of fuel. That is spoken of next.

> And the fire upon the altar shall be burning in it; it shall not be put out: and the priest shall burn wood on it every morning, and lay the burnt offering in order upon it; and he shall burn thereon the fat of the peace offerings (Leviticus 6:1).

Wood was constantly kept on the altar; and the fat of the peace offering with the wood kept the fire burning continually. It was the fat of the peace offering that fuelled the fire.

Justice fell upon Christ our Peace Offering. He bore the fire of God's fierce wrath for us. He endured the fire of hell as our Substitute. By his death under the vengeance of God's holy wrath, he obtained our peace.

129

This ever-burning fire, portraying the burning fury of God's wrath against sin, the infinite burning fury of divine wrath that fell upon our Lord Jesus Christ when he was made sin for us, was first lit by God himself (Leviticus 9:22-24).

Aaron's sons, Nadab and Abihu, despised God's sacrifice and brought strange fire before the Lord. Despising Christ, they thought to find acceptance with God by a fire of their own. When they came into the holy place, God killed them in the fury of his holy wrath. Be warned! Nadab and Abihu were justly slain because no sacrifice of man can satisfy the justice of God (Leviticus 10:1-7). The very fire that consumed God's sacrifice consumed Nadab and Abihu! And the very justice of God that consumed his darling Son, our Sacrifice, the Sacrifice he required, the Sacrifice he made, the Sacrifice he has accepted, will consume you if you despise his Sacrifice!

The Perpetuity of the Fire
The perpetuity of this fire is intended to teach us that the fire of God's wrath has no end.

> The fire shall ever be burning upon the altar; it shall never go out (Leviticus 6:13).

Throughout this instructive passage, we are constantly reminded that the fire of God's wrath has no end. Three times our Lord Jesus, no doubt referring to this passage, declared that in hell the worm dies not and the fire is not quenched (Mark 9:44, 46, 48). The eternal justice of God will never cease to find fuel for the fire of his wrath in hell. It is written, 'The wrath of God abideth'. Let every sinner tremble. The wrath of God is infinite and hell is forever.

But God has himself put out the fire for his elect. The Lord Jesus Christ forever satisfied the wrath of God. He is that one Sacrifice which, when consumed by the fire of God's holy justice in turn consumed the fire. The holy Lord God shall never cease to find complete satisfaction for his holy justice in his darling Son (Hebrews 13:10-12). Because Christ has forever satisfied the holy wrath and justice of God for sinners God's word to every believer is 'Fury is not in me' (Isaiah 27:4; Romans 8:1-4).

Chapter 16

'It Is Most Holy'

And the Lord spake unto Moses, saying, ... It shall not be baken with leaven. I have given it unto them for their portion of my offerings made by fire; it is most holy, as is the sin offering, and as the trespass offering ... Speak unto Aaron and to his sons, saying, This is the law of the sin offering: In the place where the burnt offering is killed shall the sin offering be killed before the LORD: it is most holy ... All the males among the priests shall eat thereof: it is most holy ... Likewise this is the law of the trespass offering: it is most holy ... Every male among the priests shall eat thereof: it shall be eaten in the holy place: it is most holy ... And the flesh of the sacrifice of his peace offerings for thanksgiving shall be eaten the same day that it is offered; he shall not leave any of it until the morning.

Leviticus 6:8-7:15

As you read this portion of Holy Scripture relating to the ceremonial sacrifices and services offered to the Lord God by his appointed priests, may God the Holy Spirit give you grace to focus your heart upon him who is the only true and real sacrifice for sin and 'the end of the law for righteousness to everyone that believeth', our Lord Jesus Christ, the Son of God. It is my prayer that God the Holy Spirit would also cause you to know and feel the horrid evil of sin, the sin of your own heart, before the eyes of the holy Lord God. So great is the evil of our sin that God's holy justice could never pardon and forgive it except by the blood of his own dear Son, the Lord Jesus Christ.

131

Chapters 1-7

The first seven chapters of Leviticus give us the inspired record of the law God gave to Moses on Mount Sinai regarding the sacrifices of divine worship and how they were to be offered. The burnt offering portrayed a celebration of acceptance with God by Christ. The meat offering was a sacrifice declaring the worshipper's consecration to God in Christ. The peace offering was a celebration of peace and fellowship with God in Christ. The sin offering portrayed the Lord Jesus Christ as our Substitute, our Sin Offering. The trespass offering typified Christ's effectual, sin-atoning sacrifice to God and the forgiveness of sin and restitution made by his blood.

The burnt offering, the meat offering, and the peace offering were freewill offerings. They were not required by the law but were voluntarily made. They were offerings arising from the grateful hearts of forgiven sinners for the praise of God. The Lord God never required anyone to bring them. He required only that if men and women worshipped him, they must do so in the manner he prescribed. No one worships God who does not do so with a willing heart. Yes, we are made willing by the power of his grace (Psalm 65:4; 110:3); but we are willing worshippers. In all acts of worship, 'if there be first a willing mind' – and heart – 'it is accepted' (2 Corinthians 8:12).

However, the sin offering and trespass offering were offerings God required. He required them because they portrayed redemption, the absolute necessity of redemption, by Christ our Substitute. In these two offerings, the Lord Jesus stands before us and says, 'I am the way, the truth, and the life. No man cometh unto the Father, but by me'.

Priests' Instructions

In the first chapters of Leviticus (1:1-6:7) the Lord God gave specific instructions to the people of Israel (the rulers, the common people, and the priests) about how they must come before God in worship, bringing their sacrifices to him. Beginning at Leviticus 6:8 and continuing to the end of chapter seven, all the instructions given relate to the priests, to Aaron and his sons, who offered the sacrifices, ministering before the Lord in the tabernacle. In these two chapters, the priests stand pre-eminently as types and pictures of our Lord Jesus Christ, our great High Priest before God. The entire work they performed under the law of God in offering these daily sacrifices is declared to be 'most holy'.

'It is most holy'. Those words apply not to the sacrifice alone, but to the offering of the sacrifice, the burning of the sacrifice, the eating of the sacrifice, the place of the sacrifice, and the priests who offered the sacrifice. They are specifically applied to the ceremonies relating to the meat offering, the sin offering, and the trespass offering.

I have found these seven chapters to be rich beyond measure to my own soul. I realise I can only scratch the surface of this inexhaustible mine but it is my prayer that, as I do so, you who read these lines will see the Saviour of whom the book of God speaks. May we fall at his feet and worship him. May we find in him the boundless treasures of God's free grace, flowing freely to needy sinners by his sin-atoning sacrifice. In these words of instruction given to Aaron and his sons about the sacrifices, three things stand before us like the star that led the wise men to Bethlehem, saying, 'Behold, here is the Christ of God'.

God's Holiness

The first thing to which I would direct your attention is the revelation of God's holiness. Everywhere today people talk about holiness, about being holy, and about doing holy things. The word 'holy' is thrown around by religious people with less thought than profane men use profanity. All the light talk, in very serious religious tones, about holiness reveals one certain fact. This generation knows absolutely nothing about holiness or the revelation of God's holiness.

In the book of God, men and women are described as saints, sanctified, holy men and women only because they are in Christ who is holy. Christ is our holiness. He is that 'holiness without which no man shall see the Lord'. None are described as being holy because of their own personal character and conduct.

'It is most holy.' Those four words are used only ten times in Holy Scripture (Exodus 30:10; Leviticus 6:17, 25, 29; 7:1, 6; 10:12, 17; 14:13; 24:9). Every time they are used they refer to those sacrifices that typified the sacrifice of the Lord Jesus Christ as our sin-atoning Substitute.

Without question, God's holiness is displayed in part in many ways and by many things. God revealed his holiness in the garden. He made his holiness known on Mount Sinai. His holiness is stamped upon every man's conscience by his creative hand. His holiness is displayed in his righteous judgments. But all these things reveal but a portion of his holy character. They convince us God is holy, but do not, and cannot, show us his holiness. The holiness of God is revealed and known only in the sacrificial work of the Lord Jesus Christ at Calvary.

If you would see the holiness of God go to Mount Calvary. Behold the crucified Son of God and learn something about God's holiness. Behold this burning bush that is not burned. Hear God speak. Take off your shoes here, for the place whereon you stand is holy ground. 'It is most holy.'

Beholding the floods of water over the earth, the smoke of Sodom, the plagues of Egypt, and the righteous judgments of God upon men and women in daily providence, I know the Lord God is holy, and I tremble before his holiness. Standing at the foot of Sinai's dreadful mount, beholding the fire and smoke, feeling the quaking earth and hearing the terrifying thunder, I see that God is holy and I tremble before his holiness. Lying on his deathbed, the cold sweat of death on his brow, looking into the grave and slipping into hell, the dying sinner hearing the screams of his guilty conscience, knows God is holy, and trembles with terror in his soul. But standing on Mount Calvary, beholding the bleeding, dying Lamb of God as my all-sufficient, sin-atoning Substitute, I see God in majestic, splendorous, infinite holiness forgiving sin for Christ's sake, and I love his holiness. I rejoice in his holiness.

Concerning the Lord Jesus Christ and his great sacrifice for sin, the Lord God declares, 'It is most holy'. He who undertakes the work of making an offering for sin must be holy. It is written in Leviticus 6:18, 'concerning the offerings of the LORD made by fire: everyone that toucheth them shall be holy'. The sacrifice itself must be ceremonially holy. The place where the sacrifice is made and accepted is the holy place, upon the holy altar. The One to whom the sacrifice is made is the Holy Lord God. The one for whom the sacrifice is made is, by the sacrifice, made to be holy. Everyone who touches the sacrifice shall be holy!

Behold this wondrous mystery. Here is the Holy Lord God made to be sin, punishing sin, putting away sin, and forgiving sin that sinners might forever live before him without sin in spotless holiness. That we might be made to be 'holy and without blame before him'. This Holy One who is our Substitute is the holiness we must have (1 Corinthians 1:30, 31; Hebrews 12:14).

Sacrifice Eaten
Second, notice God gave specific commandment for the eating of the sacrifice.

> And the remainder thereof shall Aaron and his sons eat: with unleavened bread shall it be eaten in the holy place; in the court of the tabernacle of the congregation they shall eat it (Leviticus 6:16).
> All the males among the children of Aaron shall eat of it. It shall be a statute forever in your generations concerning the offerings of the LORD made by fire: everyone that toucheth them shall be holy (Leviticus 6:18).
> The priest that offereth it for sin shall eat it: in the holy place shall it be eaten, in the court of the tabernacle of the congregation (Leviticus 6:26).
> All the males among the priests shall eat thereof: it is most holy (Leviticus 6:29).
> Every male among the priests shall eat thereof: it shall be eaten in the holy place: it is most holy (Leviticus 7:6).

That sacrifice made by fire unto the Lord was to be completely eaten. Remember, the sacrifice had sin imputed to it. It was to be eaten by the priest who offered it. What does that represent? It speaks of our Saviour's complete identification with sin. As the priest ate the sin offering and made it his, so our Lord Jesus Christ, the Son of God, our great High Priest, took our sins to be his own (Psalm 40:12; 69:5).

The sacrifice had to be completely eaten in one day. So in one day the Lord Jesus consumed and took away forever all the sins of all his people (Zechariah 3:9). And the sacrifice must be eaten by Aaron and his sons. 'All the males among the children of Aaron shall eat it ... The priest that offereth it for sin shall eat it ... All the males among the priests shall eat it: it is most holy'. Why were the males and only the males to eat the sacrifice of the sin offering? The females, the daughters of Aaron, were allowed to eat the wave offering as well as his sons (Numbers 18:8-11), but not the sin offering. Why?

Throughout the Scriptures, the female is presented as the weaker vessel. As such, the daughters of Aaron could never serve as priests, because the weaker vessel could never portray him who is God in human flesh. The weaker vessel portrayed weakness and need. The male here portrays a man, but a man with strength to consume and put away sin. That Man, our High Priest, is the God-man, our omnipotent Saviour. He alone is able to make our sin his own and put it away.

The Lord Jesus Christ made his people's sins his own. He bore the wrath and judgment of God against us for our sins in his own body on the cursed tree. Thus, he fully identified himself with us and with our sin, so we might know with full and blessed certainty that the matter is forever settled (Romans 8:1-4, 33, 34; Hebrews 1:1-3; 9:26).

Our salvation, peace, happiness, and eternal glory does not in any way depend on us, our works, our feelings, our goodness, or even the strength of our faith, but on the perfection of Christ's atonement alone.

Type Fulfilled

Now read 2 Corinthians 5:21 and see the fulfilment of the type.

> For he hath made him to be sin for us, who knew no sin; that we might be made the righteousness of God in him (2 Corinthians 5:21).

Never was the Lord Jesus Christ more fully seen as the Holy One of God than upon the cursed tree. Never was the holiness of God so fully revealed as when God's own dear Son was made sin for us. The vileness of our sin, with which the Son of God identified on the cross, showed him to be 'most holy'. Though he was the Sin-bearer he was sinless. Though he endured the horror of the wrath of God he was his Father's delight. Though forsaken of God when made to be sin for us he yet dwelt in the bosom of the Father. Precious mystery! Who can sound the depths of Calvary? It is the great mystery of godliness. 'It is most holy.'

> And without controversy great is the mystery of godliness: God was manifest in the flesh, justified in the Spirit, seen of angels, preached unto the Gentiles, believed on in the world, received up into glory (1 Timothy 3:16).

Come, poor, needy sinner, come touch the Sacrifice with the hand of faith, and you shall be holy. It is written, 'Whosoever shall touch the flesh thereof shall be holy'.

Chapter 17

God's People God's Priests

And this is the law of the meat offering: the sons of Aaron shall offer it before the LORD, before the altar. And he shall take of it his handful, of the flour of the meat offering, and of the oil thereof, and all the frankincense which is upon the meat offering, and shall burn it upon the altar for a sweet savour, even the memorial of it, unto the LORD. And the remainder thereof shall Aaron and his sons eat: with unleavened bread shall it be eaten in the holy place; in the court of the tabernacle of the congregation they shall eat it. It shall not be baken with leaven. I have given it unto them for their portion of my offerings made by fire; it is most holy, as is the sin offering, and as the trespass offering. All the males among the children of Aaron shall eat of it. It shall be a statute for ever in your generations concerning the offerings of the LORD made by fire: every one that toucheth them shall be holy. And the LORD spake unto Moses, saying, This is the offering of Aaron and of his sons, which they shall offer unto the LORD in the day when he is anointed; the tenth part of an ephah of fine flour for a meat offering perpetual, half of it in the morning, and half thereof at night. In a pan it shall be made with oil; and when it is baken, thou shalt bring it in: and the baken pieces of the meat offering shalt thou offer for a sweet savour unto the LORD. And the priest of his sons that is anointed in his stead shall offer it: it is a statute for ever unto the LORD; it shall be wholly burnt. For every meat offering for the priest shall be wholly burnt: it shall not be eaten.

Leviticus 6:14-23

We recognise no earthly priesthood. The very thought of calling a sinful man a priest is profane. It is the height of sinful pride and base blasphemy for any man to call himself a priest, a mediator, an advocate, or a confessor between God and men. Call no man father, because God alone is our Father. Call no man master, because Christ alone is our Master. Call no man holy or reverend, because our Saviour's name alone is 'holy and reverend'. Call no man priest, because Christ alone is our great High Priest.

One Mediator
There is only one Mediator between God and men; and that one Mediator is the Man Christ Jesus. He who is my Priest must be able to stand in the holy place on his own merit before God. He must have a sacrifice God will accept for the ransom of my soul. He must be a man who is himself God. He who is my Advocate with the Father must be perfectly righteous himself and one whose righteousness avails for me. He who is my Mediator must be the man who is God's own fellow. Christ alone qualifies!

A Royal Priesthood
Our Lord Jesus Christ is a Priest of such merit and efficacy that he has, by the merits of his blood and righteousness and by the power and grace of his Holy Spirit, made all who trust him both kings and priests unto God (Revelation 1:4-6; 1 Peter 2:9). All who are saved by the grace of God enter into that which is within the veil by the blood of atonement and do business with God himself in the holy place, being accepted in, by, and with Christ (Hebrews 4:16; 10:19-22). As God's priests we offer spiritual sacrifices well-pleasing to God (Hebrews 13:15, 16).

In this passage of Scripture the Holy Spirit gives us a beautiful, instructive picture of the believer's priesthood in Christ.[6] May God the Holy Spirit teach us how we are to live before our God and serve our God as 'a holy priesthood'.

---

[6] Aaron and his sons were primarily typical of Christ himself. However, as it is impossible to separate Christ from his people, they are also, in many ways, typical of God's servants, gospel preachers (1 Corinthians 9:13), and of God's people (1 Peter 2:9).

The Act of Consecration

In verse 14 Aaron and his sons were required to bring their meat-offering to the Lord. This was an act of publicly avowed consecration.

And this is the law of the meat offering: the sons of Aaron shall offer it before the LORD, before the altar (Leviticus 6:14).

Throughout the Scriptures those who believed God, by one means or another, publicly identified themselves with Christ, his gospel and his people. In the Old Testament era circumcision identified all the males of Israel as the seed of Abraham, God's covenant people. God's covenant people identified themselves as his people by their sacrifices and services with his people in divine worship. In this Gospel age God's elect identify themselves with him and his people by believer's baptism. Being identified by God the Holy Spirit as God's elect in the new birth (Ephesians 1:13, 14), we publicly confess ourselves his in the watery grave of baptism (Romans 6:4-6). Should anyone think such a public confession of faith in and consecration to Christ is unimportant, let him ask Moses (Exodus 4:24-26).

The priests were required to take the meat offering from the Israelite who brought it and solemnly present it before the Lord, before the altar, in view of the congregation of the Lord. This meat offering symbolized that he, the priest, and all he possessed; his body, his property, his soul, his life, belonged to God. He declared to God and all who stood before him, 'I am not my own. I have been bought with a price. I do, this day, publicly declare that I have given over the rule of my life to God my Saviour and Redeemer.'

My life, my all I give to Thee,
Thou Lamb of God who died for me.
O may I ever faithful be,
My Saviour and my God!

The Acceptance of the Worshipper

In verses 15 and 16, we see the acceptance of the worshipper in the acceptance of his offering.

And he shall take of it his handful, of the flour of the meat offering, and of the oil thereof, and all the frankincense which is upon the meat offering, and shall burn it upon the altar for a sweet savour, even the memorial of it, unto the LORD (Leviticus 16:15).

The oil was an emblem of God the Holy Spirit. Our acceptance with God is in no way the result of the Holy Spirit's work of grace in us. We were made 'accepted in the Beloved' from eternity (Ephesians 1:3-6). Our acceptance with God is the result of Christ's blood atonement, as the Lamb slain from the foundation of the world. But there is no knowledge of this acceptance, no knowledge of electing love and blood atonement, until God the Holy Spirit brings the oil of grace into our hearts in regeneration, giving us life and faith in Christ, sealing to us in the experience of grace all the blessings of the grace of God (Ephesians 1:13, 14).

The frankincense upon the meat offering represented the sweet incense of Christ's merit interceding for us in heaven. Once God the Holy Ghost has called the sinner, giving him life and faith in Christ, the believing sinner is assured of his acceptance with God in Christ, by the merit of his blood and righteousness (Romans 8:33, 34).

As the meat offering burned upon the altar with the sweet savour of the smoke of the frankincense as a memorial to the Lord, it declared both the complete consecration of the worshipper and God's acceptance of him and his sacrifice. When the memorial offering was taken and burned, the worshipper saw a sight that must have both refreshed and overwhelmed his soul. He saw the altar of God smoking and smelled the sweet incense. Breathing the smoke of the incense, he breathed the fresh air of divine approval and acceptance! Seeing God's salvation in Christ and knowing the blessedness of it, the believing sinner must have shouted for joy (Psalm 132:16).

That which remained of the meat offering, the priests' portion, was to be eaten unleavened in the holy place, as it were, upon holy ground. Since that which was burned with fire was holy, that which remained was holy. There was nothing impure or defiling in it. Here are ransomed sinners standing upon holy ground, feasting before the Lord.

And the remainder thereof shall Aaron and his sons eat: with unleavened bread shall it be eaten in the holy place; in the court of the tabernacle of the congregation they shall eat it (Leviticus 6:16).

When our Lord Jesus Christ was offered as a burnt offering and a sweet savour to God in our room and stead, what remained, his body, the church, was made pure and holy before God, being justified, and freely admitted into communion and fellowship with the holy Lord God. In Christ we are worthy worshippers (1 Corinthians 11), worthy of God's acceptance, worthy of heavenly glory (Colossians 1:12).

The 'holy place' where the priests were required to eat the meat offering was the court of the tabernacle (v. 26) where the altar and laver stood. It is called the holy place for the same reason that Peter called the mount of transfiguration 'the holy mount' (2 Peter 1:18), and the place where God revealed himself to Moses in the burning bush was called 'holy ground' (Exodus 3:5).

Like those priests of old eating the sacrifice in the holy place, you and I, God's priests, stand in the holy place, upon holy ground in Christ. This is the place of sacrifice, the Altar. It is the place of cleansing, the Laver. It is the door of heaven, the Door of the Tabernacle. It is the place of forgiveness. It is the place of God's presence. It is the place of divine revelation and instruction. It is the place of divine communion.

The Gift of God
In verses 17-23, the Lord God declares that the salvation portrayed in this and the other sacrifices is the gift of God.

It shall not be baken with leaven. I have given it unto them for their portion of my offerings made by fire; it is most holy, as is the sin offering, and as the trespass offering (Leviticus 6:17).

This bread was not to be treated as ordinary common bread. God required that no leaven be mixed with it. It was to be eaten unleavened, because it was God's gift. All its sweetness, all the relish of its taste was to be derived from this fact: 'I have given it unto them for their portion'.

Salvation is the gift of God. It takes very little thought to understand the significance of this. God's Gift is Christ. He is our Portion and our

Salvation. He is the heavenly Gift, the gift of God to his people. The sweetness and joy expressed in Hannah's song was not found in Samuel, but in God who gave him. Therefore, she sang, 'My heart rejoices in the Lord, my horn is exalted in the Lord' (1 Samuel 2:1; Psalm 16:5; 73:26; 119:57; Lamentations 3:24; James 1:17; John 4:10; Romans 5:15-18; 6:23; Ephesians 2:8, 9; 2 Corinthians 9:15).

God's salvation in Christ, indeed, Christ himself is the gift of God to be enjoyed. The Lord God declares, 'I have given it as their portion of my offerings'. He thereby declares that all that is in Christ are as community goods belonging equally to God himself and to all his people. 'All things are yours, for ye are Christ's and Christ is God's'.

What joy there is here! God and his people find satisfaction in and feed upon the same Bread Christ! If ever a sinner comes to experience the bountiful free grace of God in Christ, he will leap and dance before the Lord like David before the ark.

What grace there is here! The smallest service done for Christ, the slightest gift offered to God by him is declared by God himself to be 'most holy'. These were only cakes of flour. Yet, God counted them to be as valuable in his sight as the sin offering and the trespass offering. Do you see that? 'It is most holy, as is the sin offering, and as the trespass offering.' Even so, God looks upon the gift of a cup of cold water, a widow's mite, or an alabaster box of ointment offered to him through faith in Christ and for his glory to be as holy and valuable as Christ himself. He looks upon believing sinners and accepts us as being as holy and as valuable to him as Christ himself (Ecclesiastes 9:7).

Nothing evokes reverence and awe like a free gift of great value and sacrifice given in love, grace, and kindness. So it is with the Gift of God. Read verse 18.

> All the males among the children of Aaron shall eat of it. It shall be a statute forever in your generations concerning the offerings of the LORD made by fire: everyone that toucheth them shall be holy' (Leviticus 6:18).

This gift was eaten with great reverence. The man eating the gift knew that God reckoned him holy because of Christ. Touching the Bread of Life, eating the Bread of Life, we are holy (John 6:53-58). Nothing is more blissful than the assurance of our acceptance with God, and nothing is more awesome. Bethel was the gate of heaven, the house of God. Yet, no place was more dreadful, more consuming to proud flesh, more demanding of reverence.

> God is greatly to be feared in the assembly of the saints, and to be had in reverence of all them that are about him (Psalm 89:7).

Being reckoned holy, God's people are a holy, royal priesthood, anointed of God for holy service in the holy place (vv. 19-23). Believers are anointed as priests with that anointing only Christ can give. We have the Holy Spirit as an unction from the Holy One, and by that Spirit we offer continual sacrifice to our God day and night (Philippians 3:3).

> And the LORD spake unto Moses, saying, This is the offering of Aaron and of his sons, which they shall offer unto the LORD in the day when he is anointed; the tenth part of an ephah of fine flour for a meat offering perpetual, half of it in the morning, and half thereof at night (Leviticus 6:19, 20).

This meat offering was brought to the house of God fully baked. And believers bring their gifts of worship, 'the tenth part of an ephah of fine flour', as gifts representing their entire consecration to God. True worship is the outflow of genuine devotion. God's priests bring their gifts of worship fully prepared. Nothing about the worship and service of our God is flippant, half-hearted, or thoughtless.

> In a pan it shall be made with oil; and when it is baken, thou shalt bring it in: and the baken pieces of the meat offering shalt thou offer for a sweet savour unto the LORD (Leviticus 6:21).

Our worship, praise, gratitude, and devotion to our God arises from, and is accepted because, of an offering fully consumed upon the altar by the fire of God's holy wrath.

Verses 22, 23 tell us of another priest who offers the sacrifice. As Andrew Bonar puts it, 'The ministering high priest already in office presented the offering of the sons of Aaron on the day of their consecration'.

And the priest of his sons that is anointed in his stead shall offer it: it is a statute forever unto the LORD; it shall be wholly burnt. For every meat offering for the priest shall be wholly burnt: it shall not be eaten (Leviticus 6:22, 23).

This sacrifice was for God alone. It was not to be eaten. It pictures Christ our Saviour, who gave himself entirely and completely as a sacrifice to God for us. It refers to him alone. He who is our Substitute, our Mediator, our High Priest, our Saviour gave himself entirely, body and soul, to the consuming flames of divine justice. 'Our God is a consuming fire.' The fire of God's wrath withered our Redeemer's very soul as he was made to be sin for us and endured for us the curse of divine justice. Yet, he who was consumed by the fire consumed the fire for us. Now, we who fully deserved God's wrath have free, permanent access to God by him as priests of the most high God (Hebrews 4:16; 10:19-22; 13:15, 16).

God's people are God's priests, consecrated to God, accepted by God, possessing the gift of God, serving in the holy place, feasting upon the Bread of Life (John 6:53-58).

Chapter 18

The Sacrifice That Could Not Be Eaten

And the LORD spake unto Moses, saying, Speak unto Aaron and to his sons, saying, This is the law of the sin offering: In the place where the burnt offering is killed shall the sin offering be killed before the LORD: it is most holy. The priest that offereth it for sin shall eat it: in the holy place shall it be eaten, in the court of the tabernacle of the congregation. Whatsoever shall touch the flesh thereof shall be holy: and when there is sprinkled of the blood thereof upon any garment, thou shalt wash that whereon it was sprinkled in the holy place. But the earthen vessel wherein it is sodden shall be broken: and if it be sodden in a brasen pot, it shall be both scoured, and rinsed in water. All the males among the priests shall eat thereof: it is most holy. And no sin offering, whereof any of the blood is brought into the tabernacle of the congregation to reconcile withal in the holy place, shall be eaten: it shall be burnt in the fire.

Leviticus 6:24-30

Here we are given specific instructions concerning the sacrifice of the sin-offering and the priests, Aaron's sons, who presented the sacrifice before the Lord. The regulations relating to the sin-offering, insofar as the worshippers themselves were concerned, are given in chapter four. Here the regulations specifically relate to the priests.

Both the sacrifice and all the regulations concerning it, and all the regulations of divine worship in that legal age, were designed and given as types and pictures of redemption and grace by our Lord Jesus Christ. In reading the Old Testament, we must never forget this. The Old Testament Scriptures make sense and have application to us only as we see how they speak of Christ. But, when we see Christ in them, these pictures are instructive, comforting, and delightful.

The Place
Our attention is directed first to the place of the sacrifice.

And the LORD spake unto Moses, saying, Speak unto Aaron and to his sons, saying, This is the law of the sin offering: In the place where the burnt offering is killed shall the sin offering be killed before the LORD: it is most holy (Leviticus 6:24, 25).

Everything relating to the worship of God in the Old Testament was marked with the utmost reverence. During the Mosaic age, men and women understood that the holy Lord God was to be had in reverence by all who drew near to him. Those who did not approach him reverently, but dared to presume upon his goodness, incurred his hot displeasure (Leviticus 10:1-7; Numbers 3:4; 26:61; 2 Chronicles 26:16-21). After the Lord God killed Uzzah, he brought a breach upon Israel and David, their king, 'because', as David put it, 'we sought him not after the due order' (1 Chronicles 15:13).

If God demanded reverence in those days of types, pictures, and ceremonies, how much more ought he to be reverenced by us in this day! 'God is greatly to be feared in the assembly of the saints, and to be had in reverence of all them that are about him' (Psalm 89:7). What men and women call 'contemporary worship' is nothing but contempt for God. Reverence for God or rather, the lack of it, contempt for him, is displayed by our attitude toward his Word and ordinances, our preparation or lack of preparation for divine worship, our punctuality or carelessness, our attire, and our attitude in the house of God.

It was required that the sacrifice be brought to and slain at the place God required. It was not enough that the right sacrifice be brought; it had to be brought to the specific place and slain at the specific place God required. It must be brought before the Lord, to the door of the tabernacle, at the altar, and slain on the north side of the altar (Leviticus 1:3, 5, 11). Why all this fuss? Surely it would be acceptable, so long as the person was sincere. Ask Uzzah about that! If we are sincere in worshipping God, we will reverently worship him as he has prescribed.

Why all this fuss, and bother, and close attention to detail? Read the last line of verse 25. 'It is most holy.' The sin-offering, like the burnt-offering, pointed to the great sacrifice of our Lord Jesus Christ, by whom God has redeemed and saved his people. It had to be brought to the same place, killed on the same spot, on the north side of the altar, because it was most holy. It was most holy because it pointed to Christ, our great sin-atoning Sacrifice and his death at Calvary, which is not merely ceremonially most holy but, indeed, most holy.

The sacrifice was killed on the very spot of ground where the Lord Jesus Christ was sacrificed for us. Mount Calvary was on the north side of Jerusalem (Psalm 48:2). It was as if the priest and the worshipper were standing at the foot of the cross, where those holy women stood, watching the Saviour die in their stead. How holy that place was to them, for there God's holy Son died to satisfy God's holy justice to make them perfectly holy. It was as if they stood at the door of heaven with the heavenly host when they saw the Lord of Glory return to heaven as a man with his own blood, having obtained eternal redemption for his people by the sacrifice of himself. It was as if they stood in the presence of God himself, all his holy angels, and all the ransomed in heaven, and heard the Son of God cry, as the blood of the sacrifice was caught in the basin, 'It is finished'. It was as if they saw here the holy Lord God himself revealed in the sacrifice he required, provided, and accepted. Indeed, that is precisely what the believing worshipper saw in the sacrifice (2 Corinthians 4:6).

Never was there such an hour, such an event, such a place as that which is here portrayed. God's own dear Son was made sin for us, so that God might be just and justify chosen sinners by his grace, through the redemption that is in Christ Jesus. 'It is most holy.'

Christ is most holy as the Sacrifice that is required of God, the Sacrifice offered to God, and the Sacrifice accepted by God. This is what Isaiah saw (Isaiah 6:1-6). This is what every believer sees when he receives by faith the blessedness of redemption accomplished. This is the thing that makes us and our sacrifices (v. 17) 'most holy' before the Lord (2 Corinthians 5:21; Colossians 1:12; 2:9, 10; Ecclesiastes

9:7). It is the worthiness of our Sacrifice that makes us worthy to come to God and worship him (1 Corinthians 11:26-29).

The Eating

Verses 26 and 29 describe the eating of the sacrifice.

> The priest that offereth it for sin shall eat it: in the holy place shall it be eaten, in the court of the tabernacle of the congregation … All the males among the priests shall eat thereof: it is most holy (Leviticus 6:26, 29).

There are three things presented to us in these two verses.

1. Substitution is portrayed in the offering made by the priest. The opening words of verse 26, 'The priest that offereth it for sin' might be translated, 'The priest that makes it sin'. By receiving the sacrifice from the sinner who had come to worship God, the sacrifice upon which the sinner had laid his hands, the priest ceremonially took the sacrifice as a mass of sin to be slain.

So our Lord Jesus Christ died 'the Just for the unjust that he might bring us to God'. But when he died under the wrath of God, he was reckoned to be unjust, a horrid mass of sin, because our sins which were made his were justly imputed to him.

2. The eating of the sacrifice by God's priest is a picture of faith feeding upon Christ, and thereby drawing life from him (John 6:53-58).

3. This is also a picture of that sweet communion saved sinners have with Christ by faith. The Lord Jesus Christ, our great God and Saviour, who by himself purged our sins, holds intimate, sweet communion with those whose sins he washed away, as we feed upon his sacrifice.

The sacrifice was not eaten by one man alone, but by all the priests (v. 29) ministering in the court of the tabernacle. All God's priests (all believing sinners) feed upon the same sacrifice and have the same provision of grace. That provision is Christ.

The sacrifice was to be eaten 'in the holy place, in the court of the tabernacle of the congregation'.

Aaron and his sons feeding upon the sacrifice of the sin-offering are representatives of God's 'royal priesthood', believers in Christ, feeding and finding nourishment for their souls in the house of God, the church of the living God. Believers feed upon the bountiful provisions of God's house at his banqueting table, by the gospel, in our assemblies of worship, in the temple of God (1 Corinthians 3:16). In this place God meets with his people (Matthew 18:20). This is the place where the holy Lord God spreads his table and feeds his people (Jeremiah 3:15).

The Demands

In verses 27 and 28 we read about the demands of the sacrifice.

> Whatsoever shall touch the flesh thereof shall be holy: and when there is sprinkled of the blood thereof upon any garment, thou shalt wash that whereon it was sprinkled in the holy place. But the earthen vessel wherein it is sodden shall be broken: and if it be sodden in a brazen pot, it shall be both scoured, and rinsed in water (Leviticus 6:27, 28).

What an awesome sight the blood of the sacrifice must have been! What an awesome sight the blood of God's true sacrifice for sin is! As it was represented in the sin-offering, even those lifeless, inanimate things which came in contact with the blood of the sacrifice were revered as holy, sacred things because of the blood of the sacrifice. Once they had come into contact with the sacrifice, they were never to be used for any common, ordinary thing again.

Anything and anyone that touched the sacrifice were, by the sacrifice, made holy (v. 18). So God's elect were made holy by the sacrifice of our Lord Jesus Christ, not by our touching him in faith but by him touching us in covenant grace.

This chapter does not declare men to be holy by touching the sacrifice, but that they must be holy to touch the sacrifice (vv. 18, 27). Only those who had been sanctified could touch the sacrifice. So it is in this gospel day. Only those who have been made holy by God's work of grace can and will lay hold of Christ. Those sanctified in election by the purpose of God the Father. Those sanctified in redemption by the blood of God the Son. Those sanctified in regeneration by the grace of God the Holy Spirit.

We are manifestly made holy, we experience the blessedness of our holiness in Christ, when we lay hold of him and thereby enjoy the peace of divine acceptance and approval (Romans 4:25-5:2). Being united to Christ, being consecrated to God, having touched and having been touched by God's Sacrifice, we now must henceforth and forever serve God alone in the holy place (1 Corinthians 6:9-11, 19, 20).

The priest's garments when splattered with blood had to be washed in the holy place. I see two things here. First, the blood of Christ is precious beyond our highest thought. It must be reverenced above all things. It must never be treated as a common, ordinary thing. Second, the blood must be sprinkled upon God's altar, sprinkled toward the veil, and sprinkled upon our consciences (Hebrews 9:1-15).

The vessels that carried the sacrifice and the blood had to either be smashed to pieces or scoured. There is also much instruction here.

First, this tells us that there was a deficiency in those sacrifices. They could never take away sin (Hebrews 10:1-4). The sacrifices themselves left a defilement that had to be cleansed. There was an iniquity about the holy things themselves that had to be cleansed. But there is no deficiency in Christ's Sacrifice (Hebrews 1:1-3).

Second, the breaking of the earthen vessel which carried the sacrifice certainly showed that our Lord's holy humanity, his earthen vessel, had to be crushed in death for us.

Third, it seems obvious to me that there is a reference here to gospel preachers (2 Corinthians 4:7). God's servants are but earthen vessels, frail, broken pieces of clay.

Fourth, the treatment of these vessels also portrayed and intimated the complete restoration of all things to the glory of our God by the sacrifice of Christ, the restitution to be made unto God by the merit of Christ's blood.

That earthen vessel in which the sacrifice was offered had to be broken and never used for anything else. Why is this specified? This earth, which soaked up the blood of God's darling Son, shall be utterly destroyed and made completely new so that it shall be used for him, exclusively for him, whose blood was shed upon it.

As the brazen vessel had to be scoured and scrubbed completely clean, freed from all that dimmed its beauty, so God's creation shall, by the fire of God, be scoured and made completely clean of all that dims its beauty. This place, sanctified by the blood of God's own Son which dropped upon it 2000 years ago, shall yet be made God's holy mountain, covered with righteousness (Isaiah 11:9).

These are the demands of the sacrifice. All who touch it must be holy. The vessels carrying it must be God's alone. The earth itself, touched by the blood must be restored to God. As the earthen vessel touched by the sacrifice must be broken, so all who are touched by the crucified Christ are broken before him. As the priests' garments stained with blood had to be washed and the vessel of brass had to be scoured, so all who were redeemed by the blood of Christ at Calvary must be cleansed by the grace and power of God the Holy Ghost in the washing of regeneration and the renewing of the Holy Ghost (Titus 3:5, 6). And as the vessels sanctified by the sacrifice could never be used for any other purpose, so God's elect, once saved by his grace, are by his grace utterly consecrated to him alone (Romans 12:1, 2).

The Other Sacrifice
In verse 30 the Holy Spirit speaks of the other sacrifice, the sacrifice that could not be eaten.

> And no sin offering, whereof any of the blood is brought into the tabernacle of the congregation to reconcile withal in the holy place, shall be eaten: it shall be burnt in the fire (Leviticus 6:30).

Again, everything is spoken of and treated with the highest reverence. The blood of the sacrifice of the sin-offering has expiated the transgression. The flesh of the animal sacrificed is by virtue of its sacrifice holy, as our risen Redeemer was 'justified in the Spirit'. As such, it has been eaten in the holy place. But there was another offering, a sin-offering and a burnt-offering, by which reconciliation was made between the holy Lord God and his sinful people.

The first sacrifice was to be eaten by the priests in the court of the tabernacle, identifying themselves with the sacrifice (vv. 26 and 29). That eating portrayed our faith in Christ, faith feeding upon the Lamb of God (John 6:53-58).

This sacrifice is for God alone. The blood of this offering, on that great holy day in Israel, the day of atonement (Leviticus 16), was sprinkled on the mercy seat. The carcass of this sacrifice was not to be eaten by any man, under any circumstances, but was burned without the camp, totally consumed by the fire (Psalm 99:1-3). This other sacrifice, of course, typified our great Saviour, as did the others. The fact that it was burned without the camp spoke of the completeness of Christ's great sacrifice. He was the sacrifice of God in the totality of his holy

151

being offered up to God, utterly consumed by the fire of God's holy wrath.

But why was this sacrifice not to be eaten by any man? What is the significance of that prohibition? The writer to the Hebrews by God the Holy Spirit tells us the reason for this prohibition.

> We have an altar, whereof they have no right to eat which serve the tabernacle. For the bodies of those beasts, whose blood is brought into the sanctuary by the high priest for sin, are burned without the camp. Wherefore Jesus also, that he might sanctify the people with his own blood, suffered without the gate (Hebrews 13:10-12).

Christ is that one Sacrifice by whom justice has been fully and perfectly satisfied, by whom the veil has been ripped open, by whom sinners now have the right, yes, the right, to enter into the holiest of all, within the veil in perfect fellowship with the holy Lord God (Hebrews 10:14-22).

Our faith in Christ does not make his sacrifice effectual for the saving of our souls. The efficacy of his sacrifice is that which brings us faith and makes our faith effectual to the saving of our souls (Hebrews 13:13-15).

> Let us therefore come boldly unto the throne of grace, that we may obtain mercy, and find grace to help in time of need (Hebrews 4:16).

Chapter 19

The Priests' Portion

Likewise this is the law of the trespass offering: it is most holy. In the place where they kill the burnt offering shall they kill the trespass offering: and the blood thereof shall he sprinkle round about upon the altar. And he shall offer of it all the fat thereof; the rump, and the fat that covereth the inwards, And the two kidneys, and the fat that is on them, which is by the flanks, and the caul that is above the liver, with the kidneys, it shall he take away: And the priest shall burn them upon the altar for an offering made by fire unto the LORD: it is a trespass offering. Every male among the priests shall eat thereof: it shall be eaten in the holy place: it is most holy. As the sin offering is, so is the trespass offering: there is one law for them: the priest that maketh atonement therewith shall have it. And the priest that offereth any man's burnt offering, even the priest shall have to himself the skin of the burnt offering which he hath offered. And all the meat offering that is baken in the oven, and all that is dressed in the fryingpan, and in the pan, shall be the priest's that offereth it. And every meat offering, mingled with oil, and dry, shall all the sons of Aaron have, one as much as another.

Leviticus 7:1-10

We who believe are declared to be 'a royal priesthood'. The Lord Jesus Christ has made us kings and priests unto God. Here the Levitical law gives us instructions about our priesthood, as God's 'royal priesthood' in Christ. Specifically, these ten verses of Inspiration tell us about the priests' portion of the sacrifice offered to God.

One Law

In verse 7, the Lord God declares, 'There is one law for them'. By that statement, he tells us that all he has revealed concerning the sacrifices to this point was one law. All that has been stated in the preceding six chapters and all that is stated in these ten verses is intended by God to point us to Christ, teaching us to trust him alone as our Saviour. The lessons to be learned from these verses are of immense importance.

1. Details are important. If we would worship the holy Lord God, we must worship him in the way he has prescribed in his Word. God has given us minute details and specific directions as to how we must approach him (vv. 3, 4, 5, 7, 8, 9, 10). We worship the Triune God only by faith in Christ, with reverence, humility, and godly fear, 'in spirit and in truth' (John 4:23, 24; Philippians 3:3).

2. Sin brings death (vv. 1, 2). The trespass offering, the blood, shed and sprinkled, shows the judgment of God upon sin, the need for death, and the need of blood atonement by a justice-satisfying sacrifice.

3. What is given and consecrated to our God must be the very best (vv. 3-5). God will not accept our leftovers (Malachi 1:6-11).

4. Everything and everyone accepted by God is, through the merits of Christ, 'most holy'. We are made the very 'righteousness of God in him'. We are in Christ made to be, in the consecration of our lives to him, living sacrifices, holy and acceptable unto God by Christ Jesus (Romans 12:1, 2; 1 Corinthians 6:13, 19).

Blessed Repetition

Sometimes we think that the repetition of things is redundant. But in the book of God, nothing is redundant. The repetition of instruction concerning the offerings in this chapter shows us that the things herein described are of immense importance. This repetition of instruction, specifically being given to the priests, teaches us that the priests, those who serve as God's ministers in his house, worship him in the same way and upon the same grounds as all others. The Lord God never tires of repeating his instruction with regard to these types. Many aspects of these types are repeated in the first seven chapters of Leviticus. Because of his wondrous, infinite love to needy sinners the Lord God delights to show us these blessed pictures of redemption by Christ. Because of his infinite, indescribable love for Christ, his well-beloved, the God of heaven delights to display these pictures of him.

Precious Blood
Verses 1 and 2 tell us that God demands blood.

> Likewise this is the law of the trespass offering: it is most holy. In the place where they kill the burnt offering shall they kill the trespass offering: and the blood thereof shall he sprinkle round about upon the altar (Leviticus 7:1, 2).

The holy Lord God, whose law we have broken, whose character we have violated, whose throne we have despised, whose Son we nailed to the cross, is ever looking for blood. He demands it and he will have it, either our blood or the blood of a substitute on our behalf by whom his holy wrath and justice can be satisfied.

The blood was to be 'round about upon the altar'. Those who came to the house of God must have reckoned themselves terribly guilty, guilty sinners before the holy Lord God, because the Lord seems to have spoken to them constantly of sin and guilt in the language of blood.

The constant sight of blood in the house of God tells those who worship here two things. We are terribly guilty sinners before the holy Lord God. There is forgiveness with God!

Guilty, heavy laden sinners relished the never-ending sight of blood when they came to worship at the altar of God. Guilty, heavy laden sinners, men and women convinced by God the Holy Ghost of sin, of righteousness, and of judgment, relish the preaching of the crucified Christ. We who need him cry with Paul, 'God forbid that I should glory save in the cross of our Lord Jesus Christ, by whom the world is crucified unto me and I unto the world'. We come here to preach about the blood, hear about the blood, sing about the blood, and give thanks to God for the blood, the precious blood of Christ.

Let others, if they dare, speak lightly of the blood and deride us for preaching it. All who know and worship God count the blood of Christ precious (Galatians 2:19, 20; 1 Peter 1:18-20). It is impossible for us to speak too often or too much about the blood of God's sacrifice. The Lord God said to Israel, 'When I see the blood, I will pass over you'.

The trespass offering is declared by God to be 'most holy' (v. 1). This offering, as we have seen, was an eminent type of our Lord Jesus Christ, the perfect holy Lamb of God, who was intrinsically holy, representatively holy, and infinitely holy.

155

The blood must be shed and the sacrifice offered 'in the place where they kill the trespass offering' (Leviticus 1:3, 5, 11; 4:24, 29, 33). The sacrifice had to be offered in God's sight, at God's altar, before the tabernacle. That portrays redemption accomplished. The blood had to be 'sprinkled round about upon the altar'. What a sight! All who stood before the tabernacle observing these things were by their very worship of God compelled to reckon and confess themselves to be vile sinners, guilty and undone before the holy Lord God, but for the blood.

The blood sprinkled portrayed redemption applied. The blood sprinkled and applied 'speaketh better things than that of Abel' (Hebrews 12:24). It was this, the sight of blood; blood required, provided, shed, sprinkled, and blood accepted that made the tabernacle the place of delightful worship. In this Gospel Day it is the sight of blood; blood required, provided, shed, sprinkled, and accepted that makes the house of God the place of delightful worship.

The Fat and the Rump
The fat and rump, the richest and best parts of the sacrifice are spoken of with distinct instructions. Christ our Sacrifice is the richest and best of God's gifts, and he gives us the richest and best of all things.

> And he shall offer of it all the fat thereof; the rump, and the fat that covereth the inwards, And the two kidneys, and the fat that is on them, which is by the flanks, and the caul that is above the liver, with the kidneys, it shall he take away: And the priest shall burn them upon the altar for an offering made by fire unto the LORD: it is a trespass offering (Leviticus 7:3-5).

Again we see that the richest and best belonged to the Lord. That is Christ! That is what God required. That is what Christ gave. That is what the Lord God gives to us again (Psalm 63:5; Isaiah 55:1, 2). The Triune God sacrificed his best, his all, for us. The Lord our God gives us all things in Christ. Let us give him our all. In all our services, in all our gifts, in all things, let us give to God the richest and the best.

Burnt upon the Altar
Verse 5 tells us that the fat taken off of the sacrifice was to be burned on the altar. This, too, was typical of our Lord Jesus, our sweet-smelling

savour, who bore the fire of divine wrath for his people, for a trespass offering, an offering for trespasses committed, to make atonement for our sins. This sacrifice, the burning of the fat, was the Lord's offering.

The Priests' Portion

Now, look at the priests' portion, applying it as God intends to this gospel day and to ourselves (v. 6).

> Every male among the priests shall eat thereof: it shall be eaten in the holy place: it is most holy (Leviticus 7:3-5).

Only those who are God's priests, serving God in the holy place, only those who worship God by faith in Christ can eat of the Altar, Christ Jesus (Hebrews 13:10). Do not forget the fat and the blood of the sacrifice were never to be eaten. That is not a law forbidding us to eat fat or meat rare. It was a law concerning the sacrifices of God. The reason is clear. The sin-atoning blood of Christ cannot be eaten by man, except by faith (John 6:54, 55). The fat, which was necessary to fuel the fire, could not be eaten, because the sacrifice was offered to God alone.

By eating the trespass offering, the priest symbolically made the sins of his brother to be his own. Aaron's family alone was allowed to eat of these offerings. But every male among them was required to eat of them. Eat them every male must, but only in the holy place. The significance is beautiful and clear. Again this act is declared to be 'most holy'. It is a picture of Christ our great High Priest making our sins his own, when he was made sin for us as our Substitute (2 Corinthians 5:21; 1 Peter 2:21-24; Psalm 40:12; 69:5).

This act also portrays the brotherly love that is to rule the house of God, love which causes believers to make the sins of their brethren their own. This passage has claim upon us, who are 'holy brethren, partakers of a heavenly calling'. It is our privilege and calling to eat the meat offering and our given portion of the peace offering and the trespass offering together. We must not fail to make the sins of a fallen brother our own. To condemn such is easy and natural. But to identify ourselves with the fallen is the privilege of the priestly family. Let us bear one another's burdens, and so fulfil the law of Christ. If we are, indeed, one in Christ, we ought to deal with our fallen brethren in their weaknesses as members of our own bodies in need of help (Galatians 6:1, 2).

One Law

In verse 7 we are told there is one law for all these laws, one purpose, one object for the whole body of law given to Israel.

> As the sin offering is, so is the trespass offering: there is one law for them: the priest that maketh atonement therewith shall have it (Leviticus 7:7).

This 'one law' refers to the sacrifices. They were all designed for one purpose: to fix our hearts on Christ. He alone has made atonement for sin. He alone is accepted of God. We are accepted in him. Because Christ has redeemed us, we belong to him entirely, exclusively. 'Ye are not your own, for you are bought with a price' (1 Corinthians 6:19, 20).

'There is one law for them.' Those words should be understood in the broadest possible sense. There is one law, one purpose, one design, one intent on God's part in all the commandments, laws, ceremonies, services, holy days, sabbath days, and sacrifices of the Old Testament. The law of the law is 'Look to Christ. Believe on the Lord Jesus Christ'. The law is our schoolmaster unto Christ. It has no other purpose and serves no other purpose (Galatians 3:19-25).

Provisions for the Priests

Verses 8-10 give specific instructions regarding the priests and God's specific provisions for those who served him in the holy place. The skin of the sacrifice belonged to the priest (v. 8).

> And the priest that offereth any man's burnt offering, even the priest shall have to himself the skin of the burnt offering which he hath offered (Leviticus 7:8).

Consider what we see in Genesis 3 when the Lord clothed Adam and Eve with the skins of the slain sacrifice. In Eden, the Lord Jesus Christ acting as our great High Priest, appointed and provided the sacrifice typifying himself, and took possession of the skins. The skins belonged to him alone. He gave them to the fallen pair and put them on them; but they were his. Those skins, like the skin mentioned in Leviticus 7:8, represented his righteousness imputed to us, the garments of salvation, wherewith he clothes our naked souls with 'fine linen, clean and white'.

This is the righteousness of the saints in which we stand accepted of God (Revelation 3:18). But it is his righteousness, righteousness that could not be had but by his death as our sin-atoning Sacrifice. Still, it is our righteousness, the righteousness of God we performed in him!

The meat that was not burned as a sacrifice to God was given to God's priests for food. These were groceries for the priestly family.

> And all the meat offering that is baken in the oven, and all that is dressed in the fryingpan, and in the pan, shall be the priest's that offereth it. And every meat offering, mingled with oil, and dry, shall all the sons of Aaron have, one as much as another (Leviticus 7:9, 10).

We discover the significance of these two verses by looking at a few verses in the New Testament (1 Corinthians 9:7-14). Statutes of the law requiring a provision for the priests in Israel were given to teach us that God's servants are to be provided for by the gifts of God's people.

Three Lessons

Let us lay to heart three lessons from the last few verses of this passage.

1. In all the offerings, as here in the trespass offering, the first thing to be understood is that the offering is the Lord's. It was for the satisfaction of divine justice. God must do something for himself before he can do anything for the sinner.

2. Here the priest, as well as the offering, typified the Lord Jesus Christ, who is our great High Priest. The priest's portion on which he fed and found satisfaction, speaks of Christ our Priest and Mediator having that for which he laboured.

3. As the Holy Spirit uses this picture in 1 Corinthians 9, we are taught that those who preach the gospel shall live by the gospel. That is the way the Holy Spirit himself uses this law in the New Testament.

This matter of supporting gospel preachers, maintaining God's servants and their families in their livelihood needs to be understood in precisely the way it is presented here. The financial support of pastors, evangelists, and missionaries is not primarily to be viewed as a display of love and appreciation for them personally, though that is certainly a part of it. But, primarily, this is a matter of stewardship to God himself. It is not giving to a man, but giving as unto the Lord. If we give God his due, we will give his servants their due. If we are niggardly in the support of God's servants, we are niggardly in our attitude toward the Lord God himself, whose servants they are.

After the Lord's portions of the sacrifice were consumed upon the altar the best of the residue was given to the priests. In some cases the whole sin-offering was given to the priests. In other cases, what we would call the 'choice cuts' were the priests' portion. The priests' portion was always the best. Today it is sad but common for churches to deal with pastors, missionaries, and evangelists as businesses deal with employees. Get as much out of the man as possible for the least amount of pay. Such an attitude shows contempt for Christ, the gospel of his grace, and the church of God.

Let me be crystal clear. God's servants are not hirelings. Faithful pastors do not seek to enrich themselves. We labour not for yours, but for you. We seek no man's gold, but every man's good. Yet, as the servants of God, those men who faithfully give themselves to the work of preaching the gospel are to be highly esteemed for their work's sake and properly maintained in their work (1 Thessalonians 5:12, 13), 'for the workman is worthy of his meat' (Matthew 10:10) and 'the labourer is worthy of his hire' (Luke 10:7). God's servants, faithful gospel preachers, are to be generously maintained in their livelihood by the generosity of God's people. The Word of God teaches this plainly and emphatically (Galatians 6:6; 1 Timothy 5:17; 1 Corinthians 9:11).

When God's servants are properly esteemed as God's servants by those whom they serve, esteemed as men by whom God speaks to, ministers to, comforts, and edifies their souls, those who are served by them will count it a privilege and honour, indeed a part of divine worship and service to give them the best support they can (2 Corinthians 9:6-8, 10, 11; 8:1-5).

Let us ever give thanks to God for his unspeakable gift. Thank God for the precious, sin-atoning blood of our Lord Jesus Christ. Let us, as God's priestly family, continually feast upon the Altar Christ Jesus, and the Sacrifice of the Altar. Let us seek, like the priests of Israel, to bear one another's burdens before the Lord. Let us highly esteem God's servants and do whatever we can to maintain them in their labours, and thereby maintain the gospel and the worship of our God in this world, for the glory of Christ.

Chapter 20

'There Is One Law'

As the sin offering is, so is the trespass offering: there is one law for them: the priest that maketh atonement therewith shall have it.

Leviticus 7:7

'There is one law.' It is obvious Moses is telling us that the sin offering and the trespass offering are one law. He is also telling us that all he has said from the opening chapter of Leviticus to this point is one law. This declaration of God, 'there is one law', reaches further still. I have not counted them myself, but I am told God gave the children of Israel 613 distinct laws by his servant Moses. 613 specific commandments and 613 detailed, meticulous regulations of life and worship.

Men divide those commandments into sections, trying to fit God into their own little box. They speak of 'the moral law', 'the ten commandments', 'the Levitical law', 'the ceremonial law', 'the dietary laws', and 'the civil law'. But God says, with regard to all the sacrifices and all the laws given to Israel, 'there is one law'.

The whole law of God given in the Old Testament Scriptures is one in purpose, usefulness, and message. The law's purpose, its usefulness is to make known to us our need of Christ as our only, sin-atoning sacrifice by whom alone sinners can approach the holy Lord God and be accepted (Romans 3:19-26). The law was our schoolmaster to bring us to Christ, to shut us up to Christ. It has no other lawful purpose, no other lawful function, and no other lawful usefulness.

The Lord God told Moses and the children of Israel that all he had revealed concerning the sacrifices to this point was one law. All that has been stated in the preceding six chapters and all that is stated in this seventh chapter of Leviticus is intended by God to point us to Christ, teaching us to trust him alone as our Saviour. The message contained in this statement is of immense importance. 'There is one law'.

Many religious people have a foolish and deadly enchantment with the law of God. In many houses of worship the Ten Commandments are written out in large, bold letters and hung conspicuously on a wall, in some place for all to read. There are some churches where every Sunday the congregation mournfully chants, 'Lord have mercy upon us, and incline our hearts to keep thy law'. Some are even so foolish as to enter into a covenant for their children, and vow before God that, 'They shall keep God's holy commandments, and walk in them all the days of their lives'. The pulpit, which should proclaim freedom and liberty in Christ, lays a heavy yoke of bondage upon men, which they cannot bear. Men and women are taught from their youth up to groan under the yoke of the law and to labour after righteousness where it can never be found. If I had my way, wherever there is a plaque hanging with the Ten Commandments, I would hang another, larger plaque, inscribed with these words: 'By the deeds of the law there shall no flesh be justified'.

The law of God, including the Ten Commandments, was never intended by God to produce righteousness of any kind, to justify sinners, or to be a rule of life for God's people in this world. The law was given to convince us of our sin, condemn us for sin, and show us our need of a substitute. It was never intended to be a means of attaining righteousness. Just the opposite is true. The law was given to convince us of the impossibility of attaining righteousness by our own works. 'As many as are of the works of the law are under the curse: for it is written, cursed is everyone that continueth not in all things which are written in the book of the law to do them' (Galatians 3:10). Will men never learn the difference between the law and the gospel? Preachers make a mixture of the law and the gospel and serve out the deadly poison with such regularity that the people are so stupefied that they do not know the difference. In most places, for every ounce of gospel preached there is a pound of law! That will never do. If the message of the pulpit is not all gospel, all mercy, all grace, there is no soundness in it.

I want to turn you entirely away from yourself, and so lift up the Lord Jesus Christ before you in his redemptive, saving glory that you cannot help looking to him alone and trusting him alone to save you. I do not ask you to produce any obedience whatsoever to the law of God. I am calling you to trust the obedience of the Lord Jesus Christ, the sinner's substitute. I do not set before you commandments of the law, which you can never perform, and by which you must be condemned. Rather, I set before you the blessed commandment of the gospel.

God the Holy Ghost, gives us the one law to which the whole law of God points, the one law that must be obeyed by us.

> And this is his commandment, That we should believe on the name of his Son Jesus Christ, and love one another, as he gave us commandment (1 John 3:23).

This is what God the Holy Ghost calls 'the commandment of the everlasting God'. This is the one commandment we must obey. And if you obey this commandment you will live forever. Obedience to this commandment is called 'the obedience of faith' (Romans 16:26).

The one thing God requires of every sinner is faith in his Son, the Lord Jesus Christ. I want you who read these pages to be saved by the grace of God. And I know also that the only way you can be saved is by obeying this commandment of God. You must believe on his Son, Jesus Christ.

Must Believe
In order to be saved we must believe on the Son of God. That faith which saves the soul is believing on a Person, depending upon Jesus Christ for eternal life. We are not saved by believing certain religious dogma, no matter how true and orthodox the teaching is. We are not saved by believing certain facts about the life, death, and resurrection of Christ, no matter how accurately those facts may be perceived. We are saved by believing a Person. Saving faith is not consent to a proposition, but commitment to a Person. Specifically, John tells us three things we must believe about the Lord Jesus Christ.

1. We must believe that Jesus Christ is God the Son. 'This is his commandment, that we should believe on the name of his Son.' No one will ever trust Christ as Lord and Saviour until he or she is convinced

in heart that Christ is God. Those who deny the Godhood of our Saviour are infidels. Their religion is blasphemy. Jesus Christ our Saviour is God (Isaiah 9:6; Romans 9:5; 1 Timothy 3:16). No one but God himself can forgive us of our sins and save us.

2. We must believe that he who is God the eternal Son is also 'Jesus', the Saviour. Jesus Christ, the Son of God, became man that he might save men. Because of his great love for sinners, the Son of God came into this world as a real man to save us (2 Corinthians 8:9; 1 Timothy 1:15). He who is the sinner's substitute must be both God and man in one glorious Person. Only man could suffer. Only God could satisfy.

3. Believing that Jesus is both God and man, we must trust him as the Christ. The title 'Christ' means 'Anointed One'. He is the one ordained, anointed, and sent of the Father into this world on an errand of mercy. God sent his Son into this world, not to make it possible for sinners to save themselves, but that he might save sinners. It is his responsibility as the Christ of God to bring many sons to glory. We must believe that Jesus Christ, the Son of God, having come into this world to save sinners, has fully accomplished his mission.

Faith trusts the righteousness of Christ (Romans 5:19). His obedience to the law as a man fully satisfies the requirements of the law for all his people.

Faith trusts the blood of Christ (Hebrews 9:12). We heartily rejoice in the doctrine of the atonement; limited, effectual, blood atonement. Christ, by dying in the room, place, and instead of sinful men, bore the terror and curse of the law until justice itself was satisfied and demanded no more. Faith sees and relies upon the fact that Christ, by his one great sacrifice for sin, has put away all the sins of his people (Hebrews 9:26; 1 John 1:9).

Faith trusts the intercession of Christ (Hebrews 7:25). We rest our souls upon the fact that God our Father will not and cannot refuse the prayer of his Son (John 17:20).

Faith is something more than simply believing the truthfulness of these things. Faith is acting upon God's revelation. Faith is trusting Christ, relying upon him. Faith is looking to Christ for the healing of our souls, just as the children of Israel looked to the brazen serpent in the wilderness for the healing of their bodies (John 3:14-16).

Faith is settled, resting, confident hope in the Lord Jesus Christ.

God's Gift

In order to be saved you must believe on the Son of God. But be sure you understand that faith in Christ is the gift of God. Faith in Christ is not hereditary. It cannot be produced by human logic or religious atmosphere. Faith in Christ is not the result of providential judgment or even the terror of eternal damnation. Saving faith, true, heart faith in Christ is produced in the hearts of sinners by the gracious operation of God the Holy Spirit (Ephesians 1:10; 2:8, 9; Colossians 2:12).

No sinner will ever trust Christ until he or she hears the gospel preached in the power of the Holy Spirit (Romans 10:13-17). No one will ever trust the Lord Jesus Christ until he or she is regenerated, born again by the Spirit of God (John 3:3-7). No sinner will ever trust the Son of God until he is revealed in the heart by the Holy Spirit (2 Corinthians 4:6). Faith in Christ is produced by the revelation of Christ in the heart. It is as a person sees Christ by faith that Christ is trusted.

No Prerequisites

You must believe on Christ. Faith in Christ is the gift of God. There are no pre-requisites, conditions, or qualifications we must meet before we can trust Christ.

Self-righteousness is like a pesky mole. Drive it from one hole and it will quickly make another. We have perhaps driven it out of the den of good works as a ground of hope before God. But it has found another hiding place. These dens of darkness have many names: 'fitness for faith', 'conditions of conversion', 'suitability for salvation', and 'qualifications for grace'.

No matter what name you use, it still comes down to works and self-righteousness. The reasoning goes like this. 'Yes, salvation is by grace alone. It is not what you do, but what Christ has done that saves you. But, before you can trust Christ and be saved, you must be terrified with conviction, or you must weep and mourn over your sin, or you must desire holiness, or you must repent, or you must long after Christ, or you must come to see yourself as a lost sinner, or you must see and understand the doctrine of the gospel.'

That kind of doctrine may sound good to many; but it is only a round-a-bout way of preaching works salvation and mixing law and grace. Anything placed between the sinner and Christ as a condition or qualification for faith is works.

The gospel of Christ is addressed to sinners as sinners. 'This is his commandment, that we should believe on his Son Jesus Christ.' There are no qualifications or conditions to be met. Christ died for sinners. God saves sinners. The gospel is for sinners, not awakened sinners, not sensible sinners, not convicted sinners, not lost sinners, not repentant sinners, just sinners!

The moment a man places any condition or qualification of any kind upon the sinner before he can trust Christ and be saved, he ceases to preach a gospel of pure grace. You might ask, 'What can be wrong with using whatever means we can to make men know their desperately sinful condition, and thereby making them sense their need of Christ?' Here are seven evils of preaching conditional faith:

1. Conditional faith reverses God's order. Repentance, conviction of sin, and lamentation over sin are not pre-requisites for coming to Christ and trusting him. These things do not precede faith. They are the results of faith (Zechariah 12:10; John 16:7-14).

2. Conditional faith makes our experience, rather than the finished work of Christ, the basis of our hope before God.

3. Conditional faith keeps people from trusting Christ. Conditional faith provides sinners with a place of refuge short of Christ himself. They find hope in their feelings, their experience, or their knowledge.

4. Conditional faith gives sinners ground of boasting before God. How quick we are to boast in ourselves! I have heard and read the testimonies of men which spoke much, much more of their 'process of conversion', and their feelings, and their experience than of Christ, his redemption and the grace of God in him.

5. Conditional faith forbids any real assurance for God's elect. If true faith in Christ comes only after repentance, conviction of sin, a great sense of sin, or any other condition, then I must always be plagued with questions like these. Have I repented enough? Have I been convicted enough? Did I really sense my sinfulness enough? Did I know enough?

6. Conditional faith offers no immediate hope to perishing sinners. The gospel says, 'Today, if ye will hear his voice, harden not your hearts'. The gospel says, 'Believe on the Lord Jesus Christ, and thou shalt be saved'. But preachers of conditional faith say, 'After you feel your sin, believe. After your heart is melted, harden not your heart. If you really know your lost condition and your guilt, come to Christ'.

7. Conditional faith promotes an arrogant and judgmental attitude toward the people of God. If believers must meet certain standards and pre-requisites in order for their faith to be true faith, we must make our acceptance of a brother dependent upon his experience, rather than upon his faith in Christ. The only standard by which we can judge another man's experience is our own.

Robert Murray M'Cheyne rightly said, 'We must not close with Christ because we feel him, but because God has said it, and we must take God's Word even in the dark'. Spurgeon wrote, 'All that is of nature's spinning must be unravelled, and everything that getteth into Christ's place, however dear to thee, and however precious in itself, must be broken in pieces, and like the dust of the golden calf, must be scattered upon the water, and thou wilt be made to sorrowfully drink of it, because thou madest it thy trust'.

God's Command
God commands us to trust his Son, the Lord Jesus Christ. 'This is his commandment, that we should believe on the name of his Son.' The basis, the motive, and the reason for our faith is not our deep conviction of sin, our great remorse over guilt, or our fear of eternal ruin. Stop looking for those things, and look to Christ. I must believe because God said, 'Believe'.

If God commands you to do something, you are responsible to do it. An invitation may be accepted or rejected without fear of offending. A command must be obeyed. If God commands you to do something, you can be assured that you have the right and privilege of doing it. You may come to Christ. You may trust Christ. You may believe on the Lord Jesus Christ, because God himself commands you to do so.

The greatest evil you can commit in this world is to disobey the commandment of the gospel. If you refuse to believe on the Lord Jesus Christ, you spit in God's face and call him a liar (1 John 5:10). You are saying, 'God almighty is a liar. I do not need a Saviour. The blood of Christ cannot wash away sin. God will not save sinners'.

Law Fulfilled
By faith in Christ we fulfil the law of God. The whole purpose of God's law is to drive sinners to Christ. 'There is one law', one not ten, one not 613. 'There is one law.' When we trust Christ, we fulfil the law's

purpose (Galatians 3:24, 25). The whole requirement of the law is fulfilled in that sinner who trusts Christ's blood and righteousness (Romans 3:31; 8:4; John 6:29). The law requires righteousness. The law requires satisfaction (Exodus 13:2, 13). Believing on the Lord Jesus Christ we fulfil the law, bringing to God the righteousness and satisfaction demanded by the law (2 Corinthians 5:21).

Chapter 21

'The Law Of Consecrations'

And this is the law of the sacrifice of peace offerings, which he shall offer unto the LORD ... This is the law of the burnt offering, of the meat offering, and of the sin offering, and of the trespass offering, and of the consecrations, and of the sacrifice of the peace offerings; Which the LORD commanded Moses in mount Sinai, in the day that he commanded the children of Israel to offer their oblations unto the LORD, in the wilderness of Sinai.

Leviticus 7:11-38

Leviticus 7:11-38 is about consecration to God. The root of stedfastness is consecration to God; but the world has not yet seen what God might do with a person utterly consecrated to him. Oh, that God would give me the grace to be such a person! Oh, that God might give us grace, day by day, to consecrate ourselves to him! Consecration is not a word we hear or use very often; but it is used often in Holy Scripture. In fact, entire chapters are devoted to the subject of consecration. Here the Lord God gives us what he calls 'the law of the consecrations'. Consecration is neither more nor less than giving of ourselves to God, the dedication and devotion of our lives to our Saviour, the Lord Jesus Christ.

This consecration to God by faith in Christ is what was typified in all the Old Testament sacrifices of consecration described in Leviticus 1-7. The instruction given in this portion of Leviticus 7 is an inspired recapitulation of the instructions given in chapter three concerning the

169

sacrifice of the peace offering. However, there are some very important additions given here. Let me direct your attention to these additional words of instruction. Then, I will show you how our Lord Jesus Christ perfectly fulfilled all these typical sacrifices.

Peace Offerings

The peace offerings were sacrifices made by redeemed sinners as redeemed sinners reconciled to God. 'And this is the law of the sacrifice of peace offerings, which he shall offer unto the LORD' (v. 11). The peace offerings were offerings brought to the Lord as expressions of praise, gratitude, and thanksgiving for God's goodness in deliverance. We are taught by example to turn to our God in thanksgiving for every deliverance wrought for us by his hand of omnipotent mercy; deliverance from captivity, from sickness, from trouble, from our adversaries, from destruction. The soul overflowing with gratitude and praise, voluntarily brought a sacrifice to the Lord, by which he declared his personal consecration to God (Psalm 119:108). These were not the sacrifices of men and women seeking peace with God, but the sacrifices of those who had obtained peace. This is the position we are in in Christ.

The Lord God reconciled us to himself judicially when he sacrificed his darling Son for us at Calvary (2 Corinthians 5:17-21). We have been reconciled to God by the Holy Spirit's gracious operations in conversion. And, now, as reconciled sinners, we gladly, voluntarily give ourselves to our God (Hebrews 13:10-15). 'He is our peace'.

Leavened Bread

Next, we are told that the reconciled sinner could not bring a peace offering to the Lord, except it be brought with leavened bread.

> If he offer it for a thanksgiving, then he shall offer with the sacrifice of thanksgiving unleavened cakes mingled with oil, and unleavened wafers anointed with oil, and cakes mingled with oil, of fine flour, fried. Besides the cakes, he shall offer for his offering leavened bread with the sacrifice of thanksgiving of his peace offerings. And of it he shall offer one out of the whole oblation for an heave offering unto the LORD, and it shall be the priest's that sprinkleth the blood of the peace offerings (Leviticus 7:12-14).

The reconciled sinner brought unleavened cakes, anointed with oil. These unleavened cakes pointed to Christ in his spotless, holy purity. But why was the worshipper required to offer 'leavened bread with the sacrifice of thanksgiving of his peace offerings' (v. 13)? The answer is obvious. All who come to God in a state of reconciliation, come to him in a state of humility, confessing their sin. We joy in the knowledge and assurance of sin's complete forgiveness but we are still keenly aware of our personal sinfulness (1 John 1:8-10; Isaiah 64:6).

Must be Eaten
Then, the offering had to be eaten in the holy place by the priests, and eaten on the same day it was offered.

> And the flesh of the sacrifice of his peace offerings for thanksgiving shall be eaten the same day that it is offered; he shall not leave any of it until the morning. But if the sacrifice of his offering be a vow, or a voluntary offering, it shall be eaten the same day that he offereth his sacrifice: and on the morrow also the remainder of it shall be eaten: But the remainder of the flesh of the sacrifice on the third day shall be burnt with fire. And if any of the flesh of the sacrifice of his peace offerings be eaten at all on the third day, it shall not be accepted, neither shall it be imputed unto him that offereth it: it shall be an abomination, the soul that eateth of it shall bear his iniquity (Leviticus 7:15-18).

There are many practical things to be observed from the instructions given in these verses. First, the apostle Paul, in 1 Corinthians 9:13, 14, tells us the law here given was to teach us that those who preach the gospel are to live by the gospel. Second, observe how quickly the sacrifice must be eaten. Our Lord Jesus Christ, our Sacrifice, is to be received by faith with urgency (Hebrews 3:13, 14). Third, when the poor soul saw God's priests instantly eating his sacrifice he was assured of its acceptance by the Lord. He went home with divine approval!

Again, the Lord took great care that no part of the sacrifice see corruption. Anything left over until the third day was to be burned with fire. Why? The Lord Jesus Christ, our great Surety, after being offered as the Sacrifice for our sins, must rise from the dead on the third day. His body could not see corruption (Psalm 16:9-11).

Only the Clean

Only the ceremonially clean could come to God with a peace offering.

And the flesh that toucheth any unclean thing shall not be eaten; it shall be burnt with fire: and as for the flesh, all that be clean shall eat thereof. But the soul that eateth of the flesh of the sacrifice of peace offerings, that pertain unto the LORD, having his uncleanness upon him, even that soul shall be cut off from his people. Moreover the soul that shall touch any unclean thing, as the uncleanness of man, or any unclean beast, or any abominable unclean thing, and eat of the flesh of the sacrifice of peace offerings, which pertain unto the LORD, even that soul shall be cut off from his people (Leviticus 7:19-21).

Our works, sacrifices, and services, be they ever so great and costly, will never be accepted of God until we are washed, justified, and sanctified by Christ (1 Peter 2:5; Philippians 4:18). No ceremony, no religious ritual or church activity be it baptism, the Lord's supper, church membership, church attendance, Bible reading, prayer, or whatever, can make us clean before God (Leviticus 19:8; Haggai 2:12). Our conscience must be purged from dead works to serve the true and living God (Hebrews 9:14; 1 Corinthians 11:29). Only God the Holy Ghost can purge the guilty conscience, and only by the blood of Christ.

Personal Faith

The sacrifice of the peace offering had to be brought by the worshipper personally, with his own hands.

And the LORD spake unto Moses, saying, Speak unto the children of Israel, saying, Ye shall eat no manner of fat, of ox, or of sheep, or of goat. And the fat of the beast that dieth of itself, and the fat of that which is torn with beasts, may be used in any other use: but ye shall in no wise eat of it. For whosoever eateth the fat of the beast, of which men offer an offering made by fire unto the LORD, even the soul that eateth it shall be cut off from his people. Moreover ye shall eat no manner of blood, whether it be of fowl or of beast, in any of your dwellings. Whatsoever soul it be that eateth any manner of blood, even that soul shall be cut off from his people. And the LORD spake unto Moses, saying, Speak unto the children of Israel, saying, He that offereth the sacrifice of his peace offerings unto the LORD shall bring his oblation unto the LORD of the sacrifice of his peace offerings. His own hands shall bring the offerings of the LORD made by fire, the fat with the breast, it shall he bring, that the breast may be waved for a wave offering before the LORD. And the priest shall burn the fat upon the altar: but the breast shall be Aaron's and his sons'. And the right shoulder shall ye give unto the priest for an heave offering of the sacrifices of your peace offerings. He among the sons of Aaron, that offereth the blood of the peace offerings, and the fat, shall have the right shoulder for his part. For the wave breast and the heave shoulder have I taken of the children of Israel from off the sacrifices of their peace offerings, and have given them unto Aaron the priest and unto his sons by a statute forever from among the children of Israel. This is the portion of the anointing of Aaron, and of the anointing of his sons, out of the offerings of the LORD made by fire, in the day when he presented them to minister unto the LORD in the priest's office; Which the LORD commanded to be given them of the children of Israel, in the day that he anointed them, by a statute forever throughout their generations (Leviticus 7:22-36).

The prohibition here given forbidding the eating of fat and blood is the same law given in Leviticus 3:16, 17. As it referred to all the ceremonial sacrifices, the blood was considered sacred because of its reference to the sin-atoning blood of our Lord Jesus Christ (Genesis 9:4; Deuteronomy 12:16; Leviticus 17:11).

Still, there is more to be learned from this prohibition. The fat and the blood belonged to God. There was a spiritual significance to this command. We enjoy peace with God by giving him the best, represented by the fat and we belong to God by giving him our lives, represented by the blood.

In all things pertaining to the worship of God, personal faith is required. We must trust Christ and come to him ourselves. We must walk with him ourselves. Everyone who brought the peace-offering brought it with his own hands because salvation is a personal thing. Faith in Christ is personal (Job 19:25, 26; Galatians 2:20).

173

Fulfilled by Christ

Now, look at the last two verses of Leviticus 7. Here the Holy Spirit lumps all these sacrifices together, as if to declare that all these great sacrifices of divine worship and all the instructions concerning them are for one great purpose. The sacrifices were all given to point sinners to Christ. They were all typical of Christ and all have been fulfilled by Christ (Leviticus 7:37, 38; Hebrews 10:10-14).

This is the law of the burnt offering, of the meat offering, and of the sin offering, and of the trespass offering, and of the consecrations, and of the sacrifice of the peace offerings; Which the LORD commanded Moses in mount Sinai, in the day that he commanded the children of Israel to offer their oblations unto the LORD, in the wilderness of Sinai (Leviticus 7:37, 38).

Christ is our true Burnt Offering (Leviticus 1; Ephesians 4:32-5:2). The Lord Jesus Christ is our true Meat Offering, our Offering of Firstfruits (Leviticus 2; 1 Corinthians 15:19-23). Our Saviour is our true Peace Offering (Leviticus 3; Romans 4:25-5:11). He is our one and only Sin Offering (Leviticus 4; 2 Corinthians 5:14-21; Galatians 3:13, 14). The Lord Jesus Christ, the Son of God himself, is our only and our true Trespass Offering (Leviticus 5; Isaiah 53:1-12).

Christ is our Sacrifice, in whom alone sinners have access to and acceptance with the holy Lord God. He is the Burnt-offering, the Meat-offering, the Peace-offering, the Sin-offering, and the Trespass-offering for all his people. If we would come to God, we must come to God by him. Blessed be his name, we can come to God by him.

That is the law of consecrations. Thank God for the law of consecrations by which our Lord Jesus Christ and God's salvation in, by, and with him are portrayed so vividly!

May God the Holy Spirit now persuade you, by his sweet, irresistible grace, to come to God, to consecrate yourself to God in Christ Jesus. Christ is the one great Sacrifice who can atone for sin, give sinners acceptance with God, and bring peace to your soul forever.

Has the Son of God done this for you? Has he done this for me? The most reasonable return we can make is giving ourselves to him. He died for us that we should not henceforth live unto ourselves, but unto him who died for us and rose again (2 Corinthians 5:15).

I beseech you therefore, brethren, by the mercies of God, that ye present your bodies a living sacrifice, holy, acceptable unto God, which is your reasonable service. And be not conformed to this world: but be ye transformed by the renewing of your mind, that ye may prove what is that good, and acceptable, and perfect, will of God' (Romans 12:1, 2).

'Here, Lord, I give myself to Thee, 'tis all that I can do'. This heart, these eyes, ears, hands, feet, this mind, this life I now live in the flesh, all I am, all I have, belongs to God my Saviour. I have no claim to anything. I belong to Christ, my Redeemer.

Spirit of God, give us grace to keep our eyes stedfastly looking unto Jesus, the Author and Finisher of our faith! As we behold our Redeemer typified in this chapter of Inspiration, we give you thanks for the pictures we have of him here. As the Lord Jesus Christ was and is the minister of the sanctuary and of the true tabernacle, may our hearts rejoice and participate with him in all the sweet things here represented. May it be our portion, blessed Saviour, to feed upon you, to live unto you, and to rejoice in you! Let us never presume to bring anything of our own to mingle with the all-sufficient sacrifice of God our Saviour. Oh, may we ever be led by God the Holy Ghost in the new and living way of Christ's precious blood and make mention of his righteousness, even of his only!

Dear Lamb of God, how blessed is it to see you as our only Sacrifice, our only Priest, and our only Altar! You have made all your people kings and priests unto God and the Father. As you are our great Peace-offering and our glorious Paschal Lamb, we feed on you. By you, our Sacrifice, we live. By you we are nourished, sustained, and made partakers of everlasting life. Precious Lord Jesus, ever give us so to eat of your flesh and drink of your blood that we may have eternal life abiding in us!

'Tis not that I did choose Thee,
For Lord that could not be;
This heart would still refuse Thee,
Hadst Thou not chosen me.
Thou from the sin that stained me
Hast cleansed and set me free;
Of old Thou hast ordained me,
That I should live to Thee.

'Twas sovereign mercy called me,
And taught my opening mind;
The world had else enthralled me,
To heavenly glories blind:
My heart owns none above Thee,
For Thy rich grace I thirst,
This knowing, if I love Thee,
Thou must have loved me first!

Josiah Conder

Chapter 22

'An Holy Priesthood'

And the LORD spake unto Moses, saying, Take Aaron and his sons with him, and the garments, and the anointing oil, and a bullock for the sin offering, and two rams, and a basket of unleavened bread; And gather thou all the congregation together unto the door of the tabernacle of the congregation ... And Moses said unto Aaron and to his sons, Boil the flesh at the door of the tabernacle of the congregation: and there eat it with the bread that is in the basket of consecrations, as I commanded, saying, Aaron and his sons shall eat it. And that which remaineth of the flesh and of the bread shall ye burn with fire. And ye shall not go out of the door of the tabernacle of the congregation in seven days, until the days of your consecration be at an end: for seven days shall he consecrate you. As he hath done this day, so the LORD hath commanded to do, to make an atonement for you. Therefore shall ye abide at the door of the tabernacle of the congregation day and night seven days, and keep the charge of the LORD, that ye die not: for so I am commanded. So Aaron and his sons did all things which the LORD commanded by the hand of Moses.

Leviticus 8:1-36

Everything in the ceremonial worship of the Old Testament was typical. The whole system of carnal ordinances in Jewish worship was designed by God to show us in type and picture the way of true, spiritual worship by faith in the Lord Jesus Christ. Aaron was a type of Christ our great

High Priest, who made atonement for the sins of his people by the sacrifice of himself. The paschal lamb, slain on the day of atonement, represented Christ, the Lamb of God who, by his death, put away our sins. The tabernacle was typical of the whole work of accomplished redemption, showing the great glory of the Triune God in salvation.

It is idolatrous for men and women today to call upon any priest, other than Christ our High Priest. It is blasphemous for sinners to offer any sacrifice to God for sin other than Christ who was once sacrificed to put away sin. And it is base superstition to look upon any material building as a holy place, as though it were the tabernacle or temple of God. God's church is his temple. The church universal is the temple of God. Every congregation of true believers, gathered in the name of Christ, is the temple of God. Every individual believer is the temple of God. God dwells in his people! Our worship of God, if it is true worship, is entirely spiritual (John 4:23, 24; Philippians 3:3).

In this spiritual worship of God every believer is a priest. All who come to God by faith in the Lord Jesus Christ are themselves priests unto God (1 Peter 2:5-9; Revelation 1:6; 5:10; 20:6). Every true believer in Christ Jesus is a priest who has perpetual access to God by faith through the merits of Christ. As priests of the most high God, it is our privilege 'to offer up spiritual sacrifices, acceptable to God by Jesus Christ'. 'Ye are a chosen generation, a royal priesthood, an holy nation, a peculiar people: that ye should show forth the praises of him who hath called you out of darkness into his marvellous light.' We need no earthly priests, for we are priests ourselves.

You may not be able to read or write, but if you are converted you are a priest unto God. You may never stand at a pulpit or lead the people of God in public prayer but if you believe on Christ you are a priest unto God. You ladies are commanded of God to be silent in the public assembly of God's saints. Yet, you, too, belong to this holy priesthood.

As in the Old Testament there was one sin atoning high priest, though all the sons of Aaron were priests in the service of God, even so, the Lord Jesus Christ alone is our great, sin-atoning High Priest, and all the sons of God are priests in him. In Leviticus 8 the Holy Spirit shows us how priests were made under the Mosaic law. In this chapter we are again given many things which are richly suggestive and typical of our spiritual priesthood. Here are seven characteristics of those chosen, redeemed sinners who are 'an holy priesthood' unto God.

1. Chosen by God
Those who are priests unto God have been chosen by God himself. The Lord said to Moses,

> Take Aaron and his sons with him, and the garments, and the anointing oil, and a bullock for the sin offering, and two rams, and a basket of unleavened bread (Leviticus 8:2).

The priesthood was not something men decided upon, voted on, or chose themselves. Only the chosen and ordained by God were allowed to serve as priests (Exodus 28:1; Hebrews 5:1-5; 1 Peter 2:5-9).

If you are a part of God's 'holy priesthood', it is because God from eternity chose you, elected you, and ordained you to be his own. Salvation does not begin with man's will, but with God's will. Salvation is not caused by man's will. It is caused by God's will. Men and women are not saved because they will to be saved. We are saved because God from eternity willed to save us. All who are born of God readily confess they are debtors to sovereign grace alone.

2. Must be Cleansed
Every priest must be cleansed before God. 'And Moses brought Aaron and his sons, and washed them with water' (v. 6). That is one cleansing. It was done with water, ceremonially. But throughout the chapter we see them cleansed several times, not by water only, but by blood and water. In verse 2 we are told they brought a bullock for a sin-offering and two rams. The blood of the bullock was poured out at the bottom of the altar. The blood of one of the rams was sprinkled upon the altar. Thus the priests were cleansed before God. Without shedding of blood, none were clean. This is the way we are cleansed from sin before God.

This typical, ceremonial cleansing of these priests is full of spiritual instruction. Our cleansing from sin was accomplished at Calvary. When Christ was slain, we were cleansed from all sin and guilt before God. When Christ died, we were redeemed. When the Son of God offered his own precious blood, atonement was made and our redemption was obtained (Hebrews 9:12).

But the atonement, effectually accomplished at Calvary, must be applied to our hearts experimentally by the Spirit through the Word. Though we were cleansed of all sin before God when Christ died, we knew nothing about it until the blood was applied to our hearts by the Holy Spirit. Our consciences were yet defiled with the guilt of sin until God the Holy Ghost showed us what Christ did for us by the gospel. In regeneration, we were experimentally cleansed. This is what the washing with water represents. It does not represent baptism. It signifies the regenerating grace of God and the cleansing power of the gospel, the Word of God (Ephesians 5:26; Titus 3:4-7; Hebrews 9:13, 14).

The cleansing atonement of Christ must be received by faith.

> And he brought the ram for the burnt offering: and Aaron and his sons laid their hands upon the head of the ram. And he killed it; and Moses sprinkled the blood upon the altar round about (Leviticus 8:18, 19).

As Aaron and his sons laid their hands upon the head of the ram slain for their cleansing, we who believe lay our hands of faith upon the head of Christ, the Lamb of God, trusting him alone to cleanse us from all sin, accepting him as our sin-atoning Substitute. God will have no priests in his sanctuary who have not been cleansed by the blood of Christ. Until you trust Christ, all your religious exercises are vain oblations, unacceptable, and abominable in God's sight. Before you can serve God you must be cleansed. Go to Christ the true Altar. By faith in him lay your sin upon Christ, the true Sacrifice, as God laid your sin upon him at Calvary. Until you do, you cannot be cleansed from sin. You cannot be a part of this holy priesthood.

Another thing about the cleansing of the Aaronic priests is they had to be cleansed every day. Initially they had to be completely bathed, washed from head to toe. But each day, before they began their service, they had to wash their hands and feet. We who are the priests of God know the need of this daily cleansing (John 13:1-10).

3. Clothed with the Same Garments

All the Lord's priests are clothed with the same garments (v. 13). No matter how clean they were they had to be clothed with suitable attire, or they could not appear before the Lord. Aaron, as the high priest, was distinctly arrayed in gorgeous garments (vv. 7-12). But all the sons of Aaron were clothed alike. The garments were made for them, given to them, and put upon them by another.

And Moses brought Aaron's sons, and put coats upon them,
and girded them with girdles, and put bonnets upon them; as the
LORD commanded Moses (Leviticus 8:13).

Every priest had a coat put upon him. None had a thread of their own
stitching. These priestly coats were like the coat worn by our Lord
Jesus, all of one piece, woven from top to bottom, hanging from the
shoulder and draping the body. That coat represents the righteousness
of Christ imputed to us and given to us at the moment of conversion.
Until God puts this robe upon you, you cannot serve him. As soon as
you come to Christ he will put this robe upon you.

The priests were girded with a girdle. We are told in Revelation 1:13
that Christ, our great High Priest, is 'girt about the paps with a golden
girdle'. That is the girdle of his faithfulness, truth, and love. Christ Jesus
gives each of his own a girdle of faithfulness, truth, and love.

Girdles were used as huge belts to hold up the long, flowing
garments men used to wear, as well as to lend strength and support to
the body. Men engaged in labour, travel, or battle, strapped on a girdle
to brace themselves and hold their robes up. Every priest of Christ is
given a girdle of faithfulness to carry him through his appointed
labours. Each priest was given a bonnet, or a turban. These turbans
distinguished the priests from other men. They were given for glory and
beauty. This, too, applies to us. God has made us glorious, honourable,
and beautiful in his own eyes. We are not merely accepted but beloved,
not merely washed, but admirable, not merely free from condemnation,
but full of imparted beauty (Ezekiel 16:8-14). The Lord Jesus says to
every saved sinner, 'Thou art all fair, my love; there is no spot in thee
... Thou hast ravished my heart' (Song of Solomon 4:7, 9).

4. Only by Birth

The only way anyone could be a part of the Aaronic priesthood was by
being born into the family of Aaron. The only way you can become a
part of that holy priesthood, of which Jesus Christ is the Head, is to be
born again into the family of God. In order to be a priest, capable of
serving God acceptably, 'ye must be born again'. You cannot and will
not serve God until you are given a new heart, a new will, and a new
nature by the sovereign, regenerating power of God the Holy Ghost.

5. Anointed for Service
All this holy priesthood, washed in the blood of Christ, clothed with his righteousness, and born of God, are anointed for the service of God.

> And Moses took of the anointing oil, and of the blood which was upon the altar, and sprinkled it upon Aaron, and upon his garments, and upon his sons, and upon his sons' garments with him; and sanctified Aaron, and his garments, and his sons, and his sons' garments with him (Leviticus 8:30).

Aaron was anointed with the holy oil poured upon his head. Then all the sons of Aaron were anointed. So, the Lord Jesus Christ was anointed with the Holy Spirit without measure, and all who are in Christ by faith are anointed as priests unto God. All of God's elect have the anointing of the Holy Spirit symbolized by the holy oil (1 John 2:20, 27).

I know men talk about this anointing of the Holy Spirit, as though it were some mystical, second work of grace, which some believers have and others have not, but that is not the case. This anointing flows to all believers freely from and through the Lord Jesus Christ. According to John, the thing that distinguishes the believer from the unbeliever is this anointing of the Spirit (1 John 2:19, 20).

I do not say there are no special fillings of the Spirit, demonstrations of divine power, manifestations of the Spirit's presence, by which we are enabled to carry out the work he would have us to do. Without the power of the Holy Spirit our praying, preaching, worship, singing, witnessing, writing, all our labour for Christ is vain. We must have the Holy Spirit. I do not minimize his power or his work. Without him we are nothing and we can do nothing for Christ. But I do mean for all to understand that all of God's children are complete in Christ. The Holy Spirit is the 'Heirloom' which our Saviour passed along to his children (Galatians 3:13, 14). Thank God for the anointing of the Spirit he has given you and ever pray for the power of the Spirit to be upon you.

This anointing of the Spirit is our sanctification in the experience of grace. As Aaron and his sons were sanctified symbolically by the anointing oil poured out upon them, we are truly sanctified, made holy, by the Spirit of God's anointing in regeneration.

In election we were set apart for holy purposes, separated unto God, and sanctified (Jude 1:1). In redemption we were declared to be holy, sanctified by the blood of Christ (Hebrews 10:10). In regeneration we are made holy, sanctified, by the grace of God imparting to us and creating in us a holy nature (2 Thessalonians 2:13).

6. Consecrated to the Lord

Like Aaron's sons, every member of this holy priesthood is consecrated to the Lord. The blood of Christ, when applied to the hearts of men and women by the Holy Spirit, causes them to be consecrated to the Lord. This consecration is not perfect but it is entire. The whole man is consecrated to Christ. God's priests are not partially consecrated to Christ. They are entirely consecrated to him.

> And he brought the other ram, the ram of consecration: and Aaron and his sons laid their hands upon the head of the ram. And he slew it; and Moses took of the blood of it, and put it upon the tip of Aaron's right ear, and upon the thumb of his right hand, and upon the great toe of his right foot. And he brought Aaron's sons, and Moses put of the blood upon the tip of their right ear, and upon the thumbs of their right hands, and upon the great toes of their right feet: and Moses sprinkled the blood upon the altar round about (Leviticus 8:22-24).

The believer's ear is consecrated to God by the blood of Christ. The consecrated ear hears the voice of God. The believer hears what unregenerate men cannot hear. He hears the voice of God in his Word, in the preaching of the gospel, and in providence. He listens, not for an audible voice from heaven, but for the still, small voice within, saying, 'This is the way, walk ye in it'.

The believer's hand is consecrated to God by the blood of Christ. The hand refers to work and labour, and to all the activities of life. The believer is a person who works for God. All that he does is done with an eye to his God. Whether he eats or drinks, works in the factory or labours in the ministry, all he does, he does for the glory of God. His garments are praise. His meals are feasts unto the Lord. His work is God-service. All his days are sabbath days. The blood is upon his hand, so all he does is consecrated to God.

The believer's foot is consecrated to God by the blood of Christ. As the ear refers to hearing and the hand to working, the foot refers to your manner of life as you travel through this world. The consecrated foot follows his Master. The believer's life is governed not by pleasures or comforts, but by Christ. He seeks not wealth or even economic stability. He seeks Christ (Song of Solomon 1:7). Consecrated feet carry to the house of God, never away from it. Consecrated feet carry in the way of obedience, never in the way of rebellion. Consecrated feet pursue the cause of Christ, not the interests of self.

Anything not consecrated to and used for God must be destroyed. 'And that which remaineth of the flesh and of the bread shall ye burn with fire' (v. 32).

7. Spiritual Sacrifices

All this holy priesthood offers up spiritual sacrifices acceptable and well-pleasing to God by Christ Jesus (1 Peter 2:5-9). God's priests always come to God through the blood of Christ, the Lamb of God. They offer no sacrifice of expiation. Christ alone is our sacrifice of atonement and expiation. But we offer the sacrifices of thanksgiving and praise.

The believer first sacrifices himself to Christ (Romans 12:1, 2). Then he offers to God the sacrifices of prayer, praise, and thanksgiving, the calves of his lips (Hebrews 13:15). He sacrifices his possessions to the cause of Christ and the service of the gospel (Philippians 4:19). All the sacrifices made by believers to their God are willing, voluntary sacrifices (2 Corinthians 8:12; 9:7).

Thanks be to God there is a Priest before God, Christ our great High Priest, through whom sinners may come to God and be saved (Hebrews 7:24-27). Let us, who by the grace of God have been made 'an holy priesthood', consecrate ourselves afresh to God as priests dedicated to his service, whose ears and hands and feet have the mark of blood upon them. 'Ye are not your own. For ye are bought with a price: therefore glorify God in your body, and in your spirit, which are God's' (1 Corinthians 6:19, 20). 'Whether therefore ye eat, or drink, or whatsoever ye do, do all to the glory of God' (1 Corinthians 10:31).

Chapter 23

The Urim And The Thummim

And Moses brought Aaron and his sons, and washed them with water. And he put upon him the coat, and girded him with the girdle, and clothed him with the robe, and put the ephod upon him, and he girded him with the curious girdle of the ephod, and bound it unto him therewith. And he put the breastplate upon him: also he put in the breastplate the Urim and the Thummim. And he put the mitre upon his head; also upon the mitre, even upon his forefront, did he put the golden plate, the holy crown; as the LORD commanded Moses.

Leviticus 8:6-9

The Urim and the Thummim are mentioned only five times in the Scriptures (Exodus 28:30; Leviticus 8:8; Deuteronomy 33:8; Ezra 2:63; and Nehemiah 7:65). Yet, these two pieces in the breastplate of God's high priest were very significant and typically instructive.

Typical Priesthood

Aaron was an eminent type and picture of our great High Priest, the Lord Jesus Christ, as God the Holy Ghost tells us in Hebrews 7.

But this man, because he continueth ever, hath an unchangeable priesthood. Wherefore he is able also to save them to the uttermost that come unto God by him, seeing he ever liveth to make intercession for them. For such an high priest became us, who is holy, harmless, undefiled, separate from sinners, and made higher than the heavens; Who needeth not daily, as those high priests, to offer up sacrifice, first for his own sins, and then for the people's: for this he did once, when he offered up himself. For the law maketh men high priests which have infirmity; but the word of the oath, which was since the law, maketh the Son, who is consecrated for evermore (Hebrews 7:24-28).

As Aaron was a priest chosen and appointed by God himself, the Lord Jesus is the Priest of God's choice and God's appointment. As Aaron alone made atonement ceremonially for the sins of Israel on the day of God's appointment, the Lord Jesus by the sacrifice of himself made real atonement for God's true Israel on the day appointed by God from eternity. As Aaron ministered in the holy place, representing God's chosen nation, the Lord Jesus ministers in heaven, representing God's elect. As Aaron's priesthood was ceremonially effectual for all Israel, securing the blessing of God upon the people of Israel, Christ's priesthood is in reality effectual for all God's true Israel.

Moses put the special, holy garments of the high priest upon Aaron by God's command, those holy garments made specifically as the Lord God had prescribed; the coat, the girdle, the robe, the ephod, the breastplate, the mitre. Those holy garments put on Aaron were put on him to symbolize what our Lord Jesus Christ has done and is doing for us. Christ did not wear the ceremonial garments of a priest. He who is our High Priest made the garments of salvation and put them on us.

Moses, symbolizing the law of God, put the golden plate, the holy crown, upon Aaron's head. Though there was never a priest in Israel who was also a king, the priestly garments were not complete without this holy crown on the head of the high priest (Zechariah 3:1-5). Why? Aaron represented the Lord Jesus, who is a Priest upon a throne, a royal priest. Christ is the Priest who wears the crown as Zion's King.

There are many, many things about Aaron and his priestly garments that are highly symbolical and instructive. But, perhaps, that which is given the least consideration by the commentators is the Urim and the Thummim. Because these two aspects of Aaron's priestly attire are commonly ignored, and because they are so highly instructive, I want to show you what I can of their meaning.

Their Meaning

The word 'Urim' means 'lights'. It is always plural. The word 'Thummim' means 'perfections'. Again, it is always plural. But there is no way for us to know precisely what the Urim and Thummim were. The Scriptures never tell us what they were, only what their use and purpose was, and history gives nothing but tradition and speculation. Therefore, intriguing as it might be to look at the possibilities of what they were, I will leave that alone.

This much we know from the Word of God. The Urim and Thummim were placed along with the names of the twelve tribes of Israel in the breastplate worn by Aaron. Specifically, they were worn upon the heart of God's high-priest. By these, through the intercessory work of the high-priest, God gave direction to the children of Israel and settled all important matters of judgment and justice.

> And thou shalt put in the breastplate of judgment the Urim and the Thummim; and they shall be upon Aaron's heart, when he goeth in before the LORD: and Aaron shall bear the judgment of the children of Israel upon his heart before the LORD continually (Exodus 28:30).

Joshua was required to follow the direction of God's priest who sought God's counsel by the Urim before the Lord (Numbers 27:21). But the Urim and Thummim were lost during the Babylonian captivity and never recovered, as is apparent from the instructions given by Nehemiah in the rebuilding of the temple at Jerusalem.

> And the Tirshatha said unto them, that they should not eat of the most holy things, till there stood up a priest with Urim and with Thummim (Ezra 2:63).

Jehovah's Holy One

With those words, the Holy Spirit showed the deficiency and imperfection of the Levitical priesthood and the great need of another priest, not after the order of Aaron, but after the order of Melchizedek, a great High Priest over the house of God, with whom would be the true Urim and Thummim, the priest of whom Moses spoke.

> And of Levi he said, Let thy Thummim and thy Urim be with thy holy one, whom thou didst prove at Massah, and with whom thou didst strive at the waters of Meribah (Deuteronomy 33:8).

The Lord Jesus Christ, our Saviour and Redeemer is Jehovah's 'Holy One'. He is the holy God and the holy man. In fact, the words of Deuteronomy 33:8, 'thy holy one', might be translated 'the man, thy holy one'. Christ alone fits that character. He is 'the man, God's holy One' in his conception and birth, in his nature, in all the acts and deeds he performed. He is the High Priest for his people, 'holy, harmless, undefiled, separate from sinners, and made higher than the heavens'.

Not only is Christ the 'Holy One' spoken of here, he is also that One whom Israel 'didst prove at Massah and with whom Israel didst strive at Meribah' in the wilderness (Exodus 17:1-7).

> For he is our God; and we are the people of his pasture, and the sheep of his hand. Today if ye will hear his voice, Harden not your heart, as in the provocation, and as in the day of temptation in the wilderness: When your fathers tempted me, proved me, and saw my work' (Psalm 95:7-9).

The true Urim (Lights) and Thummim (Perfections) belong to and are found only in the Lord Jesus Christ our Saviour. Deuteronomy 33:8 might be paraphrased, as John Gill suggested, 'And of the tribe of Levi, he said, Let thy Thummim and thy Urim (or thy Perfections and thy Lights, O God) be with thy Holy One, Christ Jesus, whom thou, O Levi, with the rest of the tribes of Israel, didst tempt at Massah, and strive with at the waters of Meribah'.

Christ The Urim

Our Lord Jesus Christ is the true Urim and Thummim, the true lights and perfections of his people. All light and perfection are found in Christ and only in Christ. Apart from Christ there is no light of any kind, apart from him there is no perfection. 'For it pleased the Father that in him should all fulness dwell' (Colossians 1:19). 'In whom are hid all the treasures of wisdom and knowledge' (Colossians 2:3).

Christ is the Urim. Christ is the Light in whom all light is found and from whom all light comes. As all the light of creation from the fourth day was in the sun, so all the light of the new creation is in Christ, the Sun of Righteousness. As the light of the earth is but the reflected light of the sun, so the light that is in us is but the reflection of Christ, who is the Sun of our souls and the Light of the world. 'That was the true Light, which lighteth every man that cometh into the world' (John 1:9).

All natural light in men comes from Christ. The light of nature in fallen man is nothing compared to what it was before the fall. Yet, there is a sense in which all men are, in their natural state, enlightened by Christ. This natural light is not sufficient to save, but it does render all men without excuse before God.

It is by this natural light given by Christ to all, that all men and women know that God is, that he is holy, that he is mighty, and that he is to be worshipped. This light even causes the natural man, to some degree, to know the difference between good and evil, and the necessity of an atonement for sin to satisfy his offended Creator. This light of Christ, sometimes called 'the light of nature', also teaches natural, unregenerate men and women how to behave, at least in measure (Romans 1:20; 2:14, 15).

When John says that Christ is that true Light, 'which lighteth every man that cometh into the world', he is not talking about the light of grace that comes to regenerate men in the new creation. Christ does not give every man the light of grace. There are many who never even receive the light of the gospel, much less the light of grace. Besides, in the context, John is not talking about the new creation of grace, but about the physical creation and the things of nature (John 1:3, 4). As all men have their natural life and being from Christ, their divine Creator, the Creator of all things, so all men have all natural light from him.

Certainly, the light of grace is found in and comes from Christ as well. When I speak of the light of grace, I am talking about that light which comes upon poor sinners born in darkness, raised in darkness, living in darkness, walking in darkness, and loving darkness, causing them to be made 'light in the Lord'. The light of grace causes sinners to see what they could not see before: their lost condition, the depravity of their hearts, the guilt of sin, the necessity of a Redeemer, the fulness and glory of Christ as their Redeemer, and the accomplishment of redemption and salvation by Christ. Sinners enlightened by Christ, enlightened with the enlightenment of grace, testify with the man in John 9:25 'One thing I know, that whereas I was blind, now I see'!

God's saints are called 'children of light' because we have been called by the almighty, irresistible power and grace of God the Holy Spirit out of darkness into light, out of the darkness of depravity, death, and sin into the marvellous light of life, grace, and righteousness in Christ. If anyone receives this light, it is by the gift and grace of Christ our God (Ephesians 5:14). If any are called to light, it is by Christ. If any walk in the light, they walk in Christ. He is given of God the Father, 'a light to lighten the Gentiles' (Luke 2:32).

Christ gives us the light of the perfections, the attributes, of God. It is true as we have already seen, that some of God's perfections as God are shown forth in creation to all men. But the light of the knowledge of the glory of God is manifest and made known only in the face of Jesus Christ; our crucified, risen, exalted Substitute and Saviour (2 Corinthians 4:6). He is the brightness of the Father's glory and the express image of his Person. Salvation is more than a religious creed, experience, or feeling. Salvation is the knowledge of the living God as he is revealed and made known in Jesus Christ (John 7:3).

Unbelieving heathen and pagans know God as their Creator. Believers are people who know God in Christ. We see the wisdom of God in the scheme of salvation by and in Christ. We see the exceeding riches of his mercy, love, and grace in the mission of Christ as our Surety. We see the justice and grace, holiness and truth, faithfulness and severity of the Almighty in the sufferings and death of Christ as our Substitute. Indeed, in Christ crucified, and only in Christ crucified, we see the perfect harmony of all the attributes of God, each fully displayed, each completely satisfied, and none in conflict with another (Psalm 85:10; Proverbs 16:6).

His Own Light

It is only in his light that we see light. As we see the sun in its own light and it is impossible for us to see it in any other light than its own, so we see Christ the Sun of Righteousness in his own light and it is impossible for us to see him in any other (John 1:14). It is in his own light that we see him as the brightness of the Father's glory and the express image of his Person. It is in his own light that we see him as the only Mediator between God and men. It is in his own light that we see him as the only and all-sufficient Saviour for guilty sinners. It is in his own light that we see the glory and efficacy of his sin-atoning, precious blood, whereby he has perfected forever them that are sanctified. It is in his own light that we see the completeness and perfection of his justifying righteousness. It is in his own light that we see the immense treasures of grace and glory laid up in him for believing sinners.

The light of the knowledge of the gospel and the glorious truths of the gospel is from Christ, who is the Light and the Truth. It is Christ who, by his Spirit, opens our understanding and causes us to understand the Scriptures. It is Christ who gives regenerate men and women to understand the mysteries of the kingdom. He sends his Spirit to his elect as the Spirit of Truth, to lead us into all truth. Otherwise, the Bible would be to us, as it is to all the world, a sealed book, full of riddles, contradictions, and outdated moralisms.

David understood this. He prayed for light to understand the Word of God. We would be wise to follow his example. 'Open thou mine eyes, that I may behold wondrous things out of thy law' (Psalm 119:18).

The Light of Glory

As the light of nature and of grace is from Christ, the true Urim, so too is the light of glory. Heaven is a world, a state, a condition of blessed, glorious, eternal, satisfying light. The inheritance of God's saints is called the inheritance of light (Colossians 1:12). All the light of heaven's glory is Christ, God's Urim (Revelation 21:23). Soon we will safely arrive in our glorious, heavenly, eternal home with Christ. When we reach Canaan's fair and happy land we shall walk in perfect light forever! All the lingering darkness of infidelity, doubt, and fear that vexes us here will be completely dispelled in the twinkling of an eye. Our very souls will be radiant with the beams of light from Christ, which shall forever strike our hearts with wonder, joy, and praise.

> The sun shall be no more thy light by day; neither for brightness shall the moon give light unto thee: but the LORD shall be unto thee an everlasting light, and thy God thy glory. Thy sun shall no more go down; neither shall thy moon withdraw itself: for the LORD shall be thine everlasting light, and the days of thy mourning shall be ended (Isaiah 60:19, 20).

Christ the Thummim

Do you see this? The Urim is Lights; and Christ is the Light. He is the true Urim. The lights of nature, grace, and glory all come from him. Now, I want you to see that our Lord Jesus Christ is the true Thummim, too. All perfections are found in him completely and everlastingly. Whenever we think about perfections, let us think only of Christ. He comprehends them all and possesses them all. All the perfections of the Triune Jehovah are in him. 'For in him dwelleth all the fulness of the Godhead bodily' (Colossians 2:9).

Is eternity a divine perfection? Christ is the eternal God (Revelation 1:8). Is omnipotence a divine perfection? Christ declares himself to be the Almighty. His name is 'the mighty God'. Is omniscience a divine perfection? It is in Christ. He knows the thoughts of the heart (John 21:17). Is omnipresence a divine perfection? Christ is the everywhere present God (Matthew 18:20). Is immutability a divine attribute? Christ is the same yesterday, today, and forever (Hebrews 13:8). All the perfection of the gifts of the Spirit are in Christ and flow to us from Christ (Psalm 68:17-20).

All the perfection of grace is in Christ and comes to chosen, redeemed sinners through Christ and for Christ's sake. Our all-glorious Christ is full of grace, every kind of grace. All justifying grace is in him and comes from him. All sanctifying grace is in him and comes from him. All preserving grace is in him and comes from him. All glorifying grace is in him and comes from him. Christ is our wisdom, righteousness, sanctification and redemption. He is that holiness we must have, without which no man shall see the Lord. Indeed, in this matter of grace and salvation, 'Christ is all'!

All the perfection of the blessings and promises of God to sinners in the covenant of grace are in Christ. Christ is our Joseph. He owns and holds the keys to all the storehouses of God's grace. 'For all the promises of God in him are yea, and in him Amen, unto the glory of God by us' (2 Corinthians 1:20).

Blessed be the God and Father of our Lord Jesus Christ, who hath blessed us with all spiritual blessings in heavenly places in Christ: According as he hath chosen us in him before the foundation of the world, that we should be holy and without blame before him in love: Having predestinated us unto the adoption of children by Jesus Christ to himself, according to the good pleasure of his will, To the praise of the glory of his grace, wherein he hath made us accepted in the beloved (Ephesians 1:3-6).

We cannot come into any circumstance or condition but that there is a blessing and promise of God in Christ to meet our need, if only we had faith to see it and lay hold of it.

All perfection of life is Christ himself. With him is the fountain of life. All the streams of life, particularly spiritual, eternal, everlasting life, flow to God's elect through him, through his mediation, merit, and power. Perhaps you ask, 'How is it that all life came to be in Christ the Mediator?' The answer is found in Psalm 21:4. As our Mediator and Surety, he asked his Father for it for all his seed upon the ground of his obedience and death; and the Father granted him his request. 'As thou hast given him power over all flesh, that he should give eternal life to as many as thou hast given him' (John 17:2). It was for this purpose that the Son of God came into the world, to remove all obstacles out of the way, that the streams of life might flow freely to his people forever.

All perfection of strength is in Christ. We are poor, weak, helpless creatures of flesh. Without him, we can do nothing. But Christ is the man of God's right hand, whom he has made strong for himself and for us. Though we can of ourselves do nothing, we can do all things through Christ who strengthens us. The Lord is my Strength and my Salvation!

All perfection of wisdom is in Christ. Christ is Wisdom (Proverbs 8). Without him there is nothing but folly. He is made of God unto us Wisdom to teach us, to guide us, and to protect us.

All perfection of joy is found in our all-glorious Saviour, the Lord Jesus Christ. There is always a reason to rejoice in him, in his Person, righteousness, blood, intercession, promises, and in his providence. All who worship God in the Spirit rejoice in Christ Jesus (Philippians 3:3).

All perfection of comfort and consolation is in Christ as well. He is our Comfort and our Consolation. Any comfort and consolation found anywhere else is a deceit and a delusion (John 14:1-3).

Christ is the true Urim. All true light is in him and comes from him. And our great God and Saviour is the true Thummim. All perfections are in him and come from him.

Carried on His Heart

And Aaron shall bear the names of the children of Israel in the breastplate of judgment upon his heart, when he goeth in unto the holy place, for a memorial before the LORD continually. And thou shalt put in the breastplate of judgment the Urim and the Thummim; and they shall be upon Aaron's heart, when he goeth in before the LORD: and Aaron shall bear the judgment of the children of Israel upon his heart before the LORD continually' (Exodus 28:29, 30).

As Aaron, the typical high priest, carried the Urim and Thummim upon his heart, so Christ, God's true High Priest, carries his people upon his heart in all his priestly functions. He carries our judgment our verdict and our discernment!

Remember, the Urim and Thummim were carried upon the high-priest's breastplate where the names of the twelve tribes of the children of Israel were engraved in precious stones. Specifically, they were carried upon his heart before the Lord. This teaches us three specific, glorious, soul-cheering gospel truths.

1. God's elect are ever upon the heart of the Lord Jesus Christ, our great High Priest.

As the names of the children of Israel were upon Aaron's breastplate, so our names are engraved, not only upon the palms of his hands, but also upon our great Saviour's heart. He has set us as a seal upon his heart. We were upon his heart from eternity as the objects of his everlasting love. We were upon his heart when he came into the world to save us. We were upon his heart when he died at Calvary. We were upon his heart when he took his seat in heaven. We are upon his heart now and forever.

2. Everything our Saviour has done, is doing, and shall hereafter do as our great High Priest with the Urim and the Thummim, he does as our Representative, Mediator, and Substitute.

When Aaron made atonement by sacrifice, he made atonement for the congregation of the Lord. Christ our Passover is sacrificed for us. He obtained eternal redemption with his own blood for us. He entered into and took possession of heaven as a Forerunner for us. He appears in the presence of God for us. He makes intercession for us. That is the very language of Holy Scripture. Thank God for particular grace and distinguishing love!

3. Christ Jesus, the true Urim and the true Thummim, is that One by whom we are guided and instructed.

Remember, it was by the Urim and the Thummim that God gave direction and discernment to his servants and thus to his people.

> And he (Joshua) shall stand before Eleazar the priest, who shall ask counsel for him after the judgment of Urim before the LORD: at his word shall they go out, and at his word they shall come in, both he, and all the children of Israel with him, even all the congregation (Numbers 27:21).

None but the high-priest could ask counsel of God in the sanctuary. And Christ alone can speak to God for us. We cannot come to God without a Mediator, without a Priest, or without a Sacrifice. God's direction and blessing was sought upon the ground of Urim (Light) and Thummim (Perfection), upon the ground of God's omniscient judgment and absolute perfection being fully satisfied with Christ. Intercession was made and counsel sought for Israel alone, just as our Lord Jesus makes intercession for God's elect Israel alone. The Urim and the Thummim, all the Lights and all the Perfections of the Triune God, were engaged for a specific people. So, too, all that Christ does he does for a specific people; his redeemed, the people of his love!

As that person for whom counsel was asked stood before the high-priest, so we must each take our place before Christ, our great High Priest. We cannot come to God any other way, but by faith in his name.

If the true Urim and Thummim, all true Lights and Perfections, are found in Christ, let us go to him for them. In our darkness, let us go to him for light. In our sinfulness, let us go to him for perfection.

If we are, as the elect of God, engraved upon the very heart of the Son of God, how dear we must be to him. Upon his heart we are loved. Upon his heart we are safe. Upon his heart we ought to be free of fear.

If Christ is our Urim and Thummim, our Light and our Perfection before God, we ought to confidently trust him to manage all our affairs: spiritual, eternal affairs, temporal, earthly affairs, domestic, family affairs: all our affairs!

'How delightful it is to see Jesus thus represented', wrote Robert Hawker, 'as bearing the persons of his redeemed, in his own light and perfection, when he goes in before the presence of God for us! Sweet and precious is the thought to the believer'.

This is no trivial matter. It is of such great importance that Moses, when dying, expressly prayed, 'Let thy Thummim and thy Urim be with thy Holy One'. O precious, glorious, gracious Lord Jesus, be the Urim and the Thummim, Lights and Perfections to our souls in grace here and in glory hereafter forever!

Chapter 24

The Beauty And Glory Of Our Priest

And he put upon him the coat, and girded him with the girdle, and clothed him with the robe, and put the ephod upon him, and he girded him with the curious girdle of the ephod, and bound it unto him therewith. And he put the breastplate upon him: also he put in the breastplate the Urim and the Thummim. And he put the mitre upon his head; also upon the mitre, even upon his forefront, did he put the golden plate, the holy crown; as the LORD commanded Moses.

Leviticus 8:7-9

In Exodus 28 we are told these garments were made specifically for Aaron, to show forth the glory and beauty of his work as Israel's high priest. But they show more than that. These garments were made and put upon Aaron to reveal the glory and beauty of the Lord Jesus Christ, our great High Priest, of whom Aaron was but a type and picture.

Actually, Aaron had two sets of priestly garments. These robes, which he wore before Israel and before the Lord in his common, daily functions in the tabernacle, and the holy linen garments described in Leviticus 16:4, which he wore once a year on the Day of Atonement. On that great Day of Atonement, when he went in with the blood of the paschal lamb before the Lord God in the holy of holies, Aaron was robed only in spotless white, portraying the personal righteousness and holiness of the Lord Jesus Christ. Our Lord's righteousness showed him worthy to undertake the great work of putting away the sins of his people by the shedding of his own precious blood.

The priestly garments described here were specifically ordained of God to show Aaron's beauty and glory as priest to the people he represented and served. The garments are described in detail for us so we might discover in them something of the beauty and glory of our own great Representative.

Aaron wore seven specific, highly symbolic garments. These were a coat, a girdle. a robe, an ephod, a breastplate, a mitre, and a holy crown. We shall look at each briefly. As we do I trust God the Holy Spirit will give us eyes to behold the beauty and glory of our great High Priest, our Saviour, the Lord Jesus Christ. If ever you see him as he is here set forth, you will believe him. The more clearly we see him as he is here portrayed in Holy Scripture, the more fully we will trust him.

The Coat

Moses was commanded to put a coat upon Aaron. This was not a coat as we think of it, but an inner garment. It is described in Exodus 28:4 as 'a broidered coat' and in Exodus 28:39 as an embroidered coat of fine linen.

This embroidered coat of fine linen, along with the linen breeches or trousers, were Aaron's undergarments. They were not commonly seen by the people. I rather doubt Moses actually put these on Aaron in public, but rather gave them to him publicly, and Aaron put them on in private. They were held before all the congregation because their typical significance was important. The 'fine linen' represented purity.

> And to her was granted that she should be arrayed in fine linen, clean and white: for the fine linen is the righteousness of saints (Revelation 19:8).

Linen is a man-made material and these undergarments spoke of the personal righteousness of Christ, over which all his other perfections and glories were displayed in the outer garments of the priest.

The embroidered linen coat was a seamless garment like that worn by our Redeemer (John 19:23). It was worn next to Aaron's body as he went about his priestly functions. Here we see two things.

First, this displays our need. If we are to come to God and be accepted of him, we must have a complete clothing of righteousness, the righteousness of Christ.

Second, God supplies all our need. The Lord Jesus Christ is our righteousness and all the righteousness we require. In Revelation 19:8 the word 'righteousness' is plural and could be read 'righteousnesses'. The righteousnesses of God's saints is the righteousness of Christ imputed to us in justification and imparted to us in regeneration, the new creation of grace makes us partakers of the divine nature 'Christ in you the hope of glory', 'the new man created in righteousness and true holiness', and that 'holiness, without which no man shall see the Lord'.

The Girdle

Next, Moses was commanded of God to gird Aaron with a girdle or a sash. This was not just the ordinary sash worn by the other priests, Aaron's sons. This was 'the curious girdle of the ephod'.

> And the curious girdle of the ephod, which is upon it, shall be of the same, according to the work thereof: gold, blue, and purple, and scarlet, and fine twined linen (Exodus 28:8).

In Exodus 28:39 we learn that this sash or girdle was made of 'needlework'. It speaks of our Saviour's readiness to serve the needs of his people for the glory of God (Psalm 40; Hebrews 10). It is written, 'righteousness shall be the girdle of his loins, and faithfulness the girdle of his reins' (Isaiah 11:5).

While in this world, our Lord Jesus 'took a towel and girded himself … and then he began to wash the disciple's feet' (John 13:4, 5). Today he stands in the midst of his churches, girt about the paps with a golden girdle (Revelation 1:13), ever ready to serve his people on earth.

In Exodus 28:8 the Lord told Moses, 'It shall be of the same, according to the work thereof'. The girdle of Israel's high priest was of the same materials and the same splendorous colours as the ephod itself, indicating in picture that our Saviour's present priestly work in heaven, as well as the work he performed on earth, is according to the perfection of his character as the God-man, our Mediator. Though glorified, Christ is Jehovah's Righteous Servant still. He has gone into heaven to appear in the presence of God for us (Hebrews 9:24), having 'obtained eternal redemption for us' (Hebrews 9:12), and there he 'ever liveth to make intercession for us' (Hebrews 7:25).

My little children, these things write I unto you, that ye sin not. And if any man sin, we have an advocate with the Father, Jesus Christ the righteous: And he is the propitiation for our sins: and not for ours only, but also for the sins of the whole world (1 John 2:1, 2).

The Robe

The third garment Aaron wore was a robe. Moses clothed Aaron with the robe of the ephod, an outer apron, worn under the ephod. It had a hem of golden bells and pomegranates (Exodus 28:31-35).

This magnificent robe was blue in colour, woven of gold, blue, purple, and scarlet, and again made of fine linen. The gold represented our Saviour's divinity. The blue pointed the worshippers to heaven. The purple pictured Christ's royalty. The scarlet portrayed his precious blood. The fine linen was the display of his purity.

This robe also represented the righteousness of Christ. It is that with which Christ himself is clothed and with which we are clothed in him. It is a robe covering the whole man, from head to foot.

The golden bells portrayed the perfection and sweetness of Christ's intercession for us. As Aaron moved about inside the holy place of the tabernacle the ringing bells told the people, 'All is well. Aaron is alive. God accepts your priest'. They speak of our living, exalted High Priest and the sweet savour of his intercession in heaven for us.

The pomegranates speak of the fruitfulness of Christ's priesthood. If you cut a pomegranate open you find it full of seeds in a red fluid. Our Lord Jesus is a fruitful Priest. By the merit and efficacy of his sacrifice and his intercession, all God's elect have eternal life, faith in Christ, perfect righteousness, all grace in this world, and all glory in the world to come.

The Ephod

Next, Moses put the ephod, an outer apron, on Aaron's shoulders.

And he put upon him the coat, and girded him with the girdle, and clothed him with the robe, and put the ephod upon him, and he girded him with the curious girdle of the ephod, and bound it unto him therewith (Leviticus 8:7).

And they shall make the ephod of gold, of blue, and of purple, of scarlet, and fine twined linen, with cunning work. It shall have the two shoulder pieces thereof joined at the two edges thereof; and so it shall be joined together (Exodus 28:6, 7).

And they did beat the gold into thin plates, and cut it into wires, to work it in the blue, and in the purple, and in the scarlet, and in the fine linen, with cunning work (Exodus 39:3).

The ephod was the outer apron which hung over Aaron's robe. It was made of two parts, covering both his back and his chest. Its two pieces were joined together at the shoulders by golden clasps. These golden clasps were the setting for onyx stones. Like Aaron's robe, the ephod was made of gold, blue, purple, scarlet, and fine twined linen. The breastplate with names of the twelve tribes of Israel and the Urim and Thummim, the lights and perfections, were worn on the ephod.

Do you see the picture? Aaron is wearing his costly robe strapped over his shoulder. Then, held in place by gold clasps is this gorgeous apron. Upon his heart and shoulders hangs the breastplate with the names of God's chosen people engraved in precious stones. Somewhere on the ephod or breastplate are those mysterious emblems of lights and perfections, called the Urim and Thummim. What does all that mean?

It means that the Lord Jesus Christ constantly has his people upon his heart and carries us upon his omnipotent shoulders. He guides us according to the light and perfection of his infinite wisdom, eternal purpose, and saving grace. We are the sparkling jewels of his beauty and glory! We are totally safe, beyond the reach of any enemy.

The Breastplate
The fifth piece of Aaron's priestly garment fitted by Moses was the breastplate. Observe how this breastplate is described.

And he put the breastplate upon him: also he put in the breastplate the Urim and the Thummim (Leviticus 8:8).

And thou shalt put in the breastplate of judgment the Urim and the Thummim; and they shall be upon Aaron's heart, when he goeth in before the LORD: and Aaron shall bear the judgment of the children of Israel upon his heart before the LORD continually (Exodus 28:30).

Not only does this breastplate upon Aaron's chest portray our Saviour's constant love for and care of God's elect, it speaks of our constant, perfect, immutable acceptance with God in him.

The names of God's elect are known to our great High Priest. They are engraved upon his heart and cannot be erased. He says, 'I know them ... I give unto them eternal life; and they shall never perish'. For them he makes intercession continually (John 17). The Lord Jesus Christ, our great High Priest, bears the judgment of his people before the Lord continually. He makes intercession for his people personally and for all his saints collectively. His intercession is always effectual.

Can you see your Priest yonder in heaven with your name upon his heart? Not only are you, my brother, my sister, beyond the reach of any enemy. In Christ we are beyond the influence of any foe or any evil!

What a consolation this is to this poor sinner. The Lord God almighty always sees me and only sees me in his Son, as a sparkling jewel shining in him gloriously. In his eyes, I shine with all the lustre of Christ himself! Is he precious? We are precious in him! Is he accepted? We are accepted in him! Does he live? We live in him!

There, in heaven's glory, before the dazzling brilliance, brightness, and purity of the white light of God's holiness, things are seen clearly as they really are. That, my tempted, tried, tempest-tossed, heavy-hearted, sinning, falling, weeping brother and sister, is the very thing that ought to comfort our hearts! We are jewels in Christ, with Christ, upon his heart and in his heart in heaven. The more brilliantly the light shines upon a diamond, the more it sparkles with radiant beauty. So we shine in the radiant beauty of our Lord Jesus Christ in the brilliant light of the holiness of the Triune God. Our blessed Saviour has set us as a seal upon his heart (Song of Solomon 8:6).

Oh, what grace! What joy and peace. What cause for wholehearted devotion and consecration to God our Saviour. In Christ we are made to be partakers of his beauty and his glory!

The Mitre
Moses was commanded to put the mitre or turban upon Aaron's head.

> And he put the mitre upon his head; also upon the mitre, even upon his forefront, did he put the golden plate, the holy crown; as the LORD commanded Moses (Leviticus 8:9).

The mitre, or turban, was made of white fine linen, a symbol both of honour and humility. It was worn then, as it still is today, by Arabs of every class, by kings and by servants. When Zechariah saw the vision of Joshua the high priest standing before the Lord, the first thing the Lord commanded, after he put away his filthy garments was this holy mitre (Zechariah 3:1-5).

The Lord God has given us his own dear Son to be for us the helmet of salvation. This mitre, made of white linen, portrays that perfect righteousness which is ours in Christ (Revelation 19:8).

The Crown

Finally, Moses put the holy crown on Aaron's head. Moses, who often typifies the law, put the crown upon Aaron's head. The very law and justice of God has crowned Christ, our great High Priest, Lord and King forever.

> And he put the mitre upon his head; also upon the mitre, even upon his forefront, did he put the golden plate, the holy crown; as the LORD commanded Moses (Leviticus 8:9).

We see this crown more fully described in Exodus 28.

> And thou shalt make a plate of pure gold, and grave upon it, like the engravings of a signet, HOLINESS TO THE LORD. And thou shalt put it on a blue lace, that it may be upon the mitre; upon the forefront of the mitre it shall be. And it shall be upon Aaron's forehead, that Aaron may bear the iniquity of the holy things, which the children of Israel shall hallow in all their holy gifts; and it shall be always upon his forehead, that they may be accepted before the LORD (Exodus 28:36-38).

Here is a blessed, weighty revelation given for the comfort of our souls. This golden plate, the holy crown on Aaron's forehead pictured the perfect holiness of our Lord Jesus Christ. It is this holiness that made it possible for our Saviour to bear our iniquities. He not only put away our sins, he has washed away forever the iniquity of our 'holy things', our best deeds of righteousness, faith and worship. This holy crown is always upon our Saviour's head. The Lord Jesus wears this crown, emblazoned before the holy Lord God with 'HOLINESS TO THE LORD', that we 'may be accepted before the Lord'.

What rest there is here for our weary hearts. Amid all our failings, despite all our sin, though we may be often harassed by hell with doubts and fears, though our hearts are as cold as ice, as hard as steel, and as empty as a broken cistern, our acceptance with God is as certain, perfect and sure as Christ's.

Aaron's priestly garments represent Christ's beauty and glory as our great High Priest. In Hebrews chapters two through ten, God the Holy Ghost gives us his own interpretation of these great pictures. Do you see how beautiful a Saviour the Lord Jesus is? Child of God, his beauty and glory are yours (Ezekiel 16:8-14). If now you believe on the Son of God, his beauty and glory is yours forever. 'He shall beautify the meek with salvation' (Psalm 149:4).

Chapter 25

'The Thing Which The LORD Commanded'

And the LORD spake unto Moses, saying, Take Aaron and his sons
with him, and the garments, and the anointing oil, and a bullock for the
sin offering, and two rams, and a basket of unleavened bread; And
gather thou all the congregation together unto the door of the tabernacle
of the congregation. And Moses did as the LORD commanded him; and
the assembly was gathered together unto the door of the tabernacle of
the congregation. And Moses said unto the congregation, This is the
thing which the LORD commanded to be done ... So Aaron and his sons
did all things which the LORD commanded by the hand of Moses.

Leviticus 8:1-36

Nothing is more important to our God than his Word. In fact, the
psalmist declares, 'Thou hast magnified thy word above all thy name'
(Psalm 138:2). What is more important to you than your word? Your
word is but the reflection of you. 'Out of the abundance of the heart the
mouth speaketh'. We reveal what we are by our speech.

The same is true of our God. His Word reveals what he is. His Word
makes his character known. His Word declares his will. It is only by his
Word we know him. It is only by his Word he speaks to us, leads us,
comforts us, and teaches us. If we honour God's Word, we honour him.
If we dishonour his Word, we dishonour him. David, being a man after
God's own heart, understood how highly God had magnified his Word.
He wrote, 'Thou hast magnified thy word above all thy name'. Oh, that
we might learn this and learn to honour God's holy Word.

Because he has so greatly honoured his Word, the Lord God has given special sanctions concerning it (Deuteronomy 4:2; 12:32; Proverbs 30:6; Revelation 22:18, 19). We dare not presume to add anything to it or take anything from it.

Let us always, as we read the Scriptures, ask God the Holy Ghost to give us grace that we may read his Word applying it to ourselves. Particularly, as we read this eighth chapter of Leviticus, I want us to put ourselves into this passage. It applies as much to God's elect today as it did in the days of Moses and Aaron. As we come together in the house of God, just like Moses, Aaron, and the children of Israel, we come desiring to hear his Word and worship him through the person and work of the Lord Jesus Christ our great High Priest.

God's House

Like Israel of old, we come to the house of God to worship him. The children of Israel gathered in one place, at the door of the tabernacle of the congregation, with Aaron. There, too, was the holy anointing oil, the sin offering, and the rams and unleavened bread for offerings of thanksgiving and praise, symbols of consecration to the Lord. Similarly, God's church gathers to worship him today. As the assembly of God's saints meet for worship we come together as 'the house of God, which is the church of the living God' (1 Timothy 3:15). We meet together in the house of God with the Lord Jesus Christ, our great High Priest, our sin atoning Sacrifice, our Altar, having upon us the holy anointing oil, God the Holy Spirit, and bringing our offerings of praise, thanksgiving, and consecration to our God (Hebrews 12:22-24).

How blessed we are to have this great privilege! This is our Bethel, the House of God. 'I was glad when they said unto me, Let us go into the house of the LORD' (Psalm 122:1).' 'How amiable are thy tabernacles, O LORD of hosts' (Psalm 84:1).

How different things are in the house of God than in the places where Baal is adored. Here the whole assembly comes together as one, upon the same footing. We come to God as blood-washed sinners saved by grace. There are no big dogs or little dogs here, just dogs! All enjoy the same privileges and have the same responsibilities. Like Israel of old, we come to one place, the altar of God which is Christ, to behold him who is our divinely appointed Mediator and Priest, who has been entrusted with the everlasting care of our souls.

Each one, the lowest and the highest, the richest and the poorest, the most learned and the most unlearned, the strongest and the weakest, the most pure and the most polluted, the oldest and the youngest, the fathers, the young men, and the babes, the men and the women, each one has his place being 'fitly joined together' (Ephesians 4:16). All stand upon the same ground; the holy ground of blood atonement. All have come for the same reason; to gaze upon God's High Priest, the sacrifice which he offered, and the gorgeous robes with which he was adorned as he did his work for us.

We come to the house of God, each with our own specific and peculiar needs. The God of Israel would have us see clearly and individually how the needs of each one of us are supplied by our great High Priest. Look yonder, needy soul of mine. What need do I have that is not fully supplied in that Man who stands in the Holy Place? His blood is our atonement. His perfection is our righteousness. His shoulders are our strength. His wisdom directs our lives. His heart is touched with the feeling of our infirmities. His bounty is our supply. His power is omnipotence. His faithfulness is sure. His grace is abundant. His acceptance is indisputable.

Every aspect of our Priest's gorgeous attire is designed by God to tell us and assure us that he is both qualified and able to meet our souls' every need. He wears a coat of blue, and purple, and scarlet, interwoven with strands of beaten gold. Blue is the colour of heaven above. Purple is the colour of royalty. Scarlet represents blood. The beaten gold is God in our flesh. His golden girdle is faithfulness. Upon his very heart he carries our names. In him is all Light and Perfection! Upon his mitre there is a golden crown inscribed with 'Holiness to the Lord'. Can you hear the golden bells of the gospel ringing out the glad tidings of grace?

> The gospel bells in music tell
> The story that we love so well
> Of peace on earth, good will to men:
> Ring out sweet bells, ring out again!

Great Need
Like those worshippers of old, we come to the house of God with great need. Have you ever thought of the many needs represented in that vast

congregation in the wilderness? Some, no doubt, were so needy they were insensible to their need. Others came to the house of God with heavy hearts, grieving with bereavement, broken with sorrow, heavy with care, tortured with guilt, hungry, thirsty, weary, heavy laden.

Yes, thank God, it is true, we who belong to the Lord are one with that Man who is at his right hand. As Israel was one symbolically with Aaron in the holy place, we are really and truly one with Christ, members of his body.

Being one with Christ, we are accepted in him, accepted with him, accepted for his sake. All our sins are blotted out. In Christ, before God, we have no spot of sin, no wrinkle of infirmity, no blemish or flaw of any kind. One of the old writers put it like this, God's saints are 'all fair and lovely beneath the eye of God'. This is our joy, our consolation, and our peace (Ephesians 2:5-10; Colossians 2:6-15; 1 John 3:5; 4:17).

Yet, so long as we are in this wilderness, we are in the place of need. Needy souls need no convincing. Our need is great and we know it. We acknowledge it. We come together in the house of God because we need him. Our weakness needs his strength. Our tried souls need his grace. Our tempted hearts need the grip of his mighty hand. Our wandering affections need his correction. Falling we need his restoration. Sinning we need his forgiveness. Our filth needs cleansing. Our coldness needs his fire. Our death needs his life!

O my needy soul, look away to Christ! My dear brother, whatever your soul needs Christ is the supply. My heavy-hearted sister, whatever it is that your heart demands Christ is the supply! Poor sinner, all that you need Christ is, Christ has, Christ gives! His blood meets the demands of my troubled conscience! His life meets the demands of my soul day by day and forever!

Our Mediator
We come to the house of God to see, worship, and hear from our God through the person and work of one representative Man, the Man Christ Jesus. God will not receive us, accept us, forgive us, hear us, speak to us, or allow us to speak to him, but by a Mediator, a Priest, an Intercessor, an Advocate, a Substitute. The one Man by whom we can and do come to God, by whom God speaks, in whom God is well-pleased, in whom we see and worship God, is Jesus Christ our Lord. He is our Priest, our ever-living Priest, our Priest in the Holy Place above.

Christ's obedience in humiliation brought in everlasting righteousness for us (Romans 5:18, 19). Our Saviour's death as the Lamb of God, our sin-atoning Substitute, satisfied all the demands of God's holy law and forever put away our sins (Hebrews 9:26; 10:10-14). But it is our Saviour's life in Heaven above, as our great High Priest, which secures our souls in life (Romans 5:10, 11). Christ's priestly work is done only in heaven, in the holy place not made with hands.

Christ's presence in the sanctuary above gives us assurance and hope. His presence above causes us to rejoice. We could not stand for a second here in this world, if he did not live for us there in heaven. It is our Saviour's life yonder in heaven, the life of him who died, and rose, and ascended on high that assures us of our everlasting, immutable salvation and acceptance with the holy Lord God (Hebrews 8:3, 4; 9:11, 12, 24).

God's Word

If we would truly worship the Lord our God, if we would see and hear from the God of heaven, if we would see the glory of God, we must worship him according to the revelation he has given in his Word. As we read this eighth chapter of Leviticus, we see how everything in the worship of God is dictated by the Word of God. This we must learn. We will either come to God the way he requires, or we cannot come to him at all (Leviticus 8:5; 9:6).

Let these words sink down into our hearts. 'This is the thing which the LORD commanded to be done'. After every aspect of the holy service described in this chapter, we are told that everything was done as 'the LORD commanded'. It is repeated seven times (vv. 9, 13, 17, 21, 29, 34, 36).

Moses did not say, this is the thing that is expedient, or agreeable, or suitable. He did not say, this is what people want and expect. He did not say, this is what the fathers, the elders, and our creed requires. Moses did not say, this is what history and custom demand. The man of God recognised no such authority. He said, 'This is the thing which the Lord commanded'.

In Moses' estimation, there was but one, solitary, authoritative voice by which the kingdom of God must be governed, and that solitary voice of authority was the Word of God. It was so then, and it is so now. The Word of God alone has authority in the house of God.

All scripture is given by inspiration of God, and is profitable for doctrine, for reproof, for correction, for instruction in righteousness: That the man of God may be perfect, thoroughly furnished unto all good works (2 Timothy 3:16, 17).

The Bible alone is source of doctrine. The scriptures alone are our rule of faith and life! Our only guide for worship is the book of God. In the house of God, according to the book of God, there is nothing to be done except the worship of God by prayer, praise, and preaching. In the house of God there are two, and only two ordinances of divine worship: believers' baptism by immersion which is the confession of Christ, and the Lord's Supper which is the remembrance of Christ.

What would be the result of this strict adherence to the Word of God? 'The glory of the Lord will appear unto you.' Is God as good as his Word? Let us see ...

So Aaron and his sons did all things which the LORD commanded by the hand of Moses (Leviticus 8:36).

And Moses and Aaron went into the tabernacle of the congregation, and came out, and blessed the people: and the glory of the LORD appeared unto all the people. And there came a fire out from before the LORD, and consumed upon the altar the burnt offering and the fat: which when all the people saw, they shouted, and fell on their faces (Leviticus 9:23, 24).

Moses and Aaron, signifying truth and mercy, went in before the Lord. Moses and Aaron as truth and mercy met justice and grace and came out and blessed the people on the basis of a sin-atoning sacrifice. And the glory of the Lord appeared. 'A fire came out from the Lord and consumed' the sacrifice.

What they saw in the types and shadows before them was the glory of God in the face of the Lord Jesus Christ, our crucified Substitute. Christ crucified is the revelation of the glory of God. When the people saw it, they shouted and fell on their faces. If ever we see what these people saw we will do what they did. We will shout Jehovah's praise and fall on our face before him (Revelation 4:10, 11; 5:9, 10).

Chapter 26

The Efficacy Of The Blood

And he brought the bullock for the sin offering: and Aaron and his sons laid their hands upon the head of the bullock for the sin offering. And he slew it; and Moses took the blood, and put it upon the horns of the altar round about with his finger, and purified the altar, and poured the blood at the bottom of the altar, and sanctified it, to make reconciliation upon it ... Moses took of the anointing oil, and of the blood which was upon the altar, and sprinkled it upon Aaron, and upon his garments, and upon his sons, and upon his sons' garments with him; and sanctified Aaron, and his garments, and his sons, and his sons' garments with him.

Leviticus 8:14-30

The eighth chapter of Leviticus portrays that blessed work of redemption by Christ our Substitute which he accomplished at Calvary. It declares the certain efficacy of our Saviour's blood for the everlasting salvation of his elect, those sinners for whom he died. All were anointed with the anointing oil for whom the blood of the sin-offering was shed. All shall be born of God for whom blood atonement has been made.

The Prominence of the Blood
Christ's sin-atoning blood is set before us prominently throughout the Scriptures. The book of God is a book written in blood, the precious blood of Christ. It is all about the blood, the sin-atoning blood of Christ. Take away the blood of the Lamb from the book of God and it would

be a book utterly insignificant, void of meaning, and useless. The blood of Christ, his blood sacrifice, his blood atonement, his blood cleansing is typically unfolded in great detail in this eighth chapter of Leviticus. Throughout this chapter the thing set before us is the necessity and the efficacy of our Saviour's blood for atonement, acceptance, and reconciliation with God. On that great day when Aaron and his sons were consecrated as priests unto God, it was the blood of the sacrifice that was constantly before the eyes of the people.

Three Sacrifices
Blood is set before us by three divinely appointed sacrifices. These three sacrifices could never put away sin; but they were given by God to portray him who would put away our sins by the sacrifice of himself (Hebrews 10:1-14).

1. The Bullock of the Sin-Offering

> And he brought the bullock for the sin offering: and Aaron and his sons laid their hands upon the head of the bullock for the sin offering. And he slew it; and Moses took the blood, and put it upon the horns of the altar round about with his finger, and purified the altar, and poured the blood at the bottom of the altar, and sanctified it, to make reconciliation upon it (Leviticus 8:14, 15).

2. The Ram for the Burnt-offering

> And he brought the ram for the burnt offering: and Aaron and his sons laid their hands upon the head of the ram. And he killed it; and Moses sprinkled the blood upon the altar round about (Leviticus 8:18, 19).

3. The Ram of Consecration

> And he brought the other ram, the ram of consecration: and Aaron and his sons laid their hands upon the head of the ram. And he slew it; and Moses took of the blood of it, and put it upon the tip of Aaron's right ear, and upon the thumb of his right hand, and upon the great toe of his right foot. And he brought Aaron's

sons, and Moses put of the blood upon the tip of their right ear, and upon the thumbs of their right hands, and upon the great toes of their right feet: and Moses sprinkled the blood upon the altar round about (Leviticus 8:22-24).

It should come as no surprise to read what the writer to the Hebrews said about this.

For when Moses had spoken every precept to all the people according to the law, he took the blood of calves and of goats, with water, and scarlet wool, and hyssop, and sprinkled both the book, and all the people, Saying, This is the blood of the testament which God hath enjoined unto you. Moreover he sprinkled with blood both the tabernacle, and all the vessels of the ministry. And almost all things are by the law purged with blood; and without shedding of blood is no remission (Hebrews 9:19-22).

What does this tell us? What do these sacrifices teach us? What is their intended symbolism?

Acceptance by the Blood

These typical sacrifices teach us that sinners are accepted of God only by and because of Christ's shed blood.

In whom we have redemption through his blood, the forgiveness of sins, according to the riches of his grace (Ephesians 1:7).

Forasmuch as ye know that ye were not redeemed with corruptible things, as silver and gold, from your vain conversation received by tradition from your fathers; But with the precious blood of Christ, as of a lamb without blemish and without spot: Who verily was foreordained before the foundation of the world, but was manifest in these last times for you, Who by him do believe in God, that raised him up from the dead, and gave him glory; that your faith and hope might be in God (1 Peter 1:18-21).

We cannot come to worship, or find acceptance with the holy Lord God except by the sin-atoning blood of the Lord Jesus Christ. Only a bloodstained ear can hear God's Word. Only a bloodstained hand can do God's work. Only a bloodstained foot can walk in the courts of the Lord's house. We cannot come to God except by the blood of Christ; but, blessed be his holy name, we can come to God by that blood!

Having therefore, brethren, boldness to enter into the holiest by the blood of Jesus, By a new and living way, which he hath consecrated for us, through the veil, that is to say, his flesh; And having an high priest over the house of God (Hebrews 10:19-21).
Let us therefore come boldly unto the throne of grace, that we may obtain mercy, and find grace to help in time of need (Hebrews 4:16).

Throughout this eighth chapter of Leviticus, we see the value, the efficacy, the power, and the wide application of the blood. 'Almost all things are by the law purged with blood' (Hebrews 9:22).

Assurance by the Blood
As the whole of our acceptance with God is the blood of his darling Son shed at Calvary as our Substitute, so the whole of our assurance before God is the blood. Our Lord Jesus Christ has by his own blood entered into heaven itself. Yonder, on the throne of the Majesty on high, he sits. He sits upon that throne in heaven by the merit and virtue of all that he accomplished on the cross.
Our Redeemer's presence in heaven on the throne of grace declares the worth and efficacy of his atoning blood (Romans 8:34; Hebrews 1:3; 10:12-14). The Lord Jesus sits upon his throne for us as our High Priest. He is there for us. Blessed assurance! 'He ever liveth.' He never changes! We are in him! 'And as he is so are we in this world'!
Christ is our Substitute and High Priest; and all who are saved by the free grace of God in him are accepted upon the same ground as he is. Before Aaron could make atonement for the people, he had to first make atonement for his own sins (Leviticus 16:6-14). So, too, our Lord Jesus Christ made atonement for himself (for the sins of his people that were made to be his own 2 Corinthians 5:21; Psalm 40:12; 69:5, 9, 19). John Trapp wrote, 'As he bore our sins in his own body upon the tree,

he was first redeemed by himself, and afterwards we'. When he died and was freed from sin, so were we (1 Peter 4:1, 2). He entered in and took possession of heaven as our Mediator upon the same ground as we do, the sinless One who has put away sin by the sacrifice of himself.

The Lord Jesus presents us to the Father in his own eternal perfection. The Father delights in us so presented in his perfection, because we are in him. Yes, God our Father delights in us even as he delights in the One who presents us.

This identification of Christ with us and us with him is typically set forth in 'Aaron and his sons' laying their hands upon the head of each of the sacrifices; the bullock of the sin offering, the ram of the burnt offering, the ram of consecration (vv. 14, 18, 22). They all stood before God in the value of the same sacrifice. Whether it was the 'bullock for the sin-offering', 'the ram for the burnt-offering', or 'the ram of consecration', they jointly laid their hands on the head of the sacrifice.

Aaron First

Aaron and Aaron alone was anointed before the blood was shed. He was robed in the gorgeous garments of his priestly office and anointed with the holy oil before his sons were either clothed or anointed. Why? The reason should be obvious.

Aaron, when spoken of by himself, typifies our Lord Jesus Christ in his own peerless excellence and dignity. As such he stands alone. Our Lord Jesus Christ appeared on this earth in the unique perfection of his own personal worth. Before ever he shed his blood as our sin-atoning Substitute he was anointed by the Holy Ghost. The Father poured out the Spirit upon him without measure (John 3:34, 35). Christ is the Anointed One from eternity who was distinctly and publicly anointed by the Father from heaven at his baptism (Matthew 3:15-17).

Though Aaron was anointed alone before the blood was shed, he and his sons were united in the anointing that followed the blood-shedding.

And Moses took of the anointing oil, and of the blood which was upon the altar, and sprinkled it upon Aaron, and upon his garments, and upon his sons, and upon his sons' garments with him; and sanctified Aaron, and his garments, and his sons, and his sons' garments with him (Leviticus 8:30).

So, too, there is the fullest possible identification between Christ and his people (Ephesians 5:30; Hebrews 2:11). The Sanctifier and those who are sanctified are one. We are one with Christ. Christ and his people are distinct and yet one. We are personally distinct. Yet spiritually, representatively, we are one. This individual distinctness enhances the value of the spiritual union.

The Efficacy of the Blood

As the blood of Christ was prominent in all the sacrifices and services of the typical Levitical priesthood, so too was the efficacy of our Saviour's blood. This is the point of Satan's relentless opposition. This is the point at which self-serving prophets of deceit most quickly compromise the gospel. Let me make some plain, emphatic statements about the efficacy of our Saviour's shed blood. When I speak of the efficacy of Christ's blood, I mean just this. The shed blood of Christ effectually accomplished all it was intended to do.

1. He put away our sins. All the sins of all God's elect. All the sins of every sinner who believes on him. All the sins of every trembling soul who comes to God by him.

2. He obtained eternal redemption for all his people. That is to say, he got the job done. He purchased and secured the eternal salvation of all for whom he died at Calvary.

3. Every sinner for whom Christ shed his blood at Calvary shall be given the blessed anointing of the Holy Spirit, at God's appointed time of love. Every chosen, redeemed sinner shall be born again by the almighty, irresistible power and grace of God the Holy Ghost.

4. All for whom Christ died shall be saved by the power and grace of God the Holy Spirit. The efficacy of Christ's blood is seen in the anointing that follows it. All for whom blood was shed were anointed with the anointing oil.

This was prefigured in the anointing of Aaron and his sons (vv. 12 and 30). But between the anointing of Aaron and that of his sons several things happened. The blood was shed, the fat was consumed on the altar and the breast was waved before the Lord. Only then do we read 'And Moses took of the anointing oil, and of the blood which was upon the altar, and sprinkled it upon Aaron, and upon his garments, and upon his sons, and upon his sons' garments with him; and sanctified Aaron, and his garments, and his sons, and his sons' garments with him' (v. 30).

Here is the picture. Perfect atonement has been made by our Lord Jesus Christ. He who died at Calvary under the wrath of God as our Substitute has ascended to God in the power of his resurrection. Immanuel has taken his place in heaven by the merit of his blood. He has taken his place in heaven and has taken possession of heaven as a man for us his people. The sweet savour of Christ's blood sacrifice perpetually ascends to the holy Lord God, our heavenly Father and is accepted by him. All this comes between the anointing of the Head and the anointing of the members.

First, we see Aaron alone (vv. 8-12). The anointing oil is poured upon his head. The whole assembly was permitted to see God's high-priest gloriously arrayed, crowned, and anointed. As each garment was put on him, as each act was performed and each ceremony enacted, we read, 'as the Lord commanded'. All was done by the express revelation of God and the singular authority of the word of God. There was nothing vague, arbitrary, imaginative in it. Everything was divinely ordained and meticulously performed. All the needs of the congregation were fully met, and met in such a way that it could be said, 'This is the thing which the Lord commanded to be done'.

Aaron being anointed alone also shows us a special picture of our Saviour. Without the shedding of blood, there could be no union between Christ and his people. The Son of God could never be joined to us, and we could never be joined to him, except upon the ground of justice satisfied. Aaron's sons could not join him in the priesthood until blood was shed. There could be no union between Christ and his people except upon the ground of his death and resurrection.

Without shedding of blood there is no remission. Our Lord's righteous life would avail us nothing until his life's blood was shed. We could never be united with God in Christ until his blood had been accepted in the holy place. So, too, without shedding of blood Aaron and his sons could not be anointed together.

And Moses took of the anointing oil, and of the blood which was upon the altar, and sprinkled it upon Aaron, and upon his garments, and upon his sons, and upon his sons' garments with him; and sanctified Aaron, and his garments, and his sons, and his sons' garments with him (Leviticus 8:30).

Atonement First

The anointing oil could not be applied to Aaron's sons until the blood of the sin-offering, the burnt-offering, and the ram of consecration had been shed and the sacrifice presented in the holy place before the Lord. Why were Aaron's sons not anointed with him in verse 12? The answer is plain. The blood had not been shed. Only when atonement has been accomplished can grace be bestowed.

> And Moses took the anointing oil, and anointed the tabernacle and all that was therein, and sanctified them. And he sprinkled thereof upon the altar seven times, and anointed the altar and all his vessels, both the laver and his foot, to sanctify them (Leviticus 8:10, 11).

Aaron stands here alone. Clothed and arrayed as high priest, with his sons at his side, all eyes are fixed on him. Here is a beautiful and blessed type of Christ with his sons upon the Mount of Transfiguration. Though we could not be united to him until the blood was shed, yet, in the mind and purpose of God the blood of the Lamb was shed before the foundation of the world, and we were accepted in him from eternity.

I can almost hear the Lord God saying, 'Consider the Apostle and High Priest of your profession.' This is God's word to every believing sinner. 'Ye are complete in him.' Why should any look for acceptance anywhere else? All that can give a sinner peace is in this great High Priest, Christ Jesus. We cannot find God reconciled anywhere but in him. Only in Immanuel and all he is are our souls' needs met.

Moses has gone into the tabernacle. He is busy there. Already all things therein had been sprinkled with blood. The blood had cleansed them. Now the oil sets them apart for holy purposes, solemnly set apart to the Lord. None can ever claim the use of them again. They must be used by no one and for no one but God himself, used for nothing but the service of his will, used for no other purpose but the purpose of his glory. Thus Moses' sanctified the vessels of the tabernacle.

Sanctification Follows

Once atonement was made sanctification followed. Learn what it is to be sanctified. It is to be set apart for God alone. Our Saviour speaks of himself as a vessel set apart to be used for God alone, to accomplish

God's purpose (John 17:19). Just as the sanctuary and all its vessels were to be used only to show us the sinner's way to God, so Christ presented himself to be used by the Father entirely for the purpose of making a way for sinners to come to God. This is the glorious gospel! The use for which the incarnate Son of God was set apart was to make a way for sinners to come to God.

The Father used him in this way in coming to us. We use him in the same way in coming to the Father. Christ is a Saviour set apart for the use of sinners. No angel can ever use him for that purpose. He is not a Saviour for angels (Hebrews 2:16). But the guiltiest soul may come to God by Christ Jesus. He is the sinner's Saviour. The Lord Jesus Christ is set apart for the unlimited use of needy sinners.

Only Aaron wore the crown on his turban reading, 'HOLINESS TO THE LORD'. His sons had to look to him for everything. So it is with us. We must look to Christ alone for everything before God. We come to him, worship him, believe on him, pray to him, and offer sacrifices to him in the name of him who is our Aaron, the Lord Jesus Christ.

Seven Days
Aaron and his sons were shut up in the tabernacle for seven days.

> And Moses said unto Aaron and to his sons, Boil the flesh at the door of the tabernacle of the congregation: and there eat it with the bread that is in the basket of consecrations, as I commanded, saying, Aaron and his sons shall eat it. And that which remaineth of the flesh and of the bread shall ye burn with fire. And ye shall not go out of the door of the tabernacle of the congregation in seven days, until the days of your consecration be at an end: for seven days shall he consecrate you. As he hath done this day, so the LORD hath commanded to do, to make an atonement for you. Therefore shall ye abide at the door of the tabernacle of the congregation day and night seven days, and keep the charge of the LORD, that ye die not: for so I am commanded (Leviticus 8:31-35).

Here is Christ and his people feeding together upon the results of his atonement. Aaron and his sons, having been anointed together are shut in within the precincts of the tabernacle for 'seven days'.

This is a picture of Christ and his people now. We are shut in with God, waiting for the manifestation of the glory of God. Christ and his redeemed abide together, preserved upon the same ground, for seven days. Seven is the number of completion and perfection. The picture before us in Leviticus is a picture of complete, perfect salvation in, by, and with our blessed Saviour, the Lord Jesus Christ.

We are one with Christ, shut in with God, waiting for the day of glory, and while waiting for the glory to come, feeding upon the riches of God's abounding, free grace in Christ. Oh, for a capacity to take these things in and a heart to enjoy them! May God give us a sense of their magnitude. May he grant us grace that our hearts might be turned away from all that pertains to this present evil world, so that we may feed only upon the contents of 'the basket of consecrations', our proper food as priests in the sanctuary of God until the eighth day. The eighth day is the day that has not yet been. The eighth day is the day of the new creation, the manifestation of the glory of God (Leviticus 9).

> Behold, he cometh with clouds; and every eye shall see him, and they also which pierced him: and all kindreds of the earth shall wail because of him. Even so, Amen (Revelation 1:7).

Blessed be God, until that day we are shut in with Christ where he is in the holy place. 'That ye die not.' Shut up with Christ in the holy place we cannot perish because here we are secured by the word of God, the blood of God's Son, and the anointing of God's Spirit.

That is the saving power and efficacy of the blood, the precious blood of Christ poured out for sinners at Calvary. This is my memorial to my Substitute. HE DIED FOR ME!

> I am crucified with Christ: nevertheless I live; yet not I, but Christ liveth in me: and the life which I now live in the flesh I live by the faith of the Son of God, who loved me, and gave himself for me (Galatians 2:20).

May God the Holy Ghost make the Saviour's blood effectual to you, for Christ's sake.

Chapter 27

'On The Eighth Day'

And it came to pass on the eighth day, that Moses called Aaron and his sons, and the elders of Israel ... Aaron therefore went unto the altar, and slew the calf of the sin offering, which was for himself ... And he brought the people's offering, and took the goat, which was the sin offering for the people, and slew it, and offered it for sin, as the first ... And ye shall not go out from the door of the tabernacle of the congregation, lest ye die: for the anointing oil of the LORD is upon you. And they did according to the word of Moses.

Leviticus 9:1-10:7

Try to imagine the unimaginable. Suppose the Lord God in one swift burst of wrath and justice took two of your sons to hell today (not rebel sons but good, loyal, sons who were obedient to you and walked in your steps), and then commanded you not to weep, or mourn, or show any indication of sorrow for them.

Are you thinking, 'Impossible! God would not do such a thing. No one could be expected to endure such a thing'? Yet, it is exactly what happened to Aaron in Leviticus 10. Read Leviticus 9:1-10:7 and you will see why God killed Aaron's sons, Nadab and Abihu, see why those two young men had to die and why Aaron could not weep for them.

At the end of chapter 8 God commanded Aaron and his sons to abide in the tabernacle for seven days, until the days of their consecration were fulfilled. Chapter 9 begins 'on the eighth day'.

221

Perfected Priests

> And it came to pass on the eighth day, that Moses called
> Aaron and his sons, and the elders of Israel (Leviticus 9:1).

The priests were now made ceremonially perfect. The days of their consecration were ended. They were accepted as the priests of the most high God. Being made ceremonially perfect they could enter into the holy place before the holy Lord God as representatives of the people. As such, these priests are pictures of our great High Priest, the Lord Jesus Christ, who, when he was made perfect, or had completed all required of him, entered into heaven for us (Hebrews 5:9; 9:12).

Moses, Aaron's four sons, and the elders of Israel were special witnesses of these things. They declared to the people that they could now approach the altar of God with confidence of acceptance, because Aaron was 'made perfect', fully consecrated.

Witnesses of Christ's completeness, perfection, and acceptance as our great High Priest assure us of his acceptance with God. They proclaim, 'Being made perfect he became the author of eternal salvation unto all them that obey him' (Hebrews 5:9). The Father bore witness of his acceptance at his baptism, on the holy mount of transfiguration, in his resurrection, and by his ascension and exaltation. On earth, saved sinners witness that we have seen and felt the power of his priesthood. We have taken our sins to him and received atonement from him.

As Israel was assured of acceptance at the altar of God because Aaron was accepted, so sinners coming to God by Christ are assured of acceptance because Christ is accepted.

The Sacrifices Presented

In verses 2-6 we see the sacrifices presented to Jehovah. As you read this passage you cannot avoid seeing how that in all things, while Aaron was a picture of Christ, great care was taken that the people understood he was nothing more. Everything about him declared plainly that there must arise another greater than Aaron, with a sacrifice greater than his.

Neither Aaron nor his sons could approach God without a sacrifice, the very sacrifice God required. If we would draw near to and be accepted of God, we must have the Sacrifice he requires; the blood of his own dear Son.

And he said unto Aaron, Take thee a young calf for a sin offering, and a ram for a burnt offering, without blemish, and offer them before the LORD (Leviticus 9:2).

Robert Hawker observed, 'Some have thought that a young calf being appointed for the sin-offering of Aaron, was to remind him of his former transgression in making the golden calf: that thereby he might never lose sight of his own unworthiness, while the LORD had called him to such an exalted rank as the high priest before the people'.

Every time Aaron brought his young calf to the altar, he must have remembered his great sin and lifted his heart with gratitude and praise to God for the forgiveness of sin by the precious blood of Christ represented in the sacrifice. The Lord has graciously arranged all matters of public worship precisely according to that purpose for us in this gospel age. Our songs of praise, our prayers and especially public prayer, the hearing of his Word, confessing Christ in believer's baptism, and observing of the Lord's Supper, all are designed by our God to remind us of our sin and his salvation by the sacrifice of his dear Son.

Aaron was himself a sinner. As such, he had to bring a sin offering for himself. In doing so he was like John the Baptist, 'the voice of one crying' at the altar, 'Prepare the way of the Lord! I am not the Christ. There is One coming after me who is preferred before me, One mightier than I, the latchet of whose shoes I am not worthy to stoop down and unloose! One who shall not need daily, as I do, to offer up sacrifice, first for my own sins, and then for the people's sin. That coming One is holy, harmless, undefiled, and separate from sinners. He has no sin and needs no sacrifice for sin. He shall be the Sacrifice.'

There is another picture here, a picture repeated throughout the book of Leviticus. We saw it in chapter 8. We will see it again in chapter 16. As Aaron first had to make atonement for his own sins (Leviticus 16:11), so Christ when he was made sin for us, took our place and our sins so completely that when he made atonement for us by the sacrifice of himself, he made atonement for our sins which were made to be his own sins (Psalm 40:12; 69:5; Hebrews 7:26, 27; 2 Corinthians 5:21).

And unto the children of Israel thou shalt speak, saying, Take ye a kid of the goats for a sin offering; and a calf and a lamb, both of the first year, without blemish, for a burnt offering; Also a bullock and a ram for peace offerings, to sacrifice before the LORD; and a meat offering mingled with oil: for today the LORD will appear unto you (Leviticus 9:3, 4).

Aaron, now consecrated as Israel's priest, was commissioned to speak to the people as Moses conveyed the mind and will of God through him. Again, he stands forth as a type of our blessed Saviour.

God, who at sundry times and in divers manners spake in time past unto the fathers by the prophets, Hath in these last days spoken unto us by his Son, whom he hath appointed heir of all things, by whom also he made the worlds (Hebrews 1:1, 2).

The people had to bring all the offerings required in the law, except the trespass offering. They did not have to bring that on this occasion, because they had not yet trespassed the holy things in the worship of the Lord (Leviticus 5:15).

Foremost is the sin offering 'a kid of the goats' ceremonially bearing their sin and guilt by imputation. They also brought the burnt offering, 'a calf and a lamb, both of the first year and without blemish', to show their faith in Christ, represented in both the sin offering and the burnt offering. Next, the peace-offering, in its fullest form was brought, 'a bullock and a ram', portraying the complete reconciliation made with God by the sacrifice of Christ and peace bestowed through Christ our sin offering and the burnt offering. Last, they brought 'the meat offering, mingled with oil', by which they declared their consecration to God by blood atonement and holy anointing.

What blessed promise was given at the end of verse 4. 'For today the Lord will appear unto you.' God's way to us and our way to him is exactly the same. We come to him by the blood of Christ and he comes to us by the blood. It is as if Moses had said, 'Come to God with the blood that has been shed for you this day; and the invisible God, whom no man has seen nor can see, will this day appear unto you'. Blessed good news for sinners who know themselves far off from God.

The congregation gathered in front of the tabernacle with their offerings and 'stood before the Lord'. Then Moses said to them, 'This thing which the Lord commanded you to do, do, and in so doing expect that the glory of the Lord shall appear unto you'.

> And they brought that which Moses commanded before the tabernacle of the congregation: and all the congregation drew near and stood before the LORD. And Moses said, This is the thing which the LORD commanded that ye should do: and the glory of the LORD shall appear unto you (Leviticus 9:5, 6).

In verse 4 we saw that the Lord appears as our God reconciled and gracious when we come to him trusting Christ. Here he tells us to expect it. Yes, believing sinners have every reason to expect God to appear to them and for them as they come to him by faith in Christ. I call you this day to come to God by faith in his Son, declaring that he will be found of all who so seek him. Come to God trusting Christ and expect him to be gracious to you. That is not presumption, it is faith.

The Sinless Priest
Next, we see the Lord Jesus Christ portrayed as the sinless priest. Aaron is again presented to us as one who needs atonement, always reminding those even in the earliest days of Judaism that he was but a type of him that was to come.

> And Moses said unto Aaron, Go unto the altar, and offer thy sin offering, and thy burnt offering, and make an atonement for thyself, and for the people: and offer the offering of the people, and make an atonement for them; as the LORD commanded. Aaron therefore went unto the altar, and slew the calf of the sin offering, which was for himself. And the sons of Aaron brought the blood unto him: and he dipped his finger in the blood, and put it upon the horns of the altar, and poured out the blood at the bottom of the altar: But the fat, and the kidneys, and the caul above the liver of the sin offering, he burnt upon the altar; as the LORD commanded Moses. And the flesh and the hide he burnt with fire without the camp. And he slew the burnt offering; and Aaron's sons presented unto him the blood, which he sprinkled round about upon the altar. And they presented the burnt offering unto him, with the pieces thereof, and the head: and he burnt them upon the altar. And he did wash the inwards and the legs, and burnt them upon the burnt offering on the altar (Leviticus 9:7-14).

Behold, a greater than Aaron is here! He who is our great High Priest before God must be without sin. Therefore, Aaron first makes atonement for himself, then for the people. The Lord Jesus Christ is an effectual High Priest, because he is a sinless, everlasting High Priest (Hebrews 7:24-28).

The Sanctified People
In verses 15-21 Aaron, representing the people of Israel, brings their sacrifices to God, sacrifices by which they were sanctified and accepted as God's holy ones. Here we see the sanctified people accepted of God.

> And he brought the people's offering, and took the goat, which was the sin offering for the people, and slew it, and offered it for sin, as the first. And he brought the burnt offering, and offered it according to the manner. And he brought the meat offering, and took an handful thereof, and burnt it upon the altar, beside the burnt sacrifice of the morning. He slew also the bullock and the ram for a sacrifice of peace offerings, which was for the people: and Aaron's sons presented unto him the blood, which he sprinkled upon the altar round about, and the fat of the bullock and of the ram, the rump, and that which covereth the inwards, and the kidneys, and the caul above the liver: And they put the fat upon the breasts, and he burnt the fat upon the altar: And the breasts and the right shoulder Aaron waved for a wave offering before the LORD; as Moses commanded (Leviticus 9:15-21).

We have seen these sacrifices and their significance before. They speak of reconciliation and devotion to God by blood atonement. But look at the sin offering and the language of verse 15. 'And he brought the people's offering, and took the goat, which was the sin offering for the people, and slew it, and offered it for sin, as the first'.

The language used here is remarkable and instructive. The words 'offered it for sin' can be translated, 'sinned it' or 'made it sin'. The sin offering was the offering that distinctly had sin imputed to it. The idea seems to be that Aaron put the sins of the people on this innocent victim making it the whole mass of their sins. The victim was made the sinner and made to receive and bear all the penalty their sins deserved.

I have no doubt at all that this is precisely what both Isaiah and Paul had in their minds as they declared to us, by inspiration of God the Holy Ghost, the great work of Christ upon the cross, when he was made sin for us (Isaiah 53:4-10; 2 Corinthians 5:21). Our great Sin-offering, the Lord Jesus Christ, when slain for us, was treated as if he were the very reservoir of sin. All the curse we deserved, that flows in countless floods of wrath over man, fell on him, and fell on him all at once! Thus, the Father made him both to be sin for us and to be the curse for us.

Aaron presented the people and God accepted them for his sake. This prefigured the grand message of the gospel. Our Lord Jesus Christ has presented us, and the Triune God accepts us for his sake. In him sinners who deserve his wrath are restored and brought into fellowship with God in perfect reconciliation. By all these things, we are told two great things. First, 'there is forgiveness with thee' and next, 'without shedding of blood is no remission'.

The Satisfaction Portrayed

Read verses 22-24 and rejoice in the satisfaction portrayed. Here is the result of it all. Mercy and truth are met together. Righteousness and peace have kissed each other. Justice is satisfied. Sin is pardoned. All God's wrath is clean gone forever.

> And Aaron lifted up his hand toward the people, and blessed them, and came down from offering of the sin offering, and the burnt offering, and peace offerings. And Moses and Aaron went into the tabernacle of the congregation, and came out, and blessed the people: and the glory of the LORD appeared unto all the people. And there came a fire out from before the LORD, and consumed upon the altar the burnt offering and the fat: which when all the people saw, they shouted, and fell on their faces (Leviticus 9:22-24).

Aaron came down from the place of sacrifice and lifted up his hands, hands that were that day made wet with blood, and blessed the people for whom sacrifice had been made. In Luke 24, we find the fulfilment of this in our Saviour's ascension.

And he led them out as far as to Bethany, and he lifted up his hands, and blessed them. And it came to pass, while he blessed them, he was parted from them, and carried up into heaven. And they worshipped him, and returned to Jerusalem with great joy: And were continually in the temple, praising and blessing God. Amen (Luke 24:50-53).

Then, Aaron and Moses went back into the tabernacle.

But Christ being come an high priest of good things to come, by a greater and more perfect tabernacle, not made with hands, that is to say, not of this building; Neither by the blood of goats and calves, but by his own blood he entered in once into the holy place, having obtained eternal redemption for us (Hebrews 9:11, 12).

For Christ is not entered into the holy places made with hands, which are the figures of the true; but into heaven itself, now to appear in the presence of God for us: (Hebrews 9:24).

Afterwards, late in the evening of the eighth day, Aaron and Moses came out and blessed the people upon the basis of the sacrifice accepted (Numbers 6:24-26; Hebrews 9:26-28). 'And the glory of the Lord appeared.' When the glory of the Lord appeared, fire came out from the Lord and consumed the sacrifice. When the people saw this, they shouted and fell on their faces (Revelation 19:1-6).

What precious tokens of divine favour. The glory of the Lord appeared. The Lord Jehovah showed himself present with his people and showed himself glorified in both his sacrifice and his salvation of sinners by the sacrifice.

God answered by fire, testifying his acceptance of the sacrifice. The fire came down from heaven and consumed the sacrifice, which might justly have consumed the people for their sin. So the Holy Ghost came down in confirmation of the fact that Christ's offering for sin on the cross was accepted. Had he not died, had he not first put away our sin by the sacrifice of himself, the Holy Ghost could not have come (John 16:7). He could never have baptized us with the Holy Ghost and fire. And we could never have escaped destruction.

The Solemn Picture

Read the first seven verses of chapter 10 and pay close attention to the solemn picture. Aaron's sons, Nadab and Abihu, were slain because they sought to approach God with something other than the sacrifice he provided and accepted. This is what we must see and understand. Sinners come to God and find acceptance with him only by Christ crucified. Sinners cannot come to God in any other way or upon any other grounds. If you offer the strange fire of another sacrifice, the Lord God will destroy you with that same fire of strict justice that consumed his Son at Calvary.

And Nadab and Abihu, the sons of Aaron, took either of them his censer, and put fire therein, and put incense thereon, and offered strange fire before the LORD, which he commanded them not. And there went out fire from the LORD, and devoured them, and they died before the LORD. Then Moses said unto Aaron, This is it that the LORD spake, saying, I will be sanctified in them that come nigh me, and before all the people I will be glorified. And Aaron held his peace. And Moses called Mishael and Elzaphan, the sons of Uzziel the uncle of Aaron, and said unto them, Come near, carry your brethren from before the sanctuary out of the camp. So they went near, and carried them in their coats out of the camp; as Moses had said. And Moses said unto Aaron, and unto Eleazar and unto Ithamar, his sons, Uncover not your heads, neither rend your clothes; lest ye die, and lest wrath come upon all the people: but let your brethren, the whole house of Israel, bewail the burning which the LORD hath kindled. And ye shall not go out from the door of the tabernacle of the congregation, lest ye die: for the anointing oil of the LORD is upon you. And they did according to the word of Moses (Leviticus 10:1-7).

Come to God. Come now to God, by the merits of Christ, by the merit of his blood, trusting this great High Priest.

Let us therefore come boldly unto the throne of grace, that we may obtain mercy, and find grace to help in time of need (Hebrews 4:16).

Wherefore he is able also to save them to the uttermost that come unto God by him, seeing he ever liveth to make intercession for them (Hebrews 7:25).

My little children, these things write I unto you, that ye sin not. And if any man sin, we have an advocate with the Father, Jesus Christ the righteous: And he is the propitiation for our sins: and not for ours only, but also for the sins of the whole world (1 John 2:1, 2).

This great, glorious High Priest will perfect that which concerns us. He will put the bread on the golden table, that we may never want better angels' food. He will pour in daily the olive oil, that the lamps of his golden candlesticks may never be dim in this dark, gloomy world. He will present his incense with every prayer of ours, with every groan, with every sigh of broken, contrite sinners pouring out their hearts to him. And soon, very soon, he will come forth again, perhaps before any of us sleep with our fathers. He will come forth to bless us and to receive the shout of multitudes of adoring saved sinners confessing that he is Lord alone (Revelation 4:10, 11; 5:9-14).

Chapter 28

The Revelation Of God's Glory

And Aaron lifted up his hand toward the people, and blessed them, and came down from offering of the sin offering, and the burnt offering, and peace offerings. And Moses and Aaron went into the tabernacle of the congregation, and came out, and blessed the people: and the glory of the LORD appeared unto all the people. And there came a fire out from before the LORD, and consumed upon the altar the burnt offering and the fat: which when all the people saw, they shouted, and fell on their faces.

Leviticus 9:22-24

Bro. E. W. Johnson once made a statement that had a profound effect on me. He said, 'A lost man can see everything a saved man can see, except this: he can't see the glory of God. We do.' The lost man can see doctrine such as God's sovereignty, predestination, election, limited atonement, but he cannot see the glory of God. The unregenerate can see Bible facts but he cannot see the glory of God. Unbelievers can see good works but not the glory of God. The lost soul can see many, many things taught in the Bible such as prophecy, church order, baptism, marriage teaching, but he cannot see the glory of God. Believers do.

It is the revelation of the glory of God in the face of Christ that produces saving faith in Christ. If ever you see the glory of God in the face of Christ, you will be saved, you will believe on the Son of God.

But if our gospel be hid, it is hid to them that are lost: In whom the God of this world hath blinded the minds of them which believe not, lest the light of the glorious gospel of Christ, who is the image of God, should shine unto them. For we preach not ourselves, but Christ Jesus the Lord; and ourselves your servants for Jesus' sake. For God, who commanded the light to shine out of darkness, hath shined in our hearts, to give the light of the knowledge of the glory of God in the face of Jesus Christ. But we have this treasure in earthen vessels, that the excellency of the power may be of God, and not of us (2 Corinthians 4:3-7).

One Place

Commonly, when talking or writing about the glory of God, men tend to make it either an emotional thing with lots of sparkle and little or no substance or a mystical thing no one can really get hold of. It is neither.

The words translated 'glory', in both the Old and New Testaments, mean abundance, wealth, treasure, honour, splendour, brightness, dignity and majesty. When the Scriptures speak of God's glory, they sometimes refer to the perfection of his nature, his attributes, and his worthiness as the object of our faith, praise, and worship. The greatness, supremacy, and excellence of his eternal Being.

Yet, the revelation of God's glory is always represented as one specific thing. The Scriptures everywhere associate the revelation of God's glory with the person and work of our Lord Jesus Christ. When Moses prayed, 'Show me thy glory', the Lord God showed him Christ our Redeemer. When Manoah and his wife saw the Angel of the Lord do gloriously (Judges 13), it was the revelation of Christ crucified to them. When Isaiah saw Christ in his glory and spoke of him (Isaiah 6; John 12:41), he saw Christ enthroned by virtue of his redemptive accomplishments. The throne of grace is called 'the throne of thy glory' (Jeremiah 14:21), because Christ sits upon his throne in his glory as our Redeemer. Note the way to plead your cause with the Almighty:

We acknowledge, O LORD, our wickedness, and the iniquity of our fathers: for we have sinned against thee. Do not abhor us, for thy name's sake, do not disgrace the throne of thy glory: remember, break not thy covenant with us (Jeremiah 14:20, 21).

Our Lord Jesus Christ is the revelation of the glory of God. The glory of God is revealed in Christ, our crucified, risen, enthroned Saviour.

When the God of Glory appeared to Abraham, it was Christ who appeared to him. If the God of Glory ever appears to you, if the God of Glory ever makes himself known to you, it will be in and by the Lord Jesus Christ. The glory of God is in him. The glory of God is revealed in him. He alone is the glory of God.

The Mount of Transfiguration
God the Father and God the Holy Ghost give all glory to the Son, the Lord Jesus Christ as our Mediator and Saviour. True faith puts all the honour and glory of salvation on God's beloved Son, because God himself has placed it there (Ephesians 1:6, 12, 14). God the Father gives all glory to the Son (Colossians 1:18, 19). God the Son glorifies the Father (John 12:28). God the Holy Ghost gives glory to the Son (John 16:14). God the Son glorifies the Spirit (John 6:63; 7:38, 39). It is in his beloved Son that God the Father is well pleased. He is pleased with us in his Son. That is what Peter, James, and John saw on the Mount of Transfiguration (1 Peter 1:5-7).

> Moreover I will endeavour that ye may be able after my decease to have these things always in remembrance. For we have not followed cunningly devised fables, when we made known unto you the power and coming of our Lord Jesus Christ, but were eyewitnesses of his majesty. For he received from God the Father honour and glory, when there came such a voice to him from the excellent glory, This is my beloved Son, in whom I am well pleased (2 Peter 1:15-17).

Saving faith causes believing sinners both to imitate and obey God. It causes us to be well pleased with him in whom God is well pleased. To the eye of nature, Jesus of Nazareth appears as a mere man, in abject poverty and the lowest abasement, as Isaiah puts it, 'a tender plant, a root out of dry ground, with neither form nor comeliness that we should desire him'. Yet the Triune God gives him the highest honour and glory because he magnified his holy law and made it honourable, satisfying divine justice, and bringing in everlasting righteousness. Giving honour and glory to every attribute and perfection of the holy Lord God.

233

Trust Christ

Let us, then, with a sight and sense of our ruined nature and innumerable sins put honour and glory upon the Son of God. With him, with his person, his work, and his salvation, God is well pleased. He has satisfied heaven for our sins. Let our consciences, therefore, be satisfied with Christ and glory in him alone.

Look at Peter, the man who wrote the words above. He was with Christ on the Mountain of Transfiguration. He saw his Lord's transfiguration and heard these words from the excellent glory. Yet, he later denied he knew the man whom God the Father had honoured and glorified before his very eyes. He did so with oaths and cursing! Still, there is such an infinite, inexpressible fulness of grace in Christ that his sin was not imputed to him and could not be, for Christ died for him. Even for Peter there was immediate, free, full forgiveness through him who is the glory of God. Out of Christ's fulness Peter received grace upon grace and was recovered from his horrible fall, restored to repentance, and preserved to everlasting salvation.

May the Son of God our Saviour so move upon our hearts, yours and mine, as he did Peter's, unto godly sorrow and holy love, that we may say, 'This is my beloved Saviour, in whom I am well pleased'.

Leviticus 9 portrays God's glory in Christ. May God the Holy Spirit be pleased, by the word of the gospel, to reveal in our hearts 'the glory of God in the face of Jesus Christ'. When we read this chapter let us always leave it saying with John, 'And we beheld his glory, the glory as of the only begotten of the Father full of grace and truth'.

God's Promise

When Aaron and his sons were consecrated as God's priests and the ceremonial sacrifices began, the Lord God made a promise directly connected with the priesthood, the sacrifices, the altar, and the holy place, a promise directly connected with that which the things spoken of in this chapter portrayed. It was the same promise that is given in the preaching of the gospel today. We read the promise in Leviticus 9:6. 'And Moses said, This is the thing which the LORD commanded that ye should do: and the glory of the LORD shall appear unto you'. In other words, 'Believe and you shall see the glory of God' (John 11:40). 'Believe on the Lord Jesus Christ'. Believing, you shall be saved, you shall see the glory of God in the face of his dear Son.

That command was given, and the promise was made early in the morning as the day of sacrifice and worship began. In verses 22-24, we see the promise fulfilled at the end of the day.

> And Aaron lifted up his hand toward the people, and blessed them, and came down from offering of the sin offering, and the burnt offering, and peace offerings. And Moses and Aaron went into the tabernacle of the congregation, and came out, and blessed the people: and the glory of the LORD appeared unto all the people. And there came a fire out from before the LORD, and consumed upon the altar the burnt offering and the fat: which when all the people saw, they shouted, and fell on their faces (Leviticus 9:22-24).

In all these things, the Lord God gave Israel a picture of redemption, telling his people how he would accomplish their salvation and make his glory known in all the earth by his dear Son, the Lord Jesus Christ.

Came Down
Aaron came down from the place of sacrifice, and lifted up his hands, hands that were that day made wet with blood, and blessed the people for whom sacrifice had been made. In Luke 24 we see the fulfilment of this picture.

> And he led them out as far as to Bethany, and he lifted up his hands, and blessed them. And it came to pass, while he blessed them, he was parted from them, and carried up into heaven. And they worshipped him, and returned to Jerusalem with great joy: And were continually in the temple, praising and blessing God. Amen (Luke 24:50-53).

The Lord Jesus Christ, our great Saviour, came down. We cannot imagine how far down he came.

> For ye know the grace of our Lord Jesus Christ, that, though he was rich, yet for your sakes he became poor, that ye through his poverty might be rich (2 Corinthians 8:9).

Let this mind be in you, which was also in Christ Jesus: Who, being in the form of God, thought it not robbery to be equal with God: But made himself of no reputation, and took upon him the form of a servant, and was made in the likeness of men (Philippians 2:5-7).

The Son of God came down from heaven and entered into this world to put away sin by the sacrifice of himself, that the blessing of God might be upon his elect forever. It is written, 'Now, once, in the end of the world hath he appeared to put away sin by the sacrifice of himself' (Hebrews 9:26). What he came here to do, the Son of God has done.

Christ hath redeemed us from the curse of the law, being made a curse for us: for it is written, Cursed is everyone that hangeth on a tree: That the blessing of Abraham might come on the Gentiles through Jesus Christ; that we might receive the promise of the Spirit through faith (Galatians 3:13, 14).

Went In
Next, Aaron went in. We are specifically told that Aaron and Moses went into the tabernacle together. They went out of the outer court, away from the altar of the burnt offering, into the holy place. There, in the holy place stood the altar of incense, the table of shewbread, and the golden lampstand. Moses, representing the holy law of God, went in with Aaron, God's high priest, and turned over to him all things pertaining to the worship and service of God. Aaron represents our Saviour. Moses was saying, 'If you would come to God, Christ is the way. If you would worship God, Christ is the way. If you would find forgiveness with God, Christ is the way. If you would be accepted of God, Christ is the way. If you would be righteous, Christ is the way.'

Moses went with Aaron, taking him as it were, into the holy place to make intercession for his people Israel, to make intercession on the grounds of the sacrifice offered. Aaron went into the tabernacle, into the holy place, praying for the people, praying, I am confident, for one specific thing. He went in to pray that God would fulfil his promise and reveal his glory, that the Lord God would send his Son to his people and save them. That is exactly what the Lord Jesus is doing today.

But Christ being come an high priest of good things to come, by a greater and more perfect tabernacle, not made with hands, that is to say, not of this building; Neither by the blood of goats and calves, but by his own blood he entered in once into the holy place, having obtained eternal redemption for us ... For Christ is not entered into the holy places made with hands, which are the figures of the true; but into heaven itself, now to appear in the presence of God for us (Hebrews 9:11, 12, 24).

My little children, these things write I unto you, that ye sin not. And if any man sin, we have an advocate with the Father, Jesus Christ the righteous: And he is the propitiation for our sins: and not for ours only, but also for the sins of the whole world (1 John 2:1, 2).

Came Out

Then, Aaron came out again. Moses (the law) is still with him. Late in the evening of the eighth day, Aaron and Moses, God's priest with God's law, came out together and blessed the people together. Soon, our great Saviour will come again. When he comes we shall see the glory of God revealed in the salvation of sinners by Jesus Christ.

Now once in the end of the world hath he appeared to put away sin by the sacrifice of himself. And as it is appointed unto men once to die, but after this the judgment: So Christ was once offered to bear the sins of many; and unto them that look for him shall he appear the second time without sin unto salvation (Hebrews 9:26-28).

Soon, everybody is going to see the glory of God in the saving of his people by Christ our Substitute (Ephesians 2:7; Revelation 1:7). But this is a twofold picture. It pictures both our Lord's second coming at the end of the world and his coming to sinners in the exercise and operation of his saving grace. As the fire came out from the presence of the Lord and consumed the sacrifice here, so the Holy Spirit was poured out on the day of Pentecost as cloven tongues of fire, manifestly declaring God's acceptance of Christ's sacrifice. That is exactly what happens when God saves a sinner (John 16:7-11).

The picture before us here in Leviticus 9 is a declaration that redemption and grace through Christ reveals the glory of God (Psalm 21:5; 85:9-13; Proverbs 16:6). Do you see the picture? God's gracious and glorious presence with his people comes in consequence of the propitiatory sacrifice of the Lord Jesus Christ, the true Mercyseat. Sinners have acceptance and fellowship with the holy Lord God only by the blood of Christ (Ephesians 2:18; 3:12; 1 John 1:3).

When the glory of the Lord appeared, fire came out from the Lord and consumed the sacrifice. When the people saw this, they shouted and fell on their faces. When the glory of God is revealed in the face of the Lord Jesus Christ, when the blessings of grace are bestowed upon sinners through the power and grace of God, when God himself comes to us and makes himself known to us, our hearts are flooded with reverence, joy, and holy praise (Psalm 4:6, 7; 103:1-4).

The revelation of Christ in a sinner's heart has two profound, lasting effects. It causes us both to shout for joy and fall on our faces in humiliation, reverence and godly fear (Isaiah 6:1-8). When the glory of God is revealed in the last great day, it will have the same effect. When Aaron left the altar and went into the holy place, Moses stood with him and, as representative of Jehovah, handed over to his care all the vessels of the sanctuary and committed the ordering of all to him. Even so, the Lord Jesus in his ascension, when he left the place where he had made the sacrifice, was given dominion over all things for the salvation of his people (John 17:3-5; Psalm 68:17-20).

Our all-glorious, ever-blessed Christ has been given authority and power as our God-man Mediator, as the Captain of our salvation now made perfect (Hebrews 2:10), authority and power to administer all the affairs of the sanctuary. It was in reference to this that he said, as he was entering into heaven, 'All power is given unto me in heaven and in earth' (Matthew 28:18). Satan has no power. 'All power is given unto me in heaven and in earth.' Moses has no power. 'All power is given unto me in heaven and in earth.' The law has no power. The devil has no power. The demons of hell have no power. Man has no power. No nation in the world has any power. 'All power is given unto me in heaven and in earth.' All the nations of the earth combined have no power. 'All power is given unto me in heaven and in earth.'

See him yonder. There he is, seated on his throne in the holy place, managing all the interests of his people, managing all the affairs of the universe for us. Preparing many mansions for us. The Father has committed all things to his hands for us!

This Christ is coming out again. His coming out again will be like Aaron's. He is coming out again to bless the people anew. Try to picture the scene before us in Leviticus 9.

The people stayed in the tabernacle courtyard all day, expecting the reappearance of Aaron and Moses, expecting to see the glory of the Lord. Why shouldn't they? They had done what God commanded. They came to him in the place he required, with the blood he required, in the way he required, looking to him for the mercy he promised. Now, they expected him to do what he promised. What could be more reasonable?

We stand before God today as believing sinners, looking to Christ alone for all our salvation, in confident hope and expectation. Our eyes and hearts are fixed on the Altar, looking for that blessed hope, the glorious appearing of the great God and our Saviour, Jesus Christ, who gave himself for us, that he might redeem us unto himself. Yes, we look for and expect the second coming of the Son of God in all the glory of the Triune God, which is his own.

'And the glory of the LORD appeared to all the people' of Israel that day. Some of the bright fire of that glory shot down on the altar and consumed the pieces of the sacrifice, giving one final, grand and glorious display of divine satisfaction. What a sight it must have been.

In this I see a clear picture of Christ's second coming. 'To those that look for him' his glory will thus appear. In the evening of the world's day Christ shall come out again. The Lamb of God will give one final, indisputable display of the fact that God the Father is well-pleased with him and with all his people in him. He will appear 'without sin, unto salvation'. The sin consumed by the fire of God's holy wrath, is forever put away, forever gone, there is nothing left for us but the completion of our joy and the experience of the fulness of it in heavenly glory.

What a shout of ecstasy shall burst from us then! Yet, how deeply awed and reverent we shall be. Forgiveness produces holy awe even now wherever it is known. The people shout and fall prostrate before him. To Christ every knee shall bow, and every tongue confess, that he is Lord, to the glory of God the Father. What a day that shall be!

And after these things I heard a great voice of much people in heaven, saying, Alleluia; Salvation, and glory, and honour, and power, unto the Lord our God: For true and righteous are his judgments: for he hath judged the great whore, which did corrupt the earth with her fornication, and hath avenged the blood of his servants at her hand. And again they said, Alleluia. And her smoke rose up for ever and ever. And the four and twenty elders and the four beasts fell down and worshipped God that sat on the throne, saying, Amen; Alleluia. And a voice came out of the throne, saying, Praise our God, all ye his servants, and ye that fear him, both small and great. And I heard as it were the voice of a great multitude, and as the voice of many waters, and as the voice of mighty thunderings, saying, Alleluia: for the Lord God omnipotent reigneth (Revelation 19:1-6).

Believe and See

Believe on the Lord Jesus Christ and you shall see the glory of God. Moses said, 'This, the thing which the LORD commanded that you should do, do: and the glory of the LORD shall appear unto you.' That is exactly what our Lord Jesus said to Martha in John 11:40. 'Jesus saith unto her, Said I not unto thee, that, if thou wouldest believe, thou shouldest see the glory of God?' Believe on the Son of God and you will see the glory of God in Christ. Being born of God and taught of God, this blessing of God shall be yours (Numbers 6:24-26; 2 Corinthians 4:6). And this blessing of God shall be yours in that great day when our God shall make all things new at Christ's second coming.

For the grace of God that bringeth salvation hath appeared to all men, Teaching us that, denying ungodliness and worldly lusts, we should live soberly, righteously, and godly, in this present world; Looking for that blessed hope, and the glorious appearing of the great God and our Saviour Jesus Christ; Who gave himself for us, that he might redeem us from all iniquity, and purify unto himself a peculiar people, zealous of good works (Titus 2:11-14).

Chapter 29

Nadab And Abihu: The Worship Of God

And Nadab and Abihu, the sons of Aaron, took either of them his censer, and put fire therein, and put incense thereon, and offered strange fire before the LORD, which he commanded them not. And Aaron said unto Moses, Behold, this day have they offered their sin offering and their burnt offering before the LORD; and such things have befallen me: and if I had eaten the sin offering today, should it have been accepted in the sight of the LORD? And when Moses heard that, he was content.

Leviticus 10:1-20

The things recorded in these twenty verses of Inspiration teach us that the only way sinners can come to God, worship God, and be accepted with God is by faith in his Son, Jesus Christ. Nadab and Abihu were sons of Aaron, God's high priest. They had been ceremonially consecrated as priests unto the Lord (Leviticus 8, 9). They had seen Moses and Aaron go together into the holy place. Nadab and Abihu were among those upon whom Moses and Aaron had pronounced God's blessing. They had seen the visible symbol of the glory of the Lord in the fire that consumed the sacrifice. Then, the next day, Nadab and Abihu were consumed by the fire of God's wrath in the court of the Lord's house, as they carried out their priestly functions leading Israel in worship. That is how Leviticus chapter 10 begins.

And Nadab and Abihu, the sons of Aaron, took either of them his censer, and put fire therein, and put incense thereon, and offered strange fire before the LORD, which he commanded them not. And there went out fire from the LORD, and devoured them, and they died before the LORD (Leviticus 10:1, 2).

Obvious Lessons

What an awesome, astounding way for a day in the house of God to begin! Without question, there are many very important and obvious lessons for us to learn from this chapter. Three lessons are set before us.

1. Grace does not run in bloodlines. Though Aaron was their father, and Moses was their uncle, though Miriam was their aunt, Nadab and Abihu perished under the wrath of God. The only way anyone is born into God's family is by being born again (John 1:11-13; 3:3-8). There is no covenant family except the heaven-born family of God. There is no Christian nation except God's holy nation the church of his elect.

2. Grace cannot be obtained by the observance of religious rituals. Sacramentalism is, perhaps, the most damning heresy ever perpetrated upon the souls of men in the name of God. You cannot obtain God's salvation by the outward ordinances of divine worship. Nadab and Abihu were circumcised in their flesh, but uncircumcised at heart. They kept the passover, but did not know Christ our Passover. They wore the garments of the priesthood, but never knew God's High Priest. They went through consecration ceremonies, but knew nothing of consecration to God. They had blood on their ears, their thumbs, and their toes, but none in their hearts. Multitudes tread the courts of God's house, go through the outward services of religious devotion, and engage in the service of religion with great zeal, who yet perish under the wrath of God. Be warned! A mere form of godliness, be it ever so precisely orthodox, may carry you to hell in fine garb and with great pageantry; but it will still carry you to hell (Matthew 7:13-15; 21-23). Nadab and Abihu were priests ordained by Moses, but they are in hell.

3. In matters of doctrine and worship what God does not command is forbidden. We read in verse 1 how God the Holy Ghost describes the fatal crime of Aaron's sons. 'Nadab and Abihu, the sons of Aaron, took either of them his censer, and put fire therein, and put incense thereon,

and offered strange fire before the LORD, which he commanded them not'. They offered strange fire which the Lord forbade.

These sons of Aaron, by an act of wilful, calculated and deliberate rebellion, rejected the counsel of God and dared to approach him with strange fire, in direct violation of his Word. They came at the wrong time, according to their own whim, not on the day of atonement, the time God required that the fire be brought into the holy place (Leviticus 16:1, 2). You do not come to God on your terms, or when you decide to come. Sinners come to God when he calls (Psalm 65:4; 110:3).

They came to the wrong place, the open court (v. 4), not the holy of holies, as God required (Leviticus 16:11-13). The only place of mercy is Christ the Mercyseat! The only place of grace is the throne of grace. They came without Aaron, without God's high priest. All who vainly imagine they can come to God at their time and by their choice always come without Christ. They brought their own fire, not the fire from off the altar before the Lord, not the fire which came down from heaven (Leviticus 16:12). All will-worshippers bring strange fire to God. And these two sons of Aaron were consumed in the wrath of God. So it has always been and shall forever be. Those who come to God like Cain must forever bear the mark of Cain in hell.

Faith in Christ

Be sure you understand what the Holy Spirit here teaches us. It is a lesson repeated throughout the book of God. If we would come to God, we must come to him in the way he has prescribed, ordained, and revealed. This is exactly what we read in 1 Chronicles 13 and 15. We cannot worship God upon an altar of our own making. We cannot come to God with the fire of our own kindling. We cannot bring the censer of our own incense.

Blessed be his name, there is a way of access to God! Sinners can come to the holy Lord God with the assurance of acceptance with him by the blood of Christ. But the only way sinners can come to God and be accepted of him is by faith in his dear Son (Acts 4:12; Hebrews 10:19-22). Christ is able to save to the uttermost all who come to God by him. But if you try to climb up to heaven by any other means, or by incorporating something of your own making with Christ, God will consume you in his holy wrath for trampling under your feet the blood of his dear Son! Remember Uzza!

Christ alone is our Sin-offering and Christ alone is our High Priest. Christ alone is the Sacrifice by which the fire of God's hot wrath and holy justice is satisfied (Leviticus 9). He alone has incense acceptable to God (1 John 2:1, 2).

Peace in Believing
Faith in Christ gives us peace in the midst of heartache and trouble.

> Then Moses said unto Aaron, This is it that the LORD spake saying, I will be sanctified in them that come nigh me, and before all the people I will be glorified. And Aaron held his peace (Leviticus 10:3).

'Observe', Robert Hawker suggests, 'what effect grace had upon the mind of Moses. No doubt the awful event struck terror and dismay in every beholder. But while some trembled Moses adored. It is sweet in our afflictions to eye the Lord's appointment, and depend upon it. As long as we are enabled to keep in view divine wisdom, we shall never despond by human sufferings. Observe also the pious frame of Aaron's mind. No doubt his soul was convulsed with agony. It must have been visible in his very looks. Yet Aaron held his peace.'

Nadab and Abihu may have been very impressive to men in their religious performances, but what they did in offering their strange fire was to spit in God's face. Their religion was nothing short of painted blasphemy, because there was nothing in it that sanctified God's name, nothing in it that honoured God. There was nothing in it that glorified God before the people.

The only way we can sanctify God, the only way we can honour him, the only way we can glorify him is by faith in Christ. Yes, we would honour him in our lives; but we cannot do so. We would sanctify him in our services; but our best services are full of sin. We would glorify our God with every thought, every word, every deed, and with every second of our lives, but that we cannot do, except by faith in his Son. Nothing else honours him. Nothing else glorifies him. Nothing else sets him apart as God, but Christ and redemption by his blood (Jeremiah 9:23, 24; 1 Corinthians 1:30, 31).

God's glory is redemption by Christ. He is glorified only when we come to him by faith in Christ. All acts of will-worship are but acts of rebellion against God. We will either worship God in accordance with his Word or we will perish under his wrath (Hebrews 12:25).

Baptism, the immersion of believers in the confession of Christ, must be performed in the way he has prescribed. To alter God's ordinance is to despise his Word and pervert the gospel it portrays, proclaiming that righteousness can be had some other way. Infant sprinkling is a perversion of the ordinance and a perversion of the gospel it portrays, which is salvation by the obedience and death of the Lord Jesus Christ (Matthew 3:13-17).

The Lord's Supper must be eaten in the way he has prescribed, the unleavened bread representing the body of Christ crushed under the wrath of God and wine representing his blood poured out in death as our Substitute. To alter the ordinance is to despise his Word and pervert the gospel pictured in it, declaring the incarnation and death of Christ as our God-man Substitute was not necessary.

'And Aaron held his peace.' What an astounding statement! Aaron took one look at his lost, rebel sons and another at his glorified God, seeing, and understanding, that what God had done he had done because his sons had despised God's Son, and he held his peace.

It shall be so in the last day. Our God and Saviour shall, in that great and terrible day, point to the unbelieving as objects of his just displeasure and say, 'Depart ye cursed into everlasting fire'. And the redeemed of the Lord shall respond, as the smoke of their torments ascends up to heaven, 'Hallelujah'. Yes, the righteous shall rejoice when in righteous judgment God washes his feet in the blood of the wicked (Psalm 58:10). The glory of God will be so fully and perfectly manifest that it shall hide all else from our view. His glory will cause us to cry, 'Hallelujah'! (Revelation 19:3). The torments of the damned will cause no sorrow among the redeemed. We shall hold our peace, and more. We shall sing the praises of our God in the exercise of his righteous judgments. As it shall be in the last day, it should be now. Let us humbly bow to God our Saviour, who performs all things for us (Psalm 57:2; Romans 15:13). He is too wise to err, too strong to fail, and too good to do wrong!

The Funeral
Verses 4-7 tell us of the funeral of these two rebels. Devout men carried Stephen to his burial and made great lamentation for him (Acts 8:2).

Discovering Christ In Leviticus

But Nadab and Abihu died like Ananias and Saphira (Acts 5:6-10) and were burned by the command of God as unbelieving rebels outside the camp. How striking the difference that is made between them and the just who are translated and never taste death (John 11:25; Revelation 14:3). Of Nadab and Abihu we read,

> And Moses called Mishael and Elzaphan, the sons of Uzziel the uncle of Aaron, and said unto them, Come near, carry your brethren from before the sanctuary out of the camp. So they went near, and carried them in their coats out of the camp; as Moses had said. And Moses said unto Aaron, and unto Eleazar and unto Ithamar, his sons, Uncover not your heads, neither rend your clothes; lest ye die, and lest wrath come upon all the people: but let your brethren, the whole house of Israel, bewail the burning which the LORD hath kindled. And ye shall not go out from the door of the tabernacle of the congregation, lest ye die: for the anointing oil of the LORD is upon you. And they did according to the word of Moses (Leviticus 10:4-7).

Moses' command appears strange even harsh at first glance. But there was a specific reason for it. Verse 7 explains. Aaron, Eleazar, and Ithamar were God's priests. The anointing oil of the Lord was upon them. They were public men. They represented the people before God and God before the people. Therefore, they were not allowed to show any parental or brotherly tenderness at the loss of Nadab and Abihu. Like Ezekiel in the loss of his wife (Ezekiel 24:16-24), they stood as a sign before all Israel declaring, 'The ways of the Lord are right'. There was something more important than their great pain. The glory of God and the people of God were more important.

Lead by Example
Read verses 8-11 and learn that we must lead by example, putting a difference between that which is holy and that which is profane.

> And the LORD spake unto Aaron, saying, Do not drink wine nor strong drink, thou, nor thy sons with thee, when ye go into the tabernacle of the congregation, lest ye die: it shall be a statute forever throughout your generations: And that ye may put

difference between holy and unholy, and between unclean and clean; And that ye may teach the children of Israel all the statutes which the LORD hath spoken unto them by the hand of Moses (Leviticus 10:8-11).

How often it is that seasons of great heaviness, great sorrow, and great trouble are the times of our learning. So it was here. The Lord God came to Aaron in his great pain and taught him how to be a better, more useful servant in the house of God. The essence of the lesson was this. If we would lead others to know and worship our God, we must be calm and steady, serving him with clear minds of understanding and judgment. We must not be intoxicated with the wine of Babylon's fornications. We must not be drunk with the strong drink of self will. Rather, we must be filled with the Spirit of God, that we may in our behaviour display the distinction between the holy and the profane, between the clean and the unclean.

Sweet Assurance
In the midst of great heaviness, sorrow, and trouble, the Lord God sent Aaron and his sons a word of sweet assurance.

And Moses spake unto Aaron, and unto Eleazar and unto Ithamar, his sons that were left, Take the meat offering that remaineth of the offerings of the LORD made by fire, and eat it without leaven beside the altar: for it is most holy: And ye shall eat it in the holy place, because it is thy due, and thy sons' due, of the sacrifices of the LORD made by fire: for so I am commanded. And the wave breast and heave shoulder shall ye eat in a clean place; thou, and thy sons, and thy daughters with thee: for they be thy due, and thy sons' due, which are given out of the sacrifices of peace offerings of the children of Israel. The heave shoulder and the wave breast shall they bring with the offerings made by fire of the fat, to wave it for a wave offering before the LORD; and it shall be thine, and thy sons' with thee, by a statute forever; as the LORD hath commanded (Leviticus 10:12-15).

Why does Moses here repeat, almost exactly, instructions given in chapter six? Because he who is our God is a God full of compassion.

Picture Aaron, Eleazar, and Ithamar, as they stood speechless before God, before his servant Moses, and before the congregation of the Lord. I can almost hear their thoughts. The sin and rebellion of Nadab and Abihu was no private thing. Our household has publicly dishonoured God. We are now no longer fit to serve the Lord. How can we lead this people in the worship of God? How can we expect anyone to pay any attention to us, when our own family has despised our God and perished in a public display of his wrath?

Over the years, I have received calls from terribly troubled pastors, deacons, elders, and Bible teachers telling me of some horribly evil thing done by one in their families. Ashamed and embarrassed, they thought, or others told them, that they must resign their post, that they were unfit to serve God. My counsel to such has always been the same as Moses' counsel here to Aaron and his sons. Keep your post. God has not forsaken, and he never will.

I feel sure it was for this reason the Lord sent his prophet to Aaron, Eleazar, and Ithamar. Lest they should suppose they had forfeited their privileges by the awful sin committed by Nadab and Abihu, they were here assured that all their privileges remained as full as ever.

Sweet consolation! Aaron and his sons, in their saddest hour, were reminded that the mercy, love, and grace of the immutable God does not change. With this sweet assurance of unbroken, unbreakable acceptance, the Lord graciously bound up their wounded hearts. He wiped away their tears by assuring them of his unwavering and unchangeable love. He manifested himself in their bitterest hour as their reconciled God and poured the oil of his grace into their hearts.

Child of God, never imagine your trials, be they never so great and never so bitter, are an indication of God's displeasure. They are not!

Justice Satisfied
In verses 16-18 we see that there is only one sin offering by which the law and justice of God are satisfied; and that one offering is our crucified Christ.

And Moses diligently sought the goat of the sin offering, and, behold, it was burnt: and he was angry with Eleazar and Ithamar, the sons of Aaron which were left alive, saying, Wherefore have ye not eaten the sin offering in the holy place, seeing it is most holy, and God hath given it you to bear the iniquity of the congregation, to make atonement for them before the LORD? Behold, the blood of it was not brought in within the holy place: ye should indeed have eaten it in the holy place, as I commanded (Leviticus 10:16-18).

Moses here chides Aaron and his sons for burning and not eating the sin offering, according to the plain letter of the law. But Aaron's reply displayed the deep reverence of his heart for his God and Saviour, Christ Jesus the true Sin-offering.

And Aaron said unto Moses, Behold, this day have they offered their sin offering and their burnt offering before the LORD; and such things have befallen me: and if I had eaten the sin offering today, should it have been accepted in the sight of the LORD? (Leviticus 10:19).

Aaron said to Moses, 'The sin offering was the offering made by Nadab and Abihu, who brought with it their strange fire. If we had eaten it, we would have suggested to all the people that their offering was acceptable to God; we would have been guilty as they, and we would have been slain by the fire of God's wrath, too.' 'And when Moses heard that, he was content' (v. 20).

The letter of the law, which kills, was broken but its spirit, which is life, was fulfilled. Being circumcised in heart, Aaron worshipped God in Spirit and truth, trusted Christ alone, and placed no confidence in the flesh. He looked beyond the typical sin offering to the true Sin-offering. Moses, typifying the law and all its demands, was content.

The Lord Jesus Christ, who was made to be sin for us, is our only Sin-offering (2 Corinthians 5:21; 1 Peter 2:24; 3:18). The Son of God, our all-glorious Christ, is the effectual Sin-offering (Isaiah 53:6-11; Daniel 9:24). Like Aaron, Eleazar, and Ithamar, lay your hands upon the head of this Sin-offering, trust the Lord Jesus Christ alone, and like them you shall stand accepted in the courts of the Lord's house forever.

249

Chapter 30

Strange Fire: Counterfeit Religion

And Nadab and Abihu, the sons of Aaron, took either of them his censer, and put fire therein, and put incense thereon, and offered strange fire before the LORD, which he commanded them not. And there went out fire from the LORD, and devoured them, and they died before the LORD. Then Moses said unto Aaron, This is it that the LORD spake, saying, I will be sanctified in them that come nigh me, and before all the people I will be glorified. And Aaron held his peace.

Leviticus 10:1-3

The history of mankind is a history that should be written in tears, and read with weeping eyes. The slime of the serpent runs through every page. Ours is a history of rebellion, sin, and apostasy. Sin ruined man, and ruined man spoils everything else. Put man in a position of highest dignity and he will degrade himself. Endow him with the greatest possible privileges and he will abuse them. Shower blessings upon him and he will prove himself ungrateful. Put him in the most impressive environment and he will corrupt it.

Honesty compels anyone who reads the history of our race to acknowledge that what I have said, painful and shameful as it is, is nonetheless true. Everything touched by our foul and wicked hands is quickly defiled. The nature of man, in its fairest forms and under the most favourable circumstances, is corruption and sin, nothing more. So it has been ever since the sin and fall of our father Adam.

Ours is a history of failure, rebellion and apostasy, repeated over and over again. It has been so from the beginning. When God placed Adam in the Garden of Eden everything was perfect until Adam ruined it by disobeying his almighty, good and wise Creator (Genesis 3). When the Lord God, in electing love and sovereign mercy preserved Noah and his family from the flood of his wrath and placed them in a new world, Noah was soon found in a drunken stupor (Genesis 9). When Israel by God's outstretched arm was brought out of bondage and fed manna from heaven in the wilderness, the ransomed nation craved the leeks of Egypt. When the Lord God brought them into the land of Canaan, they 'forsook the Lord, and served Baal and Ashtaroth' (Judges 2:13). When Solomon, the wisest of our fallen race, was placed at the very summit of earthly power and glory with wealth at his feet and the resources of the world at his command, 'his wives turned away his heart after other gods' (1 Kings 11:3, 4). No sooner had the blessings of the gospel begun to be preached in all the earth than it became necessary for the Holy Spirit to warn the early church to be on guard against the 'grievous wolves' of freewill and works religion, the 'apostasy' of the professed church from the gospel of God's grace and glory in Christ, and the corrupting of the Word and worship of God in the name of righteousness and godliness (Acts 20:29; 1 Timothy 4:1-3; 2 Timothy 3:1-5; 2 Peter 3; Jude 1:4). According to the Revelation given to John, the history of our race will be concluded with greater shame than we have yet seen or imagined, as Satan is loosed for a little season to wreak havoc in the world (Revelation 20:1-10; 2 Thessalonians 2:1-12).

Man is a fallen creature who, unless God steps in to stop him, continues to fall until he falls into hell, a rebel who continues to rebel until he is cast into hell. These facts, to some degree, prepare us for the things recorded in the opening words of Leviticus 10.

What a contrast this is to the scene that closed the ninth chapter! There everything was done 'as the Lord commanded', and the result was a manifestation of God's glory. Here something is done which 'the Lord commanded them not' and the result is judgment. The echo of the shout of victory had hardly died away before the elements of apostasy and spurious worship were brought forth. No sooner were the sons of Aaron consecrated as priests of God than they deliberately abandoned the worship and service of the Almighty. No sooner were those priests instated than they failed in the discharge of their priestly duties. Nadab and Abihu 'offered strange fire before the Lord' and perished under the manifest wrath of God.

What great wonders and miraculous things these two men had seen and experienced. What great privileges they had enjoyed. They saw the wonders of God in the Land of Ham. They passed through the Red Sea. These sons of Aaron were present when the glory of the Lord was revealed, when the fire of God came down from heaven and consumed the sacrifice upon the altar. They had worshipped God on that momentous day with Moses and Aaron! Yet, they perished under the wrath of God!

Learn from them this lesson, a lesson that needs to be sounded around the world in this day of charismatic tomfoolery. Miracles will never produce grace, not even true miracles, let alone the pretend miracles of Satan's ambassadors who flood the world today. Miracles do not produce faith. Miracles cannot convince men of sin, of righteousness, and judgment. Only the Spirit of God can do that; and he does it by the preaching of the gospel. I call your attention to three things about Nadab and Abihu set before us in these three verses.

Their Sin
What was their sin? What was the failure of these two men? What was their crime? Were they spurious priests? Were they mere pretenders? By no means. Nadab and Abihu were genuine sons of Aaron, true members of the priestly family, and duly appointed priests. Their vessels of ministry and their priestly garments were exactly such as God required. What, then, was their sin? Did they stain the curtains of the tabernacle with human blood or pollute the sacred precincts with some crime to shock moral decency? No. Their sin was just this 'They offered strange fire before the Lord which he commanded them not' (v. 1).

Nadab and Abihu offered fire of their own making before the Lord. They offered what the Lord 'commanded them not', what the Lord God had expressly forbidden. Like the sacrifice of Cain, like the prayer of the Pharisee (Luke 18:11), their worship was nothing but will worship, an act of contempt for God, a trampling underfoot of the blood of Christ. Their strange fire was self-righteousness, conceit, and rebellion.

In offering the fire of their own making, Nadab and Abihu displayed an abhorrence of the gift of God. The fire that burned on the altar was God's gift, God's provision, God's work (Leviticus 16:12). As such, it was a picture and type of Christ (Romans 6:23; 2 Corinthians 9:15; John 3:16). God required the fire he provided (Leviticus 16:12). Nadab and Abihu thought their own fire was good enough. God requires Christ and only Christ but they despised Christ and said, 'Who needs a Substitute? Who needs blood atonement? Who needs an Intercessor? Who needs forgiveness, justification, pardon, reconciliation, and imputed righteousness?' Like the Jews of Paul's day and the vast majority of men and women in every age, perhaps including you who read these lines, Nadab and Abihu sought righteousness but did not obtain righteousness, because they went about to establish their own righteousness, and refused to submit themselves to the righteousness of God in Christ (Romans 9:31-10:4). Nadab and Abihu went into the great harlot, Babylon,[7] presuming they could come to God and worship him as they pleased (Proverbs 7:24-27).

Their Judgment
The Spirit of God tells us of their judgment in verse 2; the judgment of God upon them. 'And there went out fire from the Lord, and devoured them, and they died before the Lord.' How solemn! The Lord God dwelt in the midst of his people to govern, to judge and to act, according to the claims of his nature, in mercy and truth, in grace and righteousness, in love and justice. At the end of Leviticus 9 we read, 'And there came a fire out from before the Lord, and consumed upon the altar the burnt offering and the fat'. That was God's acceptance of the true sacrifice. But, here, that same fire is the fire of his wrath and judgment upon two self-righteous priests who despised his sacrifice. The burnt offering went up as a sweet odour. Their 'strange fire' was rejected as an abomination. God was glorified in the burnt offering, but was despised in their 'strange fire'.

Holiness, justice, righteousness and truth accepted and delighted in that which was a type of Christ and his sacrifice. But the fruit of man's corrupt will, never more hideous and abominable than when engaged in the pretence of worshipping and serving God, was rejected.

Nadab and Abihu perished at the hand of him whom they professed to serve. Like Ananias and Sapphira (Acts 5), they perished not because they were consumed by zeal without knowledge, but because they came

---

[7] Babylon is all freewill, works religion, and all false religion.

before God in presumption without fear. Nadab and Abihu were killed and sent to hell by the very Christ they despised (Luke 20:17, 18). That One who was offered upon God's altar as the Sacrifice for sin shall sit in judgment upon God's throne. He who was the Sacrifice consumed by the fire of God's wrath will be a consuming fire to destroy all who despise him in that great day.

Nadab and Abihu 'died before the Lord'. We read in Revelation 14:13, 'Blessed are the dead that die in the Lord'. To die in the Lord is to die in Christ in grace and faith. But Nadab and Abihu died before the Lord, without Christ, without grace, without faith, without a sacrifice, without hope. They were carried out from the presence of God, carried out from the camp of Israel (v. 4), and cast away in the place of darkness. Thus, they were made to eat the fruit of their own way and were filled with their own devices (Proverbs 1:23-33; 29:1).

Nadab and Abihu were carried out from the presence of the holy Lord God in their priestly coats (v. 5). Their priestly garments could not protect them any more than an empty religious profession and refuge of lies will protect the lost religionist from the wrath of God (Ecclesiastes 8:10; Isaiah 28:14-20).

Their Lesson
The lesson God the Holy Spirit teaches us by these two men is written in bold letters in this third verse. If we would come to God to be accepted of him, if we would live and not die, we must come to God by the merits of Christ's blood and righteousness alone, we must come to him in a way that sanctifies and glorifies him in all his holy attributes.

> Then Moses said unto Aaron, This is it that the LORD spake, saying, I will be sanctified in them that come nigh me, and before all the people I will be glorified. And Aaron held his peace (Leviticus 10:3).

If any man were permitted to defile the sanctuary of the divine presence by 'strange fire' of his own works, the very throne of God would be toppled, his honour destroyed, and his righteousness defiled. Freewill works religion is nothing less than the attempt of fallen man to creep into God's presence in impressive clothes, rape his righteousness, topple his throne, and stab him to death! We are never allowed to introduce our own devices into the worship of God. All ceremonialism, ritualism, and sacramentalism are nothing but 'strange fire', the incense of abomination, false worship and counterfeit religion.

The same is true of every effort of man to produce righteousness for himself. Man's very best attempts at righteousness and atonement by the works of his own hands and the exercise of his own will are an absolute abomination in the sight of God (Romans 9:16; Galatians 2:16; 3:1-3) are all 'strange fire', by which the followers of Nadab and Abihu are carried to hell.

Every sinner saved by the grace of God, knowing the free and full forgiveness of his sins through the precious, sin-atoning blood of Christ, worships God in spirit and in truth. He rejoices in Christ Jesus and has no confidence in the flesh (Philippians 3:1-3).

Come, weary, helpless, needy sinner. Come now to God by Christ! Come, seeking mercy, grace, and eternal life by the merits of Christ alone. 'O magnify the Lord with me, and let us exalt his name together.'

Blessed be God, the time is rapidly approaching when the 'strange fire' of freewill, works religion will be quenched forever! The throne of God shall soon cease to be insulted by the incense self-righteousness ascending from the altar of human strength and ability. Soon, all that is spurious shall be abolished, and the whole universe shall be as one great, magnificent temple, in which the only true God; Father, Son, and Holy Ghost, shall be worshipped through endless ages of eternity.

Chapter 31

Sacrifice, Submission, Stedfastness, Sobriety

And Nadab and Abihu, the sons of Aaron, took either of them his censer, and put fire therein, and put incense thereon, and offered strange fire before the LORD, which he commanded them not. And there went out fire from the LORD, and devoured them, and they died before the LORD. Then Moses said unto Aaron, This is it that the LORD spake, saying, I will be sanctified in them that come nigh me, and before all the people I will be glorified. And Aaron held his peace. And Moses called Mishael and Elzaphan, the sons of Uzziel the uncle of Aaron, and said unto them, Come near, carry your brethren from before the sanctuary out of the camp. So they went near, and carried them in their coats out of the camp; as Moses had said. And Moses said unto Aaron, and unto Eleazar and unto Ithamar, his sons, Uncover not your heads, neither rend your clothes; lest ye die, and lest wrath come upon all the people: but let your brethren, the whole house of Israel, bewail the burning which the LORD hath kindled. And ye shall not go out from the door of the tabernacle of the congregation, lest ye die: for the anointing oil of the LORD is upon you. And they did according to the word of Moses. And the LORD spake unto Aaron, saying, Do not drink wine nor strong drink, thou, nor thy sons with thee, when ye go into the tabernacle of the congregation, lest ye die: it shall be a statute for ever throughout your generations: And that ye may put difference between holy and unholy, and between unclean and clean; And that ye may teach the children of Israel all the statutes which the LORD hath spoken unto them by the hand of Moses.

Leviticus 10:1-11

We cannot and will not serve our families or the good of men's souls, or be truly useful to society as a whole, if we are not first and foremost the servants of God. If we would serve God as we make our pilgrimage through this world these four things are essential: sacrifice, submission, stedfastness, sobriety.

The Camp of Israel

As they journeyed through the wilderness, whenever Israel set up camp, whenever they set up the tabernacle, there were three distinct circles. At the centre of the camp, the innermost circle, at the very heart of the camp was the sanctuary, where the Lord God established his worship, where God promised to meet his people. That sanctuary and all it held was a type and picture of our Lord Jesus Christ (Hebrews 9:1-9).

Try to picture the camp of Israel in your minds. The outer circle of the camp of Israel was made up of those men of war appointed by God for the defence of the nation (Numbers 1, 2). Next, there was the circle of the Levites surrounding the tabernacle (Numbers 3, 4). The Levites were appointed of God to maintain his worship among his people. But in the centre, at the very heart of the camp, at the core of the nation's life, was the sanctuary and those divinely appointed priests who lived and died ministering about the holy things of the Lord, 'Everyone according to his service and according to his burden. Thus were they numbered ... as the LORD commanded Moses' (Numbers 4:49).

This divinely required order was not intended to be a model for church order, dividing 'clergy' from 'laity'. Rather, by these things the Lord gives us instructions regarding the spheres of our lives in this world as God's priests. We must never forget that as believers, as those who are born of God and adorned with the garments of salvation in Christ, we are first and foremost the servants of God, priests of the most high God. All believers are made to be God's holy nation and God's royal priesthood in Christ. That is how God the Holy Spirit describes us in the second chapter of 1 Peter. That is the same description given of God's elect in the book of Revelation (Revelation 1:4-6; 5:9, 10).

We are God's priests. Yet, we move in all the circles of the camp. The believer is and must be a man of war, constantly engaged in conflict (Romans 7:14-23; Ephesians 6:11-17; 1 Timothy 1:18; 6:12; 2 Timothy 4:7). We are Christ's soldiers, engaged in holy warfare. Yet, we are, like the Levites, ministers to God's people. Each believer walks about in the midst of God's kingdom and people serving his brethren according to the ability God has given him and in the sphere in which God has put him (Matthew 25:14, 15; Philippians 2:1-8). And every child of God is a worshipping, sacrificing priest, ministering unto God in the holy place (Hebrews 13:15, 16; 1 Peter 2:5-9), not part of the time, but all of the time, not just on Sunday, but every day.

We cannot function properly, we cannot walk aright in any sphere of life if we are not first and foremost serving God in the holy place, if we are not engaged in the business of worshipping and honouring our God. Christianity is not isolationism. Christianity does not involve hiding from the world in a cloister, a convent, or a commune. Christianity is living in this world for the glory of God, to do the will of God. Christianity is a life that worships God.

Here are four necessary things in the worship of God. This is what God taught Aaron the day he killed his sons, Nadab and Abihu. Here are four things absolutely necessary in the worship of God.

Sacrifice

If we would worship God, if we would come to God and be accepted of him, we must come with a sacrifice.

Everyone knows by the law of God written on his conscience that God must have a sacrifice. Man has demonstrated that fact throughout history. But it is not sufficient just to bring any sacrifice. We must bring the sacrifice God requires. We must bring a perfect sacrifice, a sacrifice of infinite merit, a blood sacrifice, a sacrifice of God's providing and one God has accepted. This is what the Lord God shows us here in verses 1, 2. Nadab and Abihu, like Cain (Genesis 4:3), despised God's Sacrifice, the Lord Jesus Christ who was represented in the legal sacrifice (Leviticus 9:15-24), and 'offered strange fire before the Lord'.

And Nadab and Abihu, the sons of Aaron, took either of them his censer, and put fire therein, and put incense thereon, and offered strange fire before the LORD, which he commanded them not. And there went out fire from the LORD, and devoured them, and they died before the LORD' (Leviticus 10:1, 2).

No doubt, these sons of Aaron brought a burnt-offering as God had commanded. But instead of bringing the fire of God from off the altar, they brought fire of their own with the offering of God, mixing their provision with God's provision. Symbolically, they tried to mix grace and works, law and gospel, freewill and free grace, their righteousness with the righteousness of God. Refusing to submit to the righteousness of God by faith in Christ, they went about to establish righteousness for themselves by works (Romans 9:31-10:4).

We cannot come to God, but by the blood and righteousness of the Lord Jesus Christ. Christ is the Way, the Truth, and the Life. No man comes to the Father, but by him. If you attempt to come to God by some other means, to mix your own righteousness with Christ's, your own works with the merit of his blood, you trample under your feet the blood of Christ; and God will consume you in his wrath.

Submission
The worship of God, faith in Christ, involves submission, the surrender of all things to Christ. This is what the Lord taught Aaron and teaches us in verse 3-6.

Then Moses said unto Aaron, This is it that the LORD spake, saying, I will be sanctified in them that come nigh me, and before all the people I will be glorified. And Aaron held his peace. And Moses called Mishael and Elzaphan, the sons of Uzziel the uncle of Aaron, and said unto them, Come near, carry your brethren from before the sanctuary out of the camp. So they went near, and carried them in their coats out of the camp; as Moses had said. And Moses said unto Aaron, and unto Eleazar and unto Ithamar, his sons, Uncover not your heads, neither rend your clothes; lest ye die, and lest wrath come upon all the people: but let your brethren, the whole house of Israel, bewail the burning which the LORD hath kindled (Leviticus 10:3-6).

What an astounding, instructive word we have at the end of verse three. 'And Aaron held his peace.' I find that truly remarkable.

What a solemn picture this is. Aaron's two sons are struck dead at his side, slain by the fire of divine judgment. He had only just seen them clothed in their priestly garments; washed, robed, and anointed. They had stood with him before the Lord, instated with him into the priestly office. They offered with him the divinely appointed sacrifices. They saw with him the fire of God as it fell upon the sacrifice and consumed it. They heard the shout of triumph ringing through the assembly of adoring worshippers.

Nadab and Abihu were present and witnessed all these things only the day before. Now, they lay at Aaron's feet dead, killed by the hand of God. What does he say? What does he do? Nothing. He stands in dead silence. Grieving but silent. Hurting beyond imagination, but still. 'Aaron held his peace'. 'I was dumb, I opened not my mouth, because thou didst it' (Psalm 39:9). Like Eli after him, Aaron said, 'It is the Lord, let him do what seemeth him good'.

In silent awe and reverent acquiescence, Aaron bowed his head in the house of God and worshipped. The pillars of his house were shaken. His heart was broken. His sons were dead. But Aaron knew that there was something more important than his house, his heart, and his sons. The glory of God, the people of God, the will of God, and the worship of God were more important!

Aaron stands before us here as a deeply-impressive commentary upon the words of the Psalmist. 'God is greatly to be feared in the assembly of the saints; and to be had in reverence of all them that are about him' (Psalm 89:7). 'Who would not fear thee, O King of nations? There is none like unto thee' (Jeremiah 10:7).

Aaron's sons despised God's sacrifice; they despised his Saviour, his Christ, his way of salvation. For that they were killed in the fury of God's wrath. Not only did Aaron not rebel, he bowed. He said, by his silence, God has done that which is right. In the last part of the chapter, we are told that he refused on that day to eat the burnt-offering they had brought into the holy place, saying, as it were, to Moses, 'If I eat their sacrifice, I would by that act approve of their sacrilege and sin against the Lord' (vv. 16-20).

Faith approaches God only through the merits of Christ, with the Sacrifice God requires. Faith worships God in submission, humbling itself under the mighty hand of God.

Stedfastness
The worship of God also requires stedfastness.

> And Moses said unto Aaron, and unto Eleazar and unto Ithamar, his sons, Uncover not your heads, neither rend your clothes; lest ye die, and lest wrath come upon all the people: but let your brethren, the whole house of Israel, bewail the burning which the LORD hath kindled. And ye shall not go out from the door of the tabernacle of the congregation, lest ye die: for the anointing oil of the LORD is upon you. And they did according to the word of Moses (Leviticus 10:6, 7).

The Lord God spoke plainly to Aaron, Eleazar, and Ithamar. But let us be sure we hear what he said. This is God's word to us, as well. He said to them, as he says to us, 'You are not your own. You belong to God' (1 Corinthians 6:19, 20; 2 Corinthians 5:14, 15).

As God's priests, as servants of the most high God, they must not bewail the burning which the Lord kindled.

Those who were outside, who were not the priests of God might mourn, weep, and bewail the deaths of Nadab and Abihu, but not those who served in the house of God. They were to worship, giving glory to God. Hear God my brother, my sister. We belong to God. O Spirit of God, give me that stedfastness of grace that will never let me forget for a moment that I belong to God, that the blood of Christ is upon me, upon my ear, my thumb, and my great toe, that the anointing of God is upon me.

What does this picture before us in Leviticus 10 tell us? Just this, if we are God's people, God's priests, God's servants, we are to live above the world. By the blood of Christ and the anointing of his Holy Spirit we have been brought into another world, another kingdom, another sphere of life. That does not mean we do not feel things others feel. We feel them just like they do. Indeed, we feel them more sharply than others. Aaron knew his boys died under the wrath of God. I have no doubt he felt it painfully. We are not stoics; but we are priests of the most high God! As such, we are to live above the world, even above the range of nature's influence (Colossians 3:1-3).

For the glory of God, for the gospel's sake, for Christ's sake, for the sake of men's souls, we must rise above the claims of the world, the passions of our hearts, and the influence of nature, abiding ever in the house of God, in the sanctuary.

Let me repeat Robert Hawker, commenting on Leviticus 10:3. He wrote, 'It is sweet in our afflictions to eye the Lord's appointment and depend upon it. As long as we are enabled to keep in view divine wisdom, we shall never despond by human sufferings.'

Most everyone worships God and offers him praise for recovery from sickness, any great boon of providence, and things we look upon as good. Believers, like Job of old, worship and praise the Lord God when he gives and when he takes away, in birth and in bereavement. Faith in Christ stedfastly bows to and worships God as God.

That does not mean God's saints are above or immune to pain. Sorrow commonly accompanies submission and stedfastness. Let no one imagine that sorrow and expressions of sorrow, pain, and grief imply rebellion, unbelief, or even weakness of faith. They do not. Living men and women have hearts and broken hearts weep. Aaron and his sons being God's priests were required of God to remain stedfast in their service as God's priests. But Moses specifically said, 'Let your brethren, the whole house of Israel, bewail the burning, which the Lord hath kindled' (v. 6).

I find that instructive and helpful. John Trapp stated, 'It is fit enough, ordinarily, that the body, when sown in corruption, be watered by the tears of those that plant it in the earth'. It is absurd hypocrisy for hurting people to pretend not to hurt. Pain and sorrow, weeping and tears, mourning and grief are not an indication of weakness, rebellion and unbelief. We sorrow not as those who have no hope, but God's saints do feel sorrow. When Nadab and Abihu were slain, Moses said, 'let the whole house of Israel bewail the burning of the Lord'. 'Let the whole house of Israel bewail' God's judgment upon them. 'Let the whole house of Israel bewail' their rebellion, the cause of God's judgment. And 'let the whole house of Israel bewail' Aaron's, Eleazar's, and Ithamar's painful loss'.

In verse 7, the Lord gives Aaron, Eleazar, and Ithamar a word of sweet assurance. 'And ye shall not go out from the door of the tabernacle of the congregation, lest ye die: for the anointing oil of the LORD is upon you. And they did according to the word of Moses'.

First, he warned them not to leave their place, not to go out of the tabernacle, 'lest ye die'. We must persevere. And, if we are God's, we shall persevere. Next, he assured them they were still God's priests. 'The anointing of the Lord is upon you.' God is faithful! In verses 12-15 the Lord reassured them that all the rights and privileges of priests in the sanctuary were theirs still. God does not impute our own sins to us if we are in Christ. He certainly will not impute our family's sins to us! Aaron, Eleazar, and Ithamar were chosen, redeemed, called, and accepted in, with, and by Christ, the Anointed One. Then, we read, 'And they did according to the word of Moses'.

Nothing is sweeter to the heaven-born soul in time of trouble than the sweet assurance of God's free, saving grace and immutable favour in Christ; assurance of his salvation, assurance of his sovereignty, assurance of his goodness, assurance of his care.

Nothing is more difficult, more contrary to nature than this stedfastness of faith in Christ. They not only bowed to God's will, his obvious judgment upon Nadab and Abihu, but also continued stedfast in the worship and service of God.

Sobriety

What is required in the worship of God? What is involved in this thing we call faith in Christ? Sacrifice, submission and stedfastness. And if we would worship and serve our God, we must live before him soberly, righteously, and godly in this present world.

> And the LORD spake unto Aaron, saying, Do not drink wine nor strong drink, thou, nor thy sons with thee, when ye go into the tabernacle of the congregation, lest ye die: it shall be a statute forever throughout your generations: And that ye may put difference between holy and unholy, and between unclean and clean; And that ye may teach the children of Israel all the statutes which the LORD hath spoken unto them by the hand of Moses (Leviticus 10:8-11).

While this word from God was a literal prohibition against the use of wine or strong drink by Israel's priests when they were engaged in their priestly services, it is not a prohibition against the use of such by God's people. The Word of God nowhere teaches that believers are not to use wine or alcoholic drinks. The Word of God prohibits drunkenness and intemperance, it nowhere requires total abstinence.

What, then, is the significance of these verses to us? It is just this. Wine and strong drink are things that excite and exhilarate nature. They commonly cause men and women to act according to their basest passions, losing moderation and reason. They prohibit calm action, a well-balanced state of heart and mind that is essential to walking with, worshipping, and serving God.

This is the doctrine of the passage. We must not allow our judgment or behaviour in spiritual matters to be clouded by our carnal passions. If we do, we will not be able to distinguish between holy and unholy, clean and unclean. If we are going to honour God, if we are going to serve Christ and his people in this world, if we worship God, we must be able to make that distinction. We must be not drunk with wine, wherein is excess; but, rather, we must ever be filled with the Spirit.

If we would worship God, if we would serve him as priests in his house, we must do so soberly (2 Timothy 2:15-26; James 1:27). We must flee the youthful lusts of profane and vain babblings. We must purge ourselves from all 'strange fire'. We must keep ourselves unspotted from the world. We must keep ourselves in the love of God. We must keep our hearts with all diligence.

There is a message here regarding the assembly of God's saints in public worship, too. We must studiously avoid those things that rouse passions, excite our carnal natures, and stimulate our base emotions in the house of God. When our Master overthrew the moneychangers' tables, he said, 'My house shall be called a house of prayer', not a house of politics, not a house of economics and commerce, not a house of entertainment, not a house of sensuality. My house shall be called a house of prayer; of worship, of preaching, a house of praise.

Prove all things; hold fast that which is good. Abstain from all appearance of evil. And the very God of peace sanctify you wholly; and I pray God your whole spirit and soul and body be preserved blameless unto the coming of our Lord Jesus Christ. Faithful is he that calleth you, who also will do it (1 Thessalonians 5:21-24).

For the grace of God that bringeth salvation hath appeared to all men, Teaching us that, denying ungodliness and worldly lusts, we should live soberly, righteously, and godly, in this present world; Looking for that blessed hope, and the glorious appearing of the great God and our Saviour Jesus Christ; who gave himself for us, that he might redeem us from all iniquity, and purify unto himself a peculiar people, zealous of good works (Titus 2:11-14).

This is what it is to call upon the name of the Lord. This is what it is to believe God and to worship him. It is coming to God by faith in Christ his Sacrifice. It is bowing to the Lord God in humble submission, surrendering all things to him, his will, his dominion, and his glory. It is stedfast adherence to Christ. It is living here, by the teaching of grace, in sobriety, as priests of the most high God.

Chapter 32

A Possessed People

And the LORD spake unto Moses and to Aaron, saying unto them, Speak unto the children of Israel, saying, These are the beasts which ye shall eat among all the beasts that are on the earth. Whatsoever parteth the hoof, and is clovenfooted, and cheweth the cud, among the beasts, that shall ye eat ... Ye shall not make yourselves abominable with any creeping thing that creepeth, neither shall ye make yourselves unclean with them, that ye should be defiled thereby. For I am the LORD your God: ye shall therefore sanctify yourselves, and ye shall be holy; for I am holy: neither shall ye defile yourselves with any manner of creeping thing that creepeth upon the earth. For I am the LORD that bringeth you up out of the land of Egypt, to be your God: ye shall therefore be holy, for I am holy. This is the law of the beasts, and of the fowl, and of every living creature that moveth in the waters, and of every creature that creepeth upon the earth: To make a difference between the unclean and the clean, and between the beast that may be eaten and the beast that may not be eaten.

Leviticus 11:1-47

God's elect are his own peculiar people, a divinely possessed people. We see this throughout the Scriptures. We are not our own. We have been bought with the price of our Saviour's precious blood.

Who gave himself for us, that he might redeem us from all iniquity, and purify unto himself a peculiar people, zealous of good works (Titus 2:14).

The word 'peculiar' does not mean 'odd' or 'strange'. It has the idea of ownership. It could be translated 'possessed'. However, the word 'possessed' does not fully translate this adjective by which God's elect are described. The word translated 'peculiar' in Titus 2:14 is one of those rich words that cannot really be simply translated into English accurately. It must be defined. The word means owned, held in possession, possessed lawfully, possessed powerfully, encompassed, surrounded, protected.

The Holy Ghost is teaching us about all who are born of God. This is true of all God's elect. All who believe on the Son of God are God's peculiarly and distinctly possessed people, purchased by the sin-atoning sacrifice of the Lord Jesus Christ. They are called by omnipotent grace, surrounded and encompassed by the incomprehensible God, and under his constant protection and care (Psalm 34:7).

This fact, the fact that God's people are a possessed people, his own peculiarly and distinctly possessed people set before us throughout the book of God, is the subject of the eleventh chapter of Leviticus.

And the LORD spake unto Moses and to Aaron, saying unto them, Speak unto the children of Israel, saying, These are the beasts which ye shall eat among all the beasts that are on the earth. Whatsoever parteth the hoof, and is clovenfooted, and cheweth the cud, among the beasts, that shall ye eat' (Leviticus 11:1-3).

In verses 4-42 the Lord God divides the clean from the unclean of all the animals in the skies, in the earth, in the rivers, and in the seas, giving very specific dietary laws to the nation of Israel. Then, in verses 43-47, he tells us the reason for these laws.

Ye shall not make yourselves abominable with any creeping thing that creepeth, neither shall ye make yourselves unclean with them, that ye should be defiled thereby. For I am the LORD your God: ye shall therefore sanctify yourselves, and ye shall be holy; for I am holy: neither shall ye defile yourselves with any manner of creeping thing that creepeth upon the earth. For I am the LORD that bringeth you up out of the land of Egypt, to be your God: ye shall therefore be holy, for I am holy. This is the law of the beasts, and of the fowl, and of every living creature that moveth in the waters, and of every creature that creepeth upon the earth: To make a difference between the unclean and the clean, and between the beast that may be eaten and the beast that may not be eaten (Leviticus 11:43-47).

I am sure you have read this chapter and other similar passages and thought to yourself 'Why is this in the Bible? What does all this mean? How does it apply to me?' Here is the answer to such questions.

The Setting
Mark in your mind the place of this chapter. Up to this point the book of Leviticus has been about one thing. The first 10 chapters of the book are about one subject, atonement. The Lord God shows fallen men that he is a God willing to save and that he has made a way for fallen sinners to return to him. What great, glorious good news for our cursed race! The God of glory, against whom we have sinned, has made a way whereby he can bring sinners into union with himself. The way is Christ. God has made atonement to himself for chosen sinners by the sacrifice of his own dear Son, atonement by Christ's precious blood!

In chapter 11, as if he would compel us to come to him by the blood of Christ, the Holy Spirit begins to describe our great need of grace, our great need of atonement, our great need of an effectual sacrifice and substitute. He begins to show us our utter sinfulness. The design is to shut us up to Christ and God's free grace in him. To create in our minds a sense of our corruption and sin, a sense of the corruption and sin of our race, the Lord gives us these Levitical dietary laws, laws that were binding upon the nation of Israel throughout the Mosaic economy.[8]

---

[8] Let it be clearly understood that these laws, indeed, all the law, were for the Jews only. Peter learned in Acts 10 not to call anything God has made, common or unclean. The creatures here pronounced 'unclean' were so only ceremonially, only to the nation of Israel, and only during the Old Testament dispensation. As the Holy Spirit declares in Romans 14:14, 'There is nothing unclean of itself'. In this gospel age we are totally free to eat anything we wish.

Now the Lord God laid before the nation of Israel distinctions between things clean and unclean to be carefully attended to every day. Things to be unavoidably and constantly before their minds every day, requiring them to vigilant and careful to put a 'difference between holy and unholy, and between unclean and clean' things (v. 10).

Atonement Needed

Obviously, there were no moral distinctions found in the creatures themselves. A hog is not morally or spiritually inferior to a cow. Yet, by making these ceremonial distinctions, the Lord put huge billboards throughout creation to remind the chosen nation that they were a fallen, sinful people in a fallen, sinful world, a people in need of atonement.

This is the theme of chapters 11-15. We need atonement! Chapter 11 shows us the existence of sin, the universality of corruption. Chapter 12 portrays the transmission of sin from one generation to another. The woman who brought a child into the world was ceremonially defiled by the very act of giving birth because she gave birth to a sinner. Chapters 13 and 14 display the vileness of sin in leprosy. Chapter 15 gives us a picture of original sin in all its deformity as 'a running issue'.

Shut Up To Christ

Thus, we are shut up to Christ. If we would be righteous, if we would come to God and be accepted of him, we are shut up to Christ. There is no righteousness to be had for guilty sinners except the righteousness of God in Christ, the righteousness of God given and imputed by grace through the sin-atoning death of the Lord Jesus Christ. But, blessed be God, in Christ there is righteousness of infinite merit for guilty sinners.

These laws regarding things clean and unclean, holy and unholy, were intended by God to show us spiritual things. They were given to point us to Christ and the grace of God in him. They are pictures of gospel truths.

A Difference Made

As the Lord God ceremonially made a difference in the creatures mentioned in these 47 verses, declaring some clean and others unclean, he has graciously made a difference between men, declaring some holy and others unholy. The only difference between men in this world is the difference grace has made. We are all unclean and unholy by nature.

We all deserve the everlasting wrath of God. But God has made some holy and clean by his free grace in Christ (1 Corinthians 4:7). The Lord looks on his people in Christ and says, 'Ye are clean'. He has made us clean by blood atonement; righteousness imputed in free justification, and he has made us clean by regenerating grace; righteousness imparted through sanctification of the Spirit in the new birth.

A Distinction Maintained

The Lord God has made a distinction between his people and all other people by election, redemption, and regeneration. It is a distinction to be maintained by us. Yes, it is a distinction graciously maintained by God (Philippians 1:6). But it is a distinction to be maintained by us as well. How?

The Lord gave these dietary laws to Israel, and to Israel alone, because he had made them a distinct people in the world. By observing these laws, they were to maintain themselves as a distinct and separate people from all other nations in the world. Because their diet was so strict, obedience to them would keep God's covenant people from entering into any sort of close association with any other people.

The Canaanites ate anything. They would eat an animal that had been killed by a dog and the dog itself without scruple. Arabs, Israel's nearest kinsmen, thought nothing of eating a camel, a hare, or a coney. By ceremonially preventing their social intercourse with other people, the Lord arranged and secured a distinction between his people and all other people. The things here declared unclean were commonly objects of worship and spiritual veneration among the heathen. If he could not even sit at the heathen's table the obedient Israelite would, by his obedience, be kept from other close associations with his pagan neighbours, and from worshipping and intermarrying with them.

What does that have to do with me? The Lord God would have us live in this world as his own peculiar people, as a people belonging to him, maintaining a distinction between the clean and the unclean. Though these dietary laws are not, in any way, applicable to us in this gospel age, what we eat and drink does not make us unclean, yet you and I are to studiously maintain a distinction between ourselves and the world (Titus 2:1-15; 2 Corinthians 6:14-7:1), adorning the doctrine of God our Saviour in all things. That means we are not to live like the reprobate and we are not to worship with idolaters.

271

The distinction to be maintained by us is not maintained by peculiar dress, pious sounding speech, or outward show, but by the great object of our lives, 'Whether therefore ye eat, or drink, or whatsoever ye do, do all to the glory of God' (1 Corinthians 10:31).

Look at the rule of law given in Leviticus 11:3. Here is a good picture of the believer, one who has been made clean before God by the grace of God. 'Whatsoever parteth the hoof, and is clovenfooted, and cheweth the cud, among the beasts, that shall ye eat.' The believer both chews the cud and is cloven footed. He feeds upon Christ and the gospel of his grace in his heart and soul. He does not merely hear the gospel, he relishes it! Christ is to us the Bread of Life and the Water of Life. The saved sinner is also cloven footed. He walks on the earth, but walks toward heaven. He walks as a man, but walks with God. He lives in a body of flesh, but walks in the Spirit.

In Leviticus 11:4-8 the Lord identified four unclean animals that might have been mistaken for clean ones. The camel, the coney, and the hare all chew the cud, but do not divide the hoof. They were all unclean. So, too, are those represented by them. The doctrinal purist, who has no interest in godliness, devotion, and consecration to Christ, is like the camel, plodding along in sensuality, but still chewing the cud. The coney, digging in the earth and hiding in the rocks, might well represent the self-serving religionists, the cowardly person who talks a good talk in the right company, but refuses to confess Christ openly before his enemies. The hare flying across the land in leaps and bounds, chewing the cud, but parting not the hoof, is a pretty good picture of the feel-good religionist, the shouting enthusiast and religious emotionalist. Though he chews the cud, he is but an earthling. His religion is all emotion, show, and feeling.

But why did the Lord put hogs in this list at this place? The hog seems to be set before us for a distinct reason, as an emblem of those who act right outwardly. They have profession. They are outwardly upright, devout, and zealous. But they are inwardly unclean. The hog is cloven footed and has a split hoof, but does not chew the cud.

The swine represents the religious Pharisee. No animal could be found that more accurately represents the self-righteous Pharisee than a hog. The Pharisee makes the cup and platter clean. His hoof is thoroughly divided. But inside there is nothing but vileness and corruption. All his outward religious show is but as a hog wallowing in the mire of its own excrement.

Let us walk before our God in this world as men and women who are distinctly his, for Christ's sake, with a heart of faith in and love for Christ, acknowledging and confessing our sin, in the Spirit, trusting Christ, ever separating ourselves from the world.

I do not mean we should become hermits, or we should cease to be responsible citizens in this world. I do mean we must deliberately and conscientiously come out of the world, maintaining the distinction our God has made by his grace. The world is always trying to get the Church to marry it. How sad that the Church seems so anxious for the hellish wedding! It was when the Church married the world in Genesis 6 that God sent the flood (John 15:19; 1 John 2:15-17; 1 John 3:1-3).

A Defilement Manifested

These dietary laws were so thorough, so detailed, that the Lord seems to have intended them to be a constant witness of the fact that so long as we live in this world we are defiled with sin and need the cleansing of Christ's precious blood.

Try to get the picture of a Jew living in those days with these words of God's law fixed in his heart and mind. He walks out of his house into the fields, or goes to a neighbour's, or works in the hot sun, or walks to the tabernacle to offer sacrifice to God, everywhere he goes, he sees uncleanness, defilement, sin; a caravan of camels, a dragonfly, a field mouse, a dog, a house cat, an eagle, a hawk, a bat, insects in his flowers.

All these unclean things were outward but they were numerous, universal and so inclusive that the well instructed Jew might think to himself, 'So long as I walk on this sin-cursed earth in the body of this flesh, I cannot escape defilement and sin. I cannot even breathe without inhaling some corruption of the earth and exhaling some corruption from within. Thank God for the atonement and the mercy seat. Thank God for the Sacrifice.' With those things in mind, let us ever thank God for Christ our Saviour (1 John 1:8-2:2; Romans 7:14-8:1).

A Discipline Motivated

The laws given in these 47 verses required strict, constant discipline. The life of faith, consecration to Christ, devotion to the will and glory of God requires the same strict, constant discipline. How can such discipline be motivated?

> Ye shall not make yourselves abominable with any creeping thing that creepeth, neither shall ye make yourselves unclean with them, that ye should be defiled thereby. For I am the LORD your God: ye shall therefore sanctify yourselves, and ye shall be holy; for I am holy: neither shall ye defile yourselves with any manner of creeping thing that creepeth upon the earth. For I am the LORD that bringeth you up out of the land of Egypt, to be your God: ye shall therefore be holy, for I am holy (Leviticus 11:43-45).

Here are five great, powerful arguments of mercy, grace, and love by which the Lord our God calls for and claims our hearts' devotion.

1. His sovereign Lordship – 'I am the Lord your God'.
2. His saving operations – 'I am the Lord your God that bringeth you up out of the land of Egypt.' Redemption. Regeneration. Preservation. Resurrection.
3. His immaculate holiness – 'Ye shall be holy, for I am holy.'
4. His special, covenant relationship – 'I am the Lord, your God.'
5. His gracious promise – 'Ye shall be holy.' Literally translated, 'You have become holy.'

> I beseech you therefore, brethren, by the mercies of God, that ye present your bodies a living sacrifice, holy, acceptable unto God, which is your reasonable service. And be not conformed to this world: but be ye transformed by the renewing of your mind, that ye may prove what is that good, and acceptable, and perfect, will of God (Romans 12:1, 2, see also 2 Corinthians 5:14-21).

Child of God, you and I are a possessed people, Christ's 'peculiar people', loved of God, redeemed by blood, and saved by grace. Let us seek grace from our God to conscientiously live as such every hour of every day to the glory of God our Saviour.

Chapter 33

Fallen Man An Unclean Thing

And the LORD spake unto Moses, saying, Speak unto the children of Israel, saying, If a woman have conceived seed, and born a man child: then she shall be unclean seven days; according to the days of the separation for her infirmity shall she be unclean. And in the eighth day the flesh of his foreskin shall be circumcised. And she shall then continue in the blood of her purifying three and thirty days; she shall touch no hallowed thing, nor come into the sanctuary, until the days of her purifying be fulfilled. But if she bear a maid child, then she shall be unclean two weeks, as in her separation: and she shall continue in the blood of her purifying threescore and six days. And when the days of her purifying are fulfilled, for a son, or for a daughter, she shall bring a lamb of the first year for a burnt offering, and a young pigeon, or a turtledove, for a sin offering, unto the door of the tabernacle of the congregation, unto the priest: Who shall offer it before the LORD, and make an atonement for her; and she shall be cleansed from the issue of her blood. This is the law for her that hath born a male or a female. And if she be not able to bring a lamb, then she shall bring two turtles, or two young pigeons; the one for the burnt offering, and the other for a sin offering: and the priest shall make an atonement for her, and she shall be clean.

Leviticus 12:1-8

In giving birth to her child, a young mother has to endure great pain. Often her pregnancy and labour will be full of discomfort and trouble. Yet, she is anxious to do it. Her entire family and her friends rejoice as the day nears. Our Saviour said ...

A woman when she is in travail hath sorrow, because her hour is come: but as soon as she is delivered of the child, she remembereth no more the anguish, for joy that a man is born into the world (John 16:21).

Yet, throughout the Scriptures, sin, defilement, and uncleanness are always associated with the birth of a child. We see this most clearly set forth in Leviticus 12. I think Isaiah must have had this passage in mind when he spoke of the human race in Isaiah 64:6. In Job 25:4 Bildad asked, 'How then can man be justified with God? Or how can he be clean that is born of a woman?' David said, 'Behold, I was shapen in iniquity, and in sin did my mother conceive me' (Psalm 51:5).

Fallen man is unclean, yet God has provided for the cleansing of the unclean, filthy sinners we are. Let us ever give thanks to God for that fountain opened for sin and uncleanness, Christ Jesus (Zechariah 13:1).

Humbling and Comforting

Leviticus 12 is both deeply humbling and divinely comforting. The effect of all Scripture, when applied to our souls by the efficacious power and grace of God the Holy Ghost, is to lead us out of ourselves to Christ. Wherever man appears, at whatever stage of life we contemplate our nature, be it in conception, at birth, or at any point along the way from the womb to the tomb, our entire existence, our entire being wears the double stamp of helplessness and corruption.

What poor, helpless creatures we are! We do not like to admit it. We try hard to suppress every thought of it and it is sometimes forgotten as we fill our days with frivolity and fun, seeking fortune and fame. We have many devices by which we try to cover what we are. We wear gaudy ornaments, gild ourselves with gold and silver and precious stones, we try to put on the appearance of strength, beauty, importance, and glory. But it is all a vain show (Psalm 39:4-6).

The glory of man is vanity. The pride of man is a hollow reed. We all enter into this world in exactly the same condition and leave it in exactly the same way. We come in naked and helpless and make our exit much the same way, possessing nothing and totally alone we go back to the dust.

Pastor Scott Richardson once said, 'Life in this world begins with a slap on the bottom and ends with a shovel full of dirt in your face; and there's nothing between but bumps and bruises'. They whose paths through this world are brightened by what man calls greatness and wealth, leave here just like everyone else in nakedness and alone. Helplessly they retreat like all others amid disease and death.

There is something worse than our helplessness, worse than the emptiness of our vain lives. We are as corrupt as we are helpless and then some. Our lives are as defiled as they are empty, and then some. We are a sinful race. Our entire human race is 'an unclean thing' (Psalm 14:1-3; Romans 3:12). In this twelfth chapter of Leviticus, God the Holy Spirit shows us that the birth of a child, be it male or female, is the birth of one so corrupt, defiled and unclean that the woman through whose womb the child was born was made ceremonially unclean by the law. In language that cannot be misunderstood, the Holy Spirit here teaches us that fallen man is 'an unclean thing'.

We are a people in need of atonement, cleansing, and grace. Here is the comfort of this chapter. While laying us in the dust of humiliation, portraying our helplessness and uncleanness, it points us to the gracious works of God in redemption and regeneration by which unclean sinners are made clean before him. While exposing our ruin, Moses also sets before us God's remedy.

Grace Needed

We are sinners in need of grace. That is what we see in verses 1 and 2.

> And the LORD spake unto Moses, saying, Speak unto the children of Israel, saying, If a woman have conceived seed, and born a man child: then she shall be unclean seven days; according to the days of the separation for her infirmity shall she be unclean (Leviticus 12:1, 2).

The woman under the law was made ceremonially unclean by the birth of a child, be it male or female. Why? Because every child born into this world, except he who was born of a virgin, is born a sinner and unclean before God. After giving birth to the unclean, the new mother, the unclean woman was to be separated from the congregation of Israel for a specified period of uncleanness: seven days for a son and two weeks for a daughter. This law and the instructions here given concerning the birth of a child were intended by God to teach Israel of old, and to teach the Israel of God today, three specific things.

First, by this law, preserved in his inspired Word, the Lord our God constantly holds before his people the sin and fall of our father Adam. Every time a woman is in travail with child, every time a child comes forth from the womb, every time a new born cries in a burst of life, we ought like the Jewish women of old in the days of their separation, hear the Lord our God saying, 'Thy first father hath sinned' (Isaiah 43:27).

Second, not only did our father Adam sin in the garden, we sinned in him. 'Wherefore, as by one man sin entered into the world, and death by sin; and so death passed upon all men, for that all have sinned' (Romans 5:12). Adam's sin was imputed to the entire human race. And Adam's sin is imparted to all by natural generation. It is transmitted from generation to generation in the seed of fallen men and through the wombs of fallen women.

Third, sin separates us from God. Adam and Eve were driven from the garden because of sin. The woman who gave birth to a child was ceremonially unclean and held in separation from all that was ceremonially holy, because she brought forth that which was unclean. 'We are all as an unclean thing' (Isaiah 64:6).

We try hard to convince ourselves we are clean, able to do what is good and righteous. But at heart, in the core of our being, we know we are unclean. We elevate ourselves with high thoughts and swell with pride at our good works, but still our conscience screams, 'Unclean. Unclean'. In doing so, it echoes the testimony of God's holy law (Ephesians 2:1-3).

Made Clean

The Lord our God, the God of all grace, makes sinners clean by the operation of his almighty grace.

> And in the eighth day the flesh of his foreskin shall be circumcised. And she shall then continue in the blood of her purifying three and thirty days; she shall touch no hallowed thing,

nor come into the sanctuary, until the days of her purifying be fulfilled. But if she bear a maid child, then she shall be unclean two weeks, as in her separation: and she shall continue in the blood of her purifying threescore and six days' (Leviticus 12:3-5).

Circumcision was an act of ceremonial cleansing and purification. It was the sign and seal of God's covenant and its blessings (Ephesians 1:13, 14), and it was a sign of righteousness imputed (Romans 4:11).

Under the ceremonial law by which a male child was made clean and brought into a covenant relationship with God we are given a picture of the new birth, regenerating grace and the saving operations of God the Holy Spirit[9] (Philippians 3:3; Colossians 2:11, 12).

Abraham was righteous before he was circumcised. Circumcision did not make him righteous. Nor did circumcision portray the way God made him righteous. Circumcision was a sign of righteousness received by faith. Circumcision was performed upon a child by the hands of another. It was done to him, not something he did. It was not something for which a boy volunteered, but something imposed upon him.

In all these things circumcision typified the new birth, the work of God the Holy Ghost in the hearts of chosen, redeemed sinners. Circumcision portrayed the believer's experience of grace. Like circumcision, the new birth is a painful thing. Like circumcision, the new birth is distinguishing. It is permanent. It seals us in the covenant and seals the covenant to us. It is a sign of righteousness.[10] It is cleansing (Titus 3:3-7). It is something done to us by another, the work of God wrought in us. Like circumcision, the new birth is something

---

[9] Throughout the New Testament we are taught the circumcision of the Old Testament was a picture, type and symbol of the new birth. Nowhere is there the slightest indication that circumcision was the Old Testament equivalent of New Testament baptism.

[10] As we shall see in the next section of this chapter, circumcision preceded atonement under the law in the experience of the child, because atonement cannot be known until the chosen, redeemed sinner is born again. Then, as faith is given, God the Holy Spirit sprinkles the sin-atoning blood of Christ upon the heart. Yet, just as surely as atonement was made for the child on that night when God passed through Egypt in judgment and passed over Israel because his eye was on the blood, so atonement was made for us and righteousness was accomplished for us when Christ our Passover was sacrificed for us at Calvary.

for which we are volunteered by our Father, not something for which we volunteer ourselves (John 1:11-13; James 1:18).

Circumcision was performed on the eighth day, the day of new beginning when the fulness of time was come, so the new birth is wrought in each of God's elect on the eighth day, when the fulness of time is come (Galatians 4:4-6; 2 Corinthians 5:17).

After the birth of her son, every Jewish woman was required under the Mosaic law to keep forty days of separation from the holy things, called 'the days of her purifying'. I am certain I have not yet grasped all that God has put into those words; but I am equally sure 'the days of her purifying' being forty was neither accidental nor insignificant.

God's wrath was poured out in judgment upon the earth for forty days. It rained for forty days (Genesis 7:4, 12, 17) and sin was judged. Moses was in Mount Sinai for forty days (Exodus 24:18; 34:28). There sin was identified, exposed, and condemned. Israel searched out Canaan for forty days (Numbers 13:25). During those days God's grace and salvation was both revealed and despised. Israel wandered in the wilderness for forty years, a year for every day they spied out the land, because they believed not God (Numbers 14:33, 34). Goliath berated Israel for forty days while Israel trembled in unbelief (1 Samuel 17:16). Even so, Satan, sin, guilt and condemnation berate our souls and make us tremble like Goliath did Israel until we see our great David slay the giant. When Elijah fled from Jezebel he was made to see he was no better than his fathers. He sat down under a juniper tree and wished to die. When he saw his nothingness, his weakness, his sin, the Angel of the Lord appeared to him, commanded him to arise and fed him with bread and water. He walked in the strength of that bread for forty days, all the way to Horeb, the mount of God (1 Kings 19:1-8). Ezekiel was commanded of God to lay on his right side, bearing the sins of Judah, for forty days (Ezekiel 4:6). Nineveh was under the sentence of death for forty days (Jonah 3:4). Our blessed Saviour, the Lord Jesus Christ, was driven into the wilderness by the Spirit of God and tempted of the devil for forty days (Matthew 4:2). There were forty days between the resurrection of our Redeemer and his ascension into glory (Acts 1:3).

Andrew Bonar suggested that as our Lord Jesus, the last Adam, was on the earth forty days after his resurrection, after he restored that which he took not away, so it may have been that Adam and Eve remained only forty days in innocence before the fall. This much is certain, every time 'forty days' is used in the Scriptures it seems to be like the ringing of a great bell to remind us of two things: paradise lost and paradise regained; bondage and liberty, sin and salvation, death and life.

When a Jewish mother gave birth to a daughter the days of her purification were doubled. 'But if she bear a maid child, then she shall be unclean two weeks, as in her separation: and she shall continue in the blood of her purifying threescore and six days' (v. 5).

We are not told why this was the case. Perhaps it was because the woman was the first transgressor and led Adam into transgression (1 Timothy 2:14). Perhaps it was because the woman is the weaker vessel. The serpent beguiled Eve, not Adam (2 Corinthians 11:3; 1 Peter 3:7). Perhaps it was to remind every woman and all who observed the ordinance of God of the fall and of God's promised grace and salvation in Christ Jesus to his elect (1 Timothy 2:14, 15).

Grace Come to Sinners
The Lord our God condescends to meet sinners in grace where they are. Grace does not wait for us to rise. Grace comes down to us.

> And when the days of her purifying are fulfilled, for a son, or for a daughter, she shall bring a lamb of the first year for a burnt offering, and a young pigeon, or a turtledove, for a sin offering, unto the door of the tabernacle of the congregation, unto the priest: Who shall offer it before the LORD, and make an atonement for her; and she shall be cleansed from the issue of her blood. This is the law for her that hath born a male or a female. And if she be not able to bring a lamb, then she shall bring two turtles, or two young pigeons; the one for the burnt offering, and the other for a sin offering: and the priest shall make an atonement for her, and she shall be clean (Leviticus 12:6-8).

The woman's uncleanness brought her to the altar at the appointed time. She came with a burnt offering and a sin offering, an offering for atonement and an offering of consecration. She brought the sacrifice God required, the sacrifice God provided, to the place God appointed, and offered it by the hands of the priest God accepted.

Every Jewish mother was required to do this, the rich and the poor. The Lord God graciously condescended in magnificent mercy and love to the needs of the sinner. If the woman was too poor to bring a lamb, she could bring a pair of turtledoves or a pair of pigeons.

The only remedy for our ruin, the only cleansing for our corruption, the only deliverance from our defilement is the precious blood of our Lord Jesus Christ, represented in these sacrifices.

Wherever Christ's glorious, sin-atoning work is apprehended by faith, perfect cleansing is enjoyed. The apprehension of faith may be feeble. The faith may be but the wavering finger that touches the Master's garment. The experience of faith may be shallow but it is not the depth of our experience, the stability of our faith, or the strength of our apprehension that gives us acceptance with God. Our acceptance, atonement, cleansing, and forgiveness lies wholly in the merit, value, and efficacy of our Sacrifice, Christ Jesus. Understand that and you will find rest for your soul, peace for your heart, and joy in believing.

The sacrifice of Christ is the same to every member of God's Israel. It matters not who you are, what you have done, or what your status is. God requires the same sacrifice from every sinner who comes to him for cleansing. The tenderness, compassion, love, and grace of our all-merciful God is seen in the fact that the blood of a turtledove was as efficacious for the poor as the blood of a lamb for the rich. It was not the animal that mattered, but him of whom the animal spoke, the Lord Jesus Christ.

We see the same thing in the case of the leper in chapter 14. 'And if he be poor and cannot get so much, then he shall take ... And he shall offer the one of the turtle doves, or of the young pigeons, such as he can get; even such as he is able to get ... This is the law of him in whom is the plague of leprosy, whose hand is not able to get that which pertaineth to his cleansing' (vv. 21, 30-32).

God's grace condescends to our need. He comes down to us. He never waits for us to come up to him. How I love those words, 'if he be poor', 'if she be not able'. Grace comes to those who are poor and helpless. When we cannot bring a sacrifice to God, grace brings his Sacrifice to us (Isaiah 46:13; 55:1; Romans 4:5; 10:5-9).

Chapter 34

The Law Of Leprosy

And the LORD spake unto Moses and Aaron, saying, When a man shall have in the skin of his flesh a rising, a scab, or bright spot, and it be in the skin of his flesh like the plague of leprosy; then he shall be brought unto Aaron the priest, or unto one of his sons the priests: And the priest shall look on the plague in the skin of the flesh: and when the hair in the plague is turned white, and the plague in sight be deeper than the skin of his flesh, it is a plague of leprosy: and the priest shall look on him, and pronounce him unclean ... This is the law for all manner of plague of leprosy, and scall, and for the leprosy of a garment, and of a house, and for a rising, and for a scab, and for a bright spot: To teach when it is unclean, and when it is clean: this is the law of leprosy.

Leviticus 13:1-14:59

In these two chapters the Lord God gave very specific laws regarding all manner of leprosy in men, in their garments, and in their houses. These laws we are specifically told were given to teach us to distinguish between that which is clean and that which is unclean.

The Lord God sent the horrible plague of leprosy into the earth specifically to be a type of sin. The progress of leprosy in a man shows us the utter ruin of men by sin. The cleansing of leprosy by blood atonement and the pronouncement of grace show us God's way of salvation through the sin-atoning death of the Lord Jesus Christ, our all glorious Substitute, and the pronouncement of grace in the soul by God the Holy Spirit.

Leprous Men

First, the law of leprosy deals with leprous men. The plague of leprosy in men portrays the personal depravity of all the sons and daughters of Adam by nature.

> When the plague of leprosy is in a man, then he shall be brought unto the priest (Leviticus 13:9).

Leprosy begins deep within and works its way outward. A man might have leprosy for several years before he showed symptoms of the disease. Then, he would have a rising (a boil), a scab (a small tumour), or a bright spot in his flesh. These things did not cause leprosy. They simply revealed its existence in a man.

So it is with sin. Sin is primarily an inward thing. The plague of our race is a heart plague. It is leprosy of the heart (Matthew 15:19). It is what is in us that defiles us. What is in us, at the root and core of our inmost being, is enmity against God. Religion deals with that which is outward. Grace deals with us from the inside out. Men and women look on that which is outward and physical. 'The Lord looketh on the heart.'

We are ready enough to acknowledge the guilt of our evil deeds; but we are terribly reluctant to acknowledge the inward corruption and depravity of our hearts. But it is this that must be confessed.

No one will ever be saved who does not confess his sin. We must repent of our sin, our sins, and our righteousness. Salvation cannot be had by any except those who must have it as the free gift of God's grace. And no one who confesses his sin to God will fail to receive his grace and salvation in Christ (1 John 1:8-2:2). All who must have grace shall have grace. All who must have Christ shall have Christ.

Leprosy was not a terribly painful disease. It was not something a person knew he had because he felt sharp pains or saw sudden, great changes in his health, the colour of his skin, or appetite. Rather, it simply made a person a little restless and caused some sadness, some depression, some mental anxiety. He could function just fine. He just did not feel quite right. He knew something was wrong, but did not think it was much, he was sure it would go away. So it is with sin.

But leprosy was a corrosive, cancerous disease, eating away from the inside out until life was gone. Sin is like that. It is unseen and unfelt until it has begun to consume the beauty of a person. Yet, it is always present, secretly eating away from the inside. Suddenly, it bursts forth in a mass of horrid corruption, defacing the whole person, and when it is finished it brings forth death!

I pray the Lord God will graciously show you who and what you are! That he would grant you to know the leprosy of your heart. If ever God shows you your sin, it is because he has come to grant to you his grace. Let me show you how that works.

The healing of the leper was God's work alone. Leprosy was not healed in Moses' day by medicine, only by grace. It was not cured by a doctor, but by God's priest. The leper was cleansed not by the sterile care of a surgeon, but by the blood sprinkling of a priest. Leprosy in the Old Testament could not be healed by anyone but God himself. 'Salvation is of the Lord.'

Only God's priest could help the poor leper. What grace is revealed in this fact! The examination and care of the leper was never trusted to anyone but God's priest. Moses, typifying the law, could not help a leper, but Aaron, God's priest with God's sacrifice, could; and the leper was trusted to the hands of no one else. He alone had the wisdom and skill to identify and deal with the leprosy. He alone had the experience to handle the leper's case. Only the priest could have compassion upon the poor leper because he alone knew how to make him clean.

How sweet, how blessed, is this thought. 'The Father judgeth no man, but hath committed all judgment unto the Son.' Blessed be God, we have a High Priest who has compassion upon them that are gone out of the way, upon poor lepers. That Priest is the Lord Jesus Christ, the Son of God.

The priest had to come out of the camp and come down to the leper. And the Lord Jesus came out of heaven, came down to us poor lepers, and more. He was himself made to be a leper. He took our infirmities and bore our diseases in his body on the tree (Matthew 8:17).[11] He was made to be sin for us. 'Stricken, smitten of God and afflicted.'

The leper had to be brought to the priest. The leper would not come to the priest and could not come. He must be brought to the priest by another. Sinners must be brought to Christ. None will come on their

---

[11] So great is the compassion of our great God and Saviour that he looks upon the sins of his children not as crimes to punish, but diseases to heal! 'With his stripes we are healed.'

own. Sometimes they are brought to the Saviour by a loving parent, a caring sibling, or kind friends (Mark 2:1-4). Blessed are those sinners who have others to care for them and bring them to the Saviour! But no man can bring another to Christ, except he be fetched by God the Holy Ghost in his mighty, saving operations of grace (John 5:40; 6:35-37).

The leper healed by God's intervention was made clean by divinely prescribed ceremonies and the pronouncement of the priest. Atonement had to be made for him, portraying the fact that only by Christ's atonement for sin could we be made clean before God. The atonement sacrifice was such as the leper could get: two lambs, or a lamb, or two turtledoves, or two pigeons. 'And if he be poor and cannot get so much, then such as he is able to get' (Leviticus 14:21, 22). So, too, Christ is a sacrifice at hand, available to any sinner who wants him (Romans 10:9-13). The blood was caught in an earthen vessel. And 'we have this treasure in earthen vessels, that the excellency of the power may be of God and not of us' (2 Corinthians 4:7; Ephesians 3:8).

The blood must be sprinkled upon the leper. Our hearts must be sprinkled with Christ's blood. His blood must be graciously and effectually applied to us by his Spirit working faith in us, sealing to us all the blessings of life, grace, and salvation. As the leper had to be washed, chosen redeemed sinners must be washed with the washing of regeneration and the renewing of the Holy Ghost (Hebrews 10:19-22; Titus 3:5-7). As the leper was pronounced clean, so God the Holy Spirit pronounces cleansing in the soul. As the leper was presented clean before the Lord, the Lord Jesus presents us clean before God. As the leper was restored and presented to the congregation clean, so God's elect are brought into the fold of his grace in perfect righteousness, the righteousness of Christ.

This leprosy describes the sinner's state in this world in his exclusion from the Lord's presence and his death in sin. This is your present state and condition, if you are yet without Christ. You are a leper. May God the Holy Ghost convince you of your leprosy, for Christ's sake. You have lost every principle of holiness. All your powers are withered, every sinew shrunk. Your comeliness is scarred. Streams of impurity burst forth from your soul. Your eyes betray your hopelessness. The death-like hue of your whole being proclaims the departure of the breath of God from your soul. God turns away his face from you. Your own guilty conscience compels you to cry, 'Unclean'!

'Such', Andrew Bonar wrote, 'is every convinced soul's experience in the day of the Spirit's dealing with it; when the High Priest has begun his treatment of the sin sick soul, compelling it to uncover its head and rend its garment, and with lips covered up, to take the portion of one exposed to death and curse'.

Oh, leprous soul, Christ, God's High Priest, is passing through your country this day. He can deliver you from your diseases. Come, come, though you have sat alone, shut-up in your corruption for years. Come, though you have until now looked in vain for your condition to improve. Come, though you have, like that poor woman of old, spent all your living on physicians of no value. If you come to Christ, it is because God the Holy Spirit has brought you to him.

Perhaps no man ever cared for your soul before. Perhaps you have looked everywhere on earth for help and have found none. But there is a High Priest in the land who can deliver you. He takes you as you are. He pronounces you as you really are, 'Unclean'. Then he stoops down and says, 'Look unto me and be ye saved'.

He passes by. He walks on the outside of the city where the lepers are sitting in their uncleanness. There you sit, outside the camp, wistfully looking in through the gates. Yet, you dare not enter. Christ has come to bring lepers in unto himself. Yes, the Son of God takes in lepers and pronounces them clean. He is near. 'He it is that talks with you.' Christ alone can pronounce leprous sinners clean. His blood cleanses from all sin. His touch heals. His look is life. Is there a leper reading these lines? Are you a desperate soul that needs healing grace? This great Priest heals all who have need of healing.

Leprous Garments

Second, the law of leprosy deals with leprous garments. The bulk of these two chapters deals with leprosy in men and women. But the law of leprosy also deals with leprosy in garments and in houses. This is but another indication that the leprosy God sent among the children of Israel was unlike any form of leprosy known to men in modern times and was specifically intended to be typical of spiritual things. Leviticus 13:47-59 deals with the leprosy that was found in a person's clothes.

The plague of leprosy in garments speaks of the corruption of all we touch. Our lives are corrupting in this world. Our influence is corrupting. If my leprous hand touches something, I spread leprosy.

The garment also that the plague of leprosy is in, whether it be a woollen garment, or a linen garment; Whether it be in the warp, or woof; of linen, or of woollen; whether in a skin, or in any thing made of skin (Leviticus 13:47, 48).

He shall therefore burn that garment, whether warp or woof, in woollen or in linen, or anything of skin, wherein the plague is: for it is a fretting leprosy; it shall be burnt in the fire (Leviticus 13:52).

I make no attempt to guess what this garment leprosy was. We are not told. But the leprosy found in the garments a man wore, while different from that found in a man, was also typical of defilement; sin and defilement not in the man, but in the things around him.

Anything a person wraps around himself is his garment. The circumstances of his life. The business in which he engages. All those things in which we wrap ourselves in this world. All that gives warmth, comfort, and joy to us in this world. All the events that affect our daily lives. Particularly, the garment a man wears, the garment he wraps himself in is, in Scripture, representative of his religion, his hope of salvation. A leprous garment speaks of corrupt religion, the religion a man makes for himself.

When Jude speaks of 'the garment spotted by the flesh' (Jude 1:23), he is clearly talking about the defilement of our lives, the corruption of our entire being, particularly the corruption of all false religion; the way of Cain, the error of Balaam, the gainsaying of Korah (Jude 1:11), which every believer abhors.

Our Lord commended those saints in Sardis, saying, 'They have not defiled their garments' (Revelation 3:4). Most in the Sardis church, though they had a name that they lived, were utterly dead. But even there, in that dark day, there were a few who did not defile their hope of salvation with the leprosy of freewill and works religion.

The only thing that could be done with a leprous garment was to burn it. 'It shall be burnt in the fire' (Leviticus 13:52, 57). It mattered not how costly the garment was. It had to be burned. It did not matter if the garment had belonged to a man's family for generations. It must be burned. It did not matter how beautiful the garment was. It had to be burned. If there was so much as one spot of leprosy, in the warp or in the woof, it had to be burned.

If you are yet wearing the leprous garments of freewill, works religion, tear them off at once and burn them as contemptible things. Do not be concerned about burning your garments, there is a better garment to be had. It is the robe of Christ's righteousness, the fine, white linen garments of salvation in, by, and with the Lord Jesus Christ (Revelation 3:18; 7:9, 13, 14; 16:15; 19:7, 8).

Leprous Houses

Third, the law of leprosy deals with leprous houses. The plague of leprosy in a house speaks of the defilement of the earth. In the last part of chapter 14 (vv. 33-57), the Lord gave instructions concerning the plague of leprosy he put into a person's house. To teach and remind us that the earth itself is under the curse of God. The Lord God sent leprosy into the houses of Israel because of sin.

> And the LORD spake unto Moses and unto Aaron, saying, When ye be come into the land of Canaan, which I give to you for a possession, and I put the plague of leprosy in a house of the land of your possession (Leviticus 14:33, 34).

Sin is a horrible leprosy that has defiled and continues to defile our entire race. Sin is leprosy in a man. Sin is a leprosy in us that defiles the whole world around us. Everything we touch, everything we come into contact with, everything that comes into contact with us is leprous. We defile everything. That is leprosy in the garment.

Yet, there is more. Sin reaches even to the earth itself. The very ground upon which we walk and the atmosphere in which we live is defiled by sin; leprous and unclean, and therefore cursed by God. That is what is represented by the leprosy in a house. It was as though the plagued walls of the house cried out to Israel, 'Repent! Confess your sin! Turn again to the Lord your God!' This leprosy in the houses of Israel said to the inhabitants of the houses (no matter how grand the property), 'This place is polluted. This is not your dwelling place. This is not your rest. This is not your home.' Here, we are taught to look for and anticipate a better house, 'a building of God, an house not made with hands, eternal in the heavens'.

'We look for a new heavens and a new earth, wherein dwelleth righteousness'. But, before we can have that new house, this old, earthly, leprous house must be destroyed. Is that not what is portrayed in the law of leprous houses?

The leprous house had to be emptied. The family had to move out of the house. That is what happens when God's saints drop the physical body of flesh in the grave (2 Corinthians 5:1-9). Once it was emptied, it was purged, 'scraped', by divine judgment. Being judged of God, the house had to be broken down, stone by stone, timber by timber, board by board. Even the dust of the mortar had to be carried away. Still, there was provision made for atonement for the house.

When God gets done with this leprous house we call earth, he is going to tear it down timber by timber, stone by stone, mortar joint by mortar joint, and burn the whole thing. Yes, the Lord God shall destroy this entire physical universe. But he will lose nothing to the leprosy of sin. Christ bought the earth itself; and he shall have it.

> Seeing then that all these things shall be dissolved, what manner of persons ought ye to be in all holy conversation and godliness, Looking for and hasting unto the coming of the day of God, wherein the heavens being on fire shall be dissolved, and the elements shall melt with fervent heat? Nevertheless we, according to his promise, look for new heavens and a new earth, wherein dwelleth righteousness. Wherefore, beloved, seeing that ye look for such things, be diligent that ye may be found of him in peace, without spot, and blameless (2 Peter 3:11-14).

Here is the purpose of God in giving us these two instructive chapters on the law for leprosy.

> This is the law for all manner of plague of leprosy, and scall, and for the leprosy of a garment, and of a house, and for a rising, and for a scab, and for a bright spot: To teach when it is unclean, and when it is clean: this is the law of leprosy (Leviticus 14:54-57).

There is a day coming when our Lord Jesus Christ, God's great High Priest, shall declare what is clean and what is unclean. He is the only one who can (Revelation 21:1-5, 27; 22:1-7, 10-17, 20). Blessed be his name, soon our God shall rid us of the horrid leprosy of sin forever!

Chapter 35

He Who Has The Plague Is Clean

And if a leprosy break out abroad in the skin, and the leprosy cover all the skin of him that hath the plague from his head even to his foot, wheresoever the priest looketh; Then the priest shall consider: and, behold, if the leprosy have covered all his flesh, he shall pronounce him clean that hath the plague: it is all turned white: he is clean. But when raw flesh appeareth in him, he shall be unclean. And the priest shall see the raw flesh, and pronounce him to be unclean: for the raw flesh is unclean: it is a leprosy. Or if the raw flesh turn again, and be changed unto white, he shall come unto the priest; And the priest shall see him: and, behold, if the plague be turned into white; then the priest shall pronounce him clean that hath the plague: he is clean.

Leviticus 13:12-17

What a paradox this passage seems to present! Here we are given the law of God regarding leprosy. Throughout this chapter, the person who had some symptom, or many symptoms, of leprosy was pronounced unclean. But that person whose flesh was completely covered with the plague was pronounced clean. 'The priest shall pronounce him clean that hath the plague: he is clean'! The Lord God declares that he who has the plague is clean.

Leprosy was a common disease in the Old Testament, from the time that Israel came into the land of Canaan. It was still common during the days of our Lord's earthly ministry.

However, unless I am mistaken, the leprosy described in this chapter, the leprosy we see mentioned so often in the Scriptures, is unknown in modern times. I know that leprosy, now called Hansen's Disease, though rare, is still found among men, even in our own society. It is a horrible, loathsome disease, with symptoms somewhat like the leprosy described in Leviticus 13 and 14. But the leprosy observed among men today, Hansen's Disease, is also in many ways distinct from what is described in this chapter. The leprosy described in Leviticus 13 and 14 was specifically given to Israel in the land of their possession, in the land of Canaan (Leviticus 14:34).

Real and Typical

The leprosy described in Leviticus 13 was a real disease, but it was also typical. In fact, it seems to have been sent into the world by God as a type and picture of sin. The characteristics of the disease are vivid pictures of sin. Leprosy is held before us in Scripture as a shocking picture of that horrid plague, sin, with which we are infected from the soles of our feet to the crown of our heads (Isaiah 1:6). Leprosy, as it is set forth in the book of God, was intended by God to be a picture of sin.

This can be seen first, because all the ceremonial purifications given in chapter 14, by which the stain of leprosy was removed from a man, by which the defiled leper was made clean, refer to our Lord Jesus Christ. The disease of leprosy was cleansed and removed not by medicine, but by blood atonement. This leprosy was a medically incurable malady. Its only cure was by blood and grace.

Second, no one but the priests, Aaron or one of his sons, who were typical representatives of our Lord Jesus Christ, could identify and remove the leprosy. Only the priest could pronounce the leper unclean. So, too, only Christ by his Spirit and by his Word can convince a man of his sin. Only the priest could make atonement for the leper and Christ alone could make atonement for sin. Only the priest could apply the atoning blood and pronounce the leper clean and only Christ can apply his blood to your conscience. Only Christ can speak peace to your soul and pronounce you clean.

Conviction

A careful reading of Leviticus 13 and 14 will make something else manifest. Leprosy is a picture not only of the universal sin of our race, but also of the conviction of sin by God the Holy Spirit. The leper pronounced clean by God's high priest is held before us as a picture of a sinner convinced of his sin by God the Holy Ghost and made clean by the miracle of God's saving grace.

The Fear of Leprosy

This thirteenth chapter of Leviticus sets before us the fear of leprosy. We have several examples of people coming to the high priest, fearful they might have leprosy, seeking relief from a disease they never had. They had the appearance of leprosy, but not leprosy. You might call them spurious lepers.

> When a man shall have in the skin of his flesh a rising, a scab, or bright spot, and it be in the skin of his flesh like the plague of leprosy; then he shall be brought unto Aaron the priest, or unto one of his sons the priests (Leviticus 13:2).

That is a picture of spurious sinners, spurious Christians, and spurious disciples. They have 'a rising', some stirring of the emotions, some feeling of remorse, some sense of danger, or some fear of death. They may have 'a scab', an old scar on the conscience, a sense of guilt about something long ago, or a scar from other old risings of religious wounds. They might have 'a bright spot', a boil of self-righteousness, or a pimple of religious zeal. For most people, that is all their religion amounts to: a rising, a scab, or a bright spot. It is all superficial foam and froth. There is nothing to it deeper than the skin. Nothing deeper than the flesh.

They have been told by others they are lepers. They tell themselves they are lepers. They have pronounced themselves lepers, and therefore presume they are clean. They use the language of lepers, wear sackcloth and ashes, and tear their clothes, crying, 'Unclean! Unclean!', and in doing so vainly think themselves clean.

But the disease does not spread. After seven days of being shut up, there is no spreading of the corruption. Another seven days and still no corruption. The hair of the sore has not turned white. Their beauty has not withered. Everything is at a stand. Week after week, month after month, year after year, they are the same. They have no deeper awareness of sin than they had twenty years ago. They are no more acquainted with themselves or with Christ than they were in the beginning. Their religion is like water in a tank. It knows neither ebb nor flow. It is always the same. Always stagnant.

The Gift of Leprosy

Look at verses 12 and 13. Here we see the gift of leprosy. Yes, I said, 'the gift of leprosy'. Blessed is that man whom God has made to be a leper! Blessed is that woman to whom God has given this gift!

In Leviticus 14:34, we are told it was the Lord God who made men and women lepers. It was God who put the plague of leprosy in a house. He put the plague in the house only after the children of Israel had come into the land of Canaan, the land of their promised possession, the land God gave as fulfilment of his covenant with Abraham.

> When ye be come into the land of Canaan, which I give to you for a possession, and I put the plague of leprosy in a house of the land of your possession; And he that owneth the house shall come and tell the priest, saying, It seemeth to me there is as it were a plague in the house (Leviticus 14:34, 35).

Blessed is that person whom God has made to be a leper, whom God the Holy Ghost has made a sinner. Joseph Hart wrote ...

> What comfort can a Saviour bring
> To those who never felt their woe?
> A sinner is a sacred thing;
> The Holy Ghost hath made him so.

It is what we have portrayed in Leviticus 13:12, 13.

> And if a leprosy break out abroad in the skin, and the leprosy cover all the skin of him that hath the plague from his head even to his foot, wheresoever the priest looketh; Then the priest shall consider: and, behold, if the leprosy have covered all his flesh, he shall pronounce him clean that hath the plague: it is all turned white: he is clean (Leviticus 13:12, 13).

Four Marks
God gave the high priest in Israel four distinct marks by which he was to determine whether the plague of leprosy was really in a person.

1. If the leprosy was real, the disease was deeper than the skin (v. 3). It was something more than an outward, superficial sore.

2. The hair over the sore turned white. It died at the root. Hair in the Scriptures represents beauty and glory. Long hair is a woman's glory (1 Corinthians 11:15). Absalom's attractiveness was his long, thick, heavy hair. Samson's strength was in his hair. The growth of the hair is spoken of as an emblem of beauty and excellence in a woman (Ezekiel 16:7). The Bride in the Song of Solomon speaks of Christ's beauty, saying, 'Thy locks are bushy and black as a raven'. The true leper is one whose beauty, comeliness, strength, and glory have withered before God. It is all dead at the roots (Psalm 39:11; Daniel 10:8).

3. If the leprosy was true leprosy, the disease never stopped, but constantly worsened, ever spreading until it 'covered all his flesh' (Isaiah 1:6; 64:6; Romans 7:18).

4. If the leprosy was true leprosy, there was raw flesh in the leper. 'When the raw flesh appeareth in him, he shall be unclean' (vv. 14, 15).

So it is with the experience of grace in the soul. Those who are made sinners before God, lepers before the Most High, know what it is to have raw flesh, a tender, bleeding conscience, a conscience that cannot bear being touched. Yes, when a person is made guilty before God, he cannot bear the thought of his touch, but cries and screams against it, until the touch comes.

Then all is well. Once the raw flesh was, as it were, crusted over and turned white, the leper was clean. Once the Lord God touches the sinner, that person whose screaming conscience has tormented his soul is suddenly freed from condemnation because he is clean. He is freed from sin. The conscience is silenced with the blessed peace of purity before the holy Lord God. The flesh is no longer raw (Isaiah 6:1-7).

The Humiliation of Leprosy

He is a leprous man, he is unclean: the priest shall pronounce him utterly unclean; his plague is in his head. And the leper in whom the plague is, his clothes shall be rent, and his head bare, and he shall put a covering upon his upper lip, and shall cry,

Unclean, unclean. All the days wherein the plague shall be in him he shall be defiled; he is unclean: he shall dwell alone; without the camp shall his habitation be (Leviticus 13:44-46).

Here is the humiliation of leprosy. 'The leper in whom the plague is' is the leper indeed. Our plague is an inward thing. 'In whom', not 'upon whom'. Sin is part of us. It is in us. It rises with us every morning, goes with us every step of the day, travels in every thought of our mind, and lies down with us every night. It is a plague in every living soul.

The leper's clothes were to be rent. That was a sign of humiliation and mourning. We see it in Eli's behaviour when the ark was taken, and in Jacob's actions when Joseph was gone. The leper in Israel was not allowed to mend his garments. He had to wear torn clothes all his days. So it is with God's people and sin. It is a matter of relentless grief (1 John 1:7-10). The rending of his clothes was also a sign of abhorrence, self-loathing, and contrition (2 Kings 22:11; Isaiah 66:1, 2).

The leper had no covering for his head. Blessed be God, there is a helmet of salvation, but not until the cleansing of grace is granted. The leper, like the sinner under conviction, bows naked, exposed before God. Thereby, he says, 'I have neither refuge, nor excuse, nor hope'.

He had no covering for his head; but he was required to cover his upper lip, like one covering an open grave, to keep infection in, displaying utter humility because of his corruption. The leper was compelled to cry, 'Unclean! Unclean!'. So it is with God's people in this world. Spiritual lepers we are. We are compelled from within, so long as we live in this body of flesh, to go through the world crying, 'Unclean! Unclean!'.

Perhaps you are thinking, 'I know I am a sinner; but I'm not that bad. I read my Bible. I go to Church. I pray. I am not perfect by any stretch of the imagination; but I do the best I can. And I am not so bad that I need to cover my mouth and constantly cry, 'Unclean! Unclean'!' I know you are not that bad. But I am not describing you. All you have is a little scab on the flesh, a little redness here and there, maybe an old leprosy, but you're not a leper.

Go ahead, my brother leper, cry out to the Great Physician, 'Unclean! Unclean!'. You need not tell anyone else about your plague. No one else can help. But you can tell him; and he can help (Matthew 8:1-3).

The leper, because he was a leper, all unclean, from the top of his head to the soles of his feet, was required to dwell alone. 'He shall dwell alone.' That man or woman who knows his or her uncleanness before God chooses and delights to dwell alone with God. Blessed is the soul Christ gets alone with him (Hosea 2:14; John 8:1-11; Lamentations 3:26-32). J. C. Philpot rightly observed, 'What we get alone weighs heaviest, wears best, and lasts longest'.

'Without the camp shall his habitation be.' Without question, this refers to the leper's ceremonial separation from the tabernacle, the worship of God, and the privileges of citizenship in the nation of Israel. The leper, full of the disease, knowing his uncleanness, dare not come into the camp of Israel. Until the priest came and pronounced him clean, he was not allowed, and felt himself utterly unworthy to come into the company of God's saints in his house.

This I say to you, until God's High Priest, the Lord Jesus Christ, by the power of his Spirit, pronounces you clean, you dare not come to the waters of baptism, or into the Church of God, or to the Lord's Table. Go, show yourself to God's Priest. Once the Priest, Christ Jesus, pronounces you clean, you are worthy, because you are clean through his worthiness which he has made yours.

The Cleansing of the Leper
Are you a leper, a poor soul sitting off at a distance, fearful that someone might get too close to you? Are you fearful because you know yourself thoroughly unclean, covered with the leprosy from the top of your head to the soles of your feet, unclean in heart, in soul, in mind? Does your soul cry out, 'How can I be made clean?'. I have good news for you. The Lord Jesus Christ, God's High Priest, can make you clean. Read verses 12 and 13 again. Here we see the cleansing of the leper.

> And if a leprosy break out abroad in the skin, and the leprosy cover all the skin of him that hath the plague from his head even to his foot, wheresoever the priest looketh; Then the priest shall consider: and, behold, if the leprosy have covered all his flesh, he shall pronounce him clean that hath the plague: it is all turned white: he is clean (Leviticus 13:12, 13).

The priest made him clean (14:1-33) by blood atonement and holy oil, pointing to righteousness imputed then imparted in the new birth. The priest pronounced him clean, the priest presented him clean before the Lord (14:11), and the priest presented him clean before the congregation. The Lord Jesus Christ makes lepers clean by himself alone. Christ made his people clean by the blood he shed at Calvary and he makes his people clean by the blessed pronouncement of grace when he speaks peace to the heart by his Spirit in conversion.

In chapter 14, we are told about the leper being made clean, though he was still a leper, full of leprosy. There is no mention of him being healed, only of him being pronounced clean by God's priest. Why? Because in the new birth we are not healed of our leprosy. That comes in resurrection glory. Believing on Christ, we simply hear the pronouncement of the law by the mouth of God's High Priest speaking in grace, 'He is clean'. When God's Priest, our Lord Jesus Christ, pronounces a leper clean, the Lord God declares, 'He is clean'! The Son of God presents us clean before God. The Lord Jesus presents us clean before the congregation of his saints. Once the man was completely covered with leprosy, once the plague was turned white, he was still a leper; but he was no longer corrupting. He was no longer dangerous. 'He is clean', clean before the law, clean in his conscience, because he is clean before God. May God give you faith in Christ and pronounce you clean in your own heart and conscience, as he did Enoch of old (Hebrews 11:5, 6).

Chapter 36

'In The Day Of His Cleansing'

And the LORD spake unto Moses, saying, This shall be the law of the leper in the day of his cleansing: He shall be brought unto the priest ... This is the law for all manner of plague of leprosy, and scall, and for the leprosy of a garment, and of a house, and for a rising, and for a scab, and for a bright spot: To teach when it is unclean, and when it is clean: this is the law of leprosy.

Leviticus 14:1-59

What a horrid disease leprosy is! Even what is today observed in leprosy is horrible. But, as I have shown you, leprosy in our modern world cannot be rightly compared to the leprosy God sent into the land of Canaan among the Jews as a type and picture of sin. That leprosy, dealt with in Leviticus 13 and 14, was a real disease of the most horrible kind but a disease distinctly intended by God to be typical of sin. Even more specifically, it was intended by God to represent the believer's experience of Holy Spirit conviction, by which sinners are convinced of sin, and made to know we are sinners.

Leprosy was a disease that caused a person virtually no pain. In fact, it had a numbing effect, deadening the senses. It was unidentified until the priest recognised it. Once it was identified, once the man was made to know he was a leper, he was marked as a defiled, corrupt, and unclean man.

Cut Off

The wife he loved, the brothers and sisters with whom he was raised, friends who had loved him as their own souls, all immediately cast him off. He was unclean. The leper became at once an outcast and an alien from family and friends, hearth and home. These things were painful, cutting strokes; but there was a keener and deeper stroke still in reserve.

The leper was driven from the people of God, banished from the camp of Israel. He was not allowed to come with God's people into his house. For the leper, there was no access to God, no gate open by which he might draw near to the Holy One. As far as he was concerned being shut out from the camp of Israel, the poor, unclean, corrupt leper was without hope. There was no altar for him, no sacrifice, no sweet incense, no hope. He was a man cut off, cut off from man and cut off from God.

The Picture

Leprosy was completely incurable except by a miracle of grace. So, the leper had no prospect before him but to die a miserable death, the flesh rotting from his bones, and limb dropping from limb. The leper was a dead man waiting to die. All these things show leprosy to be a vivid type and picture of sin, in the experience of it, as it is made known in the heart and conscience of the child of God by God the Holy Ghost when he convinces chosen, redeemed sinners of sin.

Once the hand of God touches a sinner, when God almighty puts leprosy in your house and sin is laid bare in the soul, the sinner finds himself cut off both from man and from God. Let a man or woman become convinced of their sin before God and family and friends, who know nothing about sin, about Christ, about the gospel will immediately cut them off. Husband or wife, sons, daughters, companions, friends will renounce you as a gloomy fanatic. The more you discuss your pain with them, the more they will distance themselves from you (Job 19:13-19; Psalm 38:11; 88:18). But, painful as these things are, what far exceeds them, what continually torments the soul awakened to a sense of sin is the separation from God which is the result of sin.

The doctrine of Leviticus 14 is obvious. As the leper in Israel was cleansed only by God's priest, and only by blood, oil, and water, so Christ alone cleanses the leprous souls of poor, guilty sinners by the blood of his sacrifice, the grace he bestows, and the Holy Spirit who brings his grace to the soul.

The Priest

Under Mosaic Law, leprosy was cleansed, and lepers were healed only by God's priests. No doctor was called. No therapy was administered. No medicine was prescribed. Moses did nothing. The people did nothing. The leper did nothing. The priest did everything. The leper was totally passive. He did not even come to the priest. The priest came out to the leper and the leper was brought to the priest.

The Place

The man was not brought into the camp of Israel lest he defile the camp. The priest came out to the place where lepers were isolated and called for the leper; and the leper was brought to him. Even so, in the sweet and blessed experience of God's saving grace, Christ comes to us. We do not come to him. Christ calls for us and God the Holy Spirit brings the sinner to the Saviour.

The Pronouncement

The priest comes out to the place where lepers are found and calls them. That speaks of the preaching of the gospel. Lepers are brought to the priest. The priest examines them one by one. He identifies their malady and pronounces them either clean or unclean. One leper is brought before God's priest and then another, and another. Try to picture the proceedings in your mind's eye.

Here comes a man with a spot like leprosy. The priest looks at him. There is a spot on him that is not leprous, a bit of raw flesh, but the rest is healthy. The priest puts him aside. He is an unclean leper.

Here is another leper. He has one or two red spots appearing beneath the skin. The rest of his body is perfectly sound. The priest puts him aside, too. He is an unclean leper.

Here is a third man. He is covered from head to foot with a scaly whiteness of the filthy disease. His hair has all turned white, for the disease has killed the roots. There is not so much as a single speck of health in him from the crown of his head to the soles of his feet. He is one ugly mass of pollution and filth. The priest says to him, 'You are clean'. After certain necessary ceremonies, he is brought into the camp, and afterwards into the very sanctuary of God.

If there had been found in him any soundness of body or any place unaffected by the disease, he would have been unclean. But when the leprosy had covered him completely, the man was made clean by the sacrificial ceremonies described in this chapter 14 of Leviticus.

Let us apply the passage to ourselves. Are you a leper? Am I? You may be ready enough and willing to confess that you have done many things that are wrong. Yet, you think, 'Though I have done much that I can neither excuse nor justify, I have done some good things. I have been charitable. I try to help the poor. Yes, I have my faults, I know. I have my sins, too. But, at the bottom, I am basically a good person'. God's High Priest says, 'You are unclean'. There is no promise for you. There is no grace for you. There is no mercy for you. There is no sacrifice for you. There is no salvation for you.

Perhaps you admit you are guilty of many things. You acknowledge many evil thoughts. You confess you have committed terrible, immoral deeds. Still, though you have no good works of which to boast and no righteous deeds to trust, you do hope by repentance and the help of God's good grace to do better. You are unclean. There is no fountain opened for you, no sacrifice for you, no cleansing for you.

I see another leper standing far off. You may be a better person than either of the others, but not in your own opinion. Your heart is heavy. Your conscience is tormenting. In brokenness you confess your sin. You cry, 'Unclean! Unclean!' You look on your righteousnesses as filthy rags. Your goodness you see to be corruption. You count all those things you once thought your most excellent distinctions but dung.

You are convinced that if ever there was a sinner who deserved the hottest depths of hell and everlasting condemnation that sinner is you. You think in your soul, 'I fear I am damned. I deserve to be damned. I am without a shred of hope. Much as I hate my sin and hate what I am, I know I can never do any better than I have done. If I am healed of this plague that consumes my soul, it must be by grace alone. I cannot change myself.' You are covered with sin from the inside out, from the top of your head to the soles of your feet.

Wait. I hear the Priest of God, Christ Jesus. What does he say? 'You are clean.' You are a clean leper. Your sins are forgiven you. Your iniquities are put away. Through the blood of Christ you are saved.

As soon as the leprosy had covered him completely, the leper of Israel was clean; and as soon as your sin is fully manifest, so that in your conscience you know yourself a sinner indeed, there is a way of salvation for you. Then, by the sprinkling of blood and the washing of water, you are made clean. Salvation is yours! As long as a man has anything to boast of, there is no Christ for him. But the moment he has nothing of his own, Christ is his. As long as you are anything, Christ is nothing to you. But when you are nothing, Christ is everything.

In the book of God, believing people speak of their personal righteousness, good works, and holiness in three distinct ways; as filthy rags (Isaiah 64:6), as dung (Philippians 3:7), and as breaking wind (Isaiah 26:18). Those are my thoughts about my personal righteousness and holiness. What are yours? Tell me honestly, and I will tell you what you think of Christ. When you discover your righteousnesses are but filthy rags, all your good works are but dung, and all your personal holiness is but breaking wind, God says you are clean.

Faith's Warrant

All the warrant a sinner needs in coming to Christ is to know that he is a sinner. For 'Christ Jesus came into the world to save sinners'. Do I know myself to be a sinner? Then he came to save me, and there I rest and there I trust. If I have any good feelings or good works which take away from me the power to call myself a sinner, or if they diminish the force and emphasis I put upon the word when I use it, then may I fear that I have no right to come to Christ. Christ died 'the just for the unjust, to bring us to God'. Am I unjust? Must I honestly declare I am? 'Christ died for the ungodly'. Am I ungodly, is this my grief and sorrow that I am ungodly? Then Christ died for me.

Use your guilt, even the greatness of it, like David of old, as the argument for mercy. Cry out, like him, 'For thy name's sake, O Lord, pardon mine iniquity, for it is great' (Psalm 25:11).

Cleansing

The leper was first healed, then he was cleansed. He was miraculously healed before he was ceremonially cleansed. The cleansing was purely a ceremonial thing intended to picture for us the sinner's experience of grace in salvation. This ceremonial cleansing had nothing to do with the leper's healing but the things pictured show us the only way sinners can ever be healed of spiritual leprosy, and made clean before God.

The cleansing of the leper who had been healed of his plague was done in three distinct stages.

The Leper's Separation

The cleansing of the leper in his separation is set before us in verses 7 and 8. This ceremonial cleansing without the camp involved the killing of a bird, the sprinkling of the bird's blood upon the leper, the shaving of the leper's hair and the washing of his clothes. This part of the ceremony portrays substitutionary redemption by our Lord Jesus Christ.

The priest took for the leper who had been healed and was to be cleansed, 'two birds alive and clean, and cedar wood, and scarlet, and hyssop' (v. 4). The leper did not bring this sacrifice. It was all brought by the priest himself. These two birds alive and clean represent the Lord Jesus Christ, our Saviour, who is both life and holiness. The cedar wood speaks of Christ's magnificent fragrance and incorruptibility. The scarlet speaks of our Saviour's precious blood. Hyssop was a herb likely used as a small, bristly brush for dipping in blood and for sprinkling the blood. We are told in Hebrews 9:19 that Moses, 'took the blood of calves and of goats, with water, and scarlet wool, and hyssop, and sprinkled both the book and all the people'. The Israelites in Egypt sprinkled the door posts and the lintels of their houses with blood, using hyssop. David cried, 'Purge me with hyssop, and I shall be clean'. The hyssop refers to 'the blood of sprinkling'.

> And the priest shall command that one of the birds be killed in an earthen vessel over running water' (Leviticus 14:5).

One of these birds had to be killed. What a blessed picture this is of Christ dying upon the cursed tree as our Substitute! The bird had to be killed 'in an earthen vessel'. Its blood was not to be spilt in vain. Every drop must be caught as a very precious thing in the earthen vessel, lest it fall upon the ground and be mingled with the dirt.

How valuable, how precious, how unspeakably precious is the blood of Christ! By his precious blood our sins are washed away. By his precious blood justice is satisfied. By his precious blood all the chosen are reconciled to God. By the blood of Christ, we are redeemed. Not one drop of Immanuel's blood falls to the ground! Particular, effectual redemption, the sweet gospel doctrine of limited atonement, is shown by the blood in the vessel. The blasphemous heresy of universal redemption, trampling the blood of Christ under foot, counting it a common thing, would be the blood in the dirt (Hebrews 10:29).

The bird had to be killed 'over running water'. This connects the substitutionary work of Christ at Calvary and the gracious work of God the Holy Spirit in regeneration and conversion. 'Running' or 'living' water commonly refers to God the Holy Ghost.

> He that believeth on me, as the Scripture hath said, out of his belly shall flow rivers of living water. This spake he of the Spirit, which they that believe on him should receive (John 7:38, 39).

The living bird was tied to the piece of cedar wood with the scarlet cord and dipped in the blood of the dead bird. Then the priest sprinkled the leper who was to be cleansed seven times with the blood, pronounced him clean, and set the living bird free.

> As for the living bird, he shall take it, and the cedar wood, and the scarlet, and the hyssop, and shall dip them and the living bird in the blood of the bird that was killed over the running water: And he shall sprinkle upon him that is to be cleansed from the leprosy seven times, and shall pronounce him clean, and shall let the living bird loose into the open field (Leviticus 14:6, 7).

The living bird was dipped in the blood of the slain bird. When he spread his wings and flew up into heaven, sin atoning blood, as it were, was scattered through the earth. He carried with him into heaven the blood of his slaughtered companion. When the Lord Jesus ascended on high, went into heaven in our nature. As our great High Priest on the Day of Atonement, he entered within the veil, with his own blood, and obtained eternal redemption for us (Hebrews 9:12).

All this was done before the leper's eyes. Every detail spoke to him. He saw all, heard all and felt all. The entire ceremony said, 'All this is for you. The bird that died, died for you. The bird flying in yonder heavens with blood on its wings, flies for you. This is your cleansing. This God has commanded that you be restored to the sanctuary.'

When by God-given faith we see Christ crucified; the blood, death, sufferings, and resurrection of the Lord Jesus, when we see him, as Paul puts it, 'crucified before our eyes', as the healed leper saw the one bird dying in agony and the other soaring upward in liberty, we hear God himself say to our souls, 'Christ died and rose again for you'.

Next, the priest had 'to sprinkle the blood upon him that was to be cleansed seven times', and then 'pronounce him clean' (v. 7). The leper not only saw the blood fall drop by drop from the slain bird. He must be sprinkled with it seven times. This points to 'the blood of sprinkling which speaketh better things than the blood of Abel'. It represents the application of atoning blood and Christ's dying love to the soul.

The man was now virtually clean, for we read, when he had been sprinkled seven times, 'The priest shall pronounce him clean'. The number seven speaks of perfection. Then, the leper, when he was pronounced clean, had to wash his clothes, shave off all his hair, and take a bath (v. 8).

He was 'to wash his clothes'. 'Having therefore these promises, dearly beloved, let us cleanse ourselves from all filthiness of the flesh and spirit, perfecting holiness in the fear of God' (2 Corinthians 7:1).

He was no longer to wear the rent garments and filthy, tattered rags of the leper, but the clean garments of God's salvation; pure and white, the garments of Christ's perfect righteousness.

He had to shave off all his hair. This was done twice. First, it was done while he was still without the camp. Then, it had to be done again on the seventh day, the day before he was presented before the Lord at the door of the tabernacle (v. 9). Let us go with the leper into the camp. This is the second stage of his cleansing.

The Leper's Restoration
The cleansing of the leper in his restoration is seen in verses 8 and 9. Once he was restored to the camp of Israel, but while he was still required to dwell outside his own tent, on the seventh day, the leper was required to shave himself again. This time he had to shave all the hair off his body, beard, eyebrows. All the hair had to be shaved off of him. He was also required to bathe himself and wash his clothes. This portrays the new birth, regeneration.

> And he that is to be cleansed shall wash his clothes, and shave off all his hair, and wash himself in water, that he may be clean: and after that he shall come into the camp, and shall tarry abroad out of his tent seven days. But it shall be on the seventh day, that he shall shave all his hair off his head and his beard and his eyebrows, even all his hair he shall shave off: and he shall wash

his clothes, also he shall wash his flesh in water, and he shall be clean' (Leviticus 14:8, 9).

In verse 8 the command is simply that he should 'shave off all his hair'. But on the seventh day (seven always speaks of grace, perfection, and completion) he had to 'shave all his hair off his head, and his beard, and his eyebrows'. Here, there is the complete removing of the old hair that there might be a fresh growth of entirely new hair. This represents old things passing away and all things becoming new in Christ in the new creation of grace (2 Corinthians 5:17). By this means, the Lord Jesus seems to have said, 'Behold, I make all things new'.

The leper was required to wash his flesh in water and be clean. This seems to signify the washing of regeneration and renewing of the Holy Ghost. I have no doubt Paul was referring to this very thing in Hebrews 10, when he wrote, 'Let us draw near with a true heart, in full assurance of faith, having our hearts sprinkled from an evil conscience, and our bodies washed with pure water'. The body washed with pure water does not refer to baptism, but to the washing of regeneration, as our Lord speaks of us being 'born of water and of the Spirit'.

The Leper's Consecration

The cleansing of the leper also speaks of his consecration (vv. 10-32). In these verses we see what the priest did to and for the leper on the eighth day at the door of the tabernacle of the congregation. The eighth day is the day of new beginning. Here we are given a picture of every believer's sanctification and consecration to Christ.

And on the eighth day he shall take two he lambs without blemish, and one ewe lamb of the first year without blemish, and three tenth deals of fine flour for a meat offering, mingled with oil, and one log of oil' (Leviticus 14:10).

On the eighth day the leper brought three lambs to the tabernacle. Two males and one female were to be selected, a male for a burnt offering, a female for a trespass offering, and a male for a sin offering. Here we see God-given faith in Christ. These things brought before the cleansed leper's eye and heart the great cost with which he had been redeemed. Let it so speak to us.

The lamb offered whole as a burnt offering represented the Lord Jesus Christ, the Lamb of God, burned in flames of divine wrath. The trespass offering represented our blessed Redeemer too, but in a different way. In the trespass offering the inward parts of the animal, primarily the fat around the kidneys and entrails, were burned in the fire. This speaks of the wrath of God we deserve. The fires of hell are fuelled by that which is in us. As the smoke and flame of the burning fat of the trespass and sin offering ascended from the brazen altar in the sight of the leper, he saw in picture the sacrifice of the Lord Jesus Christ accepted of God as a sweet savour to satisfy offended justice.

The leper also brought 'a meat offering also of one tenth deal of fine flour mingled with oil'. This was a thank-offering to be presented by the priest for the leper's cleansing, representing the thankful heart of the sinner for God's undeserved mercy by which we are saved.

Next, we are told that the blood of the trespass offering was to be taken and applied in a very special manner. It was to be 'put upon the tip of the right ear of him that was to be cleansed, upon the thumb of the right hand, and upon the great toe of the right foot'.

As we saw back in chapter 8, during the consecration of Aaron and his sons, this speaks of consecration to God. But watch this. There is a log of oil, a little less than a pint, involved in this ceremony. Oil symbolizes God the Holy Spirit and the grace of God he brings to us. Learn the meaning of the picture.

The oil was applied, like the blood, by God's priest. The oil was put on the blood, because redemption and grace have the same objects. Justification and sanctification belong to the same people. Our consecration to God is a deliberate act of faith, arising from hearts of love and gratitude to Christ. Yet, our consecration to God is the fruit and operation of his own grace. The blood and the oil are put on the tip of the right ear, the thumb of the right hand, and the great toe of the right foot of every leper. The message is clear.

> Know ye not that the unrighteous shall not inherit the kingdom of God? Be not deceived: neither fornicators, nor idolaters, nor adulterers, nor effeminate, nor abusers of themselves with mankind, nor thieves, nor covetous, nor drunkards, nor revilers, nor extortioners, shall inherit the kingdom of God. And such were some of you: but ye are washed,

but ye are sanctified, but ye are justified in the name of the Lord Jesus, and by the Spirit of our God ... What? know ye not that your body is the temple of the Holy Ghost which is in you, which ye have of God, and ye are not your own? For ye are bought with a price: therefore glorify God in your body, and in your spirit, which are God's (1 Corinthians 6:9-20).

Many years ago, I heard about a missionary serving the Lord in India. He told of an experience he had while traveling. While walking from one place to another he began to hear something. It sounded like someone groaning. As he made his way to the sound he stepped out into a field. There he saw an old man, a leper, who had been carried out and left to die. The missionary reported ...

As I made my way to that pitiful site, I saw what no words can describe. That poor old man, covered with leprosy and filth, sat on the ground with what were once his hands stretched out, crying in a raspy voice that rattled like that of a dying man, 'Help me! Help me! Won't somebody please help me.'

After telling the story, the missionary said,

As I looked at that dirty, dying leper, I thought to myself, 'If I could stretch my body over his body and put my mouth to his mouth, and draw all of his corruption and death into myself, and breath all of my life and health and strength into him, that would be a true picture of what the Lord Jesus Christ, my blessed Saviour did for me, when he who knew no sin was made sin for me, that I might be made the righteousness of God in him.

1. There is a fountain filled with blood,
Drawn from Immanuel's veins,
And sinners plunged beneath that flood,
Lose all their guilty stains.

2. The dying thief rejoiced to see
That fountain in his day;
And there have I, as vile as he,
Washed all my sins away.

3. Dear dying Lamb! thy precious blood
Shall never lose its power,
Till all the ransomed church of God
Be saved, to sin no more.

4. E'er since, by faith, I saw the stream
Thy flowing wounds supply,
Redeeming love has been my theme,
And shall be till I die.

5. But when this lisping, stammering tongue
Lies silent in the grave,
Then, in a nobler, sweeter song,
I'll sing thy power to save.

William Cowper (1731-1800)

Chapter 37

'A Running Issue'

And the LORD spake unto Moses and to Aaron, saying, Speak unto the children of Israel, and say unto them, When any man hath a running issue out of his flesh, because of his issue he is unclean ... Thus shall ye separate the children of Israel from their uncleanness; that they die not in their uncleanness, when they defile my tabernacle that is among them. This is the law of him that hath an issue, and of him whose seed goeth from him, and is defiled therewith; and of her that is sick of her flowers, and of him that hath an issue, of the man, and of the woman, and of him that lieth with her that is unclean.

Leviticus 15:1-33

Leviticus 15 speaks of corruption from within displayed in 'a running issue' in the flesh. These thirty-three verses of Inspiration, like all other portions of Holy Scripture, were written for our learning, and intended by God the Holy Spirit to be applied to each of us (Romans 15:4).

Most of what I have read from other men on this passage of Scripture treats the 'running issue' in chapter 15 as an uncleanness of far less significance than the leprosy described in chapters 13 and 14. But that is not the case at all. In fact, the corruption and defilement of this running issue portrays, in a way, something even worse than the leprosy of chapters 13 and 14.

The 'running issue' described so graphically in Leviticus 15:1-33 is a sickening, revolting type and picture of something far more sickening and revolting in us. The sin that is in us by nature, the corruption of our vile, base, depraved hearts is a foul, obnoxious puss, constantly oozing from our hearts by which we are defiled, and which defiles everything we touch. This is something worse than the leprosy seen in the flesh. This is the secret, hidden corruption and uncleanness of our hearts.

I am sometimes shocked by the comments people make with regard to the Word of God. Someone once said to me, 'I don't think the Song of Solomon should even be read in public, much less preached from. It would just be too embarrassing'. That was shocking enough, but in my study of Leviticus 15, I read this comment from a man whose writings I often find very profitable.

'We should feel strongly disposed to question the sound judgment and refined taste of a man, who could stand up and read the fifteenth of Leviticus, in the midst of an ordinary congregation. But why? Is it because it is not 'divinely inspired', and, as such, 'profitable?' By no means; but because the generality of persons are not sufficiently spiritual to enter into its pure and holy lessons.'

Such comments are shocking when made by people who rightly esteem Holy Scripture as God's inspired, infallible, inerrant Word. That is the way Roman Catholicism deals with the Word of God. Under the pretence of spirituality and piety, such expressions reveal an utter contempt for Holy Scripture. They reflect the horrid self-righteousness and pride of one who imagines he is so holy and pure that the reading of Holy Scripture might defile his mind!

May God the Holy Spirit, by whom these instructions about 'a running issue' have been preserved for us by divine inspiration, now be our Teacher as we seek to discover the message contained in Leviticus 15. I want to show you five things taught in these thirty-three verses.

Our Corruption
First, let us learn, as we are everywhere taught in Holy Scripture, that our hearts are overflowing cesspools of corruption, constantly oozing foulness, impurity, and uncleanness. If I could be more graphic in describing the corruption of our hearts, I would be. But the Holy Spirit here uses three very graphic pictures by which I hope all who read these lines will be convinced and compelled to cry before God, 'I know that in me (that is, in my flesh,) dwelleth no good thing' (Romans 7:18).

1. The corruption of our hearts is portrayed under the picture of a man with a running issue out of his flesh (vv. 1-15).

This running issue is the equivalent of what we call gonorrhoea. What a proper picture that is of our corrupt hearts! Gonorrhoea is a vile plague contracted by illicit behaviour. It is something you get from someone else. But it becomes a part of you. It is something you try to hide. But the corruption from deep within oozes foulness from your body. That pretty well describes the evil that is in us.

We became sinners by the illicit, criminal, adulterous behaviour of our father Adam. The sin of our father is now ours, so much ours that sin is what we are. Oh, how we try to hide from ourselves, from other people, and from God, what we really are! But the corruption constantly oozes foulness from within.

2. The foulness and corruption of our nature is pictured by the spilling of a man's seed (vv. 16-18).

We are not told whether the seed spilt is spilt in some profane act, or in the conjugal privileges of a husband and wife, or nocturnally. But this entire chapter describes things of the most private nature. I am therefore inclined to think that this particular passage is dealing with that which occurs nocturnally. It speaks of something that is unavoidable. Because it is unavoidable, the natural outflow of a man's body, we commonly associate nothing evil with it.

But the Lord God declares a person unclean who is in anyway touched by a man's seed. Why? The reason is clear. Everything that comes out of a man, everything is corrupt and unclean.

Everything connected with and flowing from our fallen, depraved nature is unclean. The very desires of nature are corrupt. We are so corrupt that even the multiplying of our seed is in sin (Psalm 51:5). If we read this portion of Holy Scripture spiritually and consider it as it is, a picture of the state of our very hearts, the running issues of evil from our hearts are innumerable (Isaiah 1:4-6; Hosea 4:1, 2; Matthew 15:19, 20).

How precious, how sweet, how blessed it is to sinners, conscious of their utter corruption, depravity, and sin, to read and know God's covenant grace that cleanses the soul from all its filthiness (Ezekiel 36:25-27; 1 John 1:7, 9).

3. The uncleanness presented in this chapter is the uncleanness of a woman with an issue of blood (vv. 19-24).

Isaiah declares that all our righteousnesses are as filthy rags, discarded menstrual cloths. Here, our very nature is described as the uncleanness of a woman's discharge during her monthly cycle.

This is the doctrine taught by these three disgusting examples of foulness, examples so repulsive we ordinarily do not discuss them in public, unless the matters are absolutely unavoidable. Everything that comes out of us is corrupt and corrupts everything it touches. Anything touched by the unclean man or woman, whether clothes, bed, saddle, chair, or another person, was thereby made unclean. If a person sneezed in your presence during the time of his uncleanness, though intending you no harm, the spread of his spit in the air, if it touched you, made you unclean.

This is what we are by nature, at heart, in the essence of our being. Unclean! The heart of man is a polluted fountain. Human nature is an overflowing cesspool of uncleanness, constantly oozing corruption. It is defiled and defiling. Awake or asleep, sitting, standing, or lying down, we are defiled and defiling. Our very touch conveys pollution.

This is a humbling lesson to proud creatures that we are. But it is true and faithful. Leviticus 15 is but a mirror reflecting our nature. It leaves us nothing in which to glory. We may boast of our refinement, our moral sense, our dignity, and our goodness; but God calls it as he sees it, uncleanness!

These thirty-three verses of foul ugliness accurately portray what we are by nature, all of us: young and old, men and women, rich and poor, believer and unbeliever (Matthew 15:18, 19; Romans 7:18). Fallen humanity is a polluted fountain. All its streams are polluted. It cannot send forth anything holy, pure, good, or beneficial, only corruption.

God Looks on the Heart
We are all unclean from the inside out, unclean by birth, unclean by nature, unclean at heart. In the light of this fact, the second thing taught in this passage should get the attention of all who are privileged to know it. May God drive it home! 'The Lord looketh on the heart' (1 Samuel 16:7). God is not fooled by our masks. He is not blinded by our disguises. His judgment is not perverted by our bribes. His vision is not clouded by our flattering words. The Lord God sees us as we really are at heart.

Nothing on this earth is more terrifying to a religious hypocrite than this fact. 'The Lord looketh on the heart.' Yet, nothing is more comforting to a believer (John 21:17).

God's Holiness
Third, the Lord God almighty, he who looks upon our foul, corrupt hearts is so infinitely holy and pure that he cannot and will not tolerate any uncleanness (v. 31). If a man or woman who was unclean were allowed to come into the camp of Israel and approach the tabernacle of God, the unclean would make the whole camp and the tabernacle itself unclean. Therefore, the unclean had to stay away from the camp, and were banished from the tabernacle under penalty of death. He who is God, the Triune Jehovah, is of purer eyes than to behold iniquity (Habakkuk 1:13).

If you and I are to enter into heaven at last, if we are to be accepted of the thrice holy God, if we are to be saved, we must be separated from our uncleanness; completely, utterly, absolutely separated from our uncleanness (Psalm 24:3, 4; Isaiah 35:8; 52:1; 60:21; Revelation 21:17; 22:14, 15). Lord, let me not die in my uncleanness!

A Way of Cleansing
Fourth, here in Leviticus 15, this great, infinitely holy Lord God shows us he has made a way for us to be separated from our uncleanness, a way of cleansing. Bless his holy name and rejoice! God himself, he who cannot look upon iniquity, has made a way for unclean sinners to be made clean.

> And when he that hath an issue is cleansed of his issue; then he shall number to himself seven days for his cleansing, and wash his clothes, and bathe his flesh in running water, and shall be clean. And on the eighth day he shall take to him two turtledoves, or two young pigeons, and come before the LORD unto the door of the tabernacle of the congregation, and give them unto the priest: And the priest shall offer them, the one for a sin offering, and the other for a burnt offering; and the priest shall make an atonement for him before the LORD for his issue (Leviticus 15:13-15).

The running water and the atoning sacrifice both speak of Christ's death as the sinners' Substitute. When he was pierced, both blood and water gushed out from his side upon sinful man. The blood was our atonement. The water was our cleansing. It speaks of God the Holy Spirit and the word of his grace by which sinners are made clean experimentally.

There is a way for sinners to be made clean. But the only way we can be made clean from our corruption, the only way we can be made clean from sin before God's all-seeing eye is by being washed in that fountain drawn from Immanuel's veins (Zechariah 12:10-13:1).

The unclean could not make himself clean; but he had to personally wash in the running water and bring the sacrifice God required. So it is with us. We cannot make ourselves clean. We cannot put away one sin. Christ put our sins away. But we must plunge into the fountain of his blood. We must bring God the sacrifice he requires. We must trust the Son of God. And that one who is made clean is restored. No matter how unclean he has been, no matter for how long. He is restored, perfectly and completely restored!

Have you noticed in going through the book of Leviticus, how in the ceremonies of the law, pardon was never immediately conferred? In the cases before us, those who were unclean had to wait for pardon, restoration, and cleansing for seven days. That is not so in the gospel (Mark 1:40, 41). In this gospel day, pardon and cleansing by Christ Jesus is immediate. Restoration is immediate and complete.

Touch of Faith
Here's the fifth thing taught. The only way we can be made whole from our uncleanness is by touching the Lord Jesus Christ. The Holy Spirit gives us a picture that I am sure was intended to be prophetic. He speaks of a woman whose issue of blood lasted a long, long time.

> And if a woman have an issue of her blood many days out of the time of her separation, or if it run beyond the time of her separation; all the days of the issue of her uncleanness shall be as the days of her separation: she shall be unclean. Every bed whereon she lieth all the days of her issue shall be unto her as the bed of her separation: and whatsoever she sitteth upon shall be unclean, as the uncleanness of her separation. And whosoever

toucheth those things shall be unclean, and shall wash his clothes, and bathe himself in water, and be unclean until the even. But if she be cleansed of her issue, then she shall number to herself seven days, and after that she shall be clean. And on the eighth day she shall take unto her two turtles, or two young pigeons, and bring them unto the priest, to the door of the tabernacle of the congregation. And the priest shall offer the one for a sin offering, and the other for a burnt offering; and the priest shall make an atonement for her before the LORD for the issue of her uncleanness (Leviticus 15:25-30).

Matthew, Mark, and Luke were all inspired by God the Holy Spirit to tell us of such a woman, a woman who had an issue of blood for twelve long years. For twelve years, she lived in misery, weakness, isolation, and uncleanness, as much as possible keeping aloof from family and friends lest she spread uncleanness among them. She had wasted all her substance on physicians of no value and was no better for it, but only grew worse.

What a picture of God's grace this woman is. Here is a sinner conscious of her uncleanness and her pollution. She mourns over her weak and wicked heart, trying every remedy anyone can suggest, yet remains sick, sad and broken-hearted. She cannot stop her corruption. Her soul runs out with sin. Then, someone tells her about the Lord Jesus. What a friend! She hears that just the night before he calmed the sea at its height of a storm. She hears how he had gone all the way across the stormy, treacherous sea to save a poor, lost maniac in Gadara. Then, she hears he is passing her way.

She makes her way through the crowd and sees and hears him for herself. She is persuaded that if he will, he can make her clean. She perceives he is himself the very Fountain of Life. She says within herself, 'He is so infinitely full of life and love and power and grace, that if I could but touch the hem of his garment, I would be made whole'. She did, and she was.

She brought no gift. She had spent all her living already on useless physicians. She brought nothing like a cure already begun. She was 'nothing bettered, but rather grew worse'. She had no long-waiting time to show as a plea for her sincerity. She had just come that morning. She offered no repentance. Until now, her regret was that none of her chosen physicians had been able to help her. She made no promises of love. She had no love to promise. She was only now about to see him who alone is worthy of love. She did not even offer a prayer! She just drew near and touched him.

The result was immediate cure. Sin and grace met, uncleanness and cleanness met, and the result was this. The Saviour's virtue went out of him into her and she was made immediately whole and clean. That is as clear a picture of saving faith as is to be found in the book of God.

After presenting her turtle-doves at Jerusalem, how often she might have walked the seashore with Jarius' daughter. Jarius' daughter was born the same year she had begun her issue of blood; and Jarius' daughter was raised from the dead the same day she was healed. I can almost hear them singing the Saviour's praises together as they walked in sweet fellowship. Jarius' daughter saying to her older sister, 'Who healeth all thy diseases?' This woman saying to her younger sister, 'Who redeemeth thy life from destruction?' (Psalm 103:3, 4).

Many years ago, after driving across the country preaching the gospel, Evangelist Rolfe Barnard and his wife stopped in Yellowstone National Park at Old Faithful, the famous geyser. After standing there for a while, Barnard knelt and dipped his handkerchief in the water and washed his face and his dirty hands. Then, he sang a verse of Cowper's great hymn.

> There is a fountain filled with blood,
> Drawn from Immanuel's veins,
> And sinners plunged beneath that flood
> Lose all their guilty stains.

When he had finished the first verse, someone in the small crowd behind him asked, 'Preacher, can we join you? And together they sang to God's praise what I hope you sing to his praise from your heart.

Chapter 38

The Day Of Atonement

And the LORD spake unto Moses after the death of the two sons of Aaron, when they offered before the LORD, and died; And the LORD said unto Moses, Speak unto Aaron thy brother, that he come not at all times into the holy place within the vail before the mercy seat, which is upon the ark; that he die not: for I will appear in the cloud upon the mercy seat. Thus shall Aaron come into the holy place: with a young bullock for a sin offering, and a ram for a burnt offering. He shall put on the holy linen coat, and he shall have the linen breeches upon his flesh, and shall be girded with a linen girdle, and with the linen mitre shall he be attired: these are holy garments; therefore shall he wash his flesh in water, and so put them on ... And he shall take of the congregation of the children of Israel two kids of the goats for a sin offering, and one ram for a burnt offering. And Aaron shall offer his bullock of the sin offering, which is for himself, and make an atonement for himself, and for his house ... Then shall he kill the goat of the sin offering, that is for the people, and bring his blood within the vail, and do with that blood as he did with the blood of the bullock, and sprinkle it upon the mercy seat, and before the mercy seat: ... And this shall be an everlasting statute unto you, to make an atonement for the children of Israel for all their sins once a year. And he did as the LORD commanded Moses.

Leviticus 16:1-34

The most important and most instructive of all the typical ceremonies of the Old Testament was the Day of Atonement. The Day of

319

Atonement foreshadowed and typified the sin-atoning work of our Lord Jesus Christ, our great High Priest, our substitutionary Sacrifice for sin, our Scapegoat, our Altar, and our Mercyseat, through whom alone sinners have access to, and find acceptance with, the holy Lord God.

Mercy and Truth

In order for the holy Lord God to deal with sinful men and women in mercy, grace, and peace, without compromising his character and violating his justice, there had to be a Day of Atonement. A holy, just, and true God could never allow fallen, sinful man to live before him, unless a suitable atonement is made for man's sin. Justice must be vindicated and sin punished. Else God and man can never unite in peace. Therefore, God ordained that a Day of Atonement be observed in Israel once a year, as a picture and pledge of the great Day of Atonement to be accomplished at Calvary by the slaying of the Lamb of God for the redemption of God's elect. And the Lord God gave Moses meticulous, detailed instructions about how the Day of Atonement was to be observed in this chapter sixteen of Leviticus.

1. The Day of Atonement was ordered and initiated by God himself. It was no human invention (Job 33:24; Leviticus 23:27, 28; 25:9).

2. The Day of Atonement was set for a specific time each year (v. 29). 'The seventh month, on the tenth day of the month.' God's great Day of Atonement was set, fixed, appointed, and determined by God himself. Nothing was left to chance. Nothing was left to the will of man.

3. There was only one Day of Atonement each year. Our Lord Jesus was to make only one offering for sin. 'Now once in the end of the world hath he appeared to put away sin by the sacrifice of himself ... Christ was once offered to bear the sins of many' (Hebrews 9:26, 28).

4. The sacrifices offered on the Day of Atonement were only typical. They could never put away sin (Hebrews 10:1-4).

5. All those typical sacrifices were fulfilled by Christ and have ceased (Hebrews 10:11-14, 18). 'There is no more offering for sin'.

6. Everything done on the Day of Atonement was done for a specific, chosen people and resulted in God's blessing (Leviticus 16:17, 24, 30).

The High Priest

The atonement was made by a specifically appointed man, Aaron, the great high priest of Israel. 'Thus shall Aaron come into the holy place:

320

with a young bullock for a sin offering, and a ram for a burnt offering' (v. 3). Israel's great high priest was a divinely chosen man. And the Lord Jesus Christ, our great High Priest, is a divinely chosen man, the God-man (Psalm 89:19; Isaiah 42:1-4).

On the Day of Atonement, the high priest was robed in garments of humility. 'He shall put on the holy linen coat, and he shall have the linen breeches upon his flesh, and shall be girded with a linen girdle, and with the linen mitre shall he be attired: these are holy garments; therefore shall he wash his flesh in water, and so put them on' (v. 4). On this great day Aaron laid aside his gorgeous, glorious garments and put on the garments of humility. So, too, our great High Priest, the Son of God was clothed with humility when he came to make atonement for sin as our dear Saviour (John 1:14; 2 Corinthians 8:9; Philippians 2:5-11).

> Thus shall Aaron come into the holy place: with a young bullock for a sin offering, and a ram for a burnt offering. He shall put on the holy linen coat, and he shall have the linen breeches upon his flesh, and shall be girded with a linen girdle, and with the linen mitre shall he be attired: these are holy garments; therefore shall he wash his flesh in water, and so put them on (Leviticus 16:3, 4).
>
> And Aaron shall offer his bullock of the sin offering, which is for himself, and make an atonement for himself, and for his house (Leviticus 16:6).
>
> And Aaron shall bring the bullock of the sin offering, which is for himself, and shall make an atonement for himself, and for his house, and shall kill the bullock of the sin offering which is for himself: And he shall take a censer full of burning coals of fire from off the altar before the LORD, and his hands full of sweet incense beaten small, and bring it within the veil (Leviticus 16:11, 12).

Israel's high priest was a ceremonially holy man. Though Aaron was a sinner like us, he had to be ceremonially clean to act as God's high priest. To approach God as the high priest of his people, Aaron had to have in type, and Christ had to have in reality, these four things ...

1. Personal cleanness: Aaron bathed his flesh in water, portraying our Lord Jesus Christ who had no sin and did no sin. Our Lord Jesus

was holy, harmless, undefiled, and separate from sinners. 'In him was no sin.' He 'did no sin'. He 'knew no sin'.

2. Holy garments: Aaron's garments on the Day of Atonement were linen garments, garments woven by the hands of a man. They portrayed Christ's righteous obedience to God as our Representative (John 17:4).

3. Divine approval: The incense smoke pictured Christ as a sweet-smelling savour to God, both in his merit and efficacy as our accepted sacrifice, and in his unceasing intercession for us (Romans 8:34). We are accepted because God approves of our Substitute, and us in him

4. Blood atonement: Aaron could not come into the holy of holies without blood. And Christ could not obtain redemption and remission for us without his own blood (Hebrews 9:12, 22).

And there shall be no man in the tabernacle of the congregation when he goeth in to make an atonement in the holy place, until he come out, and have made an atonement for himself, and for his household, and for all the congregation of Israel' (Leviticus 16:17).

In all his work on the Day of Atonement Aaron acted alone. No one else was present. No one but Aaron was allowed into the holy of holies. Aaron was alone with God to make atonement for the people. The whole nation was entrusted to one representative man. The nation rested on the shoulders of one man. If that man succeeds, the nation shall live. If he fails, the nation must die! So it was with our all-glorious Christ (Psalm 69:20; Isaiah 63:3-5). In all things, Aaron, the high priest, typified our great, sin-atoning High Priest, the Lord Jesus Christ.

The Slain Goat

The Holy Spirit gives us a picture of the goat slain as a victim for a sin-offering to God. This goat represents the Lord Jesus as the Lamb of God. Christ is both our High Priest and our Sacrificial Lamb, the victim not of man's will, but of God's justice!

And he shall take of the congregation of the children of Israel two kids of the goats for a sin offering, and one ram for a burnt offering (Leviticus 16:5).

And he shall take the two goats, and present them before the LORD at the door of the tabernacle of the congregation. And Aaron shall cast lots upon the two goats; one lot for the LORD, and the other lot for the scapegoat. And Aaron shall bring the goat upon which the LORD'S lot fell, and offer him for a sin offering. But the goat, on which the lot fell to be the scapegoat, shall be presented alive before the LORD, to make an atonement with him, and to let him go for a scapegoat into the wilderness (Leviticus 16:7-10).

This sacrificial lamb was an innocent victim, because no sinful man could ever make atonement for sin (Psalm 49:7). The sacrifice was taken from among the people, because divine justice must be avenged upon man and compensation must be made by man, for man sinned. The Lord's sacrifice was chosen and ordained by God (Proverbs 16:33). So, our Lord Jesus Christ was chosen and ordained of God to be his Sacrifice for us (Acts 2:23; 4:26-28; 13:29; 1 Peter 1:18-21). Like the sacrifice here in Leviticus 16:15, our dear Saviour was slain by divine order as a sacrifice for sin (Zechariah 13:7).

Thus, the Lord Jesus Christ, our Substitute, the Lamb of God, was sacrificed for us. He was a sacrifice of infinite merit, a sacrifice for a particular people, 'The Israel of God', and a sacrifice that actually made atonement and put away sin (Galatians 3:13, 14; Hebrews 10:11-14).

The blood of this goat was sprinkled on the mercy seat seven times.

And he shall take of the blood of the bullock, and sprinkle it with his finger upon the mercy seat eastward; and before the mercy seat shall he sprinkle of the blood with his finger seven times. Then shall he kill the goat of the sin offering, that is for the people, and bring his blood within the veil, and do with that blood as he did with the blood of the bullock, and sprinkle it upon the mercy seat, and before the mercy seat (Leviticus 16:14, 15).

The blood was on the mercy seat as a covering to hide God's broken law, a propitiation to cancel the sins of the people, and a reconciliation to unite God and his chosen ones. That is what Christ, our Sacrifice, the true Mercyseat, is to his redeemed (Romans 3:24-26).

Having died in our place, the Lord Jesus Christ entered into heaven and offered to the holy Lord God the merits of his own precious blood, thereby obtaining eternal redemption for us. His sacrifice was perfect and complete. His sacrifice was final and accepted. Christ's blood made a way of access for sinners to come to God. His sacrifice made certain that all for whom he died would come to him (Hebrews 9:12; 10:9-22). The sacrifice of our dear Saviour, the Lord Jesus Christ, is a sacrifice of infinite, perpetual merit and efficacy before God (Romans 8:32-35; 2 Corinthians 5:17-21; 1 John 2:1, 2).

The Lost Scapegoat
Both the high priest and the slain victim represent the Lord Jesus, who is our Saviour, our Priest and our Sacrifice, the Lamb of God sacrificed for us. Now, let us look at the lost scapegoat.

And when he hath made an end of reconciling the holy place, and the tabernacle of the congregation, and the altar, he shall bring the live goat: And Aaron shall lay both his hands upon the head of the live goat, and confess over him all the iniquities of the children of Israel, and all their transgressions in all their sins, putting them upon the head of the goat, and shall send him away by the hand of a fit man into the wilderness: And the goat shall bear upon him all their iniquities unto a land not inhabited: and he shall let go the goat in the wilderness (Leviticus 16:20-22).

The scapegoat is a picture of the complete removal of our sins by Christ. The first goat, the Lord's goat, the slain victim, gave us a picture of the atonement. The second goat, the scapegoat, gives us a picture of the result of the atonement. Both are very instructive and show, first, transfer and imputation of our sins to Christ (v. 21; Isaiah 53:4-10; 2 Corinthians 5:21), and second, removal of our sins by Christ (v. 22).

Because Christ Jesus, the Lamb of God, died in the place of his elect, suffering all the terror and wrath of God's holy law and justice against our sins, the guilt of sin is gone (Hebrews 10:14), the punishment of sin is gone (Romans 8:1), the memory of sin (insofar as God's holy law and justice is concerned) is gone (Jeremiah 50:20), and sin itself is gone, for chosen, redeemed sinners in eternal union with the Son of God (1 Peter 4:1, 2; 1 John 3:5).

Who is a God like unto thee, that pardoneth iniquity, and passeth by the transgression of the remnant of his heritage? he retaineth not his anger forever, because he delighteth in mercy. He will turn again, he will have compassion upon us; he will subdue our iniquities; and thou wilt cast all their sins into the depths of the sea. Thou wilt perform the truth to Jacob, and the mercy to Abraham, which thou hast sworn unto our fathers from the days of old (Micah 7:18-20).

The People's Response

At the close of the day, when the work of atonement was finished, Aaron took off his linen garments and put on his glorious, gorgeous garments again. Then, on the basis of atonement made, he lifted up his hands and blessed the people (Numbers 6:24-26). When the people saw what God did for them, they had a threefold response. They repented. 'Ye shall afflict your souls' (v. 29). They rested. 'Ye shall do no work at all' (v. 29). They rejoiced (Leviticus 25:9). The jubilee trumpet sounded the sweet proclamation of liberty to all who were bound, and, typifying the gospel trumpet of today, the clearing of all debt, and complete restoration of all that was lost.

The Act of Faith

May God the Holy Ghost give us now, and day by day, and hour by hour, as long as we live in this world, grace to perform the act of faith symbolized in verses 21 and 22. Lay your hands upon Christ the Scapegoat's head, confess your sins, and watch them go away.

Charlotte Elliott was a bitter woman. Her health was completely broken at thirty years of age and her disabilities had hardened her. Her parents were believers but she was full of bitterness.

On one occasion the famous Swiss preacher and hymn writer, Cesar Malan, was a guest in her parents' home. As her father and Malan spoke to one another about the goodness, mercy, grace, and love of God in Christ, Charlotte erupted in a violent outburst, in front of their honoured guest, saying, 'If God loved me, he would not have treated me this way'! Her parents left the room in embarrassment but the preacher stayed behind. 'Charlotte', he said, 'you are tired of yourself; and you are holding to your hate and anger because you have nothing else to hold to'. She replied, 'What, then, is your cure?' He answered, 'The very Christ you despise'. Charlotte softened a bit. 'What shall I do?' she asked. 'Come to Christ. Come to the Saviour, with all your fear and shame and pride. Ask him to have mercy on you and give you his grace.' She replied, 'Just come to Jesus Christ as I am?' 'Yes', he said, 'just as you are'.

Fourteen years later, Charlotte Elliott wrote her spiritual biography in one of the most well-known hymns of the English language.

> Just as I am, without one plea,
> But that Thy blood was shed for me,
> And that Thou bidst me come to Thee,
> O Lamb of God, I come, I come.
>
> Just as I am, and waiting not
> To rid my soul of one dark blot,
> To Thee whose blood can cleanse each spot,
> O Lamb of God, I come, I come.
>
> Just as I am, though tossed about
> With many a conflict, many a doubt,
> Fightings and fears within, without,
> O Lamb of God, I come, I come.
>
> Just as I am, poor, wretched, blind;
> Sight, riches, healing of the mind,
> Yea, all I need in Thee to find,
> O Lamb of God, I come, I come.
>
> Just as I am, Thou wilt receive,
> Wilt welcome, pardon, cleanse, relieve;
> Because Thy promise I believe,
> O Lamb of God, I come, I come.
>
> Just as I am, Thy love unknown
> Hath broken every barrier down;
> Now, to be Thine, yea Thine alone,
> O Lamb of God, I come, I come'.

Chapter 39

The Scapegoat

And the LORD spake unto Moses after the death of the two sons of Aaron, when they offered before the LORD, and died; And the LORD said unto Moses, Speak unto Aaron thy brother, that he come not at all times into the holy place within the vail before the mercy seat, which is upon the ark; that he die not: for I will appear in the cloud upon the mercy seat. Thus shall Aaron come into the holy place: with a young bullock for a sin offering, and a ram for a burnt offering. He shall put on the holy linen coat, and he shall have the linen breeches upon his flesh, and shall be girded with a linen girdle, and with the linen mitre shall he be attired: these are holy garments; therefore shall he wash his flesh in water, and so put them on ... And he shall take of the congregation of the children of Israel two kids of the goats for a sin offering, and one ram for a burnt offering. And Aaron shall offer his bullock of the sin offering, which is for himself, and make an atonement for himself, and for his house ... Then shall he kill the goat of the sin offering, that is for the people, and bring his blood within the vail, and do with that blood as he did with the blood of the bullock, and sprinkle it upon the mercy seat, and before the mercy seat: And he shall make an atonement for the holy place, because of the uncleanness of the children of Israel, and because of their transgressions in all their sins: and so shall he do for the tabernacle of the congregation, that remaineth among them in the midst of their uncleanness. And there shall be no man in the tabernacle of the congregation when he goeth in to make an atonement in the holy place, until he come out, and have made an atonement for himself, and for his household, and for all the congregation of Israel ... And this shall be an everlasting statute unto you, to make an atonement for the children of Israel for all their sins once a year. And he did as the LORD commanded Moses.

Leviticus 16:1-34

Types in the Bible are like our Lord's parables. They are intended to show us one specific thing, not many things, just one thing. Types usually stand on just two legs: their natural, historic meaning and their spiritual, allegorical meaning. They are bipeds, not centipedes. Adam was a type Christ our Covenant Head and Representative (Romans 5:12-21). That does not mean that there was some hidden, mystical, spiritual significance about everything we know of Adam. Sarah and Hagar and their sons, Isaac and Ishmael, were an allegory about law and grace (Galatians 4). That does not mean that everything they said, did, and experienced were typical. David's slaying of Goliath was a clear, instructive type of Christ's conquering sin and Satan in the accomplishment of our salvation. But it is unnecessary to try to find something spiritually significant in the sling he used or the five smooth stones he carried in his hand.

When we try to find more in the type than is intended by the Spirit of God in giving it we make a mess of it and cause more confusion than understanding. Yet, the types and metaphors of Holy Scripture are given to us by the Spirit of God as instructive pictures of grace and salvation in Christ. We should cherish them and seek his grace and enlightenment to understand them and profit by them.

On the day of atonement Aaron sacrificed the bullock and made atonement for himself. Then, he sacrificed the Lord's goat to make atonement for Israel. Then, God's priest was required to symbolically impute the sins of Israel to the scapegoat.

> And when he hath made an end of reconciling the holy place, and the tabernacle of the congregation, and the altar, he shall bring the live goat: And Aaron shall lay both his hands upon the head of the live goat, and confess over him all the iniquities of the children of Israel, and all their transgressions in all their sins, putting them upon the head of the goat, and shall send him away by the hand of a fit man into the wilderness: And the goat shall

bear upon him all their iniquities unto a land not inhabited: and he shall let go the goat in the wilderness (Leviticus 16:20-22).

This scapegoat beautifully portrays our dear Saviour, the Lord Jesus Christ. As the slain goat portrays him as the Lamb of God sacrificed for our sins, the scapegoat portrays him as the sacrifice accepted. This scapegoat is a picture of the removal of our sins by Christ. The first goat, the Lord's goat, the slain victim, was a picture of the atonement. The second goat, the scapegoat, gives us a picture of sin's removal, the taking away of our sins, the result of Christ's effectual atonement.

The Lost Scapegoat
We saw this previously but let me repeat what we see in these pictures. First, we see the transfer and imputation of our sins to Christ (v. 21; Isaiah 53:4-6; 2 Corinthians 5:21). Next, this scapegoat portrays the removal of our sins by Christ (v. 22). When he died at Calvary, under the wrath of God, and having satisfied God's justice, our blessed Saviour, the Lord Jesus Christ, took away our sins. He removed from his redeemed the guilt of sin (Hebrews 10:14). He took from us the curse of the law, and all punishment for sin (Romans 8:1). He even removed the memory of sin (Psalm 32:1, 2; Jeremiah 50:20; Micah 7:18-20; Romans 4:8; 1 Peter 4:1, 2).

A Fit Man
With all the sins of Israel made his, the scapegoat was taken away by a fit man. That fit man is Christ, too, God our Saviour, the Judge of all the earth who must do right, the very justice of God. The scapegoat is taken beyond the camp, beyond all sight, beyond the track of man, to the far borders of an uninhabited land. Released, it disappears into rocks and thickets of an uninhabited desert. Unseen, unknown, forgotten, it departs from mortal view and is now buried in oblivion's land.

Full Pardon
There is no brighter picture of the full pardon of all sin in Christ. Christ bore the accursed load of all my sin and guilt away, as far away as the east is from the west; and God's all-seeing eye cannot find it. Oh, precious tidings! Oh, heart-cheering revelation! Oh, wondrous grace!

God the Spirit, by the testimony of the gospel, proclaims this good news and confirms it in the soul by the gift of life and faith in Christ. God has cast our sins, all our sins, behind his back and into the depth of the sea of infinite forgetfulness. Infinite separation has separated our transgressions from us. Christ, our Scapegoat, has borne our iniquities away (Psalm 103:12; Isaiah 38:17; Micah 7:19). Blessed be his name forever, they are gone. 'Ye know that he was manifested to take away our sins; and in him is no sin' (1 John 3:5).

Can we recover what the ocean buries? No line can reach to the unmeasured depths. It has sunk downward, never to rise. Deep waters hide it; and it must be hidden. Such is the grave of sin. Our Scapegoat drowned it in a fathomless abyss. The word is sure. 'Thou wilt cast all their sins into the depths of the sea'!

Can that be seen to which the eye of omniscience is blind? Are objects visible, which are behind your back? Our Scapegoat has cast our sins behind God's back. He has blotted out, as a thick cloud, our transgressions (Isaiah 44:22), never to be found (Jeremiah 50:20).

Never was forgiveness of all our sins by our God more rightly declared than when the Lord God sovereignly forced the false prophet Balaam to declare it in Numbers 23.

> God is not a man, that he should lie; neither the son of man, that he should repent: hath he said, and shall he not do it? or hath he spoken, and shall he not make it good? Behold, I have received commandment to bless: and he hath blessed; and I cannot reverse it. He hath not beheld iniquity in Jacob, neither hath he seen perverseness in Israel: the LORD his God is with him, and the shout of a king is among them. God brought them out of Egypt; he hath as it were the strength of an unicorn. Surely there is no enchantment against Jacob, neither is there any divination against Israel: according to this time it shall be said of Jacob and of Israel, What hath God wrought (Numbers 23:19-23).

Not Remembered

That which Christ has taken away, blotted out, and removed by his precious, sin-atoning blood, God cannot and will not remember. He promised, 'I will remember their sin no more' (Jeremiah 31:34).

Do you need comfort? Drink deeply from this stream of joy. Lay down in this green pasture of delight. Your sins, so many, so vile, and so hateful, your Scapegoat has taken away. All your blemishes, defects, iniquities, transgressions, and sins are forever gone! And God your Saviour, God who cannot lie says to you, 'Thou art all fair, my love; there is no spot in thee' (Song of Solomon 4:7). With joy, every believing sinner may confidently sing with Isaac Watts ...

> Not all the blood of beasts
> On Jewish altars slain,
> Could give the guilty conscience peace,
> Or wash away the stain.
>
> But Christ, the heavenly Lamb,
> Takes all our sins away;
> A sacrifice of nobler name,
> And richer blood than they.
>
> My faith would lay her hand
> On that dear head of Thine,
> While like a penitent I stand,
> And there confess my sin.
>
> My soul looks back to see
> The burdens Thou didst bear,
> When hanging on the cursed tree,
> And hopes her guilt was there.
>
> Believing, we rejoice
> To see the curse remove;
> We bless the Lamb with cheerful voice,
> And sing His bleeding love'.

Chapter 40

The Blood

And the LORD spake unto Moses, saying, Speak unto Aaron, and unto his sons, and unto all the children of Israel, and say unto them; This is the thing which the LORD hath commanded, saying, What man soever there be of the house of Israel, that killeth an ox, or lamb, or goat, in the camp, or that killeth it out of the camp, And bringeth it not unto the door of the tabernacle of the congregation, to offer an offering unto the LORD before the tabernacle of the LORD; blood shall be imputed unto that man; he hath shed blood; and that man shall be cut off from among his people: To the end that the children of Israel may bring their sacrifices, which they offer in the open field, even that they may bring them unto the LORD, unto the door of the tabernacle of the congregation, unto the priest, and offer them for peace offerings unto the LORD. And the priest shall sprinkle the blood upon the altar of the LORD at the door of the tabernacle of the congregation, and burn the fat for a sweet savour unto the LORD. And they shall no more offer their sacrifices unto devils, after whom they have gone a whoring. This shall be a statute forever unto them throughout their generations. And thou shalt say unto them, Whatsoever man there be of the house of Israel, or of the strangers which sojourn among you, that offereth a burnt offering or sacrifice, And bringeth it not unto the door of the tabernacle of the congregation, to offer it unto the LORD; even that man shall be cut off from among his people. And whatsoever man there be of the house of Israel, or of the strangers that sojourn among you, that eateth any manner of blood; I will even set my face against that soul that eateth blood, and will cut him off from among his people. For the life of the flesh is in the blood: and I have given it to you upon the altar to make an atonement for your souls: for it is the blood that maketh an atonement for the soul. Therefore I said unto the children of Israel, No soul of you shall eat blood, neither shall any stranger that sojourneth among you eat blood. And whatsoever man there be of the children of Israel, or of the strangers that sojourn among you, which hunteth and catcheth any beast or fowl that may be eaten; he shall even pour out the blood thereof, and cover it with dust. For it is the life of all flesh; the blood of it is for the life thereof: therefore I said unto the children of Israel, Ye shall eat the blood of no manner of flesh: for the life of all flesh is the blood thereof: whosoever eateth it shall be cut off. And every soul that eateth that which died of itself, or that which was torn with beasts, whether it be one of your own country, or a stranger, he shall both wash his clothes, and bathe himself in water, and be unclean until the even: then shall he be clean. But if he wash them not, nor bathe his flesh; then he shall bear his iniquity.

Leviticus 17:1-16

There is a scarlet thread running through the Word of God, like the cord Rahab hung out of her window. That scarlet thread, by which the 66 books of Holy Scripture are bound together, a scarlet thread that unifies everything written upon the pages of Inspiration, is the blood, the precious blood of Christ.

Constant Theme of Scripture
The Scriptures speak constantly about the blood. It is written in the books of the law, 'the life of the flesh is in the blood'. God told Moses, 'the blood shall be to you for a token'. He said, 'when I see the blood, I will pass over you'. When the high priest went into the holy of holies on the Day of Atonement, he went in with blood. No one can come to God without blood atonement.

When our Lord Jesus instituted the Lord's Supper, he took the cup of wine, held it before his disciples and said, 'this is the blood of the New Testament, shed for many for the remission of sins'. In Hebrews 9:22, we read, 'without shedding of blood is no remission'. That makes the blood a matter of immense importance.

These days, it is common for preachers, churches, theologians, and hymnwriters to say as little as possible about the blood. We have become so educated, refined, and sophisticated that talking about blood is considered improper, unsophisticated and crude. But it is still true that 'without shedding of blood is no remission'. But God declares the blood of his dear Son a matter of infinite importance and something indescribably precious (Hebrews 9:12; 1 Peter 1:18-21).

> E'er since by faith I saw the stream
> Thy flowing wounds supply,
> Redeeming love has been my theme,
> And shall be till I die!

The shedding of Christ's precious blood was and is absolutely essential to the saving of our souls. Let us ever cherish the blood of Christ as that which is precious above all things. As nothing in heaven or earth is as precious to the Triune God as the blood of Christ, let nothing be so precious to us as our Saviour's blood!

Fenced in by God
In this chapter of the book of Leviticus, God put a fence around the blood, setting it apart from all other things and protecting it. This chapter has nothing to do with the imaginary sanctity of animal life or with the ordinary hunting and killing of animals, or with possible health risks involved in eating red meat, or even eating red meat rare. Leviticus 17, like all the rest of this Inspired Volume, is all about the gospel. It is all about Christ. The law of God here speaks about animals killed and offered as sacrifices to God. As such, they are sacrifices pointing to and typifying our Lord Jesus Christ and his sacrifice of himself for our sins.

There are three important lessons revealed in this chapter. We must learn them. Without the knowledge of these things, we will never understand the book of God, the gospel of God, or the work of God.

1. All worship except the worship of God through the blood atonement of the Lord Jesus Christ is idolatry, here called 'making sacrifices unto devils' (v. 7).

2. Atonement is in the blood.

3. In this gospel day, this day of grace, God's Altar can be found anywhere.

Idolatry
All worship except the worship of God through the blood atonement of the Lord Jesus Christ is idolatry. Christ is the Way. There is no other. Christ is the Truth. There is no other. Christ is the Life. There is no other. Will we ever learn this? Christ is the Door. There is no other. All who attempt to come in some other way are thieves and robbers, thieves who would rob God of his glory. God will not tolerate them. Hear what he says about this in verses 1-10. First,

> And the LORD spake unto Moses, saying, Speak unto Aaron, and unto his sons, and unto all the children of Israel, and say unto them; This is the thing which the LORD hath commanded, saying, What man soever there be of the house of Israel, that killeth an ox, or lamb, or goat, in the camp, or that killeth it out of the camp (Leviticus 17:1-3).

The idolatry Israel learned from the heathen, following the counsel of Baal, was mixing the worship of God with the worship of idols, sacrificing to devils (Numbers 25:3; Deuteronomy 32:17). Blood rituals, often involving human sacrifice and drinking of blood, have always been a part of heathen religion. The children of Israel were here forbidden such base practices.

The law given here is a law regarding the worship of God. After giving the law regarding the Day of Atonement, the Lord God gave this commandment to the children of Israel. It was a commandment he required every Israelite and every stranger who sojourned among them to observe. All who refused to do so were to be cut off from among the people of God, put out of the camp, and banished from the church and people of God.

Remember the context. The Lord God had just finished declaring to Israel how they were to observe the Day of Atonement every year on the tenth day of the seventh month. This was made as an everlasting statute, a statute to be observed throughout the Old Testament era (Leviticus 16:29-34).

Typical of Christ
Of course, everything required in this statute was typical of, and portrayed, our Lord Jesus Christ in his great work of redemption. In

those last verses of chapter 16, we are given a picture of the believer's experience of grace. On that great and glorious day, the high priest made atonement for the holy sanctuary, the tabernacle of the congregation, the altar, for himself, for the priests, and for all the people of the congregation of the Lord. It is a picture of particular redemption. By the sin-atoning blood of Christ, God's Israel has been cleansed, made clean from all sin before the Lord God (1 John 3:5).

Those for whom atonement was made were required to afflict their souls and do no work at all 'by a statute forever' (Leviticus 16:29, 31). That is a picture of faith in Christ.

That great day, when Israel saw redemption accomplished and sin put away by God's sacrifice, was 'a sabbath of rest ... by a statute forever'. It is a picture of the blessed rest of faith. Not only do we cease from our works, we rest in him who has done all for us. In those days of legal, ceremonial worship they had a sabbath day, but no sabbath rest. In this gospel day we have no sabbath day, but in Christ we have the blessed sabbath rest of faith in him (Hebrews 4:9-11).

It is in this context that God gives his commandment regarding blood. I repeat, he is not talking about the sanctity of animal life, he is talking about worship, the sanctity of his throne, the sanctity of Christ's precious blood, and the sanctity of Christ our sin-atoning Sacrifice. He is not talking about diet. He is talking about worship. He specifically mentions the killing of an ox, a goat, or a lamb, because those were the animals Israel was required to sacrifice at his altar, by which Israel worshipped him.

> And bringeth it not unto the door of the tabernacle of the congregation, to offer an offering unto the LORD before the tabernacle of the LORD; blood shall be imputed unto that man; he hath shed blood; and that man shall be cut off from among his people (Leviticus 17:4).

This is a prohibition against idolatry. God did not make a prohibition against hunting, eating the meat of animals, or wearing the skins of animals. The prohibition was against idolatry, sacrificing to devils. All false religion is sacrificing to devils. All will-worship is sacrificing to devils. All freewill and works religion is sacrificing to devils. Verse 4 is talking about the offering of a sacrifice in the open field, despising the ordinance of God.

> To the end that the children of Israel may bring their sacrifices, which they offer in the open field, even that they may bring them unto the LORD, unto the door of the tabernacle of the congregation, unto the priest, and offer them for peace offerings unto the LORD (Leviticus 17:5).

All men naturally assume it is perfectly acceptable to worship God as we please. Surely God would not object to a man offering a sacrifice to him in the open field. What could be wrong with that? It could not hurt, could it?

Yes, it could. It was an act of idolatry to offer a sacrifice somewhere else. It was despising God's altar, God's priest, God's sacrifice and God's Word. It was an act of defiance, revealing a man's contempt for God. It was nothing less than robbing the Lord Jehovah of his glory, and ascribing and giving to Satan that which was due to God alone. It is called sacrificing to devils (Deuteronomy 32:17).

A man might ask, 'But can I not offer a sacrifice in one place as well as another? May I not come to God any way I wish so long as I am sincere?' The answer is this: God promised to meet his people on the mercy seat, between the cherubs (Exodus 25:22). To offer sacrifice anywhere else showed contempt for God. He calls it devil worship, an act of the worst form of adultery in the world, whoring after other gods.

> And they shall no more offer their sacrifices unto devils, after whom they have gone a whoring. This shall be a statute forever unto them throughout their generations (Leviticus 17:7).

The lesson is plain. There is one place God has appointed where he will meet sinners. That place is the cross of Christ, the antitype of the brazen altar. There alone God's claims are met. To reject this meeting-place is to bring down judgment upon ourselves. It is to trample underfoot the blood of Christ, make the blood of God's dear Son a common thing, do despite to the Spirit of grace, and defy the just claims of God, arrogating to ourselves a right to life which we have forfeited by sin. God meets sinners on his Mercyseat, the crucified Christ!

Only the precious blood of Christ is acceptable to God. Only his sin-atoning blood is 'a sweet savour unto the Lord'.

> And the priest shall sprinkle the blood upon the altar of the LORD at the door of the tabernacle of the congregation, and burn the fat for a sweet savour unto the LORD (Leviticus 17:6).

The blood and the fat belonged to God. Our blessed Saviour fully recognised this. As a man (the God-man, our Mediator) he surrendered his life to God the Father. He voluntarily walked to the place of sacrifice and there gave up and laid down his life, poured out his precious blood, eye for eye, tooth for tooth, life for life. The fragrant sweet incense of his infinitely excellent sacrifice ascended up to God and for us satisfied his holy, infinite justice. Blessed, blessed Saviour! The incense of your precious blood shall never cease to prevail with God for us!

> Dear dying Lamb, Thy precious blood
> Shall never lose its power,
> 'Til all the ransomed church of God,
> Be saved to sin no more!

God required that the blood of the sacrifice offered anywhere except upon his altar be imputed to the man who shed it. Though it was only the blood of an animal, yet being shed as a sacrifice for man and typical of the blood of Christ shed for us at Calvary, the blood was sacred and precious to God. That blood he required to be offered to none but himself, and offered only upon his appointed altar by his appointed priest, and at his appointed time. Anyone who defied his sacrifice was to be punished as a murderer, because in God's sight idolatry is as equally heinous as murder (Isaiah 66:3).

All false worship is idolatry. Will we ever learn this lesson? God will not be worshipped except upon his Altar, through his Priest, by the merits of his Sacrifice the Lord Jesus Christ!

> And they shall no more offer their sacrifices unto devils, after whom they have gone a whoring. This shall be a statute forever unto them throughout their generations. And thou shalt say unto them, Whatsoever man there be of the house of Israel, or of the

strangers which sojourn among you, that offereth a burnt offering or sacrifice, and bringeth it not unto the door of the tabernacle of the congregation, to offer it unto the LORD; even that man shall be cut off from among his people. And whatsoever man there be of the house of Israel, or of the strangers that sojourn among you, that eateth any manner of blood; I will even set my face against that soul that eateth blood, and will cut him off from among his people (Leviticus 17:7-10).

The idolater was to be cut off from the congregation, not merely excommunicated from the church of God, deprived of the privileges of his house, but even put to death. He was guilty of blood,[12] that is, of death. Therefore, he was to be put to death, either by the hand of the congregation (when the offence was known by men), or by the immediate hand of God (v. 10), as Uzza was when he touched the ark.

The application to us in this gospel age is clear. We must worship God in the way he has prescribed and cut ourselves off from all idolatry and all idolaters (Leviticus 17:5; 2 Corinthians 6:14-7:1; Revelation 18:4). We must come to God trusting Christ alone (Ephesians 1:3-7; 1 Corinthians 1:30; Philippians 3:3).

Atonement in the Blood

For the life of the flesh is in the blood: and I have given it to you upon the altar to make an atonement for your souls: for it is the blood that maketh an atonement for the soul. Therefore I said unto the children of Israel, No soul of you shall eat blood, neither shall any stranger that sojourneth among you eat blood. And whatsoever man there be of the children of Israel, or of the strangers that sojourn among you, which hunteth and catcheth any beast or fowl that may be eaten; he shall even pour out the

---

[12] He who was guilty of blood was guilty of the blood of God's sacrifice, Christ. That blood was imputed to him. Therefore he was cut off (Hebrews 10:29), because he 'bringeth it not unto the door of the tabernacle of the congregation, to offer an offering unto the LORD before the tabernacle of the LORD; blood shall be imputed unto that man; he hath shed blood; and that man shall be cut off from among his people' (Leviticus 17:4).

blood thereof, and cover it with dust. For it is the life of all flesh; the blood of it is for the life thereof: therefore I said unto the children of Israel, Ye shall eat the blood of no manner of flesh: for the life of all flesh is the blood thereof: whosoever eateth it shall be cut off. And every soul that eateth that which died of itself, or that which was torn with beasts, whether it be one of your own country, or a stranger, he shall both wash his clothes, and bathe himself in water, and be unclean until the even: then shall he be clean. But if he wash them not, nor bathe his flesh; then he shall bear his iniquity' (Leviticus 17:11-16).

I call your attention to verse 11. Understand verse 11 and the rest of the chapter is plain enough. Look at this eleventh verse line by line.

'For the life of the flesh is in the blood.' That is stated three times in verses 11 and 14. It is not hard to figure this out. No Blood, No Life! Blood nourishes and sustains the whole of life physically. When an animal was sacrificed upon the altar of God, a life was sacrificed. When the Lord Jesus Christ poured out his life's blood upon the cursed tree for us, he gave himself. Giving his blood, he gave his life! His perfect life was sacrificed. His righteous life, a perfect righteousness, was sacrificed. A man's perfect life was sacrificed. God was sacrificed (Acts 20:28; Galatians 2:20, 21; 1 John 3:16).

These blood sacrifices in the Old Testament signified much, much more than most ever imagine. The pouring out of Christ's precious blood displays the very same thing as those sacrifices did.

The sacrifice of a life declares that life belongs to God. Life is God's prerogative. He kills and he makes alive, both physically and spiritually. He is the Lord of life. Life belongs to him. He gives it and he takes it, as it pleases him. He declares, 'I am the Lord, the God of all flesh' (Jeremiah 32:27). Man must not feast upon that which is God's. The sacrifice was not made to satisfy man, but to satisfy God. The blood of the animal slain was either to be brought to God's altar or poured out like water upon the ground, returning to God.

Coming to God, by faith in Christ, we acknowledge we have robbed God of our lives. We have taken what properly belongs to God and consumed it upon our own lusts. Bowing to him, we consecrate our lives to him, gladly taking Christ as our Lord. We lose our lives to our

Saviour. That is what faith is in its essence. It is giving up my life to Christ (1 Corinthians 6:19, 20).

The sacrifice of life declares the horrid enormity of our sin. What a horrible, infinitely evil thing sin must be if God, ever good, ever gracious, ever merciful, ever loving, should require the life of his own darling Son to put it away.

'For the life of the flesh is in the blood: and I have given it to you upon the altar.' Look yonder to Calvary. Behold, Christ's precious blood poured out upon God's altar. Hear the Lord God speak. He says, 'I have given it to you'. What a blessed word of grace! Christ is mine!

The Lord Jesus gave his life's blood for us to God the Father; but the Lord God has given his Son's precious blood to us.

We are justified by the blood (Romans 5:9).

The wrath and justice of God has been satisfied by the blood (Romans 3:24-26).

We are reconciled to God by the blood (Ephesians 2:13).

Every blessing of grace comes to us through the blood (Colossians 1:14, 20).

Our consciences are purged from the guilt of sin by the blood (Hebrews 9:12-14).

We have access to God by the blood (Hebrews 10:19, 20).

We are sanctified by the blood (Hebrews 13:12).

We are cleansed by the blood (1 John 1:7).

We will, one day soon, stand before the throne of God perfectly purified by the blood (Revelation 7:14).

We will triumph over sin and death, over hell and the grave by the blood (Revelation 12:11).

We will glorify Christ forever, singing and praising him because of the blood (Revelation 5:9).

The Token of the Blood
The Lord God says, 'the blood shall be to you for a token'. It is a token God has given us, by which he constantly speaks to us.

> And the blood shall be to you for a token upon the houses where ye are: and when I see the blood, I will pass over you, and the plague shall not be upon you to destroy you, when I smite the land of Egypt (Exodus 12:13).

I trust God's seeing of the blood more than I trust my seeing it. It is God's seeing the blood that is the token of grace. The blood is a token of God's willingness to save sinners, a token of assured acceptance, a token of God's infinite love. Ancient love! Intense love! Almighty love! Unlimited love! Immutable love! Persevering love! Free love! Indestructible love! Saving love! God's word to his chosen is, 'When I see the blood, I will pass over you'.

Blood's Efficacy
Read Leviticus 17:11 again. 'For the life of the flesh is in the blood: and I have given it to you upon the altar to make an atonement for your souls: for it is the blood that maketh an atonement for the soul'. The blood of our Lord Jesus Christ was shed at Calvary for one specific purpose. 'To make atonement for your souls.' Will it do the job? Is it enough? Let us see.

'For the life of the flesh is in the blood: and I have given it to you upon the altar to make an atonement for your souls: for it is the blood that maketh an atonement for the soul.' Yes, the blood of Christ poured out upon the cursed tree accomplished precisely what God intended. His blood made atonement for his people. Just as the blood of the paschal lamb made atonement for the whole congregation of Israel, so the blood of Christ our Passover, who was sacrificed for us, made atonement for all God's Israel (Romans 5:6-11).

Atonement is God's gift to his people. This atonement is in the blood, and only in the blood. 'It is the blood that maketh an atonement for the soul.' It is not the blood and something else. The word is most explicit. It attributes atonement exclusively to the blood. 'Without shedding of blood is no remission' (Hebrews 9:22). It was the death of Christ that rent the veil. It is 'by the blood of Jesus' we have 'boldness to enter into the holiest'. 'We have redemption through his blood, the forgiveness of sins' (Ephesians 1:7; Colossians 1:14). Christ 'made peace by the blood of his cross'. 'Ye who were afar off are made nigh by the blood of his cross.' 'The blood of Jesus Christ his Son cleanseth us from all sin' (1 John 1:7). All the saints of God have 'washed their robes and made them white in the blood of the Lamb'.

The blood of Christ is the foundation of everything and the fountain of everything. 'It is the blood that maketh an atonement for the soul.' This is conclusive. Only in this way can God be both 'a just God and a

Saviour'. Only by the blood can he be both just and the Justifier of all who believe.

Read the Bible. From Genesis through Revelation, you will find that the only ground upon which God almighty can or will deal with sinners in grace is through 'the blood that maketh atonement for the soul'. The blood of Christ is revealed as the only foundation of righteousness.

As it is the only foundation upon which we can come to God, so it is the only fountain by which grace flows to us. We get pardon, peace, life, and righteousness, all by the blood, and nothing but the blood.

Precious, precious, precious beyond expression is the blood of Christ! 'It is the blood that maketh atonement for the soul.' The blood of Christ is so precious in God's sight that he will allow nothing to be added to or mingled with it. 'The life of the flesh is in the blood, and I have given it to you upon the altar, to make an atonement for your souls: for it is the blood that maketh an atonement for the soul.'

God's Altar

In this gospel day, in this day of grace, God's Altar can be found anywhere. Before the law was given at Sinai, before the worship of God was established at the tabernacle in the wilderness and then the temple in Jerusalem, during the Patriarchal Age, men who believed God raised up altars to him wherever they were when God met them. There they worshipped (Genesis 8:20; 12:7, 8; 13:4, 18; 22:9-13; 26:25; 28:18; 35:1).

Then, after the giving of the law, God directed his worshippers to worship him only at one altar, pointing to Christ our Altar.

But in this gospel day, this day of grace, the Lord God declares that incense and a pure offering is to be offered to him in every place (Malachi 1:11), because his Israel, his elect people, is found everywhere and our Altar is Christ. I bid you, come to God's Altar where you are, every day, throughout the day, and worship God by his Sacrifice, through his High Priest, upon his Altar, the Lord Jesus Christ (Hebrews 13:10-15).

Chapter 41

'Abominable Customs'

And the LORD spake unto Moses, saying, Speak unto the children of
Israel, and say unto them, I am the LORD your God ... Therefore shall
ye keep mine ordinance, that ye commit not any one of these
abominable customs, which were committed before you, and that ye
defile not yourselves therein: I am the LORD your God.

Leviticus 18:1-30

We all have a choice to make. Will I save my life and thereby lose it;
or will I lose my life to Christ and thereby save it? Our Saviour declares
plainly and repeatedly, 'Whosoever shall save his life shall lose it: but
whosoever will lose his life for my sake, the same shall save it' (Luke
9:24; Matthew 10:39; 16:25; Mark 8:35; Luke 17:33; John 12:25).
Leviticus 16 speaks about Christ's atonement, the redemption of his
people. Chapter 17 shows us the preciousness of our Saviour's blood.
Here, in Leviticus 18, God our Saviour reveals and insists upon his
claims as our Lord. Here we are taught, as we are taught throughout
Holy Scripture, that faith in Christ involves the total surrender of our
lives to the will and rule of our Lord Jesus Christ. 'Whosoever shall
save his life shall lose it: but whosoever will lose his life for my sake,
the same shall save it.'

The Lord God knew the children of Israel, like us, were like chaff,
easily blown here and there, easily swayed, prone to every abominable

imagination, susceptible to every form of idolatry, and quick to embrace the traditions, customs, and habits of the world around them.

We all like to think of ourselves as independent, free thinking men and women, people of conviction who cannot be swayed by the opinions and approval or disapproval of others. But that is not the way things really are. We are more easily moved by the opinions of others than dandelion seeds are scattered by the wind.

It is precisely this weakness of our depraved, sinful nature that necessitated the eighteenth chapter of Leviticus. In anticipation of the trials and temptations Israel would face in the wilderness and in anticipation of the trials and temptations they would face in the land of Canaan, the Lord God here instructed and commanded his people not to practise or even participate in the 'abominable customs' they learned in Egypt, and forbids them to embrace and practise those same 'abominable customs' that would surround them in Canaan.

The subject of Leviticus 18 is the 'abominable customs' of men and women who do not know our God. Here the Lord our God teaches us we must refuse to walk in the ways of the world and walk in his way. We must refuse to practise the doings of the world and do his judgments and keep his ordinances.

Remember, the law of God was given to Israel alone. It was never given to the nations around them. It was given only to Israel. Even in the Old Testament, the law was not given to Gentiles, but to Jews only. The Lord God called the ways, the doings, the customs, the statutes, and the religions of the Egyptians and the Canaanites wickedness. But he never gave his law to them. Why? The answer should be obvious.

The statutes we read in Leviticus 18 were given to point us to Christ, our Lord and Redeemer. They are statutes of divine worship given to God's covenant people, based upon a covenant relationship, and motivated by covenant grace.

Objection Silenced
As we read through these 30 verses of Inspiration, we will see in this chapter how the Lord God deals plainly with the most personal decisions of a man's life, and the most intimate relationships of his home and family, demanding that his will be obeyed and his honour maintained in these intimate areas of life.

We resent anyone's interference in these matters. We do not want anyone telling us who we can marry, how we are to live our lives, what we may or may not do, especially in the privacy of our homes and bedrooms. We resent anyone's intrusion into these matters. We all do.

But our heavenly Father silences any possible objection to his intrusion in the most tender, loving manner possible. He prefaces his instructions, his demands, by reminding us of his sovereign mercy, love, and grace toward us, thereby silencing every possible objection to that which he here requires. Six times he reminds us, 'I am the LORD (Jehovah) your God' (vv. 1, 4, 5, 6, 21, 30). With those words, he says, 'I have loved you. I chose you. I redeemed you. I brought you up out of Egypt. I destroyed your enemies. I am bringing you into Canaan. I have the right, and I have earned the right to rule your life.'

Faith in Christ
We fulfil the law of God only by faith in Christ.

> And the LORD spake unto Moses, saying, Speak unto the children of Israel, and say unto them, I am the LORD your God. After the doings of the land of Egypt, wherein ye dwelt, shall ye not do: and after the doings of the land of Canaan, whither I bring you, shall ye not do: neither shall ye walk in their ordinances. Ye shall do my judgments, and keep mine ordinances, to walk therein: I am the LORD your God. Ye shall therefore keep my statutes, and my judgments: which if a man do, he shall live in them: I am the LORD (Leviticus 18:1-5).

First, the Lord God, our God and Saviour, commands us to strictly and conscientiously avoid the deeds and the ordinances of both the Egyptians and the Canaanites. In doing so, it is obvious our Lord is here demanding that as his people we must constantly guard against the horrid tendency of our flesh to yield to the corrupt ways and 'doings' and the corrupt religion and 'ordinances' of the world.

Rather, we are to observe his ordinances, his statutes, and his judgments. We are to live by the rule of his Word.

Our God says, 'Which if a man do, he shall live in them'. Does that mean that sinners can save themselves by obeying God's law? Of course not! But it does mean this. If you and I worship God in the way he reveals in his Word, in the way of his ordinances, statutes, and judgments, trusting Christ alone for all righteousness and redemption, we shall live forever in him. That is exactly the meaning of Romans 3:31, 1 John 3:23, 24, and 1 John 5:2-5. Read Romans 9.

> What shall we say then? That the Gentiles, which followed not after righteousness, have attained to righteousness, even the righteousness which is of faith. But Israel, which followed after the law of righteousness, hath not attained to the law of righteousness. Wherefore? Because they sought it not by faith, but as it were by the works of the law. For they stumbled at that stumblingstone; As it is written, Behold, I lay in Sion a stumblingstone and rock of offence: and whosoever believeth on him shall not be ashamed. Brethren, my heart's desire and prayer to God for Israel is, that they might be saved. For I bear them record that they have a zeal of God, but not according to knowledge. For they being ignorant of God's righteousness, and going about to establish their own righteousness, have not submitted themselves unto the righteousness of God. For Christ is the end of the law for righteousness to everyone that believeth (Romans 9:30-10:4).

Complete Dominion

Now the Lord starts to get very personal. This is a detailed prohibition of incest. Here we see that God demands universal dominion over our lives. This generation of religious infidels is ignorant of it, but faith in Christ involves the surrender of our lives to the Son of God, bowing to him as Lord. To trust Christ is to lose your life to him (Matthew 10:39).

> None of you shall approach to any that is near of kin to him, to uncover their nakedness: I am the LORD. The nakedness of thy father, or the nakedness of thy mother, shalt thou not uncover: she is thy mother; thou shalt not uncover her nakedness. The nakedness of thy father's wife shalt thou not uncover: it is thy father's nakedness. The nakedness of thy sister, the daughter of thy father, or daughter of thy mother, whether she be born at home, or born abroad, even their nakedness thou shalt not

uncover. The nakedness of thy son's daughter, or of thy daughter's daughter, even their nakedness thou shalt not uncover: for theirs is thine own nakedness. The nakedness of thy father's wife's daughter, begotten of thy father, she is thy sister, thou shalt not uncover her nakedness. Thou shalt not uncover the nakedness of thy father's sister: she is thy father's near kinswoman. Thou shalt not uncover the nakedness of thy mother's sister; for she is thy mother's near kinswoman. Thou shalt not uncover the nakedness of thy father's brother, thou shalt not approach to his wife: she is thine aunt. Thou shalt not uncover the nakedness of thy daughter in law: she is thy son's wife; thou shalt not uncover her nakedness. Thou shalt not uncover the nakedness of thy brother's wife: it is thy brother's nakedness. Thou shalt not uncover the nakedness of a woman and her daughter, neither shalt thou take her son's daughter, or her daughter's daughter, to uncover her nakedness; for they are her near kinswomen: it is wickedness. Neither shalt thou take a wife to her sister, to vex her, to uncover her nakedness, beside the other in her life time. Also thou shalt not approach unto a woman to uncover her nakedness, as long as she is put apart for her uncleanness (Leviticus 18:6-19).

The Lord forbids incestuous unions of parents and children, step-parents and step-children, siblings, step-siblings, aunts and uncles, with nephews and nieces, cousins, even step-cousins and in-laws. Though polygamy was tolerated (Matthew 19:8), a man was forbidden to marry sisters, lest they vex one another as Leah did Rachel. Temporary considerations were allowed prior to this.[13] But by this law, the Lord established a family order of stability and peace.

God calls the practice of these evils 'horrid wickedness'. Andrew Bonar rightly observed that ...

The transgression of this law is reckoned one of the marks of Israel's great corruptions (Ezekiel 22). Every sensual feeling

---

[13] Obviously, Cain and Abel had no such law as this. They married their sisters. Noah's grandchildren were not under such a law. They married either siblings or cousins. Abraham had no such law. He married Sarah, his half-sister.

must be subordinated to the Lord's will; and men must live as the Lord appoints. Their happiness consists in letting their soul flow out in the channel of the Lord's will.

Verse 20 forbids adultery. 'Moreover thou shalt not lie carnally with thy neighbour's wife, to defile thyself with her.' And verse 21 prohibits idolatry, which is the root cause of all moral corruption in society. 'And thou shalt not let any of thy seed pass through the fire to Molech, neither shalt thou profane the name of thy God: I am the LORD.'

This is the first time we read about this horrid evil in Holy Scripture. But it is frequently mentioned after this. Following the counsel of Balaam, the children of Israel, while claiming to worship God, dedicated their children to Molech, walking them through rows of fire in solemn ceremony to Jehovah, and even offered their children as sacrifices to Molech in the name of Jehovah!

In verse 22, the Lord God stamps his judgment upon homosexuality and every form of sodomy. 'Thou shalt not lie with mankind, as with womankind: it is abomination.' Verse 23 expands this denunciation to include that which is the child of homosexuality, bestiality. 'Neither shalt thou lie with any beast to defile thyself therewith: neither shall any woman stand before a beast to lie down thereto: it is confusion'. These acts of wickedness are the result of divine judgment and the cause of it.

> Defile not ye yourselves in any of these things: for in all these the nations are defiled which I cast out before you: And the land is defiled: therefore I do visit the iniquity thereof upon it, and the land itself vomiteth out her inhabitants ... (For all these abominations have the men of the land done, which were before you, and the land is defiled;) That the land spue not you out also, when ye defile it, as it spued out the nations that were before you (Leviticus 18:24-28).

In divine judgment, in judicial reprobation, the Lord God justly leaves men and women to their own lusts. Sodomy, bestiality, paedophilia, abortion and infanticide are the result of will-worship, the idolatry of freewill, works religion (Romans 1:18-32). Then, when men and women have filled the cup of their wrath, God casts them into hell, spewing them out of the earth they have defiled!

Damning Idolatry

If you and I follow the way of the wicked, the earth will soon spew us out into hell as well. If we follow the way of Balaam, if we receive the mark of the beast, if we embrace the religion of antichrist, the worship of man, the worship of self, will-worship, worshipping the work of our own hands, even if we call it worshipping Christ, we shall be damned.

> For whosoever shall commit any of these abominations, even the souls that commit them shall be cut off from among their people. Therefore shall ye keep mine ordinance, that ye commit not any one of these abominable customs, which were committed before you, and that ye defile not yourselves therein: I am the LORD your God (Leviticus 18:29, 30).
>
> And we know that the Son of God is come, and hath given us an understanding, that we may know him that is true, and we are in him that is true, even in his Son Jesus Christ. This is the true God, and eternal life. Little children, keep yourselves from idols (1 John 5:20, 21).
>
> Keep yourselves in the love of God, looking for the mercy of our Lord Jesus Christ unto eternal life (Jude 1:21).

Lessons

What does God the Holy Spirit intend for us to learn from this chapter? What is its purpose? Why was it written? Here are five things to help you to walk with God and honour him in the totality of your being.

1. The Lord God almighty is God indeed. Because he is God, he has the absolute right as God to rule you and me, to control our thoughts and our deeds. Is it not lawful for him to do with his own what he will? Because he is God, he and he alone determines and declares both the evil and the good (Isaiah 45:7).

2. The Word of God alone is our rule of life. This book and this book alone is and must be authoritative in the church and kingdom of God (2 Timothy 3:16, 17).

3. The heart of man is a thoroughly corrupt cesspool of iniquity. The horrible, shameful crimes against God and man described in this chapter are so basic to our nature that God speaks of them here as the defilement of the nations.

Such is the vileness of the human heart that all these forms of depravity were anticipated by the Lord God who knows the heart. He knows the hell that is in that poisoned spring. Men see another commit some atrocity and say, 'I cannot understand how a person can do that'. But the Lord God, looking on the hearts even of his own people Israel, knew they would be tempted to the most abominable evils imaginable. They, like us, were tempted by the pressures of the society around them and their own lusts, to incorporate into the worship and service of God the sacrifice of their children for their own sins and approval of the basest of deeds in the name of moral freedom and religious tolerance.

4. I pray God will show us the wonder of this fourth great lesson! This Holy Lord God declares himself to be our God because of his redeeming mercy, love, and grace. He begins and ends the chapter like this 'I am the Lord (Jehovah) your God' (vv. 2, 30).

Because he is the Lord our God by his great grace, by his blood atonement, because he loved us, because he chose us, because he redeemed us, because he saved us, he has the right to possess us and rule us totally. And blessed be his name, we want him to do so (1 Corinthians 6:9-11, 19, 20).

5. The Lord God demands that we take his side. There is a way that seems right to man; but it is the way of cursing, everlasting cursing. There is a way despised by men; but it is the way of blessing, everlasting blessing (Deuteronomy 11:26-29; Joshua 24:14, 15).

But the hour cometh, and now is, when the true worshippers shall worship the Father in spirit and in truth: for the Father seeketh such to worship him. God is a Spirit: and they that worship him must worship him in spirit and in truth (John 4:23, 24).

We are the circumcision, which worship God in the spirit, and rejoice in Christ Jesus, and have no confidence in the flesh (Philippians 3:3).

Chapter 42

Holiness

And the LORD spake unto Moses, saying, Speak unto all the congregation of the children of Israel, and say unto them, Ye shall be holy: for I the LORD your God am holy ... Ye shall do no unrighteousness in judgment, in meteyard, in weight, or in measure. Just balances, just weights, a just ephah, and a just hin, shall ye have: I am the LORD your God, which brought you out of the land of Egypt. Therefore shall ye observe all my statutes, and all my judgments, and do them: I am the LORD.

Leviticus 19:1-37

This is God's word to his elect. This is God's word to his elect in every place, in every generation. 'Ye shall be holy: for I the Lord your God am holy.' Because the Lord our God is holy, he requires that we also be holy. 'Follow peace with all men, and holiness, without which no man shall see the Lord' (Hebrews 12:14). May God the Holy Ghost, whose Word we have before us, be our Teacher and graciously inscribe these words upon our hearts. 'Ye shall be holy: for I the Lord your God am holy.'

A Declaration

First and foremost, this is a blessed declaration of grace. The Lord God here declares to his chosen, covenant people that they shall be a holy people, not partially holy, not mostly holy, but entirely holy, absolutely holy, perfectly holy. This is not a recommendation, but a declaration. It is a declaration of grace made to a specific people.

The word 'holy' has two distinct meanings. Both definitions of the word must be understood and applied here. First, to be holy is to be separate, distinct, peculiar, separated, and severed from all others. Second, to be holy is to be pure or purified, sanctified.

The Lord God here declares to his Israel, to all who stand before him as his covenant people, 'You shall be separate, distinct, peculiar, separated and severed from all others, pure and purified before me, sanctified'. We know this is the intent and meaning of this statement by comparing scripture with scripture (Exodus 19:6; Leviticus 11:44; 20:7, 26; 1 Thessalonians 4:7).

The Lord God almighty, by the work of his sovereign, free, distinguishing grace, takes such things as us, such things as he finds in the dung heap of fallen humanity and makes them holy. He made us holy by blood atonement, by the obedience of our Lord Jesus Christ unto death (Hebrews 10:9-14; 1 Corinthians 6:9-11, 19, 20; Titus 2:11-14; 1 Peter 2:7-10). He makes every chosen, redeemed sinner holy by the new birth, imparting to them a holy nature born of God that cannot sin (2 Corinthians 5:17; Ephesians 4:24; Colossians 1:27; 2 Peter 1:4; 1 John 3:5, 9). And in the last day the Lord God will bring us into the perfection of holiness in resurrection glory. 'Then shall I be satisfied, when I awake with thy likeness' (Psalm 17:15).

A Call
'Ye shall be holy: for I the Lord your God am holy.' This is also a call to holiness.

> Speak unto all the congregation of the children of Israel, and say unto them, Ye shall be holy: for I the LORD your God am holy (Leviticus 19:2)
> Therefore shall ye observe all my statutes, and all my judgments, and do them: I am the LORD (Leviticus 19:37).

God here calls us to holiness, godliness, and righteous behaviour in our daily lives. He calls you and me to be separate, distinct, peculiar, separated, and severed from all others, pure and purified before men in our conduct. We know that this is also the intent and meaning of these words because they are so used by the Spirit of God in the inspired writings of both the apostle Paul (1 Thessalonians 4:1-7) and the apostle Peter (1 Peter 1:13-16).

Specific Details

In Leviticus 19 the holy Lord God calls for you and me to be holy as we live in this world; and he does not leave it for us to decide what he means. In these 37 verses, he tells us specifically how we are to live in this world as his holy people.

I can hear some say, 'But, Pastor, these verses are found in Old Testament law, and we are not under the law'. You are right on both counts. Yet the fact we are free from the law in Christ does not mean we are without law, not at all. The believer's law, the believer's rule of life is the whole revelation of God in Holy Scripture. That which is here written is addressed to you and me and is just as authoritative as Ephesians 1 or Romans 9. True, it must be understood and applied in gospel terms, but it must be both understood and applied.

Here the Lord God tells us specifically how we are to live in this world in a way that honours God. We please God by faith in Christ. Without faith it is impossible to please him (Hebrews 11:6). But do not imagine that if we believe in Christ it does not matter how we live. God the Holy Ghost tells us in 1 Thessalonians 4:1 that we 'ought to walk and to please God'.

When our daughter, Faith, began to go out with friends, I almost always said to her before she left the house, 'Sweetheart, don't ever forget who you are and whose you are', often adding, 'Everything you say and do reflects on your parents, our church family, the gospel we believe, and God our Saviour'. I say the same thing to every heaven born soul. 'Don't ever forget who you are and whose you are.' As Paul put it in 1 Corinthians 10:31, 'Whether therefore ye eat, or drink, or whatsoever ye do, do all to the glory of God'.

13 Statements

Are you interested in the honour and glory of God? Would you like to know how to live in this world for the honour of God? Here are thirteen statements about this thing called holiness. If you and I would live in this world for the glory of God, we must ...

1. Give honour to whom honour is due. 'Ye shall fear every man his mother, and his father, and keep my sabbaths: I am the LORD your God' (Leviticus 19:3; Romans 13:7).

We have a saying, 'Charity begins at home'. We need to learn that reverence, respect, and honour begin at home, too. How desperately this generation needs to learn this. Children, honour your parents. Obey, yes; but there is more to honour than obedience. Honour is on the inside and shows itself on the outside. Men and women, honour your parents. Parents, if they are truly parents, are more than the people through whom you were born. They are people who have nourished, nurtured, and trained you in the knowledge of Christ.

This command extends to all divinely appointed authority. In general, the Lord commands us to simply be respectful to our superiors.

> Thou shalt rise up before the hoary head, and honour the face of the old man, and fear thy God: I am the LORD (Leviticus 19:32).

2. If we would live in this world for the honour of our God, we must worship him. In verses 3-8 the Lord deals with outward things. Though true worship is essentially an inward, heart work, where there is heart worship there is also outward, public worship.

> Ye shall fear every man his mother, and his father, and keep my sabbaths: I am the LORD your God. Turn ye not unto idols, nor make to yourselves molten gods: I am the LORD your God. And if ye offer a sacrifice of peace offerings unto the LORD, ye shall offer it at your own will. It shall be eaten the same day ye offer it, and on the morrow: and if ought remain until the third day, it shall be burnt in the fire. And if it be eaten at all on the third day, it is abominable; it shall not be accepted. Therefore everyone that eateth it shall bear his iniquity, because he hath profaned the hallowed thing of the LORD: and that soul shall be cut off from among his people (Leviticus 19:3-8).

In verse 3 the Lord God tells us to keep his sabbaths. Without question, the Old Testament sabbath days were pictures of faith in Christ, pictures of resting our souls in and upon Christ. But those Old

Testament sabbaths were divinely appointed times of worship. If we would live in this world for the honour of God, we must never neglect the worship of God in his house (Hebrews 10:25).

In verse 4, the Lord God tells us to worship him as God alone. We must not turn aside to idols. We must allow nothing to take the place of our God in our hearts' affection. Set your affection on Christ (1 Corinthians 10:14, 15; Colossians 3:1-3).

Verse 5 demands that our worship of our God be willing and free. Yes, the Lord God demands that we worship him, but we must do so because we want to, willingly (2 Corinthians 8:12; 9:7).

Yet, our worship of God must be in accordance with his Word. Our ordinances of divine worship must be divinely prescribed, and the divine order observed (vv. 6-8). In verse 30 we read, 'Ye shall keep my sabbaths, and reverence my sanctuary: I am the LORD'. All sacrifices were to be willing sacrifices. All that was given was to be used immediately. Every sacrifice, be it great or small, was to be treated as a 'hallowed thing', as what belonged to God. Thus, it is today. If we would worship God we must worship him in the way he prescribes in his Word, observing his ordinances as he prescribes and adhering faithfully to the doctrine of his Word.

3. If we would live in this world for the honour of our God, we must avoid covetousness and greed and ever care for those in need.

> And when ye reap the harvest of your land, thou shalt not wholly reap the corners of thy field, neither shalt thou gather the gleanings of thy harvest. And thou shalt not glean thy vineyard, neither shalt thou gather every grape of thy vineyard; thou shalt leave them for the poor and stranger: I am the LORD your God (Leviticus 19:9, 10).

We are not the owners of anything. We are God's stewards. We ought never get all we can for ourselves. I do not suggest, and the Scriptures do not teach that believers should not acquire wealth or that believers should not enjoy the wealth they obtain. Abraham, David, Solomon, Lydia, and Philemon were all wealthy believers. But as God's people, we are his stewards in his house. As such, we are to use that with which he entrusts us for his glory, according to his will, for the benefit of others. In a sentence, we ought to constantly go out of our way to be kind, generous, thoughtful, and caring, especially to those who are most likely to be neglected and abused.

> And if a stranger sojourn with thee in your land, ye shall not vex him. But the stranger that dwelleth with you shall be unto you as one born among you, and thou shalt love him as thyself; for ye were strangers in the land of Egypt: I am the LORD your God (Leviticus 19:33, 34).

Every needy soul we see ought to remind us that when we were strangers in need, our blessed Boaz provided us with 'handfuls of purpose', by which he brought us to himself (Ruth 2:8, 9, 16). Always deal with the poor and needy, the spiritually poor and physically poor, and the spiritually needy and physically needy, in mercy. In doing so, you may bring some of our Redeemer's Ruths to him.

4. Living for the glory of God means living in honesty, dealing with people honestly.

> Ye shall not steal, neither deal falsely, neither lie one to another. Thou shalt not defraud thy neighbour, neither rob him: the wages of him that is hired shall not abide with thee all night until the morning. Ye shall do no unrighteousness in judgment, in meteyard, in weight, or in measure. Just balances, just weights, a just ephah, and a just hin, shall ye have: I am the LORD your God, which brought you out of the land of Egypt (Leviticus 19:11, 13, 35, 36).

God's grace comes to sinners through, with, by, and in Christ by just weights and balances (Romans 3:24-26; 2 Corinthians 5:17-21; Galatians 3:13, 14). Let us, like our God, deal with all in justness and honesty, with mercy and grace.

5. Let us, for the glory of our great God cherish and reverence his name.

> And ye shall not swear by my name falsely, neither shalt thou profane the name of thy God: I am the LORD (Leviticus 19:12).

6. Honouring God means treating men and women with respect and tenderness, rather than with the harsh, beastly cruelty that is so wickedly natural to our proud hearts (v. 14).

It might seem that this verse should be properly addressed to children, but never to adults. It is, however, addressed to you and me, from whom our children learn how to be mean and cruel.

> Thou shalt not curse the deaf, nor put a stumblingblock before the blind, but shalt fear thy God: I am the LORD (Leviticus 19:14).

How base, depraved, and cruel we are. God does not build a dam where there is no water. He gives us this word because we need to hear it. Take the command as it stands. Do not curse or get upset with a person because he is deaf, and you have to repeat everything you say to him. He cannot hear you. Do not put a stumbling block before a blind man so that you can laugh at his hurt.

Take the command spiritually. Do not curse the deaf. You were just as deaf not very long ago. Do not put a stumbling block before the blind. A stumbling block is anything put between the sinner and the Saviour, any hindrance by which sinners might be kept from Christ (Romans 14:13; Deuteronomy 27:18).

He who fears God honours all men, showing neither contempt for the poor nor preference for the mighty.

> Ye shall do no unrighteousness in judgment: thou shalt not respect the person of the poor, nor honour the person of the mighty: but in righteousness shalt thou judge thy neighbour (Leviticus 19:15).

7. If we would honour our God, we must learn to bridle our tongues.

> Thou shalt not go up and down as a talebearer among thy people: neither shalt thou stand against the blood of thy neighbour: I am the LORD (Leviticus 19:16).

Slanderers, gossips, talebearers are ungodly people (Proverbs 11:13; 1 Timothy 5:13). Anytime gossip enters your ear, let your ear be its grave. To stand against the blood of a man is to falsely accuse him of evil, if even by insinuation. 'Speak evil of no man' (Titus 3:2).

8. If we would live in this world for the honour of our God, we must love our neighbours as ourselves.

> Thou shalt not hate thy brother in thine heart: thou shalt in any wise rebuke thy neighbour, and not suffer sin upon him. Thou shalt not avenge, nor bear any grudge against the children of thy people, but thou shalt love thy neighbour as thyself: I am the LORD (Leviticus 19:17, 18).

This is not, as many would like, a command to point out your brother's sins, but just the opposite. The Lord is telling us here to rebuke our brother's sin by refusing to let it affect us. The words, 'and not suffer sin upon him', could be translated, 'that thou bear not sin for him'. If you bear a grudge for an evil done to you, you are party to the evil done. Leave it alone. God will avenge his own. The thing for us to do is love the offender (Proverbs 20:22; Romans 12:20, 21; 14:19).

The coals of fire we are taught to heap upon those who would do us wrong are not coals of judgment, but coals of grace, by which the hearts of our enemies are melted. Our Saviour preached this doctrine in his Sermon on the Mount.

Nothing is more gruelling to our flesh than the exercise of kindness and love toward those who hate us. But if we would honour our Saviour and serve the souls of men, we must conquer the hearts of our enemies the same way that Christ conquered our hearts, by heaping the coals of mercy, grace, and love on their heads.

9. For the honour of our God, we must distinguish things that differ.

> Ye shall keep my statutes. Thou shalt not let thy cattle gender with a diverse kind: thou shalt not sow thy field with mingled seed: neither shall a garment mingled of linen and woollen come upon thee'[14] (Leviticus 19:19).

---

[14] John Gill wrote, 'This was to lead Israel to the simplicity and sincerity of religion, and of all the parts and doctrines of the law and Gospel in their distinct kinds, as faith and works, to mingle which together in our justification before God is forbidden; or rather to teach the saints not to mix with the men of the world, in evil conversation, or

Do not wear the woollen garment of nature, works-righteousness, and free-will salvation, with the linen garments of grace. We must not mingle the worship of God with idolatry (2 Corinthians 6:14-7:1).

10. Living for the honour of our God means that we confess our sins and find forgiveness through Christ's sin-atoning blood (1 John 1:9-2:2).

And whosoever lieth carnally with a woman, that is a bondmaid, betrothed to an husband, and not at all redeemed, nor freedom given her; she shall be scourged; they shall not be put to death, because she was not free. And he shall bring his trespass offering unto the LORD, unto the door of the tabernacle of the congregation, even a ram for a trespass offering. And the priest shall make an atonement for him with the ram of the trespass

---

in superstitious worship; to which may be added, to show that spiritual regeneration is not partly of corruptible and partly of incorruptible seed, nor partly of the will of man, and partly of the will of God; nor partly of the power of man, and partly of the power of God, but wholly of the Spirit and grace of God.

As to the mystical sense, the 'field' may represent the church of God, which is not an open but an enclosed field, enclosed by the grace of God, and separated from others by it, well manured and cultivated by the Spirit of God, and through the word and ordinances, as means, in which all manner of fruit and flowers grow, and is the property of Christ (see Song of Solomon 4:12-14 and Matthew 13:44); the seed may signify the word or doctrine of the Gospel, sown by the ministers of it, skilfully and plentifully, which should be pure and unmixed, not contradictory, nor inconsistent, but all of a piece; the doctrines of it, as those of election, justification, peace, pardon, and salvation, are to be represented, not as partly of works and partly of grace, but as entirely of the grace of God through Christ: or good and bad men may be signified by the mingled seed; good men, who are made so by the grace of God, and are the good seed, or the good ground which receives it, which hear the word, understand it, and bring forth fruit; bad men, such as are of bad principles and practices, these are not to be mixed together in a church state; bad men are neither to be received nor retained.

The design of this, as of the other, seems to be in general to caution against unnatural lusts and impure mixtures, and all communion of good and bad men, and particularly against joining the righteousness of Christ with the works of men, in the business of justification: Christ's righteousness is often compared to a garment, and sometimes to fine linen, clean and white; and men's righteousness to filthy rags (Revelation 19:8; Isaiah 64:6); which are by no means to be put together in the said affair; such who believe in Christ are justified by the obedience of one and not of more, and by faith in that obedience and righteousness, without the works of the law (Romans 5:19; 3:28; 4:6); to join them together is needless, disagreeable, and dangerous.'

offering before the LORD for his sin which he hath done: and the sin which he hath done shall be forgiven him (Leviticus 19:20-22).

11. Living for God's glory means that his will and his honour takes priority over everything else.

And when ye shall come into the land, and shall have planted all manner of trees for food, then ye shall count the fruit thereof as uncircumcised: three years shall it be as uncircumcised unto you: it shall not be eaten of. But in the fourth year all the fruit thereof shall be holy to praise the LORD withal. And in the fifth year shall ye eat of the fruit thereof, that it may yield unto you the increase thereof: I am the LORD your God. Ye shall not eat anything with the blood: neither shall ye use enchantment, nor observe times (Leviticus 19:23-26).

12. The honour of the Lord our God demands that we have nothing to do with, give no approval to, and studiously avoid the practices of the idolatry and the superstitions of the world.

Ye shall not eat anything with the blood: neither shall ye use enchantment, nor observe times. Ye shall not round the corners of your heads, neither shalt thou mar the corners of thy beard. Ye shall not make any cuttings in your flesh for the dead, nor print any marks upon you: I am the LORD (Leviticus 19:26-28).

All these things were pagan religious rites, by which ignorant barbarians hoped to gain great strength, or good luck, or drive away evil spirits. We are not to act like the heathen or give credibility to them.

Regard not them that have familiar spirits, neither seek after wizards, to be defiled by them: I am the LORD your God (Leviticus 19:31).

13. If we would honour our God, we must teach and train our children to worship and serve him.

Do not prostitute thy daughter, to cause her to be a whore; lest the land fall to whoredom, and the land become full of wickedness (Leviticus 19:29).

This is prohibition against giving one's daughter to be a prostitute for Baal. It is also a prohibition against leaving a child to her own devices, without restraint, as Eli did his sons.

By these comprehensive commands, the Lord God teaches us how we are to live in this world as his elect. We must continually sanctify ourselves just as our Lord Jesus sanctified himself for us (John 17:19). He certainly did not make himself more holy. But he did continually set himself apart to his Father's glory and bowed to his Father's will, seeking his Father's honour above all things and in all things. O Spirit of God, give me grace thus to walk in holiness, in sanctification, sanctifying myself to my God for the glory of God!

A Motive
The Lord our God gives us an irresistible motive for honouring him in our lives. No less than fifteen times in this chapter, he says, 'For I am the Lord your God'. As such, he has a rightful claim upon us. We are not our own. We have been bought with the price of Christ's precious blood. Let us, therefore, glorify God in our bodies and in our spirits, which are God's (Colossians 1:10; 1 Peter 1:13-16).

The Lord God has made us holy. He has sanctified us. Let us therefore walk before him 'in behaviour as becometh holiness'. Thereby, 'sanctify yourselves'. Soon, we shall be holy, perfectly holy, sanctified, perfectly sanctified in, by, and with Christ in glory.

The moment a sinner believes
And trusts in his crucified God,
His pardon at once he receives,
Redemption in full through His blood.

The faith that unites to the Lamb,
And brings such salvation as this,
Is more than a notion or name:
The work of God's Spirit it is.

A principle, active and young,
That lives under pressure and load;
That makes out of weakness more strong
And draws the soul upward to God.

It treads on the world and on hell;
It vanquishes death and despair;
And what is still stranger to tell,
It overcomes heaven by prayer.

Permits a vile worm of the dust
With God to commune as a friend,
To hope His forgiveness is just,
And look for His love to the end!

It says to the mountains, Depart,
That stand betwixt God and the soul;
It binds up the broken in heart,
And makes wounded consciences whole.

Bids sins of a crimson-like dye
Be spotless as snow, and as white,
And makes such a sinner as I
As pure as an angel of light'!

Joseph Hart

Chapter 43

Doing Justice

Ye shall do no unrighteousness in judgment, in meteyard, in weight, or in measure. Just balances, just weights, a just ephah, and a just hin, shall ye have: I am the LORD your God, which brought you out of the land of Egypt.

Leviticus 19:35, 36

'How can man be justified with God? Or how can he be clean that is born of a woman?' (Job 25:4). Find the answer to those two questions and you will understand the message of Holy Scripture. How can a holy, righteous, just, and true God forgive a guilty sinner, justify an ungodly man, make an unrighteous person righteous and an unholy one holy? How can the Triune Jehovah be both 'a just God and a Saviour'?

The Lord God says of himself in Exodus 34:6, 7 that he is 'The LORD, The LORD God, merciful and gracious, longsuffering, and abundant in goodness and truth, keeping mercy for thousands, forgiving iniquity and transgression and sin, and that will by no means clear the guilty; visiting the iniquity of the fathers upon the children, and upon the children's children, unto the third and to the fourth generation'.

Four Facts
Here are four facts revealed in the Word of God, facts that are stated with utter clarity, facts that cannot be gainsaid. Many try to deny them; but these four facts cannot be denied.

1. If you and I enter into heaven, we must be perfect; perfectly righteous, completely free from sin, perfectly holy. We must 'be perfect to be accepted' (Leviticus 22:21). 'The unclean shall not pass over' Zion's Highway (Isaiah 35:8-10). It is written, 'And there shall in no wise enter into it anything that defileth, neither whatsoever worketh abomination, or maketh a lie: but they which are written in the Lamb's book of life' (Revelation 21:27).

2. The God of Glory cannot and will not simply pretend a sinner is righteous and save him. 'He that justifieth the wicked, and he that condemneth the just, even they both are abomination to the LORD' (Proverbs 17:15). 'I will not justify the wicked' (Exodus 23:7).

3. God almighty cannot condemn a just man, slay a righteous man, or punish an innocent man. Holiness will not allow it. Justice will not permit it. That is an 'abomination to the LORD' (Proverbs 17:15). He will not 'condemn the innocent blood' (Psalm 94:21). The holy, just God will not 'slay the righteous with the wicked' (Genesis 18:23-25). Abraham used this as his plea with God for Lot's deliverance from Sodom.

4. The only possible way for God to save sinners is if God himself, 'the God of all grace', finds a way in mercy and truth to make the sinner perfectly righteous and holy. 'By mercy and truth iniquity is purged' (Proverbs 16:6).

Blessed be his holy name forever, God did find a way of mercy and truth to save our poor souls; and that way is the substitutionary, sin-atoning sacrifice of his own dear Son in our place at Calvary. He 'saith, Deliver him from going down to the pit: I have found a ransom' (Job 33:24). The gospel of God is the revelation of God's righteousness (Romans 3:21-31).

Weights and Balances
In Leviticus 19, the Lord God gives a command repeated and enforced by law throughout the Old Testament era. It is a command regarding weights and balances and measures.

> Ye shall do no unrighteousness in judgment, in meteyard, in weight, or in measure. Just balances, just weights, a just ephah, and a just hin, shall ye have: I am the LORD your God, which brought you out of the land of Egypt (Leviticus 19:35, 36).

In weighing and measuring out dry goods and liquids, in buying and selling, God required Israel to always use 'just balances, just weights, a just ephah, and a just hin' (Deuteronomy 25:13; Proverbs 16:11; 20:23).

Why did God, throughout the Old Testament, speak so clearly about just weights and balances? Was he merely teaching us to be honest in business when he gave these commandments? No! The Lord himself tells us in Micah 6:11 that he was by these things teaching us about his way of bestowing salvation upon chosen sinners in complete and perfect righteousness, justice, and truth in the Lord Jesus Christ.

'Doth the Almighty pervert justice?' (Job 8:3). Never. Throughout the Holy Scriptures the Lord God asserts in unequivocal terms that he abhors all injustice. If he saves, he will be 'a just God and a Saviour' (Isaiah 45:21). If he damns, it will be upon the grounds of strict justice.

He will never use wicked balances or deceitful weights. He has named himself a God who will by no means clear the guilty (Exodus 34:7). 'Behold, God will not cast away a perfect man, neither will he help the evil doers' (Job 8:20). 'He that justifieth the wicked, and he that condemneth the just, even they both are abomination to the LORD' (Proverbs 17:15). In Leviticus 19:35, 36, the Lord shows us his absolute, unbending justice in his free, saving grace in Christ Jesus.

Christ made Sin

The Lord God used just balances and weights when he punished his Son as our Substitute at Calvary. He was doing justice. If we were to be redeemed, Christ had to die in our stead. The Just must die for the unjust, the Righteous for the unrighteous, the Innocent for the guilty, the Holy for the unholy, the Sinless for the sinful. Because the Lord God is holy, just, and true, he could not and would not impute sin to his dear Son and punish him for our sins, except he make him to be sin for us who knew no sin (2 Corinthians 5:21). No court on earth can impute guilt where there is none, unless the court itself is corrupt and unjust. The court of heaven is neither corrupt nor unjust. In fact, the Lord God declares, 'By mercy and truth iniquity is purged' (Proverbs 16:6).

When the Lord Jesus Christ bore our sins in his own body on the tree, he was made sin for us. When he was made sin for us, he became guilty as our Substitute, and our sins were imputed to him, because 'He who knew no sin was made sin for us' (2 Corinthians 5:21; Psalm 40:12; 69:5).

Then, the Lord God, the Triune Jehovah, cried, 'Awake, O sword, against my Shepherd, and against the Man that is my fellow: smite the Shepherd' (Zechariah 13:7). When Christ died at Calvary, he died because he was found worthy of death. That is the clear teaching of Holy Scripture. We could never have obtained righteousness; we could never have been made the righteousness of God in Christ had not the Lord Jesus been made sin for us. Our Lord Jesus was wondrously, mysteriously, profoundly made, caused to be, sin for us, that we might be made the righteousness of God in him (2 Corinthians 5:21).

Traditionally, it is said that Christ was made sin by imputation. I have erroneously said that many, many times myself. But the Word of God never says that. There is not a place in the book of God where a legal or forensic term is used with reference to Christ being made sin. It is certainly true that our sins were imputed to our Saviour. Had they not been imputed to him, he could never have suffered the wrath of God for our sins. But he was not made sin by imputation. Our sins were justly imputed to him, because he was made sin for us.

The Bible does not say our sins were pasted on him in a legal, ceremonial way. The book of God says, 'He hath made him sin for us'. The Word of God does not say he was treated as though he were sin. It says, 'He hath made him sin for us'. The book of God does not say he was accounted a transgressor. The book of God says, 'He hath made him sin for us'. The Holy Spirit does not say that he was made a sin-offering. The book of God says, 'He hath made him sin for us'!

Our Saviour had no sin of his own. He was born without original sin, being even from birth 'that Holy One' (Luke 1:35). Throughout his life he 'knew no sin' (2 Corinthians 5:21), 'did no sin' (1 Peter 2:22), 'and in him is no sin' (1 John 3:5). But on Calvary, the holy Lord God 'made him to be sin for us, who knew no sin; that we might be made the righteousness of God in him' (2 Corinthians 5:21). Just as in the incarnation 'the Word was made flesh and dwelt among us' (John 1:14), in substitution he who was made flesh 'was made sin for us'.

I do not know how God could be made flesh and never cease to be God; but he was. I do not know how God could die and yet never die; but he did (Acts 20:28). I do not know how Christ, who knew no sin, could be made sin and yet never have sinned; but he was.

The Lord God never plays 'Let's Pretend'! I will not guess or try to explain how God became a man; but I rejoice in and hang my soul upon the reality of the fact. 'The Word was made flesh'! I will not guess or try to explain how the Jesus Christ 'who knew no sin was made sin for us' but I rejoice in it, and hang my soul on the reality of the fact. Made sin for us 'that we might be made the righteousness of God in him'.

These are mysteries beyond the reach of human comprehension. But they are facts of divine revelation to which we bow with adoration. Hard as it is for many to realise, our God is bigger than our brains! Mysteriously, profoundly, wondrously in a way that defies explanation, the Lord Jesus Christ, Son of God, Darling of heaven, who knew no sin, did no sin, and could not sin, was made sin for us! Joseph Hart wrote,

> Much we talk of Jesus' blood,
> But how little understood
> Of His sufferings, so intense,
> Angels have no perfect sense.
>
> See the suffering Son of God,
> Panting, groaning, sweating blood!
> Boundless depths of love Divine!
> Jesus, what a love was Thine!
>
> Though the wonders Thou hast done,
> Are as yet so little known,
> Here we fix and comfort take,
> Jesus died for sinners' sake'.

When our blessed Saviour, the Lord Jesus Christ, was made sin for us he was forsaken of God. All the fury of God's holy wrath and justice was poured out and spent, exhausted, upon him at once. He was slain. Justice was satisfied. And our sins were put away. Now, by the grace of God, upon the ground of justice satisfied, and of sin put away by the blood of Christ, every sinner who believes on the Son of God is 'made the righteousness of God in him'. Isaac Watts could say,

> My faith would lay her hand
> On that dear head of Thine,
> While like a penitent I stand,
> And there confess my sin.

Justice could not punish an innocent man. Therefore, Christ Jesus was made sin so that sin might be justly imputed to him, and he might be justly punished for our transgressions. By the just balances and honest weights of the court of heaven, the Son of God was justly executed upon Calvary's cursed tree as the sinner's Substitute. Wondrous mercy! Amazing grace! Incomprehensible love!

To say, as many do, that God treated Christ as though he were a sinner, that he punished Christ for sin though he was not made sin, that he imputed guilt to his Son though his Son was never made guilty, is to say that the God of heaven 'counts us pure with the wicked balances and with the bag of deceitful weights'. It cannot be. In the redemption of our souls by the substitutionary sacrifice of his dear Son, the Lord God fulfilled his own law, doing justice!

Sinners made Meet

The God of all grace uses just balances and just weights when he makes sinners the righteousness of God in Christ. He does justice. Just as the Lord Jesus Christ was so completely made to be sin for us that he fully deserved to die under the furious wrath of the holy Lord God, so all God's elect, all for whom Christ was made sin, all for whom he died at Calvary, are made the very righteousness of God in him (2 Corinthians 5:21). Our great and righteous God accepts his elect, embraces us, and assures us of everlasting blessedness in heaven righteously and justly.

As all human beings were made sinners by Adam's disobedience, so all God's elect were made righteous before God by Christ's obedience unto death (Romans 4:25-5:2). God does not count us pure with wicked balances and a bag of deceitful weights. He does not bend his law and compromise his justice to save his chosen. He does not simply pretend that we are righteous.

Rather, by the wondrous works of his grace, he makes his chosen people righteous. By the obedience of his Son as our Representative, we have fulfilled all righteousness. By the sin-atoning death of the Lord Jesus Christ as our Substitute, justice has been satisfied in us, for we were crucified with him (Romans 5:19; Galatians 2:20).

In the new birth, God the Holy Spirit makes every chosen, redeemed sinner a new creature in Christ (2 Corinthians 5:17). All who believe on the Lord Jesus Christ have been made 'partakers of the divine nature' (2 Peter 1:4). That new man created in us is 'Christ in you, the hope of

Glory' (Colossians 1:27). He is that new man 'created in righteousness and true holiness' (Ephesians 4:24). That new man is not going to be righteous and worthy of heaven someday. He was 'created in righteousness and true holiness'. He is right now born of God and 'cannot sin, because he is born of God' (1 John 3:9).

Because we have been made righteous by redemption and regeneration, all who believe on the Lord Jesus Christ are 'meet to be partakers of the inheritance of the saints in light' (Colossians 1:12). If I am in Christ and Christ is in me, I am really and truly righteous, so perfectly righteous in him that I am worthy of God's approval, worthy of heavenly glory, worthy of eternal life. Yes, we who live in hope of eternal life have a good hope through grace, a confident 'assurance of hope', because in our Saviour we are worthy of heaven!

In Christ

Read 1 Corinthians 1:30 and 31, and rejoice. Here we see what the Lord God has made Christ to be to us and what he has made us in Christ in the sweet and blessed experience of his grace. 'Of him are ye in Christ Jesus, who of God is made unto us wisdom, and righteousness, and sanctification, and redemption: That, according as it is written, he that glorieth, let him glory in the Lord.'

Paul is talking here about things we experience in Christ. He is talking about every believer's blessed experience of grace. All true believers, all who are born again by the Spirit of God, are in Christ. We are, in Christ, vitally united to him by a living union of grace. As the branches are in the vine, drawing life from and entirely dependent upon the vine, we are in Christ Jesus. We are in Christ, not by an act of our free will, but by the work of God's free, sovereign, almighty grace. Meditate often, child of God, upon this glorious theme, 'What does it mean to be in Christ?'.

To be in Christ is to be blessed of God (Ephesians 1:3-6). In the everlasting covenant of grace, God blessed all his people with all spiritual blessings in Christ before the world began. All with which God can or will bless man, he has freely bestowed upon chosen sinners in Christ from eternity, in infinite fulness, and without measure. All who are in Christ have been blessed of God eternally with all spiritual blessings according to God's electing love. In Christ, we are chosen, adopted, redeemed, forgiven, and accepted of God. But we knew nothing of this great blessedness until we came to be in Christ experimentally by God's gift of faith, uniting us to our Saviour.

To be in Christ is to be favoured of God, the objects of God's blessing and pleasure. With whom is God well pleased? Only Christ (Matthew 17:5). If we are in Christ and one with Christ, God is well pleased with us for Christ's sake. He cannot be displeased with the body if he is well pleased with our Head. As the smile of the Father is on his Son unceasingly and justly, so it is upon us in him!

To be in Christ is to be complete (Colossians 2:10). In Christ Jesus we are complete, full, lacking nothing, perfect. He is all our wisdom, all our righteousness, all our sanctification, and all our redemption.

To be in Christ is to be free, freed from the curse of the law (Galatians 3:13); freed from the yoke of the law (Romans 10:4), and freed from all possibility of condemnation by the law (Romans 8:1). It is no more possible for a believer to be condemned by God than it is for Christ to be condemned again, for we are in him. Because we are in him, because God has made us righteous, the very righteousness of God in Christ, he will not impute sin to us (Romans 4:8), and we can never be condemned. If the Lord God will not impute sin to us, he can never, for any reason, condemn us for sin. We are in Christ! I repeat, when Paul tells us Christ is made of God to us wisdom, and righteousness, and sanctification, and redemption, he is telling us what transpires in the experience of grace when we believe on the Lord Jesus Christ.

Our experience of grace does not make Christ our wisdom, and righteousness, and sanctification, and redemption. Nor does our faith in Christ make him our wisdom, and righteousness, and sanctification, and redemption. But you will never know Christ to be your wisdom, and righteousness, and sanctification, and redemption until you trust him, until you believe on the Son of God.

That is what God the Holy Ghost tells us when he describes Abraham's faith as an illustration of saving faith. When Abraham believed the record of God concerning his Son, the Lord Jesus, it was imputed to him for righteousness (Romans 3:24-26; 4:3-11; 6:11). As our Lord Jesus was 'numbered' with transgressors when he experienced being made sin for us, so we are numbered with him when we experience being made the righteousness of God in him.

To say, as many do, that God treats sinners as though they were righteous, but does not actually make sinners righteous by his grace is to declare that the God of heaven counts them pure with the wicked balances and with the bag of deceitful weights. He does not. The Almighty never perverts justice. In saving his people he does justice.

Everlasting Damnation

The Lord God will use just balances and just weights when he casts the wicked into hell at the last day. He will do justice. It is written,

> The soul that sinneth, it shall die (Ezekiel 18:4). The soul that sinneth, it shall die. The son shall not bear the iniquity of the father, neither shall the father bear the iniquity of the son: the righteousness of the righteous shall be upon him, and the wickedness of the wicked shall be upon him (Ezekiel 18:20).

Be assured, poor sinner, be assured, the Lord God will not count you pure with wicked balances and deceitful weights. He will judge you in the last day according to the record of heaven. You shall receive wages commensurate to your works when you stand before the Great White Throne (Revelation 20:11-15). 'The wages of sin is death' (Romans 6:23). Everlasting hell will be your just portion forever.

Flee away to Christ! Trust the Son of God. He is the only refuge for your soul. 'Believe on the Lord Jesus Christ, and thou shalt be saved.' Trust Christ, and the righteousness of God is yours forever. He has made you the very righteousness of God, just as he was made sin for you. God will, with the true balances of his strict justice and the honest weights of his holy law, count you pure in that great day. In that great day he will do justice.

Heavenly Glory

Our great God, the God of all grace, will use just balances and just weights when he brings his chosen into heavenly glory on the day of judgment, saying, 'Well done, thou good and faithful servant; ... enter thou into the joy of thy Lord' (Matthew 25:21-23). He will do justice (Jeremiah 23:6; 33:16; 50:20).

Consider that! Our eternal salvation in, by, and with the Lord Jesus Christ is the Triune God justly honouring His own character and fulfilling his own law.

Chapter 44

Biblical Separation

And the LORD spake unto Moses, saying, Again, thou shalt say to the children of Israel, Whosoever he be of the children of Israel, or of the strangers that sojourn in Israel, that giveth any of his seed unto Molech; he shall surely be put to death: the people of the land shall stone him with stones ... Ye shall therefore put difference between clean beasts and unclean, and between unclean fowls and clean: and ye shall not make your souls abominable by beast, or by fowl, or by any manner of living thing that creepeth on the ground, which I have separated from you as unclean. And ye shall be holy unto me: for I the LORD am holy, and have severed you from other people, that ye should be mine. A man also or woman that hath a familiar spirit, or that is a wizard, shall surely be put to death: they shall stone them with stones: their blood shall be upon them.

Leviticus 20:1-27

What is biblical separation? Is it separation from sinful people? Is it dressing differently from other people? Is biblical separation not going to the movies, not watching television, not playing card games, not dancing, etc.? Is biblical separation talking differently from other people, or eating different foods and drinking different beverages? Is biblical separation living in such a way that people recognise us as a holy, godly people?

Actually, biblical separation is none of those things. What does this world know about holiness and godliness? But the Bible does teach us to be a separate people. In fact, the Bible declares plainly that all who are born of God, all who trust the Lord Jesus Christ, are a separate people, separated and separating themselves from all others. In Leviticus 20:26 the Lord our God declares that we who are his are his because he has separated or severed us from all other people. By sovereign election, by particular redemption, by special providence, by effectual calling, and by gracious preservation, the Lord our God severs his own from the rest of the world as his peculiar people, as a people who are distinctly his.

Context

This section of the book of Leviticus begins in chapter 18. In Leviticus chapters 18-20 the Lord God commands his Israel to walk before him in the land of Canaan as a holy people, separated and consecrated to him. He is commanding us to walk before him in the world today as a holy people, a people separated and consecrated to him.

Throughout the Scriptures the Lord God constantly calls us to live in this world for the honour of his name. His appeal is irresistible. His demands are most reasonable. His authority is unquestionable.

His Appeal is this. I am the Lord your God. I have brought you out of Egypt. I am bringing you into the land of your inheritance. He first identifies himself with us. Then he reminds us of his matchless mercy, love, and grace toward us distinctly.

His demands are truly reasonable. What could be more reasonable than living our lives in this world constantly renewing our consecration to our great God and Saviour?

His authority is unquestionable. He is God. He has given his Word to us his people. This Word is absolutely, totally authoritative in his house. It is not expected that the Egyptians and the Canaanites should live in submission to and in accordance with his Word. But his people are not only expected to do so, he also sees to it that they do. His people live by the rule of his Word.

We live in an age of such ignorance and degradation that the whole world denies there is any such thing as authority, any unchangeable, immovable standard by which we must determine right and wrong. But that is not the case for believers. For us the Word of God is authoritative

(2 Timothy 3:16, 17). In this twentieth chapter of Leviticus the Lord God our Saviour tells us precisely how we must live in this world if we would live for his honour. This chapter gives God's own instruction to his people about separation. This is true biblical separation.

A Warning to Idolaters

In verses 1-6 the Lord our God speaks with unmistakable clarity, as he gives a warning to idolaters. Perceiving that which his people would soon face, he forewarns them of the evil of idolatry, and does so with startling words of condemnation.

> And the LORD spake unto Moses, saying, Again, thou shalt say to the children of Israel, Whosoever he be of the children of Israel, or of the strangers that sojourn in Israel, that giveth any of his seed unto Molech; he shall surely be put to death: the people of the land shall stone him with stones. And I will set my face against that man, and will cut him off from among his people; because he hath given of his seed unto Molech, to defile my sanctuary, and to profane my holy name. And if the people of the land do any ways hide their eyes from the man, when he giveth of his seed unto Molech, and kill him not: Then I will set my face against that man, and against his family, and will cut him off, and all that go a whoring after him, to commit whoredom with Molech, from among their people. And the soul that turneth after such as have familiar spirits, and after wizards, to go a whoring after them, I will even set my face against that soul, and will cut him off from among his people (Leviticus 20:1-6).

The Lord God declares that he will use the people of the land as the executioners of his justice, though the execution of his justice is always a work over which he presides. 'They shall stone him, and I will cut him off, setting my face against him'. The sentence appears extreme, even barbaric in the minds of men who imagine they are wiser and more compassionate than God. The idolater was to be stoned to death.

What crime demanded such a sentence from the Judge of all the earth? The crime that demanded such fearful punishment was idolatry. It was the worship of Molech, the fire god of the Canaanites. As is the case with all false religion, Molech worship was horribly cruel.

Molech was an image of red-hot glowing brass. Men and women, to appease this worthless idol, laid their living children in his arms and watched as the god of fire, whose only fire was the fire they kindled and kept burning, consumed their own children! Everything was savage and demonic to the extreme. The Canaanites invented and the Jews accepted a hellish fiend of hatred in preference to the Lord of Glory. The toleration of idolatry led to the murder of children, even babies! Therefore, the idolaters were to be destroyed.

What a contrast to Jehovah. 'God is love'. His everlasting arms of omnipotent mercy take up little children to bless and to save them. His heart is never satisfied until the objects of his love know his love to them. Rather than casting us into the fiery pit of hell that we so fully deserve, our great God, Jehovah-Jesus, stretched out his arms on the cross, opened his side to the spear, and took all the fire of God's holy wrath against us into his own soul. Rather than requiring satisfaction from us, our God has made satisfaction for us.

That, in its essence, is the difference between Jehovah and Molech. Molech is nothing. Christ is everything. Molech does nothing for his worshippers without their contribution. Christ did everything for us without any contribution. Molech makes his worshippers pay. Christ paid for us. Molech stands in scripture representing all false gods. The worship of Molech represents all false religion.

In case you missed my point and are wondering, 'How does all this about Molech apply to anyone today?' I lay this charge of Molech against every false, idolatrous misrepresentation of God our Father, of his Son Jesus Christ, and of God the Holy Spirit. I call all doctrine Molech that requires for salvation any satisfaction or contribution from the sinner. Such a worthless, cruel, useless god is worse than Molech. Molech could, at least, have been beaten down and sold for bread!

Those who choose Molech in preference to Jehovah prove themselves to be in a state of utter enmity against God. By their pretended worship of Jehovah, they are 'defiling his sanctuary'. They stand in the house of God, calling themselves the people of God, while worshipping another god. Their worship is an expression of contempt for God. Choosing Molech as their god is 'defiling his (Jehovah's) name'. The phrase, 'whoredom with Molech', is intended to show the contempt of man for God's mercy and grace by every invention and act of idolatry, by every invention and act of freewill, works religion. God's saving grace is compared throughout Scripture as the marriage union of his own darling Son to our souls (Jeremiah 3:14; Hosea 2:19; Ephesians 5:25-30). But the Lord God declares, 'Judah ... hath married the daughter of a strange god' (Malachi 2:11). In the New Testament John calls it making God a liar.

In verse 6 the Lord God continues to condemn idolatry; but here he speaks of another form of it. Verse 6 condemns every form of wizardry or witchcraft. But there is more here than going to a psychic, reading your daily horoscope, or watching 'Harry Potter'. This verse speaks of a form of idolatry more common among us than we like to admit.

> And the soul that turneth after such as have familiar spirits, and after wizards, to go a whoring after them, I will even set my face against that soul, and will cut him off from among his people (Leviticus 20:6).

The message of this verse is clear. We must never rely upon man's wisdom and humanistic counsel to solve our problems rather than our great God, whose very name is 'Wonderful Counsellor'. He has wisdom enough to direct us. His grace is sufficient to sustain us. His love revealed to us in Christ ought to be sufficient to make us perfectly content to leave that which we do not know in his hands.

A Call to Sanctification

In verses 7 and 8, the Lord God issues a call to sanctification.

> Sanctify yourselves therefore, and be ye holy: for I am the LORD your God. And ye shall keep my statutes, and do them: I am the LORD which sanctify you (Leviticus 20:7, 8).

Our God calls for us to sanctify ourselves and be holy. This holiness and sanctification, as we shall see in the following verses, is not a work by which we make ourselves holy before God. It is the separation of ourselves from the worship and ways of the world around us. The way we sanctify ourselves, set ourselves apart from the world around us, is by obeying his Word. He is our great God and his greatness is our motive to honour and serve him. Then, the Lord our God assures us that it is he who sanctifies us, who sets us apart from the world.

A Display of Depravity
In verse 9 a dark, dark scene of dismal corruption begins, by which the Lord God sets before us a display of depravity that is as chilling as it is true. It is a scene of blackness that continues through verse 21.

For everyone that curseth his father or his mother shall be surely put to death: he hath cursed his father or his mother; his blood shall be upon him (Leviticus 20:9).

Here is a people who have lost all 'natural affection' (Romans 1:31). When the strongest tie of respect, friendship, and obligation is broken, all are broken. When the first and most important representation of divine authority is despised, all authority is despised. When authority is gone and affection turns only to self, chaos and corruption run rampant.

These words more perfectly describe Adam's fallen race than anyone imagines. 'He hath cursed his father.' They mark the crime as eminently heinous. They describe the utter renunciation of all ties to God our Father, who has nourished and brought up children. The son has become a prodigal. The son has gone to a far country. The son wishes to erase the very memory of his father's home. 'Be astonished, O ye heavens, at this, and be very desolate' (Jeremiah 2:12).

Who can read verses 10-21 and not be embarrassed, if not shocked? Are these things so? Do men and women actually perform such evils as these, these things of which it is a shame even to speak? Surely, God's Israel needs not be warned against these things. Horrible as it is to face this fact, we need the warning just like all other men and women. These things were not written to the Canaanites, but to God's covenant people.

Amazing, truly amazing is the grace of our God! Our great God has chosen for the fellowship of his bosom throughout eternity people whose nature he knows to be capable of the foulest, filthiest, darkest profligacy imaginable! What depth of meaning there is in the fact that the Son of God 'saves his people from their sins', in the fact that God, for Christ's sake, 'is faithful and just to forgive us our sins and cleanse us from all unrighteousness.' Read the catalogue of our corruption.

And the man that committeth adultery with another man's wife, even he that committeth adultery with his neighbour's wife, the adulterer and the adulteress shall surely be put to death. And the man that lieth with his father's wife hath uncovered his father's nakedness: both of them shall surely be put to death; their blood shall be upon them. And if a man lie with his daughter in law, both of them shall surely be put to death: they have wrought confusion; their blood shall be upon them. If a man also lie with mankind, as he lieth with a woman, both of them have committed an abomination: they shall surely be put to death; their blood shall be upon them. And if a man take a wife and her mother, it is wickedness: they shall be burnt with fire, both he and they; that there be no wickedness among you. And if a man lie with a beast, he shall surely be put to death: and ye shall slay the beast. And if a woman approach unto any beast, and lie down thereto, thou shalt kill the woman, and the beast: they shall surely be put to death; their blood shall be upon them. And if a man shall take his sister, his father's daughter, or his mother's daughter, and see her nakedness, and she see his nakedness; it is a wicked thing; and they shall be cut off in the sight of their people: he hath uncovered his sister's nakedness; he shall bear his iniquity. And if a man shall lie with a woman having her sickness, and shall uncover her nakedness; he hath discovered her fountain, and she hath uncovered the fountain of her blood: and both of them shall be cut off from among their people. And thou shalt not uncover the nakedness of thy mother's sister, nor of thy father's sister: for he uncovereth his near kin: they shall bear their iniquity. And if a man shall lie with his uncle's wife, he hath uncovered his uncle's nakedness: they shall bear their sin; they shall die childless. And if a man shall take his brother's wife, it is an unclean thing: he hath uncovered his brother's nakedness; they shall be childless Leviticus 20:10-21).

What sins these are. What wrath! 'Put them to death.' 'Their blood shall be upon them.' 'Burn them with fire.' 'Cut them off in the sight of their people' that all may see and fear. 'Cut them off from among the people.' Drive them out of holy fellowship (Revelation 18:10). 'They shall die childless', standing as living monuments of wrath to be seen by all, like a leafless, fruitless tree which the lightning of God has blasted. Many are the arrows in his quiver, shot forth even now on earth upon transgressors. What, then, shall the fulness of his wrath be when his 'bow is made quite naked?'

What horrid sins are here described, sins corrupting the whole earth, causing the earth itself to cry up to heaven. Children cursing their parents. Neighbours and relatives living in adultery with each other. The son dishonours the bed of his step-mother, the father-in-law that of his daughter-in-law. Men burn in unnatural lust (Romans 1:27). The same man takes mother and daughter as his wives. Men and women go to the very beasts to gratify their lusts. Brothers despise and defile their own sisters and step-sisters to gratify their lusts. Fornication, adultery, incest, sodomy, bestiality, the murder of one's own babies. All these evils are here set before us as evils arising directly from idolatry (Romans 1:18-32). Evils arising from man worshipping himself as God (2 Thessalonians 2:4) and from will worship (Colossians 2:23). Everything on earth, including the dearest relationships of men are used only as fuel for the raging lust of depraved hearts when men and women are taught to worship at the altar of their own free will!

Canaan was a land of enormous guilt. Its people were rooted out. The only wonder is that the Lord God put up with it for so long. Should he not blot it out from his creation? He did so to Sodom and Gomorrah.

But here is grace, amazing, abounding grace! Instead of destroying it, he purged it, and peopled it with a new race. Thereby the God of all grace gave a token of his purpose for his creation. He will not utterly annihilate it. Instead, he will cause the earth to be purged with fire, create it new, and people it with a holy people to stand forever as monuments to his goodness, wisdom, and grace. Soon our great Joshua, the Lord Jesus Christ, shall appear in flaming fire. Then shall there be 'a new heavens and a new earth wherein dwelleth righteousness'.

So it shall be with every sinner saved by the grace of God! O sinner, O polluted soul, hear the Word of God! Though every hideous sin, vile vice, lurid lust, and perverse passion has ruled you all your life, though you may have hidden what you are from all around you, yet the Lord God, instead of destroying you, can cleanse and save you. He has promised salvation to all who call upon him. When Christ our God and Saviour, the Priest on his throne, comes into your soul, you are washed, you are clean, you are righteous, you are justified, you are sanctified, you are holy! Thanks be unto God for blood atonement by his dear Son.

A Separated People

In verses 22-26 the Lord God declares that his elect are and must be a separated people. He declares we are a separated people and calls for us to separate ourselves unto him. This is a call to holiness, a call to separate ourselves from the people of the land, to separate ourselves from the religion of this world. This is what Paul refers to when he speaks of us 'perfecting holiness in the fear of God'. Sinai's thunder could never cause fallen men to come to God. It only drives them from him. But free, unconditional grace causes redeemed sinners to trust, love, worship, and walk with God. 'The love of Christ constraineth us'.

Ye shall therefore keep all my statutes, and all my judgments, and do them: that the land, whither I bring you to dwell therein, spue you not out. And ye shall not walk in the manners of the nation, which I cast out before you: for they committed all these things, and therefore I abhorred them. But I have said unto you, Ye shall inherit their land, and I will give it unto you to possess it, a land that floweth with milk and honey: I am the LORD your God, which have separated you from other people (Leviticus 20:22-24).

Be ye not unequally yoked together with unbelievers: for what fellowship hath righteousness with unrighteousness? And what communion hath light with darkness? And what concord hath Christ with Belial? Or what part hath he that believeth with an infidel? And what agreement hath the temple of God with idols? For ye are the temple of the living God; as God hath said, I will dwell in them, and walk in them; and I will be their God, and they shall be my people. Wherefore come out from among them, and be ye separate, saith the Lord, and touch not the unclean thing; and I will receive you, and will be a Father unto you, and ye shall be my sons and daughters, saith the Lord Almighty (2 Corinthians 6:14-18).

Having therefore these promises, dearly beloved, let us cleanse ourselves from all filthiness of the flesh and spirit, perfecting holiness in the fear of God (2 Corinthians 7:1).

And I heard another voice from heaven, saying, Come out of her, my people, that ye be not partakers of her sins, and that ye receive not of her plagues (Revelation 18:4).

God's people are a severed people. Therefore, we must sever ourselves from the world around us, not from the people of the world, but from the religion and ways of the world. This is biblical separation.

> Ye shall therefore put difference between clean beasts and unclean, and between unclean fowls and clean: and ye shall not make your souls abominable by beast, or by fowl, or by any manner of living thing that creepeth on the ground, which I have separated from you as unclean. And ye shall be holy unto me: for I the LORD am holy, and have severed you from other people, that ye should be mine (Leviticus 20:25, 26).

A Deserved Reverence

In verse 27 our great and gracious God demands of us a deserved reverence.

> A man also or woman that hath a familiar spirit, or that is a wizard, shall surely be put to death: they shall stone them with stones: their blood shall be upon them (Leviticus 20:27).

This is not a mere repetition of verse 6. Here the Lord speaks of the wizards themselves, not of those who go to consult them. When found, witches and wizards, and all of that class were to be put to death. Israel was required to remove the stumbling-blocks of religious superstition and expunge from their borders all such wickedness. This law in Canaan is to be applied spiritually in the church of God today as fully as it was in Israel of old. None but God shall be honoured in God's house (1 Timothy 6:3-5; 2 John 1:9-11).

God's Israel must live in open and avowed enmity with the serpent and the seed of the serpent. There can to be no compromise. Such devotion to our God and the gospel of his free grace in Christ throws us entirely upon him for help and strength. We are to wage war with Satan, to storm the very gates of hell, to crush the adder and dragon in their den, refusing to offer peace to any who refuse to worship God our Saviour, and refusing any terms of peace for ourselves with the enemies of our God.

Hell assaulted no portion of earth so intensely as Canaan in the days of believing Israel. Yet, no region on earth was so secure as that land where God was worshipped as God. The strength of heaven was Israel's strength. The breadth of heaven was her shield. The edge of heaven's keen sword was her safety. 'The Lord alone did lead him, and there was no strange god with him' (Deuteronomy 32:12). 'Happy art thou, O Israel! O people saved by the Lord' (Deuteronomy 33:29).

Have no fellowship with the unfruitful works of darkness, but rather reprove them. For it is a shame even to speak of those things which are done of them in secret. But all things that are reproved are made manifest by the light: for whatsoever doth make manifest is light. Wherefore he saith, Awake thou that sleepest, and arise from the dead, and Christ shall give thee light (Ephesians 5:11-14).

God the Holy Ghost tells us to 'prove all things; hold fast that which is good. Abstain from all appearance of evil'. If any doctrine looks Arminian, smells like free will, or tastes like works, run from it as fast as you can, and as far as you can.

And the very God of peace sanctify you wholly; and I pray God your whole spirit and soul and body be preserved blameless unto the coming of our Lord Jesus Christ. Faithful is he that calleth you, who also will do it (1 Thessalonians 5:23, 24).

That is biblical separation. See that you practise it always 'perfecting holiness in the fear of God'.

Jesus, in thee our eyes behold
A thousand glories more
Than the rich gems and polished gold
The sons of Aaron wore.
They first their own burnt offerings brought
To purge themselves from sin;
Thy life was pure without a spot,
And all thy nature clean.

Fresh blood, as constant as the day,
Was on their altar spilt;
But thy one offering takes away
For ever all our guilt.
Their priesthood ran through several hands,
For mortal was their race;
Thy never-changing office stands
Eternal as thy days.

Once in the circuit of a year,
With blood (but not his own),
Aaron within the veil appears,
Before the golden throne.
But Christ, by his own powerful blood,
Ascends above the skies,
And, in the presence of our God,
Shows his own sacrifice.

Jesus, the King of Glory, reigns
On Zion's heavenly hill;
Looks like a lamb that has been slain,
And wears his priesthood still.
He ever lives to intercede
Before his Father's face;
Give him, my soul, thy cause to plead,
Nor doubt the Father's grace.

Isaac Watts

Chapter 45

God's Priests And God's Priest

And the LORD said unto Moses, Speak unto the priests the sons of Aaron, and say unto them, There shall none be defiled for the dead among his people ... And Moses told it unto Aaron, and to his sons, and unto all the children of Israel.

Leviticus 21:1-24

This chapter deals with and gives specific instructions to the priests of Israel, the sons of Aaron. In verses 1-6, the priests were forbidden to mourn the dead as other people do. In verses 7 and 8, the Lord tells them that even in the selection of their wives, God's honour was to be paramount. In verse 9, God required that any priest's daughter who profaned her father by playing the harlot was to be put to death. Verses 10-15 give specific instructions to the high priests throughout their generations. The high priest was not to mourn as others might, even for his own parents (vv. 10, 11). He who served as God's high priest was to live always in the service of God's sanctuary (v. 12). His wife was to be neither a widow nor a divorced woman, but only a virgin of the daughters of Israel (vv. 13, 14). In a word, he was to so order his life and household that God was honoured in it (v. 15). Verses 16-24 are addressed specifically to Moses, the lawgiver, and required that none of the priests (none of the males in Aaron's family) who had a blemish of any kind be allowed to serve as God's priests.

What does this have to do with any of us? There are no Aaronic or Levitical priests today. We have no material altar or rituals of sacrifice today. Such things are forbidden of our God in this gospel age. So how do these things apply to you and me?

We must conclude one of two things. Either this portion of God's Word has nothing to do with us and can be ignored, or the instructions given have a far wider, spiritual, gospel application than most imagine.

Obviously, Leviticus 21 was written by divine inspiration for our instruction, learning, edification, and consolation (Romans 15:4). These instructions concerning God's priests were written 'that we through patience and comfort of the Scriptures might have hope'.

There are no priests today who minister in the sanctuary of our God, who serve in the tabernacle, and offer sacrifices at God's altar. Yet, if we would come to God and have our sins forgiven, and be accepted of him, if we would be saved, we must have an altar, a sacrifice, and a priest, an altar appointed by God, a sacrifice accepted by God, and a priest anointed by God

The Lord Jesus Christ is our great High Priest. Christ is our Melchizedek, our ever-living High Priest, touched with the feeling of our infirmities, 'who also maketh intercession for us' and is able to save to the uttermost all who come to God by him (Hebrews 7:25).

The Scriptures also tell us every believer is a priest unto God, one who does business in the holy place, offering up spiritual sacrifices acceptable to God by Christ (1 Peter 2:5-9). And God's servants, those men who preach the gospel of Christ, though we have no mediating priestly function and are in no sense priests between God and men, are also typified by Aaron and his sons, and the Levitical priesthood.

Let me be clear. Gospel preachers and pastors are not priests. The only mediator between God and men is Christ. Yet, in the New Testament, the Holy Spirit uses the laws given in the Old Testament to illustrate the work of the gospel ministry and to enforce the pastor's separation of himself to the gospel, as well as the local church's maintenance of pastors and missionaries in the work of the gospel.

When Canaan was divided by Joshua, he gave no inheritance to the tribe of Levi, the priestly tribe. This was done by divine command, because those who served in the house of God, who ministered for the souls of men in holy things for the glory of God, were to be maintained in their livelihoods by the gifts and sacrifices of God's people. The

Apostle Paul, by divine inspiration, tells us that those revealed facts teach that God has ordained that those who preach the gospel are to be financially supported and maintained by the people they serve (Numbers 18:20, 23, 24; Deuteronomy 10:9; 18:1, 2; Joshua 13:14, 33; 18:7; 1 Corinthians 9:13, 14; 1 Timothy 5:17, 18). With these things in mind, let us look at Leviticus 21 and see what the Lord teaches us in this chapter about our great Saviour and about ourselves.

'And'

Leviticus 21 begins with the word 'And'. The instructions of this chapter are directly connected with the last verse of chapter 20.

> A man also or woman that hath a familiar spirit, or that is a wizard, shall surely be put to death: they shall stone them with stones: their blood shall be upon them (Leviticus 20:27).

In chapters 19 and 20, the Lord frequently and specifically warns us never to consult with wizards, witches, and the like, never to seek counsel at the hands of palm readers, soothsayers, astrological interpreters, today's psychologists, psychiatrists, or psychics, or at the altar of any idol. God's people are to seek direction at God's hand, by the mouth of his servants, in his house. Therefore, in chapter 21 he tells us what kind of men his servants must be. Leviticus 21 is in many ways the Old Testament equivalent of Titus 1:6-9, where the Holy Spirit tells us what a pastor must be.

God's Servants

Never forget that we belong to God. That is the message of Leviticus 21:1-9). We who are saved by God's amazing, free grace in Christ are the sons and daughters of God. Let us never forget who we are and whose we are. Those servants of God who are gospel preachers and minister about holy things must not forget that the treasure entrusted to our hands is and must be first and foremost in our lives. Let us ever live as men separated unto the gospel, devoted to the glory of God.

> And the LORD said unto Moses, Speak unto the priests the sons of Aaron, and say unto them, There shall none be defiled for the dead among his people: But for his kin, that is near unto him,

that is, for his mother, and for his father, and for his son, and for his daughter, and for his brother, and for his sister a virgin, that is nigh unto him, which hath had no husband; for her may he be defiled. But he shall not defile himself, being a chief man among his people, to profane himself (Leviticus 21:1-4).

In verse 4 God tells the priest why he must not behave as other men, even if someone he loves dearly has died. He must not defile himself; he must not mourn as those who have no hope, because he was 'a chief man among his people' a guardian of the people. All eyes were on him.

So it is with you and me, both you who are my fellow labourers in the gospel and you who are our brothers and sisters in Christ. We are guardians of God's people. That makes us public people. The eyes of God's people are upon us, looking to us for direction and we are responsible to care for one another.

Aaron's sons were not permitted to defile themselves, that is to mourn as those who do not believe God; but they were permitted to mourn. If one of Aaron's sons lost one of his family, he was not expected to act without feeling. God's people are still people. God's servants are still men. That which causes others sorrow causes us sorrow, too. But we 'sorrow not as others who have no hope'.

Our Lord wept at Lazarus' tomb. He wept because Mary and Martha wept. He who was the perfect man entered into their sorrow. So may we. Grace does not make people hard. It makes them tender. But even in sorrow, we must never forget we belong to God. We worship God. We serve God and his people. That is first and foremost.

The Lord God made particular allowance for expressions of tenderness, care, and love of the priest for his own family. We often feel guilty and beat ourselves because we do not love and pray for others like we do for our own. No doubt, this is an evil of our nature. Yet, it is an evil attributable to the weakness of our nature. And our God here specifically allows it. God's family is our first concern. Yet, concern for God's family does not make men and women indifferent toward their own. Grace makes us more diligent in all the tender relations and responsibilities connected with our families. Grace does not weaken natural affection. It increases it.

There is something else here. The priest was not permitted to mourn for any but his own, immediate family, to teach us that we ought not display greater regard and tenderness for some of God's people than we do for others. Our hearts are to be devoted to the whole family of God, concerned for the welfare of each brother and each sister in the household of God. Let there be no cliques in God's house, among God's people. Let each brother and sister in Christ make it their business to look out for and minister to the most overlooked among us. As for pastors, the pastor must be pastor to all the congregation, the weak and the strong, the most devoted and the most wavering, the most pleasing and the most displeasing. Let us learn to pray as Andrew Bonar, 'Lord, keep us from selfish joys. Teach us to live for others and for you'.

They shall not make baldness upon their head, neither shall they shave off the corner of their beard, nor make any cuttings in their flesh. They shall be holy unto their God, and not profane the name of their God: for the offerings of the LORD made by fire, and the bread of their God, they do offer: therefore they shall be holy (Leviticus 21:5, 6).

'They shall be holy unto their God, and not profane the name of their God.' God requires that you and I walk before him as a holy people, that is, as a people separated, distinct and distinguished from all other people as his own peculiar people.

Even when we mourn the loss of a loved one or experience any of those things in this sin cursed world that cause us grief and pain, we are not to be like the heathen. We are not to display uncontrollable anguish and grief. In all things, let us bow to the will and wisdom and goodness of our God. And let us see to it that all around us know that we do, not by our speech, but by our demeanour.

Gospel preachers, pastors, elders, and teachers, those who are employed in the service of Christ publicly, are doubly bound to abstain from all appearance of evil in these matters. We are the King's attendants in his palace, cupbearers at his table, representatives of our God to his people. Let us take care that we do not profane his name by behaving as those who worship other gods. If we, by our behaviour in times of heavy trial, leave upon those around us the impression that our God is not doing us good, that he is not in control of our affairs, that he has abandoned us, we profane his name before them.

As priests of old, we stand before God's people as men sent of God to point them to Christ's effectual sacrifice, declaring that since Christ has redeemed us and reconciled us to God, God is for us and his love for us is unceasing. But that which we teach and preach with our lips will fall on deaf ears if it is not demonstrated by our calm acquiescence before him when he sends us through deep waters and fiery trials.

> They shall not take a wife that is a whore, or profane; neither shall they take a woman put away from her husband: for he is holy unto his God. Thou shalt sanctify him therefore; for he offereth the bread of thy God: he shall be holy unto thee: for I the LORD, which sanctify you, am holy (Leviticus 21:7, 8).

The priests of Israel were not allowed to marry any woman who was unchaste or divorced. Clearly, this is not a law to be literally enforced upon men today, any more than sabbath keeping and laws regarding animal sacrifices. This applies neither to believers in general nor to those who serve as gospel preachers in a literal way. The spirit of the law points to and teaches something far higher.

Typical of Christ
The priest was typical of our Lord Jesus Christ in all his public acts. He points us to our great High Priest. Even in his choice of a bride, the Lord God took care that the priest set forth another Priest.

Our Savour's bride is 'without spot or wrinkle', 'undefiled', 'the choice one of her that bare her; the daughters saw her and blessed her' (Song of Solomon 6:9). That is not what we are by nature; but that is what Christ makes us. By nature, we are all like Hosea's wife Gomer, people of ill repute (Hosea 1-3). But the Lord Jesus has made all his holy bride chaste virgins (Revelation 14:4).

God 'hateth putting away' (Malachi 2:16), the priest must not marry a divorced woman. The Saviour chose us for eternity. There must be nothing to hint to his bride that she may again be separated from him.

The Gospel Preacher
Certainly, there is an application to the gospel preacher, to that man who stands before God's people to lead them in the knowledge and worship of God. We are God's servants. For his name's sake, for the

honour of the gospel, our whole lives are to be devoted to our God and Saviour. The same is true of all believers. But in as much as our God has put us in trust with the gospel, since he has given us this great work to do, we are all the more responsible. To whom much is given much is required. Let us honour our God. No demand is too great. No sacrifice is too costly. No work is too difficult.

> Let no man despise thy youth; but be thou an example of the believers, in word, in conversation, in charity, in spirit, in faith, in purity. Till I come, give attendance to reading, to exhortation, to doctrine. Neglect not the gift that is in thee, which was given thee by prophecy, with the laying on of the hands of the presbytery. Meditate upon these things; give thyself wholly to them; that thy profiting may appear to all. Take heed unto thyself, and unto the doctrine; continue in them: in doing this thou shalt both save thyself, and them that hear thee (1 Timothy 4:12-16).
> And the daughter of any priest, if she profane herself by playing the whore, she profaneth her father: she shall be burnt with fire (Leviticus 21:9).

As in the case of New Testament pastors it is written, 'having faithful children not accused of riot, nor unruly' (Titus 1:6), so it was with the priest's family. The conduct of the family reflects upon the father. God would not have us burn our daughters at the stake for such behaviour. Rather, he teaches us to forgive and help. But I am sure of this. If any who now wear the name of Christ, if any who profess faith in the Son of God go awhoring after other gods, they shall be burned forever with the fire of God's wrath in hell.

We are to sanctify ourselves unto our God. We are to seek his honour in all things, devoting everything, our entire lives, even our families to his glory. It is a reasonable thing that we should do so (1 Corinthians 6:9-11, 19, 20; Romans 12:1, 2).

Christ Our Priest
It is most reasonable, if you consider this. The Lord Jesus Christ, as our great High Priest, sanctified himself, consecrated himself entirely to the will and glory of God for the saving of our souls (John 17:17-19). We see this portrayed in verses 10-15.

And he that is the high priest among his brethren, upon whose head the anointing oil was poured, and that is consecrated to put on the garments, shall not uncover his head, nor rend his clothes; Neither shall he go in to any dead body, nor defile himself for his father, or for his mother; Neither shall he go out of the sanctuary, nor profane the sanctuary of his God; for the crown of the anointing oil of his God is upon him: I am the LORD' (Leviticus 21:10-12).

The words 'high priest' are used here for the first time in the book of God. Another translation could be 'great priest' or 'great high priest'. Our great High Priest, the Lord Jesus Christ, is the one of whom the passage speaks. In all things, he is our example. Even in the typology of this chapter, it is the High Priest, the Lord Jesus, who is the eminent example of devotion to God. The holy anointing oil is upon him. The words 'anointing oil' might be translated, as some suggest, 'the crown of the anointing oil'. You see, our great High Priest is the King, the King of glory, a Priest upon his throne. He is called the great High Priest, because he is infinitely better than all others, because there was never a priest like him (Exodus 28:36; 29:6; 39:30). Christ was consecrated to put on garments of salvation. He made them. He wore them. He puts them on us. Jehovah's Righteous Servant never rent his clothes or uncovered his head as one in mourning (Isaiah 42:1-4).

Never Defiled Himself
He never touched the dead, except to give life. Even when his mother was before him as a bereaved widow, as she beheld his anguish upon the cursed tree, he was her High Priest and Mediator, and showed tenderness, concern and care not for himself but for her. In the midst of his woes as the smitten Shepherd, he took time to recommend her to John, and then, so to speak, resumed his work of suffering. And what he did for her, he did for all his chosen family (Psalm 69:4-9).

Never Went Out
Our great High Priest never went 'out of the sanctuary', and who never 'profaned it' by the introduction of personal concerns. He ever felt the streams of the anointing oil on his head. He 'saved' not, but 'hated and lost' his own life for us. He stood entirely as our Substitute and Surety.

The Bride Chosen

And he shall take a wife in her virginity. A widow, or a divorced woman, or profane, or an harlot, these shall he not take: but he shall take a virgin of his own people to wife. Neither shall he profane his seed among his people: for I the LORD do sanctify him (Leviticus 21:13-15).

Here he is again. God's elect, the Church of Christ is espoused to him 'as a chaste virgin' (2 Corinthians 11:2), and he calls her, 'my undefiled' (Song of Solomon 6:9). When we stand with him before the throne of God, he declares that we are chaste, undefiled virgins (Revelation 14:1-5). As he calls us his undefiled, we look upon the Son of God and say, Thou art 'my first husband' (Hosea 2:7). These things are not so by nature, but blessed be God, they are so, nevertheless.

The Lord Jesus Christ is married to his church in perfect holiness. 'She cometh to the king in robes of needle-work' all glorious. She was not thus fair when he found her; but she is 'all fair', 'undefiled', 'the choice one' when he marries her. The marriage of the Lamb is on the day of his coming out of the Holy Place to bless his redeemed. We are his holy people in whom he rejoices, over whom he rejoices with singing! No spot or wrinkle, no blemish, nor any such thing appears on his redeemed when he is their Bridegroom (Ephesians 5:27).

The blood of our all-glorious Christ, our great High Priest's sacrifice and his righteousness demand and absolutely secure our everlasting glory and perfection as his chosen bride. It is written of God's High Priest, 'Neither shall he profane his seed among his people' (v. 15). Aaron was not to mix his seed with the wicked. Neither shall Christ. He shall never profane one of his own, by charging them with sin, as he shall the damned forever (Romans 4:8; 8:33, 34).

Our Effectual Priest
We know all the work of our great High Priest will certainly secure this blessed end because our Priest is the Priest God required. In verses 17-21, the Lord God speaks not to Aaron personally, but to Moses, the lawgiver, telling him the kind of man the high priest must be.

Speak unto Aaron, saying, Whosoever he be of thy seed in their generations that hath any blemish, let him not approach to offer the bread of his God. For whatsoever man he be that hath a blemish, he shall not approach: a blind man, or a lame, or he that hath a flat nose, or anything superfluous, or a man that is brokenfooted, or brokenhanded, or crookbackt, or a dwarf, or that hath a blemish in his eye, or be scurvy, or scabbed, or hath his stones broken; No man that hath a blemish of the seed of Aaron the priest shall come nigh to offer the offerings of the LORD made by fire: he hath a blemish; he shall not come nigh to offer the bread of his God (Leviticus 21:17-21).

The man God requires, the man we need, the man God accepts as our great High Priest is the God-man. Christ Jesus is exactly the priest we need. He is the perfect man, the God-man, our Saviour. None other could save us (Hebrews 7:25-28).

The Bread of God

Who can read those words, 'the bread of God', and not think of our Lord Jesus Christ? Those specific words are used only seven times in Holy Scripture (Leviticus 21:6, 8, 17, 21, 22; 22:25, John 6:33). It seems obvious to me that our Lord Jesus referred to this twenty-first chapter of Leviticus when he said, 'The bread that I will give is my flesh, which I will give for the life of the world' (John 6:51). 'The Bread of God is he which cometh down from heaven' (John 6:33).

The shewbread the priests offered continually upon the table of shewbread pointed to him, our Lord Jesus Christ, who is 'The Bread of God'. He is the Bread that satisfies God. He is the Bread God gives by which our souls are satisfied. He is the Bread God's servants constantly spread on the table in his house. Christ is our daily Bread, the Bread we must have, the Bread we must eat, and the Bread we want.

The Perfect Priest

All of these precepts concerning the men who might be allowed to serve as God's High Priest were necessary because the high priest in Israel was a type of Christ throughout the Old Testament. As such, he must always appear as one who was altogether without blemish or fault of any kind.

The Song of Solomon chapter 5 gives us some light on this passage. In setting forth Christ's purity, beauty and perfection in figurative terms, it uses almost all the references to the body that are found here in Leviticus 21. Here the defects are spoken of, there the excellences.

1. If the priest had been 'blind', the people would be led to misapprehend the type. He could not represent him whose 'eyes are as a flame of fire'.

2. If the priest had been 'lame', he could not represent him whose 'legs are as pillars of marble'.

3. If the priest had been 'flat nosed', he could not be the type of him whose bride has this said of her, 'Thy nose is as the tower of Lebanon'.

4. If the priest had been 'superfluous in any limb', if one limb was longer than the other, he could not be a type of him who 'cometh leaping on the mountains'.

5. If the priest had been 'broken-footed', he could not have typified him whose feet are 'sockets of fine gold'.

6. If the priest had been 'broken-handed', he could not have typified our Lord Jesus, whose hands we are told are 'as gold rings, set with beryl'.

7. Our Redeemer, our great High Priest, was to stretch out his whole body on the cross. The nails were to pierce his hands and feet. Yet, not a bone of his body would be broken. If the priest had been 'crookbackt', he would have represented the High Priest of the church as inferior to the church herself, 'whose stature is like the palm-tree'.

8. If the priest had been 'a dwarf', he could not have reached up to the altar's height. He could not have been a type of him whose 'countenance is as Lebanon, excellent as the cedars'.

9. If the priest had had 'a blemish in his eye', he could never have typified our Saviour whose 'eyes are as doves by rivers of waters, washed in milk, and fitly set'.

10. If the priest had been diseased, having the 'scurvy' or 'scabbed', he could not have typified him 'who is all fair', who has 'no spot or wrinkle'.

11. If in the most secret, hidden spot of his frame, the priest had had the slightest blemish or defect, he could not have been a type of our great Saviour who is 'all glorious within'.

Our great High Priest is just such a High Priest as we need, altogether perfect, altogether lovely. Virtue flows out of him when he is but touched by a sinner's hand. And this all-glorious Christ was the Sacrifice as well as the Priest. 'He offered up himself' (Hebrews 7:27).

> He shall eat the bread of his God, both of the most holy, and of the holy. Only he shall not go in unto the veil, nor come nigh unto the altar, because he hath a blemish; that he profane not my sanctuaries: for I the LORD do sanctify them (Leviticus 21:22, 23).

The common, deformed, defiled men among Aaron's sons were provided for. They were allowed to feed upon the holy things. But only the unblemished, faultless man could go into the holy place, only God's appointed High Priest could go into the holy of holies and make atonement for the people.

The high priest had to be a man who had no fault or blemish, because he typified that Man who is our great High Priest of infinite worth, beauty, and glory, the God-man, who gives all his beauty to us, and yet retains it all in himself. Oh, how fair he is! 'Thou art all fair, my Beloved. Thou art all fair'. He who offered the bread of perfect righteousness in the holy place, the outer sanctuary, must be himself perfect. He who offered the blood of complete satisfaction in the most holy place, behind the veil, must himself be perfect.

> And Moses told it unto Aaron, and to his sons, and unto all the children of Israel (Leviticus 21:24).

By these things all Israel knew what sort of priest to expect. Their eyes were fixed on One who was to be 'altogether lovely', by whose merit, virtue, and sacrifice God would accept his people, by whose merit, virtue, and sacrifice God could not but accept and bless his people.

Chapter 46

'Profane Not My Holy Name'

And the LORD spake unto Moses, saying, Speak unto Aaron and to his sons, that they separate themselves from the holy things of the children of Israel, and that they profane not my holy name in those things which they hallow unto me: I am the LORD. Say unto them, Whosoever he be of all your seed among your generations, that goeth unto the holy things, which the children of Israel hallow unto the LORD, having his uncleanness upon him, that soul shall be cut off from my presence: I am the LORD ... Therefore shall ye keep my commandments, and do them: I am the LORD. Neither shall ye profane my holy name; but I will be hallowed among the children of Israel: I am the LORD which hallow you, That brought you out of the land of Egypt, to be your God: I am the LORD.

Leviticus 22:1-33

There is a struggle in the hearts and minds of all men and women, a struggle many try to silence but a struggle from which none can escape. It is a struggle arising from the fact that God has stamped upon all a God consciousness by which all know that God is, that God is holy, and that mankind is both corrupt and condemned (Romans 1:18-20).

The Struggle
Here is the struggle. How can I come to God? He is infinitely holy. I am a sinner. How can I approach the holy Lord God and find acceptance with him? This I know. If we would come to God and find acceptance with him, we must do so in a way he specifies and in a way that will not profane his holy name.

> And the LORD spake unto Moses, saying, Speak unto Aaron and to his sons, that they separate themselves from the holy things of the children of Israel, and that they profane not my holy name in those things which they hallow unto me: I am the LORD (Leviticus 22:1, 2).

The Lord God will not be worshipped by any who profane his holy name in their approaches to him. He will not accept any who profane his name in coming to him. His commandment is plain. 'Profane not my holy name.' But how? How can sinners come to God without profaning his holy name? Leviticus 22 gives the answer to that question.

Leviticus 22 records God's law regarding the households of his priests. These thirty-three verses reveal for us the reverence God requires of his people. If we would worship God we must reverence him in the details of our lives. If we do not reverence him and worship him in the privacy of our homes, at our dinner tables and in our closets, in the house and in the field, we cannot reverence him and worship him in his house. Believers are men and women who worship and serve the Lord God in the totality of their lives.

That is the teaching of God the Holy Spirit in this chapter. As we go through this chapter, five things are clearly set before us, five lessons about the worship of God that need to be inscribed upon our hearts. May God be pleased to teach us these five, vital lessons.

1. Total Consecration

God requires total consecration. None but priests, chosen, consecrated, anointed priests, can approach God and offer sacrifice to him. Read 2 Chronicles 26 and see how King Uzziah learned that. All who are God's are made to be priests unto God in Christ. And God's priests are God's priests in all places and at all times.

> And the LORD spake unto Moses, saying, Speak unto Aaron and to his sons, that they separate themselves from the holy things of the children of Israel, and that they profane not my holy name in those things which they hallow unto me: I am the LORD (Leviticus 22:1, 2).

When I speak of God's elect as his priests, I am not talking about the priestcraft of religious idolatry practised by deceived men and women who call other men and women their priests. We have only one Mediator between us and God, Christ the Lord. Christ alone is our sin-atoning High Priest, Mediator and Advocate, by whom we have access to and acceptance with the holy Lord God.

When I speak of God's elect as his priests, I am talking about saved sinners, men and women who are accepted of God in the holy place, upon his throne. If we are God's, if we are saved by his almighty grace, if we are believers, we are the consecrated, anointed servants of the Most High God by his almighty grace, through the merits of Christ's blood and righteousness. Christ has made us priests of the Most High God (Exodus 19:4-6; 1 Peter 2:5-10; Revelation 1:5, 6; 5:9, 10).

God's priests are to act like God's priests in all circumstances, at all times, in all things. The requirement here given to separate himself from the holy things, means that he must keep aloof from them at home, as if the holy things were placed away from him to show reverence. The priests at home were not to handle holy things familiarly; they must act even there with deepest reverence. Even though the man was a priest, if he was ceremonially unclean in any way, he was to separate himself from the holy things, lest he profane God's holy name.

We must always acknowledge and confess our sin, trusting Christ alone as our Salvation, ever bathing our souls in his precious blood (1 John 1:9). We must never treat sacred things lightly or irreverently. We who are the Lord's priests ought always to think and speak of our God and the things of God with utmost reverence and sobriety.

We who have been made the priests of God by Christ, who are born of God, who worship, serve and live for God must be separated to the Lord. Moses learned this lesson at great cost (Deuteronomy 32:49-51).

The Lord my God, the Triune Jehovah, is totally consecrated to me. Let me, therefore, be totally consecrated to him.

2. No Uncleanness
Only those who are altogether perfectly clean can approach the holy Lord God and be accepted of him. All believers are God's priests, living in the holy place all the time, accepted in the holy place, brought nigh by the blood of Christ, being made clean in him, by him, and with him.

Say unto them, Whosoever he be of all your seed among your generations, that goeth unto the holy things, which the children of Israel hallow unto the LORD, having his uncleanness upon him, that soul shall be cut off from my presence: I am the LORD. What man soever of the seed of Aaron is a leper, or hath a running issue; he shall not eat of the holy things, until he be clean. And whoso toucheth anything that is unclean by the dead, or a man whose seed goeth from him; Or whosoever toucheth any creeping thing, whereby he may be made unclean, or a man of whom he may take uncleanness, whatsoever uncleanness he hath; The soul which hath touched any such shall be unclean until even, and shall not eat of the holy things, unless he wash his flesh with water. And when the sun is down, he shall be clean, and shall afterward eat of the holy things; because it is his food. That which dieth of itself, or is torn with beasts, he shall not eat to defile himself therewith: I am the LORD. They shall therefore keep mine ordinance, lest they bear sin for it, and die therefore, if they profane it: I the LORD do sanctify them (Leviticus 22:3-9).

These priests were never to be careless, especially regarding the worship of God. If one went into the tabernacle in a careless state, unclean through some ceremonial pollution, the Lord God would cut him off (v. 3) as he did Nadab and Abihu. Let us apply the law, here given, to ourselves. Believers are men and women purified and made clean by the blood of Christ (Titus 2:11-14).

God's object in giving these laws was to keep the priesthood from the very appearance of evil, even in their homes (vv. 4-7). Many of the causes of defilement were such as could be known only by the man himself and the Lord his God. It might be only the very slightest pollution, pollution from 'creeping things'. But even the slightest pollution meant banishment. In his most private situations, the priest must be ceremonially holy, undefiled, and clean. He could not eat of the holy things, even at his own table, until he was ceremonially purified. Why? Because he was a type of Christ, our High and Holy Priest. But he is also set before us here as a type and representative of believers as God's priests, sinners sanctified by God's grace in Christ.

Those 'holy things' were the portions of the sacrifices that were the priest's due. They were pledges of God's fellowship and communion.

But because he is the holy Lord God, he cannot allow even a ceremonial symbol of fellowship share a part with one defiled. Before he could eat the food of divine fellowship the unclean priest must wash his flesh in water and wait for the setting of the sun. Even so, we cannot come to God until we have been washed by his Spirit in regenerating grace, washed in the blood of Christ (Zechariah 12:10-14; 13:1). Once the sun of God's fury has set, we can enjoy communion with him. The sun of God's wrath went down forever after those three hours of darkness at Calvary when our Saviour finished the work of redemption for us.

In his home, the priest was never to serve on his table anything that died a natural death or was torn, anything that spoke of decay and violence. Even in the food he provided for his family and ate himself, God's priest was to have an eye to God's worship and honour. The neglect of God's honour, even in the privacy of his family dining room, was rewarded with death (v. 9). That brings us to the next lesson.

3. Absolute Holiness

God requires absolute holiness. Any who profane God's ordinance shall be put to death.

> They shall therefore keep mine ordinance, lest they bear sin for it, and die therefore, if they profane it: I the LORD do sanctify them (Leviticus 22:9).

We read in Hebrews 12:14 that we must 'follow peace with all men, and holiness, without which no man shall see the Lord'. That holiness we must pursue, without which we cannot see the Lord, is Christ. He is our holiness, our sanctification. We pursue and seek him by faith.

These ordinances of divine worship spoken of in the book of Leviticus were all typical of Christ, his person, his work, his priesthood, his obedience, his righteousness, his sacrifice, his salvation. To profane God's ordinance was to profane his name and his Son. For that, God still sends people to hell. Uzza put his hand to God's ark, Uzziah assumed the work of God's priest. Both were killed, because they profaned God's name, assuming God's salvation, portrayed in the ark and in the priestly sacrifices needed assistance from men, and they were the men to provide it. I repeat, God sends people to hell for profaning of his name. All freewill, works religion is profaning God's name.

403

We are all guilty. We have profaned his ordinance, presuming upon his goodness, attempting to come to him and find acceptance with him upon the ground of our own worth and merit. We would yet, at this very moment, as we attempt to worship him, profane his name and his holy ordinance, except for one blessed fact of grace. He declares, 'I the Lord do sanctify them'. See Hebrews 10:9-14. By sovereign election, by blood atonement, by gracious regeneration he sanctifies his people.

4. Perfect Sanctification

Now we learn we cannot come to God except we be perfectly sanctified. We must have a perfect sanctification. All who are sanctified and made holy by God's grace are accepted of him. They can and do come to him, worship him, and serve him.

> There shall no stranger eat of the holy thing: a sojourner of the priest, or an hired servant, shall not eat of the holy thing. But if the priest buy any soul with his money, he shall eat of it, and he that is born in his house: they shall eat of his meat. If the priest's daughter also be married unto a stranger, she may not eat of an offering of the holy things. But if the priest's daughter be a widow, or divorced, and have no child, and is returned unto her father's house, as in her youth, she shall eat of her father's meat: but there shall no stranger eat thereof. And if a man eat of the holy thing unwittingly, then he shall put the fifth part thereof unto it, and shall give it unto the priest with the holy thing. And they shall not profane the holy things of the children of Israel, which they offer unto the LORD; Or suffer them to bear the iniquity of trespass, when they eat their holy things: for I the LORD do sanctify them (Leviticus 22:10-16).

No strangers, none who were not priests of God, were allowed to eat of the holy things. Why? Because, as we learn in 1 Corinthians 11, when unconverted people partake of the things of God and intrude into holy things such as baptism, the Lord's supper, church membership, they eat and drink damnation to themselves, not discerning the Lord's body, not knowing their need of a Substitute.

All who were members of the priestly family were given the right to the holy things of the priest's table; his sons, his daughters, his servants, even a daughter who had departed from his house and was returned. And all who are in the household of faith have a right in Christ to all things in the house of God (Ephesians 2:11-22).

If a man unknowingly participated in and ate of the holy things of the priesthood, he was required to make restitution and add to it a fifth part, acknowledging he had defrauded God, taking what he had no right to take (v. 14). If he refused, he was to be put to death. Why? Because the holy Lord God will have no fellowship with man except upon the grounds of perfect holiness, righteousness and satisfaction. The fifth part spoke of restitution made by Christ our Substitute at Calvary (Leviticus 5:15, 16). By adding the fifth part, the transgressor admitted and confessed Christ alone could make restitution to God (Psalm 69:4).

This perfect sanctification involves three things. The priests of God are chosen of God. That is eternal election. Only those born into the priestly family are God's priests. This is the new birth. All of God's priests are washed in the blood. This is redemption effectually accomplished by Christ and applied to the redeemed by the Holy Spirit.

5. Willing Heart

God requires a willing heart. God will not be worshipped except by those who worship him in the way he has prescribed with willing hearts.

> And the LORD spake unto Moses, saying, Speak unto Aaron, and to his sons, and unto all the children of Israel, and say unto them, Whatsoever he be of the house of Israel, or of the strangers in Israel, that will offer his oblation for all his vows, and for all his freewill offerings, which they will offer unto the LORD for a burnt offering; Ye shall offer at your own will a male without blemish, of the beeves, of the sheep, or of the goats (Leviticus 22:17-19).

When an Israelite or a proselyte who had joined himself to Israel made a vow or resolved to bring a free-will offering, one essential condition was that it be unblemished and that it be a male.

> But whatsoever hath a blemish, that shall ye not offer: for it shall not be acceptable for you. And whosoever offereth a sacrifice of peace offerings unto the LORD to accomplish his

vow, or a freewill offering in beeves or sheep, it shall be perfect to be accepted; there shall be no blemish therein. Blind, or broken, or maimed, or having a wen, or scurvy, or scabbed, ye shall not offer these unto the LORD, nor make an offering by fire of them upon the altar unto the LORD (Leviticus 22:20-22).

Christ, the 'holy, harmless, undefiled' One is ever set before our eyes. The Lord God never tires of the sight. Let us never tire of the sight. Surely saved sinners will never get tired of the sight of him who brings us life by his death. There could be no blemish in the offering, because a holy God can have no fellowship with man, except in a blameless way. There can be no peace or reconciliation, except through an unblemished sacrifice. That Sacrifice is our blessed Saviour, the Lord Jesus Christ (2 Corinthians 5:21).

Our Sacrifices

Either a bullock or a lamb that hath anything superfluous or lacking in his parts, that mayest thou offer for a freewill offering; but for a vow it shall not be accepted (Leviticus 22:23).

The sacrifices for atonement and for a vow must be perfect, without blemish. But here an exception is made for sacrifices of free-will offerings. If the sacrifice was a free-will offering, it showed the offeror's view of things and not the Lord's view. Therefore, if his sacrifice from his herd or flock was an animal that was in some way maimed, lacking an eye or an ear, or the like, it showed and expressed his present state of weakness, sin, and failure as a sinner in this world. Yet, it was accepted of God.

Why was this allowance made? 1 Peter 2:5 has the answer. The Lord God accepts our feeble efforts at serving and honouring him through the infinite merits of our perfect Substitute and Sacrifice. Our free-will offerings of thanksgiving and praise, of worship and work, of ourselves, of life, are always maimed sacrifices at best.

The Lord has measured the narrowness of man's soul. But who has measured the unlimited fulness of the mind of God? 'It is as high as heaven; what canst thou do? deeper than hell; what canst thou know? The measure thereof is longer than the earth, and broader than the sea'

(Job 11:8, 9). Who can measure his infinite love? Who can comprehend what is the breadth, and length, and depth, and height, and know the love of God which passes knowledge (Ephesians 3:18, 19)?

Perfect Male

Verse 24 speaks of the sacrifice being one that was not bruised, crushed, broken, or cut or castrated, because Christ our Surety was a man, fully man in all things, sin alone excepted. There was no weakness or unmanliness in him.

> Ye shall not offer unto the LORD that which is bruised, or crushed, or broken, or cut; neither shall ye make any offering thereof in your land (Leviticus 22:24).

A Stranger's Sacrifice

God's priests could not offer the bread of God at a stranger's hand. A stranger's sacrifice was never to be offered to God by his priests.

> Neither from a stranger's hand shall ye offer the bread of your God of any of these; because their corruption is in them, and blemishes be in them: they shall not be accepted for you (Leviticus 22:25).

Why could they not offer on the altar of God that which their heathen neighbours gave them to offer him? Because their neighbours were idolaters! They were never to mix or incorporate into the worship of God the worship of idols. There can be no mixture of law and grace in the worship of God. There can be no mixture of free will and free grace, no mixing of Christ and Belial, no mixture of merit and mercy!

God will not accept the sacrifice or worship of a stranger's hand, because whatever the corrupt hand of an unsanctified man touches it pollutes. 'The plowing of the wicked is sin' (Proverbs 21:4).

The Ewe and the Lamb

> And the LORD spake unto Moses, saying, When a bullock, or a sheep, or a goat, is brought forth, then it shall be seven days

under the dam; and from the eighth day and thenceforth it shall be accepted for an offering made by fire unto the LORD. And whether it be cow or ewe, ye shall not kill it and her young both in one day (Leviticus 22:26-28).

Many suggest that this was meant to discourage cruelty. I do not doubt it had that effect. But the typical reason for this is more precious.

God the Father was to give up his darling Son. The Son was to be, as it were, torn from the Father's care by the hands of wicked men. How could this be represented if both the ewe and her young were offered together? It is written, and must never be forgotten, 'God so loved the world that he gave his only begotten Son'. The bleating of the tender lamb in its parent's ears, as it was taken from the fold, filling the air with the sad, mournful sound, represented the bleating of 'the Lamb of God led to the slaughter', who so sadly, mournfully wailed, 'Eli, Eli, lama sabachthani! My God! My God, why hast thou forsaken me?'

These laws applied to domestic, household things, arrangements about what they were to carry out of their houses and herds for the altar. Thus, a picture was hung in every house in Israel of this grand, gospel truth, 'God spared not his Son, but delivered him up to us all'.

Perfection Demanded

Now, learn how we can and must worship our God.

But whatsoever hath a blemish, that shall ye not offer: for it shall not be acceptable for you. And whosoever offereth a sacrifice of peace offerings unto the LORD to accomplish his vow, or a freewill offering in beeves or sheep, it shall be perfect to be accepted; there shall be no blemish therein. Blind, or broken, or maimed, or having a wen, or scurvy, or scabbed, ye shall not offer these unto the LORD, nor make an offering by fire of them upon the altar unto the LORD. Either a bullock or a lamb that hath anything superfluous or lacking in his parts, that mayest thou offer for a freewill offering; but for a vow it shall not be accepted. Ye shall not offer unto the LORD that which is bruised, or crushed, or broken, or cut; neither shall ye make any offering thereof in your land. Neither from a stranger's hand shall ye offer the bread of your God of any of these; because their corruption is in them, and blemishes be in them: they shall not be accepted for you. And the LORD spake unto Moses, saying, When a bullock, or a sheep, or a goat, is brought forth, then it shall be seven days under the dam; and from the eighth day and thenceforth it shall be accepted for an offering made by fire unto the LORD. And whether it be cow or ewe, ye shall not kill it and her young both in one day. And when ye will offer a sacrifice of thanksgiving unto the LORD, offer it at your own will. On the same day it shall be eaten up; ye shall leave none of it until the morrow: I am the LORD. Therefore shall ye keep my commandments, and do them: I am the LORD. Neither shall ye profane my holy name; but I will be hallowed among the children of Israel: I am the LORD which hallow you, That brought you out of the land of Egypt, to be your God: I am the LORD (Leviticus 22:20-33).

We must worship God with a perfect sacrifice (v. 21). We cannot bring a sacrifice to God which costs us nothing. God will not be worshipped without self-denial. A stranger's sacrifice is a sacrifice that costs nothing. 'Neither from a stranger's hand shall ye offer the bread of your God' (v. 25). We must worship the Lord our God with a willing heart (v. 29). And the sacrifice must be eaten. The whole sacrifice was to be eaten on the day it was offered (v. 30; John 6:48-58).

Five Motives
In verses 31-33 the Lord gives us five motives for worshipping him, five words of inspiration to stir up and inspire our hearts in his worship.

1. 'I am the Lord.'
2. 'I will be hallowed among the children of Israel.'
3. 'I am the Lord which hallow you.'
4. 'I am the Lord which brought you out Egypt.'
5. 'To be your God.'

'Profane not my holy name'! If you attempt to come to God in any way other than by Christ, his blood, his righteousness, his merit, his intercession, his sacrifice, you profane the name of God in doing so. You trample the blood of his Son under your feet. You do despite to the

Spirit of grace. You mock God and attempt to rob him of his glory. His commandment is clear. 'Profane not my holy name'!

How can I, a vile sinner, come to God without profaning his name? How can I hallow his name and still come to him? How can I honour, sanctify, and glorify the King of Heaven and still come to him? I must come to him trusting his Son. I must come to him with his Son. I must come to him by his Son. I must come to him in his Son (John 14:6).

If you come to God by Christ, you can never profane his name. Faith in Christ honours his name. Faith in Christ honours God (John 6:28, 29). This is how God's priests live. By faith in Christ, God accepts us as his holy priesthood and accepts us entirely (Ecclesiastes 9:7).

Chapter 47

'Shall Be Perfect To Be Accepted'

And whosoever offereth a sacrifice of peace offerings unto the LORD
to accomplish his vow, or a freewill offering in beeves or sheep, it shall
be perfect to be accepted; there shall be no blemish therein.

Leviticus 22:21

How many times have you heard people use this statement to justify
their behaviour 'Well, nobody's perfect'? How many times have you
used it yourself? Of course, the statement is true. None of us is perfect.
But what an understatement! We are all sinners. Sinners by birth, by
nature, by choice, by practice, at heart. In the very core of our being we
are sin, nothing but sin, a constant, growing mass of iniquity. We are
transgressors in all things at all times (1 John 1:8-10). The Bible does
not only tell us we make mistakes, we are less than perfect, and we have
sinned. The Word of God declares and we must acknowledge that we
are sin, and there is never a time when we are not sinning. So long as
we live in this body of flesh, we are an ugly, hideous mass of sin.

The holy Lord God demands perfection. He will accept nothing less
than perfection. The perfect God demands perfection. It is written, 'It
shall be perfect to be accepted'.

Ceremonial Worship
During the days of legal ordinances, under the ceremonial law, the
children of Israel were taught to exercise great care in coming to the

house of God. The law and the sacrifices and ceremonies associated with divine worship were meticulous. They were designed to inspire reverence for the holy Lord God, while reminding the worshipper of his sin and pointing him to Christ as his only, all-sufficient hope before God. Nothing was to be done thoughtlessly. In every detail the Lord God showed himself to be God and declared, 'I the Lord thy God am a jealous God'. He said, 'I will be sanctified in them that come nigh me'. He commanded, 'Profane not my holy name'.

The glorious perfections of the infinite, thrice holy God demand reverence. No Israelite could come to God's altar aright who did not carefully consider what he was doing and how it was to be done. No doubt, much fear was involved in the worship of those ancients. God's law and its ordinances inspired fear in the people who approached him: fear of carelessly omitting something, fear of bringing an unacceptable sacrifice, fear of intruding where one was not permitted, and putting a hand where it was forbidden. If one would worship God great care must be exercised. It is written of every ceremony, every sacrifice, every act and every work. 'It shall be perfect to be accepted.' That was the law; and God would not budge from it.

The holy, perfect Lord God cannot and will not accept anything less than absolute perfection.

The Lesson
This is no easy lesson to learn; but learn it we must. I fear in our worship we are often terribly thoughtless. How careless and indifferent, how half-hearted we are. We are commonly careless in preparing to worship God, thoughtless in prayer, in the reading of Holy Scripture, in our songs of praise, in hearing the Lord's message, in preaching, in seeking God's presence, his power, and his blessing.

When we gather with God's saints in his house to worship him, we are coming to God. Our Saviour said, 'Where two or three are gathered together in my name, there am I in the midst of them'. The Spirit of God tells us as we gather in Christ's name, 'Ye are the temple of the living God'. The church of God is 'an habitation of God through the Spirit'. Of every gospel assembly, we are assured, 'The Spirit of God dwelleth in you'. Those facts ought to inspire reverence.

The glory of God, his grace toward us, and our love for him ought to make us whole-hearted in worship. When we come into the house of

God, when we gather with God's saints in the presence of God, we ought to behave ourselves as men and women in the immediate presence of Jehovah. We ought to strive with the utmost watchfulness of holy care to honour God our Saviour. Our God requires and deserves our best in attitude, behaviour, approach and dress (Malachi 1:1-14).

Priests and Sacrifices
The priests who stood for the people before God and represented Christ, must be in bodily presence the perfection of manhood; men without physical blemish. When old age crept upon them, they must give place to one who showed no such sign of decay. Their garments must be white and clean in their daily service. On the Day of Atonement, for glory and beauty, God's high priest appeared in all the dignity and radiance the purest gold and most precious stones could put upon him.

The sacrifice offered must be without blemish, as seen throughout the book of Leviticus. Every sacrifice offered for atonement had to be examined before its blood was spilt. 'It shall be perfect to be accepted'.

Blood
Under the law, the guilt of sin and the need of atonement were constantly before the eye. Everywhere within the holy place was the marks of blood. If a man went into the tabernacle, he would see the floor, the curtain, the altar, and every piece of furniture stained with the blood of slaughtered lambs, and calves, and doves. Blood was poured by bowlfuls on the floor and sprinkled on almost every holy thing. Everywhere you looked, you would be compelled to read and hear this Word from God. 'Without shedding of blood there is no remission.'

There can be no approach to a thrice-holy God without the remission of sin. That remission must be obtained through the atoning blood. The Israelite, if he thought about what he was doing and what he observed, must have been keenly aware that he worshipped a God who is terrible in holiness, a God who hates and punishes sin, a God who will by no means clear the guilty, or pardon sin without atonement. As he observed the unblemished sacrifice, its blood gushing from its slit throat, he could not help hear God declare, 'It shall be perfect to be accepted'.

He saw in the necessity for a perfect sacrifice a declaration of the holiness of God. He must have felt his sin was no trifling matter. God required the blood of a perfect sacrifice before sin could be forgiven and removed. A life must be sacrificed. Blood had to be shed. The life and the blood had to come from a perfect, unblemished victim.

The Law

God's holy law was constantly ringing in the ears of his people in those days, declaring incessantly, 'The soul that sinneth, it shall die'. The law showed a man his sin, exposed his guilt, and condemned him for sin. The sacrifice showed him a door of hope, but hope altogether outside himself, for 'it shall be perfect to be accepted'.

Yes, we preach the law. It is holy, just, and good. We do not preach the law as a rule of bondage. We preach the law as God intended it, to shut sinners up to Christ. I pray that God the Holy Ghost will lay his holy law, like an axe, at the root of all our self-righteousness and cut it down. I pray he will make the law a mirror to us and make us see ourselves in it as we really are, exposing all our warts, spots, blemishes, and all the inward foulness of our hearts and souls. Only then will we be driven outside ourselves to Christ for cleansing.

God always kills before he makes alive. He wounds before he heals, gets us lost before he saves, shows us our foulness before he cleanses, and strips us naked before he clothes us. He always makes people miserable before he comforts, and abases before he exalts.

God says, 'It shall be perfect to be accepted'. That unbending declaration shuts you and me up to Christ altogether. I want us to hear this word from God for the rest of our lives. When we rise in the morning and go to God in prayer, when we go to work, or school, or go about our daily employment, when we come into our homes in the evening, and bow with our families before the throne of God at our table, when we lay down to sleep, when we come to the house of God to worship him, when we leave to serve him, I want us to hear our God speaking these words to us. 'It shall be perfect to be accepted.'

Perfection Demanded

God demands perfection. The holy, perfect Lord God will never accept anything or anyone that is not perfect. He says, 'It shall be perfect to be accepted'. The thrice holy Jehovah would not have a blemished priest before his altar, or a blemished sacrifice on it. He demands perfection (Leviticus 21:21; 22:20, 21). 'It shall be perfect to be accepted.'

Put this plummet to your wall and see how straight it is. 'It shall be perfect to be accepted.' That fact shuts out all those faulty offerings by which multitudes hope to find acceptance with God. It totally nullifies any hope you have of attaining acceptance with God by something in you or something done by you. Salvation cannot be attained by good works, no matter how good they appear to be. For a work to be good the person performing it must be good and the book says, 'None is good but one, that is, God'. Because we are all corrupt, we are all without ability to do good (Job 8:20; 9:1-3, 20; 14:4; 15:12-16; 25:4-6). 'There is none that doeth good, no not one.'

If the bed on which you rest and the covers you wrap yourself with are made with the material and fabric of your works, 'the bed is shorter than that a man can stretch himself on it: and the covering narrower than that he can wrap himself in it' (Isaiah 28:20). Your 'good works' can no more commend you to God, give you acceptance with him, and save your soul than adultery, rape, or murder (Isaiah 65:2-7).

God will not accept the worship, service, or sacrifice of any man who has any pollution of iniquity, any blemish of infirmity, any stain of sin upon him (Isaiah 1:11-15). Hear what God says about the most devout services of self-righteous men (Isaiah 66:3). God demands perfection (Isaiah 1:16, 17). 'It shall be perfect to be accepted.'

That is what God demands, but I cannot do it. I cannot give it. 'It shall be perfect to be accepted.' It is not written, 'It shall have no great and grievous blemish' but 'there shall be no blemish therein'. That is the standard, absolute perfection. Let the plummet hang straight and see whether you can build to it. By this standard examine the walls of that house you have built upon the sand of your own works. It is a bowing wall and a tottering fence, altogether out of line as tested by God's uncompromising requirement. 'It shall be perfect to be accepted; there shall be no blemish therein'.

Why do you continue to look for salvation by what you do? You cannot be saved by your works; by what you do, what you feel, what you experience, or by what you know. Your nature is tainted. God's Word assures us it is so. There is evil in your heart from the very beginning. You are not perfect. You are not without blemish. This sad fact spoils all at the very beginning. You are blemished and imperfect.

Who can bring a clean thing out of an unclean? Not one. If the fountain is tainted, can the streams be pure? Do you think it possible

415

that you, a fallen sinner in whom there is a decided bias toward evil, can possibly render perfect service to the holy Lord God? Your hands are foul. How can your work be clean? Darkness cannot produce light. Sin cannot produce righteousness. Death cannot bring forth life. If we are rotten at the core, how can our thoughts, words, ways be perfect? And yet all must be perfect to be accepted.

As for this poor excuse for a man who writes these words, I dare not claim that the best deed I have ever done, or the most fervent prayer I have ever prayed could have been accepted in and of itself before God. I know I have no perfection in my best things, much less in my worst. My best deed, my best prayer, my best preaching, my best thought, my best feeling, my best emotion, my best love, my best faith, my best aspiration, my highest devotion, my most costly sacrifice, my most useful service is utterly vile and forbids my acceptance with God upon the basis of it! God says, 'It shall be perfect to be accepted. There shall be no blemish therein.' Do you hear him? 'It shall be perfect to be accepted; there shall be no blemish therein.'

Our Hope
Are we, then, without hope? Is there hope for a sinner? Oh, blessed be God, there is 'a good hope through grace'. There is no hope in ourself. But there is hope for such sinners as we are in Christ. This word from God, 'It shall be perfect to be accepted', shuts us up entirely to Christ.

After telling us how vile and helpless we are in ourselves before him who demands such perfection as we can never give, the Lord God, by his prophet Isaiah, bids us come to him for grace and find perfection in his darling Son (Isaiah 1:18-20; 45:20-25).

Perfection in Christ
I call you now to come to Christ and find in him that perfection God requires, that holiness without which no man shall see the Lord. He is absolutely perfect. There is no blemish in him.

He is perfect in his nature as God and man. No stain defiled his birth. No pollution touched his body. No evil soiled his soul. The prince of this world himself, with keenest eyes, came and searched the Saviour, but found nothing sinful in him, who 'was in all points tempted like as we are, yet without sin'. There was not even a possibility of sinning in our holy Saviour. He had no tendency toward transgression. He had no desire for iniquity. Nothing that could be construed into evil ever came upon his character. Our perfect sacrifice is without spot or wrinkle.

As he was perfect in his nature, so he was in his motive. What brought him from above but love to God and man? You can find no trace of ambition in Christ Jesus. In him there is no thought of self. No sinister or sordid motive ever lingered in his breast, or crossed his mind. He was purity and holiness in the highest degree. Even his enemies have nothing to allege against the purity of the motive of Jesus of Nazareth.

As his nature was perfect, so was his spirit. He was never sinfully angry, nor harsh, nor untrue, nor idle. The air of his soul was the atmosphere of heaven rather than of earth.

Look at his life of obedience, and see how perfect that was. Which commandment did he ever break? Which duty of relationship did he ever forget? He honoured the law of God and loved the souls of men. He gave the character of God perfect reflection in his human life. You can see what God is as you see what Christ is. He is perfect, even as his Father who is in heaven is perfect. There is no redundancy, or excess, or superfluity in his character. There is nothing omitted in any point.

Look at the perfection of his sacrifice. It was and is forever infinite, meritorious, and effectual. He gave his body to be tortured and his mind to be crushed and broken, even unto the agony and death of the cross. He gave himself for us a perfect sacrifice. All that the law could ask was in him. He has given to his Father double for all our sins. He has given him suffering for sin committed, and yet a perfect obedience to the law. The Lord God is well pleased with him. He rests in the Son of his love. For Christ's sake, he smiles upon all the multitudes of sinners who are in him and represented by him.

Our Sacrifice
Come with me now to God. Bring this perfect sacrifice to God. By faith take it to be yours. You may. Christ belongs to every believer. If you trust him, he is yours. Poor guilty soul, whether you have been a believer fifty years, ten years, or ten seconds, if you believe on the Son of God, you may now come with Christ in your hand and say to the Father, 'O my Lord, you have given all that your law requires, a perfect sacrifice. There is no blemish in it. Behold, I bring it to you as my own.'

With that God is satisfied. What joy! God is satisfied. The Father is well pleased. He has raised Christ from the dead and set him at his own right hand in the heavenly places in token of that satisfaction. Let us be satisfied too. My soul, when your eyes are full of tears because of sin and your heart is disturbed by countless infirmities and imperfections, look away, look away from yourself to the full atonement made and the utmost ransom paid. Christ is perfect; and Christ is accepted. His atonement is perfect; and his atonement is accepted. His righteousness is perfect; and his righteousness is accepted.

Perfect and Accepted

Christ has made us perfect in himself; and in him we are accepted, 'accepted in the beloved'. He was manifested to take away our sins; and he has done it (1 John 3:5). He came here to bring in everlasting righteousness for us; and he has done it. He came here to make us holy, unblameable, unreproveable, and utterly without spot, or blemish, or wrinkle before God. And he has done it (Colossians 1:12; 2:9, 10; Ephesians 5:25-27; Hebrews 10:9-14; Jude 1:24, 25).

When the Israelite sprinkled the blood on the door posts and the lintel of his house, he then shut the door. He was inside. He could not see the blood. The blood was outside on the posts. Was he safe? Yes. God said, 'When I see the blood, I will pass over you'!

It is God's sight of the blood of his dear Son that is the everlasting safeguard of all who are in Christ. It is precious, and sweet beyond expression to me, to look at that blood once shed for many for the remission of sins. I look upon it with delight. Yet, if ever there should come a dark night to me in which I cannot see it, God still sees it, and all is well. I am safe. I am saved because it is not, 'when you see the blood', but 'when I see the blood, I will pass over you'. It is the perfection of the sacrifice, not of our sight, which is our safeguard. It is the absence of all blemish from the sacrifice, not the absence of blemish from your faith that makes you to be 'accepted in the Beloved'.

God will never accept anything any sinner does for him until he is accepted by the merits of a perfect, unblemished sacrifice. But once he has accepted us by the perfect, unblemished sacrifice of his dear Son, he accepts even our blind, maimed, broken, scurvy, scabbed, superfluous, and seriously-lacking sacrifices of praise and thanksgiving as sacrifices holy and well-pleasing to him (Leviticus 22:21-23; 1 Peter 2:5; Ecclesiastes 9:7-10).

Chapter 48

Inspiration To Worship

Therefore shall ye keep my commandments, and do them: I am the LORD. Neither shall ye profane my holy name; but I will be hallowed among the children of Israel: I am the LORD which hallow you, that brought you out of the land of Egypt, to be your God: I am the LORD.

Leviticus 22:31-33

God's saints come to the house of God to worship God, not just to go through the motions of regular religious activity, but to worship our God. The Holy Spirit tells us that 'bodily exercise profiteth little' (1 Timothy 4:8). That is to say, the mere exercise of religious activity and ceremonies, the mere performance of religious duty, is of little benefit to our souls. What we must have is godliness; living, vital godliness. It is the duty of all to worship the holy Lord God. But it is our privilege to do so because God has made us his own in Christ Jesus.

Seven Requirements
In this instructive chapter the Lord God shows us seven things he requires of those who would worship him. These are things revealed throughout the Scriptures; but they are specifically required of God in this twenty-second chapter of Leviticus. If we would worship the eternal, infinite, omnipotent, ineffably glorious, sovereign Lord God:

1. We must stand before him in perfect cleanness (v. 4).

None can eat the holy things of God's altar 'until he be clean'. Christ is our Altar and our Sacrifice; but none can feast upon the things of Christ, none can enjoy and partake of the boundless mercy, grace, and love of God in Christ 'until he be clean'. There is only one way for sinners to be made clean before God. If we would be clean before God, we must plunge into that Fountain God himself has opened for uncleanness and sin (1 Corinthians 6:9-11, 19, 20).

2. We must worship him willingly (vv. 19, 29).

Anything we offer to God must be offered willingly because we want to. No sinner ever truly wants to worship the true God until he is made willing by the work of God's omnipotent grace. But once God puts his grace in us, we worship him willingly, we want to worship him. Mark this down and take it to the bank. God almighty will never receive or honour anything done for him, or given in his name, that does not arise from a willing heart (2 Corinthians 8:12).

3. What we bring to God must be our best (v. 24).

God will not have our leftovers! He will not honour that which does not honour him. If we would worship God, we must worship him with our best; be it time, efforts, gifts, or service (Malachi 1:6-14)

4. Worship of God requires personal sacrifice (v. 25).

Like David (2 Samuel 24:24), we must never offer God that which costs us nothing. Most people are busy with all kinds of things. The cares and pleasures of life in this world consume almost all their time and attention. When it is convenient they attend church, give God a little tip and sing, 'Oh, how I love Jesus'! But any time something more important comes up; a good football game, a special television show, a visiting relative, or a sick dog, they absent themselves from the house of God with little regret. They say to themselves, 'I can always go to church next week. The Lord knows my heart'. Of that much you can be sure: the Lord does know our hearts, and he will judge us accordingly!

Those who are truly God's people love the house of God and the worship of God. They arrange their lives around his worship. Nothing comes up, over which they have control, to keep them from the house of God. They see to it that when the saints of God gather for worship, they are among them, unless their absence is genuinely unavoidable.

Our faithfulness in the matter of public worship is much more than a matter of duty. It is our delightful choice. Public worship is the single most important aspect of the believer's life in this world. Nothing is more important to believers in this world than the public assembly of the saints for worship. The public assembly of the saints for worship is the local church, the congregation of the Lord, the house of God.

5. If we would worship the Lord our God, we must do so by feasting upon his sacrifice in his house (v. 30).

Worship requires the feast of faith. The Sacrifice must be eaten. The whole Sacrifice must be eaten. The Sacrifice upon which we feast is Christ Jesus, our crucified Saviour (John 6:48-58).

6. God requires we worship him after the divine order (v. 31).

If we would worship God, we must worship him in the way he has prescribed, adding nothing to it and taking nothing from it. God's servant, David, shows us this by his own painful example in 1 Chronicles 13 through 15.

The worship of God in his house involves the reading of his Word, prayer, preaching, and praise, the frequent remembrance of Christ at the Lord's Table and the practice of believer's baptism which is the believer's confession of faith in Christ by immersion. Any addition to or omission from those things is the perverting of the ordinance of God.

7. And God requires we honour him in the purpose of our hearts and in the exercise of worship (v. 32).

He says, 'I will be hallowed ... Neither shall ye profane my holy name'. Let us take care that we honour God in what we do in his house. In attitude, in doctrine, in song, in prayer, in praise, and in preaching our object must be the glory of God. Nothing is to be done or tolerated for self-gratification, the pleasing of the flesh, or to impress men.

Without question, when we come to the house of God to worship the King of Heaven, we ought to dress for worship. It seems beyond ridiculous to me that this matter even needs to be addressed. But in this day of self-centred contempt for anything showing respect for others it must be addressed. I am not about to establish a dress code for our worship services; yet there are principles for the way we dress and sadly immodest attire has become common in many places. In the house of God, attending the worship of God in the assembly of his saints, we ought to dress for worship, as people who take the worship of God seriously and come to the house of God respectfully. I know everything today is geared toward casual attire but let us, out of reverence for our God, respect for one another, and the honour of the gospel of the grace of God, dress with thought and dignity when we come to the house of God. Do not over-dress, calling attention to yourself; do not under-dress, showing a disregard for the worship of God. In the house of God especially, let us all adorn ourselves in 'modest apparel'.

Five Motives
In verses 31-33 the Lord our God gives us five reasons why we ought to worship him with such whole-hearted devotion. Here are five great motives by which our God stirs our hearts to worship him, in our hearts, in our lives, in our homes, and in his house.

> Therefore shall ye keep my commandments, and do them: I am the LORD. Neither shall ye profane my holy name; but I will be hallowed among the children of Israel: I am the LORD which hallow you, that brought you out of the land of Egypt, to be your God: I am the LORD (Leviticus 22:31-33).

All men ought to worship God; but none can worship him except he does so of his own will, with a willing heart. Let none be induced to bring a sacrifice to God, pretend to worship him, or take up a profession of faith in Christ because someone pressures you to do so, or you might thereby please a friend, or your family, or because you want to make a good impression upon others, appearing to be what you are not. All true worship, all service to God, must be 'at your own will'. It must flow spontaneously from the heart. God will not have it any other way.

1. The Lord our God inspires us to worship him because of who he is. 'I am the Lord.'
He who is alone the worthy object of worship and praise, he who is alone the worthy object of faith and devotion is he who is the Lord, Jehovah, the sovereign Monarch of the universe.
No one will ever truly worship until he worships at the footstool of an absolute Sovereign. Divine sovereignty is not the last thing God's people learn, but the very first thing learned in the experience of grace. The first thing John saw in Revelation 4, when he was taken up to heaven by the Spirit of God was God on his throne. Men bargain with an equal, trample upon an inferior, and bribe a superior. We worship only one who is Sovereign (Deuteronomy 4:39; Leviticus 19:37).

2. This great, glorious, omnipotent sovereign, the Lord God, the Almighty, inspires us to worship him by stooping to be worshipped by us. He says, 'I will be hallowed among the children of Israel'.

What majestic condescending grace! God wills to be worshipped by us! Yes, he demands that we profane not his name. Yes, he demands we worship him in the precise way he prescribes. But he wills to be worshipped by us! He says, 'I will be hallowed among the children of Israel' (John 4:23, 24; Philippians 3:3).

3. The Lord God inspires us to hallow and sanctify him as the Lord God by reminding us he alone has sanctified us by his grace. 'I am the Lord which hallow you.'

The Lord our God has many distinct names by which he reveals himself to us in the Old Testament. Particularly, his great redemptive name, Jehovah, the name by which he first revealed himself to Moses. Jehovah is used at least fourteen times in a compound form. Those fourteen compound names of our God are intended both to show us who he is and to assure us of his great works of mercy and grace in saving our souls. But of all those great names, none is greater, or more inspiring to our hearts than that which describes the work mentioned here 'I am the Lord which hallow you'. His name is Jehovah-M'kaddesh. He says, 'I am the Lord that doth sanctify you' (Exodus 31:13; Leviticus 20:8). The Lord our God has set us apart from all men by election, redemption, effectual calling, and regeneration. Let us set him apart from all the gods of men by worship, faith, and devotion.

4. Our great God and Saviour inspires us to worship him as God our Saviour by reminding us of his great deliverance of our souls. 'That brought you up out of the land of Egypt' (v. 33).

Just as he saved Israel out of Egypt, he has saved us by special providence, by blood atonement, by omnipotent power, and by his word of grace. Soon, he will complete his work for us, in us, and with us by the resurrection of our bodies at the last day.

5. We are here inspired and motivated to worship our God by him reminding us of his great reason for all he has done. He has done all this and much, much more 'to be your God'!

Who is a God like our God? Who would not worship such a God, if only they knew him? 'Who would not fear thee, O King of nations? For to thee doth it appertain: forasmuch as among all the wise men of the nations, and in all their kingdoms, there is none like unto thee' (Jeremiah 10:7).

Who is a God like unto thee, that pardoneth iniquity, and passeth by the transgression of the remnant of his heritage? He retaineth not his anger forever, because he delighteth in mercy. He will turn again; he will have compassion upon us; he will subdue our iniquities; and thou wilt cast all their sins into the depths of the sea. Thou wilt perform the truth to Jacob, and the mercy to Abraham, which thou hast sworn unto our fathers from the days of old (Micah 7:18-20).

Chapter 49

The Chain Of Grace

Therefore shall ye keep my commandments, and do them: I am the LORD. Neither shall ye profane my holy name; but I will be hallowed among the children of Israel: I am the LORD which hallow you, that brought you out of the land of Egypt, to be your God: I am the LORD.

Leviticus 22:31-33

In the eighth chapter of the book of Romans, the Apostle Paul sets forth the great purpose of God in grace. He shows us that the purpose of God is the salvation of his people. In verse 28, he tells us all the works of providence come to pass by his all-wise omnipotence in pursuit of that end. 'And we know that all things work together for good to them that love God, to them who are the called according to his purpose'.

When David thought upon this great, glorious, soul-cheering fact that our God rules the universe in absolute sovereignty for the salvation of his people, he said, 'O God ... my soul trusteth in thee: yea, in the shadow of thy wings will I make my refuge ... I will cry unto God most high; unto God that performeth all things for me. He shall send from heaven, and save me' (Psalm 57:1-3).

Paul sets before us the great mystery of providence in Romans 8:28. Then, in verses 29 and 30, he shows us how God accomplishes the salvation of his people, according to his sovereign, eternal, unalterable purpose.

425

For whom he did foreknow, he also did predestinate to be conformed to the image of his Son, that he might be the firstborn among many brethren. Moreover whom he did predestinate, them he also called: and whom he called, them he also justified: and whom he justified, them he also glorified (Romans 8:29, 30).

Five Works of Grace

Here we have the grace of God set before us in five great works. These works of grace Matthew Henry compared to a golden chain with five unbreakable links, reaching from the everlasting past to the everlasting future, from eternity to eternity.

1. Divine Foreknowledge: 'Whom he did foreknow.' God's foreknowledge is his everlasting love for his elect (Jeremiah 31:3).

2. Sovereign Predestination: 'He also did predestinate to be conformed to the image of his Son, that he might be the firstborn among many brethren.'

3. Effectual Calling: 'Moreover, whom he did predestinate, them he also called.' God adopted his elect and named us as his children from eternity. Then, at the appointed time of love, he called us to be his children and made us his children in the sweet experience of his grace (Galatians 4:4-6; 1 John 3:1, 2).

4. Eternal Justification: 'Whom he called, them he also justified.' As here stated by the Spirit of God, God's elect were justified from eternity in his eternal purpose. We were justified by the obedience unto death of Christ at Calvary. And we are justified consciously in the experience of grace by the testimony of the Spirit by the gift of faith in Christ.

5. Everlasting Glorification: 'And whom he justified, them he also glorified.' Here God the Holy Ghost tells us that all God's elect, being one in Christ, were glorified with him eternally as the Lamb of God slain and accepted before the world began. We were glorified with him when he was glorified and took his seat in heaven as our Forerunner (Ephesians 2:4-6). We shall be glorified with him in resurrection glory at the last day.

Five Challenges

In response to this great revelation of God's sovereign purpose and saving grace in Christ, the Apostle Paul raised five bold challenges of faith. Because he believed what God revealed, he lifted his eyes to heaven, scanned the experiences of time, and peered into the very depths of hell and said in Romans 8:31-39:

1. 'What shall we then say to these things? If God be for us, who can be against us?'

2. 'He that spared not his own Son, but delivered him up for us all, how shall he not with him also freely give us all things?'

3. 'Who shall lay anything to the charge of God's elect? It is God that justifieth.'

4. 'Who is he that condemneth? It is Christ that died, yea rather, that is risen again, who is even at the right hand of God, who also maketh intercession for us.'

5. 'Who shall separate us from the love of Christ? shall tribulation, or distress, or persecution, or famine, or nakedness, or peril, or sword? As it is written, For thy sake we are killed all the day long; we are accounted as sheep for the slaughter. Nay, in all these things we are more than conquerors through him that loved us. For I am persuaded, that neither death, nor life, nor angels, nor principalities, nor powers, nor things present, nor things to come, nor height, nor depth, nor any other creature, shall be able to separate us from the love of God, which is in Christ Jesus our Lord.'

In Romans 8 Paul describes God's great purpose of grace. It is eternal, absolute, unalterable, and shall be accomplished. 'He shall not fail'! When time shall be no more, God's elect in glory shall be exactly those whom he loved with an everlasting love, those whom he chose and predestinated before time began.

Our Experience of Grace

There is another aspect of grace that is as important as God's purpose of grace. In fact, it is this other aspect of grace that makes God's purpose of grace glorious in our eyes and gives the confidence to raise the bold, confident challenges of faith we have just read. That other aspect of grace is the experience of it, as we shall see.

Therefore shall ye keep my commandments, and do them: I am the LORD. Neither shall ye profane my holy name; but I will be hallowed among the children of Israel: I am the LORD which

427

hallow you, that brought you out of the land of Egypt, to be your God: I am the LORD (Leviticus 22:31-33).

Commenting on this passage, Robert Hawker wrote, 'Here is God's authority as God. Here is added to this his gracious character as their covenant God. And as if these were not enough, here is added that striking instance of his covenant-mercy in their redemption from Egypt.' It is by his authority as God that our God and Saviour demands our reverence, our faith, our obedience, and our consecration to himself.

This is also a picture of grace in experience, a picture of that which every chosen, redeemed sinner experiences when God saves him by his omnipotent mercy. Here are seven things experienced by every saved sinner in this wondrous thing we call 'salvation'. As Matthew Henry saw Romans 8:29 and 30 as five links in the golden chain of grace purposed. I see Leviticus 22:31-33 as setting before us seven links in the equally golden chain of grace experienced.

God's purpose of grace is a theme of worship and praise. But God's purpose of grace will never motivate anyone to worship him until grace is experienced. In these three verses the Lord our God uses our experience of grace to motivate us in his worship and praise.

Revelation
The first link in this chain of grace is revelation, God's revelation of himself. Here, in verse 31, he says, 'I am the LORD'. As the Lord God spoke to Moses out of the bush and revealed himself to him, as he revealed himself to Abraham, Isaac, and Jacob, so he must reveal himself to us if ever we come to know him in the glorious experience of grace. There is no salvation apart from the knowledge of God (John 17:3). And there is no knowledge of God apart from God's revelation of himself.

God is known and reveals himself in and by creation, providence, judgment, and the written Word, so all are without excuse (Romans 1 and 2). But the Lord savingly reveals himself only in these three ways.

1. The Man Christ Jesus, the God-man our Saviour, the Lord Jesus Christ is the revelation of the eternal God (John 1:14, 18; 14:6-9).

2. The Lord God reveals himself to men and women by the preaching of the gospel (2 Corinthians 4:3-7; Ephesians 1:13, 14).

3. But it takes more than hearing any other man preach the gospel for a sinner to know the living God. It takes more than the preaching of the gospel to save an immortal soul. If ever you are saved, if ever you come to know God, the Lord Jesus Christ must be revealed in you, not just to you, but in you by God the Holy Ghost (Galatians 1:15, 16; Colossians 1:27).

Once the Lord God makes himself known, if ever the Lord God is pleased to reveal himself, that sinner to whom and in whom he is revealed will reverence him as God. 'Neither shall ye profane my holy name'. The second link in this chain of grace is:

Reverence

Reverence for God has something to do with what the Bible calls 'the fear of God'. When the Lord God comes in the saving operations of his grace, the first thing, the very first thing that happens is fear, reverence for God as God; sovereign, just, and holy (Isaiah 66:1, 2; Ezekiel 1:28; Revelation 1:17, 18). That is what Moses experienced at the burning bush, what Isaiah experienced in the year that king Uzziah died, and what Saul of Tarsus experienced on the Damascus Road. And that is what every elect sinner experiences in salvation.

Worship

The third link in this chain, the third thing involved in the experience of grace is worship. The Lord God declares, 'I will be hallowed among the children of Israel'. Once God makes himself known, those who know him worship him. They not only bow before him acknowledging and confessing their guilt and sin, utterly withered, without strength, and helpless before his august majesty and holiness, they worship him alone as God, and worship as God alone, the only true God; sovereign, holy, righteous, just, gracious, and true.

Sanctification

Then, fourth, comes the blessed experience of sanctification, the new birth. Read the last line of verse 32, 'I am the Lord which hallow you'. Only when we are made to know who God is and worship him will we hear him declare, 'I am the LORD which hallow (sanctify) you'. God's elect were sanctified by him eternally in Christ (Jude 1:1) and sanctified by the blood of Christ at Calvary (Hebrews 10:9-14). And all those sanctified from eternity and at Calvary are sanctified by God the Holy Spirit in the new birth when Christ is formed in them and they are made partakers of the divine nature.

Deliverance

Read the last part of verse 32 and the first part of verse 33 together, and you will see the fifth link in this chain of grace as it is experienced. 'I am the LORD which hallow you. That brought you out of the Land of Egypt.' Here is the declaration of deliverance by grace. When you find yourself at the footstool of his throne, worshipping him as God, you will hear God declare deliverance to your soul. You were in bondage, and in darkness, in the land of the cursed, but he brought you out by the blood of the Lamb and by his mighty arm of omnipotent mercy and irresistible grace.

Conversion

Sixth, 'I brought you out of the land of Egypt, to be your God'. Once a sinner hears God's declaration of salvation, of deliverance, he is made to experience the wondrous, life changing blessedness of conversion. If ever God makes himself known to you in grace, you will have no other God. When you hear the law cry, 'Who is on the LORD'S side', you will take your place on his side with great delight and gratitude, renouncing every false way and every false god. That's called 'conversion'.

Consecration

The seventh link in the chain of grace is consecration. Once a sinner experiences this mighty operation of grace that we call salvation, he is forever more a person of consecration. All who know God, all who experience his grace in Christ, all who have been delivered by him from the curse of the law and the bondage of guilt and sin, all who have been snatched as brands from the burning are forever God's. He says, in light of all he has done for us, 'Therefore shall ye keep my commandments, and do them: I am the LORD'.

This is not a matter of legal obedience. Not one of us ever keeps even one of his commandments by our own effort or work. As everywhere else in the law, this is a promise of grace. It is talking about faith in Christ (Romans 3:31; 8:1-4; 1 John 3:23). The only way sinners like us keep his commandments is by trusting God's Son, our Saviour, our justice-satisfying, commandment-keeper, the Lord Jesus Christ.

By his gracious gift of faith in Christ, God the Holy Ghost continuously turns our hearts Godward, consecrating us by his grace to our Saviour (Colossians 3:1-3; 1 Corinthians 6:9-11, 19, 20; Romans 12:1, 2; 1 Corinthians 10:31).

Many years ago, in the reign of Queen Victoria, the Punjab Province of India came under the British Crown. The young Maharajah, then only a boy, sent an offering to his new monarch, the wonderful Koh-i-noor diamond (105.6 carets). It was placed in the Tower of London with the other crown jewels.

Several years later, the Maharajah, now a full-grown man, came to see the Queen. During his visit, he asked if he could see the Koh-i-noor diamond. Somewhat bewildered at his request, the Queen, courteously, gave orders that the jewel be brought under armed guard from the Tower to Buckingham Palace. When it arrived and was handed to the Maharajah. Everyone present eagerly watched to see what he would do. Taking the priceless jewel in his hand, he walked to the window, where he examined it carefully. Then as the onlookers still wondered, he walked back with it clasped in his hand and knelt before the Queen. 'Madam', he said, 'I gave you this jewel when I was a child, too young to know what I was doing. I want to give it again, in the fulness of my strength, with all my heart's affection and gratitude, now and forever, fully realising all that I do.' O Spirit of God, give me grace to so consecrate myself to Christ my God, now and forever, realising all I do!

As we read the instructions of God's holy law in the many typical ordinances and sacrifices of the Old Testament, we should earnestly pray that God the Holy Ghost would enlighten our understanding that we might be led, again and again, to our blessed Saviour, the Lord Jesus Christ. In this chapter, by the sanctity required of God's priests, we see him who is our Priest. In the unblemished object of every sacrifice, Christ's spotless nature is set before us.

May it be my portion, in every approach to God, to bear in the arms of my faith none and nothing but Christ! Gracious Spirit of God, keep me from bringing anything of my own to my God for acceptance with him! All that is in me, all that comes from me, is, as the prophet describes, torn, and lame, and sick. Let me never sacrifice to the Lord a corrupt thing. But looking wholly to Christ, the Lamb of God, in his infinite holiness, purity, and soul-cleansing oblation, may the Lord God accept this one all-sufficient offering at my hand and sanctify my soul by the precious merits of his obedience and death for me.

Could our zeal know no respite, could our prayers know no pause, could our efforts know no relaxation, could we give all we have of time, wealth, talent, and opportunity, could we die a martyr's death a thousand times over, would not the Lord Jesus Christ, the best beloved of our souls, deserve far more?

Chapter 50

'The Feasts Of The LORD'

And the LORD spake unto Moses, saying, Speak unto the children of Israel, and say unto them, Concerning the feasts of the LORD, which ye shall proclaim to be holy convocations, even these are my feasts ... And Moses declared unto the children of Israel the feasts of the LORD.

Leviticus 23:1-44

In the Old Testament throughout the legal, Mosaic dispensation, the Lord God required his people to keep seven distinct feasts called 'holy convocations' every year. These 'holy convocations' were solemn assemblies of God's people for worship. They were to be observed in a specific order, on specific days, and in specific ways. Like all things in the law and worship of the Triune Jehovah, these seven feasts were typical of things spiritual and typical of our Lord Jesus Christ and God's great salvation in him. The feasts are described in Leviticus 23.

This twenty-third chapter of Leviticus is a chapter of tremendous importance full of typical gospel instruction. The seven feasts were seasons of joyful solemnity appointed by God to point to Christ's coming and the salvation he would accomplish. Each feast pointed the children of Israel back to something they had experienced and pointed them forward to things yet to come.

433

The Order

One cannot avoid noticing how one feast led to another and how each seemed to suggest its successor. In other words, the feasts were given by divine command specifically to teach by type and shadow the order of things to come. They were commemorations of grace.

Israel's feasts seem to represent the course of time, from creation to the final end of all things. The Lamb slain, the Passover, begins it, while the eighth day of the Feast of Tabernacles is its close. The Sabbath, symbolizing rest and pointing to God's rest in himself and our rest in him, precedes and follows each in this course of history.

These feasts also appear to be representative of the great works of our God in redemption, grace, and salvation, ultimately culminating in the Tabernacle of God being with men forever.

The Sabbath

As you read the chapter, you cannot help noticing that the opening three verses appear to be out of place. They deal with the observance of the Sabbath. Then, the next 41 verses describe 'the feasts of the LORD'. Why are these first three verses put here? What was God's intention in opening this chapter with Sabbath instruction?

It is obvious the Sabbath occupied a very prominent place in Old Testament worship. Each of these feasts is associated with Sabbath observance. Before Moses gives instruction about keeping the feasts, he gives specific instruction from God about keeping the Sabbath. It is as if the Lord is saying, 'These feasts which I give are typical of my great salvation which shall give you everlasting rest in me, and will give me everlasting rest in you'.

Israel's first great feast was the Feast of Passover. Their last annual feast was the Feast of Tabernacles. Strip away their typical dress and you have full, complete redemption and eternal resurrection glory. This everlasting salvation in Christ is the great rest of which the Sabbath was typical in Old Testament.

And the LORD spake unto Moses, saying, Speak unto the children of Israel, and say unto them, Concerning the feasts of the LORD, which ye shall proclaim to be holy convocations, even these are my feasts. Six days shall work be done: but the seventh day is the sabbath of rest, an holy convocation; ye shall do no work therein: it is the sabbath of the LORD in all your dwellings (Leviticus 23:1-3).

The Sabbath was to be kept every week. It was a constant reminder to Israel of the sweet rest Adam lost in the Garden of Eden. It pointed to the rest found in Christ. The Sabbath was intended to typify salvation in Christ, the blessed rest of life, faith and reconciliation to God in him.

'No work' was to be done on the Sabbath because salvation is a matter of grace alone enjoyed by faith in Christ, without our works of any kind. No other festival in the Old Testament had such a strict injunction put on it except the Day of Atonement. Do you see the significance of that? The rest of faith in Christ is the rest of complete, perfect atonement, and the rest of complete reconciliation to God. This is what was typified in the beginning when the Lord God rested from all his works on the seventh day.

Is it so with your soul? Do you have such rest in Christ with God as if you had never sinned? Do you have no more conscience of sin? This is the rest Christ has won for all who trust him. Come to the Lord Jesus Christ and rest. Cease from all work and labour and rest in him (Matthew 11:28-30; Hebrews 4:3, 7). The rest of faith is good, and the rest of heaven will be glorious (Hebrews 4:9).

The Feast of Passover

The first Holy Convocation God required Israel to keep every year was the Feast of Passover.

> These are the feasts of the LORD, even holy convocations, which ye shall proclaim in their seasons. In the fourteenth day of the first month at even is the LORD'S passover (Leviticus 23:4, 5).

This feast was a reminder of God's great work of grace in bringing Israel out of Egypt by his mighty power and stretched out arm, by the blood that was shed for them (Exodus 12-14). But it was more. The Passover was a picture and reminder of God's promise to send a Redeemer, Christ our Passover, sacrificed for us (1 Corinthians 5:7).

This feast is called 'the LORD'S passover' because the whole of the work was his. Three things were prominent in the first Passover, a lamb, blood and deliverance. It was pre-eminently 'the LORD'S passover'. He ordained it. He provided the lamb. He accepted the lamb. He passed over the people. He brought them out of Egypt and across the Red Sea. And he was praised for it (Exodus 15). 'Salvation is of the LORD'.

As often as we eat the bread and drink the wine at the Lord's Table, like Israel of old, we show forth the Lord's death until he comes again, in remembrance of him.

> Forasmuch as ye know that ye were not redeemed with corruptible things, as silver and gold, from your vain conversation received by tradition from your fathers; But with the precious blood of Christ, as of a lamb without blemish and without spot: Who verily was foreordained before the foundation of the world, but was manifest in these last times for you (1 Peter 1:18-20).

> Not unto us, O LORD, not unto us, but unto thy name give glory, for thy mercy, and for thy truth's sake (Psalm 115:1).

The Feast of Unleavened Bread
God required his people to observe the Feast of Unleavened Bread.

> And on the fifteenth day of the same month is the feast of unleavened bread unto the LORD: seven days ye must eat unleavened bread. In the first day ye shall have an holy convocation: ye shall do no servile work therein. But ye shall offer an offering made by fire unto the LORD seven days: in the seventh day is an holy convocation: ye shall do no servile work therein (Leviticus 23:6-8).

The Feast of Unleavened Bread was really a continuation of the Feast of Passover. On the Passover night the children of Israel ate the lamb with their coats on their backs, their shoes on their feet, and their staffs in their hand, ready to go out of Egypt. The passover sacrifice represented the cause, means, and accomplishment of redemption by Christ. The Feast of Unleavened Bread represented the effects of redemption. The sacrifice of the paschal lamb, Christ and his shed blood, is the effectual means and cause of pardon. The sweet fellowship of faith, represented in the Feast of Unleavened Bread, is the effect, the sure and certain result of Christ's death as our Substitute. The Feast of Unleavened Bread pictures faith in Christ, eating his flesh and drinking his blood (John 6:53-56).

Do not miss the connection of the Feast of Unleavened Bread with the Feast of Passover. The Feast of Unleavened Bread began the next day after the Passover was ended. The gift of life and faith in Christ follows the accomplishments of Christ at Calvary. All who were redeemed by blood shall be made to live and feed upon Christ at God's appointed time (Galatians 3:13, 14).

As one great family the children of Israel kept the first day of this feast as a 'Holy Convocation'. No servile work was done. It was a blessed time of rest. Faith in Christ is a perpetual Sabbath rest. The people were all joined together, united as one holy body of redeemed souls, remembering what God had done for them (Ephesians 3:17-19; 4:1-7). They were all bought with the same blood, saved by the same power and going to the same homeland. They all ate the same bread.

The Feast of Firstfruits
The third feast, the third holy convocation the children of Israel were required to observe every year was the Feast of Firstfruits.

> And the LORD spake unto Moses, saying, Speak unto the children of Israel, and say unto them, When ye be come into the land which I give unto you, and shall reap the harvest thereof, then ye shall bring a sheaf of the firstfruits of your harvest unto the priest: And he shall wave the sheaf before the LORD, to be accepted for you: on the morrow after the sabbath the priest shall wave it. And ye shall offer that day when ye wave the sheaf an he lamb without blemish of the first year for a burnt offering unto the LORD. And the meat offering thereof shall be two tenth deals of fine flour mingled with oil, an offering made by fire unto the LORD for a sweet savour: and the drink offering thereof shall be of wine, the fourth part of an hin. And ye shall eat neither bread, nor parched corn, nor green ears, until the selfsame day that ye have brought an offering unto your God: it shall be a statute forever throughout your generations in all your dwellings (Leviticus 23:9-14).

In 1 Corinthians 15:23, God the Holy Spirit tells us plainly this feast speaks of Christ's glorious resurrection and of our resurrection with him, in him, and by him (Romans 11:16; James 1:18; Revelation 14:4).

The sheaf of firstfruits was offered to God with the lamb of burnt offering. This portrayed the fact that God's elect are accepted in Christ by the merit of his precious blood. Our offerings, works, worship, praise, and prayers are accepted in Christ by the merit of his blood.

The Feast of Pentecost

The Feast of Weeks described next was held fifty days, or seven weeks and a Sabbath day, after the Feast of Firstfruits. This feast is called the 'Feast of Pentecost' because it was held on the fiftieth day. It is the harvest feast and speaks of the ingathering of God's elect by Christ.

> And ye shall count unto you from the morrow after the sabbath, from the day that ye brought the sheaf of the wave offering; seven sabbaths shall be complete: Even unto the morrow after the seventh sabbath shall ye number fifty days; and ye shall offer a new meat offering unto the LORD. Ye shall bring out of your habitations two wave loaves of two tenth deals: they shall be of fine flour; they shall be baken with leaven; they are the firstfruits unto the LORD. And ye shall offer with the bread seven lambs without blemish of the first year, and one young bullock, and two rams: they shall be for a burnt offering unto the LORD, with their meat offering, and their drink offerings, even an offering made by fire, of sweet savour unto the LORD. Then ye shall sacrifice one kid of the goats for a sin offering, and two lambs of the first year for a sacrifice of peace offerings. And the priest shall wave them with the bread of the firstfruits for a wave offering before the LORD, with the two lambs: they shall be holy to the LORD for the priest. And ye shall proclaim on the selfsame day, that it may be an holy convocation unto you: ye shall do no servile work therein: it shall be a statute forever in all your dwellings throughout your generations. And when ye reap the harvest of your land, thou shalt not make clean riddance of the corners of thy field when thou reapest, neither shalt thou gather any gleaning of thy harvest: thou shalt leave them unto the poor, and to the stranger: I am the Lord your God (Leviticus 23:15-22).

The risen Christ gave us a delightful picture and foretaste of the ingathering of his elect in Acts 2:1-4. When the Day of Pentecost was fully come, he poured out his Spirit upon all flesh and 3000 souls were gathered into the fold of his grace at one time. Just as the harvest follows the firstfruits, so the salvation of God's elect follows the resurrection of Christ. Indeed, all the redeemed shall be gathered unto God (Isaiah 43:5-7; John 10:15-18; Romans 11:26).

Robert Hawker said, 'As gleanings of the harvest were to be left in the corners of the field for the poor and the stranger, so in every corner of the earth there are gleanings of grace for poor and miserable sinners'.

Even in requiring Israel never to gather all their harvest, the Lord is teaching us about his grace. Boaz left some 'handfuls of purpose' for Ruth and the Lord God always provides for his own. In the Old Testament there was a remnant according to the election of grace among the Gentiles. The Lord said, 'Take care that you provide for them'. Even now, in this gospel age, there is a remnant according to the election of grace among both Jews and Gentiles. The Lord says, 'Take care that you provide for them'. Our God would have us ever mindful of the needs of others, specifically that he has a people to whom he will be gracious. He gives us the privilege of serving their souls' needs.

The Feast of Trumpets

The Feast of Trumpets represented the glorious triumph of Christ proclaimed by the gospel.

> And the LORD spake unto Moses, saying, Speak unto the children of Israel, saying, In the seventh month, in the first day of the month, shall ye have a sabbath, a memorial of blowing of trumpets, an holy convocation. Ye shall do no servile work therein: but ye shall offer an offering made by fire unto the LORD (Leviticus 23:23-25).

'The joyful sound' mentioned in Psalm 89:15 likely referred to the Feast of Trumpets. 'Blessed is the people that know the joyful sound: they shall walk, O LORD, in the light of thy countenance' (Psalm 89:15). Every saved sinner enters into the joyful sound of grace proclaimed in the gospel. We hear the sweet sounds of mercy and grace, justice and judgment, righteousness and peace blended together in blessed harmony, and rejoice. Do you know the joyful sound of justice satisfied, redemption accomplished, sin pardoned, righteousness brought in, God glorified, salvation sure, grace abundant, and eternal salvation in, by, and with the Lord Jesus Christ? Read Psalm 89:14-37!

The Feast of Atonement
The Lord God graciously required his worshippers to celebrate for a holy convocation the Feast of Atonement once a year, every year.

> And the LORD spake unto Moses, saying, Also on the tenth day of this seventh month there shall be a day of atonement: it shall be an holy convocation unto you; and ye shall afflict your souls, and offer an offering made by fire unto the LORD. And ye shall do no work in that same day: for it is a day of atonement, to make an atonement for you before the LORD your God. For whatsoever soul it be that shall not be afflicted in that same day, he shall be cut off from among his people. And whatsoever soul it be that doeth any work in that same day, the same soul will I destroy from among his people. Ye shall do no manner of work: it shall be a statute forever throughout your generations in all your dwellings. It shall be unto you a sabbath of rest, and ye shall afflict your souls: in the ninth day of the month at even, from even unto even, shall ye celebrate your sabbath (Leviticus 23:26-32).

The word 'atonement' in verse 27 can be translated 'expiation'. This feast has reference to our perfect, complete restoration to our God and the restitution of all things when our great Saviour shall have gathered all things together in one for the glory of God (Acts 3:21; Ephesians 1:10, 11; 1 Corinthians 15:24-28). The Feast of Trumpets was a prelude to and a proclamation of 'the glorious liberty of the sons of God' (Romans 8:18-24).

The Feast of Tabernacles
The seventh holy convocation God required his people to observe every year was the Feast of Tabernacles. 'This Feast of Tabernacles, which was', Hawker tells us, 'one of the highest in points of enjoyment to Israel, very mercifully follows five days after the Day of Atonement.

And is there not this gospel mercy typified in it, that the conviction of sin by the Spirit is sweetly followed by the conviction of the righteousness of Christ; whereby the soul is made glad in righteousness, and peace, and joy in the Holy Ghost?'

And the LORD spake unto Moses, saying, Speak unto the children of Israel, saying, The fifteenth day of this seventh month shall be the Feast of Tabernacles for seven days unto the LORD. On the first day shall be an holy convocation: ye shall do no servile work therein. Seven days ye shall offer an offering made by fire unto the LORD: on the eighth day shall be an holy convocation unto you; and ye shall offer an offering made by fire unto the LORD: it is a solemn assembly; and ye shall do no servile work therein. These are the feasts of the LORD, which ye shall proclaim to be holy convocations, to offer an offering made by fire unto the LORD, a burnt offering, and a meat offering, a sacrifice, and drink offerings, everything upon his day: Beside the sabbaths of the LORD, and beside your gifts, and beside all your vows, and beside all your freewill offerings, which ye give unto the LORD. Also in the fifteenth day of the seventh month, when ye have gathered in the fruit of the land, ye shall keep a feast unto the LORD seven days: on the first day shall be a sabbath, and on the eighth day shall be a sabbath. And ye shall take you on the first day the boughs of goodly trees, branches of palm trees, and the boughs of thick trees, and willows of the brook; and ye shall rejoice before the LORD your God seven days. And ye shall keep it a feast unto the LORD seven days in the year. It shall be a statute forever in your generations: ye shall celebrate it in the seventh month. Ye shall dwell in booths seven days; all that are Israelites born shall dwell in booths: That your generations may know that I made the children of Israel to dwell in booths, when I brought them out of the land of Egypt: I am the LORD your God. And Moses declared unto the children of Israel the feasts of the LORD (Leviticus 23:33-44).

This Feast of Tabernacles was a time when Israel was reminded that they dwelt in booths in the wilderness and God dwelt with them in the cloud and fiery pillar. But it spoke of more than that. It spoke of that time when God the Son came here and tabernacled in human flesh that he might at last bring God and man together in everlasting glory and perfect fellowship, with sin and every evil consequence of it forever expiated, put away, purged and forgotten (John 1:14; 2 Corinthians 8:9; Philippians 2:5-9; Psalm 72:16-19; Revelation 21:1-7).

The Eighth Day
Let me show you one more thing. The eighth day was considered the great day of the Feast of Tabernacles (John 7:37). On the eighth day all grapes and fruits were gathered in (Exodus 23:16). The harvest was completed. What a time of celebration it was! The joy of harvest and the shouting and dancing associated with the treading of the winepresses must have been something to behold.

Who knows? It just may be that this is the eighth day of the feast. This may just be the last day there is. So I want you to hear the Son of God as he speaks on the eighth day, the great day of the feast.

In the last day, that great day of the feast, Jesus stood and cried, saying, If any man thirst, let him come unto me, and drink. He that believeth on me, as the Scripture hath said, out of his belly shall flow rivers of living water (John 7:37, 38).

And he that sat upon the throne said, Behold, I make all things new. And he said unto me, Write: for these words are true and faithful. And he said unto me, It is done. I am Alpha and Omega, the beginning and the end. I will give unto him that is athirst of the fountain of the water of life freely. He that overcometh shall inherit all things; and I will be his God, and he shall be my son (Revelation 21:5-7).

That is the message of 'the feasts of the Lord'.

Chapter 51

'The Sabbath Of Rest'

And the LORD spake unto Moses, saying, Speak unto the children of Israel, and say unto them, Concerning the feasts of the LORD, which ye shall proclaim to be holy convocations, even these are my feasts. Six days shall work be done: but the seventh day is the sabbath of rest, an holy convocation; ye shall do no work therein: it is the sabbath of the LORD in all your dwellings.

Leviticus 23:1-3

This twenty-third chapter of Leviticus describes the seven feasts the Lord God required Israel to keep as 'holy convocations' throughout the Old Testament. These 'holy convocations' were typical, ceremonial feasts by which the whole work of redemption is pictured.

1. The Feast of Passover (v. 5) is a picture of redemption by Christ.

2. The Feast of Unleavened Bread (vv. 6-8) signifies faith in Christ.

3. The Feast of Firstfruits (vv. 9-14) typifies the resurrection of Christ and our resurrection with him.

4. The Feast of Weeks or Pentecost (vv. 15-22) is a portrayal of the ingathering of God's elect by the irresistible power and omnipotent grace of God the Holy Spirit.

5. The Feast of Trumpets (vv. 23-25) is typical of the proclamation of the gospel.

6. The Feast of Atonement or Expiation (vv. 26-32) typifies 'the times of the restitution of all things, of which God hath spoken by the mouth of all his holy prophets, since the world began' (Acts 3: 21).

7. The Feast of Tabernacles (vv. 33-43) portrays the glory awaiting us when the work of grace is complete and God's elect are brought into heavenly glory, when the Lord God shall forever be our Tabernacle.

Sabbath Observance Prominent

As we have seen, each of these feasts involved the observance of the sabbath. The opening verses of the chapter (vv. 1-3) show the sabbath was prominent in all Old Testament worship. There was no worship of God without the observance of the sabbath in the Old Testament.

If you will read the rest of the chapter, carefully marking the instructions given for sabbath observance, you will see at least seven things were required for the keeping of the sabbath.

1. Affliction of soul and cessation of work (vv. 7, 8, 21, 25-36).
2. Atonement (vv. 27, 28).
3. Consecration (v. 38).
4. Remembrance (v. 43).
5. Celebration (vv. 40, 41).
6. Feasting.
7. Worship.

That the sabbath is given such a prominent place and is closely connected with all these feasts of worship is very important. The Lord is giving us a very instructive picture of redemption and grace.

These seven feasts give us a vivid type of all God's saving operations of grace for his elect. The sabbath portrayed that rest which remains for the people of God. Yes, it was a ceremonial day to be observed by Israel. But it was also a type of what was and in a sense is yet to come. The sabbath overshadowed all the feasts of worship. It typically encompassed all that great and glorious work of God's salvation in Christ, which this chapter foreshadows, when it is finished.

God's Rest

The sabbath is God's rest into which all who believe enter by faith in Christ, but which, as to its full and actual accomplishment, yet remains (Hebrews 4:1-11). Soon we shall enter into our everlasting rest that shall never be disturbed.

In one sense the believer enters into rest yet in another sense he labours to enter into it. We have found our rest in Christ and we labour to enter into rest in glory. We have found full repose in what Christ has done for us, yet our eye rests on that everlasting sabbath into which we shall enter when all our present toils and conflicts are over. We rest in Christ by faith, yet living in this world, day by day, we labour to enter into rest, to truly rest in Christ by faith. We are compelled to pray, like the poor father who brought his demon possessed son to the Lord Jesus, 'Lord, I believe. Help thou, mine unbelief' (Mark 9:24).

We rest in Christ and labour as workers together with God in full assurance that when our earthly toil is over we shall enjoy unbroken, eternal rest in those mansions of unfading light and perfect blessedness where labour and sorrow can never enter. Blest prospect! Blest hope! Here we have but a foretaste of the eternal sabbath awaiting us when time shall be no more, that sabbath which shall never be broken, that 'holy convocation' which shall never be dissolved.

First Sabbath

The weekly sabbath began at the end of creation. The Lord God worked six days then rested on the seventh day. God did no work on the sabbath. It was the Lord God himself who kept the first sabbath (Genesis 2:2, 3).

The sabbath is not mentioned again in Holy Scripture until the book of Exodus. Only after Israel's deliverance from Egyptian bondage do we find men observing the sabbath day (Exodus 16:23-29). Then, when he gave his law on Mount Sinai, the Lord God reminded his people that the sabbath was at the heart of all his work (Exodus 20:8-11).

Only a Shadow

We often hear Sunday referred to as the sabbath. Perhaps you think that sabbath is just another word for Sunday. But that is completely wrong. Sunday is the first day of the week. Saturday is the seventh day. That was the sabbath day. Sunday is not the sabbath. It never was the sabbath, and never can be the sabbath.

I stress this fact because many would bring us under the yoke of legal bondage by constraining us to keep a carnal, legal sabbath in this gospel age. Such legal sabbath keeping is strictly and purposefully forbidden in the New Testament.

The sabbath was but a shadow, a symbol of something yet to come. What does God teach us in giving all the laws regarding sabbath observance in the Old Testament? What are all those Old Testament sabbath laws intended to portray? Let me show you from the Scriptures.

As there was no worship of God without the observance of the carnal sabbath in the Old Testament, so there is no worship of God without the observance of the true sabbath today.

Sabbath Observance Forbidden

Sabbath keeping is not a matter of indifference. It is not one of those areas about which the Scriptures give no specific instructions. In fact, the instructions given in the Word of God about sabbath keeping are very specific and very clear.

Like circumcision, the Passover, and all other aspects of legal, ceremonial worship during the Old Testament, the legal sabbath day was established by our God to be a sign, picture, and type of grace and salvation in Christ. This is not a matter of speculation and guesswork.

> Speak thou also unto the children of Israel, saying, Verily my sabbaths ye shall keep: for it is a sign between me and you throughout your generations; that ye may know that I am the LORD that doth sanctify you (Exodus 31:13).

Sabbath keeping was a legal type of our salvation in Christ during the age of carnal ordinances, like the Passover and circumcision, once Christ came and fulfilled the type, the carnal ordinance ceased. In the New Testament, we are strictly and directly forbidden to keep any of those carnal ordinances (Colossians 2:8-23). In fact, we are plainly told that those who attempt to worship God by observing carnal, legal ordinances are yet under the curse of the law. They have not yet learned the gospel.

Circumcision is forbidden as an ordinance of divine worship (Galatians 5:2, 4). Those who have their babies sprinkled to bring them into the church and kingdom of God, to seal them into the covenant of grace, attempting to symbolically retain the carnal ordinance of circumcision, by their act of sprinkling that child, deny the gospel of salvation by grace alone. They deny the necessity of heart circumcision by the Spirit of God, the new birth, which circumcision symbolized.

Passover observance is forbidden since Christ our Passover has been sacrificed for us (1 Corinthians 5:7). All who continue to offer up sacrifices to God, either for atonement, or as acts of penance, or to gain a higher degree of divine favour, or to prevent God's anger, do by their sacrifices deny that Christ's death at Calvary was an effectual satisfaction of divine justice for the sins of his people. If something must be added to his blood and his righteousness by me, then his blood and his righteousness are totally useless.

In exactly the same way, those who attempt to sanctify themselves by keeping a carnal sabbath day, deny that Christ is enough to give us perfect acceptance with the thrice holy God.

Christ our Sabbath

As Paul puts it in Colossians 2:23, those who pretend to keep a carnal sabbath in this gospel age make an outward show of spirituality and wisdom; but it is all will-worship. Such pretences of humility are nothing but the satisfying of the flesh. Not only that, the whole matter of sabbath keeping is specifically and strictly forbidden by the Holy Spirit in Colossians 2:16, 17. Since the Lord Jesus Christ has, by his death at Calvary, blotted out the handwriting of the ordinances that was against us, since he nailed God's broken law to the cross and put away our sins, he alone is our Sabbath. We rest in him.

> Let no man therefore judge you in meat, or in drink, or in respect of an holyday, or of the new moon, or of the sabbath days: Which are a shadow of things to come; but the body is of Christ (Colossians 2:16, 17).

All carnal sabbath keeping, any form of it, is strictly forbidden because in Christ all who are born of God are totally free from the law (Romans 7:4; 10:4). Yet, the New Testament does speak of a sabbath keeping that remains for the people of God.

The children of Israel perished in the wilderness because of unbelief. They could not enter into God's rest in the land of Canaan. They could not enter into that typical picture of God's salvation because of unbelief (Hebrews 4:1-6). Though that generation perished in unbelief, the purpose of God was not, and could not be hindered. There is an elect multitude who must and shall enter into his rest (Hebrews 4:6).

That typical rest given by Joshua in the land of Canaan was not the rest purposed and purchased for God's elect. It was only typical of that blessed rest of faith which is ours in Christ (Hebrews 4:7, 8).

> There remaineth therefore a rest to the people of God. For he that is entered into his rest, he also hath ceased from his own works, as God did from his. Let us labour therefore to enter into that rest, lest any man fall after the same example of unbelief (Hebrews 4:9-11).

The word translated 'rest', which is used over and over in Hebrews 3 and 4, means to lie back, lay down, be at peace, cease from work, be at home. But if you have a marginal reference in your Bible, you will notice that the word translated 'rest' that is used in verse 9 is different. Here the word means 'a keeping of a sabbath'. This remaining sabbath rest is the blessed rest of faith in Christ. Christ is our Sabbath. I want you to see from the Scriptures how the Old Testament sabbath day finds its fulfilment and complete accomplishment in Christ. I want you to see how we who believe keep the sabbath by faith in him.

Christ's Rest

The Lord Jesus Christ has entered into his rest, and his rest is glorious, because he has finished his work (Isaiah 11:10; 2 Corinthians 5:17-21; Romans 8:34; Hebrews 10:11-14). Our Saviour's rest in heaven is his glory. Again, I call your attention to the marginal translation of the last sentence of Isaiah 11:10. It reads, 'His rest shall be glory'.

God the Father rested on the seventh day after creation as his work of creation was finished, so God the Son rested in the seventh day of time, and entered into his rest forever because he finished his work of making all things new for his people (Romans 8:34; Hebrews 10:9-14).

Matthew 28:1 is a very remarkable verse of Scripture. 'In the end of the sabbath, as it began to dawn toward the first day of the week, came Mary Magdalene and the other Mary to see the sepulchre.' The literal translation of Matthew 28:1 is, 'In the end of the sabbath, as it began to dawn toward the sabbath'. In other words, when the Lord Jesus Christ died at Calvary and rose again, the old sabbath of the law ended and the new sabbath of grace began.

Behold our exalted Saviour! Do you see him seated yonder upon his throne in heaven? He sits in the undisturbed serenity of his absolute sovereignty. His rest is his glory (John 17:2; Philippians 2:9-11; Isaiah 45:20-25). He has finished his work (John 17:4; 19:30). Having finished his work, the salvation of his redeemed is certain (Hebrews 9:12). 'Therefore it remaineth that some must enter therein' (Hebrews 4:6). The works were finished before the foundation of the world in God's purpose (Romans 8:29, 30; Ephesians 1:3-6; Hebrews 4:3) and finished in time when the God-man took his seat in heaven as our forerunner (Hebrews 6:20). There is no more work to be done. Christ did it all. Having finished his work he sat down in his glory. There he is resting.

Our Sabbath

Every sinner who believes on the Lord Jesus Christ keeps the sabbath by faith, by entering into his rest.

> For we which have believed do enter into rest, as he said, As I have sworn in my wrath, if they shall enter into my rest: although the works were finished from the foundation of the world ... There remaineth therefore a rest to the people of God. For he that is entered into his rest, he also hath ceased from his own works, as God did from his (Hebrews 4:3, 9, 10).

We keep the sabbath of faith, a spiritual sabbath, not a carnal one. We rest in Christ, trusting his finished work, by faith entering into his rest. The believer's life is a perpetual keeping of the sabbath.

None of us keeps it perfectly. Our best faith in this world is still unbelief. But we do keep this blessed sabbath rest sincerely, ever looking to Christ, ever coming to Christ, ever resting in Christ. Our all-glorious Christ gives rest to every sinner who comes to him in faith. He says, 'Come unto me, all ye that labour and are heavy laden, and I will give you rest' (Matthew 11:28).

The Lord Jesus Christ has given and continually gives us rest: the rest of complete pardon (Isaiah 45:22; Ephesians 1:6), perfect reconciliation (2 Corinthians 5:17; Colossians 1:20, 21), absolute security (John 10:27-30; Philippians 1:6; 1 Thessalonians 5:24), and his special providence (Romans 8:28).

As the ceremonial sabbath portrayed a strict, universal consecration to God, this blessed sabbath of faith involves the perpetual consecration of ourselves to our God and Saviour, the Lord Jesus Christ (Matthew 11:29, 30). We keep the sabbath of faith when we wilfully, deliberately take the yoke of Christ. If you would keep the sabbath, it involves much, much more than living in religious austerity one day a week. To keep the sabbath is to bow to Christ's dominion, to learn of him what to believe, how to live, what to do, how to honour God. To keep the sabbath is to bow to his will. How can a troubled, weary, heavy laden sinner obtain this blessed sabbath rest? I can tell you, both from experience and from the Word of God, there is only one way you can enter into his rest. You've got to quit working! You have to trust Christ alone for everything!

> Ye shall do no manner of work: it shall be a statute forever throughout your generations in all your dwellings. It shall be unto you a sabbath of rest, and ye shall afflict your souls: in the ninth day of the month at even, from even unto even, shall ye celebrate your sabbath (Leviticus 23:31, 32).

Labour to Rest

> There remaineth therefore a rest to the people of God ... Let us labour therefore to enter into that rest, lest any man fall after the same example of unbelief (Hebrews 4:9, 11).

There is a great, eternal sabbath to be obtained; an eternal remembrance of redemption, an eternal, perfect consecration to Christ, an eternal rest, an eternal feasting, an eternal 'holy convocation' of worship, an eternal celebration of grace. Some have already entered into that rest (Hebrews 4:10). Many could not enter in because of unbelief. But those who have entered in have ceased from their own works. Christ has entered into his rest. We who have entered into his rest by faith shall enter into his rest in heaven. And there are some who 'must enter therein'. All of God's elect, all whom Christ purchased with his precious blood must enter into his rest. 'Let us therefore labour (strive) to enter into that rest, lest any man fall after the same example of unbelief' (Hebrews 4:11; 2 Corinthians 5:5-9).

The salvation and eternal rest of God's elect is not, John Gill wrote,

> ... a precarious thing. God has promised it and provided it for his people. Christ is in the possession of it and is preparing it for them. And the Spirit of God is working them up for the selfsame thing. And Christ will give them an abundant entrance into it. But the Gospel rest is here meant, that rest which believers now enter into and is at this present time for them (Hebrews 4:3). And though true believers are entered into it, yet their rest, peace, and joy in Christ, is not full. They enter by degrees into it and by believing enjoy more of it. And this is to be laboured for by prayer, hearing the Word, and attendance on ordinances. And this requires strength, diligence, and industry, and supposes difficulties and discouragements through the corruptions of the heart and the temptations of Satan. And this is designed to quicken and awaken a godly jealousy in God's people, over themselves.

The Apostle Paul tells the Corinthians,

> Now he that hath wrought us for the selfsame thing is God, who also hath given unto us the earnest of the Spirit. Therefore we are always confident, knowing that, whilst we are at home in the body, we are absent from the Lord: (For we walk by faith, not by sight:) We are confident, I say, and willing rather to be absent from the body, and to be present with the Lord. Wherefore we labour, that, whether present or absent, we may be accepted of him (2 Corinthians 5:5-9).

The penalty for not keeping the sabbath is still death, everlasting death in hell (John 3:36; Romans 6:23). If you would be saved, you must keep and satisfy the whole of God's law. And there is only one way you can do that. Sinners keep the law only by faith in Christ (Romans 3:31). Faith in Christ is the blessed sabbath rest of grace. Come to Christ and rest forever.

.

Chapter 52

'The Lord's Passover'

These are the feasts of the LORD, even holy convocations, which ye shall proclaim in their seasons. In the fourteenth day of the first month at even is the Lord's passover.

Leviticus 23:4, 5

The first feast, or 'holy convocation', God required Israel to keep, and with which they began every new year, was 'the Lord's passover'. The first Passover coincided with the last of the Egyptian plagues. The Lord God determined to kill the firstborn son in every family in Egypt. The Israelites would be spared the judgment of God. But we must never imagine that they were spared simply because of their bloodline. They were spared because of the blood.

God gave explicit instructions in Exodus 12 for the slaughtering of year-old male sheep or goats and the sprinkling of the blood of the lamb slain upon the doorposts and lintel of each house. Then, the destroying angel 'passed over' any house covered by that blood, for the Lord God declared, 'When I see the blood, I will pass over you'.

The firstborn of the believing Israelites were saved because of the blood. It pictures our Lord Jesus and the efficacy of his blood atonement as the Lamb of God. The blood by which we are redeemed, justified, cleansed from all sin, made righteous, accepted with God, and saved. By divine arrangement our Lord Jesus Christ, the true Passover, was sacrificed at the time of the Jews' Passover feast (1 Corinthians 5:7, 8).

The Passover was the annual commemoration of God's deliverance of Israel out of Egyptian bondage. It was a time of remembrance, reflection, and celebration. The Lord God found Israel in Egypt in bondage and set them free that they might worship and serve him.

The Lamb Slain

The Lamb is always at the forefront in the book of God. 'The lamb slain' was the first object held up to the view of Israel when they were about to be delivered. The same is true today. 'Behold the Lamb of God' is still the cry that first reaches a sinner's ear, the very first message a sinner hears. Christ, the Lamb of God, our sin-atoning Saviour, is the very first thing the chosen, redeemed sinner sees in his experience of grace.

The very first feast with which God would have his people to worship him, the very first feast which the God of all grace required fallen, sinful men to keep, the very first day of every year was a display of God's infinite mercy, love, and grace to sinners in Christ. It was a feast of redemption. It was the feast of the lamb.

How gracious our God is. 'He delighteth in mercy'! What grace meets the sinner. God meets us with the Lamb; and that Lamb is his own beloved Son. 'Behold, the Lamb of God.' In the Lamb, God shows us life out of death, life for sinners rising out of the death of his own darling Son!

The first death recorded on the pages of history was the death of a sacrificial lamb (Genesis 3). The first altar erected upon the earth was an altar covered with the blood of a lamb slain (Genesis 4). The first act of God for Israel is the slaying of the lamb. The first deed of the new dispensation was presenting the true Lamb to the view of all, and then the offering up of that Lamb to God. The first opening of the door in heaven above presents us with the Lamb that was slain seated upon his throne in heaven (Revelation 4 and 5).

See him yonder, seated in glory upon his throne. See him in lofty majesty with the book of God in his hand. Heaven gazes upon him with admiration. All the redeemed sing his praise with delight and gratitude.

The People Delivered

Be sure you see the connection between the Lamb slain and the people delivered. We rejoice to see Christ as the Lamb of God slain from the foundation of the world, slain in the types and shadows of the law, slain for the satisfaction of justice. But the slaying of the Lamb, the pouring out of his life's blood would be utterly without comfort to our souls if any for whom his blood was shed were yet left to perish under the wrath of God. That can never be. The Lamb of God did not die in vain. Christ did not shed his blood for nothing. Israel came out of Egypt, all Israel was saved, not so much as a hoof of one cow was left in the land of God's curse. Israel went out of Egypt with a high hand, carrying the spoils of Egypt with them.

The picture of the Passover feast could never be complete without all God's elect saved, without every blood bought sinner and ransomed soul together with Christ in heaven, our Lord Jesus told us plainly that it would be fulfilled only then (Luke 22:16). Only when Christ comes again and gathers all his people to glory will the Passover feast be fulfilled. Then, when our salvation is complete, we will keep the Lord's Passover forever (Revelation 4:10, 11; 5:1-14).

The Place of Feasting
Without question, the children of Israel kept the Passover feast in the land of Canaan, just as we shall keep the feast forever in heaven. But the feast had to be kept in Egypt before it could be kept in Canaan. The children of Israel were required to keep the feast while they were still in Egypt (Exodus 12:11). Everything that took place on that memorable night when God brought Israel out of Egypt with a high hand and stretched out arm, and everything involved in the Jews' annual feast of the Passover in the Old Testament was designed by God to be a typical picture of our Lord Jesus Christ and the redemption of our souls by him.

As Israel was preserved from death and delivered out of Egypt by the blood of the paschal lamb and the mighty arm of God, so God's true Israel, all the host of his elect, has been delivered from death and hell by the sacrifice of Christ our Passover, and shall be delivered from all bondage by the arm of God's omnipotent and irresistible grace.

The first Passover feast was a feast of faith. Israel had not yet been delivered. There were no signs or indications they would be delivered. All they had to go on was the Word of God, the naked Word of God.

There were four things essential to the Lord's Passover. These four things are still essential things. It is my prayer that the Lord God will now cause you to keep this blessed feast. If you now, for the first time, begin keeping 'the Lord's passover', this day shall be to you the very beginning of life!

Slaughtered Lamb

First, the Passover feast required slaughter of a lamb (Exodus 12:3-6).

Israel could not come out of Egypt, except a sacrifice be made on their behalf. They deserved the wrath of God just as fully as the Egyptians did. Moses' sons deserved to die just as much as Pharaoh's. They could not escape the judgment of God, except blood be shed, except the life of an innocent victim be given.

The teaching of the type is obvious. No sinner could ever be saved by the grace of God except by the death of the Lord Jesus Christ as the sinner's Substitute (1 Peter 3:18).

Blood Sprinkled

Second, the blood of the lamb had to be sprinkled (Exodus 12:7).

Before any sinner can eat the feast, before any sinner can trust the Lord Jesus Christ, the blood must be sprinkled upon his heart, and effectually applied to his conscience, by God the Holy Ghost (Hebrews 9:11, 12; 9:14; 10:22). The blood of the sacrifice must be applied as well as spilt. An unapplied ransom is no ransom. An unapplied Saviour is no Saviour (Hebrews 9:19, 20). Only God the Holy Spirit can do this for us. When he sprinkles the guilty conscience with the blood of Christ, guilt is removed, because he makes us to see and know the Saviour's blood is enough, that by his blood alone justice is satisfied and iniquity purged. The blood sprinkled speaks peace to our souls!

> But Christ being come an high priest of good things to come, by a greater and more perfect tabernacle, not made with hands, that is to say, not of this building; Neither by the blood of goats and calves, but by his own blood he entered in once into the holy place, having obtained eternal redemption for us. How much more shall the blood of Christ, who through the eternal Spirit offered himself without spot to God, purge your conscience from dead works to serve the living God? Let us draw near with a true heart in full assurance of faith, having our hearts sprinkled from an evil conscience, and our bodies washed with pure water (Hebrews 9:11, 12, 14; 10:22).

Let me tell you about the sin-atoning blood of Christ.

1. It is distinguishing blood. The blood was sprinkled on the doorpost and lintel and by it Israel was separated from Egypt. The only difference between Israel and Egypt was the blood. The only difference between God's elect and the reprobate of the earth is the blood.

The world has always hated this fact. From Cain on, the unbelieving of the world have always despised the blood of Christ as the sinner's only door of access and acceptance with God. The people of God, like Abel, acknowledge this distinction, rejoice in it, and give thanks to God for it. Israel is distinguished from Egypt by blood.

2. It is protecting blood. The Lord God said, 'When I see it, I will pass over you'. The blood was Israel's shield. The sword of justice can never pierce that shield. The blood is ever before God. We do not see it. It is outside, beyond our vision, shed 2000 years ago. But God sees it and that is our security. We trust the blood which God sees and know ourselves secure (Isaiah 31:5).

3. It is delivering blood. The blood did not merely protect Israel in Egypt. It delivered Israel out of Egypt. It was the blood that saved. The Lord God declares to his redeemed, 'I gave Egypt for thy ransom' (Isaiah 43:3). There is death for Egypt, but life for Israel. Pardoned and set free, Israel turns its back on the land of bondage. The blood was the opening of the prison doors. It is still the blood that sets sinners free. Freedom by the blood is what we preach, it is the only freedom there is.

Lamb Eaten
Third, the lamb had to be eaten (Exodus 12:8-11).

There is no deliverance for our souls until Christ is believed, until the sacrifice is eaten by faith (John 6:53-56). The sacrifice had to be eaten with bitter herbs, portraying repentance toward God. It had to be eaten without mixture, not 'sodden with water', and eaten entirely, all at once. So it is that the heaven-born soul eats and drinks Christ Jesus, trusting his obedience and blood for all our salvation.

> Then Jesus said unto them, Verily, verily, I say unto you, Except ye eat the flesh of the Son of man, and drink his blood, ye have no life in you. Whoso eateth my flesh, and drinketh my blood, hath eternal life; and I will raise him up at the last day. For my flesh is meat indeed, and my blood is drink indeed. He that

eateth my flesh, and drinketh my blood, dwelleth in me, and I in him (John 6:53-56).

All Went Out

Fourth, 'All the hosts of the Lord went out of the land of Egypt' (Exodus 12:40-42).

Every Israelite for whom blood was shed, all upon whom blood was sprinkled, all who ate the sacrifice, all went out upon the same ground and for the same reason. And they took the riches of Egypt with them.

Every person in the house was required to eat the roasted lamb for himself (Exodus 12:8). Only those who ate the lamb were delivered from death. All who ate the lamb were delivered. All for whom blood was shed ate the lamb and walked out of Egypt, Moses leading the way.

> Truth and justice cry as loud
> As God's love with Jesus' blood,
> 'Every sinner bought with blood
> Must escape the wrath of God'.
>
> Justice, mercy, truth and love,
> Shining bright in Jesus' blood,
> Make secure our place above,
> One with Christ! Approved of God!
>
> Let His praise forever swell
> Jesus has done all things well!
> By His sin-atoning blood
> He both saves and honours God!

God commands us to eat the Lamb. That means it is alright for us to do so. If you eat the Lamb, his blood was shed for you, but it is something only you can do. You must eat the Lamb for yourself. 'The Lord's passover' is the celebration of redemption accomplished by Christ, redemption experienced by grace, and redemption sure for all of God's Israel, redemption certain for all of God's elect (Romans 11:26, 27; Revelation 14:1-5; 15:3).

Chapter 53

'The Feast Of Unleavened Bread'

And on the fifteenth day of the same month is the feast of unleavened bread unto the LORD: seven days ye must eat unleavened bread. In the first day ye shall have an holy convocation: ye shall do no servile work therein. But ye shall offer an offering made by fire unto the LORD seven days: in the seventh day is an holy convocation: ye shall do no servile work therein.

Leviticus 23:6-8

In Leviticus 23 God the Holy Ghost gives us Jehovah's instructions to Moses and to Israel about the seven annual feasts, or 'holy convocations', he required the children of Israel to keep throughout their generations. These were, 1. The Feast of Passover; 2. The Feast of Unleavened Bread; 3. The Feast of Firstfruits; 4. The Feast of Weeks (Pentecost); 5. The Feast of Trumpets; 6. The Feast of Atonement; 7. The Feast of Tabernacles.

These 'holy convocations' are called 'the feasts of the Lord' because they were feasts of worship required by the Lord, feasts of worship by which men and women symbolically came to the Lord; primarily, they were feasts of worship that portrayed and typified the person and work of the Lord Jesus Christ and the salvation we have in him.

These were material, carnal feasts, but they pointed to that which is altogether spiritual. We no longer keep the symbol but all who believe God, and are born from above as the Israel of God keep these feasts spiritually and continually in the exercise of faith in Christ.

Sabbath Rest

This chapter begins with instructions about the keeping of the sabbath (v. 3). This, of course, speaks of the blessed rest of faith in Christ. When sinners come to God by faith they cease from their works of self-righteousness and find rest in Christ's finished work as our all-sufficient Substitute (Matthew 11:28-30; Hebrews 4:9-11). We keep the sabbath by faith in Christ. 'He that is entered into is rest, he also hath ceased from his own works, as God did from his' (Hebrews 4:10).

The Lord's Passover

In verses 4 and 5 we are given instructions about the feast of passover, which portrayed Christ our Passover, who is sacrificed for us. The only way sinners can ever find rest in their souls and peace with God is by the sin-atoning blood and substitutionary death of our Lord Jesus Christ, the Lamb of God.

The Feast Of Unleavened Bread

In verses 6-8 the subject is the feast of unleavened bread. Note the very close connection between the feast of unleavened bread and the feast of passover. The feast of passover was to be kept on the fourteenth day of the month of Abib (the first month of the Jewish calendar). The feast of unleavened bread began the very next day, on the fifteenth day of the month.

There is a reason for this. The two feasts refer to two things that can never be separated: the death of Christ in the room and stead of his people and the deliverance of his people.

The feast of unleavened bread was a continuation of the feast of passover. In fact, the New Testament frequently uses the terms unleavened bread and passover as synonyms of one another (Matthew 26:17; Mark 14:12; Luke 22:1, 7).

The passover portrayed the cause of deliverance. The feast of unleavened bread portrayed the experience and the effects of deliverance. The passover was a picture of redemption and pardon by the blood of Christ. The feast of unleavened bread portrayed the believer's life of faith in Christ, our experience of grace in this world.

Purge out therefore the old leaven, that ye may be a new lump, as ye are unleavened. For even Christ our Passover is sacrificed for us: Therefore let us keep the feast, not with old leaven, neither with the leaven of malice and wickedness; but with the unleavened bread of sincerity and truth (1 Corinthians 5:7, 8).

Paul's exhortation here is often applied to the observance of the Lord's Supper. But that is not what Paul is referring to when he says, 'Therefore let us keep the feast, not with old leaven, neither with the leaven of malice and wickedness; but with the unleavened bread of sincerity and truth'. We know this does not refer to the Lord's Supper precisely because Paul tells us in 1 Corinthians 11 that the Lord's Supper is not a feast. It is a remembrance of redemption and has connection with the Jews' passover and the feast of unleavened bread, in the sense that the Lord's Supper is the remembrance of that which those Old Testament ceremonies typified, the sacrifice of Christ and our salvation by him. But the connection ends there.

When Paul says, 'Therefore let us keep the feast, not with old leaven, neither with the leaven of malice and wickedness; but with the unleavened bread of sincerity and truth', he is telling us that since Christ our Passover has been sacrificed for us and we are 'unleavened' in him, we are to spiritually keep the feast of unleavened bread in sincerity and truth, by faith in Christ.

When God the Holy Spirit inspired Paul to pen those blessed words, 'ye are unleavened', this is what he meant for us to understand. Believing on the Lord Jesus Christ, we are pure, holy, and righteous. 'In him is no sin'. Christ our Passover is sacrificed for us. We are redeemed by his precious blood. He has, by himself, purged our sins by his sin-atoning sacrifice. We are by him, in him, and with him 'unleavened', because we are now new creatures in Christ. By the new birth, we have been 'made partakers of the divine nature', and have in us that 'new man created in righteousness and true holiness' which cannot sin. We have been made the righteousness of God in him.

We keep the feast of unleavened bread, not one week a year, but spiritually, 'in sincerity and truth', living by faith in Christ, feeding upon him. The feast of unleavened bread pictures faith in Christ, eating his flesh and drinking his blood (John 6:53-56). We must have a whole unleavened Saviour for salvation. Christ is our whole Saviour. Anything of ours mingled with his pure and perfect sacrifice would pollute it. We feed upon him alone.

461

Then Jesus said unto them, Verily, verily, I say unto you, Except ye eat the flesh of the Son of man, and drink his blood, ye have no life in you. Whoso eateth my flesh, and drinketh my blood, hath eternal life; and I will raise him up at the last day. For my flesh is meat indeed, and my blood is drink indeed. He that eateth my flesh, and drinketh my blood, dwelleth in me, and I in him (John 6:53-56).

The feast of unleavened bread began the next day after the Passover was ended. So, too, the gift of life and faith in Christ follows the accomplishments of Christ at Calvary. All who were redeemed by blood shall be made to live and feed upon Christ at God's appointed time (Galatians 3:13, 14). Feasting upon our crucified Redeemer, we glory in him and glorify him (Galatians 6:14, 15; Philippians 3:3).

Five Aspects
Leviticus 23:6-8 gives the five specific words of instruction given about the feast of unleavened bread.

1. The feast began with a sabbath day observance, portraying the rest of faith. 2. No servile work was to be done. This cessation of work was to be maintained throughout the seven days of the feast. No works of our own could ever bring us to God. We must never look upon our works as in anyway commending us to God. 3. Throughout the feasts, every day an offering made by fire was to be brought to the Lord (Romans 12:1, 2). 4. The feast of unleavened bread lasted for seven days. The number seven represents grace, perfection, and fulness. Here, it speaks of the full age of a man, the whole span of our lives in this world. 5. The feast ended with another sabbath day observance, portraying the rest of heavenly glory.

How does all of this apply to us? The Apostle Paul tells us to keep this feast. But how are we to keep this feast? Spiritually, of course. But how do we keep it spiritually? The feast of unleavened bread typified the life of faith, the believer's whole experience of grace in this world.

It begins with the experience of deliverance from the curse of the law by the blood of Christ. Everything in our experience of grace is based upon and arises from the sin-atoning sacrifice of our Lord Jesus Christ. We cannot worship God, we cannot come to God, we cannot have peace with God, except upon the ground of Christ's sacrifice as our Substitute. Once we have received the atonement by faith in Christ, we enter into the blessed sabbath of faith, cease from our own works, and find rest in Christ.

Resting in Christ, being accepted in the Beloved, we are unleavened, without sin, before God, because 'Christ our Passover is sacrificed for us' (1 Corinthians 5:7). But Israel's redemption did not stop with deliverance from Egypt. It continued until Joshua brought them into the possession of Canaan. Likewise, our redemption is more than just deliverance from the curse of the law. It is also deliverance from our vain conversation, our empty, meaningless way of life (1 Peter 1:18), as well as from our state of condemnation and death (Titus 2:14).

We keep the feast of unleavened bread as those who stand before God as unleavened in Christ. Being received in Christ, by virtue of his blood, we feed on and apprehend the unleavened perfection that is ours in him. 'As he is so are we in this world.' Yet, we are required to put away the old leaven, that we may keep the feast.

And on the fifteenth day of the same month is the feast of unleavened bread unto the LORD: seven days ye must eat unleavened bread. In the first day ye shall have an holy convocation: ye shall do no servile work therein. But ye shall offer an offering made by fire unto the LORD seven days: in the seventh day is an holy convocation: ye shall do no servile work therein (Leviticus 23:6-8).

Two Sabbaths were always involved, plus the weekly sabbath. It did not make any difference on which days of the week they fell. It was the day of the month which counted. It began on the fifteenth day, lasted seven days, then ended. This feast, like the feast of passover, looked back to Egypt to the command God gave in Exodus 12 that the Israelites purge all leaven from their houses. To this day orthodox Jews meticulously do this in preparation for the passover season.

Constant Purging
In this life of faith, we must constantly purge out the old leaven of malice and wickedness. Obviously, all who are born of God know that we cannot, so long as we live in this world, purge sin from our lives (1 John 1:8-10). Yet, it is our responsibility and our hearts' desire to put

away sin, put off the old man, say 'no' to ungodliness and worldly lusts, and put on the Lord Jesus Christ. This is what Paul means when he says, 'purge out the old leaven' (1 Corinthians 5:7; Ephesians 4:21-24).

Leaven comes in many forms. It is yeast. It is a symbol of that which tends to puff us up. That is what yeast does in bread. It makes it swell. There is in us, God says, that which makes us swell up, and puffs us up. Someone once said, 'The strangest thing about the human body is that when you pat a person on the back, the head swells up'.

Why is that? It is because there is a principle at work in us constantly driving us to be self-sufficient. One of the earliest struggles we have with our children is in this area. Who has not had a child push him away saying, 'I can do it myself'? We do not want help. We do not even like to tell people our problems, to let them know we are not sufficient in ourselves. We all have this tendency within us to want to protect our image and to look as if we are fine by ourselves. That is leaven. Our Saviour often spoke of leaven. He said, 'Beware of the leaven of the Pharisees, which is hypocrisy' (Luke 12:1). Nothing swells a man like the hypocrisy of self-righteousness.

The Master also warned us to beware of the leaven of the Sadducees; rationalism, self-sufficiency, denial of the supernatural, and a proud assumption everything can be explained in terms of what you can see, taste, touch, smell, hear and feel. This leaven says there is no power beyond man, that man is sufficient in himself and has no need of God, does not need grace, and does not need a Saviour (Matthew 16:5-12).

The doctrine of the Pharisees and the Sadducees, though expressed with rigidly maintained distinctions, was in essence one doctrine. Self-salvation! Legalism, rationalism, free-willism, and decisionism, with all manmade religion is essentially the same. All teach self-salvation, dependent upon and determined by man. Then our Lord also warns of the leaven of the Herodians (Mark 8:14-21). These were materialists. They lived for pleasure and self-indulgence, for status and prestige. The Herodians lived to be seen, recognised, and applauded by men.

Paul tells us to keep the feast without the leaven of malice, that is without that natural, sinful, proud self-love that makes other people contemptible and disposable to us. He also tells us to keep it without the leaven of wickedness. The leaven of wickedness refers specifically to those sensual lusts of our hearts that are reflected in ungodly attitudes and behaviour (Ephesians 4:17-5:21).

If we would worship and serve God our Saviour, we must put away the old leaven of malice and wickedness, materialism, self-sufficiency, and hypocrisy. We must cease to live for ourselves, after the lusts of our flesh and live for God. Perhaps you are thinking, 'How can anyone be expected to do that? It makes for good, pious sounding religious talk; but surely no one is really expected to live like that'. Not so! Indeed, this is not only what is expected, it is normal, everyday Christianity.

Constant Offering

You see, the keeping of the feast of unleavened bread involved a daily offering of fire unto the Lord for seven days. 'Ye shall do no servile work therein. But ye shall offer an offering made by fire unto the Lord seven days' (vv. 7, 8). The life of faith, true Christianity, is a continual offering made by fire unto the Lord. It involves the constant giving up of ourselves to our Saviour. To trust Christ is to cease from all servile work for acceptance with God. There is no faith in Christ where there is no denunciation of all personal righteousness.

Faith in Christ is giving up my life to him, and surrendering to Christ as my Lord (Mark 8:34, 35: Luke 14:26-33). Voluntary, lifelong surrender of life to Christ is the most reasonable thing in the world to the believing heart (Romans 11:33-12:2; 1 Corinthians 6:9-11, 19, 20).

Continual Feast

Living in this world by faith in Christ is portrayed as a continual feast of unleavened bread. The feast of unleavened bread speaks of our continual feast of faith, feeding on Christ the Bread of Life, the Manna which came down from heaven. In Deuteronomy 16:3, this unleavened bread is called 'the bread of affliction'. Why? It is thick and heavy, hard to digest, unsavoury, and unappealing.

Certainly all those things are true. But there is more to this than the physical characteristics of unleavened bread. It is here called 'the bread of affliction', because it represents the same thing as was represented in the bitter herbs with which the passover lamb was to be eaten.

The believer's life, the life of faith, so long as we live in this world is eating 'the bread of affliction'. This does not refer to outward, providential affliction, but to inward grace, the affliction of our souls. That is it. That is what it is to keep the feast of unleavened bread. It is continually eating 'the bread of affliction'.

Yes, we rejoice in Christ. We live in this world in the joy of faith. This is not the bread of doubt and despair, but 'the bread of affliction'. It is bread we delight to eat, but it is heavy and hard to digest. It is the very bread of life to our souls, but it is still 'the bread of affliction'. We eat 'the bread of affliction' when we cease from legal works and legal hopes before God.

We eat 'the bread of affliction' when we, under the weight of Holy Ghost conviction, confess our sin with mournful hearts. There is more to this than the remembrance of our sins, more than looking to the hole of the pit from whence we were digged. To eat 'the bread of affliction', this keeping of the feast of unleavened bread, involves the unceasing, growing, bitter-sweet remembrance of the price of our ransom. It begins in conversion, but continues throughout our days in this world (Zechariah 12:10; Philippians 3:10; Galatians 6:14).

Nothing is so humbling as the realisation of the cost of our redemption, the sacrifice of Christ. Nothing produces contrition before God like the cross. Nothing produces consecration of heart like Christ crucified. Nothing produces sincerity and reflects truth like this.

Another Sabbath
At the end of the feast of unleavened bread, the Jews kept another sabbath. The feast began with sabbath observance and ended with sabbath observance. So it is with us. Soon we will eat the bread of affliction no more and there shall be another sabbath (Revelation 14:13; 21:4, 5). Our gospel feast of unleavened bread began with the sabbath rest of faith in Christ. It shall end with the blessed sabbath rest of eternal heavenly glory with Christ.

And I heard a voice from heaven saying unto me, Write, Blessed are the dead which die in the Lord from henceforth: Yea, saith the Spirit, that they may rest from their labours; and their works do follow them (Revelation 14:13)
And God shall wipe away all tears from their eyes; and there shall be no more death, neither sorrow, nor crying, neither shall there be any more pain: for the former things are passed away. And he that sat upon the throne said, Behold, I make all things new. And he said unto me, Write: for these words are true and faithful (Revelation 21:4, 5).

Chapter 54

The Feast Of Firstfruits

And the LORD spake unto Moses, saying, Speak unto the children of Israel, and say unto them, When ye be come into the land which I give unto you, and shall reap the harvest thereof, then ye shall bring a sheaf of the firstfruits of your harvest unto the priest: And he shall wave the sheaf before the LORD, to be accepted for you: on the morrow after the sabbath the priest shall wave it. And ye shall offer that day when ye wave the sheaf an he lamb without blemish of the first year for a burnt offering unto the LORD. And the meat offering thereof shall be two tenth deals of fine flour mingled with oil, an offering made by fire unto the LORD for a sweet savour: and the drink offering thereof shall be of wine, the fourth part of an hin. And ye shall eat neither bread, nor parched corn, nor green ears, until the selfsame day that ye have brought an offering unto your God: it shall be a statute forever throughout your generations in all your dwellings.

Leviticus 23:9-14

Did you ever notice in reading the Scriptures that our God wisely and graciously revealed the gospel progressively? First, he spoke to Adam and Eve of the bruising of the serpent's head by One who would be the Seed of woman, promising a man to be our Saviour. Then, he killed an innocent victim, portraying the sacrifice of our all-glorious Christ as our Substitute, dying that we might live by his blood. Then, he clothed our first parents with the skins of that slain victim, typifying Christ's righteousness, that righteousness in which every redeemed sinner, being made the righteousness of God in him, by him, and with him, stands accepted before God in Christ, forever justified.

Throughout the book of God, we see the unfolding drama of redemption, act by act, scene by scene, until at last the Son delivers up the kingdom to the Father, saying, 'Lo, I and the children which thou hast given me', and presents all the myriads of his elect holy, unblameable, and unreproveable before the presence of his glory.

Seven Feasts
In the progressive revelation of his purpose of grace, the Lord God established seven annual feasts to be observed by the children of Israel, each one building upon the other, each revealing a specific aspect of our God's operations of grace and mercy for the salvation of his people.

The first feast established by God was the feast of the passover. This typified Christ our Passover who is sacrificed for us and by whom we are redeemed. Then, the feast of unleavened bread was established to portray our life of faith in this world. There could be no life and no faith without redemption by the blood of Christ. All the redeemed, all for whom the paschal lamb was slain, kept the feast of unleavened bread, because all who were redeemed by the blood of Christ are born of God and given faith in him at the appointed time of love. Now, in verses 9-14, we come to the feast of firstfruits, which speaks of Christ our Resurrection and our future, bodily resurrection, which will follow this life of faith in Christ. We know that this is what the feast of firstfruits referred to and typified because God the Holy Spirit specifically tells us that in 1 Corinthians 15:19-28.

The Feast of Firstfruits
The feast of firstfruits was a celebration of God's provision in the Land of Canaan. The feast was established by divine law while Israel was in the wilderness; but it was not observed until they came into possession of the Land of Canaan.

For forty years, they ate manna, the food of their wilderness journey. Then, when they arrived in Canaan it was time to celebrate the promise of God's abundant harvest in the land of provision. So they observed this feast, as they did the feast of passover and unleavened bread, just as soon as Joshua brought them into Canaan (Joshua 5:9-12).

For the believing Israelite, the harvest represented all God's elect, all who shall be saved in time. The firstfruits of the harvest represented the Lord Jesus Christ risen from the dead, the pledge of the full harvest.

The Ceremony

The ancient ceremony itself is described in this portion of Holy Scripture. When they planted their crops, the Israelites marked off a specific section in their barley fields. When the harvest was ripe, the men carried their sickles into the field and gathered one sheaf of barley each, the firstfruits of the field. They carried that sheaf to the tabernacle and gave it to God's priest. The priest then waved the sheaf along with the burnt offering and the meal offering.

The priest, of course, speaks of Christ our Priest and Mediator, by whom we come to God. The sheaf of firstfruits, as we have seen, speaks of Christ. This was waved before the Lord for the acceptance of the people and of their sacrifices. The burnt offering of the he lamb typified Christ, the Lamb of God, by whom we have atonement. The meal offering mingled with oil, which was double the usual amount, represented the very life of the people. They brought that upon which they depended for sustenance to God as an expression of faith, trusting him to provide everything for them. This was to be offered with a drink offering of wine, which demonstrated that the offering was made willingly, joyously, without reluctance (Psalm 104:15).

All this was done before they were allowed to gather anything from the fields for themselves. This firstfruits offering represented the whole harvest yet in the field. They gave thanks to God for the harvest while it still stood in the field, before they had so much as one bite of corn from the ear in their mouths.

How forcibly this taught and demonstrated their utter dependence upon the Lord God for everything. Yet, it also displayed, ceremonially, a willing, joyful consecration of all things to their God. They dipped every temporal blessing in the fountain of life before ever tasting it. That made it sweet to taste. God accepted the people and their sacrifice as a sweet savour with which he was well-pleased (Ecclesiastes 9:7).

God's Claim

May God the Holy Spirit graciously enable us to see and acknowledge our God's rightful claim upon the firstfruits because he is God. The firstfruits belong to him, even before they are harvested. God still claims the firstfruits of everything. He has first claim on our lives. Everything on the earth, both man and beast, was to be presented before the Lord as firstfruits to him. The firstborn of both man and beast were sanctified, made holy, and presented to the Lord (Exodus 13:2; 22:29). The firstfruits of all the earth were presented to the Lord at his altar with praise and thanksgiving (Deuteronomy 26:1-11).

The Message
The message of the feast of firstfruits is resurrection and salvation by Christ. All who know and worship God, who have been washed in the blood of Christ, born of God, saved by God's free grace in Christ ought to bring the firstfruits of all things to God. The giving of the firstfruits is a picture of faith in Christ, trusting God our Saviour for all things.

> That thou shalt take of the first of all the fruit of the earth, which thou shalt bring of thy land that the LORD thy God giveth thee, and shalt put it in a basket, and shalt go unto the place which the LORD thy God shall choose to place his name there (Deuteronomy 26:2).
> Trust in the LORD with all thine heart; and lean not unto thine own understanding. In all thy ways acknowledge him, and he shall direct thy paths. Be not wise in thine own eyes: fear the LORD, and depart from evil. It shall be health to thy navel, and marrow to thy bones. Honour the LORD with thy substance, and with the firstfruits of all thine increase: So shall thy barns be filled with plenty, and thy presses shall burst out with new wine (Proverbs 3:5-10).

But there is more represented here than our faith in Christ and our devotion to him. The feast of firstfruits points us to Christ and his devotion to God and to us as our Saviour.

There are many very important and significant things recorded in the Scriptures which took place on the very day the Lord God set as the day his people would keep the feast of firstfruits. Here are five with which you are familiar.

1. Noah's ark rested on Mount Ararat (Genesis 8:4), picturing redemption finished by Christ.

2. Israel came out of Egypt and crossed the Red Sea (Exodus 13:3, 4), portraying deliverance by God's outstretched arm and omnipotent hand.

3. Israel ate the firstfruits of the Promised Land (Joshua 5:10-12), which represented God's elect obtaining heavenly glory with Christ.

The manna God gave from heaven during the days in the wilderness ceased the 16th day of Nisan after the people ate of the old corn of the land. The day following was the 17th of Nisan, the day when the children of Israel ate the firstfruits of the Promised Land. Nisan means 'new beginning'. In Christ every saved sinner experiences a new beginning (2 Corinthians 5:17).

4. Haman was defeated and slain (Esther 3:1-8:2), even as all our foes are vanquished by our God, and Satan and antichrist shall forever be overthrown by our mighty Man of War, the Lord Jesus Christ.

In the book of Esther, Haman plotted to kill all the Jews in Persia and Media. Haman had ten sons. He was a picture of the false Messiah, Antichrist. A decree was sent out on the 13th of Nisan that all the Jews would be killed. Upon hearing this news, Esther proclaimed a three-day fast, which would be Nisan 14-16.

On the 16th of Nisan, Esther risked her life when she came to King Ahasuerus. The king asked her, in effect, 'Tell me, what you want?' Esther replied, 'If it seem good unto the king, let the king and Haman come this day unto the banquet that I have prepared for him' (Esther 5:4). This was the 16th day of Nisan. At the banquet, the king again asked Esther what she wanted, and she asked the king to come to another banquet to be held the next day, the 17th of Nisan. On this day, Haman, a picture of antichrist and Satan, was hanged on the gallows he had built for Mordechai.

5. The resurrection of Christ took place on this very day (John 12:24, 1 Corinthians 15:16-20).

The Lord Jesus celebrated the festival of firstfruits by presenting himself as the Firstfruits of his elect. According to the Jews' own calculation, our Saviour's resurrection from the dead was accomplished on the day the firstfruits were appointed to be offered (John 12:23, 24).

On the next day after the sabbath, the Son of God arose from the dead. Standing upon the earth, the risen Christ waved himself before God as the true Wave Offering of Firstfruits by whom, with whom, and in whom we are accepted as a sweet savour to God (Matthew 27:52, 53;

28:1-6; Romans 4:25). He was for us the Lamb of sacrifice. He stands before the Triune Jehovah as the wave sheaf of harvest for his ransomed. He is our sweet savour of acceptance (Ephesians 1:6).

The Lord Jesus Christ is the firstfruits, the one who has preeminence in all things and over all things (Colossians 1:18). He is the firstborn of Mary (Matthew 1:23-25). He is the first-begotten of God the Father (Hebrews 1:6). He is the firstborn of every creature (Colossians 1:15). He is the first-begotten from the dead (Revelation 1:5). He is the firstborn among many brethren (Romans 8:29). He is the firstfruits of the resurrected ones (1 Corinthians 15:20, 23). He is the beginning of the creation of God (Revelation 3:14). He is the preeminent One, Jehovah's Firstborn (Colossians 1:18). The Lord Jesus Christ, our all-glorious Saviour, is indeed the Holy One of God, sanctified by the Father as his Firstborn. He is the first, the choicest, the preeminent One. Behold the crucified, risen, exalted Christ, our Saviour, Jehovah's Firstborn as he is held before us in the book of God.

> I was in the Spirit on the Lord's day, and heard behind me a great voice, as of a trumpet, Saying, I am Alpha and Omega, the first and the last: and, What thou seest, write in a book, and send it unto the seven churches which are in Asia; unto Ephesus, and unto Smyrna, and unto Pergamos, and unto Thyatira, and unto Sardis, and unto Philadelphia, and unto Laodicea. And I turned to see the voice that spake with me. And being turned, I saw seven golden candlesticks; and in the midst of the seven candlesticks one like unto the Son of man, clothed with a garment down to the foot, and girt about the paps with a golden girdle. His head and his hairs were white like wool, as white as snow; and his eyes were as a flame of fire; and his feet like unto fine brass, as if they burned in a furnace; and his voice as the sound of many waters. And he had in his right hand seven stars: and out of his mouth went a sharp twoedged sword: and his countenance was as the sun shineth in his strength. And when I saw him, I fell at his feet as dead. And he laid his right hand upon me, saying unto me, Fear not; I am the first and the last: I am he that liveth, and was dead; and, behold, I am alive for evermore, Amen; and have the keys of hell and of death (Revelation 1:10-18).

What is thy beloved more than another beloved, O thou fairest among women? What is thy beloved more than another beloved, that thou dost so charge us? My beloved is white and ruddy, the chiefest among ten thousand. His head is as the most fine gold, his locks are bushy, and black as a raven. His eyes are as the eyes of doves by the rivers of waters, washed with milk, and fitly set. His cheeks are as a bed of spices, as sweet flowers: his lips like lilies, dropping sweet smelling myrrh. His hands are as gold rings set with the beryl: his belly is as bright ivory overlaid with sapphires. His legs are as pillars of marble, set upon sockets of fine gold: his countenance is as Lebanon, excellent as the cedars. His mouth is most sweet: yea, he is altogether lovely. This is my beloved, and this is my friend, O daughters of Jerusalem (Song of Solomon 5:9-16).

Our Saviour, the Lord Jesus, is both the Firstborn of God and the Firstfruits unto God. He is the sheaf of the firstfruits, the pledge and promise of the full harvest. The firstfruits represent the whole.

But now is Christ risen from the dead, and become the firstfruits of them that slept. For since by man came death, by man came also the resurrection of the dead. For as in Adam all die, even so in Christ shall all be made alive. But every man in his own order: Christ the firstfruits; afterward they that are Christ's at his coming. Then cometh the end, when he shall have delivered up the kingdom to God, even the Father; when he shall have put down all rule and all authority and power. For he must reign, till he hath put all enemies under his feet (1 Corinthians 15:20-25).

I would not have you to be ignorant, brethren, concerning them which are asleep, that ye sorrow not, even as others which have no hope. For if we believe that Jesus died and rose again, even so them also which sleep in Jesus will God bring with him. For this we say unto you by the word of the Lord, that we which are alive and remain unto the coming of the Lord shall not prevent them which are asleep. For the Lord himself shall descend from heaven with a shout, with the voice of the archangel, and with the trump of God: and the dead in Christ shall rise first: Then we which are alive and remain shall be caught up together with them in the clouds, to meet the Lord in the air: and so shall we ever be with the Lord. Wherefore comfort one another with these words (1 Thessalonians 4:13-18).

As if that great expectation were not enough, Paul tells us about another great 'firstfruits' that all who trust Christ have already experienced, which is the first resurrection, the new birth (Revelation 20:6). He wrote to the saints at Rome, 'And not only they, but ourselves also, which have the firstfruits of the Spirit, even we ourselves groan within ourselves, waiting for the adoption, to wit, the redemption of our body' (Romans 8:23).

We have received the pledge, the promise, the down payment, the firstfruits of the Holy Spirit. That means there is more to follow. Can you imagine what it is going to be like in heaven in the presence of the Christ, our God and Saviour, for all eternity? We cannot even begin to imagine it! We have only tasted what it is going to be like when Christ comes for us. The presence of the Holy Spirit guarantees the promise.

The apostle John was permitted to see what is taking place in heaven, around the throne of God. He heard the new song they are singing about the throne. He saw the Lamb and those who follow him wherever he goes. 'These were redeemed from among men, being the firstfruits unto God and to the Lamb' (Revelation 14:4). He goes forth with a golden crown on his head and a sharp sickle in his hand.

Immediately after the tribulation of those days shall the sun be darkened, and the moon shall not give her light, and the stars shall fall from heaven, and the powers of the heavens shall be shaken: And then shall appear the sign of the Son of man in heaven: and then shall all the tribes of the earth mourn, and they shall see the Son of man coming in the clouds of heaven with power and great glory. And he shall send his angels with a great sound of a trumpet, and they shall gather together his elect from the four winds, from one end of heaven to the other' (Matthew 24:29-31).

Even so, come Lord Jesus, even today!

Chapter 55

The Feast Of Pentecost

And ye shall count unto you from the morrow after the sabbath, from the day that ye brought the sheaf of the wave offering; seven sabbaths shall be complete: Even unto the morrow after the seventh sabbath shall ye number fifty days; and ye shall offer a new meat offering unto the LORD. Ye shall bring out of your habitations two wave loaves of two tenth deals: they shall be of fine flour; they shall be baken with leaven; they are the firstfruits unto the LORD. And ye shall offer with the bread seven lambs without blemish of the first year, and one young bullock, and two rams: they shall be for a burnt offering unto the LORD, with their meat offering, and their drink offerings, even an offering made by fire, of sweet savour unto the LORD. Then ye shall sacrifice one kid of the goats for a sin offering, and two lambs of the first year for a sacrifice of peace offerings. And the priest shall wave them with the bread of the firstfruits for a wave offering before the LORD with the two lambs: they shall be holy to the LORD for the priest. And ye shall proclaim on the selfsame day, that it may be an holy convocation unto you: ye shall do no servile work therein: it shall be a statute forever in all your dwellings throughout your generations. And when ye reap the harvest of your land, thou shalt not make clean riddance of the corners of thy field when thou reapest, neither shalt thou gather any gleaning of thy harvest: thou shalt leave them unto the poor, and to the stranger: I am the LORD your God.

Leviticus 23:15-22

Studying the book of Leviticus, I keep praying that the Lord will be pleased to be my Teacher and show me his message for our souls in each type and picture it describes. I want us to behold the wonders of his law. May he be pleased to anoint our eyes, yours and mine, with the eye-salve of his grace and lead us as he led John through the wonders of the streets of the New Jerusalem. I want us to see the fine gold and every precious stone. May our Lord, the Lamb, be our light, as we open his Word, who promised ...

> And I will pray the Father, and he shall give you another Comforter, that he may abide with you forever; Even the Spirit of truth; whom the world cannot receive, because it seeth him not, neither knoweth him: but ye know him; for he dwelleth with you, and shall be in you. I will not leave you comfortless: I will come to you (John 14:16-18).

May he be pleased, once more, to come to us and lead us again to fountains of living waters as we seek to understand by his teaching and grace God's message to us in the Old Testament feast of Pentecost.

In the passage before us we are given instructions concerning the feast of Pentecost. In the Old Testament it was called 'the feast of weeks' (2 Chronicles 8:12, 13); but we know it best as the feast of Pentecost because that is how it is referred to in the New Testament (Acts 2:1; 20:16; 1 Corinthians 16:8). It was called 'the feast of weeks' in the Old Testament because it was observed seven weeks and a day after the feast of passover. It is referred to as the feast of Pentecost in the New Testament because it was observed seven weeks and a day or fifty days, after the Jews' passover. 'Pentecost' means 'fiftieth'.

The feast of firstfruits was held at the beginning of the barley harvest. This feast, the feast of Pentecost, was held seven weeks later at the beginning of the wheat harvest. We cannot help noticing significant differences between the two feasts. The firstfruits of the wheat, like the firstfruits of the barley, were to be offered to the Lord, but not as a sheaf. The wheat offering was to be offered in the form of two loaves of bread. This offering must be made of leavened bread, which the priest would eat (v. 20). This offering was to be made with specific animal sacrifices.

The two loaves of leavened bread were to be waved with two lambs of the first year before the Lord by God's appointed priest.

What is the significance of all these things? Why are they given? What does the Holy Spirit teach us by this typical ceremony of divine worship? It was an offering of thanksgiving to God, acknowledging that all our daily provisions come from him (James 1:17). But there is more here than an act of thanksgiving. The feast of Pentecost was a picture of the ingathering of God's elect by the mighty operations of God the Holy Ghost (Joel 2, Acts 2).

The two loaves of leavened bread represent God's elect, gathered from the four corners of the earth by the Holy Ghost and presented before him in connection with all the perfection and preciousness of Christ our Passover, who was sacrificed for us. In the passover, we see the sacrificial death of Christ, the Lamb of God. In the sheaf of firstfruits, we see the resurrection, ascension, and acceptance of Christ as our sin-atoning Substitute. Here, in the feast of Pentecost, we see the outpouring of the Holy Spirit upon all flesh to gather in God's elect, the prize of Christ's accomplished redemption (Galatians 3:13, 14).

Christ had to die, redemption had to be accomplished, sin had to be put away, before we could be brought to God and accepted of him. The sheaf must first be offered. Only then could the loaves be baked and presented to God upon the basis of the slain Lamb's atonement. Let us look at this feast of Pentecost more closely.

The Time of the Feast
We should note the time of the feast. The Jews have, from ancient times, contended that the feast of Pentecost was to be observed 50 days after the passover because this was precisely the time that God gave the law to Israel by the hand of Moses. Though the Scriptures do not verbally connect the two, there is an obvious connection. The Israelites left Egypt on the day of passover. They arrived at Mount Sinai sometime during the third month, (Exodus 19:1), which begins about a week before Pentecost. It was then that Moses was called up into Mount Sinai to receive the law of God, the revelation of God's holiness and justice.

I find those things significant. The law was given to shut us up to Christ, to make us know our sin and our need of Christ as our Substitute. The law's revelation of God could not be complete without its fulfilment by Christ. That fulfilment could not be known without our

Lord's resurrection, ascension, and acceptance as our Substitute in heaven, declaring that he has fulfilled all the law in putting away our sins by the sacrifice of himself. Yet, this glorious fact, by which God is revealed in all the splendour of his glorious holiness, can never be known by any sinner until he has been brought in, gathered in by God the Holy Spirit in regenerating grace.

Two Loaves of Leavened Bread

Be sure you do not miss this. We are told that the sacrifice of this feast of Pentecost must be a sacrifice of two loaves of leavened bread. 'They shall be baked with leaven' (v. 17). Why was this?

These loaves were to be baked with leaven and presented to the Lord as leavened loaves because they were intended to represent us, God's people in this world. There were two loaves because God's church is made up of both Jews and Gentiles. The loaves were leavened loaves because saved sinners are sinners still.

Though born of God, justified by blood and sanctified by grace; though filled with the Spirit and walking in the Spirit; though adorned with the gifts of his grace; believers are still people personally defiled with the leaven of sin. We constantly acknowledge that painful, sad fact (1 John 1:7-2:2; Romans 7:14-24).

On the day of Pentecost the Spirit-filled church stood before God in the full perfection and acceptance of Christ's blood and righteousness, crowned with the gifts of the Holy Ghost. Yet, they were leavened with the flesh. The regenerating grace of God the Holy Spirit in us does not eradicate or change the old man in us. Indwelling sin is something we must live with and war with as long as we live in this world.

Acts of sin may be suppressed and kept out of view but sin is in us. Our natural hearts are just as depraved as ever! This fact is portrayed in the type before us by the leaven in the two loaves. It is set forth in the history of the church, and in the life experience of every ransomed soul.

The fact is, 'that which is born of the flesh is flesh'. The flesh will never be anything but flesh. The Holy Spirit did not come down on the day of Pentecost, and does not come down in saving power and grace, to improve nature or remove its incurable evil. Not at all! He came on the day of Pentecost to put God's church into an entirely new realm of life. On that day, the King of Glory baptized his church and kingdom in the Holy Spirit. He comes in saving grace to give us a new nature, to bring us into one body, and unite us with Christ, our living Head in heaven, that we might 'walk in the Spirit', that is, live by faith, and no longer, 'fulfil the lusts of the flesh'.

These two waved loaves were made out of the wheat seed, the fruit of that which had been sown in the earth (John 12:20-32). The two leavened loaves were accepted, though leavened, by the holy Lord God, as an offering of sweet savour because of another sacrifice (v. 18).

I have already shown you how the leavened loaves portrayed God's people in this world, saved by grace, yet sinners still. Clearly, there is an indication in that fact that our God knows and acknowledges the evil that is in us. But, blessed be his matchless name, the evil that is divinely recognised is divinely provided for.

> And ye shall offer with the bread seven lambs without blemish of the first year, and one young bullock, and two rams: they shall be for a burnt offering unto the LORD, with their meat offering, and their drink offerings, even an offering made by fire, of sweet savour unto the LORD (Leviticus 23:18).

Here is an immediate connection between the leavened loaves and the presentation of an unblemished sacrifice, typifying the great truth that it is Christ's perfection and not our sinfulness that is ever before the eye of God (Ephesians 1:3-7; Colossians 1:12; 2:9-17).

Here is rest and joy for our hearts and souls, even as we acknowledge our sin. God knows exactly what we are. 'He remembereth that we are dust'! He knows the worst of us. Yet, he does not deal with us after our sins. He does not reward us according to our iniquities. He deals with us in grace and rewards us according to Christ's righteousness. Our great God, who delights in mercy, has made provision in his wisdom, according to his justice and truth, according to his goodness and grace, according to his mercy and love, according to his holiness and righteousness, not according to our merit.

'Ye shall offer with the bread, seven lambs without blemish.' Seven is the number of perfection and the number of grace. Seven represents the work of God, the number of completion and the number of rest.

This is not religious theory and speculation. It is exactly what this type was intended by God to teach us. As I said before, this is obvious.

Two Lambs and a Priest

In verses 19 and 20 we see that these two leavened loaves were offered and accepted because of two lambs of the first year offered by God's appointed priest as a peace offering, waved before God with the lambs.

> Then ye shall sacrifice one kid of the goats for a sin offering, and two lambs of the first year for a sacrifice of peace offerings. And the priest shall wave them with the bread of the firstfruits for a wave offering before the LORD with the two lambs: they shall be holy to the LORD for the priest (Leviticus 23:19, 20).

The priests took the two lambs and the two leavened loaves and waved them as one before God, and God accepted them as one. Christ is our Priest. He is our sacrifice, our peace offering, our priest. Christ presents us in union with himself to God upon the basis of his sacrifice. God accepts us as one with Christ. C. H. Mackintosh well observed,

> Thus, on the day of Pentecost, the church was presented, in all the value and excellency of Christ, through the power of the Holy Ghost. Though having in itself the leaven of the old nature, that leaven was not reckoned, because the divine sin offering had perfectly answered for it. The power of the Holy Ghost did not remove the leaven, but the blood of the Lamb had atoned for it.

The work of the Spirit in the believer does not remove indwelling evil. It enables us to detect it, judge, and reckon it as God does, put away by the blood of the Lamb (Romans 6:11; 1 Peter 4:1).

Our sin is never under the eye of God. It has been put out of sight, purged, removed, put away and forgotten by God forever; and we are accepted in Christ, who offered himself to God as a sweet-smelling sacrifice, that he might glorify him in all things (Numbers 23:21).

These two leaven loaves were for the priest and were the priest's food (v. 20). John explains this part of our typical picture. Christ says,

> ... I have meat to eat that ye know not of. Therefore said the disciples one to another, Hath any man brought him ought to eat? Jesus saith unto them, My meat is to do the will of him that sent me, and to finish his work (John 4:32-34).

Rest Proclaimed

Next, we see rest proclaimed.

> And ye shall proclaim on the selfsame day, that it may be an holy convocation unto you: ye shall do no servile work therein: it shall be a statute forever in all your dwellings throughout your generations (Leviticus 23:21).

That is what happens when the gospel of Christ is preached. Preaching Christ crucified, God's servants proclaim rest, rest for weary sinners in Christ. He says,

> Come unto me, all ye that labour and are heavy laden, and I will give you rest. Take my yoke upon you, and learn of me; for I am meek and lowly in heart: and ye shall find rest unto your souls. For my yoke is easy, and my burden is light (Matthew 11:28-30).
> Rest in the LORD, and wait patiently for him: fret not thyself because of him who prospereth in his way, because of the man who bringeth wicked devices to pass (Psalm 37:7).
> Return unto thy rest, O my soul; for the LORD hath dealt bountifully with thee (Psalm 116:7).
> This is my rest forever: here will I dwell; for I have desired it (Psalm 132:14).

Gleanings for Poor Strangers

Verse 22 speaks of gleanings God required the Jews to leave in their fields for poor strangers.

> And when ye reap the harvest of your land, thou shalt not make clean riddance of the corners of thy field when thou reapest, neither shalt thou gather any gleaning of thy harvest: thou shalt leave them unto the poor, and to the stranger: I am the LORD your God (Leviticus 23:22).

This is a picture of God's provision for us, both Jews and Gentiles. As gleanings of the harvest were to be left in the corners of the field for the poor and the stranger, so in every corner of the earth there are gleanings of grace for poor, miserable sinners, 'handfuls of purpose' left by our great Boaz, Christ our Kinsman Redeemer, to bring us to himself. 'And of his fulness have all we received, and grace for grace' (John 1:16).

We are by nature poor, needy, bankrupt sinners; strangers far off from God. Our Boaz scatters his grace through the four corners of the earth for strangers far off from God.

Our inheritance with Christ is the inheritance of Christ, bestowed by grace and bestowed upon all God's elect alike. The gleanings of grace, the gleanings of heaven, the gleanings of the fields of glory are boundless, infinite bounties of grace in Christ. The gleanings of Canaan represent the glories of heaven, the glories of Christ. God's Church is not merely blessed by Christ, but with Christ and in Christ. The Bride of Christ in heaven shall possess and enjoy her own wealthy and happy home in heaven, the home she rightfully holds as her own, the home to which she belongs, her Husband's house.

We are one with Christ! Can you get hold of that? God's Church is the King's Bride, the Queen of his throne, and the sharer of his joys, his dignities and his glories. The eternal mansions of the Father's house on high is the church's rightful portion in and with Christ. May we ever bear this in mind, and live worthy of such a holy, elevated destination.

Come, poor sinner, glean in Canaan's boundless fields. Come, strangers to grace and to God, come and welcome. What boundless blessedness we shall possess when all the Lord's wheat has been gathered into his garner (Ephesians 2:7; 5:25-27; Hebrews 2:13; 1 Corinthians 15:24-28; Jude 1:24, 25).

Chapter 56

The Feast Of Trumpets

And the LORD spake unto Moses, saying, Speak unto the children of Israel, saying, In the seventh month, in the first day of the month, shall ye have a sabbath, a memorial of blowing of trumpets, an holy convocation. Ye shall do no servile work therein: but ye shall offer an offering made by fire unto the LORD.

Leviticus 23:23-25

Gospel preachers are trumpeters and in the Scriptures the preaching of the gospel is often likened to the blowing of a trumpet. Sometimes it is compared to a trumpet sound making a joyful announcement, other times to a sound of alarm in preparation for war. 'If the trumpet give an uncertain sound, who shall prepare himself to the battle?' But throughout the book of God, gospel preaching is compared to the blowing of a trumpet (Psalm 81:1-4; 89:1-18). The first mention of a trumpet is found in connection with the giving of the law at Mount Sinai when God called Moses up into the mount (Exodus 19:13, 19; 20:18). In the Old Testament, the Lord God used the blasts of trumpets to summons his people to himself: 1. To call for solemn assemblies; 2. In preparation for journeys; 3. To prepare for war; 4. To announce the new moons; 5. In the year of jubilee. All were highly symbolic and typical of things to come in this gospel age.

One of the annual feasts of worship was the Feast of Trumpets. It is described here in Leviticus 23:23-25. We are given a little more detail in Numbers 10:1-10 and Numbers 29:1-6.

And the LORD spake unto Moses, saying, Make thee two trumpets of silver; of a whole piece shalt thou make them: that thou mayest use them for the calling of the assembly, and for the journeying of the camps. And when they shall blow with them, all the assembly shall assemble themselves to thee at the door of the tabernacle of the congregation. And if they blow but with one trumpet, then the princes, which are heads of the thousands of Israel, shall gather themselves unto thee. When ye blow an alarm, then the camps that lie on the east parts shall go forward. When ye blow an alarm the second time, then the camps that lie on the south side shall take their journey: they shall blow an alarm for their journeys. But when the congregation is to be gathered together, ye shall blow, but ye shall not sound an alarm. And the sons of Aaron, the priests, shall blow with the trumpets; and they shall be to you for an ordinance forever throughout your generations. And if ye go to war in your land against the enemy that oppresseth you, then ye shall blow an alarm with the trumpets; and ye shall be remembered before the LORD your God, and ye shall be saved from your enemies. Also in the day of your gladness, and in your solemn days, and in the beginnings of your months, ye shall blow with the trumpets over your burnt offerings, and over the sacrifices of your peace offerings; that they may be to you for a memorial before your God: I am the LORD your God (Numbers 10:1-10).

And in the seventh month, on the first day of the month, ye shall have an holy convocation; ye shall do no servile work: it is a day of blowing the trumpets unto you. And ye shall offer a burnt offering for a sweet savour unto the LORD; one young bullock, one ram, and seven lambs of the first year without blemish: And their meat offering shall be of flour mingled with oil, three tenth deals for a bullock, and two tenth deals for a ram, and one tenth deal for one lamb, throughout the seven lambs: And one kid of the goats for a sin offering, to make an atonement for you: Beside the burnt offering of the month, and his meat offering, and the daily burnt offering, and his meat offering, and their drink offerings, according unto their manner, for a sweet savour, a sacrifice made by fire unto the LORD (Numbers 29:1-6).

The Feast of Trumpets was a representation of the spiritual joy and gladness that belongs to God's elect, the gladness of redemption and the joy of grace found in Christ (Isaiah 35:10) when we are made to know the joyful sound of the gospel (Psalm 89:14-18).

God's Voice

The trumpet sounded as God's voice calling his people to himself, so the preaching of the gospel is God's voice to his people. 'See that ye refuse not the voice of him that speaketh.' The trumpet at Sinai represented the voice of the Almighty and when the Apostle John heard the Lord Jesus speaking to him on the Isle of Patmos, his voice was as the voice of a great trumpet (Revelation 1:10). What a gracious God we have. He who spoke in terror at Sinai calls us to everlasting bliss by the gospel (2 Corinthians 5:17-6:2; Hebrews 12:25).

God's voice is the voice of two trumpets (Numbers 10:2): the Old Testament and the New. Yet, these two trumpets are one. They were made of one 'whole piece' of silver. The message of the Old Testament and the message of the New is one message 'Jesus Christ and him crucified'. The gospel is one message.

These trumpets were typical of the gospel. The blowing of the trumpets symbolized gospel preaching called 'the great trumpet' (Isaiah 27:13). Gospel preachers are to lift up their voice like a trumpet, both to sound an alarm to perishing sinners, warning of wrath to come, and to call them to Christ for salvation (Isaiah 58:1).

The trumpets were made of silver and the gospel of God is comparable to silver because it is fetched out of the rich mines of the sacred Scriptures, pure and free from the dross of errors and human inventions. It will bear to be tried by the standard of the Word, and is lasting and durable. It is the everlasting gospel. It is compared to silver because it is of great value and precious. Here we find the unsearchable riches of Christ and all the treasures of divine truth, called 'gold, silver, and precious stones', by which God builds his church.

These two trumpets, like the preaching of the gospel, were used 'for the calling of the assembly', for the gathering of God's elect (Romans 10:13-17; 1 Peter 2:23-25). These same trumpets, like the gospel of Christ, were used to inspire and direct the children of Israel in their journey to the land of promise. They were the weapons of Israel's warfare along the way, by which they prevailed over their enemies

(Numbers 10:9; 2 Corinthians 10:3-5). And the two silver trumpets were to be blown only by the sons of Aaron, only by divinely appointed men (Numbers 10:8).

Numbers 10:10 tells us these silver trumpets of grace were to be blown over the sacrifices, for there is no good news for sinners but by the sacrifice of Christ. The trumpets were blown at the beginning of their months.[15] They were blown as the children of Israel offered God their sacrifices and as a memorial before the Lord. They were memorials of faith, joy, and gratitude, remembering the past and in hope of the future.

Redemption Accomplished

The feast of trumpets was symbolical of God's mercy, love, and grace proclaimed in the gospel. The blowing of the trumpets portrayed the preaching of the gospel, a finished redemption and salvation obtained by the sacrifice of Christ.

There is no good news in the gospel of will-worshippers and works-mongers. Good news is the declaration of justice satisfied, sin put away, righteousness brought in, and eternal redemption obtained by the doing and dying of the Son of God. It was in realization of that which was signified by the blowing of these trumpets that David wrote Psalm 89.

Justice and judgment are the habitation of thy throne: mercy and truth shall go before thy face. Blessed is the people that know the joyful sound: they shall walk, O LORD, in the light of thy countenance. In thy name shall they rejoice all the day: and in thy righteousness shall they be exalted. For thou art the glory of their strength: and in thy favour our horn shall be exalted. For the LORD is our defence; and the Holy One of Israel is our king (Psalm 89:14-18).

---

[15] Charles Simeon observed, 'The Jews had two calendars and observed two new years each year. When the Lord brought Israel out of Egypt, he proclaimed that their new year (Exodus 12:2). That was the day of spiritual beginnings. But their civil, legal, political new year was the first day of the seventh month. 'This day then was *the first day in the new year;* and the feast of trumpets was to them 'a memorial'; a memorial of *mercies received,* and of *mercies promised.*'

In this Psalm David sets before us those gracious, covenant promises made between the Father and the Lord Jesus Christ; eternal promises and certain promises (Psalm 89:3, 28, 34, 37). Commentators have called this psalm, 'The Glorious Covenant Psalm', and truly it is that. We read here about covenant mercies and the covenant faithfulness of Christ our Surety. Psalm 89 is about our covenant God who rules over all and his promised grace to the covenant seed being established forever in Christ Jesus (Psalm 89:4, 29, 36). He is a covenant God; therefore his covenant people must be blessed (Ephesians 1:3-6). God gives us a clear description of his people in verses 15-17 of this psalm.

They know the joyful sound of the gospel. The sheep of Christ know the effectual voice of the Good Shepherd and they delight to follow him (John 10:27-30). It is the sound of victory over sin through his blood. It is the sound of mercy, grace, love, peace, and pardon in and through Christ Jesus (Ephesians 1:3-14).

They shall walk in the light of his countenance. Our darkened hearts have been illuminated through the preaching of the gospel and the quickening of God the Holy Ghost to see the beauty, glory, and necessity of our great Redeemer and King (2 Corinthians 4:6). Christ is our Light (John 9:5).

God's saints shall rejoice in his name all the day. Believers have every reason to rejoice in Christ alone having no confidence in the flesh (Philippians 3:3). We are redeemed, justified, and sanctified in him.

They shall be exalted in his righteousness. The perfect righteousness Jesus Christ worked out for his elect has been freely, eternally, and fully imputed to them that believe. We have been made the righteousness of God in him (Romans 4:6; 2 Corinthians 5:21). Christ Jesus is the Lord our Righteousness (Jeremiah 23:5; 33:16; Philippians 3:7-9).

The Lord Jesus Christ is our glory and strength. Without him we are nothing, we can do nothing, we know nothing (John 15:5). Any spiritual strength or spiritual knowledge we enjoy and experience is and must be because of his grace worked within us (Philippians 1:6; 4:13).

The Lord Jesus Christ, our Saviour, our Covenant Surety, our God, is our defence. We are unable to defend ourselves against our spiritual enemies. There are too many of them and they are too powerful for us even to begin to fight. However, our Lord Christ, our Man of War, stood face to face and toe to toe with all our enemies and won the glorious victory for us (Psalm 98:1). He defeated sin by making atonement for it (Hebrews 9:26). He magnified and honoured the law for us (Galatians 3:13). He defeated Satan by crushing his dominion and power (Hebrews 2:14). He defeated death by rising from the dead (Revelation 1:18).

Call to Rest

Like the blowing of these silver trumpets, the preaching of the gospel is a call to rest.

> And the LORD spake unto Moses, saying, Speak unto the children of Israel, saying, In the seventh month, in the first day of the month, shall ye have a sabbath, a memorial of blowing of trumpets, an holy convocation. Ye shall do no servile work therein: but ye shall offer an offering made by fire unto the LORD (Leviticus 29:23-25).

What gracious, sweet words those are which fall from the lips of him who is the Gospel, from the lips of him who is our blest Sabbath Rest!

> Come unto me, all ye that labour and are heavy laden, and I will give you rest. Take my yoke upon you, and learn of me; for I am meek and lowly in heart: and ye shall find rest unto your souls. For my yoke is easy, and my burden is light (Matthew 11:28-30).

The trumpet sound was like the word 'behold' so commonly used in the New Testament, that word by which we are called to Christ. May God the Holy Spirit, whose word we have before us, graciously call both writer and reader by his almighty, omnipotent grace and irresistible mercy to Christ and give us rest in him.

Chapter 57

The Feast Of Atonement

And the LORD spake unto Moses, saying, Also on the tenth day of this seventh month there shall be a day of atonement: it shall be an holy convocation unto you; and ye shall afflict your souls, and offer an offering made by fire unto the LORD. And ye shall do no work in that same day: for it is a day of atonement, to make an atonement for you before the LORD your God. For whatsoever soul it be that shall not be afflicted in that same day, he shall be cut off from among his people. And whatsoever soul it be that doeth any work in that same day, the same soul will I destroy from among his people. Ye shall do no manner of work: it shall be a statute forever throughout your generations in all your dwellings. It shall be unto you a sabbath of rest, and ye shall afflict your souls: in the ninth day of the month at even, from even unto even, shall ye celebrate your sabbath.

Leviticus 23:26-32

Leviticus 16 describes the day of atonement God required Israel to observe in Old Testament worship. Everything relating to that great day was typical, portraying the sin-atoning work of our Lord Jesus Christ at Calvary. The picture of atonement given in that chapter involved many, many things. Here are six things that stand out in that chapter about the day of atonement.

1. Aaron, God's high priest, was the only one who could make atonement for the sins of the people. None but Christ, our great High Priest, of whom Aaron was but a type, could make atonement for us.

2. Atonement was made for Israel alone, God's chosen people. Christ died for and redeemed God's elect alone. The book of God universally teaches the sweet and blessed gospel doctrine of limited atonement, or particular and effectual redemption.

3. The sins of the people were ceremonially imputed to two goats, the Lord's goat and the scapegoat. The sins of God's elect were made our Saviour's sins and carried away by him (2 Corinthians 5:21).

4. The Lord's goat was slain, and his blood was sprinkled upon the mercy seat in the holy of holies. We read of our ever-blessed Christ, 'Neither by the blood of goats and calves, but by his own blood he entered in once into the holy place, having obtained eternal redemption for us' (Hebrews 9:12).

5. The scapegoat was carried away by a fit man and forever lost. Our sins were forever put away by the Lord Jesus Christ.

6. All for whom atonement was made were blessed of God, even as all for whom Christ died and made atonement are blessed of God with blessings of grace and salvation.

Atonement Experienced
It is a very great mistake to imagine that instructions given in one portion of Holy Scripture and repeated in another is merely a matter of repetition. That is not the case. There is always a reason when directions are given about something more than once. The passage before us in Leviticus 23:26-32 is a very clear example of this.

Leviticus 16 describes the day of atonement for the purpose of showing in type how the Lord Jesus Christ accomplished redemption by the sacrifice of himself at Calvary. Leviticus 23 sets before us the feast of atonement or the feast of expiation, as one of Israel's annual holy convocations.

Notice that this feast, the feast of atonement, follows the feasts of passover, unleavened bread, firstfruits, Pentecost, and trumpets. Those are all feasts portraying our experience of grace and salvation by Christ.

The redemption of our souls was accomplished for us altogether outside our experience, long before we were born, when the Son of God died in our room and stead upon the cursed tree. That accomplished redemption is what Leviticus 16 portrays.

Leviticus 23:26-32 portrays the believer's experience of grace in receiving the atonement by faith in Christ. The ceremony, the holy assembly for worship, described in Leviticus 23:26-32 is not talking about what Christ did at Calvary, but about what goes on in our souls when God the Holy Ghost reveals Christ in us and gives us a saving interest in what he did at Calvary (Romans 5:6-11; 2 Timothy 1:9, 10).

When God the Holy Spirit comes to chosen, redeemed sinners in the saving operations of his grace, when he sprinkles the conscience with the blood of Christ and gives us faith in Christ, he convinces us of Christ's glorious, effectual redemption accomplished for us (Hebrews 9:11-14; John 16:7-11). The feast of atonement was Israel's annual day of repentance, portraying God's gift of repentance wrought in our souls by his almighty grace.

Repentance

I have read countless sermons and articles on repentance. I have read a good many books on the subject. But I have never read anything that more blessedly explains what repentance is than Leviticus 23:26-32.

The feast of atonement was intended to show us the character of true repentance. It was, in fact, a call to the whole congregation to repent and be reconciled to God. There are several different words translated 'repent' and 'repentance' in the Hebrew text of the Old Testament and in the Greek text of the New Testament. There are two words translated 'repent' in the Old Testament and two in the New. The one means to sigh, be sorry, or regret bitterly. The other means retreat, turn back, or return. There are also two different words in the New Testament which are translated 'repent'. The one means think differently, reconsider, or change your mind. The other means regret.

The one time the word 'repentance' is found in the Old Testament (Hosea 13:14), it means 'to deeply regret'. In the New Testament, the word translated 'repentance' also means 'to deeply regret'. Repentance is sorrow and contrition before God because of sin (Zechariah 12:10). Repentance is returning to God, being reconciled to God by faith in Christ (2 Corinthians 5:17-21). Repentance is a change of mind about yourself and God, about sin and righteousness, about redemption and grace. Repentance is having the mind of Christ (1 Corinthians 2:12-16).

The feast of atonement was Israel's annual day of repentance, portraying God's gift of repentance wrought in our souls by his almighty grace.

The Numbers

It is probably unwise to overemphasize the importance of numbers used in the Bible. The Scriptures do not give us explicit direction for doing so. However, I am certain that numbers and numerals in the Word of God do have significance. One seems clearly to represent unity (Ephesians 4:4-6; John 10:30). Two speaks of division (Genesis 1:6-8). Three is the number for the Triune God and the resurrection.

Four is the number for creation, the four corners of the earth and the four winds (Revelation 7:1). Five is the number representing grace, as in the five burnt offerings. Six is the number of man, who was created on the sixth day.

Seven speaks of completeness and perfection. Creation was completed on the seventh day. The Holy Spirit is referred to as seven spirits to display the completeness and perfection of his Being, his knowledge and his work. The seven churches in the opening chapters of Revelation refer to the whole church of God.

Eight is the number of new beginning, new birth, and new creation. Nine represents fruitfulness. The fruit of the Spirit and gifts of the Spirit are nine. Our Saviour gave nine beatitudes in his Sermon on the Mount. Ten speaks of bounty, wealth, riches, and fulness.

This feast of atonement began on the tenth day of the seventh month and was consummated with a sabbath observance on the ninth day of the month. The number seven represents completion and perfection, the believer's completion and perfection in Christ. The number nine represents fruitfulness, the fruit and gifts of the Holy Spirit and the number ten represents all the bounty, wealth and riches of grace that are ours in Christ.

I do not know just how much weight should be placed upon these numbers, but I do know when God gives sinners faith in Christ, he gives us all the fulness, completion and perfection of his grace, all the fulness of his Spirit, and all the treasure of heaven. It is written, 'All things are yours, for ye are Christ's'.

Here are six things involved in repentance, six characteristics of true faith, as they are portrayed in the feast of atonement.

Worship

The feast of atonement was a holy convocation, an assembly of divine worship. 'It shall be an holy convocation unto you' (v. 27). And the very first characteristic of repentance toward God and faith in Christ is worship. Saved sinners worship God. We call upon the name of the Lord. We worship toward his holy hill of Zion, gathering on Zion's hill with the general assembly and church of the firstborn (Philippians 3:3). To call upon the name of the Lord is to worship God as he is, as he makes himself known in the person and work of his dear Son, the Lord Jesus Christ (Genesis 4:26; Romans 10:8-13).

Affliction

This feast of atonement was a time of soul affliction. 'Ye shall afflict your souls' (v. 27). As soon as a sinner has Christ revealed in him, he is broken, contrite and afflicted in his soul (Job 42:5, 6; Isaiah 6:5; 66:1, 2; Zechariah 12:10-12; 13:1; Matthew 5:3, 4).

Burnt-Offering

The feast of atonement involved burnt offerings of consecration to God. 'Ye shall afflict your souls, and offer an offering made by fire unto the Lord' (v. 27). True repentance and faith, arising from the revelation and knowledge of Christ, compels every saved sinner to consecrate himself to God (Romans 11:33-12:3; Colossians 3:1-3).

Expiation

When the Lord God gives you faith in Christ, it shall be for you the day of atonement, expiation and full, free, everlasting forgiveness of sin. 'It is a day of atonement, to make an atonement for you before the Lord your God' (v. 28). The word 'atonement' means expiate, cover, cancel, placate, appease, pacify, purge, put away, forgive, reconcile (Isaiah 43:25; 1 John 1:9).

Sabbath Rest

During the feast of atonement the children of Israel were to cease from all work of any kind and keep a sabbath of rest unto the Lord (vv. 28-32). True repentance and faith involves a total cessation of works of any kind for acceptance with God, a keeping of sabbath rest before him, a continual affliction of our souls.

It is an affliction to our proud flesh to cease from our works, to cease trusting in ourselves and trust Christ alone for all forgiveness, righteousness, holiness, and sanctification. That is the very 'foundation of repentance from dead works, and of faith toward God' (Hebrews 6:1). Faith in Christ is the true keeping of the sabbath. Any manner of work performed to win God's favour, improve God's favour toward us, or keep God's favour will bring God's everlasting destruction (v. 31; Galatians 5:1-4).

Celebration
This affliction of soul during the feast of atonement was a time of celebration. Ye shall 'celebrate your sabbath' (v. 32). True repentance and faith in Christ brings us into the blessed celebration of grace. The life God gives us in Christ is a life of celebration. Faith celebrates the character of God set forth in all his glorious attributes. We celebrate God's salvation in Christ, the peace he gives, the pardon we receive, the freedom of grace, and the hope of eternity.

The Lord our God has sent his church into the world as his voice to preach to needy sinners 'repentance and remission of sins' by the blood of Christ, calling upon sinners everywhere to be reconciled to God by faith in his dear Son (Luke 24:47; 2 Corinthians 5:17-21).

May God the Holy Spirit be pleased to bring you into this blessed celebration of grace by faith in Christ! 'Except ye repent, ye shall all likewise perish.' Worship him. Afflict your soul. Consecrate yourself to God. May this be for you a day of expiation, atonement, forgiveness. Come to Christ and rest. Celebrate the grace of God.

Chapter 58

The Feast Of Tabernacles

And the LORD spake unto Moses, saying, Speak unto the children of Israel, saying, The fifteenth day of this seventh month shall be the feast of tabernacles for seven days unto the LORD. On the first day shall be an holy convocation: ye shall do no servile work therein. Seven days ye shall offer an offering made by fire unto the LORD: on the eighth day shall be an holy convocation unto you; and ye shall offer an offering made by fire unto the LORD: it is a solemn assembly; and ye shall do no servile work therein. These are the feasts of the LORD, which ye shall proclaim to be holy convocations, to offer an offering made by fire unto the LORD, a burnt offering, and a meat offering, a sacrifice, and drink offerings, everything upon his day: Beside the sabbaths of the LORD, and beside your gifts, and beside all your vows, and beside all your freewill offerings, which ye give unto the LORD. Also in the fifteenth day of the seventh month, when ye have gathered in the fruit of the land, ye shall keep a feast unto the LORD seven days: on the first day shall be a sabbath, and on the eighth day shall be a sabbath. And ye shall take you on the first day the boughs of goodly trees, branches of palm trees, and the boughs of thick trees, and willows of the brook; and ye shall rejoice before the LORD your God seven days. And ye shall keep it a feast unto the LORD seven days in the year. It shall be a statute forever in your generations: ye shall celebrate it in the seventh month. Ye shall dwell in booths seven days; all that are Israelites born shall dwell in booths: That your generations may know that I made the children of Israel to dwell in booths, when I brought them out of the land of Egypt: I am the LORD your God. And Moses declared unto the children of Israel the feasts of the LORD.

Leviticus 23:33-44

The Lord God required the children of Israel to observe seven great, annual feasts by which he was to be worshipped: 1. The Feast of Passover; 2. The Feast of Unleavened Bread; 3. The Feast of Firstfruits; 4. The Feast of Pentecost; 5. The Feast of Trumpets; 6. The Feast of Atonement; 7. The Feast of Tabernacles.

These feasts, called 'holy convocations', were solemn assemblies of worship. Each feast was highly symbolic, portraying specific aspects of our redemption by Christ Jesus. Three of these feasts stand out from the others. For the feasts of Passover, Pentecost, and Tabernacles, God required every man in Israel to go up to Jerusalem to keep them (Deuteronomy 16:13-15). These three feasts specifically portrayed three great aspects of redemption and grace that cannot be separated.

The feast of passover, of course, portrayed our redemption by the sacrifice of Christ our Passover. The feast of Pentecost was typical of the ingathering of God's elect, the harvest of redeemed souls by the effectual, irresistible work of God the Holy Spirit. The feast of tabernacles typified the consummation of redemption in resurrection glory, the gathering of all the redeemed into heaven in the resurrection, at the second coming of our Lord Jesus Christ. When the Lord God has finished his work, when all his purpose of grace has been accomplished, every chosen sinner shall be with him in glory. Every sinner for whom Christ obtained eternal redemption, every ransomed soul, called by God the Holy Ghost, shall be brought into the heavenly glory.

And the LORD spake unto Moses, saying, Speak unto the children of Israel, saying, The fifteenth day of this seventh month shall be the feast of tabernacles for seven days unto the LORD. On the first day shall be an holy convocation: ye shall do no servile work therein. Seven days ye shall offer an offering made by fire unto the LORD: on the eighth day shall be an holy convocation unto you; and ye shall offer an offering made by fire unto the LORD: it is a solemn assembly; and ye shall do no servile work therein (Leviticus 23:33-36).

496

These verses do not give us a full description of the feast of tabernacles. Rather, they show its place among the other feasts of the Lord in the Old Testament.[16] This was the last feast, the feast by which the year was brought to its final conclusion. It speaks of that time John describes in Revelation 10, when the Lord Jesus, the mighty Angel of the Covenant, shall have fulfilled all the purpose of God, everything written in the book of divine predestination, and shall come again, make all things new, lift his hand to heaven, and declare time shall be no more. The mystery of God is finished (Revelation 10:1-7).

> These are the feasts of the LORD, which ye shall proclaim to be holy convocations, to offer an offering made by fire unto the LORD, a burnt offering, and a meat offering, a sacrifice, and drink offerings, everything upon his day: Beside the sabbaths of the LORD, and beside your gifts, and beside all your vows, and beside all your freewill offerings, which ye give unto the LORD (Leviticus 23:37, 38).

These two verses conclude the Lord's instructions about the solemn feasts of divine worship and service. But the conclusion is announced before further instruction is given about the feast of tabernacles. The feast is announced in verses 33-36. Then, Moses gives a summary of all 'the feasts of the LORD'. Then, he returns to the feast of tabernacles giving more detailed instructions about how it is to be observed.

I cannot help wondering, 'Why did Moses appear to interrupt himself?' It was not that he suddenly realised he had forgotten to mention a few things. The arrangement of the passage is by divine purpose. By writing as he does, the Holy Spirit here calls special attention to that feast which represents the most joyful prospect of heavenly, everlasting bliss, in that day called 'the times of restitution of all things' (Acts 3:21).

> Also in the fifteenth day of the seventh month, when ye have gathered in the fruit of the land, ye shall keep a feast unto the LORD seven days: on the first day shall be a sabbath, and on the

---

[16] For a more detailed description of the feast of tabernacles read Exodus 23:14-17, Numbers 29:13-39, and Deuteronomy 16:13-15.

eighth day shall be a sabbath. And ye shall take you on the first day the boughs of goodly trees, branches of palm trees, and the boughs of thick trees, and willows of the brook; and ye shall rejoice before the LORD your God seven days. And ye shall keep it a feast unto the LORD seven days in the year. It shall be a statute forever in your generations: ye shall celebrate it in the seventh month. Ye shall dwell in booths seven days; all that are Israelites born shall dwell in booths: That your generations may know that I made the children of Israel to dwell in booths, when I brought them out of the land of Egypt: I am the LORD your God. And Moses declared unto the children of Israel the feasts of the LORD (Leviticus 23:39-44).

The Time of the Feast

The feast of tabernacles was to be observed on the fifteenth day of the seventh month, at the time of full harvest, when all the fruit of the land was gathered and the grapes were in the wine press. It was held at this season of the year because it typified the full harvest of the earth in the resurrection, when the Lord Jesus Christ comes again and gathers his elect up to glory in the resurrection.

This is not a matter of speculation. Zechariah 14 shows us this is the typical meaning of the feast of tabernacles.

The feast of tabernacles was kept during the rainy season in Israel. Had the feast been held in the Spring, it would not be unusual to see people camping out in booths. But during the rainy season, it was not an expected sight to those who were not Jews. So it shall be when our Lord returns. He shall come again at an hour when he is not expected.

No one knows the day or hour of Christ's second advent. No one even knows the approximate time of our Redeemer's appearance. Learn this fact and learn it well. No one knows when the Lord Jesus is coming again. The language of Scripture in this regard is crystal clear (Mark 13:32; Acts 1:4-11).

No one knows, or even has a hint of an idea, when the Lord Jesus will come again to this world. And no one knows when Christ is coming to take him or her out of this world to meet God in judgment. I find it utterly amazing that we so blatantly ignore this fact. David said, 'There is but a step between me and death'. We all say we realise that; but very few people live like they realise it. There is but a step between you and death. My soul, hear the Word of God and learn. 'There is but a step between me and death.' God has, from eternity, fixed the moment and means by which he will take you out of this world. As soon as God takes you out of this world, you are going to stand before him in judgment. I know, there is a day of judgment at the end of time. Following the general resurrection, there will be a general judgment (John 5:28, 29; Revelation 20:11-15). But you will meet God in judgment as soon as you draw your last breath (2 Corinthians 5:10, 11; Hebrews 9:27). 'How wilt thou do in the swelling of Jordan?'

The Purpose of the Feast
God's purpose in establishing the feast of tabernacles was to remind Israel of their time in the wilderness when they dwelt in tents, or booths, as pilgrims, and the Lord God dwelt in their midst in the pillar of cloud. For this purpose, the Lord required them to dwell in booths for seven days during the feast (vv. 42, 43). In keeping the feast, the Lord would have his people remember continually that as they journeyed through the wilderness he spread his covering over them and journeyed with them every step of the way.

But there is more. The feast of tabernacles also typically spoke of another, better, more glorious day for the Israel of God. It typified that blessed, endless day of eternal glory when our God has made all things new and tabernacles with men forever. That day when the Lamb shall lead us to living fountains of water. The beginning of the new creation was the incarnation of Christ and the accomplishment of redemption by him (John 1:14; Hebrews 9:6-12). The full accomplishment of the type will take place when our Lord Jesus comes again in his glory (Revelation 7:15-17; 21:1-7; 22:1-7).

A Time of Great Joy
This feast of tabernacles was a celebration of God's goodness. It was kept with joyful remembrance of his wondrous works and observed in hope of eternal life and resurrection glory. Believers in those days were as fully convinced as we are of Christ's second coming, that our God shall make all things new, and that we shall be raised from the dead. Job declared this hope as his own back in Job 19:25-27. Enoch spoke of these things (Jude 1:14, 15), as did Isaiah, Zechariah, and others.

The Significance of the Booths

The booths they made displayed a picture of the new creation, when the earth shall be covered with rich, luxurious vegetation, where men and women shall forever live in righteousness and peace, sending up songs of praise to God continually. Try to get a picture of this celebration and the booths the people made in which they dwelled during the seven days of the feast. Reading Nehemiah 8:14-18 and Leviticus 23:33-44 together we see a picture of the new creation, when God's creation is restored to him and fully restored by him.

> And ye shall take you on the first day the boughs of goodly trees, branches of palm trees, and the boughs of thick trees, and willows of the brook; and ye shall rejoice before the LORD your God seven days (Leviticus 23:40).

1. 'Every good tree' provided boughs of fruit for the occasion.
2. 'Branches of palm trees', symbols of victory and joy, were used for the booths.
3. 'The boughs of thick trees', that is to say, 'bushy' trees, like the myrtle tree spoken of by Nehemiah, were used. They took the high, lofty palm branches and the lower thickets for their booths.
4. 'The willows of the brook', willows that grow by the streams, with their thick, hangings under which men find refuge from the heat of the sun were employed in making these booths.
5. Nehemiah tells us they used 'the olive and the pine'. The olive tree provided both fruit and oil, symbolizing the Spirit of God. The pine provided strong, massive beams needed to hold their booths together and pleasant fragrance, portraying the Lord Jesus.

They dwelt in these booths for seven days, rejoicing before the Lord and rejoicing in the Lord. So we shall dwell with our God forever in resurrection glory, possessing all the earth, rejoicing before him.

Still, there is more. These booths, being made of these trees, portray the matchless love of the God of Jeshurun, in which we have dwelt from eternity, in which we dwell now, and in which we shall forever dwell (Deuteronomy 33:26-29). The love of God, like the bough of every good tree, feeds us continually. Like the palm tree, it is lofty and triumphs over all obstacles. Like the pine, it is strong and fragrant. Like the myrtle, the love of God reaches down to the lowest and is thick, immense, substantial. Like the olive tree, it is rich and full. Like the willow by the brook, God's infinite, immutable love bends over us and protects us continually, refreshing our souls in the heat of the day.

> There is none like unto the God of Jeshurun, who rideth upon the heaven in thy help, and in his excellency on the sky. The eternal God is thy refuge, and underneath are the everlasting arms: and he shall thrust out the enemy from before thee; and shall say, Destroy them. Israel then shall dwell in safety alone: the fountain of Jacob shall be upon a land of corn and wine; also his heavens shall drop down dew. Happy art thou, O Israel: who is like unto thee, O people saved by the LORD, the shield of thy help, and who is the sword of thy excellency! And thine enemies shall be found liars unto thee; and thou shalt tread upon their high places (Deuteronomy 33:26-29).

Two Sabbaths
Did you notice the feast of tabernacles involved the observance of two sabbaths? One was to be kept on the first day and the other on the eighth day (v. 39). Eternal life in, by, and with Christ, God's great salvation, involves two great sabbaths: the sabbath-rest of faith in Christ and the sabbath-rest of eternal glory with Christ (Hebrews 4:3-11).

The Addition of Men
The Jews added another superstitious element to the feast of tabernacles of their own religious invention. They added the ceremony of drawing water out of the pool of Siloam, to which they attached magical healing powers (John 9). They claimed it represented the water that flowed from the smitten Rock. They would draw up their 'magic' water and pour it out in the temple. As they did, they sang and rejoiced, as if the angel of the Lord had come down among them.

But their addition turned 'the feast of the LORD' into nothing but 'the Jews' feast of tabernacles' (John 7:2). What a sad commentary that is on all the additions of men to the worship of God! Instead of worshipping God, they were will-worshipers. Instead of looking to Christ and trusting him of whom the feast spoke, they worshipped water drawn from a pond. Instead of finding satisfaction for their souls in keeping the feast, they went away as dry and thirsty as they came. That makes the words of our Lord in John 7 all the more striking.

> In the last day, that great day of the feast, Jesus stood and cried, saying, If any man thirst, let him come unto me, and drink. He that believeth on me, as the scripture hath said, out of his belly shall flow rivers of living water (John 7:37, 38).

The Sacrifices of the Feast

In Numbers 29:12-40 the sacrifices of this feast are described. There were many, many sacrifices made throughout the week of the feast. But each day the number of sacrifices diminished. The sacrifices, of course, all pointed to Christ, the Lamb of God, who is our sin-atoning sacrifice. That the sacrifices diminished every day is more than interesting. They were, like the whole of divine revelation in Holy Scripture, focusing more and more clearly upon the fact that there is but one sacrifice for sin. That sacrifice is Christ. Truly Christ is All, and all we need!

The Solemn Closure

In verse 36 the closing of the feast of tabernacles is called 'a solemn assembly'. The marginal reading is 'solemn restraint'. An even better rendering might be 'a solemn shutting up', or 'a solemn closure'. The feast of tabernacles portrayed God's solemn closure of all things. When Christ comes again, raises the dead, makes all things new, brings us into that state of glory wherein the tabernacle of God is forever with men, that will be God's solemn closure (Psalm 96:9-13; Isaiah 25:6-9; 35:1, 2). Then, we will say what Peter did on the Mount of Transfiguration, 'Master, it is good for us to be here'.

The Servant of God

Here is a picture of God's servant. 'And Moses declared unto the children of Israel the feasts of the LORD' (v. 44). The Lord God testifies of his servant Moses that he was faithful. He faithfully declared all God told him to declare. He faithfully obeyed the revealed will of God. May God give each of us grace to do the same, following his example, following the Lord fully, for Christ's sake.

Chapter 59

The Golden Candlestick

And the LORD spake unto Moses, saying, Command the children of Israel, that they bring unto thee pure oil olive beaten for the light, to cause the lamps to burn continually. Without the vail of the testimony, in the tabernacle of the congregation, shall Aaron order it from the evening unto the morning before the LORD continually: it shall be a statute for ever in your generations. He shall order the lamps upon the pure candlestick before the LORD continually.

Leviticus 24:1-4

It was the intention of our God that the tabernacle, the priesthood, the sacrifices, the ceremonies, the sabbaths, holy days, and the events of the Old Testament be types and pictures of heavenly things. When I say all these carnal things were pictures of spiritual things, and specifically, that they were types of Christ and the gospel of God's free grace in him, I am not just pulling these things out of the air. Hebrews 9:1-12 speaks particularly of the tabernacle in the wilderness, its furnishings, and the sacrifices offered upon God's altar at the tabernacle, telling us these things were given as things typical of and portraying our Lord Jesus Christ and God's salvation of his elect by him. In Hebrews 9:23 we are told these carnal things were 'patterns of things in the heavens'. In Hebrews 10:1 we read explicitly, they were 'a shadow of good things to come'.

The Tabernacle

If you were to approach the Tabernacle the very first thing that strikes your eye is the brazen altar, the place of sacrifice. Between that brazen altar and the door of the tabernacle stands the laver of brass, the place of cleansing.

If you pull back the curtain you would enter the outer court of the tabernacle, 'which is called the sanctuary'. In the sanctuary, the holy place, there were three pieces of furniture. On your right is the golden table of shewbread with twelve loaves of bread and incense on it. In the back, just before you get to the veil separating the sanctuary from the 'Holiest of all', is the golden altar of incense. On the left side is the golden candlestick, a candelabra with seven candles burning constantly.

Then, if you could go with Aaron behind the veil on the day of atonement into the inner sanctuary, 'which is called the Holiest of all', you would see just one piece of furniture, the centre of Israel's worship, the ark of the covenant, overlaid with pure gold. Inside the ark of the covenant is a golden pot of manna, Aaron's rod that budded, and the tablets of God's broken law. Over the ark, completely covering it, is the mercy seat, the place of atonement, symbolising the very throne of God, the throne of grace. At each end of the mercy seat are cherubs facing one another, looking constantly upon the mercy seat. This is where God declared he would meet with and commune with men (Exodus 25:22). This is what Isaiah saw in his vision of the enthroned Christ (Isaiah 6:1-8). This is what Ezekiel saw in his vision of the wheels of providence (Ezekiel 1-10). This is what Daniel saw in his vision of our Saviour (Daniel 7:9-14). And this is what John saw when he saw heaven opened (Revelation 4:1-5:14).

If you wish to read about these articles of furniture in greater detail, you can find a full description of each piece in Exodus 37 and 38.[17] Leviticus 24:1-4 describes just one of the three pieces of furniture in the outer court of the sanctuary, the golden candlestick.

We do not have to guess what this candlestick represents. The Holy Spirit specifically tells us that this candlestick represents the church of God in this world (Revelation 1:20). More particularly, it represents the Lord Jesus Christ, the Light of the world, in glory and his mystical body, the church, which is the light of the world on earth.

---

[17] See also my book *Discovering Christ in Exodus* from Go Publications.

The Oil

The first thing mentioned is the oil God required for the candlestick.

> And the LORD spake unto Moses, saying, Command the children of Israel, that they bring unto thee pure oil olive beaten for the light, to cause the lamps to burn continually (Leviticus 24:1, 2).

God required the children of Israel to bring the oil from the olives of their own olive trees to the priests to be burned in the candlestick. It must be 'pure', the very best, undiluted, and clear. It must be oil 'beaten' from the olive and prepared with the greatest of care. There are at least four very important lessons here.

1. The oil represents God the Holy Spirit and the grace he gives.

2. True worship always involves personal cost. It always involves time, effort and money. There is no such thing as worship without sacrifice (2 Samuel 24:24).

3. In all things, we are to bring our best to our God.

4. Our great and gracious God would have us worship him in the full assurance of acceptance with him by Christ.

By requiring the children of Israel to bring the oil used by the priests to be burned in the candlestick, the Lord gave them assurance of acceptance. In accepting their oil, he said, 'I have accepted you'. By this seemingly insignificant gesture, he was saying to his people, 'This candlestick and the light it gives burns for you. Though you are not in the holy place personally, you are there representatively in your priest; and all that goes on in that holy place, all the transactions of the sanctuary are for you. You have an interest in them.' That is precisely what God the Holy Spirit tells us in Hebrews 10:16-22 that these things meant.

The Lamps in the Candlestick

The 'pure candlestick', of verse 4, was made of pure gold (Exodus 37:17). It had seven lamps at the ends of seven branches, upheld by one shaft. As such, it was typical of God's church in this world, upheld by Christ, the shaft of gold, and being constantly supplied with light, life, and grace by God the Holy Spirit.

Put this together with John's vision in Revelation 1, and we learn that Christ upholds and sustains his church in all its branches. As we have seen, the number seven suggests the fulness and completion of the church. Every true gospel church is represented in the seven branches of the candlestick. God the Holy Spirit indwells his church, each individual believer and each local assembly, which is 'an habitation of God through the Spirit'. Christ not only dwells in his church by the Spirit and upholds it, he walks in the midst of the seven golden candlesticks, protecting both his church and the angels of the churches.

I was in the Spirit on the Lord's day, and heard behind me a great voice, as of a trumpet, Saying, I am Alpha and Omega, the first and the last: and, what thou seest, write in a book, and send it unto the seven churches which are in Asia; unto Ephesus, and unto Smyrna, and unto Pergamos, and unto Thyatira, and unto Sardis, and unto Philadelphia, and unto Laodicea. And I turned to see the voice that spake with me. And being turned, I saw seven golden candlesticks; And in the midst of the seven candlesticks one like unto the Son of man, clothed with a garment down to the foot, and girt about the paps with a golden girdle. His head and his hairs were white like wool, as white as snow; and his eyes were as a flame of fire; And his feet like unto fine brass, as if they burned in a furnace; and his voice as the sound of many waters. And he had in his right hand seven stars: and out of his mouth went a sharp twoedged sword: and his countenance was as the sun shineth in his strength. And when I saw him, I fell at his feet as dead. And he laid his right hand upon me, saying unto me, Fear not; I am the first and the last: I am he that liveth, and was dead; and, behold, I am alive for evermore, Amen; and have the keys of hell and of death. Write the things which thou hast seen, and the things which are, and the things which shall be hereafter; The mystery of the seven stars which thou sawest in my right hand, and the seven golden candlesticks. The seven stars are the angels of the seven churches: and the seven candlesticks which thou sawest are the seven churches (Revelation 1:10-20).

The lamps in the candlestick were to be kept burning continually (v. 4). That does not mean they were never allowed to go out, they were.

The priests did not keep them burning when they were moving from place to place in the wilderness, but only when they were encamped in a specific place for a time.

The lamps were trimmed, filled with oil, and lit every morning. They burned until nightfall. In the evening they were trimmed, filled with oil, and lit again, and burned until the next morning. You may recall that the Lord first called Samuel after he and Eli had laid down in their beds, 'and ere the lamp of God went out in the temple' (1 Samuel 3:3).

The lamps were kept burning continually to tell us that the grace of God and the supply of it to our souls is constant, both in the day when the sun shines brightly, and in the night when our vision is dim. Our experience does not, in any way, affect or alter God's goodness. 'He abideth faithful' (2 Timothy 2:13).

The lamps were permitted to go out to teach us our need of the light and grace of God's Spirit, and to keep us ever mindful of the fact that all light and grace bestowed upon us comes through the sanctuary work, the intercession, of our great Priest, the Lord Jesus Christ. Our great Aaron orders the light and the candlestick from evening until morning.

> Without the vail of the testimony, in the tabernacle of the congregation, shall Aaron order it from the evening unto the morning before the LORD continually: it shall be a statute forever in your generations. He shall order the lamps upon the pure candlestick before the LORD continually (Leviticus 24:3, 4).

We have God's ordained means of grace, the preaching of the gospel. But only Christ, our great High Priest, can make the means subservient to the purpose intended. Ordinances of divine worship are precious things, but if the Lord of ordinances is not in them the lamp of grace will not burn. The lamps were kept burning all through the day to teach that something more than the light of nature is needed to lead us out of this wilderness to the throne of God. Blessed Spirit of God keep alive your own work in our hearts, so that in times of languishing your holy oil of grace is sweetly conveyed to our souls (Zechariah 4:2-6).

The candlestick was kept burning throughout the night, until the dawning of the new day, to teach us that the church of God in this world of darkness gives light and shall continue to give light, be it ever so dim or bright, until the Daystar, Christ Jesus, comes. The candlestick shall continue to burn in this dark world until all God's elect are born of God with Christ the Daystar shining in their hearts (2 Peter 1:19; 2 Corinthians 4:4-6). God's church will continue shining forth the Light of God until Christ comes again (Revelation 2:28; 22:16).

Take a careful look at this pure candlestick as it is presented here in Leviticus 24. This candlestick stands not in the most holy place, which refers to heaven itself, but in the sanctuary, which refers to heavenly things enjoyed on earth. Our Lord Jesus Christ, our High Priest after the order of Melchizedek, uses this candlestick to speak of himself and his churches in this world (Revelation 1:20). So it is clearly his intention that we should see it in this sense. The seven lamps of fire burning before the throne of God are the sevenfold Spirit of our God.

> After this I looked, and, behold, a door was opened in heaven: and the first voice which I heard was as it were of a trumpet talking with me; which said, Come up hither, and I will show thee things which must be hereafter. And immediately I was in the spirit; and, behold, a throne was set in heaven, and one sat on the throne. And he that sat was to look upon like a jasper and a sardine stone: and there was a rainbow round about the throne, in sight like unto an emerald. And round about the throne were four and twenty seats: and upon the seats I saw four and twenty elders sitting, clothed in white raiment; and they had on their heads crowns of gold. And out of the throne proceeded lightnings and thunderings and voices: and there were seven lamps of fire burning before the throne, which are the seven Spirits of God (Revelation 4:1-5).

The shaft, as seen before, speaks of Christ. The seven lamps, we saw in Revelation 1:20, represent the church. But here, in Revelation 4, we are told they represent the seven Spirits, or sevenfold Spirit, of our God. There is no contradiction here, but a delightful, instructive picture.

Christ is the Candlestick. He upholds the lamps, his church and each member of it. Without him, we would all fall and come to utter ruin in a heartbeat (John 10:28-30; Jude 1:24, 25). The light we have, the oil of grace we enjoy, is ours because we are in him and one with him.

Here is a great wonder. The Lord Jesus gives light, life, and grace in this world by his Spirit; but he does so through the instrumentality of his church, using such things as we are, to carry the light of his grace and glory into the four corners of this dark world. The olive oil feeding the flame is God the Holy Spirit. He is the unction, the anointing, in and upon us, giving us light and knowledge and understanding (1 John 2:20-27). He is given to us by Christ, by the merit, mediation, and power of our Saviour (Revelation 3:1). As all the light shining from the lamp comes from the oil, so all grace is the gift and operation of God the Holy Ghost. Christ pours out his Spirit upon us by the merit of his sacrifice (Galatians 3:13, 14) continually, as the priest poured oil into the lamp in the tabernacle. He gives us his oil in the day and in the night.

The care of the lamps, the churches, is all his. He upholds them. He feeds them with oil, the grace of his Spirit. He lights them and keeps them burning. He trims them. He carries away the ashes.

The priest setting the lamps in order daily portrays our great Saviour's unceasing work of grace causing his people to receive and give forth light. You and I are the representatives of Christ, who shined as light in the midst of darkness (Philippians 2:15; Matthew 5:16). Let us faithfully shine forth his light by the preaching of the gospel, that men everywhere might trust the Son of God and glorify our Father which is in heaven.

The candlestick shined only upon the golden table of shewbread and the golden altar. It shined to give light only upon those two things. The bread on the table speaks of Christ, the Bread of Life, who gave his life for us. The golden altar of incense speaks of Christ, exalted and accepted, and of full salvation in him. God give us grace to hold before men the light of the gospel and the adorable name of Christ. We must never cover the light with religious ceremony, carnal reason, historic traditions, customs, and denominational creeds, confessions, and rules.

Let it be ours ever to hold forth that word of life, not to set up new lights or to defend old ones, but by faithfully proclaiming the gospel of God's boundless free grace in Christ. Let the light of our lamp be the light of the pure candlestick; pure, free, sovereign grace.

There is a blessed unity about this candlestick and its lamps. The candlestick is one (Ephesians 4:1-7). The light of each lamp is exactly the same. The oil was pure, without mixture. The light of God, the gospel, is all grace. There is no sputter of works or free will in it.

God's Interpretation

Zechariah 4 gives us God the Holy Spirit's own interpretation of this typical picture in Zechariah's vision. The third chapter of Zechariah gives us a picture of a sinner saved by the grace of God. Such men are men who shall never cease to be 'men wondered at', wondered at because of the wonderful work of God for us, in us, and by us.

If we would see the light of the gospel, the light of this candlestick, we must be awakened by the Spirit of God.

> And the angel that talked with me came again, and waked me, as a man that is wakened out of his sleep, And said unto me, What seest thou? And I said, I have looked, and behold a candlestick all of gold, with a bowl upon the top of it, and his seven lamps thereon, and seven pipes to the seven lamps, which are upon the top thereof (Zechariah 4:1, 2).

The Lord God tells us plainly that the meaning of the candlestick's light is salvation by grace alone in Christ alone.

> So I answered and spake to the angel that talked with me, saying, What are these, my lord? Then the angel that talked with me answered and said unto me, Knowest thou not what these be? And I said, No, my lord. Then he answered and spake unto me, saying, This is the word of the LORD unto Zerubbabel, saying, Not by might, nor by power, but by my spirit, saith the LORD of hosts. Who art thou, O great mountain? Before Zerubbabel thou shalt become a plain: and he shall bring forth the headstone thereof with shoutings, crying, Grace, grace unto it. Moreover the word of the LORD came unto me, saying, The hands of Zerubbabel have laid the foundation of this house; his hands shall also finish it; and thou shalt know that the LORD of hosts hath sent me unto you (Zechariah 4:4-9).

It is my prayer that God will bring you to the Light and cause you to behold his righteousness in Christ. All who are born of God love the Light of God, 'Jesus Christ and him crucified'. Believing on the Lord Jesus Christ, we do the truth and come to the Light (John 3:19-21).

Chapter 60

The Table Of Shewbread

And thou shalt take fine flour, and bake twelve cakes thereof: two tenth deals shall be in one cake. And thou shalt set them in two rows, six on a row, upon the pure table before the LORD. And thou shalt put pure frankincense upon each row, that it may be on the bread for a memorial, even an offering made by fire unto the LORD. Every sabbath he shall set it in order before the LORD continually, being taken from the children of Israel by an everlasting covenant. And it shall be Aaron's and his sons'; and they shall eat it in the holy place: for it is most holy unto him of the offerings of the LORD made by fire by a perpetual statute.

Leviticus 24:5-9

You will remember there were three pieces of furniture in the first section of the tabernacle, the outer sanctuary. As the priest walked into that holy place, before the veil that separated the holy place from the holy of holies containing the ark of the covenant, he would see those three pieces of furniture. Standing in the back, right in front of the veil, he would see the golden altar of incense. On his left, he would see the golden candlestick. On his right, he would see the table of shewbread, with its twelve loaves of bread in two rows, with golden dishes, golden bowls, and golden spoons, and frankincense upon each row of bread.

This third piece of furniture, the table of shewbread, is described in detail in Exodus 37:10-16. There the Holy Spirit has recorded the physical description of the table. In Leviticus 24:5-9 we have the instructions Aaron was given concerning the table and its bread. This golden table of shewbread and the bread upon it give us much typical instruction concerning our Lord Jesus Christ and his bounteous provisions of grace for his people.

The Table
First, I want you to see that the golden table of shewbread is itself typical of our great Saviour. The name given to this table, 'the table of shewbread' (Numbers 4:7), can be translated, 'the table of the bread of presence'. It speaks of Christ ever present with God and ever present with us. The materials of the table clearly speak of our Redeemer. It was made of shittim wood, overlaid with pure gold. The very same materials used to make the ark of the covenant.

The shittim wood, a wood like our cedar that did not decay or rot, portrays our Saviour's humanity, which never saw corruption. In order to redeem and save us, the Son of God took on himself our nature. He became one of us. Yes, Jesus Christ, our God, is a real man. He has taken our nature into union with himself, indivisibly and permanently. He who would redeem man must himself be a man. But this man was born of a virgin, and had no sin. He had no sin, did not sin, and knew no sin. Yet, he was made sin for us, that we might be made the righteousness of God in him (2 Corinthians 5:21).

Sin is what has corrupted God's universe, corrupts our race, and shall at last corrupt our bodies in the grave, but not Christ's! Though he was made sin for us, when he had put away our sins by the sacrifice of himself, he arose from the grave before his body could see corruption. Now, yonder in heaven, seated upon the throne of God is God in our nature, the God-man, the Lord Jesus Christ. It is written, 'He that hath suffered in the flesh hath ceased from sin'.

The shittim wood overlaid with pure gold speaks of our Saviour's perfect and eternal divinity. That man who is our Saviour is God, perfectly and fully God, shining forth from eternity, and for evermore, in the golden brilliance of his divinity. Though he were a perfect man, though he had died as our Substitute, his sacrifice could never have availed for our eternal salvation, except he be himself God incarnate.

The table, wearing a crown of pure gold, speaks of Christ's exaltation and glory as our great King. God the Father has made him both Lord and Christ. He has placed upon the head of the God-man, our Mediator, the crown of universal monarchy. He has given him power and dominion over all flesh, that he might give eternal life to all his redeemed ones. Yes, the God-man, our Saviour, holds the reins of the universe in his hands. He rules the entire universe, absolutely, for the salvation and everlasting good of his people to the glory of God.

The Table's Place
Second, the table of shewbread, the bread of presence, stood in the holy place in the tabernacle, before the presence of the Lord. The bread was symbolically set before God himself. It stood there before the Lord God continually, as bread fit for God, offered to God, honoured by God, and accepted by God. It stood there symbolically as the Bread of God.

The shewbread was typical of our Saviour. 'For the bread of God is he which cometh down from heaven, and giveth life unto the world' (John 6:33). The Lord Jesus Christ, the Bread of Life for our souls, is the very Bread of God. He is the Food of heaven. That is to say, our all-glorious Christ, in his person and work, is he upon whom God feasts, delights, and finds satisfaction.

The Loaves
Third, we are told that twelve cakes or loaves of bread were to be set upon the golden table.

> And thou shalt take fine flour, and bake twelve cakes thereof: two tenth deals shall be in one cake. And thou shalt set them in two rows, six on a row, upon the pure table before the LORD (Leviticus 24:5, 6).

Twelve is the number of God's Israel, the number of his elect, the 144,000 John saw with the Lamb of God in heaven (Revelation 7:4; 14:1-3). These twelve loaves of bread typify our Lord Jesus Christ, the Bread of Life, as we have seen. But the fact that the bread is here specifically required to be in twelve loaves makes it clear that the loaves represent Christ in connection with his people, represented in the twelve tribes of Israel, the twelve names inscribed upon Aaron's breastplate, the twelve stones of the altar erected by Joshua when Israel crossed over Jordan, the twelve stones of Elijah's altar on Mount Carmel before the prophets of Baal, the twelve apostles, the twelve foundations of the New Jerusalem, and the twelve gates of the city.

The twelve loaves in the holy place, upon the table before God, tells us that Christ Jesus, the High Priest of God, has an abundant supply for all whose names are inscribed upon his breastplate. Therefore, none shall perish. In our Father's house there is 'bread enough and to spare' (Luke 15:17). The supply is abundant, super-abundant.

Notice each loaf had 'two tenth deals' of fine flour, two omers. That was double any man's daily provision of manna in the wilderness. In other words, in each loaf of bread, sitting on the table in the holy place, there was symbolically twice as much bread for every person in Israel as he needed. 'Where sin abounded, grace did much more abound.' Our Saviour's supply is infinite, boundless. And it is ours. All grace is ours (Ephesians 1:3). All glory is ours (John 17:22). All things are ours, because Christ is ours (1 Corinthians 3:21).

Bread for Sinners
In Christ, there is bread enough for every poor sinner who is made hungry by his grace. If you hunger and thirst after righteousness, hunger and thirst to be righteous before God, Christ is Bread for your soul, all the bread you need. There is such an infinite sufficiency and abundance of life, mercy, love, and grace in Christ that, though untold multitudes live by eating this Bread, the Bread is undiminished. There is still just as much as in the beginning. There is plenty of Bread on God's table, plenty of Bread for our needy souls in Christ, and we are welcome to it.

Yet, we are told that none were allowed to touch the bread except priests. The Bread of Life is for sinners who need a Priest. The Priest alone must manage the table and keep bread on it all the time. The Bread of God is in the holy place, where sinners may get it as they come to God by faith in Christ, the only Mediator between God and men.

Priests' Bread
There is much typical instruction in the fact that only God's priests were allowed to eat the shewbread, and that they were to eat it only in the holy place. The shewbread was God's provision for his servants, the Levites and even so those who preach the gospel are to live by the

gospel (1 Corinthians 9:14). That which is represented in the table and its bread is the salvation of God's elect by the will of God. That is our dear Saviour's bread, the satisfaction of his soul.

Still, the shewbread is for us. It speaks of Christ, our Bread. None but God's priests could eat this bread. If I come to the Bread of Life, and eat him, I am, I must be one of those made to be in him 'a chosen generation and a royal priesthood' before God. We often say, 'the proof is in the pudding'. In this case, the proof is in eating the Bread of God.

Whoso eateth my flesh, and drinketh my blood, hath eternal life; and I will raise him up at the last day. For my flesh is meat indeed, and my blood is drink indeed. He that eateth my flesh, and drinketh my blood, dwelleth in me, and I in him. As the living Father hath sent me, and I live by the Father: so he that eateth me, even he shall live by me. This is that bread which came down from heaven: not as your fathers did eat manna, and are dead: he that eateth of this bread shall live for ever (John 6:54-58).

Two Rows

Then we are told that the bread was to be set on the table in two rows (v. 6). There is a priest, Aaron or one of his sons, standing before this table with twelve loaves of bread before him. There is Christ, standing in the holy place, ever busy, never idle, his hands constantly and bountifully providing Bread for his people. He gives us our daily bread; the bread of grace, providence, consolation, of his presence and care.

Taken from Israel

The bread was to be taken from the children of Israel (v. 8), because the Lord God would have all his people know that it was for them. So, too, the Lord Jesus Christ, the Bread of Life, is Bread taken from among men, that we might know that all he is, he is for us, and all he does, he does he does on our behalf.

Then thou spakest in vision to thy holy one, and saidst, I have laid help upon one that is mighty; I have exalted one chosen out of the people (Psalm 89:19).

For every high priest taken from among men is ordained for men in things pertaining to God, that he may offer both gifts and sacrifices for sins: Who can have compassion on the ignorant, and on them that are out of the way; for that he himself also is compassed with infirmity (Hebrews 5:1, 2).

The Frankincense

Fourth, God required that each row of bread have some frankincense upon it for a memorial of burnt offering to the Lord.

And thou shalt put pure frankincense upon each row, that it may be on the bread for a memorial, even an offering made by fire unto the LORD (Leviticus 24:7).

The bread was to be eaten; but the frankincense was to be burned. The frankincense speaks of our acceptance with God and the acceptance of our worship, praise, and sacrifices. The acceptance of our very prayers by Christ. All God's spiritual Israel, typified by the twelve loaves, are made through Christ a sweet savour to him. Our prayers and sacrifices, worship and service come up before God for a memorial of a sweet, acceptable savour to him (Acts 10:4; 1 Peter 2:5).

Renewed Weekly

Fifth, the Lord required Aaron to set fresh bread on the golden table every sabbath (v. 8). There is more here than this, I am sure, but this is distinctly a word of instruction to God's servants. The bread was to be prepared before it was brought to the tabernacle. Yet, it was to be freshly prepared. Then, every Saturday the priest was required to set fresh bread on the table in the house of God.

Gospel preachers must come to the house of God with fresh Bread, and set that upon the table before the Lord, feeding his children with the Bread of God. God's servants dare not bring stale bread to his people, and dare not bring any other food to feed them. Displays of eloquence, great learning, philosophical or theological speculation, denominational dogma, religious ceremony, history, moralism, and civic duty are all a breach of this perpetual statute. The only bread with God's servants are to feed his children is Christ the Bread of Life.

The Sabbath

Sixth, as the bread was brought out before the people and placed in the holy place on the golden table on the sabbath day, so our Lord Jesus, the Bread of God, shall be brought out on the morning of that great eternal sabbath awaiting us and set gloriously before his people forever.

Blessed Fellowship

Seventh, the two rows of bread, six loaves to a row, set upon that golden table, suggests the blessed fellowship, unity, and oneness of God's church. God's Israel in this gospel age is just one tribe. All who are born of God are one with Christ and one in Christ.

> The cup of blessing which we bless, is it not the communion of the blood of Christ? The bread which we break, is it not the communion of the body of Christ? For we being many are one bread, and one body: for we are all partakers of that one bread (1 Corinthians 10:16, 17).

Those loaves sat on the table one beside the other, each closely connected with the other. We read in Colossians 3 the words 'one another' again and again. 'Lie not one to another; forbearing one another, and forgiving one another;' 'in all wisdom teaching and admonishing one another'. That is the way believers are to live. We live not for ourselves, but to love and serve one another (Ephesians 4:1-5:2).

God's Israel, his church, is ever one before him. These twelve loaves, covered with pure frankincense, arranged in divine order on the table of pure gold, standing in the holy place before the Lord, in the light of the golden candlestick, display the unity of God's Israel. Even after the revolt of the ten tribes there were twelve loaves on the table (2 Chronicles 13:11), because, 'the purpose of God according to election' stands unaltered (Romans 9:11; 2 Timothy 2:19). The Church of God is one body, the body of Christ, already seated with him in glory. Not one member shall be severed from that body. All Israel shall be saved.

This is the everlasting memorial of God's honour and glory. These twelve loaves in the tabernacle declare to the glory of God our Saviour, whose name is called Jesus, 'He shall save his people from their sins'.

Chapter 61

The Death Of A Blasphemer

And the son of an Israelitish woman, whose father was an Egyptian, went out among the children of Israel: and this son of the Israelitish woman and a man of Israel strove together in the camp; And the Israelitish woman's son blasphemed the name of the LORD, and cursed. And they brought him unto Moses: (and his mother's name was Shelomith, the daughter of Dibri, of the tribe of Dan:) And they put him in ward, that the mind of the LORD might be shewed them. And the LORD spake unto Moses, saying, Bring forth him that hath cursed without the camp; and let all that heard him lay their hands upon his head, and let all the congregation stone him. And thou shalt speak unto the children of Israel, saying, Whosoever curseth his God shall bear his sin. And he that blasphemeth the name of the LORD, he shall surely be put to death, and all the congregation shall certainly stone him: as well the stranger, as he that is born in the land, when he blasphemeth the name of the LORD, shall be put to death. And he that killeth any man shall surely be put to death. And he that killeth a beast shall make it good; beast for beast. And if a man cause a blemish in his neighbour; as he hath done, so shall it be done to him; Breach for breach, eye for eye, tooth for tooth: as he hath caused a blemish in a man, so shall it be done to him again. And he that killeth a beast, he shall restore it: and he that killeth a man, he shall be put to death. Ye shall have one manner of law, as well for the stranger, as for one of your own country: for I am the LORD your God. And Moses spake to the children of Israel, that they should bring forth him that had cursed out of the camp, and stone him with stones. And the children of Israel did as the LORD commanded Moses.

Leviticus 24:10-23

You are either a worshipper of the Lord Jesus Christ, or you are a blasphemer. There is no in between ground. I am either a worshipper of Christ, or I am a blasphemer. There is no in between ground. Blasphemy is the cursing of God, and cursing God brings death, eternal death, under the wrath of God.

Three Events
We have previously noted there are only three historical events mentioned in the book of Leviticus. Each of these is very significant and directly connected with God's instructions concerning his worship.

1. The first historical event recorded in this book is the consecration of Aaron and his sons as the priests of Israel (Leviticus 8, 9).

The Aaronic priesthood represented the priesthood of our Lord Jesus Christ. Aaron, as the high priest of Israel, foreshadowed the Lord Jesus, our great High Priest before God. He was divinely chosen, equipped, anointed, and approved. Only Aaron could make atonement in the holy of holies, because he represented Christ who alone could and would put away sin by the sacrifice of himself (Hebrews 7:23-28).

Aaron's sons represented the church and kingdom of God, as that 'holy priesthood' of believers who serve God in the holy place day and night. Everything about these priests typifies and represents believing sinners in this world. These men were specifically chosen by God. They were God's priests because they were Aaron's sons. They wore the garments of the priesthood, representing the garments of salvation that are ours in Christ. They were accepted as priests because of a slain sacrifice, just as we are accepted because of Christ's sacrifice. They were anointed with holy anointing oil and washed with pure water, portraying God the Holy Ghost and our new birth by him. They were men who deliberately and voluntarily consecrated themselves to God. These priests lived continuously upon the sacrifice of God's altar, serving God and his people continually (1 Peter 2:5-9).

2. The second historic event recorded in Leviticus is the death of Nadab and Abihu by the hand of God, for offering 'strange fire before the Lord' (Leviticus 10).

Let all who worship God understand the powerful lesson set before us. If we would worship God and find acceptance with him, we must come to him with that which he has provided, Christ alone, and no mixture of anything with Christ (Leviticus 10:1-3; Galatians 5:1-4).

3. The third historic event recorded in the book of Leviticus is the stoning of the son of the Shelomith for blasphemy (Leviticus 24:10-23). Those who blaspheme the name of God curse him and deny he is God alone. Though this unnamed wretch had a Hebrew mother, his father was an Egyptian; and he preferred both the gods and the people of Egypt to the God of Glory and his people.

Moses has been, by divine inspiration, giving us instructions about the worship of God. He spoke of the golden candlestick, typifying our Lord Jesus Christ, who is the Light of the world, the only light that truly reveals us as we are and the only light by which we see the way to God.

Then he spoke about the golden table of shewbread, and Christ the Bread of life. Only as we eat the Bread from heaven, and live by Christ's blood and righteousness, do we have everlasting life.

On that table, there were twelve loaves of bread. In Christ there is bread for all God's Israel. There is in him an infinite fulness and sufficiency of bread. In our Father's house there is bread enough and to spare. Here is bread for all who are hungry. The bread was ordered and maintained by God's priests. It is Christ, our great High Priest, who provides all we need and constantly feeds our souls.

On those loaves of bread the Lord required that the priests place pure frankincense. The bread speaks of Christ but it also speaks of us, his people (1 Corinthians 10:16, 17). We are truly one in him and one with him. The frankincense speaks of our acceptance with God by the merit and efficacy of Christ's mediation. Our God accepts us as he accepts our Substitute, and because he accepts our Substitute.

The oil in the lamps and the bread on the table were to be taken from the children of Israel. Among other things, this symbolized our consecration to God. Bread, being the very staff of life, portrayed that faith in Christ involves us giving up our lives to our Redeemer as our Lord and King (Luke 14:25-33). All that was done in the tabernacle, all access to God, was by his appointed priests. The whole tabernacle service was a constant display of man's separation from God by reason of sin and God's holiness. It displayed God's absolute right of sovereignty, dominion and authority as God. God alone has the right to prescribe law. The tabernacle displayed salvation by God's free, sovereign grace through the merits of Christ, the Substitute God has accepted. The light, the bread, the frankincense were in the priest's hands alone. Our need of grace is supplied by our Substitute alone.

Instructive Interruption

In verses 10-23 Moses seems to tell us something that has nothing to do with the context. He has been giving us instructions about the worship of God, using pictures of Christ, redemption, grace, and salvation. When we get to chapter 25, he returns to the same message. But right in the middle of these wonderful pictures of Christ, we have this story of one man's blasphemy and his punishment (Leviticus 24:10-23).

Here the Spirit of God tells us of a nameless mongrel Israelite; part Jew, part Egyptian, who openly blasphemed the Lord God in the camp of Israel and was put to death because of it. Why this interruption? Why is this recorded here by inspiration of God the Holy Spirit? Surely, the death of this blasphemer by order of God must have something to do with Moses' message of Christ, the gospel of God, the worship of God, redemption, grace, and salvation by Christ Jesus.

The Offender

The man described in this story is not named. We do not know who he was. His father's name is not revealed either, only his mother's. Her name was Shelomith, of the tribe of Dan. He is an unnamed blasphemer, an Egyptian who claimed a place among the children of Israel. When the sons of God marry the daughters of men, nothing good can be expected as a result of their union. Here is an Israelite, one of God's covenant children, who married an Egyptian idolater. What could be expected from such a union, except a blaspheming child?

Disobedience is always costly. Disobedience of parents is often manifested in the ruin of children. Being depraved by nature, children are always more apt to follow the influences of evil than of good, to follow the way of an Egyptian father in blasphemy than the way of an Israelite mother in the faith, worship, and praise of God. Yet, this man was a man, not a child. He alone stood responsible for his actions.

The Strife

The son of Shelomith got into a heated argument with one of God's children. The fight may have been violent, we are not told. But it was, to say the least, heated. The camp of Israel was a mixed multitude. The mixed multitude was a mixture of Egyptians with Israelites. Egyptians who came out of Egypt with Israel (Exodus 12:38). This mixed multitude was often a source of strife and division in the camp of Israel.

So it is today. The church of God on this earth is always a mix of believers and unbelievers who profess to be believers, wheat and tares, sheep and goats, Egyptians who claim to be a part of Israel. Mongrels always cause trouble. Mongrels are always demanding. Mongrels never promote peace. They always have a bone to pick.

Once a quarrel begins, who knows what evil will be done before it ends? How great a fire a little matter kindles! When passion is hot, people forget both their reason and their religion. They are never satisfied to fight with another alone. They try to get others involved in the quarrel, so they can justify themselves. We would be wise to avoid it altogether. The beginning of strife is like the letting forth of water. Once the dam breaks, you cannot get the water back (Proverbs 6:12-19; Ephesians 4:29-5:2; 2 Timothy 2:24-26).

The Blasphemy
The Spirit of God does not tell us what this strife was about that ended in a man being stoned to death by the whole camp of Israel, stoned by the direct command of God. Whatever it was about, it ended in an eruption of blasphemy. I must confess I have always read this passage, perhaps as you have, thinking this man, in the heat of anger said to the Israelite, 'God damn you'! I have read dozens of commentaries and sermons giving that interpretation. Such language is crude and offensive. But that is not what happened here.

Remember, this event is related to us. It probably occurred just after Moses gave the instructions recorded in this chapter about the worship of God. When the mongrel heard and understood Moses' doctrine, God's requirements and the things signified by these ordinances of divine worship, this Egyptian free-willer, this idolater who claimed to have embraced the gospel and the Israelite who loved free grace, got to it. When the debate was over, the Egyptian cried, 'Jehovah be damned!' That was his blasphemy, the blasphemy of all wilful unbelief. He did not say, Ra be damned, Horus be damned, but Jehovah be damned.

He was enraged that the God of Glory demands to be worshipped as God alone. He was enraged that Moses declared salvation by grace alone, through faith alone, in Christ alone. What enraged this Egyptian Israelite was the gospel doctrine set forth by Moses in every piece of furniture, sacrifice, ceremony, priestly task, and every sabbath day connected with the tabernacle.

Everywhere he looked, in everything connected with tabernacle worship, the son of the Egyptian saw displays of God's total sovereignty and his utter depravity. He saw demonstrations of God's sovereign election of his people, special atonement accomplished for them alone, free justification, perfect, full, complete salvation in, by, and with Christ alone, righteousness, holiness, sanctification, acceptance with God by the doing and dying of the Son of God. The offense of the cross enraged him; and his rage moved him to blasphemy.

The name God gives to Babylon, the name God gives to all Arminian, free-will, works religion is 'Blasphemy' (Revelation 17:1-3). That is what will-worship is. It is what unbelief is. Blasphemy!

The Name
This man 'blasphemed the name of the LORD' (v. 11). What was this mongrel's blasphemy? Remember, God's name is what he is. It is his character, the revelation of his being. The name of the Lord is Christ. The word 'blasphemed' means 'pierced, bored through, punctured, violently perforated, struck through, cursed'.

> And Moses said unto God, Behold, when I come unto the children of Israel, and shall say unto them, The God of your fathers hath sent me unto you; and they shall say to me, What is his name? What shall I say unto them? And God said unto Moses, I AM THAT I AM: and he said, Thus shalt thou say unto the children of Israel, I AM hath sent me unto you (Exodus 3:13, 14).

Our Lord Jesus Christ is the 'I AM'. Though the priests in Israel in Jesus' day had a favoured place in the temple of God (vv. 1-9), they showed utter contempt for the Lord of the temple when he came among them, blaspheming him just as the son of Shelomith did (Luke 22:63-65). Christ is the revelation of God, the embodiment of God, the name of God. To despise him and his work is to blaspheme God (Acts 4:12; Philippians 2:5-11; Hebrews 1:1-4; Psalm 111:1-9).

I try to never miss an open display of divine providence. This is a wonderful display of it. The fact that this thing took place just as Moses was giving the children of Israel God's law regarding his worship is not insignificant. It shows God's providence working together with his revelation of himself.

The Sentence

The Lord God himself gave the sentence of the law for this blasphemy, the sentence of divine justice that must be executed upon all who refuse to trust his dear Son.

> And the LORD spake unto Moses, saying, Bring forth him that hath cursed without the camp; and let all that heard him lay their hands upon his head, and let all the congregation stone him. And thou shalt speak unto the children of Israel, saying, Whosoever curseth his God shall bear his sin. And he that blasphemeth the name of the LORD, he shall surely be put to death, and all the congregation shall certainly stone him: as well the stranger, as he that is born in the land, when he blasphemeth the name of the LORD, shall be put to death (Leviticus 24:13-16).

Moses put the man in prison that he might know the mind of God in the matter. He sought God's will and the Lord revealed his will to his servant (Proverbs 3:5, 6). Moses waited on the Lord to direct him. He did not act hastily, and would not be pushed into acting hastily.

The sentence given was not the sentence of Israel, or the sentence of Moses, but the sentence of God, whose name was blasphemed. 'He that blasphemeth the name of the LORD shall surely be put to death.' He who cursed God was cursed of God.

He must be stoned outside the camp, away from the place of blessing, in the place of cursedness and uncleanness. Every Israelite who heard his blasphemy must lay his hands upon him, imputing his guilt to him. All the congregation must stone him, all must show their approval of, and agreement with, God's justice. The execution was done before all Israel, a public execution. The law applied equally to all. Thus it shall be with all who blaspheme the name of the Lord, who despise the Lord Jesus Christ and the gospel of the grace of God.

Civil Law

Before the sentence was executed, the Lord commanded Moses to set before Israel the code of civil law. This Mosaic code of civil law is the code of law recognised in all civil societies to this day, though few acknowledge it as God's law, and few adhere to the code.

And he that killeth any man shall surely be put to death. And he that killeth a beast shall make it good; beast for beast. And if a man cause a blemish in his neighbour; as he hath done, so shall it be done to him; Breach for breach, eye for eye, tooth for tooth: as he hath caused a blemish in a man, so shall it be done to him again. And he that killeth a beast, he shall restore it: and he that killeth a man, he shall be put to death. Ye shall have one manner of law, as well for the stranger, as for one of your own country: for I am the LORD your God (Leviticus 24:17-22).

The law was made for and given to man, for the good of man, to protect society. Moses, in executing the sentence of the law, did not act as a private person seeking revenge, but as a civil magistrate executing justice for the protection of society. That is the purpose of law (Romans 13:1-5).

The Substitute

I cannot leave this chapter without telling you again that he whom we have blasphemed and cursed by our unbelief, esteeming him 'stricken of God, smitten, and afflicted', the Lord Jesus Christ, died at Calvary to save blaspheming sinners like you and me. He was made a curse that we might escape the curse of God's holy law.

And Moses spake to the children of Israel, that they should bring forth him that had cursed out of the camp, and stone him with stones. And the children of Israel did as the LORD commanded Moses (Leviticus 24:23).

Behold the condemned blasphemer executed that day in Israel. His execution was done before all Israel. His execution was approved of by all. His mother, all Israel, and even his own conscience approved of God's just and righteous sentence. Where he was stoned, there he was left, outside the camp.

Behold the condemned sinner in the Day of Judgment. His execution shall be done before all Israel. His execution shall be approved of by all. His mother, all Israel, his own conscience, all men, all angels, and all devils will approve of and say, 'Amen', to God's just and righteous sentence upon the wicked in that day. And their final place shall be hell, the bottomless pit, the place of outer darkness, outside the camp where they can do no harm.

Behold the Lord Jesus Christ, the Son of God, the sinners' Substitute, who was made to be sin for us, that we might be made the righteousness of God in him. If we would escape the wrath of God, we must go forth unto him, without the camp, to the place of cursing, bearing his reproach, trusting him alone as God our Saviour (Isaiah 53:4-6; 2 Corinthians 5:21; 1 Peter 3:18; Galatians 3:13, 14).

You are either a worshipper of the Lord Jesus Christ, or you are a blasphemer. There is no middle ground. I am either a worshipper of Christ, or I am a blasphemer. There is no place in between. Which are you? To trust Christ is to worship him. Unbelief is blaspheming him, blaspheming the name of the Lord. God will forgive any sin and all sin. But if you die in your unbelief, blaspheming the name of the Lord, there shall be no forgiveness for you! May God the Holy Spirit graciously grant you faith in Christ.

Before the throne of God above
I have a strong, a perfect plea,
A great High Priest, whose name is Love
Who ever lives and pleads for me.
My name is graven on His hands,
My name is written on His heart;
I know that while in heav'n He stands
No tongue can bid me thence depart.

When Satan tempts me to despair
And tells me of the guilt within,
Upward I look, and see Him there
Who made an end of all my sin.
Because the sinless Saviour died,
My sinful soul is counted free,
For God the just is satisfied
To look on Him and pardon me.

Behold Him there! the risen Lamb!
My perfect, spotless righteousness,
The great unchangeable I AM"
The King of glory and of grace!
One with Himself, I cannot die;
My soul is purchased by His blood;
My life is hid with Christ on high,
With Christ my Saviour and my God.

Charitie Lees Bancroft

Chapter 62

The Year Of Jubilee

Thou shalt number seven sabbaths of years unto thee, seven times seven years; and the space of the seven sabbaths of years shall be unto thee forty and nine years. Then shalt thou cause the trumpet of the jubile to sound on the tenth day of the seventh month, in the day of atonement shall ye make the trumpet sound throughout all your land. And ye shall hallow the fiftieth year, and proclaim liberty throughout all the land unto all the inhabitants thereof: it shall be a jubile unto you; and ye shall return every man unto his possession, and ye shall return every man unto his family. A jubile shall that fiftieth year be unto you: ye shall not sow, neither reap that which groweth of itself in it, nor gather the grapes in it of thy vine undressed. For it is the jubile; it shall be holy unto you: ye shall eat the increase thereof out of the field. In the year of this jubile ye shall return every man unto his possession.

Leviticus 25:8-13

'The year of my redeemed is come' (Isaiah 63:4). 'There remaineth therefore a rest to the people of God' (Hebrews 4:9).

Sabbath Days
In the Old Testament everything revolved around the sabbath. At the end of creation, the Lord God rested on the seventh day, the sabbath. In the giving of the law, the Lord commanded Israel to keep the sabbath day holy. But, did you ever notice how many sabbath days the Lord

required the children of Israel to keep? He required them to keep a seventh day sabbath, a seventh week (fiftieth day) sabbath, a seventh year sabbath, and a fiftieth year sabbath.

Fiftieth Year Sabbath

This fiftieth year sabbath is discussed in great detail in Leviticus 25. It was a year-long sabbath called 'the year of jubilee'. I have little hope of expounding this text or this subject satisfactorily. I will simply draw your attention to seven things involved in this year of jubilee and show you how this sabbatical year, which the Lord God required the nation of Israel to observe every fifty years, was typical and prophetic of our Lord Jesus Christ and the gospel of God's free grace in him.

The year of jubilee was a season appointed by God during which the children of Israel were required to adjust their social affairs once every fifty years, setting their brethren free from bondage and free from all debt, and restoring lost possessions, lost property, and lost inheritances to those who had lost them.

The year of jubilee portrayed and typified the great work of our Lord Jesus Christ in restoring chosen sinners to God and to one another, and bringing us at last into that great sabbath of eternal rest in 'the glorious liberty of the sons of God'.

To many throughout the land the year of jubilee was 'the accepted time' and 'the day of salvation'. It was announced by the blowing of a trumpet throughout all the land. That is, of course, a representation of gospel preaching (Isaiah 27:13). 'Blessed is the people that know the joyful sound: they shall walk, O LORD, in the light of thy countenance' (Psalm 89:15). Pause, my soul, adore and wonder. Rejoice, give thanks! Blessed are these ears that have been made to hear the joyful sound of God's free grace, of God's great, free, everlasting salvation in Christ.

Four Trumpets

There were four distinct and special sounds of the trumpet in the camp of Israel. Each one distinctly portrayed the preaching of the gospel. Memorial trumpets were sounded to announce the new moon and call the people together in a joyful assembly of worship (Leviticus 23:24; Psalm 81:3). Battle trumpets, trumpets of war (Judges 3:27), were sounded to gather the people to battle (1 Corinthians 14:8). Trumpets of alarm warned men of impending judgment and called them to repentance (Joel 2:1). The jubilee trumpet spoken of here in Leviticus 25 announced liberty, forgiveness and restoration throughout the land.

The jubilee trumpet was different from the others. This trumpet's sound was never heard except once every fifty years. Yet, its sound was so sweet and so distinct that no poor captive in the land of Israel was at a moment's loss to know its music and its gracious meaning.

That is just exactly the way it is when God the Holy Spirit causes poor, needy, captive sinners to hear the gospel. When he proclaims pardon to the guilty, pardon by the blood of Christ, he causes the sinner to understand that atonement has been made and accepted. At that very moment, jubilee commences. The soul, long held captive to sin, to Satan, and to the law, is set free and walks and dances in liberty. What a joyful sound! What a joyful day! When the gospel jubilee trumpet first sounded in my soul, the acceptable year of the Lord began (Isaiah 61:1, 2; 63:4). Charles Wesley wrote the lovely hymn,

> Oh for a thousand tongues to sing
> My great Redeemer's praise!
> The glories of my God and King,
> The triumphs of His grace!
>
> He breaks the power of cancelled sin
> And sets the prisoners free!
> His blood can make the foulest clean
> His blood availed for me!

Atonement
The year of jubilee began on the day of atonement.

> Then shalt thou cause the trumpet of the jubilee to sound on the tenth day of the seventh month, in the day of atonement shall ye make the trumpet sound throughout all your land (Leviticus 25:9).

This is where the preaching of the gospel begins. The gospel has not been preached until atonement has been proclaimed. There can be no joyful sound apart from the sin-atoning blood of Christ. The jubilee trumpet declared atoning-blood shed, atonement-blood accepted, atonement finished. The Lord Jesus Christ, the Son of God, was delivered unto death under the wrath of God because our sins were made his sins and our guilt was made his guilt. He was raised again the third day because our justification was accomplished, because our sins were forever put away. This trumpet was blown by a man. It proclaimed the year of jubilee. And the trumpet was blown throughout the land.

Liberty

Here is the second thing revealed in Leviticus 25. The year of jubilee began on the Day of Atonement, and it began with the proclamation of liberty, liberty according to the very demands of God's holy law.

> And ye shall hallow the fiftieth year, and proclaim liberty throughout all the land unto all the inhabitants thereof: it shall be a jubilee unto you; and ye shall return every man unto his possession, and ye shall return every man unto his family (Leviticus 25:10).

Our Lord Jesus Christ tells us plainly that he is the Liberator and the One who proclaims liberty (Luke 4:17-21). This liberty proclaimed in the year of jubilee, the liberty proclaimed in the gospel, is the blessed liberty of grace; but it is liberty demanded by God's holy law. Unlike the ceremonies we read about in the previous chapters of Leviticus, this law concerning the year of jubilee was given at Sinai, at the very time God gave the law to Moses (Leviticus 25:1). The ceremonial requirements described in the preceding chapters of Leviticus were given at the door of the tabernacle.

The law of God, being totally satisfied by the blood of our Substitute, the Lord Jesus Christ, demands the liberty of every redeemed sinner. Grace reigns through righteousness unto eternal life, by Jesus Christ our Lord (Romans 5:20, 21). It demands judicial liberty, spiritual liberty, and glorious eternal liberty.

Forgiveness

Third, the year of jubilee was a time of forgiveness.

And if thy brother be waxen poor, and fallen in decay with thee; then thou shalt relieve him: yea, though he be a stranger, or a sojourner; that he may live with thee (Leviticus 25:35).

The poor wretch who had lost everything, who had incurred such a tremendous load of debt that he sold his land, then his house, and at last sold himself into bondage, when the jubilee trumpet sounded, was released from bondage, released from debt, forgiven completely, freely, and forever. His debt did not bar him from the joy of jubilee. His debt qualified him as the one for whom the trumpet sounded.

God sends his servants to preach the gospel, to blow the jubilee trumpet to the poor. His blood has cancelled my debt. I am entirely, forever forgiven. That is liberty!

Rest
Fourth, the year of jubilee was a year of rest.

Six years thou shalt sow thy field, and six years thou shalt prune thy vineyard, and gather in the fruit thereof; But in the seventh year shall be a sabbath of rest unto the land, a sabbath for the LORD: thou shalt neither sow thy field, nor prune thy vineyard. That which groweth of its own accord of thy harvest thou shalt not reap, neither gather the grapes of thy vine undressed: for it is a year of rest unto the land (Leviticus 25:3-5).

The gospel of Christ is a proclamation of rest, calling weary sinners to rest, promising eternal rest (Matthew 11:28-30; Hebrews 4:1-11; Psalm 116:7).

How their Gentile neighbours must have mocked and derided the Jews during the year of jubilee. Perhaps they thought they were being lazy. They had no idea what they were doing. But what they were doing was worshipping, depending on God alone for everything. Resting (Galatians 5:1-4).

Bounty
The fifth thing Moses was inspired of God to tell us about the year of jubilee was that it was a year of great, unparalleled bounty.

And the land shall yield her fruit, and ye shall eat your fill, and dwell therein in safety (Leviticus 25:19).

Oh, what a gospel we have! In Christ we are made to dwell in complete safety in a land of infinite bounty. Here we lie down in green pastures and fear no evil. Our treasury is the unsearchable riches of Christ. 'All things are yours, for ye are Christ's'. We who have been brought by the grace of God into the liberty of the gospel have been brought into his fulness. Let us therefore be careful for nothing, but in all things give thanks.

Restoration

Sixth, in the year of jubilee every man who had lost his inheritance had it returned to him in its totality; free and clear, with no mortgage of any kind, no lien of any kind against it.

In the year of this jubilee ye shall return every man unto his possession (Leviticus 25:13).

All we lost in Adam, Christ has restored. All we lost by our own wilful rebellion and sin, Christ has restored. David understood this. He sang, 'He restoreth my soul'. We who 'were by nature children of wrath, even as others', are now made to be 'heirs of God and joint-heirs with Jesus Christ'.

Brotherly Love

Here is the seventh thing. In the year of jubilee the children of Israel were required by law to love their brethren.

Ye shall not therefore oppress one another; but thou shalt fear thy God: for I am the LORD your God (Leviticus 25:17).

In the gospel jubilee saved sinners are constrained and taught by grace to love one another. 'By this shall all men know that ye are my disciples, if ye have love one to another.'

Be ye kind one to another, tenderhearted, forgiving one another, even as God for Christ's sake hath forgiven you. Be ye therefore followers of God, as dear children; And walk in love, as Christ also hath loved us, and hath given himself for us an offering and a sacrifice to God for a sweetsmelling savour (Ephesians 4:32-5:2).

Have I been loved freely? Let me love freely. Have I received freely? Let me give freely. Have I been forgiven freely? Let me forgive freely. We read in Matthew 18 of a forgiven servant who took his fellow servant by the throat and demanded payment on the spot. He was obviously bold enough to deal with the man face to face; but he was utterly destitute of the grace, compassion, and forgiveness he had experienced from his master. Let all who know the love of God in Christ walk in love for their brethren in Christ. Ask God for grace ever to show to your brothers and sisters the love of Christ in all your thoughts of, speech to and about, and dealings with them.

Another Jubilee Trumpet

There is another jubilee trumpet we will soon hear. Let us live in its hope and expectation, listening for its sound (1 Corinthians 15:51, 52; 1 Thessalonians 4:13-18; Revelation 11:15-19). Once that trumpet blows announcing the glorious coming of our Saviour, and our eternal jubilee has commenced, we shall forever enjoy atonement to its fullest. Here is liberty beyond imagination, forgiveness in its greatest magnificence, rest in perfection, bounty beyond measure, restoration such as eye has not seen, ear has not heard, and the heart of man has never conceived, and brotherly love in unfailing perfection!

Have you heard this joyful sound? Has the Son of God made you free? Has the Lord Jesus caused you to return to your long lost, long ago forfeited inheritance? Let us never forget his unspeakable mercy. Hail, Almighty Deliverer, blessed Redeemer of your captives! I had sold my possession, and sold myself for nothing; you have redeemed it for me again without money. I had sold it, but could not destroy it, because the right of redemption was with my Kinsman Redeemer.

Blest Son of God, your brethren shall praise you! You are the next of kin, the nearest of all relations, and the dearest of all brothers. You have redeemed both body and soul, both lands and inheritance by your blood. You, blessed Christ, have so completely redeemed all that it can never be lost again, and never forfeited.

Let the jubilee trumpet sound and be heard through all the land in this gospel day! Give liberty to the captive and sight to the blind. Bring forth the prisoners out of the prison, and them that sit in darkness into your great light.

Cause us to know the joyful sound and daily to walk in the light of your countenance. Cause us, by the sweet influences of your Holy Spirit, to live in the constant expectation of the year of the everlasting jubilee, when the trumpet of the archangel shall finally sound, and all the redeemed shall return to Zion with songs and everlasting joy upon their heads. Oh, blessed, blessed hope! Then we shall obtain joy and gladness, and sorrow and sighing shall flee away. Hallelujah!

Chapter 63

The Sabbath That Remains

And the LORD spake unto Moses in mount Sinai, saying, Speak unto the children of Israel, and say unto them, When ye come into the land which I give you, then shall the land keep a sabbath unto the LORD. Six years thou shalt sow thy field, and six years thou shalt prune thy vineyard, and gather in the fruit thereof; But in the seventh year shall be a sabbath of rest unto the land, a sabbath for the LORD: thou shalt neither sow thy field, nor prune thy vineyard. That which groweth of its own accord of thy harvest thou shalt not reap, neither gather the grapes of thy vine undressed: for it is a year of rest unto the land. And the sabbath of the land shall be meat for you; for thee, and for thy servant, and for thy maid, and for thy hired servant, and for thy stranger that sojourneth with thee, and for thy cattle, and for the beast that are in thy land, shall all the increase thereof be meat ... Wherefore ye shall do my statutes, and keep my judgments, and do them; and ye shall dwell in the land in safety. And the land shall yield her fruit, and ye shall eat your fill, and dwell therein in safety. And if ye shall say, What shall we eat the seventh year? behold, we shall not sow, nor gather in our increase: Then I will command my blessing upon you in the sixth year, and it shall bring forth fruit for three years. And ye shall sow the eighth year, and eat yet of old fruit until the ninth year; until her fruits come in ye shall eat of the old store.

Leviticus 25:1-22

Are you weary in your soul, labouring under the heavy, heavy load of guilt and sin? Would you like to be free of your burden? Would you like to lie down and rest? What would you give if your very heart and soul could find rest before God? Are you carrying a heavy load, a crushing weight of burden that seems too great to bear, a yoke too hard to wear, a load you just cannot carry any longer? What would you give if your very heart and soul could find rest before God? The Son of God calls weary, labouring, heavy-laden sinners to himself, and promises rest to all who come to him (Matthew 11:28-30).

It is this rest, promised in the gospel to all who come to Christ, promised to all who believe on the Son of God, that was typified and portrayed in the Old Testament sabbath. It was God's purpose in giving all the sabbatical laws of the Old Testament that they should be signs, types, and pictures of this blessed rest that is found in Christ. It was never God's intention that people throughout the world should perpetually keep a sabbath day, any more than it was his intention that we should observe the passover! The law was given to point us to Christ.

Like circumcision, the passover, and all other aspects of legal, ceremonial worship during the Old Testament, the legal sabbath day was established by our God to be a sign, picture, and type of grace and salvation in Christ. This is not a matter of speculation and guesswork. This is exactly what God says about the matter himself.

> Speak thou also unto the children of Israel, saying, Verily my sabbaths ye shall keep: for it is a sign between me and you throughout your generations; that ye may know that I am the LORD that doth sanctify you (Exodus 31:13).

Christ's Rest

First, I want you to see that our great Saviour, the Lord Jesus Christ, has entered into his rest; and his rest is glorious because he has finished his work (Isaiah 11:10; 2 Corinthians 5:17-21; Romans 8:34; Hebrews 10:11-14). We have seen this previously in an earlier chapter, but let me remind you. Our Saviour's rest in heaven is his glory. Once again, I call your attention to the marginal translation of the last sentence of Isaiah 11:10. It reads, 'His rest shall be glory'.

As God the Father rested on the seventh day because his work of creation was finished, so God the Son rested in the seventh day of time entering into his rest forever because he has finished his work of making all things new for his people (Romans 8:34; Hebrews 10:11-14). Matthew 28:1 literally reads, 'In the end of the sabbath, as it began to dawn toward the sabbath'. I take the verse to mean that when the Lord Jesus Christ died at Calvary and rose again, the old sabbath of the law ended and the new sabbath of grace began.

Christ's rest is his glory (John 17:2; Philippians 2:9-11; Isaiah 45:20-25). He has finished his work (John 17:4; 19:30). Because he has finished his work, the salvation of his people is certain (Hebrews 9:12). There is no more work to be done. Christ did it all. Since he has finished his work, he sat down in his glory. There he is resting. We ought to be just as restful.

Sabbath Keepers
Second, I want you to see from the Scriptures that every sinner who believes on the Lord Jesus Christ keeps the sabbath by faith by entering into his rest (Hebrews 4:3, 9, 10). We do not keep a literal, carnal sabbath of any kind. Ours is a sabbath of faith, a spiritual sabbath. Because sabbath keeping was a legal type of our salvation in Christ during the age of carnal ordinances, like the passover and circumcision, once Christ came and fulfilled the type, the carnal ordinance ceased. We are not carnal sabbath keepers, but spiritual sabbath keepers, true sabbath keepers.

The New Testament strictly forbids keeping any of those carnal ordinances of the law. Any who attempt to worship God on the grounds of legal ordinances are yet under the curse of the law and have not yet learned the gospel. Paul says in Colossians 2:23 that pretending to keep a literal, legal, sabbath in this gospel age is an outward show of spirituality and wisdom; mere will-worship. Our sabbath is a spiritual sabbath, not a carnal one. We rest in Christ, trusting his finished work, by faith entering into his rest. The believer's life is a constant keeping of the sabbath because Christ is our Sabbath. None of us keeps this sabbath of faith perfectly. Our best faith in this world is still unbelief. But we do keep this sabbath rest sincerely, looking to Christ, coming to Christ, resting in Christ. Our all glorious Christ gives rest to every sinner who comes to him in faith (Matthew 11:28).

Seventh Year Sabbath

Third, I want to show you that there is a sabbath that yet remains, a sabbath that is yet to come, the eternal rest of glory. This sabbath that is yet to come, that sabbath Paul refers to when he says, 'There remaineth therefore a rest to the people of God' (Hebrews 4:9), is typically set before us in Leviticus 25:1-22. Here the Lord God in giving the law to Israel required them to keep a sabbatical year every seven years.

Every seventh day the children of Israel were required to keep a sabbath day. At the end of every seventh week, they were required to keep a sabbath. In the seventh month of every year, as they observed the feast of tabernacles, they were required to keep a sabbath week. Every seventh year they were required to keep a sabbath year. And at the end of every seven years, the Lord God required Israel to keep a year long sabbath. That seventh year sabbath portrayed two things: the gospel rest of faith and the eternal rest of heaven.

How insistent our God is for us to be assured of the rest awaiting us! In the Mosaic age of types and ceremonies, he held it constantly before the eyes of his people. In this gospel age, he keeps before us the blessed hope of that eternal sabbath yet to come called 'the glorious liberty of the children of God'. How we ought to long for that day of our God, when we shall at last rest forever (2 Thessalonians 1:7).

Leviticus 25 stands before us as a beacon, a lighthouse, drawing us to that blessed haven of eternal rest awaiting our souls in heaven. As we sail through the tempest tossed, troubled seas of time, may our hearts be ever more encouraged with hope and drawn toward that rest.

1. This sabbath year could not be kept until the Jews came into the possession of Canaan (v. 2).

Remember, this law was given at Sinai. But it was a law that God would not allow the children of Israel to keep until they were in possession of their land of promise. They kept other sabbath days, week after week, throughout their wilderness journey, as we now keep the sabbath of faith, resting in Christ. But this great sabbath year could not be kept in the wilderness. It must be kept only in Canaan. So it is with us. We rest in Christ now, by faith. But there is an eternal sabbath yet to be fulfilled in heavenly glory, when our God makes all things new, in which we shall rest perfectly forever.

2. This sabbath year, like the weekly sabbath, was a sabbath to 'keep unto the Lord'. The Lord God delighted in the picture; and he would have his people delight in the prospect, too.

3. Here is a picture of full, complete rest, an utter cessation of labour and toil (vv. 3-5).

'Six years shalt thou sow thy field.' Until the sabbath year comes, we must work and toil. The sweat must ever drop from our brow while we live in this sin-cursed earth. These six years represent the days of our lives here. Here we serve our God and serve one another. We do so gladly; but there is toil and labour in our work. Not so in eternity! The sixth year was a time of great expectation. What hope the Israelites had the sixth year as they sowed their seeds. They expected, because God promised it, that the harvest at the end of the sixth year would be a harvest of three years!

'But in the seventh year shall be a sabbath of rest unto the land, a sabbath for the Lord'. The seventh year rang out the glad tidings of heavenly glory, saying to all the people, 'There is a day coming when there shall be no more curse'. No work was to be done in that year. No seed could be sown. No vines could be pruned. No one was allowed to reap anything, not even that which grew of itself.

Everything involved in this sabbath year was designed to give a picture of complete, total rest. It was a typical picture of that which shall be our state when the Prince of Peace has made a new heavens and a new earth. Try to get the picture.

Walk through Israel's land during the seventh year. Every man is sitting with his family under his vine and fig tree. No ox is in the yoke. No wine is in the winepress. No man is in the field. There is a strange stillness throughout the land. Everyone is resting, meditating upon the goodness of God, reflecting upon deliverance, giving praise and thanks to him who brought them into this good land. The whole year round, month after month, for twelve sweet months, they leisurely worship God without a care in the world. Yes, in eternity, 'his servants serve him'. They never cease serving him. Yet, there is no labour, no toil, no sweat to their labour.

> They shall have linen bonnets upon their heads, and shall have linen breeches upon their loins; they shall not gird themselves with any thing that causeth sweat (Ezekiel 44:18).

4. In addition to these instructions, the book of Deuteronomy tells us that in this year there was to be a general release of debts (Deuteronomy 15:1, 2). We have been released from all our debts. How we rejoice in the free and total forgiveness of our sins through the blood of Christ in the experience of grace. But what shall it be to be released from all the consequences of them!

5. There was to be a public reading of the law (Deuteronomy 31:10, 11) for the instruction of the people. All Israel, men, women, and children, were taught of God as his law was opened to them. Eternity will be for our souls an ever-increasing learning of Christ!

6. The seventh year sabbath portrayed the blessed oneness, unity, and communion of God's saints when he has made all things new (vv. 6-8). In this great sabbath year no one claimed anything as his own. The rich and the poor, the stranger and the sojourner, as well as the children of Israel, even the cattle and beasts fed alike upon that which grew of itself throughout the land. In glory, blessed be God, we shall be made perfect in one. We shall be in perfect harmony with our God, with one another, and with all God's creation.

7. Still, there is more. Look at verses 18-22. Here, after speaking about the jubilee year, Moses picks up the matter of the sabbath year again, showing us God's gracious, absolute promises concerning it. 'Wherefore ye shall do my statutes, and keep my judgments, and do them; and ye shall dwell in the land in safety. And, and ye shall eat your fill, and dwell therein in safety.' Yes, these words stand as a command of law at Sinai, but I cannot avoid reading them in the light of the gospel as promises of grace. 'Ye shall do my statutes.' 'Ye shall dwell in the land in safety.' 'The land shall yield her fruit.' 'Ye shall eat your fill.'

Promised Abundance

In preparation for this great sabbath year observance, the Lord God inspired Israel's faith with a promise from which we ought to learn.

> And if ye shall say, What shall we eat the seventh year? behold, we shall not sow, nor gather in our increase: Then I will command my blessing upon you in the sixth year, and it shall bring forth fruit for three years. And ye shall sow the eighth year, and eat yet of old fruit until the ninth year; until her fruits come in ye shall eat of the old store (Leviticus 25:20-22).

Israel's unbelief and ours was anticipated by our gracious God, who knows our frame and remembers that we are dust. These verses read much like our Saviour's admonition in Matthew, 'Seek ye first the kingdom of God and his righteousness, and all these things shall be added unto you'. Here, the Lord God promises his special providence and bounteous blessing to supply everything for his own. He assures us that he is both able and willing to protect us and provide for us now and forever. His heart is full of love for us. His arm is full of strength for us. The Lord God would not allow those who trusted him enough to commit all things to him to lose anything by doing so (Exodus 34:24).

Let us serve our God in the six years of labour he has given us. As we serve him, he will keep us, provide for us, and protect us. And, soon, very soon, we shall enter into his rest (2 Peter 3:10-14).

Chapter 64

Let Us Start Over

And thou shalt number seven sabbaths of years unto thee, seven times seven years; and the space of the seven sabbaths of years shall be unto thee forty and nine years. Then shalt thou cause the trumpet of the jubile to sound on the tenth day of the seventh month, in the day of atonement shall ye make the trumpet sound throughout all your land. And ye shall hallow the fiftieth year, and proclaim liberty throughout all the land unto all the inhabitants thereof: it shall be a jubile unto you; and ye shall return every man unto his possession, and ye shall return every man unto his family. A jubile shall that fiftieth year be unto you: ye shall not sow, neither reap that which groweth of itself in it, nor gather the grapes in it of thy vine undressed. For it is the jubile; it shall be holy unto you: ye shall eat the increase thereof out of the field. In the year of this jubile ye shall return every man unto his possession. And if thou sell ought unto thy neighbour, or buyest ought of thy neighbour's hand, ye shall not oppress one another: According to the number of years after the jubile thou shalt buy of thy neighbour, and according unto the number of years of the fruits he shall sell unto thee: According to the multitude of years thou shalt increase the price thereof, and according to the fewness of years thou shalt diminish the price of it: for according to the number of the years of the fruits doth he sell unto thee. Ye shall not therefore oppress one another; but thou shalt fear thy God: for I am the LORD your God.

Leviticus 25:8-17

How often have you heard someone say, 'I wish I could undo the past. If only I could start over, I would sure do things different'? Such sentiments are usually expressed by those who are getting on in years. But, then, with a sigh of resignation, the person returns to reality and says, 'but of course I can't'. Of course, we all know it is impossible to undo the past and start over. Or is it?

In ancient Israel the Lord God established a law that required a new beginning every fifty years. It is called 'the year of jubilee'. I want to show you how this great ordinance of God in the Old Testament finds its fulfilment in the gospel of Christ. May God the Holy Spirit, whose Word we have before us, be our Teacher.

Time of Restoration

Of all the solemn, typical ordinances of the Old Testament held up to the eye of faith, which foreshadowed good things to come by Christ, none was more blessed to behold and contemplate than the year of jubilee. The year of jubilee was ordained of God to be a time of restoration, rest, and rejoicing. The jubilee sabbath was designed to be the highest, most glorious, most anticipated of all the Old Testament sabbaths. In the year of jubilee all the woes of the previous forty-nine years were undone, all debts were cancelled, lost property was restored, and families were reunited. There was a complete reversal and renewal of life given to all in Israel who had, by any cause or circumstance, come into debt, lost their heritage, or been subjected to bondage. In all these things, the year of jubilee was a picture of God's great salvation in Christ (2 Corinthians 5:17).

The Jubilee Trumpet

Some have debated whether the jubilee trumpet (vv. 8, 9) prefigured the preaching of gospel liberty in Christ or the trump of God that will announce the glorious second advent of Christ and the consummation of liberty for the sons of God in him. There is no need for the debate. It very suitably refers to both. New life by Christ's death and the future resurrection glory of the elect are both aspects of one great salvation.

The jubilee trumpet was typical of the preaching of the gospel. Our Saviour makes this abundantly clear by applying the words of Isaiah 61 to himself in the fourth chapter of Luke, verses 16-21. 'Blessed is the people that know the joyful sound: they shall walk, O LORD, in the light of thy countenance' (Psalm 89:15). The jubilee trumpet also refers to the trump of God that shall announce our Saviour's second coming and resurrection glory (1 Corinthians 15:51-58). The jubilee gospel trumpet refers primarily to our Saviour's first advent, proclaiming redemption accomplished by the blood of Christ and deliverance from both the guilt of sin and the dominion of sin. The jubilee trumpet, as it refers to our Lord's second advent and the sounding of the trump of God, will proclaim that great day when all the ransomed of God shall eternally enjoy deliverance from the very existence of sin, and deliverance from all the evil and bitter consequences of it!

Day of Atonement
The jubilee trumpet could not be sounded, liberty could not be proclaimed and the yearlong jubilee sabbath rest could not begin, until the passover sacrifice had been slain, atonement made, and the blood of the lamb sprinkled on the mercy seat (v. 9).

Israel was taught by this requirement that no blessing, mercy, or grace can come down to sinners from heaven, except by the merit, efficacy, and accomplishment of Christ's blood atonement. His blood must be poured out upon the cursed tree, his blood must be sprinkled upon the mercy seat, his blood must be accepted in the holy place, he must come forth out of the tomb, without sin unto salvation, he must ascend to the throne of God and sit down, before grace can come down to sinners.

Salvation is altogether by God's free grace but God's free grace comes to us only through the redemption that is in Christ Jesus. 'Without shedding of blood is no remission.'

Does that mean no grace was given to sinners until two thousand years ago when Christ died and rose again? No. This great work was finished in the mind and purpose of God before the world began (Revelation 13:8; 1 Peter 1:18-20; Romans 8:29, 30). Yet it was a work executed in time by the wisdom, providence, and grace of our God.

So precise and detailed is the order of God's providence that even the cycles of the solar system were set by him and are maintained by him so that the Jews and Romans, with their wicked wills crucified the Lord of Glory, according to the calculations of those who calculate such things, at the time of passover, at the time of the evening sacrifice, in Jerusalem, at the place where God required the sacrifice to be made, in the year of jubilee (Acts 2:23). This work of redemption by God our Saviour shall be the matter of our souls' amazement, contemplation, and joy to eternity.

Jubilee Work

There are eight specific things given in this portion of Scripture that were to be done in the year of jubilee (Leviticus 25:10-13).

1. Liberty was to be proclaimed throughout the land.

2. The exiles returned.

3. The captives were emancipated.

4. The debtor was set free and his debts cancelled.

5. Each family opened its arms to embrace and receive once more its long-lost members.

6. Everyone received his inheritance again. None of God's chosen, not one soul redeemed by Christ's precious blood can ever, by any circumstance, be deprived of possessing forever his inheritance with the Son of God (Ephesians 1:3-14). The very law of God demands it.

7. Everybody in God's Israel enjoyed a time of blessed rest, feasting upon the provisions of grace.

The sound of the trumpet was the welcome and soul-stirring signal for the captive to escape his prison, for the slave to cast off the chains of his bondage, for the manslayer to return to his home, and for the ruined and poverty-stricken to rise to the possession of their forfeited inheritance. No sooner had the trumpet's welcome sound been heard than the mighty tide of blessing rose majestically and sent its refreshing undulations into the most remote corners of Canaan's happy land.

8. Everyone in Israel was required to measure the value of all things in the prospect of that great day when the year of jubilee would come (vv. 14-17).

> And if thou sell ought unto thy neighbour, or buyest ought of thy neighbour's hand, ye shall not oppress one another: According to the number of years after the jubilee thou shalt buy of thy neighbour, and according unto the number of years of the fruits he shall sell unto thee: According to the multitude of years thou shalt increase the price thereof, and according to the fewness of years thou shalt diminish the price of it: for according to the number of the years of the fruits doth he sell unto thee. Ye shall

not therefore oppress one another; but thou shalt fear thy God: for I am the LORD your God (Leviticus 25:14-17).

The year of jubilee reminded both buyer and seller that the land belonged to Jehovah, and was not to be sold. 'The fruits' might be sold, but not the land. It all belonged to God. They were just temporary tenants. Houses in walled cities could be bought and sold at any time, because they were just houses (vv. 29, 30). But the little cottages in the country villages were to be redeemed in the jubilee, because they were part of the land itself (vv. 31, 32). The scale of prices was to reflect and be regulated by the jubilee. All human contracts regarding land, trade and money were torn up the moment the jubilee trumpet was heard.

Loose Hand
This teaches us a great lesson. If our hearts cherish the abiding hope of Christ's return, we must hold all earthly things with a loose hand, valuing them altogether in the light of eternity. 'Let your moderation be known unto all men. The Lord is at hand' (Philippians 4:4; 2 Corinthians 4:17-5:11). May God give us grace to live every moment in the immediate prospect of eternity.

If we can do this, valuing all things in the light of eternity, we will not oppress our brethren, but serve them and use what the Lord puts in our hands to serve them and him.

All Things New
Yes, the clock can be turned back. Old things can be put away. All things can be made new. Not by you. Not by me. But by the God of all grace through the sin-atoning blood of the Lord Jesus Christ (2 Corinthians 5:17-6:2). May God graciously cause you this very day to hear the jubilee trumpet of his matchless free grace in Christ and give you liberty; blessed, eternal liberty, for Christ's sake.

> The Gospel trumpet, blow!
> Good news from heaven sound
> Let all the nations know,
> To earth's remotest bound:
> The year of jubilee is come!
> Return, all ransomed sinners, home.

Christ Jesus, our High Priest,
Has full atonement made;
Come, weary sinners, rest;
You need not be afraid:
The year of jubilee is come!
Return, all ransomed sinners, home.

Extol the Lamb of God,
The sin-atoning Lamb;
Redemption through His blood
Through all the world proclaim:
The year of jubilee is come!
Return, all ransomed sinners, home.

Enslaved to sin and hell,
Christ's liberty embrace,
And safe forever dwell,
Saved by His wondrous grace:
The year of jubilee is come!
Return, all ransomed sinners, home.

Though you have sold for naught
Your heritage above,
Come, have it back unbought,
The gift of God's free love:
The year of jubilee is come!
Return, all ransomed sinners, home.

Soon, we the trump shall hear,
And Christ will come again!
In glory He'll appear,
And say to us again.
The year of jubilee is come!
Return to your eternal home.

Chapter 65

Is It Safe And Wise To Trust The Lord?

Wherefore ye shall do my statutes, and keep my judgments, and do them; and ye shall dwell in the land in safety. And the land shall yield her fruit, and ye shall eat your fill, and dwell therein in safety. And if ye shall say, What shall we eat the seventh year? behold, we shall not sow, nor gather in our increase: Then I will command my blessing upon you in the sixth year, and it shall bring forth fruit for three years. And ye shall sow the eighth year, and eat yet of old fruit until the ninth year; until her fruits come in ye shall eat of the old store.

Leviticus 25:18-22

The wise man, Solomon, said, 'Trust in the LORD with all thine heart; and lean not unto thine own understanding. In all thy ways acknowledge him, and he shall direct thy paths' (Proverbs 3:5, 6). Is it safe and wise to trust the Lord, to trust him in all things and for all things? Is it prudent to trust in the Lord with all your heart?

I know this. Faith in Christ is nothing less than willing, deliberate, voluntary surrender of my very life to the rule and dominion of the Son of God as my Lord and Saviour. It is trusting Christ alone for my salvation, trusting him as my sin-atoning Substitute, trusting him as all my righteousness before God, trusting him alone to keep me by his grace and bring me at last into the everlasting bliss of heavenly glory.

But Christ is more than a fire escape from hell. Salvation is more than the hope of going to heaven and having eternal life when we die. We often speak of Christ saving our souls; but that is not Bible

551

language. The Son of God did not die at Calvary to save souls. He will never save your soul. Christ saves sinners: body, soul, and spirit. He will either save you, all of you, or damn you, all of you. The Lord Jesus Christ demands all of you. If he is not Lord of all, he is not Lord at all.

I am calling on you to give up yourself to Christ, to believe on the Son of God, to acknowledge you are his, that you are from this day forward his servant. I am calling upon you to devote your life, your entire life; your family, time, talents, money, everything, to the service of his kingdom, his glory, and his cause alone. Acknowledge you have no right to claim anything for yourself, no right to use anything for yourself, no right even to have a thought or will of your own.

Perhaps you think, 'That sounds great. It seems to be the right thing to do. But it's just not practical and reasonable. Surely, the Lord does not expect me to totally give myself up to him. Surely, he does not expect anyone to trust him absolutely?'

Again, I ask, 'Is it safe and wise to trust the Lord?' I cannot tell you it is physically, mathematically, economically, or philosophically safe and wise to trust him. What is demanded by God can never be made to fit any human graph or scale. In fact, I tell you honestly that in earthly terms, faith in Christ is anything but reasonable. Martin Luther once said, 'The first thing that faith does is to knock the brains of reason out'.

Listen to our Saviour. When he calls us to believe God, to trust him, he says, If the Lord God, your heavenly Father, watches over and feeds the sparrow, do you not know he will watch over and feed you? He who has numbered the hairs of your head will meet your every need. If your heavenly Father clothes the worthless lilies of the field in splendour, he will never fail to supply your needs. Trust him.

> Therefore take no thought, saying, What shall we eat? or, What shall we drink? or, Wherewithal shall we be clothed? (For after all these things do the Gentiles seek:) for your heavenly Father knoweth that ye have need of all these things. But seek ye first the kingdom of God, and his righteousness; and all these things shall be added unto you. Take therefore no thought for the morrow: for the morrow shall take thought for the things of itself. Sufficient unto the day is the evil thereof (Matthew 6:31-34).

Can we really be expected to put Christ first in everything? Not only is it expected, it is demanded that we trust him for everything. I do not suggest, imply, think, or imagine that this trust is perfect. Far from it! Our best faith in God is so full of unbelief it would sink us to the lowest hell were it not bathed in Jesus' blood and robed in his righteousness.

Faith is never perfect in us, but true faith is what trusts the Son of God in all things and for all things, absolutely. Such faith compels the believing soul to surrender all things to his dominion.

If I so trust Christ that I devote my entire life to him, how can I live in this world? How can I provide for my family? If I allow nothing to keep me from worshipping God and obeying him, what will happen to my business? Is that safe and wise? Let us look into the book of God, and see what he says about these very practical things.

Exodus 34:24
Look at Exodus 34. You will remember that in the Old Testament the Lord God required every male Israelite to leave his land, herds, fields, business, home, and everything else three times a year to travel to Jerusalem and spend a week there worshipping him.

Their pagan neighbours would soon be aware that these people not only refused to allow anything to interfere with their daily worship and their weekly sabbaths, these Jews are such religious zealots that they leave everything three times a year to go to Jerusalem to worship for a week. We can mark our calendars and take everything they have without resistance when they are away worshipping their God. The Jews might reasonably fear that their worship of God would make them vulnerable to such people, except for one thing.

Thrice in the year shall all your menchildren appear before the Lord GOD, the God of Israel. For I will cast out the nations before thee, and enlarge thy borders: neither shall any man desire thy land, when thou shalt go up to appear before the LORD thy God thrice in the year (Exodus 34:23, 24).

We have a similar situation here in the twenty-fifth chapter of Leviticus. In this passage of the law, the Lord God does not require the children of Israel to neglect their livelihoods for a week, but for a year, once every seven years (vv. 1-7). During this sabbath year, they were not allowed to gather crops from the previous year, or sow their fields. It meant they had to trust the Lord whom they worshipped, the God they served, and him alone to provide them with food for three years. God required them to trust him and obey him because they trusted him. Is that safe? Is that wise? Read the passage again and see.

> Ye shall do my statutes, and keep my judgments, and do them; and ye shall dwell in the land in safety. And the land shall yield her fruit, and ye shall eat your fill, and dwell therein in safety. And if ye shall say, What shall we eat the seventh year? Behold, we shall not sow, nor gather in our increase: Then I will command my blessing upon you in the sixth year, and it shall bring forth fruit for three years. And ye shall sow the eighth year, and eat yet of old fruit until the ninth year; until her fruits come in ye shall eat of the old store (Leviticus 25:18-22).

Three Promises

The Lord God here gave his people assurance that they would lose nothing by observing these years of rest. In fact, rather than losing by obedience, they would gain much. Look at what the Lord promised.

1. He promised them safety. 'You shall dwell in the land in safety' (vv. 18, 19). The word 'safety' means more than physical safety and security. It means, you shall both be safe and inwardly confident and secure. You shall neither experience evil nor fear it.

2. He promised them plenty. 'You shall eat your fill' (v. 19). When we are obedient to our Saviour, obedient to the revealed will of God, we may cheerfully and confidently trust him to provide for us all we need (Philippians 4:19).

3. He promised they would not lack provisions during that year in which they neither sowed nor reaped. 'I will command my blessing in the sixth year, and it shall bring forth fruit for three years' (v. 21).

This was a standing miracle of providence. At other times, one year yielded food for the next. But in the sixth year, the fields would yield enough to last for three years. The blessing of God upon our provisions makes a little go a long way. Our Saviour still multiplies loaves and fishes for his own. He who gave manna every other day of the week, gave none on the sabbath. But he gave twice the daily provision on

Friday, so his people could give themselves without concern on the sabbath to worship him.

All of this is intended to be an encouragement from our God to us. Here he teaches you and me to obey him in all things, to put him first in all things, confidently trusting him and casting all our care upon him. He assures us nothing is ever lost by faith in and obedience to our God. He declares, 'Them that honour me I will honour'.

I see five very important spiritual lessons in this portion of Holy Scripture. May God the Holy Spirit drive them home to our hearts.

The Obedience of Faith
First, the Spirit of God here speaks about the obedience of faith, and teaches us obedience arises from faith in Christ. 'Wherefore ye shall do my statutes, and keep my judgments, and do them; and ye shall dwell in the land in safety' (v. 18). There is no keeping of God's statutes and judgments apart from faith in Christ (1 John 3:23).

Throughout the book of Leviticus, the Lord God calls for obedience to that which is revealed in the book upon one basis. It is repeated throughout the book and again in the last verse of this chapter.

> For unto me the children of Israel are servants; they are my servants whom I brought forth out of the land of Egypt: I am the LORD your God (Leviticus 25:55).

Here the Lord God says, I call for you to obey me because you are my servants, I am the Lord your God, and I brought you out of the land of Egypt. I redeemed you and saved you. I bought you and you are mine. That is exactly what he tells us in 1 Corinthians 6:9-11, 19, 20.

The Lord demands we acknowledge he is our God and we belong to him. Nothing is exempted. All must be consecrated to him. That is his right as our God. Obedience to the will of God is always costly and causes problems. It requires we make choices that are painful. But as we obey him he takes care of the problems because of our obedience.

The Danger of Worldliness
Second, this passage speaks clearly about the danger of worldliness, and teaches us we must never allow the cares of the world to keep us from worship of our God and obedience to our God.

When I speak of worldliness, I am not talking about wearing stylish clothes, watching television, or going to the movies. I am talking about something far more serious. I am talking about the love of the world. Nothing is so dangerous, nothing is more powerful poison to our souls than 'the care of this world and the deceitfulness of riches'.

Love of the world, more than anything else, keeps people who profess to love Christ from doing what they know is the will of God, what they know is best for their souls, and what they know most serves the interests of God's glory (1 John 2:15-17; Ecclesiastes 3:10, 11; Matthew 13:22).

It is my constant prayer for you, for my children, for my wife, and for myself, that God will never set the world in our hearts. It is written of the reprobate, 'He hath set the world in their heart, so that no man can find out the work that God maketh from the beginning to the end' (Ecclesiastes 3:11).

The Promise of Providence

Third, the promise given of God's special providence teaches us that the Lord God our Saviour pledges his providence to protect and provide for us as we seek to worship, serve, and honour him in this world.

> Wherefore ye shall do my statutes, and keep my judgments, and do them; and ye shall dwell in the land in safety. And the land shall yield her fruit, and ye shall eat your fill, and dwell therein in safety ... Then I will command my blessing upon you in the sixth year, and it shall bring forth fruit for three years (Leviticus 25:18, 19, 21).

Our Lord Jesus seems to refer to this passage in Matthew 6 and Luke 12. He tells us to seek first the kingdom of God and his righteousness, and all these things will be supplied. Our Master tells us that our primary purpose on this earth must be the will and glory and kingdom of God, and assures us he will take care of us.

The Lord pledges his providence in our behalf. Surely, this should be enough for every believing heart. Our Saviour said, 'Your heavenly Father knoweth that ye have need of these things'. Yet, how often we are overcome by fear of losing money, or friends, or the good opinion of family, or some little toy, should we devote ourselves to his cause.

How little we credit God's faithfulness. We should leave in his hands all our difficulties as to the matter of our provision and his method of providing it. He has promised he will work all things together for our good. 'He that spared not his own Son, but delivered him up for us all, how shall he not with him also freely give us all things?'

Besides, it is God's blessing, not our industry, or skill, or foresight, that is the source of all our safety and provision. There is nothing to sustain faith but the assurance here given that the Lord our God is able and willing to do for us all we need. His heart is full of love for us. His holy arm is full of strength for us. It is most reasonable that we should trust him implicitly and obey him completely.

The Hindrance of Fear

Fourth, we see in verse 20 that it is fear, more often than not, that hinders us from obeying our God without hesitation. 'And if ye shall say, What shall we eat the seventh year? Behold, we shall not sow, nor gather in our increase'.

Carnal reason says. 'If I worship God rather than working today, I may not be able to meet my obligations. If I worship God rather than spend the evening socialising with my family or friends, what will they think of me? If I give my money to support the gospel of Christ, how can I wisely and prudently expect to provide for my family?'

Zedekiah, king of Judah, was a weak man. He discovered he would have been far safer and far wiser to obey God than to have been kept from obedience by his fear of the Jews and Babylon's king.

> Then said Jeremiah unto Zedekiah, Thus saith the LORD, the God of hosts, the God of Israel; If thou wilt assuredly go forth unto the king of Babylon's princes, then thy soul shall live, and this city shall not be burned with fire; and thou shalt live, and thine house: But if thou wilt not go forth to the king of Babylon's princes, then shall this city be given into the hand of the Chaldeans, and they shall burn it with fire, and thou shalt not escape out of their hand. And Zedekiah the king said unto Jeremiah, I am afraid of the Jews that are fallen to the Chaldeans, lest they deliver me into their hand, and they mock me (Jeremiah 38:17-19).

In the eleventh year of his reign, Babylon invaded Judah and destroyed Jerusalem. And they 'put out Zedekiah's eyes, and bound him with chains, to carry him to Babylon. And the Chaldeans burned the king's house, and the houses of the people, with fire, and brake down the walls of Jerusalem (Jeremiah 39:7, 8).

The Assurance of Grace
Fifth, in verse 21, God gave his people the assurance of his grace, and thereby teaches us we will never impoverish ourselves, or suffer any loss by honouring him.

> Then I will command my blessing upon you in the sixth year, and it shall bring forth fruit for three years (Leviticus 25:21).
>
> I have been young, and now am old; yet have I not seen the righteous forsaken, nor his seed begging bread (Psalm 37:25).
>
> And he said unto them, When I sent you without purse, and scrip, and shoes, lacked ye anything? And they said, Nothing (Luke 22:35).
>
> Be not deceived; God is not mocked: for whatsoever a man soweth, that shall he also reap. For he that soweth to his flesh shall of the flesh reap corruption; but he that soweth to the Spirit shall of the Spirit reap life everlasting. And let us not be weary in well doing: for in due season we shall reap, if we faint not (Galatians 6:7-9).

Our God has promised us safety in the path of faith and obedience; and he has promised us plenty. God is as good as his Word. That fact ought to forever eliminate from our minds every doubt, fear and hesitation.

Chapter 66

Strangers And Sojourners With God

The land shall not be sold for ever: for the land is mine; for ye are strangers and sojourners with me. And in all the land of your possession ye shall grant a redemption for the land. And if a man sell a dwelling house in a walled city, then he may redeem it within a whole year after it is sold; within a full year may he redeem it. And if it be not redeemed within the space of a full year, then the house that is in the walled city shall be established for ever to him that bought it throughout his generations: it shall not go out in the jubile. But the houses of the villages which have no wall round about them shall be counted as the fields of the country: they may be redeemed, and they shall go out in the jubile. Notwithstanding the cities of the Levites, and the houses of the cities of their possession, may the Levites redeem at any time. And if a man purchase of the Levites, then the house that was sold, and the city of his possession, shall go out in the year of jubile: for the houses of the cities of the Levites are their possession among the children of Israel. But the field of the suburbs of their cities may not be sold; for it is their perpetual possession.

Leviticus 25:23-34

The year of jubilee was established by God at the time he gave the law to Israel on Mount Sinai. As we have seen, it was distinctly a picture of God's great grace in Christ, a picture of the salvation of God's elect. The blowing of the jubilee trumpet was symbolic of the preaching of the gospel. Jubilee itself portrayed the grace and glory God promises to chosen sinners in Christ. As jubilee began on the Day of Atonement, the whole of God's salvation comes to chosen sinners by and because of the atonement Christ made for our sins at Calvary.

God's Blessings

The blessings of grace and glory, all the blessings of God's salvation in this world and in the world to come, are free gifts of grace (Ephesians 1:3-6; 2 Timothy 1:9). They are gifts of God's free grace bestowed upon chosen sinners through the blood of Christ (Ephesians 1:7), and by the demands of God's holy law (Romans 3:24-26). Neither the blessings of grace we enjoy now in the experience of salvation, nor the blessings of our God in heavenly glory to come depend on, or are in any way determined by our works. Salvation is, in its entirety, the gift of God.

We have seen in this chapter 25 that in the year of jubilee all debts were immediately cancelled, all who had been in bondage were set free, every man who had lost his inheritance had it returned, and all the children of Israel were to keep a yearlong sabbath. That is exactly what Christ has done for us in salvation; and exactly what we shall enjoy in glory, because he redeemed us with his precious blood at Calvary.

Oh, poor soul, if you are yet labouring in bondage under sin's dominion, hear the jubilee trumpet today, and go free! Believe on the Lord Jesus Christ and walk in liberty.

God's Reason

After giving the jubilee law and declaring what was to be done in the year of jubilee, the Lord God explains the reason why he gave such specific and strict laws about this great year of liberation. The Lord God established this Jubilee law for the children of Israel as a perpetual reminder they were strangers and sojourners with him in this world.

> The land shall not be sold for ever: for the land is mine; for ye are strangers and sojourners with me. And in all the land of your possession ye shall grant a redemption for the land (Leviticus 25:23, 24).

After mentioning the law of the kinsman redeemer in verses 25-28, he continues talking about houses and lands in Leviticus 25:29-34.

Sabbath Laws

As a ceremonial institution the year of jubilee completed the picture of the sabbatical laws of the Old Testament. The seventh day sabbath, seventh week sabbath, and the seventh year sabbath all spoke of the rest of faith in Christ (Matthew 11:28-30). They were all connected with the institutions of divine worship on earth in the Mosaic age, portraying our present enjoyment of God's grace and salvation in Christ.

The jubilee or fiftieth year sabbath was different. Though God commanded it, there is no record Israel ever observed it. This sabbath portrayed the great sabbath that yet remains, the everlasting sabbath of eternal glory. It was God's promise, in type to those who were strangers and sojourners with him, of a better sabbath beyond this vale of tears.

The Land

In verse 23 the Lord states, 'The land shall not be sold forever'. Why? What was the purpose of this command? The land of Canaan represented our heavenly inheritance, the gift of God's free grace in Christ, an inheritance that cannot be lost, forfeited, or destroyed, either by the fierceness of our foes, nor by the failures of our flesh (Romans 11:29; Ecclesiastes 3:14). Then, the Lord makes a specific exception.

And if a man sell a dwelling house in a walled city, then he may redeem it within a whole year after it is sold; within a full year may he redeem it. And if it be not redeemed within the space of a full year, then the house that is in the walled city shall be established for ever to him that bought it throughout his generations: it shall not go out in the jubilee (Leviticus 25:29, 30).

In verses 31-34 the Lord God declares that the houses in the country villages and the houses of the Levites were to be counted as part and parcel with the land. Being built upon the ground, joined to the ground, they were counted one with the land. They could not be sold forever. The houses in the country villages, among the vines and fig trees, were considered one with the land. The houses of the Levites were, like the land, the Lord's provision for the priestly tribe. Like the land itself, these could never be lost permanently.

But the houses of the walled cities were looked upon differently. They could be bought and sold repeatedly. Why? Because the land of Canaan was the heritage of redemption and grace by covenant promise. It was a grant of redemption (v. 24). But the walled cities of the land and the houses built upon the walls that men had erected were the works of men. The works of men, no matter how noble and impressive, have nothing to do with the gifts of grace.

Strangers and Sojourners

There is another reason why the land was not to be sold forever.

> The land shall not be sold for ever: for the land is mine; for ye are strangers and sojourners with me (Leviticus 25:23).

Though the land of Canaan was typical of our eternal inheritance with Christ, it was still but an earthly parcel of ground. It was no more permanent than any other part of the earth; and the Lord God reminded Israel of this by declaring that so long as they lived on the earth, they were strangers and sojourners; but importantly, they were strangers and sojourners with him. Let us learn this lesson well. We are strangers and sojourners with God in this world.

> Hear my prayer, O LORD, and give ear unto my cry; hold not thy peace at my tears: for I am a stranger with thee, and a sojourner, as all my fathers were (Psalm 39:12).

We are pilgrims passing through the earth for a brief time. Here, we have no abiding city. Everything is temporary. But land to which we go is permanent and eternal (2 Corinthians 4:18-5:1; Hebrews 11:8-10).

God's people are strangers in this world. A stranger is a person who is away from home and away from his homeland. A sojourner is one who is moving through one place on his way to another. That is our state in this world. Our Father is there, our Elder Brother is there, most of our family is there, our inheritance is there. Soon, we shall be there.

A stranger is one who never quite fits in with the crowd around him. He can never really be comfortable in their company; and they are not comfortable in his. 'The world knoweth us not.'

With God

We are strangers and sojourners in this world; but that is not the end of the matter. The Lord says, 'ye are strangers and sojourners with me'. We are strangers and sojourners with God our Saviour. That means that we are always under our heavenly Father's watchful eye, omnipotent protection and tender care. We are ever in the company of our God and Saviour. We live in Christ and with Christ, but more: Christ is our Life (Philippians 4:4-7; Colossians 3:1-3; Ephesians 2:4, 5).

John 13

At the end of John 13, God the Holy Spirit tells us of the conversation our Lord Jesus had with Peter about his fall, the fall that would occur that very night, as the Saviour was about to be crucified in Peter's place, bearing his sins in his own body under the wrath of God.

> Simon Peter said unto him, Lord, whither goest thou? Jesus answered him, Whither I go, thou canst not follow me now; but thou shalt follow me afterwards. Peter said unto him, Lord, why cannot I follow thee now? I will lay down my life for thy sake. Jesus answered him, Wilt thou lay down thy life for my sake? Verily, verily, I say unto thee, The cock shall not crow, till thou hast denied me thrice (John 13:36-38).

Read on. Ignore the chapter break. As soon as the Saviour told Peter how horribly he would fall, he gave him a word of sweet assurance, 'Let not your heart be troubled: ye believe in God, believe also in me. In my Father's house are many mansions: if it were not so, I would have told you. I go to prepare a place for you. And if I go and prepare a place for you, I will come again, and receive you unto myself; that where I am, there ye may be also' (John 14:1-3).

When I Fall

There is a great mercy of God we commonly overlook, a mercy for which none of us are sufficiently thankful. It is that the Lord God graciously hedges us about with strong restraints of providence and grace, keeping his people from those grave, outward sins, that give Zion's enemies occasion to blaspheme the name of our God and mock his gospel. He plants his fear deep in the heart, and causes a well of living water to flow through the soul, and keeps us, for the most part, from great acts of iniquity in our outward lives. How we ought to thank him for this great mercy every day, every hour, every moment.

Yes, it is true, sometimes a man who has found grace in the eyes of the Lord, as Noah did, will be found in a drunken stupor, with his shame uncovered, in naked sin before the reprobate. Sometimes a godly man of faith, like righteous Lot, will choose to pitch his tent toward Sodom and choose to stay in the chosen place of wickedness. Sometimes the mighty Samson will lay his head in Delilah's lap. It has happened that a man after God's own heart has committed adultery and even murder. Sometimes even the wisest man will bow to the will of a wicked wife and worship at the altar of an idol, as Solomon did. Sometimes a great preacher, like Peter, will deny the Lord Jesus. Sometimes the most soundly orthodox and most useful preacher will shave his head and take a Jewish vow, like the Apostle Paul did.

Sad falls do occur. They are plainly recorded in Holy Scripture for our learning and admonition; but they are not common occurrences. For the most part, God's saints in this world are graciously kept from such outward displays of iniquity and sin by the restraint of his grace and the restraints of his providence.

That said, I hasten to declare that though we are usually kept from grave and gross outward wickedness, the righteous do fall; and all who are righteous know they fall seven times in a day. 'A just man falleth seven times' (Proverbs 24:16). That is to say, in the totality of his being, in all he is and does, the righteous man, the just continually falls.

Let us hear the words of God's prophet Micah. 'Rejoice not against me, O mine enemy: when I fall, I shall arise; when I sit in darkness, the LORD shall be a light unto me' (Micah 7:8)

My Refuge Still
Yes, I do fall seven times in a day! I lament the fact and wish it were not so. My life is a constant series of falls and failure. But when I fall, Christ is my Refuge. In the midst of all our falling, failure and sin, still God, the Triune Jehovah, declares to his Israel, 'Ye are strangers and sojourners with me'. We are strangers and sojourners but we walk in good company. We are strangers and sojourners with God our Saviour.

Chapter 67

Christ Our Kinsman Redeemer

If thy brother be waxen poor, and hath sold away some of his possession, and if any of his kin come to redeem it, then shall he redeem that which his brother sold. And if the man have none to redeem it, and himself be able to redeem it; Then let him count the years of the sale thereof, and restore the overplus unto the man to whom he sold it; that he may return unto his possession. But if he be not able to restore it to him, then that which is sold shall remain in the hand of him that hath bought it until the year of jubile: and in the jubile it shall go out, and he shall return unto his possession.

Leviticus 25:25-28

And if a sojourner or stranger wax rich by thee, and thy brother that dwelleth by him wax poor, and sell himself unto the stranger or sojourner by thee, or to the stock of the stranger's family: After that he is sold he may be redeemed again; one of his brethren may redeem him: Either his uncle, or his uncle's son, may redeem him, or any that is nigh of kin unto him of his family may redeem him; or if he be able, he may redeem himself.

Leviticus 25:47-49

The Old Testament is full of pictures of the gospel; of grace and salvation in Christ. One of the most instructive, delightful, and thrilling pictures of our Saviour in the Old Testament is that of the kinsman redeemer.

Given at Sinai
The law of the kinsman redeemer is found in Leviticus 25:25-55. Remember, this law was given on Mount Sinai (v. 1) at the very time God gave the law by which sin is condemned, he gave this law by which he shows how he saves his people from their sins. Remember, too, that the context is describing the year of jubilee.

The Lord Jesus Christ, the Son of God, became our Kinsman, our next of kin, our nearest Kinsman. He became one of us so he might redeem us and set us free from bondage. Read the verses in this passage that specifically talk about the kinsman redeemer and his work.

The Redeemed
The first thing we see in this passage is the redeemed. If one of the Jews had fallen into deep poverty by neglect, carelessness, foolishness or any other means, and sold his land to another, and at last sold himself to a stranger, the Lord God here made a way for him to be redeemed.

This is a powerful picture of Adam selling himself and all his race into sin and bondage. When this happened, God made provision for his redemption. Verse 48 says, 'After that he is sold he may be redeemed again'. God gave this law in Israel before anyone needed it, so our great God found a way to redeem his lost ones long before we fell in our father Adam. Redemption was not an after-thought with God, but the eternal purpose of his grace (Romans 8:28-30). The words 'redeemed again' speak of getting something back that has been lost. We were his before we fell. We belonged to him from eternity!

The Redeemer
Second, this chapter speaks about the redeemer. The nearest kinsman had the responsibility of redeeming his brother and his brother's lost property. If a person was forced into slavery, his redeemer purchased his freedom. When debt threatened to overwhelm him, the kinsman stepped in to redeem his homestead and preserve the family. If a family member died without an heir, the kinsman gave his name by marrying the widow and raising a son unto his brother (Genesis 38:8; Deuteronomy 25:5; Ruth 3, 4). When death came at the hands of another man, the redeemer acted as the avenger of blood and pursued the killer (Numbers 35:12-34; Deuteronomy 19:1-3).

The word translated 'redeemer' is the same word translated 'avenger' in Numbers 35:12, where God gave the law concerning the avenger of blood and the cities of refuge. This word is used throughout the Old Testament by the Lord God to describe himself as our Redeemer (Exodus 6:6; Job 19:25; Psalm 103:4; Isaiah 41:14; 43:1; 44:6, 22; 48:20). The implication is clear. He who is our Kinsman Redeemer, the true Kinsman Redeemer, is himself God.

But even God himself could not be our Redeemer except he become our Kinsman; and that is exactly what he did when Christ came into the world. Jesus Christ is God our Kinsman (Hebrews 2:16, 17).

When the Lord Jesus was born, his birth was different from that of any other man. When you begin reading in Matthew chapter one, you read that so and so begat so and so until you come to verse 18, and there is a definite change. The book of God says, 'Now the birth of Jesus Christ was on this wise: When as his mother Mary was espoused to Joseph, before they came together, she was found with child of the Holy Ghost'. He became a man to be our Kinsman Redeemer.

Requirements

Five things were required of the kinsman-redeemer.

He must be near of kin (Leviticus 25:25, 48; Ruth 3:12, 13). He must be able to redeem (Ruth 4:4-6). He must be free of any calamity or need of redemption himself. He must be willing to redeem (Ruth 4:6). Redemption was completed when the price was completely paid (Leviticus 25:27; Ruth 4:7-11). He was required to redeem. If he, for any reason, failed to do so, it was to his open shame.

Christ had the right to redeem us for he is our nearest Kinsman by the incarnation. 'For what the Law could not do, in that it was weak through the flesh, God sending His own Son in the likeness of sinful flesh, and for sin, condemned sin in the flesh' (Romans 8:3). He was like us in every way except he knew no sin. To identify with us he 'made himself of no reputation, and took on him the form of a servant, and was made in the likeness of men' (Philippians 2:7).

The Lord has the power to redeem us as God. That gives infinite merit and efficacy to all his work (2 Corinthians 8:9; Hebrews 1:1-3). Blessed be his name, our nearest Kinsman was willing to redeem us, too (Titus 2:14; 1 Peter 2:24; Hebrews 10:5-15; John 10:16-18).

The Son of God has paid the price for our redemption. Not only is he qualified, willing, and able to redeem, not only has he paid the price of redemption, he has effectually redeemed us by his blood Galatians 3:13; Hebrews 9:12; Ephesians 1:7. Job understood this (Job 19:23-27). He knew that Christ was his Kinsman Redeemer.

The Redemption
But there is one more thing revealed in Leviticus 25 about our Lord Jesus Christ as our Kinsman Redeemer. Verses 26 and 49 speak of the possibility of one being sold into bondage being able to redeem himself. But that cannot possibly have reference to any of us (Psalm 49:7).

What, then, does this refer to? To our great Saviour. For our sakes, the Lord Jesus Christ sold himself into bondage, took our sin and our debt to be his own, and was made to be sin for us. Then, when he died, he redeemed himself from all the debt he had incurred as our Substitute.

Commenting on Psalm 40:12 John Trapp wrote that Jesus Christ was

> ... maximus peccatorum, the greatest of sinners by imputation (2 Corinthians 5:21; Isaiah 53:6), for our sins (which here he calleth his) he suffered. And here his bitter agony in the garden is graphically described. Neither is it absurd to say, that as he bore our sins in his own body upon the tree, he was first redeemed by himself, and afterwards we.

Go back to ancient Israel in the time of the Judges. Can you see Naomi holding her grandson in her arms? Her neighbours said, 'A son has been born to Naomi'! They named him Obed, the father of Jesse, the father of King David (4:17), of the lineage of the Messiah, Jesus Christ (Matthew 1:5). God had redeemed her.

The words of Naomi's friends are a fitting reminder of God's grace in our lives. 'And the women said unto Naomi, Blessed be the LORD, which hath not left thee this day without a kinsman, that his name may be famous in Israel' (Ruth 4:14). We who had lost everything are the redeemed. Let us rejoice in the redemption our great Saviour, the Lord Jesus Christ, our Kinsman Redeemer has obtained for us. He has paid our debt. He has redeemed us from poverty. He has redeemed us from bondage. He has redeemed us from death. He has recovered all we had lost. He did it all that his name may be famous in Israel.

Chapter 68

God's Slaves

And if thy brother be waxen poor, and fallen in decay with thee; then thou shalt relieve him: yea, though he be a stranger, or a sojourner; that he may live with thee. Take thou no usury of him, or increase: but fear thy God; that thy brother may live with thee. Thou shalt not give him thy money upon usury, nor lend him thy victuals for increase. I am the LORD your God, which brought you forth out of the land of Egypt, to give you the land of Canaan, and to be your God. And if thy brother that dwelleth by thee be waxen poor, and be sold unto thee; thou shalt not compel him to serve as a bondservant: But as an hired servant, and as a sojourner, he shall be with thee, and shall serve thee unto the year of jubile: And then shall he depart from thee, both he and his children with him, and shall return unto his own family, and unto the possession of his fathers shall he return. For they are my servants, which I brought forth out of the land of Egypt: they shall not be sold as bondmen ... For unto me the children of Israel are servants; they are my servants whom I brought forth out of the land of Egypt: I am the LORD your God.

Leviticus 25:35-55

I call you to the most ennobling, honourable, and honouring of all service. I am recruiting slaves. I am calling upon you to voluntarily put yourself into slavery, taking the Lord Jesus Christ as your Master

(Matthew 11:28-30). Since the Lord God has redeemed us, since he has saved us by his grace, he claims us as his slaves (vv. 42, 55).[18]

Read this chapter carefully and you will see that the Lord claimed rule over the children of Israel, dictating to them what they were to be and do in all things. He claimed the rule of their property, their families, their time, their money, their affections, even their attitude toward one another and their enemies.

Such a claim is only reasonable. It is only reasonable that we consecrate ourselves to him as voluntary slaves, devoted in all things to him, his honour, his will, and his glory (Romans 12:1, 2). The Holy Spirit tells us exactly what this slavery is in 1 Corinthians 6.

> Know ye not that the unrighteous shall not inherit the kingdom of God? Be not deceived: neither fornicators, nor idolaters, nor adulterers, nor effeminate, nor abusers of themselves with mankind, nor thieves, nor covetous, nor drunkards, nor revilers, nor extortioners, shall inherit the kingdom of God. And such were some of you: but ye are washed, but ye are sanctified, but ye are justified in the name of the Lord Jesus, and by the Spirit of our God (1 Corinthians 6:9-11).
>
> What? know ye not that your body is the temple of the Holy Ghost which is in you, which ye have of God, and ye are not your own? For ye are bought with a price: therefore glorify God in your body, and in your spirit, which are God's (1 Corinthians 6:19-21).

Blessed Fact

Here is a blessed fact. 'Ye are bought with a price.' You are bought. It is this idea of redemption that modern heretics dare to style 'mercantile' and 'commercial'. Mercantile redemption is scriptural. The expression 'bought with a price' is a double declaration of that idea. Christ bought

---

[18] This passage is not an endorsement of slavery by God. The Lord God used what was the custom of the day to teach us the gospel of his grace. The Word of God addresses men and women where they are. He does the same thing in 1 Corinthians 11, using the customary veil of the day as a symbol of a woman's modesty and submission to her husband. This passage no more teaches us to practise slavery than that passage requires women to wear a veil in public worship.

us out from under the law. All he bought with his blood, the Lord has sought out, is seeking out, and will seek out by the almighty, irresistible grace of his Holy Spirit. Those who are sought out by him shall be brought out from among the fallen sons of Adam to experience his grace and mercy at the appointed time of love.

'Ye are bought with a price.' How great the cost! How great the sacrifice! The Father gave his darling Son. The Son of God gave himself for us. The Lord Jesus Christ gave everything for us even to the laying down of his life.

> For ye know the grace of our Lord Jesus Christ, that, though he was rich, yet for your sakes he became poor, that ye through his poverty might be rich (2 Corinthians 8:9).
>
> Forasmuch as ye know that ye were not redeemed with corruptible things, as silver and gold, from your vain conversation received by tradition from your fathers; but with the precious blood of Christ, as of a lamb without blemish and without spot: Who verily was foreordained before the foundation of the world, but was manifest in these last times for you (1 Peter 1:18-20).

How can we measure the price of our redemption? Measure it in the light of dark Gethsemane and the agony there experienced by our Saviour, as he anticipated the horror of being made sin for us. Measure the price of our souls' ransom by the pain of our Lord's betrayal by Judas, by his humiliation in Pilate's judgment hall. Ever measure the cost of your soul's redemption by the light of Calvary. There the Lord Jesus was made sin for us, made a curse for us, punished for us, and died for us, that we might be made the righteousness of God in him!

Both our body and spirit are bought with the precious blood of Christ. This is either a fact, or it is not. 'Ye are bought', or you are not. Are you redeemed? If you are, if this is a fact, it is the fact of your life. Wonder of wonders I am redeemed! If you are redeemed, your redemption will remain to you eternally the grandest of all benefits and blessings. If true at all, it will never cease to be true; and it will never be outdone in importance by any other event.

This fact, the fact we are redeemed by the precious blood of Christ, ought to operate powerfully upon our lives. This ought to be the most powerful influence there is upon our hearts, the most powerful governing principle of our lives.

Blessed Loss

Here is a blessed loss. 'Ye are not your own.' You are not your own provider. Sheep are fed by their shepherd. You are not your own guide. Ships are steered by their pilot. You are not your own father. Children are loved, nurtured and cared for by their parents. We are not our own to waste in idleness, amusement, or making ourselves rich. We are not our own to use, not our own to rule. We belong to God.

We read in Deuteronomy 26:17, 'Thou hast avouched the LORD this day to be thy God ... And the LORD hath avouched thee this day to be his peculiar people'. How honoured we are to avouch that the Triune Jehovah is our God, declaring by our baptism and our confessed faith that we are his; chosen, redeemed, called, and devoted by faith to him. But how indescribably more blessed it is to have the Triune Jehovah avouch that we are his! As soon as the sinner looks to Christ in faith, trusting him as his only Wisdom, Righteousness, Sanctification, and Redemption, he has within him God's own avouched assurance that he is God's. The blood of Christ sprinkled on the conscience, the love of God shed abroad in our hearts by the Holy Ghost gives assurance that 'I am my Beloved's, and my Beloved is mine' (Song of Solomon 6:3). It is this avouchment, that we are God's property, that was confessed in the tithes of the law, and is confessed in the free, voluntary gifts of God's saints in the house of God week by week.

Blessed Slavery

Here is a blessed slavery. 'Your body and your spirit, which are God's'. My brother, my sister in Christ, we belong to God our Saviour. By creation, by sovereign predestination, by eternal election, by special redemption, by irresistible grace, by voluntary surrender, we are altogether God's. Body and spirit include the whole man. We are God's people and God's property. We are always God's. The price having once been paid means we are forever his.

Blessed Responsibility

Here is a blessed responsibility. 'Glorify God in your body, and in your spirit, which are God's.' Glorify God in your body (1 Corinthians

10:31; Colossians 3:12-17), and glorify God in your spirit. It is both our privilege and our desire, as well as our responsibility, to live in this world for the glory of God, only for the glory of God, and always for the glory of God.

Let us daily seek his help that our God may give us wisdom and grace day by day to honour him, honour the gospel of free salvation, and to bring no reproach upon his name, his word, or his church. Compel me by the sweet, irresistible constraint of your Spirit, my God, to 'have a perfect balance and just weight, a perfect and just measure' in all my dealings with men in this world.

Blessed Example

Here is a blessed example of what it is to be God's slave (Isaiah 42:1-4). Our dear Saviour, the Lord Jesus Christ, God's own darling Son, voluntarily became the Servant of the Triune God that he might save us by his grace.

Yes, Jehovah's righteous Servant is God the Son, the Lord Jesus Christ (Exodus 21:5, 6; Psalm 40:6-10; Isaiah 50:5-7; Philippians 2:5-11; Hebrews 10:5-14). The Lord Jesus Christ voluntarily became his Father's Servant to redeem and save his people (Isaiah 50:5-7). He is that One to whom the law of God referred in Exodus 21:5, 6. The bond slave who refused his freedom because he loved his master, his wife, and his children, was typical of our Saviour. In the covenant of grace, before the world began, the Son of God voluntarily made himself his Father's Servant, because he loved his Father, and his chosen family.

It was in this capacity that he spoke in Psalm 40:6-10. Hebrews 10:5-14 explains that the words of our Lord in Psalm 40 referred to his obedience unto death as our Substitute, by which the Lord of glory obtained the everlasting salvation of his chosen. Our great Saviour came into the world in the fulness of time to fulfil his covenant engagements as Jehovah's Servant. And when he had fulfilled those covenant engagements, his people were redeemed, sanctified, and perfected forever by his finished work.

This is the basis of our Lord's exaltation and glory, the means by which he obtained the monarchy of the universe as the God-man, our Mediator (Psalm 2:8; John 17:1-5; Romans 14:9; Philippians 2:5-11). And this is the basis of my appeal to you. Volunteer to be God's slave forever!

O the depth of the riches both of the wisdom and knowledge of God! how unsearchable are his judgments, and his ways past finding out! For who hath known the mind of the Lord? or who hath been his counsellor? Or who hath first given to him, and it shall be recompensed unto him again? For of him, and through him, and to him, are all things: to whom be glory for ever. Amen (Romans 11:33-36).

I beseech you therefore, brethren, by the mercies of God, that ye present your bodies a living sacrifice, holy, acceptable unto God, which is your reasonable service. And be not conformed to this world: but be ye transformed by the renewing of your mind, that ye may prove what is that good, and acceptable, and perfect, will of God (Romans 12:1, 2).

Chapter 69

A Blessing And A Curse

Ye shall make you no idols nor graven image, neither rear you up a standing image, neither shall ye set up any image of stone in your land, to bow down unto it: for I am the LORD your God. Ye shall keep my sabbaths, and reverence my sanctuary: I am the LORD. If ye walk in my statutes, and keep my commandments, and do them; then I will give you rain in due season, and the land shall yield her increase, and the trees of the field shall yield their fruit ... But if ye will not hearken unto me, and will not do all these commandments; and if ye shall despise my statutes, or if your soul abhor my judgments, so that ye will not do all my commandments, but that ye break my covenant: I also will do this unto you; I will even appoint over you terror, consumption, and the burning ague, that shall consume the eyes, and cause sorrow of heart: and ye shall sow your seed in vain, for your enemies shall eat it. And I will set my face against you, and ye shall be slain before your enemies: they that hate you shall reign over you; and ye shall flee when none pursueth you ... But I will for their sakes remember the covenant of their ancestors, whom I brought forth out of the land of Egypt in the sight of the heathen, that I might be their God: I am the LORD. These are the statutes and judgments and laws, which the LORD made between him and the children of Israel in mount Sinai by the hand of Moses.

Leviticus 26:1-46

Hear the Word of the Lord. 'I set before you this day a blessing and a curse' (Deuteronomy 11:26-28). This is God's Word to you and me. It is a word about obedience and disobedience, about great promises of grace and great threatenings of wrath. This twenty-sixth chapter of Leviticus is God's own commentary on his holy law. Here, the Lord God himself tells us the doctrine of all the Levitical Law.

A Fence of Protection

In verses 1, 2 the Lord God graciously sets up a fence of protection for our souls, a fence for which we can never be sufficiently thankful. The fence he has cast around our souls is the blessed fence of public worship. I say, without hesitancy, that this is our greatest earthly blessing, our greatest privilege, the most important aspect of every believer's life.

The Lord God demands that we worship him, and worship him only, because he alone is God.

> Ye shall make you no idols nor graven image, neither rear you up a standing image, neither shall ye set up any image of stone in your land, to bow down unto it: for I am the LORD your God (Leviticus 26:1).

Our God demands our whole heart, our entire soul, our undivided devotion. He will have no rival. Salvation is neither more nor less than knowing and owning the Lord God our Saviour as our God. It is bowing to and worshipping him as he is revealed in Christ, as 'a just God and a Saviour', confessing Christ as Lord (Romans 10:1-13).

If we would worship this holy Lord God, we must worship him in the way he requires. We must worship him in spirit and in truth, without rival (John 4:23; Philippians 3:3). Our worship of God must be spiritual, not carnal worship. All idols, all images, all religious relics, all religious icons such as crosses, pictures of angels, or any representation of God, are prohibited.

In verse 2, the Lord tells us what this worship is. 'Ye shall keep my sabbaths, and reverence my sanctuary: I am the LORD.' This Old Testament requirement of sabbath keeping was a portrayal of faith in Christ. The only way a sinner can know and worship God is by this blessed rest of faith in Christ, by ceasing from his own works and trusting the finished work of Christ, the sinner's Substitute (Matthew 11:28-30; Hebrews 4:9-11). Come to Christ, and rest. In this gospel age we must not keep a legal sabbath of any kind (Colossians 2:16-23). Our Sabbath is Christ. We rest in him.

This commandment to reverence his sanctuary is a great commandment of mercy. The sanctuary in the Old Testament was the place of worship, instruction, and pronounced blessing; the place where God met with men and men met with God, the place of God's dwelling, the house of God. All spiritual declension, all spiritual decay begins with the neglect of public worship. This is the fence the Lord has put around us to keep us from idolatry, to keep us believing, worshipping, and loving him (Hebrews 10:22-27). This is exactly what John and Jude are referring to in 1 John 5:21 and Jude 1:21.

How I give thanks to God for establishing this blessed ordinance of public worship for the honour of his name and the benefit of our souls.

> Thus will I magnify myself, and sanctify myself; and I will be known in the eyes of many nations, and they shall know that I am the LORD (Ezekiel 38:23).

In verses 3-39 the Lord God promises bounteous blessings of grace upon all who obey his commandments and threatens terrible wrath upon all who disobey. Without question, our obedience or disobedience to the revealed will of God are matters of great importance. Let no one imagine otherwise. If we are disobedient to what the Lord God has revealed in his Word, we bring upon ourselves great trouble. He will manifest his disapproval in chastisement. If we are obedient we walk in the path of blessing.

But this passage is not teaching conditional grace. Leviticus 26 is God's explanation of his law. He is here declaring how he always deals with sinners in absolute, strict, unbending justice. The text reaches beyond temporal, earthly blessedness and temporal, earthly wrath.

Promises of Bounteous Grace
In verses 3-13, the Lord God promises bountiful grace to all who obey his commandments. Note that the blessings here promised are seven, the number of perfection and completion; the number of grace. These are 'the precious things of heaven' (Deuteronomy 33:13, 14) promised

to all the sons of Joseph. Understand them spiritually as referring to gospel blessedness and you understand them correctly. The things here promised, using carnal, earthly symbols to portray spiritual, heavenly truths, are blessings of grace promised to the obedience of faith in Christ.

1. Fruitfulness: Our Saviour ascended his throne, having obtained eternal redemption for us, by the sweet, irresistible grace and power of his Spirit. Now he is gathering in his redeemed from the four corners of the earth (vv. 3, 4).

2. Satisfaction and safety: 'Ye shall eat your bread to the full, and dwell in your land safely' (v. 5).

3. Peace: 'And I will give peace in the land, and ye shall lie down, and none shall make you afraid: and I will rid evil beasts out of the land, neither shall the sword go through your land' (v. 6). Where sin abounded grace much more abounds. God not only promises plenteous redemption and plenteous grace, he promises peace with it!

4. Triumph: 'Ye shall chase your enemies, and they shall fall before you by the sword. And five of you shall chase an hundred, and an hundred of you shall put ten thousand to flight: and your enemies shall fall before you by the sword' (vv. 7, 8). 'We are more than conquerors through him that loved us' (Romans 8:37). We overcome and shall overcome all our foes, 'because greater is he that is in you, than he that is in the world' (1 John 4:4). 'No weapon that is formed against thee shall prosper; and every tongue that shall rise against thee in judgment thou shalt condemn. This is the heritage of the servants of the LORD, and their righteousness is of me, saith the LORD' (Isaiah 54:17).

5. Divine favour: 'For I will have respect unto you, and make you fruitful, and multiply you, and establish my covenant with you' (v. 9). When God the Holy Ghost gives us life and faith in Christ, in the sweet experience of his grace, he who is the Seal of the covenant, seals to us all the blessings of the covenant of grace (Ephesians 1:13, 14; Galatians 3:13, 14).

6. Blessings upon the old and the new: 'And ye shall eat old store, and bring forth the old because of the new' (v. 10). Our Saviour promises, 'at our gates are all manner of pleasant fruits, old and new, which I have laid up for thee, O my beloved' (Song of Solomon 7:13).

7. Divine presence: 'And I will set my tabernacle among you: and my soul shall not abhor you. And I will walk among you, and will be

your God, and ye shall be my people. I am the LORD your God, which brought you forth out of the land of Egypt, that ye should not be their bondmen; and I have broken the bands of your yoke, and made you go upright' (vv. 11-13). That is God's promise of salvation to his covenant people. 'Remember me, O LORD, with the favour that thou bearest unto thy people: O visit me with thy salvation' (Psalm 106:4).

What do the commandments of God require? The law, all of it, requires that we love God with all our hearts and our neighbours as ourselves. Remember, Israel's neighbours were their ruthless enemies. There is but one way we can keep God's commandments; and he tells us exactly what that way is. It is believing on the name of his Son, Jesus Christ (1 John 3:23; Romans 3:31; 10:4).

These blessings of grace, promised to all who believe on the Lord Jesus Christ, speak of the perfect, full inheritance of grace in salvation, the blessedness of heaven's eternal glory, the blessedness of eternal life (Ephesians 1:3-7). They speak of that grace and glory God promises to give his people.

There is a day coming when we shall enjoy the rain of heaven, the former and the latter rain, perfectly, by the gift of God (James 1:17). In that day, there will be no barrenness in the earth. The earth shall yield her fruit to the full satisfaction of our souls (Amos 9:13). In that day when our God makes all things new, there shall be nothing to cause us pain or tears, sorrow or sighing. The former things shall be passed away forever, never to rise again (Zechariah 12:8; Revelation 20:6; 21:1-5).

'My soul shall not abhor you' (v. 11). The holy Lord God would have us remember, and forever remember, that all the blessedness we shall enjoy in heaven is a matter of free grace, established to us and given to us by covenant love. We deserve his wrath; but he has given us his grace for Christ's sake; because he loved us with an everlasting love (Psalm 47:1-9).

Threats of Indescribable Wrath

Some who read these lines will not enjoy such blessedness. Infinite bounties of everlasting mercy are reserved for sinners who obey God, who believe on the Lord Jesus Christ. But to you who believe not, the Lord God promises all the horrid terror of his wrath and justice (vv. 14-39).

If you are yet without Christ, without faith, without God, without hope, your rebellion and unbelief have brought misery of heart and soul to you already. Your life is a wreck. You are constantly terrified. But your present misery and terror are only forerunners of hell's everlasting woe! That is what these verses describe. Look at verse 18, and learn this. In hell you shall reap exactly what you have sown. You shall eat the fruit of your own way and be filled with your own devices. 'And if ye will not yet for all this hearken unto me, then I will punish you seven times more for your sins.'

Notice that the Lord promises seven plagues to all who despise his Word. In verse 21 he promises seven more. In verse 24 he promises seven more. In verse 28 he promises seven more. Yet, if you count them, there is not a single time when the number seven is succeeded by seven plagues. There are six, then four, then ten, but never seven. Why? These plagues are symbolic of the complete, perfect justice of God in punishing men according to their deserts. In other words, the greater the light you despise, the greater will be your condemnation. The Lord God says, 'I will appoint over you terror' (v. 16; 2 Corinthians 5:10, 11).

In hell you will experience the everlasting consumption of your soul. A burning ague, burning fever consuming your eyes and that shall everlastingly consume your hope with eternally increasing sorrow of heart. The Triune Jehovah says, 'I will set my face against you' (v. 17). All that you have sought, laboured for, and spent your life to gain will prove vanity and vexation. Wild beasts of darkness, famine in your soul, pestilence in your body, unsatisfied lusts, divine fury, and mockery by your refuge of lies will torment you forever (vv. 18-30).

The Lord God will rid the earth of you and of all evil and cause all his creation to rest. 'Then shall the land enjoy her sabbaths' (vv. 34-36). The wicked and unbelieving, having been cast into hell, will fall upon, trample upon, and devour one another. You shall perish among the heathen.

Read verse 29. Maybe, you will begin to see what awaits you. Behold the wrath of the Lamb! 'And ye shall eat the flesh of your sons, and the flesh of your daughters shall ye eat.' In hell the lost mother shall curse her lost daughter, the lost son will curse his lost father, the lost sinner shall curse his lost pastor forever, wishing them to be damned with whom they are damned!

Such is the death you have chosen. Such is the wrath you deserve. Such is the end to which you run. But this does not have to be your end. In verses 40-46 the Lord God himself, the God whose honour you trample under your feet, whose character you attempt to impugn, whose very being you despise, opens to sinners like us a door of hope.

A Marvellous Call to Repentance
Here the Lord God himself calls hell-bent, hell deserving sinners to repentance, and promises eternal salvation to all who turn to him, confessing their sin, trusting his Son.

> If they shall confess their iniquity, and the iniquity of their fathers, with their trespass which they trespassed against me, and that also they have walked contrary unto me; and that I also have walked contrary unto them, and have brought them into the land of their enemies; if then their uncircumcised hearts be humbled, and they then accept of the punishment of their iniquity: Then will I remember my covenant with Jacob, and also my covenant with Isaac, and also my covenant with Abraham will I remember; and I will remember the land. The land also shall be left of them, and shall enjoy her sabbaths, while she lieth desolate without them: and they shall accept of the punishment of their iniquity: because, even because they despised my judgments, and because their soul abhorred my statutes. And yet for all that, when they be in the land of their enemies, I will not cast them away, neither will I abhor them, to destroy them utterly, and to break my covenant with them: for I am the LORD their God (Leviticus 26:40-44).

There is yet a remnant according to the election of grace who must and shall be saved. Robert Hawker wrote,

> Of this we may be very confident, that wherever a soul is made a partaker of the riches of his grace, most heartily and fully will that soul subscribe to the rights of God's justice. This is accepting the punishment of our iniquity.

But I will for their sakes remember the covenant of their ancestors, whom I brought forth out of the land of Egypt in the sight of the heathen, that I might be their God: I am the LORD. These are the statutes and judgments and laws, which the LORD made between him and the children of Israel in mount Sinai by the hand of Moses (Leviticus 26:45, 46).

That is the message of God in the commandments of the law he gave by the hand of Moses at Sinai. 'He that believeth on the Son hath everlasting life: and he that believeth not the Son shall not see life; but the wrath of God abideth on him' (John 3:36).

Who is a God like unto thee, that pardoneth iniquity, and passeth by the transgression of the remnant of his heritage? He retaineth not his anger forever, because he delighteth in mercy. He will turn again, he will have compassion upon us; he will subdue our iniquities; and thou wilt cast all their sins into the depths of the sea. Thou wilt perform the truth to Jacob, and the mercy to Abraham, which thou hast sworn unto our fathers from the days of old (Micah 7:18-20).

Chapter 70

The Old Store And The New

Ye shall make you no idols nor graven image, neither rear you up a standing image, neither shall ye set up any image of stone in your land, to bow down unto it: for I am the LORD your God. Ye shall keep my sabbaths, and reverence my sanctuary: I am the LORD. If ye walk in my statutes, and keep my commandments, and do them; Then I will give you rain in due season, and the land shall yield her increase, and the trees of the field shall yield their fruit ... And ye shall eat old store, and bring forth the old because of the new. And I will set my tabernacle among you: and my soul shall not abhor you. And I will walk among you, and will be your God, and ye shall be my people. I am the LORD your God, which brought you forth out of the land of Egypt, that ye should not be their bondmen; and I have broken the bands of your yoke, and made you go upright. But if ye will not hearken unto me, and will not do all these commandments; And if ye shall despise my statutes, or if your soul abhor my judgments, so that ye will not do all my commandments, but that ye break my covenant: I also will do this unto you ... I will break the pride of your power; and I will make your heaven as iron, and your earth as brass: And your strength shall be spent in vain: for your land shall not yield her increase, neither shall the trees of the land yield their fruits.

Leviticus 26:1-20

Our great and glorious God is ever gracious, ever good, constantly displaying himself as a God who, unlike all the imaginary gods men have invented, 'delighteth in mercy'. He is a God ready to pardon. We see this even at Mount Sinai, when he gave Moses the tables of his holy law.

Given at Sinai

Remember, what we have before us are the commandments of God given at Mount Sinai, at the very time God gave his law to Moses and to Israel. From chapter 1 through chapter 24, the laws and instructions are things given to the children of Israel while they were in the wilderness. They are commands spoken at the door of the tabernacle. But that which we read in chapters 25-27, we are specifically told, was given at Mount Sinai (25:1, 2; 26:46; 27:34).

We are given all that is revealed in chapter 25 about the sabbatical year to be observed every seven years, the year of jubilee to be observed every fifty years, and the kinsman redeemer. In chapter 26 he declares both the blessing he promised to all who keep his statutes and the curse that shall fall upon those who despise them.

The Lord God is talking here specifically about the statutes regarding the sabbath year, the year of jubilee, and the kinsman redeemer the gospel of Christ. And he tells us that all that is written in this chapter was also given at Sinai (v. 46).

In chapter 27, the Lord summarizes all the Levitical law he gave at Sinai by the hand of Moses. Everything in that law, everything in the law of the Old Testament pointed to and typified our Lord Jesus Christ and his great salvation. Though the specific commands (chapters 1-24) were not given until Israel was in the wilderness, the whole Levitical law was summarized at Sinai (Leviticus 27:34).

Mercy's Voice

The voice of mercy sounds throughout the book of Leviticus. Mercy is God's remedy for woe. At the very foot of Mount Sinai grace sweetly smiles. What is grace but the recovery of lost sinners? Even here, as God gives his holy law, the very law that condemns our race, the gospel shines brightly. What is the gospel, but the revelation of God's salvation in Christ? In saving sinners by his free grace, through the redemption that is in Christ Jesus, justice remains just, truth continues true, and holiness appears holy. Honour bends not from its highest throne. We see these things in the book of Leviticus in a long parade of types and pictures of redemption and grace by Christ.

As we walk through the hallowed ground of these twenty-seven chapters, we see something of the depths of redemption. Here we drink from the cup of wisdom and see clearly that 'where sin abounded grace did much more abound'. Here we see grace reigning through righteousness by Jesus Christ our Lord. Here we see our God in his great glory as 'a just God and a Saviour'.

Sinai's Message

At the giving of his law in Sinai, before the children of Israel started their wilderness wandering, the Lord God graciously impressed upon them not only the perfection and strictness of the law they had broken, but also the method of mercy, salvation, and deliverance from its curse and condemnation. Even at Sinai's fiery mount, the Lord God set before hell-bent sinners the wonder and grace of redemption by Christ. He says to a fallen people, 'I have found a ransom'.

If you go to hell you do so pushing the God of all grace out of your way, hardening your proud neck, setting your face like a flint, sticking your fingers in your ears, covering your eyes, and wilfully choosing death instead of life, wrath instead of mercy, perdition instead of pardon.

The last three chapters of Leviticus are full of instruction for eternity bound sinners. Hear and heed the message of God in these chapters. May the pen of the Almighty write their message upon the table of your heart and mine, for Christ's sake!

Read the first thirteen verses of Leviticus 26. Here we are given the commands of God; the sovereign, holy Lord God against whom we have incessantly sinned from our youth. Yet, they are given in the tender words and phrases of a loving father's counsel to his erring child. In these thirteen verses the Lord God shows us what great blessings of grace he will bestow upon all who obey his Word, upon all who believe on the Lord Jesus Christ.

In verses 14-46 we read about the eternal miseries that will befall the unbelieving rebel. Emphatic pictures are drawn to deter rebellion and persuade the rebel to reconciliation. Two signposts are raised before our eyes. One points to peace and urges us to follow its way. The other warns of misery, wrath, and everlasting torment, and cries, 'Flee! Flee! Flee for your life.'

Believe

The chapter begins by telling us that we must call upon the name of the Lord, we must worship God alone, acknowledging him as the Lord our God, finding rest in him (vv. 1, 2). Salvation is believing God. It is knowing God, trusting God, worshipping God as God, as he reveals himself in his Son, the Lord Jesus Christ (John 17:3).

> Ye shall make you no idols nor graven image, neither rear you up a standing image, neither shall ye set up any image of stone in your land, to bow down unto it: for I am the LORD your God. Ye shall keep my sabbaths, and reverence my sanctuary: I am the LORD (Leviticus 26:1, 2).

The only way of life and peace is faith in Christ. Salvation, eternal life, and rest for our souls is found in Christ. Believing on the Son of God is worshipping God alone in Christ Jesus (Matthew 11:28-30; Romans 10:9-13).

Promises of Grace

The Lord God himself courts rebel sinners, calling us to himself, by promises of bounteous riches of goodness and grace in Christ. In verses 3 to 13 are God's promises of grace given at Mount Sinai.

> If ye walk in my statutes, and keep my commandments, and do them; Then I will give you rain in due season, and the land shall yield her increase, and the trees of the field shall yield their fruit. And your threshing shall reach unto the vintage, and the vintage shall reach unto the sowing time: and ye shall eat your bread to the full, and dwell in your land safely. And I will give peace in the land, and ye shall lie down, and none shall make you afraid: and I will rid evil beasts out of the land, neither shall the sword go through your land. And ye shall chase your enemies, and they shall fall before you by the sword. And five of you shall chase an hundred, and an hundred of you shall put ten thousand to flight: and your enemies shall fall before you by the sword.

For I will have respect unto you, and make you fruitful, and multiply you, and establish my covenant with you. And ye shall eat old store, and bring forth the old because of the new. And I will set my tabernacle among you: and my soul shall not abhor you. And I will walk among you, and will be your God, and ye shall be my people. I am the LORD your God, which brought you forth out of the land of Egypt, that ye should not be their bondmen; and I have broken the bands of your yoke, and made you go upright (Leviticus 26:3-13).

What a dazzling catalogue of goodness this is! Henry Law observed,

It is a picture in which plenteousness abounds. The earth in season yields luxuriant crops. Scarceness and need are buried in deep graves. Peace waves her gentle sceptre. Invading hosts scare not the quiet valleys. No ravening beasts watch for their prey. And if assailing armies make attack, they move to sure defeat. A little band puts multitudes to flight. A happy progeny rejoices in each house.

These things are spoken of in the language of external, earthly things but they convey spiritual blessedness and spiritual delights for our souls, delights scattered by God's infinite hand. These bounties of God are promised to all who walk in his commandments and keep his statues. That is to say, to all who believe on his Son. That is not a fanciful claim. That is exactly what God says obedience to his law is (Romans 3:31; 10:1-4; Galatians 3:19, 24; 1 John 3:23; 5:1-3).

Twelve Sinai Promises

Here are twelve Sinai promises of grace. What the law of God requires, the grace of God supplies, and the gospel of God proclaims.

1. God promises us he will send his rain from heaven, symbolizing his Word, his Holy Spirit, and his grace, at the appointed season (v. 4).

2. God promises his grace toward us will be bounteous and satisfying to our souls. He says, 'My grace is sufficient for thee'.

Then I will give you rain in due season, and the land shall yield her increase, and the trees of the field shall yield their fruit.

And your threshing shall reach unto the vintage, and the vintage shall reach unto the sowing time: and ye shall eat your bread to the full (Leviticus 26:4, 5).

In that day will I make a covenant for them with the beasts of the field, and with the fowls of heaven, and with the creeping things of the ground: and I will break the bow and the sword and the battle out of the earth, and will make them to lie down safely (Hosea 2:18).

We know that all things work together for good to them that love God, to them who are the called according to his purpose (Romans 8:28).

Ho, everyone that thirsteth, come ye to the waters, and he that hath no money; come ye, buy, and eat; yea, come, buy wine and milk without money and without price. Wherefore do ye spend money for that which is not bread? and your labour for that which satisfieth not? hearken diligently unto me, and eat ye that which is good, and let your soul delight itself in fatness (Isaiah 55:1, 2).

3. The Lord God promises safety and security to all who trust his Son. 'And dwell in your land safely' (v. 5).

My sheep hear my voice, and I know them, and they follow me: And I give unto them eternal life; and they shall never perish, neither shall any man pluck them out of my hand (John 10:27, 28).

4. Then God promises peace.

And I will give peace in the land, and ye shall lie down, and none shall make you afraid: and I will rid evil beasts out of the land, neither shall the sword go through your land (Leviticus 26:6).

Therefore it is of faith, that it might be by grace; to the end the promise might be sure to all the seed; not to that only which is of the law, but to that also which is of the faith of Abraham; who is the father of us all, As it is written, I have made thee a father of many nations,) before him whom he believed, even God, who quickeneth the dead, and calleth those things which be not as though they were. Who against hope believed in hope, that he might become the father of many nations, according to that which was spoken, So shall thy seed be. And being not weak in faith, he considered not his own body now dead, when he was about an hundred years old, neither yet the deadness of Sara's womb: He staggered not at the promise of God through unbelief; but was strong in faith, giving glory to God; And being fully persuaded that, what he had promised, he was able also to perform. And therefore it was imputed to him for righteousness. Now it was not written for his sake alone, that it was imputed to him; But for us also, to whom it shall be imputed, if we believe on him that raised up Jesus our Lord from the dead; Who was delivered for our offences, and was raised again for our justification.

Therefore being justified, by faith we have peace with God through our Lord Jesus Christ: By whom also we have access by faith into this grace wherein we stand, and rejoice in hope of the glory of God. And not only so, but we glory in tribulations also: knowing that tribulation worketh patience; And patience, experience; and experience, hope: And hope maketh not ashamed; because the love of God is shed abroad in our hearts by the Holy Ghost which is given unto us. For when we were yet without strength, in due time Christ died for the ungodly. For scarcely for a righteous man will one die: yet peradventure for a good man some would even dare to die. But God commendeth his love toward us, in that, while we were yet sinners, Christ died for us. Much more then, being now justified by his blood, we shall be saved from wrath through him. For if, when we were enemies, we were reconciled to God by the death of his Son, much more, being reconciled, we shall be saved by his life. And not only so, but we also joy in God through our Lord Jesus Christ, by whom we have now received the atonement (Romans 4:16-5:11).

5. The Lord God, our Saviour, promises that all who trust him shall prevail and triumph over their enemies, all of them.

And ye shall chase your enemies, and they shall fall before you by the sword. And five of you shall chase an hundred, and an hundred of you shall put ten thousand to flight: and your enemies shall fall before you by the sword (Leviticus 26:7, 8).

You, being dead in your sins and the uncircumcision of your flesh, hath he quickened together with him, having forgiven you all trespasses; Blotting out the handwriting of ordinances that was against us, which was contrary to us, and took it out of the way, nailing it to his cross; And having spoiled principalities and powers, he made a shew of them openly, triumphing over them in it (Colossians 2:13-15).

And we know that all things work together for good to them that love God, to them who are the called according to his purpose. For whom he did foreknow, he also did predestinate to be conformed to the image of his Son, that he might be the firstborn among many brethren. Moreover whom he did predestinate, them he also called: and whom he called, them he also justified: and whom he justified, them he also glorified. What shall we then say to these things? If God be for us, who can be against us? He that spared not his own Son, but delivered him up for us all, how shall he not with him also freely give us all things? Who shall lay anything to the charge of God's elect? It is God that justifieth. Who is he that condemneth? It is Christ that died, yea rather, that is risen again, who is even at the right hand of God, who also maketh intercession for us. Who shall separate us from the love of Christ? Shall tribulation, or distress, or persecution, or famine, or nakedness, or peril, or sword? As it is written, For thy sake we are killed all the day long; we are accounted as sheep for the slaughter. Nay, in all these things we are more than conquerors through him that loved us. For I am persuaded, that neither death, nor life, nor angels, nor principalities, nor powers, nor things present, nor things to come, nor height, nor depth, nor any other creature, shall be able to separate us from the love of God, which is in Christ Jesus our Lord (Romans 8:28-39).

O my soul, believe God, and chase away your enemies! All who assail and accuse you. All who would condemn you. All who would charge you with evil. All who would separate you from his love, and Satan too (Romans 16:20).

6. God promises to bless us with his favour. 'I will have respect unto you' (Leviticus 26:9). He says, I will look upon you with delight and pleasure. My eye will be upon you to care for you, watching over you to do you good and protect you from all evil. I will turn myself away from all others to you, having a distinct and particular regard for you. Cast all your care on me, and I will care for you.

7. Then he promises to make you fruitful. 'I will have respect unto you and make you fruitful' (v. 9).

But the fruit of the Spirit is love, joy, peace, longsuffering, gentleness, goodness, faith, meekness, temperance: against such there is no law (Galatians 5:22, 23).

They shall still bring forth fruit in old age; they shall be fat and flourishing (Psalm 92:14).

Henceforth I call you not servants; for the servant knoweth not what his lord doeth: but I have called you friends; for all things that I have heard of my Father I have made known unto you. Ye have not chosen me, but I have chosen you, and ordained you, that ye should go and bring forth fruit, and that your fruit should remain: that whatsoever ye shall ask of the Father in my name, he may give it you (John 15:15, 16).

8. Next the Lord graciously promises to multiply us. 'I will have respect unto you and make you fruitful, and multiply you' (v. 9).

Sing, O barren, thou that didst not bear; break forth into singing, and cry aloud, thou that didst not travail with child: for more are the children of the desolate than the children of the married wife, saith the LORD. Enlarge the place of thy tent, and let them stretch forth the curtains of thine habitations: spare not, lengthen thy cords, and strengthen thy stakes; For thou shalt break forth on the right hand and on the left; and thy seed shall inherit the Gentiles, and make the desolate cities to be inhabited. Fear not; for thou shalt not be ashamed: neither be thou confounded; for thou shalt not be put to shame: for thou shalt forget the shame of thy youth, and shalt not remember the reproach of thy widowhood anymore. For thy Maker is thine husband; the LORD of hosts is his name; and thy Redeemer the Holy One of Israel; The God of the whole earth shall he be called (Isaiah 54:1-5).

9. Then, he promises to establish his covenant with you. 'I will have respect unto you and make you fruitful, and multiply you, and establish my covenant with you' (v. 9), his everlasting covenant of grace, ordered in all things and sure (Isaiah 55:3; Jeremiah 31:31-34; 32:38-40).

10. 'And ye shall eat old store, and bring forth the old because of the new' (v. 10).

With those words, the Lord our God promises to every believing sinner a constant supply of grace; grace to our souls forever, grace sufficient to meet our soul's needs without fail. His supplies of wisdom, love, joy, peace, and power to our souls are always more than enough for our needs. The flow of his grace is uninterrupted. If it comes to us in fits and starts, it is because we have put some obstacle in the way, to choke the channel and quench his Spirit.

Why should we have these dismal times of famine in our souls, these times of spiritual deadness and paralysis? In our Father's house there is bread enough and to spare. He promises, 'Ye shall eat of the old store, and bring forth of the old because of the new'.

> Oh how great is thy goodness, which thou hast laid up for them that fear thee; which thou hast wrought for them that trust in thee before the sons of men (Psalm 31:19).

We must not be satisfied with just the old store. Yes, we rejoice in past experiences of grace. Let us never look upon past goodness with contempt. But there is a sense in which we must forget those things that are behind, pull out the old grain to make room for the new. Let us constantly cast away old experiences and come to Christ with empty hearts to be filled anew with the bounty of heaven (Philippians 3:10).

11. The Lord God promises us his constant, abiding presence.

> And I will set my tabernacle among you: and my soul shall not abhor you. And I will walk among you, and will be your God, and ye shall be my people (Leviticus 26:11, 12).

12. The Lord promises to grant to every believer the blest assurance of redemption, grace, and salvation.

> I am the LORD your God, which brought you forth out of the land of Egypt, that ye should not be their bondmen; and I have broken the bands of your yoke, and made you go upright (Leviticus 26:13).

Oh, come to Christ and live! Come, taste and see that the Lord is gracious! Believe on the Lord Jesus Christ, and you are welcomed home as God's child and God's heir. Your seat is at his table. Hear his assuring voice, 'All things are yours ... all are yours, for you are Christ's, and Christ is God's' (1 Corinthians 3:21-23). At every moment you may draw near. You may tell out your every sorrow and your every need. The ears of love receive. The hand of power relieves. Supplies of grace are given largely. Heaven comes down in showers of goodness.

The gift of Christ leaves no gift withheld. 'He who spared not his own Son, but delivered him up for us all, how shall he not with him also freely give us all things?' (Romans 8:32).

Faith finds abundance in the land of grace. For every sin there is a fountain to cleanse. For all unrighteousness there is a glorious robe. 'In the Lord have I righteousness and strength'. For every burden a support is at hand. 'Casting all your care upon him, for he cares for you'. Light, guidance, and peace shine upon our souls from the throne of grace! When Satan terrifies, the cross is seen. When conscience trembles, the dying Saviour shows his hands and side. When the law thunders, Calvary spreads its sheltering wings. When heart-corruptions vex, the Spirit comes with reviving grace.

The past is a wide flood of mercy, the present a river of grace, the future is an ocean of glory. When the end comes and the freed spirit wings its upward flight, who can conceive the rapture? Then our all-glorious Christ is revealed. No distance intervenes. No separation can again occur. If faith finds him so dear, what will be the sight!

When the grave restores its prey and this poor body puts on immortality's attire and shines more brightly than a thousand suns, we shall be like Christ, exactly like Christ forever. One with him in perfection! What then? God then shall be fully known, and fully loved, and fully praised, while endless ages build the glory higher.

Eternal love planned all this blessedness. The blood of Christ purchased it. His promise seals it. His Spirit fits us for it. His power will bring us to it.

Terror, Nothing But Terror

It is sweet joy to linger on this scene. But God in faithfulness presents a contrast. The scene now changes. In verse 14 begins a scene of woe, wrath and terror to you who will not believe on the Son of God.

> But if ye will not hearken unto me, and will not do all these commandments; And if ye shall despise my statutes, or if your soul abhor my judgments, so that ye will not do all my commandments, but that ye break my covenant: I also will do this unto you; I will even appoint over you terror, consumption, and the burning ague, that shall consume the eyes, and cause sorrow of heart: and ye shall sow your seed in vain, for your enemies shall eat it. And I will set my face against you, and ye shall be slain before your enemies: they that hate you shall reign over you; and ye shall flee when none pursueth you. And if ye will not yet for all this hearken unto me, then I will punish you seven times more for your sins. And I will break the pride of your power; and I will make your heaven as iron, and your earth as brass: And your strength shall be spent in vain: for your land shall not yield her increase, neither shall the trees of the land yield their fruits (Leviticus 26:14-20).

God's Word is as fixed as heaven's high throne. He speaks. Performance is at hand. You have madly scorned his rule. You have rashly followed your own heart's desire. Except you repent, nothing but judgment awaits you. The gospel prized is everlasting joy. The gospel scorned is everlasting woe. O Holy Spirit of God, grant that these who now read these lines may hear the voice of the Son of God by your power and live!

> He that believeth on the Son hath everlasting life: and he that believeth not the Son shall not see life; but the wrath of God abideth on him (John 3:36).

Chapter 71

Public Worship

Ye shall make you no idols nor graven image, neither rear you up a standing image, neither shall ye set up any image of stone in your land, to bow down unto it: for I am the LORD your God. Ye shall keep my sabbaths, and reverence my sanctuary: I am the LORD. If ye walk in my statutes, and keep my commandments, and do them; Then I will give you rain in due season, and the land shall yield her increase, and the trees of the field shall yield their fruit.

Leviticus 26:1-4

Leviticus 26:1-4 gives us instruction about worship, specifically about public worship. Worship is, at least in part, the act of paying honour to God as God. The words used in the Word of God for worship speak of a bowing or falling down, of reverence and obeisance, of humility and surrender, of praise and honour to God. But there is nothing in the average church service that is even remotely related to the honour of God.

In the typical 'worship service' of the modern church everything is done for the exaltation of the flesh, the pampering of human pride, and the recognition and praise of men. We greet men, turn around and shake hands, recognise everything men do. In general, churches and preachers do everything possible to bow and scrape before human flesh as though man were God and God Almighty were a beggar, pleading with us to get a little attention. Today, we praise men and women for blessing us with their presence in the house of God. In the Bible, men praised God for the privilege of coming.

Most 'worship services' today are nothing more than religious pep rallies designed to get more people to come, raise more money, perform more baptisms, and build bigger buildings than the next church around the corner. There are few who worship God!

Can a local church have a true worship service? We can, indeed. I am no expert. I do not pretend to know a great deal about this business of worship. But I do have some suggestions about what we can do, some things that may help us to worship God when we gather for public worship.

1. Make the entire service a 'worship service'. You cannot have both religious promotions and divine worship. We cannot entertain men and worship God. It is impossible to honour man and glorify God. Let God's glory be the theme in all our services, from the first hymn to the final Amen. Maybe, just maybe, if we seek the glory of God, we will be privileged to see the glory of God.

2. Eliminate all excess baggage. Everything that interferes with the worship of God must go. How important are the announcements? Could they be pinned up or written in a bulletin? There is no need to work up people's interest and enthusiasm by exciting church promotions and programs. Spiritual enthusiasm (if you will permit me to use such a word) is found in and maintained by the gospel of Christ. It is inspired by God the Holy Ghost. It is derived from the knowledge of the love, mercy, grace, and glory of God in Christ. Enthusiasm, faithfulness, or generosity stirred by any other means but the gospel itself is not genuine and will sour, not enhance, true worship.

3. Stick to the gospel. Heresy in music is just as bad as heresy in the pulpit. A hymn or special music that is not thoroughly consistent with the gospel is out of place in the house of God. Anything short of the gospel does not belong in a worship service. Even our prayers and perhaps especially our prayers, should be filled with the gospel. It is amazing what the gospel will do for men when it is the sum and substance of their worship.

Oh, that men would worship God! Let us deliberately and continually clean the house of the Lord, taking everything that has nothing to do with the worship of our God, the glory of God, and the preaching of the gospel out to the garbage dump.

Worship is never defined in the Word of God. But there are several words used in the book of God that give us an indication of what is involved in the business of worship. I have already hinted at this. The different words translated 'worship' in the Bible mean 'to bow down in reverence, awe, and obeisance', 'to prostrate one's self before the Lord', 'to stand in awe before God', 'to supplicate the throne of grace', and 'to serve the one true and living God of heaven and earth', 'to kiss the hand of our Master'.

We recognise there is no sense in which believers are under the law. We do not observe holy days, new moons, and sabbath days. We do not offer sacrifices on material altars. We do not recognise any place on earth as a holy place. We have no earthly priesthood, no earthly altar, and no earthly sanctuary. We do not practise circumcision as a matter of obedience to God, or observe any of the carnal ordinances of the Mosaic Age. We do not live under the rule of the law's terror. Why? Because 'Christ is the end of the law'.

But that does not mean that the types and shadows of the law are of no value to us. The types and shadows of the law are full of instruction. In this passage we are given very clear words of instruction concerning the worship of our God in the assembly of his saints.

Great Privilege

The greatest privilege men and women have this side of eternity is the privilege of worshipping God in the assembly of his saints. There is nothing on this earth so important to your soul as the worship of God in the assembly of his saints. 'As for me, I will come into thy house in the multitude of thy mercy: and in thy fear will I worship toward thy holy temple' (Psalm 5:7).

Multitudes who profess to be Christians, lovers of God, believers in the Lord Jesus Christ, and promoters of righteousness, wilfully absent themselves from the house of God and despise the blessed privilege of public worship. They justify their actions and excuse their disobedience by pointing to personal responsibilities, inconveniences, or objectionable things connected with the local church. A person determined to walk in a course of disobedience never lacks for excuses to do so. But you will never find justification for neglecting the worship of God in Holy Scripture.

In Nehemiah's day, the children of Israel, who had long been without the privileges of worship in the house of God, made a covenant and took an oath saying, 'We will not forsake the house of our God' (Nehemiah 10:39). The Shunammite woman rode a donkey every sabbath day to hear God's prophet at Carmel, though her husband objected to it (2 Kings 4:23). In David's time, the saints of God 'passed through the valley of Baca' to worship God at Zion (Psalm 84:6). In Daniel's day, the children of God ran here and there 'to increase knowledge', to know more of the Lord God (Daniel 12:4). Zechariah tells us that in his days, the inhabitants of one city went to another, saying, 'Let us go speedily to pray before the Lord, and to seek the Lord of hosts' (Zechariah 8:21). Our Lord and his disciples went to considerable trouble and inconvenience to meet together and worship God. On the day appointed, he and his disciples were found in the house of God, worshipping (Mark 1:21; Luke 4:16). The Ethiopian Eunuch journeyed from Ethiopia to Jerusalem to worship God, seeking to know him of whom the prophets spoke (Acts 8:25-35).

Call it fanaticism if you choose, I say anyone who talks about being a Christian, who talks about worshipping God and about being a believer, and yet wilfully neglects the worship of God ought to blush with shame for his obvious hypocrisy. All who know God in the experience of his grace delight in worshipping him.

David's Example
David, the man after God's own heart, was cut from a different bolt of cloth. He found pleasure and satisfaction in daily prayer and meditation. Daily, private, personal worship was a characteristic of his life. With the rising of the morning sun, his heart was lifted up to God. Every morning he directed his prayer to the throne of grace and looked to his Lord with a heart of faith. Every evening he gave thanks to God and laid his head on his pillow in the sweet rest of faith. That is the way to begin and end every day!

Blessed is the man or woman who worships God in private. Let all who know and trust the living God worship him daily. Let all who follow Christ in the path of faith and obedience follow him also to the solitary place of private prayer. I would do everything within my power to promote and encourage private worship among the saints of God. Let every priest of God offer the daily sacrifices of prayer and praise to the Lord. But there is something even more important than private worship. Does that surprise you? I know most people who are genuinely concerned for the glory of God and the worship of God rank personal, private worship above all things in the life of faith. But I am convinced that public worship, if it is true worship, is even more important than private worship. David, the sweet singer of Israel, gave the highest possible regard to the matter of public worship (Psalm 5:7).

Without neglecting private worship, he said, 'As for me, I will come into thy house in the multitude of thy mercy: and in thy fear will I worship toward thy holy temple'. He could not force others to worship God, and would not if he could. 'But', he says, 'as for me, I will come into thy house'. That is to say, 'I will come into the place of public worship in the assembly of God's saints, to worship the Lord my God'.

When he came into the place of worship with the saints of God, David was determined truly to worship the Lord. He says, 'In thy fear will I worship toward thy holy temple'. David resolved in his heart, at every appointed time to come with God's saints into the place of public worship, there to worship God in heaven, in the temple of his holiness.

Look at David's words a little more closely and ask the Spirit of God to apply them to your heart, that his words may become the expression of your own hearts' resolve. 'I will come into thy house.' The house of God is the congregation of the saints wherever they gather in public assembly to worship God (1 Timothy 3:15).

'I will come into thy house in the multitude of thy mercy.' It is not enough merely to 'go to church'. We must come into the house of God in faith, trusting the Lord's mercy. There is a multitude of mercies with God in Christ. Sinners need mercy. We must come to the place of public worship as sinners trusting God's abundant mercy in Christ. If we do not come as sinners seeking mercy, we will not worship. But sinners looking to Christ for mercy always find a multitude of mercy in him (Luke 18:13, 14). In him we find everlasting, covenant mercy (Jeremiah 31:31-34), sin-atoning, redeeming mercy (Romans 3:24-26), effectual, saving mercy (Micah 7:18-20), immutable, preserving mercy (Malachi 3:6), and daily, providential mercy (Romans 8:28). Truly, 'It is of the Lord's mercies that we are not consumed, because his compassions fail not' (Lamentations 3:22). Every worshipper in God's house finds it so.

599

'And in thy fear will I worship toward thy holy temple'. We must come to the house of God with reverence and godly fear to worship him; that is, to see him, to hear him, to adore him, to praise him, and to obey him. This was David's resolve. May it ever be yours and mine. May God give us grace to make public worship our delight and truly to worship him in the assembly of his saints.

I want, by the Spirit of God and by the Word of God, to show you that public worship is the single most important aspect of the believer's life. When David was banished from Jerusalem, the place of public worship, he envied even the sparrows who made their nests in the house of God. His heart longed not for the throne, the riches, or the power that had been taken from him, but for the assembly of God's saints in public worship. When the blessed privilege of public worship was taken from him for a short time, nothing was more important or precious to God's child (Psalm 84:1-4, 10).

The fact is, all who are born of God love the assembly of God's saints in public worship, and love the ministry of the gospel. There are no exceptions. God's people will not willingly absent themselves from the worship of God.

It is true, there are many who very strictly attend, and even love, the outward service of public worship, who do not know the Lord. Their outward worship is nothing but a show of hypocrisy, for they never worship God in private. But anyone who wilfully neglects and despises the public assembly of the saints for worship, also neglects and despises private worship. And those who do not worship God, do not know God.

Most of us are very busy with countless cares and responsibilities. The cares and pleasures of life in this world consume almost all our time and attention and reveal our priorities. For those things that are really important to us such as work, a dinner engagement, a social visit, a golf game, a fishing trip, we set dates, make appointments, and arrange our lives accordingly. But when it comes to the worship of God, people have a different attitude. The difference is obvious. You care about those other things.

Those who are truly God's people love the house of God and the worship of God. They arrange their lives around the worship of God. Nothing ever comes up, over which they have control, to keep them from the house of God. They see to it that when the saints of God gather for worship, they are among them, unless their absence is genuinely unavoidable. Their faithfulness in the matter of public worship is much more than a matter of duty. It is their delightful choice. Public worship is the single most important aspect of their lives in this world. Nothing is more important to the children of God in this world than the public assembly of the saints for worship; and that public assembly of the saints for worship is the local church, the congregation of the Lord, the house of God.

Five Reasons
Why do God's people place such importance upon the public worship of the local church? Let me show you five reasons for this.

1. This is the place where God meets sinners in saving mercy. It is true God uses personal witnessing, tracts, recordings, books, and other instruments of gospel instruction to call his elect to life and faith in Christ, but generally God saves his sheep in the congregations of his saints when they are gathered for worship (Acts 2:1, 37-41). Sinners in need of mercy should seek mercy where mercy is always found in great abundance; and mercy is always found in the house of God. God's saints know themselves to be sinners in need of mercy; so they come, with all their needs, to the house of mercy, seeking the Lord.

2. This is the place where our family gathers. Every true local church is a family of believers. When the church gathers for worship, it is the gathering of our family for sweet and blessed fellowship in the gospel. Family members need each other, comfort each other, and help each other, because they love each other.

3. This is the place where the Lord Jesus Christ meets with his people. Our Saviour promised that wherever his people gather in his name, he will be with them (Matthew 18:20). To gather in Christ's name is to gather by faith in his name, for the honour of his name, and to worship in his name. If only two or three gather to worship the Son of God, he will meet with them. The old man, Simeon, found God's salvation, the Lord Jesus Christ, in the temple, the appointed place of public worship (Luke 2:25-32). If we would see Christ, we must come with his saints when they gather in the place of public worship.

4. This is the place where God deals with men. Each local congregation of believers is the house and temple of the living God (1 Corinthians 3:16, 17; 1 Timothy 3:15). God reveals his glory, gives out his law, makes known his will, bestows his blessings, and instructs his

people in his temple, his church. It is in this place that God speaks to men by his Spirit through his Word.

In all ages the people of God have been known and identified by their public gatherings for worship. Wherever God has had a people in this world, he has had a congregation to worship him. Sheep are always found in flocks. The only sheep who are alone are either lost or sick. God's elect are his sheep. No matter how few they have always gathered together in public worship. In the public assembly they bear public, united testimony to the world of their Saviour's grace and glory. As an assembled gathering and body of believers they strengthen, cheer, comfort, encourage, edify, and help one another by prayer, praise, and the preaching of the gospel.

From the beginning of the Bible to the end, there is a clear line of succession in this matter of public worship. Cain and Abel came to worship God in a public assembly. Noah's first act after the flood was an act of public worship to celebrate God's saving grace. Wherever the patriarchs pitched their tents in days of old, they erected an altar for worship. Throughout the Mosaic economy, the Israelite who did not worship God in the tabernacle or temple was cut off from the congregation. Throughout the book of Acts, wherever God's children were scattered by persecution, they soon gathered in public assemblies for the worship of God.

Public worship is an identifying mark of true believers. With David, every saved sinner is resolved to worship God, saying, 'As for me, I will come into thy house in the multitude of thy mercy: and in thy fear will I worship toward thy holy temple'. By this let each examine himself. Those who willingly and habitually absent themselves from the worship of God do not know God. A person may faithfully attend the church of God who does not know God; but no one is faithful to Christ who is not faithful in public church assembly for worship.

5. The neglect of public worship is the first step towards total apostasy (Hebrews 10:23-31). Seldom do men and women turn away from Christ and the gospel of his grace suddenly. Usually the charms of the world take people by degrees, gradually. Apostasy is usually so gradual that those who forsake Christ do not even realise they have forsaken him. How many there are who never attend, or seldom attend, the worship of God, who yet foolishly presume they are children of God. Their continued forsaking of the assembly of God's saints is proof

they never really knew the Lord Jesus Christ in saving faith (1 John 2:19). Those who wilfully neglect the assembly of God's saints for public worship, though they may know the truth of God, yet tread underfoot the Son of God, counting the blood of the covenant a useless thing, and despise the Spirit of grace (Hebrews 10:25, 26, 29).

Our Duty and Choice

The Worship of God is the duty of all men. Leviticus 26:1-4 is not a kindly, wise recommendation. It is the command of God. Yet, no one can worship the Holy Lord God who does not worship him freely.

The Lord God commands us to worship him and him alone, because he is God. 'For I am the Lord your God.' We are to worship him and worship him exactly according to his Word, in precisely the way he requires. The reference here to graven images, standing images, and images of stone appears to have direct reference to what is recorded in Exodus 20:22-26.

We are to set aside a fixed time to worship our God. 'Ye shall keep my sabbaths.' The Jews of old were required to arrange their lives around the appointed day for the worship of God. No excuses were accepted. It mattered not who came visiting, what came up, or what pressing demands arose. God said, 'Ye shall keep my sabbaths'.

No, we do not keep sabbath days of any kind in this gospel age. The Lord strictly forbids that in Colossians 2:16. Christ is our Sabbath. We rest in him. Yet, just as the Jews of old marked their calendars by fixed days of divine worship, we are to worship God at appointed, fixed times, arranging our lives around those times.

There is no precept in the Word of God requiring that we worship on Sunday; but that has been the day set aside for public worship since apostolic times. John calls it 'the Lord's day'. In the book of Acts the disciples met on the first day of the week. Probably, they did so because the Lord Jesus arose from the dead on Sunday. It is important for us to have a set time for our worship services so everyone knows when to come, and because we are apt to neglect that for which we do not set a time. We set a time for those things that are important to us so that we will not allow other things to interfere with them. If we do not set a time for the worship of God, we will not worship him. From the beginning of human history, God's saints have had set times for public worship.

Not only does the Lord require we set aside a fixed time to worship him, allowing nothing to interfere with it, he also requires we do so with reverence. 'Ye shall reverence my sanctuary' (Ecclesiastes 5:1, 2; Habakkuk 2:20; Hebrews 12:28). Our great, all-glorious God deserves our utmost reverence; and he demands it. What is reverence? The definition is broad. Reverence involves awe, respect, love, adoration, esteem, special regard, and honour. When the Lord commands us to reverence his sanctuary, he is telling us to stand in awe in his sanctuary.

How do we reverence God's sanctuary? How do we reverence God in his sanctuary? The building in which we meet is a house of worship, but it is not a sanctuary, a holy place, it is the place where we come together to worship our God. As such, it ought to be reverenced by us. It is to be maintained, adorned, and used with reverence for our God.

The assembly of God's saints, every local church, is God's house, his temple, his sanctuary (1 Corinthians 3:16; Ephesians 2:22). When we come together to worship God, we do so with reverence. Everything about us ought to display reverence for our God and his worship.

I do not mean we should cringe before God, but we should respect him. I do not mean we should put on a show of respect for men, but we should truly be respectful and reverent in the house of God. We should always be punctual in attendance, attentive in hearing, singing, and prayer, and appropriate in attire.

Yes, it is our duty, as well as our privilege, to worship God, to celebrate his praise, to confess our faith in Christ, to encourage, comfort, and edify his people, and to spread his gospel. Yet, in its very essence, worship is a free, voluntary thing. It is something that cannot be forced, except by the sweet force of irresistible grace (Ezra 2:68, 69).

As the grace of God operating towards his people is free, so the grace of God operating in his people is free. We know and rejoice in the fact that every blessing of grace and providence, as well as every blessing of heavenly glory, is free (Romans 8:32; 1 Corinthians 2:12; 3:21; Ephesians 1:3). What God does for us he does simply because it is his will to do so. He gains nothing by it and would lose nothing if he did not do it. Grace is God's good pleasure, the good pleasure of his will toward us. Even so, whatever the believer does for his God he does simply because it is his good pleasure to do so. He is not motivated by either the fear of punishment or the hope of reward. All he offers to God is offered freely.

As we have freely received the grace of God, so we must freely proclaim the grace of God to all men (Matthew 10:7, 8). Paul said, 'I have preached to you the gospel of God freely' (2 Corinthians 11:7). God's servants are worthy of their hire (Luke 10:7; 1 Corinthians 9:7-14; 1 Timothy 5:18). But God's servants are not hirelings. I cannot imagine anything more offensive to a gospel preacher than to have someone ask him how many people, or how much money he would have to have to go anywhere to preach the gospel. Neither can I imagine a gospel preacher asking for anything as a condition for his services as a preacher. We preach the gospel freely, trusting God to supply our needs as he sees fit. God's saints worship him freely (Psalm 54:6, 7).

Both private worship and public worship are to God's people free, uncoerced acts. Worship forced, or performed in dread of punishment or desire of gain, is not worship at all. It is the pretentious act of a mercenary servant. Sinners saved by the grace of God give freely of their means to maintain and promote the worship of God (Ezra 2:68, 69; 7:13-15; 2 Corinthians 9:7). Those to whom much is forgiven love much; and love is manifest in two ways: doing and giving. God does not need any of us. What can a man do for God? Nothing! But the Lord allows us the privilege of giving to the cause of Christ, ministering to his people, maintaining the repair of his house, and caring for his servants. These God receives as done to himself, and his people do freely, as unto the Lord.

> I was glad when they said unto me, Let us go into the house of the LORD (Psalm 122:1).

I was glad because there was a place to go, someone asked me to go, I wanted to go, I could go, and I did go. I was glad because there I met God my Saviour!

Our Own Best Interest

We do not worship and serve our God for gain. Yet, it is in our own best interest to worship him. All spiritual declension and decay in our souls begins with the neglect of divine worship. Our souls' fatness and prosperity comes as a direct result of worshipping our God. We cannot grow in the grace and knowledge of our Lord Jesus Christ, except by feeding at his banqueting table, spread in his house. We cannot walk with God, if we refuse to walk with him in his house.

> If ye walk in my statutes, and keep my commandments, and do them; Then I will give you rain in due season, and the land shall yield her increase, and the trees of the field shall yield their fruit (Leviticus 26:3, 4).

Solomon teaches us the wisdom in heeding this instruction (Proverbs 3:1-18). Let me remind you of that which we have seen in the book of Leviticus which is essential to the worship of our God.

We must worship God, celebrating all his attributes, giving thanks and praise to him for all his wonderful works. We must worship at his Altar, Christ. We must worship through the mediation of his Priest, Christ. We must worship through his Sacrifice, Christ. We must come with a need he alone can fill. We must have a prophet to deliver his Word. We must keep his sabbath resting in Christ (Matthew 11:28-30).

Chapter 72

A Call To Voluntary Consecration

And the LORD spake unto Moses, saying, Speak unto the children of Israel, and say unto them, When a man shall make a singular vow, the persons shall be for the LORD by thy estimation ... These are the commandments, which the LORD commanded Moses for the children of Israel in mount Sinai.

Leviticus 27:1-34

As the Lord God our Saviour, the Triune Jehovah, has proved himself utterly consecrated to us in redeeming and saving us by the sacrifice of his own dear Son, so we ought to utterly consecrate ourselves to our God. That is the message of this last chapter of Leviticus.

This twenty-seventh chapter is all about vows and gifts made to God. Whether you call them vows, or resolutions, or determinations, or promises, they all amount to the same thing, and in this chapter, the Lord God gives specific instructions which we need to understand.

I must point out immediately that in all the Scriptures, both Old and New Testaments alike, God never commands a vow. Vows are never mandatory, never obligatory upon the people of God. We do not have to promise God anything in order to get something from him. God is a Giver. He delights in giving. That is his nature (James 1:17). Because God is love, he delights in giving.

> Love ever lives
> And ever stands with open hands
> And while it lives, it gives
> For this is love's prerogative
> To give and give and give.

The Lord God is always giving. His gifts are voluntary. All we do for God our Saviour must be voluntary, constrained by nothing but his love for us and in us. 'The love of Christ constraineth us.'

Yet, there is something innate in human beings that makes us want to vow, to promise, to make resolutions to God. When he left home, Jacob made a vow to God. Jephthah made a vow and sacrificed his only child to the Lord. Hannah made a vow and consecrated her only son, Samuel, to the Lord.

The Scriptures speak of many others who made vows to the Lord. The Lord never requires such vows. But the Scriptures everywhere teach that once a vow is made before God, it is to be kept (Numbers 30:1, 2).

Christ's Vow
Assuredly, these laws have reference to our Lord Jesus Christ, the one who honoured God, swearing to his own hurt as our covenant Surety and changed not (Psalm 15:4; Proverbs 6:1, 2). Our all-glorious Redeemer consecrated himself to God as his righteous Servant and swore he would do his will, laying down his life as our sin-atoning Substitute, thereby saving us from our sins and reconciling God's elect to him (Hebrews 9:12; 10:1-14).

Voluntary Consecration
But Leviticus 27 is specifically talking about you and me. The vows spoken of here are matters of voluntary consecration. The firstlings of the flocks and herds, the firstfruits of the fields, and the tithes are specifically exempted as things belonging to God already (vv. 26-30). The book of Leviticus closes with a call to voluntary consecration.

Leviticus is truly, a radiant jewel in the crown of Holy Scripture. It stands as a fruitful tree in a rich garden of delight. Blessed are they who gather wisdom from its heavy boughs.

These last words of the book come from Moses' pen with solemn weight. They set us down, as it were, on a high mountain, from which we survey the traversed plain through which we have come.

These are the commandments, which the LORD commanded Moses for the children of Israel in mount Sinai (Leviticus 27:34).

These commandments bring the whole book into view, urging us to survey the entire thing and count our gains before we move onward. Let us do that. Let us look over the book and count up our gains. Then, I will give you the message of this twenty-seventh chapter.

Christ the Theme
One fact is as obvious as it is paramount. The book of Leviticus is about our Lord Jesus Christ and his great work of redemption. We read it aright only when we read it in the light of his presence, see him upon each page, hear him identify himself in each picture.

Have we found him and walked with him upon this fruitful ground? Is he more clearly seen, more fully known? Is he more fully enshrined in our hearts? Is he the mainspring of our lives? Henry Law said, 'Christ is the juice, the life, the heart-blood of Leviticus'. If we do not read the book this way, a veil is over our eyes and we grope in darkness amid the glorious rays of the Sun of Righteousness who shines upon these pages of Inspiration. Christ is our Sacrifice, Altar, Priest, Satisfaction, Mercyseat, Light, Guide, Bread, Acceptance, Wisdom, Righteousness, Sanctification, Redemption, God and Saviour,

God is Love
Seeing Christ as the theme of this book, we see that our God is love. The Son reveals the Father. The gift proclaims the Giver. Here golden letters write God's name of love. Hear it, O Heaven! Rejoice O Earth! God's infinite mercy, grace, and love for perishing sinners shines forth brightly in redemption's plan. He calls his Son to bear the sinner's sins. He lays all help upon one mighty Helper. Such a scheme is as a flood of grace bursting from springs of love. The first thought and the last is love. Because this blessed book of Leviticus exhibits Christ, it calls us to adore our God as Love (John 3:16; Romans 5:8; 1 John 3:16; 4:9, 10, 19).

God is Just

But there is more to the gospel than the love of God. The love of God chose us. The love of God sent his Son to die for us. But God's love could never have saved us apart from the satisfaction of his justice. The book of Leviticus, with all its sacrifices; highlighting and describing the altar, the priest, and the mercy seat, tell us that he is both 'a just God and a Saviour' (Isaiah 45:20-25; Romans 3:24-26).

Desire To Bless

This book is a marvellous display of God's desire, determination, and delight in blessing sinners with grace who fully deserve his wrath. Commandment after commandment, picture after picture, ceremony after ceremony, sacrifice after sacrifice, promise after promise sets before us the gospel of God.

Types and figures are profusely given. Every method imaginable is used to picture Christ. Here are clear models of his saving work. Part after part moves like a procession of grace before our eyes. One is exhibited. Another comes, then another follows. But all have one purpose and design, to set Christ crucified before our eyes, that we may behold him. In every portion of this book, 'Christ is All'. We cannot read it aright and doubt God's mind. Throughout these 27 chapters the God of all grace says, 'I will be gracious, forgiving iniquity, transgression and sin', because 'He delighteth in mercy'.

Who can harden his heart against such mercy? Who can draw back from such grace? Who can resist such love? Who can read these pages and follow the signposts at every intersection pointing to Refuge, and yet go to death and eternal destruction in hell? Only he that being often reproved hardens his heart.

God's Method of Grace

Leviticus also graphically displays God's method of grace. It shows us our Saviour and shows us how he saves. This is a blood-stained book. Its ceremonies are full of death. Its pages groan with the cries of slaughtered beasts.

Behold, Christ is here! He cries not, nor lifts up his voice in the streets. He makes no effort to compromise justice. He seeks neither mitigation nor reprieve. He grants his poor, ruined, doomed people are lost; totally and helplessly undone and writes 'condemned' on each one.

He acknowledges that each has justly earned eternal hell, endless agony, everlasting destruction from the presence of the Lord. He acknowledges, in every type, Jehovah's glory in demanding death.

Yet, he claims the right to save by substitution. He pleads the covenant, which gives him the right of redemption as Kinsman and Surety. He comes as our representative man by eternal compact. The sinful seed are flesh and blood, so he takes our nature. He assumes our flesh and thus becomes our Kinsman-redeemer. If flesh must suffer, he is flesh. If the soul must agonize, a human soul is his, he is wholly fit to bear our sins in his body, to suffer, and to die.

He leaps into the place of the guilty. With eager heart he mounts the altar. His people's sins are piled upon him and made his. The hateful load is bound upon his back and strapped to his shoulders. He endures all the shame, ignominy, and torment of God's holy, unmitigated wrath and justice that we deserved, until every debt is fully paid, every crime is completely cancelled, and every sin totally blotted out of the book of God's remembrance! He drinks the cup until every dreg is drained. The sword of justice is sheathed within his heart, and he cries, triumphantly, 'It is finished'.

Salvation hangs upon him: his person, his obedience, his death. Until this is seen, our souls drift hopelessly toward shores of woe. Oh, it is worth ten thousand times ten thousand worlds, to be assured that death has died, that vengeance is satisfied, and our sins are all gone, our debt fully paid, and that he who did it all is the Lamb of God, who 'shall see of the travail of his soul and shall be satisfied'.

Here, in Leviticus, in this book of law, other words like mercy, grace, and love are written in blazing gospel letters, shining brightly in the face of our crucified Saviour. There is the altar, prominently standing before all. What is that, but the cross of Christ? Victims without number are slain. What are they but pictures and types of the Lamb of God? A stream of blood flows constantly. Each drop displays the wounded Saviour and the dying Lamb. Priests spare not the death blow. The uplifted arm shows justice with the avenging sword. The blazing fire consumes the sacrifice. Here all demands of wrath and justice are met. God meets sinners in the tabernacle at the mercy seat, declaring, 'God has reconciled sinners to himself by the sacrifice of his own darling Son'. All that is here revealed points directly to the Curse-bearer hanging upon the tree. The whole book speaks of Christ taking away guilt, of God inflicting wrath upon him, of sinners ransomed by his death, and of wrath drowned in the God-man's blood.

A Question

Here is a question with which I pray the Holy Spirit will pierce your heart and melt it to repentance, granting you faith in Christ. What is your profit from this book? Each sacrifice allures you to Christ. Each ceremony brings the Saviour before your eyes. Each altar is a call to Calvary. 'Why will ye die?' Are there no charms in the crucified Christ for you?

> Is it nothing to you, all ye that pass by? Behold, and see if there be any sorrow like unto my sorrow, which is done unto me, wherewith the LORD hath afflicted me in the day of his fierce anger (Lamentations 1:12).

Is the all-lovely unlovely in your eyes? Is the all-precious vile to you? Do you scorn the gift of God? Dare you cast heaven's glory to the wind? Dare you trample underfoot the blood of heaven's Darling?

Here is Christ. Here is the Saviour you need. Believe on him and live forever. Read this book again. Its pages cry, 'Sin need not be your ruin'. There is a death which saves from death. There is a stream which cleanses every stain. There is a blood sacrifice that redeems and a Saviour who saves. If by his grace you lay hold on him, all is pardoned. Do not leave Leviticus, until you see salvation's glorious scheme, until you see the God-man bleeding in your place, until you see all your transgressions laid on him, punished in him, and put away by him.

Assurance, Comfort, and Joy

If you have eyes to see, thrice-happy you are! Blessed of God you are! You are God's child, heir of God, and joint-heir with Jesus Christ! Here you pant, you long, you strive, you thirst, you hunger, you pray for deeper knowledge of the Saviour. More and more intensely you pursue him. For you, Leviticus is a boundless mine. The more you dig, the richer is the ore.

When Satan whispers that your sins are vile, these many sacrifices come into view. Each puts a seal to the reviving truth that God's own Lamb has borne your guilt away.

You hear of coming judgment and wrath? You know hell is a terrible reality? Yet every altar shows the fierce flame of justice consuming an offering, that the offender may go free. You see here that all the vengeance, fury, and wrath you deserved expired in Immanuel's agony.

You seek renewed assurance that God's smile is upon you? These sacrifices forever declare that enmity is no more, and reconciliation is complete.

Would you read the language of Christ's heart? These types and pictures unfold it. Each death proclaims Christ's death for you. He counted no suffering too great to redeem you. He waded through all the billows of God's wrath, through all the flames of hell, through all the depths of torment, to set you free and cleanse you from all stains; rescue you and to save you. His love for you exceeds all bounds. Leviticus displays its costly deeds and proves its truth. Faith claps her hands at every ordinance and shouts, 'Behold, how he loves me'!

Voluntary Consecration
By these things, by all these commandments, sacrifices, and ordinances revealing our Saviour, the Lord God calls us to consecrate ourselves to him. That is what we have come to in chapter 27. This chapter speaks of the 'singular vow', or the voluntary act whereby a person would devote himself or his property to the Lord (vv. 1-3).

If a person consecrated himself, his beast, his house, his field, or his child to the Lord, the gift was to be valued by Moses. What it is worth was to be determined by his estimation. Moses, representing the claims of God, was called upon to estimate each case according to the standard of the sanctuary. If a man made a vow, he must be tried by the standard of righteousness.

In Exodus 30:15, we read, in reference to the atonement money, 'The rich shall not give more, and the poor shall not give less than half a shekel, when they give an offering unto the Lord, to make an atonement for your souls'.

In the matter of atonement all stood upon one common level. Thus it shall ever be. High and low, rich and poor, learned and unlearned, old and young, male and female, bond and free, Jew and Gentile, black and white, all have one common title. 'There is no difference.' All stand alike before God on the same ground, by the same merit, by the infinite merit and value of Christ's precious blood. There are vast differences in us all by nature and by providence; but our title to divine acceptance is Christ's blood. 'The rich shall not give more, and the poor shall not give less.' Nothing more could be given, nothing less could be taken. 'We have boldness to enter into the holiest by the blood of Jesus.' What mercy! The blood of Christ makes heaven ours!

But, in Leviticus 27 the issue is the worth of the gift brought to God. Moses had a certain standard from which he could not descend. He had a rule from which he could not swerve. If anyone could come up to that, he and his gift were accepted. If not, he was rejected with his gift.

What about those who could not meet the standard, who could not rise to the height of the claims set forth by the representative of divine righteousness? Read verse 8 and rejoice.

> But if he be poorer than thy estimation, then he shall present himself before the priest, and the priest shall value him; according to his ability that vowed shall the priest value him (Leviticus 27:8).

In other words, if a sinner undertakes to meet the claims of righteousness, then he must meet them. But if he knows himself to be poor, utterly incapable of meeting those claims, he has only to fall back upon the redemption and grace represented in God's priest, Christ and his Sacrifice. And the priest would receive him and his gift, though they are altogether unworthy in themselves of God's acceptance.

Moses represents the claims of divine righteousness. The priest represents the provisions of divine grace through the blood of Christ. The poor man who was unable to stand before Moses fell back into the arms of the priest.

Thus it is today and forever. If I cannot 'dig', I can 'beg'. I take my place before God; a beggar, a mercy beggar. Will you? The issue is not, 'what can I do, but what will God do?'

> Grace all the work shall crown,
> Through everlasting days.
> It lays in heaven the topmost stone,
> And well deserves the praise!

God is glorified in giving grace. We are blessed in the gift (Ephesians 1:3-7). God accepts us in his Son (Ecclesiastes 9:7-10). 'Blessed are the poor in spirit, for theirs is the kingdom of heaven.' When our poverty causes us to seek the boundless riches of God's grace in Christ, we will gladly echo our Master's doctrine. 'Blessed are the poor in spirit, for theirs is the kingdom of heaven.'

Grace will never allow anyone to go away empty. It meets the very deepest need of our souls and is glorified in meeting it. Moses, the Lawgiver, has proved us poorer than his estimation. Christ, the Grace-giver, takes us upon the merit of his blood atonement, the priest's estimation. Upon that basis, I call upon myself and you to freely, voluntarily consecrate ourselves to God (Romans 11:33-12:3).

That is what the book of Leviticus is all about. It is God's call to sinners by the sacrifice of Christ, upon the basis of his finished work, to consecrate themselves to him by faith.

> No drops of grief can e'er repay
> The debt of love I owe.
> Here, Lord, I give myself away,
> 'Tis all that I can do!

Amen

Index Of Bible Verses

Old Testament

Genesis

1:6-8	492
2:2, 3	445
3	158, 252, 454
3:15	45
3:15, 21	45
3:24	125
4	454
4:3	259
4:3-5	45
4:26	493
6	273
7:4	280
7:12	280
7:17	280
8:4	470
8:20	344
8:20-22	45
9	252
9:4	173
12:7, 8	344
13:4, 18	344
14:3	74
15:9, 10	42
15:9-11	45
15:17, 18	125
18:23-25	366
19:26	74
22	125
22:8	45, 77
22:9-13	344
26:25	344
28:18	344
35:1	344
38:8	566
45:18	83
47	114
47:18-26	115

Exodus

3	126
3:5	141
3:13, 14	524
4:24-26	139
6:6	567
12	453, 463
12-14	435
12:1-13	45
12:2	486fn
12:3-6	456
12:7	456
12:8	458
12:11	455
12:13	52, 342
12:38	522
12:40-42	458
13:2	470
13:2, 13	168
13:3, 4	471
15	436
16:23-29	445
17:1-7	188
19:1	477
19:4-6	401
19:6	16, 354
19:13, 19	483
20:8-11	445, 457
20:18	483
20:22-26	603
21-23	118
21:5, 6	573
22:29	470
23:7	366
23:14-17	497fn
23:16	442
24:18	280
25:22	338, 504
28	197

28:1	179
28:4	198
28:6, 7	201
28:8	199
28:29, 30	194
28:30	185, 187, 201
28:31-35	200
28:36	394
28:36-38	203
29:6	394
30:10	133
30:15	613
30:34	62
31:13	423, 446, 538
34:6, 7	365
34:7	367
34:23, 24	71, 553
34:24	543, 553
34:28	280
37	504
37:10-16	512
37:17	505
38	504
39:3	201
39:30	394

Leviticus

1:1, 2	23
1:1-9	21
1:3	24, 25, 147, 156
1:4, 5	29, 30
1:5	49, 51, 147, 156
1:5-9	26
1:7, 8	27
1:10-13	37

Discovering Christ In Leviticus

Leviticus cont'd					
1:10-17	35	5:15, 16	405	8:1-36	177, 205
1:11	147, 156	5:16-6:7	117	8:2	179
1:12, 13	40	5:17, 18	113	8:5	209
1:14-17	41, 43, 45	6:1	129	8:6-9	185
2:1	58	6:2	112	8:7	200
2:1-16	56	6:8	132	8:7-9	197
2:2, 3	60, 64	6:8, 9	127	8:8	185, 201
2:4	60, 61	6:8-13	125	8:9	202, 203
2:7	60	6:8-7:15	131	8:10, 11	218
2:9, 10	64	6:10	128	8:13	181
2:11	62	6:11	129	8:14, 15	212
2:11, 12	76	6:13	130	8:14-30	211
2:12	68	6:14	139	8:18, 19	180, 212
2:12-16	67, 68	6:14-23	137	8:22-24	183, 213
2:13	63, 68, 73, 75	6:16	135, 141	8:30	182, 215, 217
2:14	69	6:17	133, 141	8:31-35	219
2:15, 16	71	6:18	134, 135, 142	8:36	210
3:1	92	6:19, 20	143	9:1	222
3:1-17	79, 90	6:21	143	9:1-10:7	221
3:2	93	6:22, 23	144	9:2	223
3:3, 4	93	6:24-30	145	9:3, 4	224
3:5	94	6:24, 25	146	9:5, 6	225
3:6	95	6:25	133	9:6	209, 234
3:7, 8	95	6:26	135	9:7-14	225
3:9, 10	96	6:26, 29	148	9:15-21	226
3:11	96	6:27, 28	149	9:15-24	259
3:12, 13	96	6:29	133, 135	9:22-24	130, 227, 231, 235
3:12-17	82	6:30	151	9:23, 24	210
3:14-16	97	7:1	133	10:1, 2	242, 260
3:16	84	7:1, 2	155	10:1-3	14, 251, 520
3:16, 17	173	7:1-10	153	10:1-7	14, 130, 146, 229
3:17	97	7:3-5	156	10:1-11	258
4:1-35	99, 100	7:6	133, 135	10:1-20	241
4:10-12	105	7:7	158, 161	10:3	244, 255, 263
4:14	101	7:8	158	10:3-6	260
4:24	156	7:9, 10	159	10:4-7	246
4:29	156	7:11-21	80	10:6, 7	262
4:33	156	7:11-38	169	10:8-11	247, 264
5:1	111	7:12-14	170	10:12	133
5:1-6:7	100, 109	7:15-18	84, 171	10:12-15	247
5:4	111	7:19-21	172	10:16-18	249
5:11	62	7:21, 22	86		
5:11, 12	110fn	7:22-36	173		
5:15	113, 224	7:29-34	80, 86		
		7:37, 38	174		

Leviticus cont'd

10:17	133	16:16-14	214	19:20-22	362
10:19	249	16:7-10	323	19:23-26	362
10:20	249	16:11	223	19:26-28	362
11:1-3	268	16:11, 12	321	19:29	363
11:1-47	267	16:11-13	243	19:31	362
11:3	272	16:12	243, 253, 254	19:32	356
11:4-8	272			19:33, 34	358
11:4-42	268	16:14, 15	323	19:35, 36	358, 365, 366, 367
11:43-45	274	16:15	140, 323		
11:43-47	269	16:17	320, 322	19:37	354, 422
11:44	16, 354	16:20-22	324, 329	20:1-6	377
12:1, 2	277	16:21	31, 33	20:1-27	375
12:1-8	275	16:24	320	20:6	379
12:3-5	279	16:29, 31	337	20:7	16
12:6-8	281	16:29-34	336	20:7, 8	379
13:1-14:57	283	16:30	320	20:7, 26	354
13:2	293	17:1-3	336	20:8	423
13:9	284	17:1-16	334	20:9	380
13:12, 13	294, 297	17:4	337, 340fn	20:10-21	381
13:12-17	291			20:22-24	383
13:44-46	296	17:5	338, 340	20:25, 26	384
13:47, 48	288	17:6	339	20:26	15, 376
13:47-59	287	17:7	338	20:27	384, 389
13:52	288	17:7-10	340	21:1-4	390
13:52, 57	288	17:11	52, 173, 343	21:1-9	389
14:1-57	299			21:1-24	387
14:5	304	17:11-16	341	21:5, 6	391
14:6, 7	305	18:1-5	347	21:6	396
14:8, 9	307	18:1-30	345	21:7, 8	392
14:10	307	18:6-19	349	21:8	396
14:13	133	18:24-28	350	21:9	393
14:21, 22	286	18:29, 30	351	21:10-12	394
14:33, 34	289	19:1-37	353	21:13-15	395
14:34	292, 294	19:1, 2	15, 354	21:17	396
14:35	294	19:3	356	21:17-21	396
14:54-57	291	19:3-8	356	21:21	414
15:1-33	311	19:8	172	21:21, 22	396
15:13-15	315	19:9, 10	357	21:22, 23	398
15:25-30	317	19:11	358	21:24	398
16:1, 2	243	19:12	358	22:1, 2	400
16:1-34	319, 328	19:13	358	22:1-33	399
16:3, 4	321	19:14	359	22:3-9	402
16:4	197	19:15	359	22:9	403
16:5	322	19:16	359	22:10-16	404
16:6	321	19:17, 18	360	22:17-19	405
		19:19	360	22:20, 21	414

Leviticus cont'd	
22:20-22	406
22:20-33	409
22:21	366, 411
22:21-23	418
22:23	406
22:24	407
22:25	396, 407
22:26-28	408
22:31-33	419, 422, 425, 428
23:1-3	435, 443
23:1-44	433
23:4, 5	435, 453
23:6-8	436, 459, 462, 463
23:9-14	437, 467
23:15-22	438, 475
23:18	497
23:19, 20	480
23:21	481
23:22	481
23:23-25	439, 483
23:24	530
23:26-32	440, 489, 490, 491
23:27, 28	320
23:33-44	441, 496, 500
23:37, 38	497
23:39-44	498
23:40	500
24:1, 2	505
24:1-4	503, 504
24:3, 4	507
24:5, 6	513
24:5-8	62
24:5-9	511, 512
24:7	516
24:9	133
24:10-16	14
24:10-23	519, 521, 522
24:13-16	525
24:17-22	526
24:23	526

25:1	532
25:1-22	537, 540
25:3-5	533
25:8-13	529
25:8-17	545
25:9	320, 325, 531
25:10	532
25:10-13	548
25:13	534
25:14-17	549
25:17	534
25:18-21	556
25:18-22	551, 554
25:19	534
25:20-22	542
25:21	558
25:23	562
25:23-34	559, 560
25:25	567
25:25-28	565
25:25-55	566
25:27	567
25:29, 30	561
25:29-34	560
25:35	533
25:35-55	569
25:47-49	565
25:48	567
25:55	555
26:1	576
26:1, 2	586
26:1-5	595, 603
26:1-20	583
26:1-46	575
26:3, 4	606
26:3-13	587
26:4, 5	588
26:6	588
26:7, 8	590
26:9	591
26:11, 12	592
26:13	593
26:14-20	594
26:40-44	581
26:45, 46	582

27:1-34	607, 614
27:34	584, 609
Numbers	
1, 2	258
3, 4	258
3:4	146
4:7	512
4:49	258
5:15	62
6:24-26	50, 228, 240
7	38
10:1-10	483, 484
10:2	485
10:8	486
10:9	486
10:10	486
13:25	280
14:33, 34	280
18:8-11	135
18:12	83
18:19	68, 76
18:20	389
18:23, 24	389
23:19-23	330
23:21	480
24-26	325
25:3	336
26:61	146
27:21	87, 195
29:1-6	483, 484
29:12-40	502
29:13-39	497fn
30:1, 2	608
35:12	567
35:12-34	566
Deuteronomy	
4:2	206
4:39	422
10:9	389
11:26-28	576
11:26-29	352
12:16	173
12:30-32	63

Deuteronomy cont'd		1 Samuel		Job	
12:32	206	2:1	142	5:23	69
15:1, 2	542	3:3	507	6:6	78
16:3	465	16:7	314	8:3	367
16:13-15	496,	17:16	280	8:20	367, 415
	497fn			9:1-3	415
18:1, 2	389	2 Samuel		9:20	415
19:1-3	566	24:24	420, 505	9:25, 26	106
25:5	566			11:8, 9	407
25:13	367	1 Kings		14:4	415
26:1-11	470	11:3, 4	252	15:12-16	415
26:2	470	19:1-8	280	19:13-19	300
26:17	572			19:23-27	568
27:18	359	2 Kings		19:25	567
31:10, 11	542	2	73	19:25, 26	173
32:8-12	106	4:23	598	19:25-27	499
32:12	385	22:11	296	25:4	276, 365
32:17	336, 338			25:4-6	415
32:49-51	401	1 Chronicles		33:24	110, 320,
33:8	185, 188	13	243, 421		366
33:13, 14	577	15	243, 421	42:5, 6	493
33:26-29	500, 501	15:13	146		
33:29	385	16:29	17	Psalms	
				2:8	573
Joshua		2 Chronicles		4:6, 7	238
5:9-12	468	8:12, 13	476	5:7	597, 599
5:10-12	471	13:5	68, 76	9:17	126fn
13:14, 33	389	13:11	517	14:1-3	277
18:7	389	20:21	17	15:4	608
24:14, 15	352	26	400	16:5	142
		26:16-21	146	16:9-11	68, 171
Judges		36:16	74	17:15	85, 354
2:13	252			21:4	193
3:27	530	Ezra		21:5	238
13	232	2:63	185, 187	22:1	52
		2:68, 69	604, 605	22:14	69
Ruth				22:14, 15	60
2:8, 9	358	Nehemiah		22:22	52
2:16	358	7:6	185	22:25-27	52
3, 4	566	8:14-18	500	24:3, 4	315
3:12, 13	567	10:39	598	25:11	124, 303
4:4-6	567			29:2	17
4:7-11	567	Esther		31:19	592
4:14	568	3:1-8:2	471	32:1, 2	329
		5:4	471	34:7	268

Psalms cont'd

37:7	481
37:25	558
38:11	300
39:4-6	276
39:9	261
39:11	295
39:12	562
40	199
40:6-10	573
40:12	135, 157, 214, 223, 367, 568
47:1-9	579
48:1-3	39
48:2	147
49:7	323, 568
51:1-4	32, 111
51:5	276, 313
51:7	62
54:6, 7	605
57:1-3	425
57:2	245
58:10	245
62:3, 4	87
62:11, 12	87
63:5	156
65:4	132
68:17-20	192, 238
69:4	119, 405
69:4-9	394
69:5	135, 157, 214, 223, 367
69:9	214
69:19	214
69:20	322
72:16-19	442
73:25, 26	85
73:26	142
76:10	116, 123
81:1-4	483
81:3	530
84:1	206
84:1-4	600
84:6	598

84:10	600
85:9-11	121
85:9-13	238
85:10	190
88:7	50
88:18	300
89:1-18	483
89:3	487
89:4	487
89:7	143, 146, 261
89:14	110
89:14-18	485, 486
89:14-37	440
89:15	439, 530, 547
89:19	97, 110, 321, 515
89:28	487
89:29	487
89:34	487
89:36, 37	487
92:14	591
94:21	366
95:7-9	188
96:9	17
96:9-13	502
98:1	487
99:1-3	151
102:4	69
103:1-4	238
103:3, 4	318
103:4	567
103:12	330
104:15	469
105:1	58
106:1	58
106:4	579
107:34	74
110:3	132
111:1-9	524
115:1	436
116:7	481, 533
116:16, 17	92
119:18	191
119:57	142

119:108	170
119:160	127
122:1	206, 605
130:3-8	100
132:14	481
132:16	140
138:2	205
141:3	112
149:4	204

Proverbs

1:23-33	255
3:1-18	606
3:5, 6	525, 551
3:5-7	70
3:5-10	470
6:1, 2	608
6:12-19	523
7:24-27	254
8	193
11:13	359
16:6	110, 120, 190, 238, 366, 367
16:11	367
16:33	323
17:15	366, 367
20:22	360
20:23	367
21:4	407
24:16	564
28:17	101
29:1	255
30:6	206

Ecclesiastes

3:10, 11	556
3:11	556
3:14	561
5:1, 2	604
5:2	112, 113
8:10	255
9:7	42, 142, 147, 410, 469
9:7-10	418, 615

Song of Solomon
2:12   41
3:6   62
4:6   62
4:7   181, 184,
            331
4:9   181
4:12-14   361fn
4:14   62
5   397
5:9-16   473
5:12   41
6:3   572
6:9   392, 395
7:13   578
8:6   202

Isaiah
1:4-6   313
1:6   292, 295
1:11-15   415
1:16, 17   415
1:18   62
1:18-20   416
6:1-6   147
6:1-7   295
6:1-8   238, 504
6:5   493
9:6   164
11:5   199
11:9   150
11:10   448, 538
21:34   94
25:6-9   502
26:18   303
26:19   68
27:4   18, 130
27:13   485, 530
28:14-20   255
28:20   415
31:5   457
33:4   126fn
35:1, 2   502
35:8   315
35:8-10   366
35:10   485

38:17   330
40:1-5   119
40:31   106
41:14   567
42:1   95
42:1-4   321, 394,
            573
43:1   567
43:3   457
43:5-7   439
43:25   100, 114,
            495
43:27   278
44:6   567
44:22   114, 330,
            567
45:7   351
45:20-25   416, 449,
            539, 610
45:21   53, 367
45:22   449
46:13   282
48:9   114
48:20   567
50:5-7   573
52:1   315
53:1-12   18, 174
53:4-6   329, 527
53:4-10   227, 342
53:4-11   32, 102
53:6   19, 568
53:6-11   249
53:7   38
53:9-11   19, 85
53:10   100
53:10, 11   47
53:10-12   68
53:12   52
54:1-5   592
54:17   578
55:1   282
55:1, 2   156, 588
55:3   592
58:1   485
60:8   108
60:19, 20   191

60:21   315
61   546
61:1, 2   531
63:3-5   322
63:4   529, 531
64:6   171, 276,
            278, 296,
            303,
            361fn
65:2-7   415
66:1, 2   296, 429,
            493
66:3   30,   339,
            415

Jeremiah
2:12   380
3:14   379
3:15   149
9:23, 24   244
10:7   261, 424
14:20, 21   232
17:6   74
23:5   487
23:6   373
31:3   121, 426
31:31-34   592, 599
31:34   330
31:40   129
32:27   341
32:38-40   592
33:16   373, 487
38:17-19   557
39:7, 8   558
50:20   114, 324,
            329, 330,
            373

Lamentations
1:12   612
3:22   599
3:24   142
3:26-32   297

Ezekiel
1-10   504

Ezekiel cont'd
1:28   429
4:6   280
16:7   295
16:8-14   181, 204
18:4   373
18:20   373
20:40-42   77
22   349
24:16-24   246
36:25-27   313
38:23   577
44:18   541
47:11   74

Daniel
7:9-14   504
9:24   249
10:8   295
12:4   598

Hosea
1-3   392
2:7   395
2:14   297
2:18   69, 588
2:19   379
4:1, 2   313
13:4   491

Joel
2   477
2:1   531

Amos
5:22   90
9:13   579

Jonah
3:4   280

Micah
6:11   367
7:8   564

7:18-20   325, 329,
            424, 582,
            599
7:19   330

Nahum
1:6   18

Habakkuk
1:13   315
2:20   604

Zephaniah
2:9   74
3:17   95

Haggai
2:12   172

Zechariah
3:1-5   186, 203
3:9   135
4:1, 2   510
4:2-6   507
4:4-9   510
8:21   598
12:8   579
12:10   166, 466,
            491
12:10-13:1 316, 403,
            493
13:7   27, 39,
            323, 368
14   498

Malachi
1:1-14   413
1:6-11   154
1:6-14   420
1:11   344
1:14   70
2:11   379
2:16   392
3:6   599
3:6-11   96

New Testament

Matthew
1:1-18   567
1:5   568
1:20   61
1:23-25   472
3:13-17   46, 245
3:15-17   215
3:16   61
3:17   59, 95
4:2   280
5:3, 4   493
5:13   64
5:16   509
5:19, 20 313
6   556
6:31-34   552
7:13-15   242
7:21-23   242
8:1-3   296
8:17   285
10:7, 8   605
10:10   160
10:39   345, 348
11:28   449, 539
11:28-30 435, 460,
          481, 488,
          533, 538,
          561, 570,
          577, 586,
          606
11:29, 30 450
13:16   118
13:22   556
13:44   361fn
15:18, 19 314
15:19   284
16:5-12   464
16:24   63
16:25   345
17:5   59,   95,
          372
18   535

18:20   149, 194,
          601
19:8   349
24:8   106
24:29-31 474
25:14, 15 259
25:21-23 373
27:46   60
27:52, 53 471
26:17   460
28:1   448, 539
28:1-6   472
28:18   238

Mark
1:21   598
1:40, 41 316
2:1-4   286
8:14-21   464
8:34, 35 465
8:35   345
9:24   445
9:44   130
9:46   130
9:48   130
13:32   498
14:12   460

Luke
1:35   61, 368
2:21-30   46
2:25-32   601
2:32   190
2:34   74
4:1   61
4:14   61
4:16   598
4:16-21   546
4:17-21   532
4:18   61
9:24   345
9:59-62   63
10:7   160, 605

12   556
12:1   464
14:25-33 521
14:26-33 465
15:17   514
17:33   345
17:37   106
18:11   253
18:13   101, 105
18:13, 14 599
20:17, 18 255
22:1   460
22:7   460
22:16   455
22:35   558
22:63-65 525
24:45   118
24:47   494
24:50-53 228, 235

John
1:3, 4   189
1:9   189
1:11-13   33,   242,
          280
1:14   190, 321,
          368, 428,
          442, 499
1:16   482
1:18   428
1:29   96
3:3-7   165
3:3-8   242
3:14-16   164
3:16   121, 254,
          609
3:19-21   510
3:34, 35 215
3:36   451, 582,
          594
4:10   142
4:13, 14 85
4:23   576

John cont'd
4:23, 24   154, 178, 352, 423
4:32-34   480
4:34   57
5:28, 29   499
5:40   286
6:28, 29   410
6:29   168
6:33   396, 513
6:35-37   286
6:37   38
6:48   85
6:48-58   409, 421
6:51   396
6:53-55   85
6:53-56   437, 457, 458, 461, 462
6:53-58   142, 144, 148, 151
6:54, 55   157
6:54-58   515
6:63   63, 233
7:2   501
7:3   190
7:37   442
7:37, 38   442, 502
7:38, 39   233, 305
8:1-11   297
8:29   59
8:46   59
9   501
9:5   487
9:25   189
10:15-18   439
10:16-18   567
10:27, 28   588
10:27-30   449, 487
10:28-30   508
10:30   492
11:25   246
11:40   234, 240
11:47-52   97
12:20-32   479
12:23, 24   471

12:24   51, 69, 471
12:25   345
12:28   233
12:32   106
12:41   232
13   563
13:1-10   180
13:4, 5   199
13:36-38   563
14:1-3   193, 563
14:6   15, 410
14:6-9   428
14:16-18   476
14:27   87
15:5   487
15:15, 16   591
15:19   273
16:4   233
16:7   228
16:7-11   237, 491
16:7-14   166
16:8-11   101
16:9   105
16:21   276
17   202
17:1-5   57, 573
17:2   193, 449, 539
17:3   428, 586
17:3-5   238
17:4   322, 449, 539
17:17-19   393
17:19   219, 363
17:20   164
17:22   514
19:23   198
19:30   57, 449, 539
21:17   192, 315

Acts of the Apostles
1:3   280
1:4-11   498
2   46, 477

2:1   476, 601
2:1-4   439
2:23   323, 548
2:37-41   601
3:18-21   119
3:21   440, 444, 497
4:12   243, 524
4:26-28   323
5   254
5:6-10   246
8:2   245
8:25-35   598
10:4   516
10:38   61
13:29   323
13:38, 39   114
20:16   476
20:28   341, 368
20:29   252

Romans
1:18-20   43, 399
1:18-32   350, 382
1:20   189
1:23-25   44
1:27   382
1:31   380
2:14, 15   43, 189
3:12   277
3:19-26   45, 161
3:21-31   366
3:24-26   53, 323, 342, 358, 372, 560, 599, 610
3:25, 26   123
3:28   361fn
3:31   168, 348, 430, 451, 579, 587
4:3-11   372
4:5   282
4:6   361fn, 487

Romans cont'd

4:8	329, 372, 395
4:11	279
4:16-5:11	589
4:25	54, 92, 472
4:25-5:2	71, 104, 149, 370
4:25-5:11	129, 174
5:1	85
5:1, 2	92
5:5-11	25
5:6-8	121
5:6-11	36, 343, 491
5:8	609
5:9	342
5:10, 11	102, 209
5:12	278
5:12-21	32, 328
5:15-18	142
5:18, 19	209
5:19	164, 361fn, 370
5:20, 21	514, 532
6:4-6	139
6:7	53
6:11	372, 480
6:23	139, 142, 373, 451
7:4	447
7:9	101
7:14-23	16, 259
7:14-24	478
7:14-8:1	273
7:18	295, 312, 314
8	81, 427
8:1	324, 329, 372
8:1-4	45, 96, 130, 136, 430
8:3	567

8:4	168
8:7	61
8:17-21	85
8:18-24	440
8:22, 23	70
8:23	474
8:28	69, 84, 91, 425, 449, 588, 599
8:28-30	16, 70, 566
8:28-39	85, 590
8:29	472
8:29, 30	33, 426, 428, 449, 547
8:31-39	427
8:32	593, 604
8:32-35	324
8:33, 34	136, 140, 395
8:34	214, 322, 448, 538, 539
8:37	578
9	348, 355
9:5	164
9:11	517
9:15, 16	24
9:16	256
9:30-10:4	348
9:31-10:4	254, 260
10:1-4	587
10:1-13	576
10:4	372, 447, 579
10:5-9	282
10:8-13	493
10:9-13	286, 586
10:13-17	165, 485
11:16	438
11:26	439
11:26, 27	458
11:29	561
11:33-36	120, 574
11:33-12:2	465

11:33-12:3	493, 615
12:1, 2	54, 65, 151, 154, 175, 184, 274, 393, 431, 462, 570, 574
12:20, 21	360
13:1-5	526
13:7	356
14:9	573
14:13	359
14:14	269fn
14:19	360
15:3	63
15:4	311, 388
15:13	245
16:5	70
16:20	591
16:26	163

1 Corinthians

1:21-23	106
1:30	84, 340
1:30, 31	34, 134, 244, 371
2:12	604
2:12-16	491
3:16	149, 604
3:16, 17	601
3:21	514, 604
3:21-23	593
4:7	84, 271
5:7	435, 447, 463, 464
5:7, 8	453, 461
6:9-11	16, 115, 150, 352, 354, 393, 420, 431, 465, 555, 570
6:9-20	309
6:13	154
6:19	154

1 Corinthians cont'd
6:19, 20   58,   115,
            150, 158,
            184, 262,
            342, 352,
            354, 393,
            420, 431,
            465, 555
6:19-21   570
9   159
9:7-14   159, 605
9:11   160
9:13   138fn
9:13, 14   171, 389
9:14   515
10:14, 15   357
10:16, 17   517, 521
10:31   184, 272,
            355, 431,
            572
11   141, 404,
            461,
            570fn
11:15   295
11:26-29   148
11:29   172
14:8   530
15:16-20   471
15:19-23   174
15:19-28   468
15:20-23   70, 472
15:20-25   473
15:20-28   16
15:23   71, 438
15:24-28   440, 482
15:49-58   16
15:51, 52   535
15:51-58   71, 547
16:8   476

2 Corinthians
1:20   192
2:14-16   74
4:3-7   232, 428
4:4-6   120, 508

4:6   147, 165,
            190, 240,
            487
4:7   150, 286
4:17-5:11   549
4:18-5:1   562
5:1-9   290
5:5-9   451
5:10, 11   74,   499,
            580
5:14   34, 54
5:14, 15   262
5:14-21   174, 274
5:15   174
5:17   16,   280,
            307, 354,
            370, 449,
            471, 546
5:17-21   48,   170,
            324, 358,
            448, 491,
            494, 538
5:17-6:2   485, 549
5:18-21   126
5:21   33, 36, 45,
            97,   100,
            102, 136,
            147, 157,
            168, 214,
            223, 227,
            249, 324,
            329, 367,
            368, 370,
            406, 487,
            490, 512,
            527, 568
6:14-18   383
6:14-7:1   271, 340,
            361
7:1   306, 383
8:1-5   160
8:9   164, 235,
            321, 442,
            567, 571
8:12   132, 184,
            357, 420

9:6-8   160
9:7   184, 357,
            605
9:10, 11   160
9:15   142, 254
10:3-5   486
11:2   395
11:3   281
11:7   605

Galatians
1:15, 16   429
2:16   256
2:19, 20   155
2:20   34,   173,
            220, 370
2:20, 21   341
3:1   40
3:1-3   256
3:10   162
3:13   372, 488,
            568
3:13, 14   36,   174,
            184, 236,
            323, 358,
            437, 462,
            477, 509,
            527, 578
3:19   587
3:19-25   158
3:24   587
3:24, 25   168
4   328
4:4-6   280, 426
5:1-4   494, 520,
            533
5:2   446
5:4   446
5:22, 23   591
6:1, 2   157
6:6   160
6:7-9   558
6:14   466
6:14, 15   462

Ephesians
1   355
1:3   514, 604
1:3-6   25, 33, 84,
             140, 193,
             371, 449,
             487, 560
1:3-7   340, 479,
             579, 615
1:3-14   116, 487,
             548
1:6   233, 449,
             472
1:7   102, 213,
             343, 560,
             568
1:10   165
1:10, 11   440
1:12   233
1:13, 14   139, 140,
             279, 428,
             578
1:14   233
2:1-3   278
2:4, 5   563
2:4-6   426
2:4-7   119
2:5-10   208
2:7   116, 237,
             482
2:8, 9   142, 165
2:11-22   405
2:13   342
2:18   238
2:22   604
3:8   286
3:12   238
3:17-19   437
3:18, 19   407
4:1-7   509
4:1-5:2   517
4:4-6   492
4:16   207
4:17-5:21   464
4:21-24   464
4:24   354, 371

4:29-5:2   523
4:32-5:2   174, 535
5:2   27, 42, 48,
             57, 78
5:11-14   385
5:14   190
5:25, 26   16
5:25-27   418, 482
5:25-30   379
5:26   27, 180
5:27   395
5:30   216
6:11-17   259

Philippians
1:6   271, 449,
             487
2:1-8   259
2:5-7   236
2:5-9   442
2:5-11   321, 449,
             524, 573
2:7   567
2:9-11   539
2:15   509
3:1-3   256
3:3   143, 154,
             178, 193,
             279, 340,
             352, 423,
             462, 487,
             493, 576
3:7   303
3:7-9   487
3:10   70,   466,
             592
3:21   70
4:4   549
4:4-7   563
4:7   91
4:13   487
4:18   64, 172
4:19   184, 554

Colossians
1:10   363

1:12   141, 147,
             191, 371,
             418, 479
1:14   102, 342,
             343
1:15   472
1:18   472
1:18, 19   233
1:19   188
1:20   342
1:20, 21   449
1:27   354, 371,
             429
2:3   188
2:6-15   208
2:8-23   446
2:9   192
2:9, 10   18,   34,
             147, 418
2:9-17   479
2:10   372
2:11, 12   279
2:12   165
2:13-15   53, 590
2:16   603
2:16, 17   447
2:16-23   577
2:23   282, 447,
             539
3   517
3:1-3   262, 357,
             431, 493,
             563
3:12-17   573
4:6   64

1 Thessalonians
4:1   355
4:1-7   355
4:7   16, 354
4:13-18   71,   474,
             535
5:12, 13   160
5:21-24   265
5:23, 24   98, 385
5:24   449

2 Thessalonians
1:6-10   126fn
1:7   540
2:1-12   252
2:4   382
2:13   183

1 Timothy
1:15   164
1:18   259
2:14   281
2:14, 15 281
3:15   206, 599,
          601
3:16   136, 164
4:1-3   252
4:8   419
4:12-16   393
5:13   359
5:17   160
5:17, 18 389
5:18   605
6:3-5   384
6:12   259

2 Timothy
1:9   560
1:9, 10   491
2:13   507
2:15   40
2:15-26   265
2:19   517
2:24-26   523
3:1-5   252
3:16, 17 210, 351,
          377
4:7   259

Titus
1:6   393
1:6-9   389
2:1-15   271
2:11-14   16, 240,
          266, 354,
          402

2:14   268, 463,
          567
3:2   360
3:3-7   279
3:4-7   180
3:5   27
3:5, 6   151
3:5-7   286

Hebrews
1:1, 2   224
1:1-3   136, 150,
          567
1:1-4   524
1:3   214
1:6   472
2:10   70, 238
2:11   216
2:13   482
2:14   488
2:16   219
2:16, 17 567
3   448
3:13, 14 171
4   448
4:1-6   447
4:1-11   444, 533
4:3   33, 45,
          435, 449,
          451, 539,
          577
4:3-11   501
4:6   447, 449
4:7   435
4:7, 8   448
4:9   435, 529,
          540
4:9, 10   449, 539
4:9, 11   450
4:9-11   337, 448,
          460
4:10   450, 460
4:11   451
4:16   138, 144,
          152, 214,
          229

5:1, 2   516
5:1-5   179
5:9   222
6:1   494
6:10   64
6:20   449
7:11   15
7:23-28   14, 520
7:24-27   184
7:24-28   186, 226
7:25   22, 164,
          199, 230,
          388
7:25-28   396
7:26, 27 223
7:27   398
8:34   209
9:1-9   258
9:1-12   503
9:1-15   150
9:6-12   499
9:11, 12 209, 228,
          237, 456
9:11-14   491
9:12   27, 52,
          129, 164,
          179, 199,
          222, 305,
          322, 324,
          335, 449,
          490, 539,
          568, 608
9:12-14   342
9:13, 14 180
9:14   27, 46, 53,
          61, 70,
          172, 146
9:19   304
9:19, 20 456
9:19-22   213
9:22   44, 52,
          214, 322,
          334, 343
9:23   503
9:24   199, 209,
          228, 237

Hebrews cont'd
9:26   19, 136,
            164, 209,
            236, 488
9:26, 28   320
9:26-28   228, 237
9:27   499
10   199, 307
10:1   503
10:1-4   53, 150,
            320
10:1-14   45, 212,
            608
10:5-14   573
10:5-15   567
10:9-14   354, 404,
            418, 429,
            448
10:9-22   324
10:9-23   129
10:10   183
10:10-14   54, 174,
            209
10:11-14   320, 323,
            448, 538,
            539
10:12-14   214
10:14   324, 329
10:14-22   15, 152
10:16-22   505
10:18   320
10:19, 20   342
10:19-21   214
10:19-22   24, 138,
            144, 243,
            286
10:22   456
10:22-27   577
10:23-31   602
10:25   357
10:25, 26   603
10:29   304,
            340fn,
            603
11:5, 6   298
11:6   355

11:8-10   562
12:2   85
12:14   16, 134,
            353, 403
12:22-24   206
12:24   156
12:25   245, 485
12:28   604
13:8   192
13:10   157
13:10-12   130, 152
13:10-15   108, 170,
            344
13:12   342
13:13-15   152
13:15   58, 64, 94,
            184
13:15, 16   65, 138,
            144, 259

James
1:17   83, 142,
            477, 579,
            607
1:18   70, 280,
            438
1:27   265

1 Peter
1:5-7   233
1:13-16   355, 363
1:18   463
1:18-20   155, 436,
            547, 571
1:18-21   213, 323,
            335
2:5   58, 64,
            172, 406,
            418, 516
2:5-9   14, 178,
            179, 184,
            259, 388,
            520
2:5-10   401
2:7-10   16, 354

2:9   138,
            138fn
2:21-24   157
2:22   368
2:23-25   485
2:24   249, 567
3:7   281
3:18   97, 249,
            456, 527
4:1   480
4:1, 2   215, 324,
            329

2 Peter
1:4   16, 354,
            370
1:15-17   233
1:18   141
1:19   508
3   252
3:10-14   543
3:11-14   290

1 John
1:3   238
1:7   342, 343
1:7, 9   313
1:7-10   296
1:7-2:2   99, 478
1:8-10   171, 411,
            463
1:8-2:2   273, 284
1:9   31, 101,
            164, 401,
            493
1:9-2:2   361
2:1, 2   62, 200,
            230, 237,
            244, 324
2:15-17   273, 556
2:19   603
2:19, 20   182
2:20   182
2:20-27   509
2:27   182
3:1   121

1 John cont'd

3:1, 2	426
3:1-3	273
3:5	19, 208, 324, 330, 337, 354, 368, 418
3:9	16, 354, 371
3:16	121, 341, 609
3:23	163, 430, 555, 579, 587
3:23, 24	348
4:4	578
4:9, 10	121, 609
4:17	208
4:19	54, 122, 609
5:1-3	587
5:2-5	348
5:10	167
5:20, 21	351
5:21	577

2 John

1:9-11	384

Jude

1:1	182, 429
1:4	253
1:11	288
1:14, 15	499
1:21	351, 577
1:23	288
1:24, 25	16, 20, 418, 482, 508

Revelation

1:4-6	138, 258
1:5	472
1:5, 6	401
1:6	178
1:7	220, 237
1:8	192
1:10	485
1:10-18	472
1:10-20	506
1:13	181, 199
1:17, 18	429
1:18	488
1:20	504, 508
2:28	508
3:1	509
3:4	288
3:14	472
3:18	159, 289
3:20	69
4	422, 454
4:1-5	508
4:1-5:15	504
4:10, 11	210, 230, 455
5	454
5:1-14	455
5:9	342
5:9, 10	210, 258, 401
5:9-14	230
5:10	178
6:9	47
7:1	492
7:14	342
7:15-17	499
7:4	513
7:9	289
7:13, 14	289
10:1-7	497
11:15-19	535

12:11	342
12:14	106
13:8	45, 547
14:1-3	513
14:1-5	395, 458
14:3	246
14:4	71, 392, 438, 474
14:10, 11	127
14:13	255, 466
14:18	127
15:3	458
16:15	289
17:1-3	524
18:4	340, 383
18:10	381
19:1-6	228, 240
19:3	245
19:7, 8	289
19:8	128, 198, 199, 203, 361fn
20:1-10	252
20:6	71, 178, 474, 579
20:11-15	373, 499
21:1-5	290, 579
21:1-7	442, 499
21:4, 5	466
21:5-7	442
21:17	315
21:23	191
21:27	290, 366
22:1-7	290, 499
22:10-17	290
22:14, 15	315
22:16	508
22:18, 19	206
22:20	290

www.ingramcontent.com/pod-product-compliance
Lightning Source LLC
Chambersburg PA
CBHW030942150426
42812CB00062B/2691